ISBN 978-1-330-38992-8
PIBN 10048874

# 1 MONTH OF
# FREE
# READING

## at
## www.ForgottenBooks.com

By purchasing this book you are eligible for one month membership to ForgottenBooks.com, giving you unlimited access to our entire collection of over 700,000 titles via our web site and mobile apps.

To claim your free month visit:
www.forgottenbooks.com/free48874

English
Français
Deutsche
Italiano
Español
Português

# www.forgottenbooks.com

**Mythology** Photography **Fiction**
Fishing Christianity **Art** Cooking
Essays Buddhism Freemasonry
Medicine **Biology** Music **Ancient
Egypt** Evolution Carpentry Physics
Dance Geology **Mathematics** Fitness
Shakespeare **Folklore** Yoga Marketing
**Confidence** Immortality Biographies
Poetry **Psychology** Witchcraft
Electronics Chemistry History **Law**
Accounting **Philosophy** Anthropology
Alchemy Drama Quantum Mechanics
Atheism Sexual Health **Ancient History**
**Entrepreneurship** Languages Sport
Paleontology Needlework Islam
**Metaphysics** Investment Archaeology
Parenting Statistics Criminology
**Motivational**

# RIMITIVE CATHOLICIS

BY

## Mgr. PIERRE BATIFFOL, Litt.D.

RANSLATION BY HENRI L. BRIANCEAU, OF ST. MARY'S SEMINAR
BALTIMORE, FROM THE FIFTH FRENCH EDITION OF "L'EGLISE
NAISSANTE," REVISED BY THE AUTHOR)

LONGMANS, GREEN AND CO.
39 PATERNOSTER ROW, LONDON
NEW YORK, BOMBAY AND CALCUTTA
1911

𝕹ihil obstat:

F. Thos. Bergh, O.S.B.
*Censor deputatus*

𝕴mprimatur:

Edm. Can. Surmont
*Vicarius generalis*

Westmonasterii, *die* 1 *Junii*, 1911

# INTRODUCTION
## TO THE FIFTH FRENCH EDITION (1911).

THE subject I am proposing to treat, and which, if God permit, I intend at some future day to pursue down to the epoch of St. Augustine and St. Leo, is the history of the formation of Catholicism, that is to say, of the Church in so far as it is a visible, universal society, built upon the framework of a rule of faith and a hierarchy.

In the present volume on "Primitive Catholicism," I study the origins of this formation, taking the time of St. Cyprian as the term of these origins. It might indeed be contended that their real term was reached more than half a century before his time, but his writings and the discussions in which he took a leading part, show so clearly that the doctrines and institutions of Catholicism were then generally accepted, and, on the other hand, the historical continuity that had governed the development of these doctrines and institutions up to his day, makes itself so sensibly felt in these same writings, that they complete for us in an admirable manner the knowledge we are able to acquire of the two hundred years of previous Christianity.

We must confess, however, that it is not without some timidity we approach the study of these two centuries of primitive history, seeing that the documentary evidence, abundant as it is, gives us but a faint idea of the early Christian life, so varied, so complex, so deep! How much light we should be deprived of, had not the Epistles of St. Ignatius and the Apologies of St. Justin been preserved!

On the other hand, how much more light we should have, were the " De Ecclesia " of Melito and the " Memorabilia " of Hegesippus still extant! The discovery of the " Didachè " has been a genuine revelation and has obliged scholars to correct many an inference. So too has the discovery of the Odes of Solomon. The preservation of the texts, as well as their loss, is something accidental. For this reason history, when dealing with centuries concerning which we have few and scanty documents, is a science of only approximate correctness, always susceptible of revision, except as regards certain manifest facts, and some general features inferred from several series of concordant observations. Such is the condition of primitive ecclesiology. Its history is made up of a few features which, clearly marked from the beginning, acquire with each successive generation a more vigorous and expressive prominence. Thus for instance, as early as the Apostolic age, Christianity presents itself as a corporate religion, a brotherhood which swarms over the earth without diminishing its cohesion, which everywhere forms itself into co-operating societies of exactly the same character. These little Christian communities have the same faith, the same worship, the same authorities. That such a phenomenon should constantly recur in Mithraism, for instance, would not seem strange to us; but it surprises us in the case of Christianity, because we are little accustomed to look at the latter from this point of view. The best definition ever given of our religion is that drawn up by Tertullian, when he writes: " *Corpus sumus de conscientia religionis et disciplinae unitate et spei foedere,*" meaning to say that the whole Christian community is this association, this *corpus*, and that in each particular Christian community there is identity of hierarchy as well as of discipline and of faith. Now this is nothing but concrete, living and historical Catholicism; and what is true of the Christianity of Tertullian's time is equally true of the Christianity of St.

Clement's time, and of the Christianity of the earliest Christian generation. Christianity was born Catholic, for there is identity of structure between Apostolic Christianity and the Christianity of about the year 200.

That, between the early days of the Christian community and the year 200 or 250, there were elements which developed, and that there were also *sinkings*, so to speak, is beyond dispute: St. Thomas Aquinas states more than once that the Minor Orders were implicit in the diaconate, and were separated from it at the proper moment, which came comparatively late; on the other hand, charisms disappeared at the proper time, prophecy was regulated with religious care for the discernment of the spirits by which it was inspired, and in such a manner as to preserve the deposit of revealed faith, which, after the Apostles, was susceptible of no new acquisitions, and which was, by divine right, entrusted to the guardianship of the bishops, the successors of the Apostles. Heresies, of which we know names and specific doctrines, appeared now and then: but the Church was so constituted that by the very fact of their springing up they differentiated themselves from her, and only served to give her the opportunity to define herself more firmly and distinctly. Built by the Apostles who knew only Jesus and Him crucified, the Church knew that only which she held from the Apostles: she was not, in this first period of her existence, in an amorphous state; history does not represent her as a mere spiritual movement whose institutions and doctrines were determined by or even borrowed from the civilization through which it passed: she was a Gospel, an apostolate, a tradition, a worship, an hierarchical society, *one* Church made up of *many* Churches, a unity preserved by the unity of the *cathedra Petri*. All this she was conscious of being. Far from being an ever-advancing and progressive evolution, she was from her origin a living and divinely assisted preservation of the gift made by God to

BQX

men in the Incarnation. All this and only this she continues to be.

In speaking thus I draw the doctrinal conclusions which form the leading portions of my book, but these conclusions are only conclusions, and my investigation remains an investigation, and is conducted, as no one has ventured to deny, in full accordance with the historical method.

\* \*
\*

In the " Theologische Literaturzeitung " for 16 Jan., 1909, Professor Harnack, has given a notice of " Primitive Catholicism " which I feel I must transcribe here almost in its entirety. I could not have wished my essay to receive more attention and favourable consideration than it has received in this notice from the most illustrious Protestant historian of the present time.

" . . . The author," he writes, "has rendered to his Church . . . a most signal service, for one could not undertake with greater special knowledge of the subject to establish the original identity of Christianity, Catholicism, and the Roman primacy. He does not seek to prove his thesis by means of metahistoric speculation which does not concern itself with the chronology of events, but confines himself to the territory of facts and their consequences, and seeks to furnish a truly historical demonstration.

" That *Roman* and *Catholic* are identical I proved as a Protestant historian some twenty-two years ago, in my ' History of Dogma,' though with certain reserves which the author strives, of course, to discard in most cases. In that work I had likewise endeavoured to prove that, in the history of the development of Christianity, we must assign to the rise of the Catholic element an earlier date than Protestant historians have generally admitted. Since then this thesis has been still more strongly accentuated (see the well-known work of Wernle,[1] for instance), and well-informed

---

[1] [Wernle's work may be found in an English translation, under the title, " The Beginnings of Christianity ".]

Protestant historians of the Church will no longer feel scandalized at the statement that some of the principal elements of Catholicism go back to the apostolic age and belong to its very heart. Thus the view of Church history taken by Catholics would seem to triumph, without their having themselves done anything to secure their victory.

"Yet, they have hardly any reason—in fact, absolutely no reason—for crying out victory.

"For, first the chasm that separates Jesus from the Apostles has not yet been bridged over, nor can it be. Secondly, the same must be said in regard to the movements which were beginning or ending in their time. Thirdly, the value, the sphere of action, and the hierarchy of the factors at work within the complex organism of Christian thought and the forms of ecclesiastical life were constantly changing until by the third century the dominant note of these factors became displaced. Fourthly and lastly, an abnormal element which was active in the beginning, later on died away, namely the element of the immediate subjection to the Divine (πνεῦμα), and the element of individual liberty which resulted therefrom. As a consequence of all this, the Church underwent unceasing and essential changes in spite of her continuity: changes the successive stages of which began about the years 30, 60, 90, 130, 160, and 190.

"But the facts recalled in the third and in the fourth place are such that one may be unacquainted with them and yet not be taxed with ignorance, in the ordinary sense of the word. They are imponderables that cannot be referred to definite and special sources. As to the chasm that separates the Apostles from all that, during their lifetime, made its appearance in the Church, it can be filled up by invoking their authority which extended to all ; and as to the conformity between Jesus and the Apostles, the old arsenal of exegesis can seem to account for it in a satisfactory manner. Hence it is possible to establish, by impressionist arguments, that the Catholic concept of the infant Church is historically the true one, i.e. that Christianity, Catholicism, and Romanism are, in the light of history, perfectly identical. This is what Batiffol has done, by availing himself of the best results of Protestant scholarship in this direction, and by using them in a calm and scientific exposition, with that solid competence which is his characteristic and which has made his name so well known.

"In this exposition there are few inaccuracies, in the worst sense of the term (except in what he says of Jesus). But, in tracing the line of historical development, he has, at every stage, overlooked the slight deviations which, taken together, cause most momentous changes of direction. We have thus, instead of a curve, a straight line which, with such a method, it would be easy to prolong even to the Catholicism of the 'Syllabus' and of the Encyclical letter of 1907. To the exulting words of the introduction, proclaiming that Catholicism is still to-day what it was in the first century, and that Protestantism, on the contrary 'may claim to be a modern ideology, but has in its essence nothing in common with the Infant Church,' we may oppose the following historical estimate: The Catholicism of the year 250—to say nothing of the year 1908—possesses, in common with primitive Christianity, a number of elements which are all lacking in Protestantism. But these elements have gradually acquired in Catholicism a value, a sphere of action, a proportion that greatly differ from what they had at the beginning, and have changed the essence of piety and the life of religion to such an extent *that Roman Catholicism can justly claim to be an ancient state with an ancient ideology, and yet in its essence it has little in common with infant Christianity.*

"However, I would earnestly recommend those Protestants who are interested in the history of the Church, not to overlook this work, but to study it thoroughly, to draw from it all that it can give, and carefully to notice, page after page, the various places where Batiffol has failed to observe, in tracing out the line of evolution, this or that small break. For instance, it is easy—and I must say, it is most important—to prove that, even in the first letter of Clement, there is a very big dose of Roman Catholicism; but it is at least equally important to show clearly in what Christianity as set forth and described by Clement differs from Cyprian's Catholicism. The chasm between them is almost immeasurable, and yet Batiffol tells us nothing about it, whilst—of course—he does not fail to emphasize the points on which both agree. The eyes of this investigator —great as is his courage and honesty—are 'held' so that he does not see what there is to see. While it is his earnest wish that the study of history should give us a yearning for unity and the intuition of the true faith, we may express the more reasonable and perhaps more hopeful wish, that *he* may learn to perceive the shades of thought and of discipline, to notice the differences, and to sum up the total effect in which they issue.

"The author's researches are partly carried on in the form of a dialogue with me, because, on many points, I am closer to him than most Protestant historians, and also because, on other points, I stand particularly in his way. I thank him for his high appreciation of my works, and I need not assure him that I shall make a thorough and detailed examination of all these topics. I am very sorry that the new edition of my 'History of Dogma' is already in the press, and that I am unable there to discuss the matter with him."

In the Preface to my third French edition, I had occasion to define my attitude towards this criticism of Professor Harnack's, which marks out so neatly and so courteously our reciprocal positions. If I return to this same passage now it is because the views it expresses have undergone fresh

developments in a recent book by the same author, "Entstehung und Entwickelung der Kirchenverfassung und des
Kirchenrechts in den zwei ersten Jahrhunderten".[1]

*<br>**

In this new book Professor Harnack adheres to the contention which underlies his "What is Christianity?" namely
that between Jesus and His Apostles a deep ditch runs, to
fill up which, though the task is in reality impossible, an
attempt has been made by casting in arguments drawn from
"the antiquated arsenal of exegetics". It will not be expected of me that I should speak of the value of exegetics
with such detachment. But in regard to this particular
point I desire to indicate the kind of value which, as it appears to me, any one endowed with the true instinct of a
historian must needs attach to the texts which Professor
Harnack sacrifices, and the considerations he neglects.

In the first place, he conceives that the famous text in
Matthew xvi. 18-19 is condemned "by all the rules of historical criticism" ("Entstehung," p. 3). To me, on the
contrary, this text appears to be in the strictest relation
with the plan of the first Gospel, and I note that criticism
is inclining to recognize, much more categorically than it
would have ventured to do as late as ten years ago, the
"ecclesiastical" character of the Gospel of St. Matthew, and
the interest it takes in the ἐκκλησία, in an ἐκκλησία
which is taught, and is governed by those who teach it,
above all by the Apostle Peter. The promise made by
Jesus to Peter (Matt. xvi. 18-19) is not then an intrusive
text, introduced into the narrative of Matthew surreptitiously, as an after-thought, and at a very late date, as Dr.
Resch contended; it is in close harmony with the spirit of
the first Gospel, as has been argued by no one better than

---

[1] Leipzig, 1910. An English translation of this work has since appeared under the title of "The Constitution and Law of the Church in
the First Two Centuries'. Translated by F. L. Pogson, M.A., edited by
H. D. A. Major, M.A.

by Dr. Wellhausen, unless it be Dr. Jülicher.[1] The fact is the first Gospel is by no means a document of uncertain origin. Professor Harnack this time has shown better than any one else that it has Palestine for its near horizon, that it is the work of the Palestinian Church now liberated from the Law and favourable to converts not of Jewish race, that it is a community-book, a "Gemeinde-buch"; that it keeps the community in the foreground, and might well be called the first liturgical book of the Christian Church, drawn up for it in the days when it had but recently disengaged itself from its Judeo-Christian bonds.[2] But if so, are we not entitled to infer that the promise of Jesus to Peter, through its incorporation in St. Matthew's Gospel, is attested as belonging to the Jerusalem tradition which went back to the first Christian generation? And if so, its claim to be historical, instead of having against it, "all the rules of historical criticism," has, in reality, nothing against it save that it oversteps the limits of what a certain system of exegetics, if it is to hold its ground, is able to accept in the contents of the recorded teaching of Jesus.

Secondly, Professor Harnack insists that, when we have set aside Matt. XVI. 18-19 as unhistorical, there remains no other direct external bond to connect Jesus with the Church, however we may strive to magnify the inappreciable by pleading the highly embryonic condition of the Church in the first hour of its existence. We must reply, however, that at least one other fact remains which Professor Harnack has acknowledged to be undeniable, namely

---

[1] J. WELLHAUSEN, "Einleitung in die drei ersten Evangelien" (Berlin, 1909), p. 70. A. JÜLICHER, "Einleitung in das Neue Testament," Tübingen, 1906), p. 265 : "He [the author of the first Gospel] has written a Catholic Gospel and it is its genuine Catholic character which gained for it the first place among the Gospels. . . . In it the fundamental elements of ancient Catholicism are ready prepared."

[2] A. HARNACK, "Lukas der Arzt" (Leipzig, 1906), pp. 118-20. "Neue Untersuchungen" (Leipzig 1911), p. 94.

that the disciples of Jesus and the men who believed in Him were those who formed the Church, and further that the " Twelve " had been appointed by Jesus to propagate His teaching and to be one day the judges of the " twelve tribes ". There remains too another fact equally undeniable, namely, the place held by Peter amongst the Twelve. Professor Harnack has observed that, in a purely Messianic perspective, there could have been no room for a chief among the Twelve, and this observation is just ; but from the time when Jesus was still with His disciples, Peter was the first, and was spokesman for the rest ; he was " an der Spitze," at the head. Again, just as in the Palestinian environment in which the Gospel of St. Matthew was edited, it was held to be certain that Jesus at Cæsarea Philippi had designated Peter as the rock on which He would build His Church, so in the Johannine environment it was held to be certain that the risen Christ had entrusted His flock to him that he might be its Pastor. Peter then had a unique office. Professor Harnack reproaches the " Protestant exegetists and historians for their disposition to underestimate the importance of the place held by Peter among the Apostles and in the primitive community " (" Entstehung," p. 6), but does he not himself underestimate it when he endeavours to explain this place of precedence by the natural qualities which can be ascribed to St. Peter ? Again, in the Christian community of the Apostolic age Professor Harnack finds that there must have been the following elements working—something of the communism of the Quakers, and of a " mild pneumatic anarchism," but likewise, as a counter-force, the Jewish spirit of order, of magistracy, of law, which was then all-potent, together with the ideal of the Kingdom of God which was striving for realization. By way of hypothesis, let us suppose that this was so. But Professor Harnack concedes to us that, in addition to the authority of the Old Testament from which this Jewish spirit was derived, there was potent also " the authority of the words of the Lord " which was the source of the maxims of the Christian life.   This is most true, but it is not all, and Professor Harnack further concedes to us that there was another and last element " the prerogative of the Twelve and the infallible authority (thanks to the abiding aid of the Holy Spirit) of the community '".   These were " *the absolute authorities which rigidly limited and curbed the liberty of the individual*," and assured the " conformity " of all (" Entstehung," p. 18).   This concession is of capital importance, but we must insist on its going a step further.   How could the prerogative of the Twelve have succeeded in establishing its own authority as an intermediary between authorities so holy and absolute, had it not been based on a commission emanating from Christ in person?

In this way then we can connect the Church with Christ through the Apostles.   The theory on which we rest may be " an old theory " but none the less it is valid, and Professor Harnack appears to have nothing better to substitute in its place than a peculiarly fragile modernity, for such surely is his theory that the Church came to its birth " automatically," being born of " the fraternal community of men who through Jesus had found God, of men who felt themselves to be led by the Spirit of God, and who, faithful to the theocratic ideal of the Jews, believed in its realization through Jesus " (" Entstehung," p. 3).   It is surely astonishing that these disciples of the first hour should have had a religious conscience so modern as to impel them " to find God through Jesus " (it is Ritschl's formula),[1] seeing that, as Jews and children of Abraham, they needed no longer to find God, but only to find the Messiah.   How too could their expectation of the realization of the kingdom, even

---

[1] W. Sanday, " Christologies Ancient and Modern " (Oxford, 1910), p. 82.

when eked out by the charismatic inspiration of individuals among them, give birth "automatically" to a society? But the real fact is these disciples believed that Jesus was the Messiah, the Son of God; and straightway they were in possession of a truth which caused their Judaism to strain and burst the bonds of its older organization, like new wine in an old bottle. It was this truth which was the immediate cause that created the fraternity which separated them from the other Jews, and rendered them indifferent to the privilege of being Jews; and it was in this truth and this fraternity that they found an authority in which that of Christ was continued, namely, that of the Apostles appointed by Christ. Thus from the very outset of its historical existence, Christianity was a formed faith, a visible society, a living authority.

\* \*
\*

Of these three terms, to which for the purposes of the present discussion we may limit the description of Catholicism, at all events in the abstract, the second is firmly maintained by Professor Harnack against Professor Sohm.

I have explained in my book (pp. 130, 143 and foll.) the position taken up by this eminent jurist in his "Kirchenrecht" (1892). Professor Harnack ("Entstehung," p. 122) does not hesitate to say that "next to the Catholic theory, that of Professor Sohm is the most coherent that has been propounded" as a solution of the problem of the Church's origins. Professor Sohm, I should add, has quite recently resumed his advocacy of this theory in a new essay.[1]

Professor Sohm's theory is a curious product of the Lutheran and juristic minds in combination. As a jurist he cannot but represent to himself Catholicism as a legal organism, the legitimacy of which is guaranteed by its his-

---

[1] R. Sohm, "Wesen und Ursprung des Katholizismus". Abhandlungen der Philol. Histor. Klasse d. K. Sächs. Gesellsch. d. Wiss. B. 27, H. 3 (1909).

torical continuity, which continuity, however, he assures us, is verified only in the Roman Catholic Church. Professor Sohm deduces the whole of Catholicism from one initial postulate, just as one deduces each separate corollary from one and the same theorem—for every jurist is in his way a geometrician. As a Lutheran, he postulates as the initial fact from which this logical development has issued a certain state of mental confusion which was not deliberate but arose inadvertently and inevitably. Primitive Christianity ("Urchristentum") could not fail to transform itself into Catholicism because it was not as yet in a condition to distinguish between the body mystical of Christ and the *corpus* or "empirical" association of the faithful among themselves. It had only one word, the word *ecclesia*, to denominate the invisible Church of faith, and that legal and contingent institution which is the visible Church. This supposed confusion involves that Christianity, though it passed thus quickly into Catholicism, was not Catholic at the very first; but, strange to say, when this confusion had arisen, "it was necessary to wait till Luther came, before the distinction, lost sight of so soon after the beginning, between the invisible and visible Church could be recovered."

Let us come, however, to a summary of the facts, to see how Professor Sohm presents them. The faith of the first believers, whether they were dispersed over the world, or resident in the same city, or gathered together in the same house, had, we are assured, its expression in the maxim: "Where two or three are gathered together in my name, there am I in the midst of them". Initial Christendom had no other conception of the Church than this, and that is why it knew only of the Church and not of the Christian community. But soon the presence of the Spirit of Christ begins to manifest itself by means of charismata: the Spirit inspires, the Spirit speaks, the faithful are taught and led by the Spirit, and he who has received the charisma of the

Spirit becomes the presbyter. It is then that for the first time the mutual interpenetration of the Spirit and the community reveals itself, and we touch upon the identification of the invisible with the visible. The order of legality is about to appear. The religious gatherings in which Christians came together " for the word " were delivered over to a " pneumatic anarchy "; but the gatherings in which they celebrated the Eucharist required that order should be observed, and hence that there should be a president, and ministers, and that there should be an investiture of offices : in short the life of the community required a hierarchy. As soon as this investiture came to be regarded as giving "the Spirit," Catholicism was born ; and this development was completed at the time when the " Prima Clementis " was written.

We perceive that for Professor Sohm the " Church " cannot rightly claim to be more than a purely religious, spiritual entity, a soul without a body; in proportion as it takes to itself a body it tends to become Catholic. There is this of piquancy in the theory that the larger the part in history it accords to " Catholicism," the more it requires of Lutheranism to liberalize and enfeeble itself. But there is also this of error in it that it represents the first Christian meetings as displays of " pneumatic anarchy "; for I have shown in my book (pp. 28-30) what part the outpourings of the Spirit took in that earliest phase of Christian life, and I have shown that the charismatic element appears invariably as one that is subordinated; and Professor Harnack has likewise said : " The reception of a charisma exempted no one from the necessity of having his mandate recognized and controlled by the community " (" Entstehung," p. 19). It is a further error in Professor Sohm's theory that it allows no place for the prerogative of the Apostles. The common life, he acknowledges, required a hierarchy, but what caused this common life to spring up? Was it not the

fruit of the apostolic preaching? And was the Apostolate a
charisma, and did it tolerate anarchy? All primitive history
answers, No. The gravest, however, of the errors into
which Professor Sohm falls is that of supposing initial Christianity to have been a soul without a body. Professor Harnack fastens on this error with a sharpness which is not
undeserved: Sohm, he says, may profess what faith he
pleases in regard to this point, but as for the Church of the
first hour being what he imagines, we can only say, No it
was not: had that Church been deprived of every terrestrial
element, what else could it have been "save a mere idea, the
object of the faith of each separate Christian in isolation from
all the others" ("Entstehung," p. 148). The reader who
will refer to my book (pp. 146, 151) will find that I have
not been more severe than Professor Harnack in my criticism
of this theory of the priority of the invisible Church, classical
as it has been up to the present day in the schools of Protestant scholasticism. But what an accession of force this
criticism now receives under the pen of Professor Harnack!
The invisible Church, he writes, is nothing more than a
*numerus praedestinatorum et credentium*, the units of which
are nothing for one another, more than are parallel lines
which only meet at infinity. He who speaks of a Church,
speaks of an assemblage, an assemblage of the called and
the chosen, and this implies "something of a social character, which is already a present reality on earth, for on
earth the called are the Church of God, and only in this
character have they intercourse with one another". In fact,
the word of Christ: "Where two or three are gathered together in my name there am I in the midst of them," turns
against Professor Sohm, since it promises that Christ will be
wherever there is a concrete society, even if it be one of only
two or three of His disciples; it is an invitation to join such
societies. Hence "to associate is for those who bear the
name of Christ not a secondary or unessential feature in the

*b* *

idea of the Church, it is a feature essentially involved in the idea itself which is only realized through the fact of the faithful thus associating themselves " (" Entstehung," p. 149). The Church is essentially visible and social.

Primitive Christendom is then a visible society, as Professor Harnack agrees with me in maintaining. Moreover, this visible society bears in its womb a living authority; a living authority, that is, by contrast with a written authority. This living authority, if we are to believe Professor Sohm, is nothing more than the outcome of an evolution of charismata; the gifts of the Spirit are transformed eventually into "liturgies," in the Greek sense of the term, that is, into local and permanent liturgies which become offices for life. The " Prima Clementis " reveals to us the evolution at this stage. But here again Professor Harnack is before us in his criticism. The " Prima Clementis " marks a very instructive moment in the development of the hierarchy, but it reveals to us "nothing which is essentially new". It claims an ecclesiastical right which is not of human origin but divine, since it declares that the office of the ἐπισκοπή is for life, in virtue of the divine will and the divine revelation. But in this respect the " Prima Clementis " does not differ from the decree of the Apostles in Acts xv. (" Entstehung," p. 159). In reality, concludes Professor Harnack, " the divine origin of ecclesiastical right is as old as the Church itself " (p. 161). I take note of this concession without however wishing to exaggerate its bearing; for this divine right which Professor Harnack opposes to Professor Sohm has over the human and contingent right imagined by the latter no other advantage than that of historical priority. Professor Harnack makes it as ancient as the Church, and makes " the Church " congenital with primitive Christianity, and this is a great advance on his part. Nevertheless this right which he claims to call divine springs, if thus conceived, only from the requirements of Christendom regarded as a visible society, and it springs from it merely as a legal and formal element that is necessarily postulated by the Christian life which has to propagate and establish itself. It is divine for this sole reason that the new religion is theocratic. Thus, ultimately, Professor Harnack does not, any more than Professor Sohm, stand for the doctrine of any such juridical organisation as the Christian life has required, as is clear from the formal assent he gives to this proposition which he quotes from Professor Sohm : " The natural desire of man is to externalize his religion " (p. 177). Man by his nature demands a law, an authority, and by demanding it he has created it ; such is the sense in which Professor Harnack speaks of divine right.[1] We, however, cannot but observe how full is the evidence that the Church from the first hour was a society under a government. It was not governed by any mere abstract authority ; or by the imperious requirements of charismata, which were variable, obscure, intermittent, always needing to be verified, quickly discredited ; nor by any statute spontaneously elaborated and embodying the experience of all the Churches, for such experience would have produced

---

[1] Professor Harnack has written elsewhere in the same book : "The Reformation [of the sixteenth century] not only destroyed the ecclesiastical constitution ('Kirchenverfassung') of the Middle Ages, but also broke off all connexion with the 'Kirchenverfassung' of the second and first centuries ". He adds : "The people of West Europe are still either Catholic or Protestant. *Tertium adhuc non datur.* It is Luther who created for them this alternative, and it is an alternative which concerns us more than all the philosophical and scientific culture of the present time, or all its technical applications. The people are, however, on the look out for a *tertium genus Ecclesiae* under which they may find shelter for their higher life " ("Entstehung," p. 120). It is indeed interesting to have from Professor Harnack this acknowledgment of the bankruptcy of the Reformation in regard to all its historical and religious pretensions, and this appeal from it to an unlimited modernism. For it is just what I myself said (Fourth French Edit. p. xiii) when I wrote the words against which Professor Harnack has protested : "This being the historical conception of the Church, Protestantism may claim to be a modern ideology, but it has in its essence nothing in common with the Infant Church ". But I have no wish to insist on these considerations.

only a universal variation; but by a living authority emanating we know from what quarter, and alone able to explain the unity of the institutions founded and the credit they enjoyed. The " Prima Clementis " declares all this in plain terms, and what else is the " Decree of the Apostles " save the most striking manifestation of the existence of this authority, and of the lawfulness of its claims?

The prerogative of the Apostles is then the true key to the question of the origin of the Church : by this prerogative is explained the initial fact that Christianity is a society and not a mere preaching, a society ordered and governed and not a " charismatic anarchy " ; by this prerogative is explained the fact that the preaching of the Gospel was fixed and defined as a " rule of faith " and as an " Apostolic tradition ". The second century did not create doctrinal statements at the bidding of its needs ; it only acquired a clearer understanding of those doctrines, of which the " presbyters " had preserved the remembrance. What Professor Sohm holds to have been an initial confusion, and Professor Harnack holds to have been an initial logic, we hold to have been a thing intended. Let the reader decide which of these three theories is most in accordance with the facts.

In treating of the Infant Church I have spoken of the rule of faith only in so far as it is of the nature of a rule, without touching on its contents, on the doctrines which the faith affirms, that being a subject the study of which belongs properly to the history of dogma. I do not overlook that in those histories of dogma which are the most widely circulated, " Catholicism " is described as the faith which found expression at the end of the second century, in a form which Professor Harnack is pleased to regard as the outcome of Hellenistic syncretism (" Entstehung," p. 184). I have not touched on this discussion, my purpose being to treat not of the object of this official ecclesiastical teaching, but of its essential character and origin. Professor Harnack, on the other hand, prefers to consider Catholicism under the former of these aspects. Let me take note, however, that, in his sketch of the main outlines of Tertullian's doctrine, which he takes as the expression of this Catholicism, he does not hesitate to write : " All these points of doctrine, as we can prove texts in hand, manifest their presence already in the first century and in the writings of the New Testament : the only difference is that some of them manifest it more distinctly, others more faintly. . . . Catholicism is thus, if we include in it its embryonic phases, as ancient as the Church itself." (" Entstehung," p. 182). I repeat that the question treated in this passage is as to the contents of the rule of faith ; moreover, affirmations of this kind when made by Professor Harnack are never unaccompanied by revisions and attenuations which must not be disregarded. If, however, we call attention to these particular affirmations, it is because they have their bearing on my own present thesis of the continuity and tenacity of the rule of faith in the Infant Church.

PARIS, 15 *March*, 1911.

# TABLE OF CONTENTS.

PAGE

INTRODUCTION TO THE FIFTH FRENCH EDITION (1911) . . . . . v

## CHAPTER I.

### THE JEWISH DISPERSION AND CHRISTIANITY.

I. Had the Judaism of the Dispersion any tendency to become a Church ?—
Legal and social status of the Dispersion—Religious and national
institutions—Jewish hellenization, nothing apart from the religious
and national life—Proselytism aims at imposing circumcision, and un-
circumcized proselytes do not belong to God's people—In what way the
body of proselytes paved the way for Christianity . . . . 1

II. Political confusion of Christianity with Judaism—In the year 64 this
confusion comes to an end—Testimony of Tacitus—Christianity is
legally forbidden—Pliny and Trajan—Nero, the first to interdict Christianity : testimony of Tertullian and of Suetonius . . . . 17

III. Christianity, no mere spiritual movement—Subordination of the outpourings of the Spirit, i.e. of charisms, to the good order of the communities and to the received faith—Christianity, no mere brotherhood
of love and of mutual aid—Christianity, a religion of cities—Christianity, not a religion of colleges—Christianity, a *religio illicita* and
a *corpus* or association . . . . . . . . 28

## CHAPTER II.

### THE INFANT CHURCH.

I. The apostolate of the first Christian generation, not an institution
borrowed from Judaism—Various meanings of the word *Apostle*—The
apostolate, not a charism—Notion of the apostolate, in St. Paul—The
Apostles of the circumcized—The Twelve—There are not three contradictory notions of the apostolate—The apostolate, a principle of
unity and authority laid down by Christ Himself . . . . 37

II. Churches and the Church in the first Christian generation—The earliest
missions to the Gentiles—The decree of the Apostles—Peter and Paul
at Antioch, and the principle of the unity of the new people in Jesus
Christ . . . . . . . . . . . . 55
    Christianity, not a "wisdom," but a catechesis—Notion of the de-
posit of faith, and of the Apostle as pledge for the divine authority of
the Gospel—The initiation, baptism in the name of Christ—Worship
in common, Sunday synaxis, Eucharist—Mutual supervision, expulsion of the sinner—Those who preside . . . . . . 64

PAGE

The assembly of the faithful of the same city, called a Church—The Churches of Christ—The Church of God—The Church, Christ's mystical body—The *tertium genus* inaugurated upon earth by Christianity . . . . . . . . . . . . 69

EXCURSUS A.

The Church in the Gospel, value of Matt. XVI. 18-19 . . . . . 75

## CHAPTER III.

### THE INFANT; CHURCH (CONTINUED).

I. The second Christian generation—The Pauline Epistles of the captivity —The saints, the *episcopi*, and the deacons of Philippi—Ecclesiology of the "Didachè—Ecclesiology of the "Prima Petri"—St. Paul's last instructions, ecclesiology of the Pastoral Epistles—Johannine ecclesiology . . . . . . . . . . . . . . 97

II. The Epistle of St. Clement of Rome—Transformation of the notion of charism—Discipline by means of authority—The received faith—The canon of tradition—The hierarchy—The intervention of Rome at Corinth—Criticism of Sohm's theory . . . . . . 122

III. The Epistles of St. Ignatius of Antioch—Discipline—The hierarchy— The unity of each Church—Heresy—The "dogmas" of the Lord and of the Apostles—The bishop makes the unity of each Church—Jesus makes the unity of the "Catholic Church"—The primacy of the Roman Church . . . . . . . . . . . . 131

Conclusion, the Infant Church is Catholic . . . . . 142

EXCURSUS B.

Critical examination of Protestant theories on the formation of Catholicism . . . . . . . . . . . . . . . 143

## CHAPTER IV.

### THE CATHOLICISM OF ST. IRENÆUS.

The ecclesiological principles of Irenæus, not his creation . . . 164

I. St. Polycarp of Smyrna: discipline and tradition—Solidarity of Churches —Irenæus and Polycarp—Anicetus and Polycarp—The *Martyrium Polycarpi* and the word "Catholic"—Papias: his notion of tradition —Hegesippus: succession of bishops, the justification of the tradition —Catholicity of tradition—Abercius: the same criterion of faith— Pantænus and the presbyters, on the true tradition—Is the epilogue of the Epistle to Diognetus by Pantænus?—The *Secunda Clementis* and the "Pneumatic" Church—Dionysius of Corinth and the Roman Church—Ecclesiology of the "Shepherd" of Hermas—St. Justin: the deposit of faith, apostolic tradition, heresies—The catholicity of the Church—Christendom, as seen by Celsus: heresies and the "great Church"—Synthesis of the preceding testimonies . . . 164

II. Importance of the ecclesiology of St. Irenæus—Catholicity and unanimity of Christendom—Sources of unanimity: the Prophets, the Lord, the Apostles—The succession of bishops authenticates the tradition of the Apostles—The Holy Ghost and the indefectibility of the Church—The primacy of the Roman Church—Criticisms of Gnosticism: it is a reaction against the existing Church—Synthesis of the principles of Irenæus . . . . . . . . . . . . . 197

PAGE
III. Contemporary facts—The Church and the spirit of prophecy—In what way Montanism is a novelty—How it is eliminated without any general crisis—The question of Easter—Conflict between Pope Victor and Polycrates of Ephesus—Nature of Victor's intervention . . . 217
Catholic and Roman, a criticism of Harnack . . . . . . 228

EXCURSUS C.

Marcionism and Catholicism . . . . . . . . . 230

EXCURSUS D.

The end of Judæo-Christianity . . . . . . . . . 238

## CHAPTER V.

### THE CASE OF CLEMENT OF ALEXANDRIA.

Clement's so-called characteristic . . . . . . . . . 246
Clement and the apostolic canon of the New Testament—Clement and the ecclesiastical canon of faith—The tradition of the Apostles, through the presbyters—Apostolicity of the episcopate—Presbyters, deacons and laity—The bishop's supremacy—The Church, a condition of salvation . . . . . . . . . . . . . . . 247
Unity and catholicity of the Church—Economy of Clement's doctrine; philosophy, faith, gnosis—Faith rests on authority and on tradition—Heresies are many, various, new—Clement does not depart from the common tradition . . . . . . . . . . . 254

## CHAPTER VI.

### TERTULLIAN'S VARIATIONS.

Tradition in Tertullian . . . . . . . . . . . 264
I. The treatise on prescription—Animosity against philosophy—The rule of faith—It is justified by tradition—Tradition is apostolic—Heresies are subsequent to the Apostles—The *praescriptio longi temporis*—Tertullian's argument, properly speaking, an argument of discussion, not of prescription—Bearing of Tertullian's discussion—Detailed features of Tertullian's ecclesiology—The hierarchical Church . . . 264
II. The evolution of Tertullian—Opposition between tradition and truth—The working of the Spirit in the Church—Revelation continued by the new prophecy—Rome condemns this principle—Tertullian's revolt—His invective against the hierarchy and against Callistus—New and anarchical character of Tertullian's paradox—Tertullian's final isolation . . . . . . . . . . . . . . 281

## CHAPTER VII.

### ORIGEN AND GREEK ORTHODOXY.

Doctrine, in Origen . . . . . . . . . . . . 295
The Church, a close society—The Church, a society in which there is a hierarchy—The bishop's supremacy—His eminent dignity—Duties of the clergy and their remissness—Origen's error regarding the subordination of the power of Orders to the holiness of the minister . . . 298

PAGE

The ecclesiastical doctrine is apostolic tradition—Canon of Holy Scripture—
Baptismal symbol—Living magisterium—Function of the *doctores*
*Ecclesiae*—Heretics or heterodox condemned in the name of tradition
—Refuted by the teaching of the *doctores*—Bishops, judges of doc-
trine . . . . . . . . . . . 319
Why Origen says "the Churches" rather than "the Church"—Analogy
between the Church and the city—Visible unity of all the Churches—
Origen and St. Peter's primacy—The Roman primacy . . . 322
Shortcomings of Origen's ecclesiology . . . . . . . 329

## CHAPTER VIII.

### ST. CYPRIAN AND ROME.

Tradition in St. Cyprian . . . . . . . . . . 332
I. Ecclesiastical organization in Cyprian's time—The *plebs* and the *ordo*—
The bishop, successor of the Apostles ; his election and supreme power
—Office of priests and deacons—Lectorate and minor orders—Maintenance of the clergy—Share of the *plebs* in the government of the
Church—The Church, a social community—Excommunication of the
disobedient and of sinners—Provincial councils—Had Carthage the
primacy in Africa?—Relations between the Churches of the whole
world—Unity of the whole episcopate—Is the hierarchical conception
of the Church peculiar to Cyprian? . . . . . . . 333
II. No reconciliation of the *lapsi*, without the bishop—The bishop, the
foundation of his Church—Outside the Church, no reconciliation, no
sacrifice, no priesthood—Revolt of Felicissimus at Carthage, and of
Novatian at Rome—The Council of Carthage (May, 251) condemns
Felicissimus—Cyprian writes the "De Unitate ecclesiae," against
Novatian and the Roman schism—Analysis of the treatise—The
Church, a condition for the validity of the sacramental powers—The
promise made by Christ to St. Peter—Imperfection of Cyprian's
ecclesiology . . . . . . . . . . . . 350
The two editions of the "De Unitate ecclesiae" . . . . . 366
III. Felicissimus appeals to Rome—Cyprian's protest—Claim of the Council
of Africa to supreme power in Africa—The case of the Spanish bishops
—The subordination of the power of Orders to the holiness of the
minister—The case of Marcianus of Arles—Cyprian's unexpected recourse to Rome—Gallicanism and Donatism in germ, in the doctrine
of the Africans . . . . . . . . . . . 373
IV. The baptismal controversy—Cyprian's position : outside the Church, no
baptism, because outside the Church, no Holy Ghost—Similar decision
of the Council of Carthage of 255 and 256—Rome declares against
Carthage—Pope Stephen's letter : reassertion of the Roman primacy,
and of the validity *ex opere operato* of baptism—Protest of the Council
of Carthage, in September 256—Rome lays the subject before the Catholic world—Firmilian unites with Cyprian against Pope Stephen—
Firmilian's ecclesiology—Death of Cyprian and of Stephen—Principles
raised by the baptismal controversy—Cyprian's contradictions : traditional character of Rome . . . . . . . . . 381
General conclusions . . . . . . . . . . . 403

# CHAPTER I.

## THE JEWISH DISPERSION AND CATHOLICISM.

### I.

PRIMITIVE Catholicism first impresses the historian as a dispersion of local churches, united by the identity of their faith and the solidarity, spiritual and social, which binds them all together. Considered under this aspect, it has considerable resemblance to that Judaism from which it detached itself in the course of the first century. The latter has even been looked upon as a sort of pre-existing Church, for critics who are averse to recognizing any ecclesiastical elements in the Christianity of the Apostolic Age, willingly speak of the " Jewish Church ". It is one of the themes of Bousset's brilliant book on the religion of Judaism in New Testament times.[1] Bousset has, it seems, already somewhat modified his views on the subject.[2] But whether or not the Judaism which was contemporaneous with the Gospel was a rough draft of the Church realized in Christianity, it is not without interest to compare the two. The study of those features in which they are alike, as well as those in which they differ, will conduce to a better understanding of the peculiar and original character of the new Dispersion.

\* \*
\*

The geographical expansion of Judaism has been brought into full light by recent critical studies. Palestine was now entirely judaized though this had been brought about only in the period of the Hasmonæan restoration, when Idumæa, Peræa, and Galilee were annexed to Judæa. But long be-

---

[1] W. BOUSSET, " Die Religion des Judentums in Neutestamentlichen Zeitalter " (Berlin, 1903).

[2] In the second edition of his book (Berlin, 1906). See the Preface, p. vii.

fore the Hasmonæan rule, the Jews had found their way into every part of the Hellenic world.

This spread of Judaism in the Greek cities began at the time of Alexander, and reached its climax in the age of Julius Cæsar and of Augustus: the time of Herod's rule was its Golden Age. There were jewries in all the Roman provinces washed by the Mediterranean and by the Black Sea; some could be found in Mesopotamia, Arabia, Babylonia, Media, so that, towards the year 140 B.C., a Jewish poet could write of his race this emphatic, but truthful verse: "Every land and every sea is filled with thee!"[1]

More than once scholars have drawn up statistics of this Jewish expansion by noting carefully the traces of the then existing jewries of the Dispersion, as revealed both by the texts of written works and by those of inscriptions.[2] A study of these statistics shows that the expansion of Judaism does not exactly coincide with the earliest expansion of Christianity. The centres are, indeed, the same for both: Antioch, Damascus, Smyrna, Ephesus, Thessalonica, Athens, Corinth, Alexandria, Rome; and how could it be otherwise? But there were regions where Judaism was already established —at Palmyra, Nisibis, Seleucia, Ctesiphon, on the shores of the Black Sea, in the interior and in the southern part of Egypt, and in Roman Africa—but where Christianity did not at first find a home.

A second point to be borne in mind is the numerical importance of the jewries of the Dispersion, especially in Syria and in Egypt, in the provinces of Asia Minor, and in Rome. It has been calculated that in the time of Philo the Jews made up a seventh of the whole population of Egypt; this writer estimates at one million the number of the Jews then dwelling in Egypt. During the reign of Tiberius, under pretext of forcing them into military service, some

---

[1] "Orac. Sibyll." III. 271: Πᾶσα δὲ γαῖα σέθεν πλήρης καὶ πᾶσα θάλασσα. Kautzsch, "Die Apokryphen und Pseudepigraphen des A. T." Tom. ii. (Tübingen, 1900), p. 190. Cf. Père LAGRANGE, "Le Messianisme chez les Juifs" (Paris, 1909), pp. 273-84.

[2] E. SCHÜRER, "Geschichte des jüdischen Volkes," vol. III.[3] pp. 2-70. See too, art. "Diaspora" in the extra volume of HASTINGS' "Dictionary of the Bible". HARNACK, "Mission und Ausbreitung des Christentums," second edition (1906), vol. I. pp. 1-16.

4000 Jews were banished from Rome to Sardinia: a fact from which we may conclude that the Jewish colony of Rome counted at least 10,000 men, besides the women and the children.   According to Harnack's calculations, the Jews formed above 7 per cent of the whole population of the Roman Empire under Augustus.   This numerical consideration, conjectural though it is, might account for the rapid expansion of Christianity in the Empire, if Christianity had spread easily and exclusively in the jewries.   But it is beyond dispute that, even as early as the year 64, the imperial legislation distinguished the Christians from the Jews; and this makes it clear that the Christians as a whole were no longer Jews by race, whilst it was on account of their race that the Jews formed a people apart.

Indeed, a third well-ascertained historical fact is that the Jewish population could not be absorbed or assimilated by the nations in whose midst it settled and grew.   Several centuries before, Aman had said to Assuerus : "There is a single people scattered and living apart from the other races in all the provinces of thy kingdom, and their laws differ from those of every race.   And it is not expedient for the King to tolerate them." [1]   The Jewish race was bound to a faith the rigorous prescriptions of which tended to isolate it : it forbade all part in idolatrous worship, "*gens contumelia numinum insignis,*" in the words of Pliny; [2] it forbade mixed marriages; it forbade Jews to frequent theatres, circuses, gymnasia, baths, to sit down at the same table as a Pagan, to enter military service, or to take charge of public affairs.   The Jews enjoyed many important legal privileges pertaining to the free exercise of their religion: they could meet in their synagogues, they could have their own judges who would pronounce according to their Law ; they could keep the Sabbath and practise circumcision; [3] but all these privileges made their isolation the greater. Finally, Antisemitism, which was even then abroad, and displayed itself in sarcasms, often in massacres or proscriptions,

---

[1] Esther III. 8.          [2] "Hist. Nat." XIII. 4, 46.
[3] On the legal status of Judaism, see SCHÜRER, vol. III. pp. 56-78. Cf. V. CHAPOT, "La province romaine proconsulaire d'Asie" (Paris, 1904), pp. 182-6.

set the seal on their exclusion. From whatever point of view they may be considered, the Jews, by reason of their race, formed a city within the city. "The Jews," says Strabo, "have places assigned them in Egypt, wherein they dwell apart; the quarter specially allotted to this nation at Alexandria is a large part of the city. There is also an ethnarch allowed them, who governs the nation, administers justice for them, supervises their contracts, and sees to the observance of their laws, just as if he were the ruler of an independent city."[1] The title *ethnos* or *laos*, the Jews actually claim in some inscriptions as the official name of their communities of Smyrna, and of Hierapolis, for instance.[2]

This thorough penetration of the race by its faith is a phenomenon of which Bousset does not seem to realize the full importance. In his eyes, the facts which characterize the transformation of Judaism into the Church are these: first, the dissociation of religion from the national life; next, the fact that this dissociation does not result in the establishment of pure individualism, but in the rise of community forms which are religious without being national; thirdly, the fact that these community forms overflow the boundaries of the nation. "It is only when these three symptoms manifest themselves that we can rightly speak of a tendency towards the formation of a Church."[3]

There seems to be in this statement some confusion between autonomy and national life. Under the Hasmonæan rule, the Jews enjoyed a kind of autonomy, which consisted in their being governed by princes of their own blood and faith; for them, these were the conditions of political legitimacy. But their national life was not bound up with these conditions; for according to the remark of the historian

[1] STRABO, quoted by JOSEPHUS, "Antiq.," XIV. 7. 2. TH. REINACH, "Textes d'auteurs grecs et romains relatifs au judaïsme" (Paris, 1895), p. 92. Notice, in the "Papyrus of Alexandria," published by BRUNET DE PRESLES, how the Jews of Alexandria complain before a Roman emperor (Commodus ? 181 ?) that their "king" had been ill-treated. This king of the Jews is a mere ethnarch. REINACH, p. 226.

[2] SCHÜRER, vol. III.[4] pp. 14 and 17.

[3] BOUSSET, "Religion des Judentums (1903)," p. 55. Harnack's "Dogmengeschichte," vol. I.[4] (1897), pp. 53-56.

Josephus,[1] the special characteristic of the Jewish people lay in the fact that its national constitution was neither monarchical nor oligarchical nor democratic, but theocratic. We must add, that this theocracy was not of necessity exercised by a prince, nor by an established and traditional body of priests; the Law alone was supreme; it alone exercised and expressed God's sovereignty; and since, leaving aside the case of individual defections, nothing whatever could part the Jews from the Law of God which ruled in its least detail their private, social, and religious life, it follows that there was for the Jews no possibility of separating their religion from their national life, to whatever corner of the world this life might immigrate.[2]

That the Jews emigrated so easily, and that, when once they had emigrated, they settled down and multiplied so fast without ever becoming absorbed by the surrounding population, is to be explained by the fact that, turning their back on any claim to political existence, they found everywhere what they sought—the possibility of living their own national life, i.e. a life in keeping with the institutions given by God to His people.

Unlike the Greeks, the Jews were, as a nation, the least liable to individualism. The more their religion isolated them from the nations in whose midst they dwelt, the more did it join them together among themselves: "*Quia apud ipsos fides obstinata,*" Tacitus writes, "*misericordia in promptu, sed adversus omnes alios hostile odium.*" [3] Everywhere treated with contempt, or threatened, they met together in separate quarters, so as more effectively to defend themselves and to help one another. They had their own synagogues where they met on the Sabbath. They had their own cemeteries where they were buried side by side.

In this way corporate institutions unforeseen by the Law forced themselves upon the Jews. Rightly do scholars

---

[1] "Contra Apion." II. 164-5 ; BOUSSET, p. 71.

[2] As to the supremacy of the Law, see SCHÜRER, vol. II.[3] pp. 305-12.

[3] TACIT. "Histor." v. 5. Compare the text of Philostratus in the Life of Apollonius of Tyana, v. 33 (REINACH, p. 176), and that of Quintilian, "Instit. Orat.," III. 7 (REINACH, p. 284). The same thought is found in St. Paul, 1 Thess. II. 15.

speak in this connexion of the synagogue service—any synagogue was also called "a prayer" (προσευχή),—a service
made up of prayer and teaching, a comparatively late institution, since it dated only from the second century B.C., and
yet an institution necessary for the existence of jewries both
in Palestine and among the Dispersion. Every synagogue
was ruled by a president (ἀρχισυνάγωγος), whose duty it was to
preside over the prayer, reading, and ministry of preaching:
a presidency which did not imply any priestly dignity. The
ruler of the synagogue was assisted by a servant, called ḥazan,
whose help was merely material. The ruler had charge
only of the religious services and was not the leader of the
jewry. In every jewry there were two kinds of existence,
the one religious, the other social: they interpenetrated each
other to such an extent that the term synagogue had actually become synonymous with that of nation (ἔθνος, κατοικία).
Hence in every synagogue there was a deliberative assembly
of the ancients (πρεσβύτεροι). These were men of note to
whom authority had been entrusted by the community itself:
they formed a board of temporal administration and of
judicature; they were the archons of the jewry (ἄρχοντες,
γέροντες). In large cities like Rome (Alexandria apparently
had a very exceptional organization) there were many synagogues; and each formed a distinct jewry, with its own
presbyteral board, its own chief presbyter, its own archons.[1]
These institutions were fashioned after the model of the
communal institutions of the Greek cities. Taken together,
synagogue and presbyteral board were inseparable institutions, at once religious and national, that had grown out of
the special conditions in which Jewish life was placed in the
Dispersion.

*\*
\*

Ever since it had spread in the midst of Hellenic civilization, and especially in Alexandria, Judaism had been constrained to present itself as a "wisdom" (σοφία), so as to
be able to defend itself and to find a place for itself. The
Jewish wisdom could claim to be more ancient than any
other wisdom. The synchronisms of Greek and Jewish

---

[1] SCHÜRER, vol. III.[3] pp. 44-51.

history laid the first foundations of universal history, and in this universal history everything contributed to set forth the wonderful antiquity of the Jewish people and its part in the rise of civilization. The contradictions of Greek philosophy and the absurdities of Greek paganism furnished the advantage of a striking contrast to the unity, purity and solidity of the Jewish faith, which, considered in its essential contents—its monotheism and its ethics—could claim to be the primitive and normal wisdom of mankind. In the eyes of unbiassed Greeks, the Jews were a "race of philosophers".[1] For three centuries, a school of Jewish thinkers—most unlike the Pharisees of Jerusalem—devoted the best efforts of their minds to this hellenization, to this universalizing of Judaism.[2] The Hebrew Bible, which until then had been a closed and inaccessible book for the Greeks, was translated into Greek during the third century. This was indeed a great novelty, which was held in the utmost abhorrence by the fanatic Zealots, nor did the version succeed in obtaining their approval even when it was supported by the legend of the Pseudo-Aristeas. But on the other hand, what a wonderful source of new ideas it proved for the Greeks! The Hellenizing Jewish exegetes rivalled one another in exploiting it by interpreting it. During the second century, Aristobulus, one of the Alexandrian commentators and philosophers, gave currency to the idea that the leading masters of Greek philosophy, Heraclitus, Pythagoras and others, were merely the disciples of Moses: a suggestion which was destined to appeal rather too much to Clement of Alexandria. This was, according to Bousset, the fundamental dogma of Judaism thus hellenized: and to confirm it, Jewish scholars attributed to Orpheus, Homer, Hesiod, Pindar, Æschylus, Sophocles, Euripides . . . many apocryphal or adulterated texts, in which these poets were made to agree with Moses, for the greater glory of Judaism. Allegorism, applied to the Biblical narratives,

---

[1] REINACH, p. 8, text of "Porphyry" quoting THEOPHRASTUS (3rd cent. B.C.); p. 40, text of Hermippos of Smyrna (same cent.). Cf. VARRO, quoted by St. Augustine, "De Civ. Dei," IV. 31 (REINACH, p. 242). ORIGEN, "Contra Celsum," IV. 51.

[2] SCHÜRER, vol. III.[3] pp. 304 and ff. P. WENDLAND, "Die hellenistich-römische Kultur" (Tübingen, 1907), pp. 109 and foll.

completed this work of hellenization. Those interpreters who still clung to the literal sense were "μικροπολῖται" ("citizens of small countries"), small countries being much given to myth-making: the allegorizing Jews, on the contrary, like the Stoics, were "citizens of the world". "One word sums up Philo's purpose, when he uses the allegorical method: the universalization of the Jewish Law."[1] And Philo, who is a contemporary of Jesus, Philo who is an encyclopædist, represents this new Judaism at its best.

There was in Judaism another, deeper tendency: the tendency more and more to minimize the part of worship. It would be a mistake to look upon this as a result of hellenization. It is beyond question that the worship monopolized by the Temple, became every day less and less attractive, in proportion as the religious service conducted in the synagogues became the true aliment of Jewish piety. However, with this phenomenon hellenization had nothing to do, for piety without altars was against the tendency of the Greek mind: it had arisen out of the historical conditions in which the Jews had been placed at the time when the Temple was in ruins, out of the fact of the Dispersion itself, and also from the very ancient and most religious sentiment that mercy is better than sacrifice. Nor was the unpopularity of the priests of Jerusalem a consequence of hellenization—but the reaction of Pharisaism with its political and doctrinal grievances against the Sadducees, who had then full control of the Priesthood. On the other hand, whilst the Temple and the Priesthood gradually lost their influence and eventually disappeared—a disappearance which did not at all shake the faith of Judaism—the personal duties imposed by the Law, such as circumcision, kept all their hold, nor were they affected in any way by hellenization, even though the latter tried to discover an allegorical meaning for them.[2] In this way hellenization shows what it truly was, a philosophy of religion within religion itself.

Pharisaic Judaism claimed to be in possession of the key of knowledge and of the chair of Moses: it rested its

[1] E. Bréhier, "Les idées philosophiques et religieuses de Philon d'Alexandrie" (Paris, 1908), p. 65.

[2] Bousset, p. 110.

claim on a tradition, which, by means of a continuous succession, was traced back to Moses himself, through Josue, the Ancients, the Prophets, the Great Synagogue and its latest representatives, among whom Simon the Just, his disciple Antigonus of Socho, and later on Hillel and Shammai, were to be numbered. This was the essence of Rabbinism : it stood by a tradition untouched by speculation or criticism or increment, and hence without life, and yet not without an imposing and respectable authority, which no Jew ever dreamt of disobeying, so severely might the disobedient be dealt with ! [1]

Hellenized Judaism had none of these features ; and, even though it had also a theology, theologians, and a theological literature, yet that theology had not the authoritative character of the Palestinian theology ; on the contrary it was a kind of private concern, and, in this respect, did not differ from popular Greek philosophy : it was something spontaneous, brought about by the need of defining the Jewish position in presence of Hellenism ; it was an argumentative defence of that position, and the apologists had become the intellectual leaders of the Dispersion, even though they had been invested with no other authority than that conferred on them by the confidence of general opinion. As regards authority, Aristobulus and Philo cannot be compared with Hillel and Shammai, still less with Melito and St. Irenæus : we can compare them at most with St. Justin, who was a philosopher and a layman.

We may then rightly conclude that hellenization was an intellectual current in Judaism, caused by Hellenic civilization, but that this current did not amount to a schism apart from the national and religious life of the Jews of the Dispersion.

\* \*
\*

[1] See the prayer against heretics, the *Birkath ha-Minim*, in the *Shmone Esre*, i.e. the daily prayer of the pious Jews, of which the redaction may date from the year 80-100. SCHÜRER, vol. II.[4] p. 961. Lagrange, " Messianisme," p. 294, and Hönnicke, " Das Judenchristentum " (Berlin, 1908), p. 381. Regarding the "dogma of tradition," as it is called by Bousset, see BOUSSET, pp. 133-6, and LAGRANGE, pp. 137-47. On the heretics of the Synagogue, FRIEDLÄNDER, " Synagoge und Kirche in ihren Anfängen " (Berlin, 1908), pp. 64-78.

There still remains proselytism: does it not represent a peculiar Jewish status distinct from Jewish national life?

At the most prosperous period of the Dispersion, the proselytes, i.e. the Gentiles who embraced the Jewish faith, constituted in every jewry an important element. For the Jew had but to read the Prophets, to perceive that in his Law he could find the light that was to enlighten the Gentile world. Conscious as he was of the superiority of his Law, he looked upon the conversion of a Greek to Judaism as a recognition of this superiority. Hence both Pharisees and Hellenists rivalled each other in propagandism. " Thou who art called a Jew and restest in the Law, and makest thy boast of God, and knowest His will, and approvest the more profitable things, being instructed by the Law; thou who art confident that thou thyself art a guide of the blind, a light of them that are in darkness, an instructor of the foolish, a teacher of infants, having the form of knowledge and of truth in the Law; thou therefore that teachest another, teachest not thyself! . . . Thou that abhorrest idols committest sacrilege! Thou that makest thy boast of the Law, by transgression of the Law dishonourest God!"[1] Although less than the number of those who had been initiated into the worship of Isis or of Mithra, the number of proselytes was very great. These proselytes, it is true, constituted a more or less fluctuating and uncertain category: for, as we know from Josephus himself, many did not persevere. Nevertheless, there were proselytes in èvery synagogue. When St. Paul at Antioch of Pisidia calls his hearers: " Children of the stock of Abraham, and whosoever among you fear God," let us bear in mind that these φοβούμενοι τὸν θεόν are proselytes.[2] The author of the Acts also gives them the synonymous title of σεβόμενοι [τὸν θεόν], which is found quite often in the inscriptions.[3]

[1] Rom. II. 17-23.

[2] Acts XIII. 16, 26, 43, 50. See also Acts x. 2, 22, XVI. 14, XVII. 4, 17, XVIII. 7. Cf. A. DEISSMANN, " Licht vom Osten " (Tübingen, 1908), p. 326.

[3] SCHÜRER, vol. III. pp. 115, 124. See also J. LÉVI, " Le prosélytisme juif " in the " Revue des études juives," vol. L. (1905) and vol. LI. (1906).

These pagans converted to the fear of Yahweh were not indeed proselytes in the rabbinical sense of the term. The latter, few in number it is believed, were those who had submitted to circumcision and strictly kept the Law. They were in fact incorporated into the Jewish people. "Yea, I testify to every man that receiveth circumcision that he is a debtor to do the whole Law," St. Paul says to the Galatians.[1]  These converts who have been circumcised and who live up to their faith, are the "proselytes of right-eousness," the only genuine proselytes, the only ones who are admitted "under the wings of the Shechina!"[2]

To be incorporated into the people of Israel, such prose-lytes had to submit to circumcision, to offer sacrifice in the Temple, and to pass through a kind of baptism.  It goes without saying that circumcision was only for men, and that the obligation to sacrifice ceased altogether, after the ruin of the Temple.  But what was this baptism?[3]

We must confess that the texts in which it is mentioned enter into few details and are not always very reliable.  See-berg brings forward a description of the proselyte's initiation taken from the treatise *Jebamoth* of the Talmud which dates, at the earliest, from the third century of our era.  He cites also another description taken from the treatise *Gerim*, and dating from the second half of the second century.  These two descriptions agree: in both the candidate has to answer some questions regarding the status and condition of the Jews, which he is about to embrace; after his answers, he is

---

[1] Gal. v. 3.  SCHÜRER, vol. III. pp. 127-8 opposes the view which identifies the σεβόμενοι with the "proselytes of the gate". The "prose-lytes of the gate" are the pagans who dwell within the confines of Israel and who must observe those precepts of the Law which regard the Gentile world. Then, too, the expression "proselytes of the gate" is comparatively recent: it is not found in the Rabbinical literature before the thirteenth century.

[2] B. Meinertz, "Jesus und die Heidenmission" (Münster, 1908), pp. 42, 43.

[3] Regarding the baptism administered by John the Baptist, Origen writes : "Christus a Ioanne baptizatus refertur, non eo baptismate quod in Christo est, sed eo quod in lege est" ("Comment in Rom." v. 8). The ablutions performed by the Jews were also called "baptisms". Cf. Luke, XI. 38, and GRENFELL-HUNT, "Fragment of an Uncanonical Gospel" (Oxford, 1908), pp. 15-17.

circumcised, then immediately passes through a bath, which is styled by the treatise *Gerim* " a bath of levitical cleansing," or " a bath of cleansing ". In the treatise *Jebamoth*, there are recorded the answers of R. Eliezer and of R. Josua, two rabbis who lived about the year A.D. 100. The former says: " A proselyte, who is circumcised but not baptized, is already a proselyte, for we know regarding our fathers, that they were circumcised, but not that they were baptized." The latter says: " Whoever is baptized, but not circumcised, is already a proselyte, for we know regarding our mothers, that they were baptized, but not circumcised." The wise men conclude: " Any one who is baptized, but not circumcised, and any one who is circumcised, but not baptized, is not a proselyte, so long as he is not circumcised and baptized ".[1]

Those sayings of R. Eliezer and of R. Josua seem to imply that this " baptism " was not a very ancient institution, since R. Eliezer alleges that his " fathers " were only circumcised. The solution given by the " wise men " is a conciliatory solution, a compromise between the practice of baptism and the rejection of baptism. Would it not seem that the dispute about the necessity of baptism took place at the time of R. Eliezer and of R. Josua, i.e. toward the year 100 ? A fact of capital importance in this connexion is the silence of Philo and of Josephus:[2] from it we may conclude that baptism had not in their times the importance which it acquired later on owing perhaps to the rivalry of Christianity and of Mithraism.

---

[1] A. SEEBERG, "Das Evangelium Christi " (Leipzig, 1905), pp. 98-101. W. Brandt, "Die jüdischen Baptismen " (Giessen, 1910), pp. 57-62 and SCHÜRER, vol. III. p. 129 and ff.

[2] A text of Arrian (about 150), "Dissert. Epicteti," II. 9, is quoted (REINACH, p. 155): ὅταν δ' ἀναλάβῃ τὸ πάθος τὸ τοῦ βεβαμμένου καὶ ᾑρημένου, τότε καὶ ἔστι τῷ ὄντι καὶ καλεῖται Ἰουδαῖος. " But if any one adopts the mode of life required of one who has been baptized and elected, then is he really a Jew and entitled to be called such." REINACH remarks that the exact meaning of this phrase is disputed ; and he is inclined to think that in it there is a confusion between the Jews and the Christians. A verse of the " Oracula Sibyllina," (IV. 165) is also quoted as referring to the Jewish baptism ; but it is rather vague. Still more so is the allusion of the Epistle of Barnabas (XI. 1). Cf. LAGRANGE, "Messianisme," p. 281.

In reality, a pagan became a Jew only through circumcision.[1]  But baptism was also necessary.  He who received circumcision was still legally impure, until he was baptized, even were he born of Jewish parents.  This resulted from his having been uncircumcised.  There is a rabbinical answer[2] to the following case: supposing a Gentile is circumcised on the eve of the Passover, may he eat the Pasch on the morrow?  Yes, the school of Shammai answers: he takes the bath and he eats the Pasch.  No, the school of Hillel replies, for whoever has just come forth from the state of incircumcision is like one who comes forth from the grave: which means that he is unclean for seven days (Num. xix. 16).  In the eyes of a Jew, a pagan was unclean: therefore, before circumcision could incorporate him into God's people, he must needs be purified by means of an ablution.

Since, then, these proselytes, now become Jews, and Jews most faithful to the religious practices of Judaism, these proselytes of righteousness, are incorporated into the Jewish people and are no longer distinct from it, we cannot say that they form a church: as yet we have only a people.

*<br>* *

Shall we find an incipient church in the group of those who are proselytes in the broader sense of the word, i.e. those who are not circumcised, and who do not practise the Law in all its strictness?

Here, Jewish propagandism found a powerful help in hellenization, which set forth Judaism as the most ancient of all systems of wisdom, cared but little for worship and ritual, and professed what was essential in the Jewish faith— monotheism and moral righteousness.  In this the religious-minded Greek found a justification of his own revolts against mythology and polytheism: "*Iudaei mente sola unumque numen intellegunt. . . . Igitur nulla simulacra urbibus suis nedum templis sistunt: non regibus haec adulatio, non Caesaribus honor.*"[3]  Considered merely in these essential

---

[1] Cf. Petronius (a contemporary of Nero), quoted by REINACH, p. 266.
[2] SCHÜRER, vol. III. p. 131, note 86.
[3] TACIT. "Hist." v. 5.

teachings, Judaism gave more than philosophy, for while it was philosophical it did not cease to be a religion. It had the attractiveness of a negation although it remained a positive faith. Judaism has been compared by some to the oriental worships, those of Isis, of Sabazios, and of Mithra, for instance, which recruited so many followers in the Greek and Roman world ; but the comparison is hardly appropriate : it would be much nearer to the truth, to say that Judaism was a reaction against these licentious and mythological worships, against these worships replete with pompous ceremonies and displays that appealed to the senses. As conceived and propounded by its hellenizing apologists, Judaism was far more like Stoicism, but a Stoicism imbued with the idea of God and bound to certain observances without which there can be no external religion.

According to the historian Josephus, the Sabbath-rest was everywhere observed by some, both in Greek cities and among the barbarians : this he says was also the case with fasting and precepts regarding food.[1] This penetration of heathen environments by Jewish customs, is described in the passage of Seneca quoted by St. Augustine : *" Cum interim usque eo sceleratissimae gentis consuetudo convaluit, ut per omnes iam terras recepta sit, victi victoribus leges dederunt. . . . Illi tamen causas ritus sui noverunt : maior pars populi facit quod cur faciat ignorat."* [2]

From this it may be inferred that, in the eyes both of Josephus and of Seneca, it is a question of a mere " infiltration " of the Jewish customs into Greek, barbarian, or Roman surroundings. On the other hand, what we are inquiring after is a real adhesion to Judaism as characterizing this broader species of proselytism.

One case of this kind we find in Juvenal : the case of a Roman who keeps the Sabbath and abstains from pork : this Roman is a φοβούμενος τὸν θεόν : he is called *metuens* by Juvenal. The son of this *metuens* embraces Judaism. He has himself circumcised, he gives up Roman ways altogether,

[1] "Contra Apion." II. p. 282. Cf. the texts of Tibullus and Ovid, quoted by REINACH, pp. 247-9, FRIEDLÄNDER, pp. 34-5, LAGRANGE, p. 276.
[2] SENECA, *apud* AUGUSTINE, "De Civ. Dei," VI. 11 (REINACH, p. 262). Cf. TERTULLIAN, "Ad Nation." I. 13.

and knows no other law than that of the Jews: he hates any one who is not a Jew.

*Non monstrare vias eadem nisi sacra colenti!*

This son is a true proselyte of righteousness, duly incorporated into the Jewish people, whereas his father was a Jew but vaguely.[1]   A similar contrast can be seen in the history of the conversion of the king of Adiabene, Izatis.[2]   At the preaching of a Jewish merchant named Ananias, Izatis becomes converted to the Jewish faith and wishes to be circumcised.   But Ananias tells him that to observe God's commandments is more important than to be circumcised, and that even without that ceremony one can be a good Jew.   Some time later, a Galilæan Jew, named Eleazar, finding the king reading the Pentateuch, shows him, by texts, that he cannot observe the Law unless he be circumcised. Izatis yields to Eleazar's persuasions and is circumcised. At Cæsarea, we find Cornelius, a centurion of the cohort Italica, who is not a Jew, since he is engaged in the military service.   However, he is "a religious man and fearing God" (εὐσεβὴς καὶ φοβούμενος τὸν θεόν), with all his house, giving much alms to the people, and always praying to God.  He is a just man, and "one that feareth God (δίκαιος καὶ φοβούμενος τὸν θεόν), and having good testimony from all the nation of the Jews at Cæsarea" (τοῦ ἔθνους τῶν ᾿Ιουδαίων): when he is visited by the Apostle St. Peter, he invites to his house, "his kinsmen and special friends".[3]   When Peter goes back to Jerusalem, some will upbraid him vehemently for having entered the house of one who does not belong to God's people and is unclean: "Thou didst go into men uncircumcised, and didst eat with them!"[4]

These are three striking and typical instances of proselytism in the broad sense, as opposed to the proselytism of righteousness: the person attached to Judaism in this sense

---

[1] JUVENAL, "Sat." XVI. 96-106 (REINACH, pp. 292-3).   LAGRANGE, p. 278.

[2] JOSEPH. "Antiq." XX. 2, 4.   SCHÜRER, vol. III. p. 119.   LAGRANGE, p. 280.

[3] Acts x. 2, 22, 24.

[4] Acts XI. 1, 3.   Compare SUETON. "Domitian," 12 (REINACH, p. 333).

is not circumcised and does not keep the Law in its rigour, but he professes monotheism and is pious, i.e. has nothing to do with heathenism, fulfils the moral precepts of the Law, and observes some of its prohibitions.  Still, well as he may be disposed towards the Jews, and well as the Jews may be disposed towards him, he remains an unclean alien. This kind of interdict ceases only when he accepts circumcision and the whole Law.

Shall we look upon this floating contingent—which after all is not acknowledged by Judaism—as a spiritual society, as a church?   This multitude, which so rouses our sympathy, was, in the eyes of authentic Judaism, alien and unclean. Shall we identify it with Judaism and call it a Jewish Church?   To do so would be a mere abuse of words.

*
* *

Hence, what is true is most probably this.   Historical Judaism, that best typified by the Pharisees, was based on the idea of a People and on that of the Law: a man either was or was not a child of Abraham, either did or did not observe the Law of God, the whole Law.

Hellenized Judaism had indeed the intuition of a religious universalism: but it conceived it less as a reformed faith than as a defence of the traditional faith, an argument that was meant to command the respect of the Greeks. As some one has fitly observed, hellenized Judaism defended its religion *by means of* Hellenism, whilst Pharisaism defended its religion *against* Hellenism.   Hellenized Judaism did not broaden the idea of a People of God any more than it restricted the function of the Law; whilst proselytism was an application of that apologetical idea and like it ended in imposing circumcision.   Any one who did not ultimately submit to the latter, was an "allophylian," an unclean person, because the People of God and its Law were supreme.

Proselytism was destined to survive the ruin of Jerusalem only by a few years.   The recollections of it that survived in the Talmudic tradition are not unlike the recollections which Conservatives preserve of those Liberal tendencies and movements which they had once feared would succeed. R. Helbo, a Palestinian rabbi of the third century, writes:

"Proselytes are as painful for Israel as is leprosy for the skin,"[1] and Helbo's view was not solitary.

At the same time it cannot be doubted that these proselytes who were drawn to Judaism by its teaching about God and its ethical doctrine, formed a class well prepared—although they were not the only class so prepared—and disposed to esteem the Church: the Puritan exclusivism of Judaism contributed to make the Church the more desirable, precisely because it was not itself a Church.

## II.

Tacitus has gathered and summed up in a few lines the history of the beginnings of Christianity: "*Auctor nominis eius Christus Tiberio imperitante per procuratorem Pontium Pilatum supplicio adfectus erat ; repressaque in praesens exitiabilis superstitio rursum erumpebat, non modo per Iudaeam originem eius mali, sed per Urbem etiam, quo cuncta undique atrocia aut pudenda confluunt celebranturque*".[2]    Christus, after whom the Christians are called, was condemned to death, under Tiberius, by the procurator Pontius Pilate.    Repressed then, this execrable superstition was again overflowing—about the year 64, under Nero—not only in Judæa where it had arisen, but in Rome itself, where all forms of wickedness and infamy flow in and find adepts.

We cannot take in its strict meaning this statement of Tacitus, who, because of his great artistic taste, is always to be suspect of artificial composition and presentation.    In this particular instance, he describes the facts as though, from the death of Jesus to the burning of Rome in 64, Christianity had passed through a protracted period in which it was apparently crushed, and then, a short while before the year 64, had suddenly begun to expand, not only in Judæa but even at Rome.    That Christianity suddenly expanded, is not correct; what is correct is that, towards the year 64, Christianity appeared as distinct from Judaism.

Roman legislation did not allow freedom of worship.

---

[1] Lévi, vol. li. pp. 1 and 5.    Lagrange, p. 270.
[2] Tacit. " Annal." xv. 44.

Tertullian mentions an ancient law, "*vetus decretum*," which forbade the Emperor to sanction the worship of any god, without the previous assent of the Senate:[1] he may allude to the law quoted by Cicero: "*Separatim nemo habessit deos ; neve novos sive advenas, nisi publice adscitos privatim colunto*".[2] Hence even domestic worship was subject to the interdiction. Still great was the practical tolerance shown, less prompted by irreligion than by the fear of angering unknown divinities by the ill-treatment of their followers. But Christianity could not expect that tolerance, precisely because the heathen looked upon the new religion as a kind of atheism.[3] The profession of Christianity was long an heroic risk as much as it was an act of faith, and we cannot properly understand the special character of the Christianity of the first three centuries unless we see in it an exhortation to martyrdom.[4] But, before the year 64, it spread under the shadow of the laws that protected Judaism, with which so far it had been confounded.

As a proof of the primitive confusion of Judaism with Christianity, we may mention a fact related as follows by Suetonius in his "Vita Claudii": "*Iudaeos impulsore Chresto adsidue tumultuantes Roma expulit*".[5] This statement of Suetonius is confirmed by the Acts of the Apostles (XVIII. 2). On leaving Athens, St. Paul arrives at Corinth, and there he "finds a certain Jew named Aquila, a native of Pontus, lately come from Italy, with his wife Priscilla, *because Claudius had commanded all the Jews to depart from Rome*". The expulsion of the Jews from Rome may have dated from the year 51 or 52. The assertion of Suetonius is obscure only as regards the mention of the instigator, named Chrestus. Some have proposed to take these words

---

[1] TERTULL. "Apolog." 5.   Cf. Acts XVI. 21.

[2] CICERO, "De legib." II. 8.   The religious policy of the Romans is strikingly expressed in a speech attributed to Mæcenas when addressing Augustus, in DION CASSIUS, "Hist. roman." LII. 36 (Dion wrote about the year 240).   Cf. G. BOISSIER, "La religion romaine," vol. I. p. 347.

[3] "Martyr. Polycarpi," 9 : Christians are insulted with the cry, "Away with the atheists !"

[4] HARNACK, "Die Mission und Ausbreitung," vol. I. p. 404.

[5] SUETON. "Claud." 25.

literally, and have conjectured that some person of the name of Chrestus—a name which was quite common among slaves or freedmen—had perhaps raised a riot among the Jews, his co-religionists.[1]  Others incline to believe that Suetonius mistook the name *Chrestus* for *Christus*—as a matter of fact, Tertullian charges the Romans with pronouncing wrongly *Chrestianus*.[2]  Some controversies probably arose in the jewries of Rome, about "the author of the" Christian "name," controversies like those which, as we know from the book of the Acts, the introduction of Christianity caused in all the jewries.[3]

If then, as is generally held, the Roman jewries were deeply disturbed by the introduction of Christianity, *impulsore Chresto*, the fact that Claudius re-established order, by banishing the Jews from Rome—and with them the Christians, like Aquila and Priscilla—proves that the Roman police had not as yet come to distinguish the Christians from the Jews or was unwilling to take cognizance of what distinguished them.  Viewed in the same light, what occurred at Corinth at the same time or shortly after, is most significant.  When St. Paul was dragged by the ruler of the synagogue and by the Jewish Zealots before the proconsul— Annaeus Novatus Gallio, the brother of Seneca—and was charged with being an apostate from the Law, the proconsul said: "Jews, these are questions about your own Law,

---

[1] REINACH, "Textes," p. 329.  True, Χρηστός is not an uncommon name in the Greek onomasticon.  But, were this the name of some obscure personage, Suetonius would probably have written, "impulsore Chresto quodam," or omitted it altogether.  Cf. Philip. I. 15-18: τὸν Χριστὸν κηρύσσουσιν. . . . Χριστὸς καταγγέλλεται.  The *jeu de mots* (χριστός—χρηστός) is found again in St. Justin, "Apol." 41 ; in Theophilus, "Ad Autolyc." I. 1 : perhaps already in 1 Petr. II. 2, 3.

[2] TERTULL. "Apol." 3 : ". . . perperam Chrestianus pronuntiatur a vobis, nam nec nominis certa est notitia penes vos. . . . "  In the text of TACITUS, "quos vulgus christianos adpellabat," a recent revision of the manuscript shows that we must read *chrestianos* (HARNACK, "Mission," vol. I. p. 348).  TACITUS meant to say that the common people said *chrestiani*, but the founder of the sect was called *Christus*.

[3] Acts xxv. 19.  EUSEB. "H. E." II. 17. 1, records a legendary rumour according to which, in the time of Claudius, Philo, then in Rome, had an interview with St. Peter who was preaching the gospel to the Romans.

look to them yourselves; I am not minded to be a judge in these matters ".[1]

On the contrary, some ten years later, the separation of the Jews from the Christians had taken place; and this tends to show, on the one hand, that most of the recruits of Christianity were no longer of Jewish birth, and, on the other, that the Jews themselves had not only obtained the repeal of the edict of expulsion, enacted against them at Rome by Claudius, but had even profited by Nero's favour to forestall any return of the confusion which had caused them so much trouble. How clear the distinction had become we may see from the events of the year 64.

On July 19, A.D. 64, a fire broke out in the neighbourhood of the Great Circus, at Rome: for six days and seven nights, it raged in the Velabrum, the Forum, and a part of the Palatine; then it started again at the other end of the city, and within the space of three days laid waste the Quirinal, the Viminal, and the Campus Martius. Out of the fourteen sections of the city, only four were spared, among them those (the Capena Gate and the Trastevere) where the Jewish element was predominant. In their intense excitement, the people accused Nero of setting fire to Rome in order to have an opportunity of remodelling the plan of the city. Anxious to put an end to these rumours, the Emperor "announced as the true culprits and visited with the most cruel punishments those who were called Christians by the mob and are hated for their moral enormities ".[2]

Even though they suffered least from the fire, the Jews were not suspected for an instant of having started it; but the accusation fell on the Christians:[3] they were, then, notoriously and personally distinct from the Jews. Some Christians were seized, and unhesitatingly confessed they were Christians; then, a very large multitude of the dis-

---

[1] Acts XVIII. 12-17. Cf. XXIII. 29. In Acts XXIV. 5, the rhetorician Tertullos denounces to Felix the Apostle Paul as the leader of "the seditious sect of the Nazarenes". For him Christianity is but a Jewish sect.

[2] TACIT. "Annal." xv. 44.

[3] HARNACK, "Mission," vol. I. pp. 51, 400, surmises that Nero punished the Christian community at the instigation of the Jews.

ciples of Christ was gradually found: "*Igitur primum correpti qui fatebantur, deinde indicio eorum multitudo ingens, haud perinde in crimine incendii, quam odio humani generis coniuncti sunt*".[1]    This name Christian is not unknown to the rabble: they are those "*quos per flagitia invisos vulgus Chrestianos adpellabat*".    Theirs is an odious name, associated with wicked and infamous deeds: the definite complaints made against it do not recall the popular grievances against the Jews.    We no longer hear of a race which is hated and persecuted, and which can easily be recognized because of its peculiar customs and physiognomy; but of a worship which is owned (*fatebantur*) or denounced (*indicio*).    The Christians are an immense and defenceless multitude; while the Jews live apart, and their race is both a sign by which they can be recognized and a title to protection.    Tacitus, who wrote about the year 115, had for the chief source of his narrative of Nero's reign, a history, now lost, of that reign, composed by Cluvius Rufus in the time of Galba and of Vespasian, i.e. between the years 68 and 79.[2]    The testimony of Tacitus receives a confirmation from the authority of its source.

The same testimony is also confirmed by a passage that many believe to be taken from the lost fragment of the "History" of Tacitus—which is found in the "Chronicle" of Sulpitius Severus.    In a meeting held on August 9, 70, the eve of the burning of the Temple of Jerusalem, Titus puts the question whether or not the Temple is to be destroyed: several of his officers agree with him in considering the destruction expedient, in order more completely to do away with the religion both of the Jews and of the Christians: "*Quo plenius Iudaeorum et Christianorum religio tolleretur: quippe has religiones, licet contrarias sibi, iisdem tamen ab auctoribus profectas: Christianos ex Iudaeis extitisse: radice sublata, stirpem facile perituram*".[3]    Here we have another and still more explicit affirmation both of the Jewish origin of Christianity,

---

[1] The current text is *convicti*. But (on the authority of the MS. "Mediceus") the reading *coniuncti* is preferred.

[2] P. FABIA, "Les sources de Tacite" (Paris, 1893), p. 403.

[3] SULP. SEVER. "Chron." II. 30 (REINACH, p. 325).

and of the distinction and opposition between the two religions.

We may go even further; this distinction was not only known to all; it was, we think, as early as the year 64 sanctioned by law.[1]

\* \*
\*

Certain it is that, at the beginning of the second century, the profession of Christianity was forbidden by the Roman legislation, as is well known from the correspondence between Pliny the Younger and Trajan. Pliny was the imperial legate in the province of Bithynia and Pontus, from the autumn of the year 111 to the spring of the year 113. Scarcely had he arrived in his province, when he had to take cognizance of prosecutions against the Christians. Strangely enough, although he had been a lawyer, a prætor, and a consul, he does not seem to have as yet had occasion to meet, or to undertake, prosecutions of this kind. This fact goes to show that prosecutions of Christians are local and intermittent. At all events, in Bithynia and Pontus, they have started, and a great many persons are actually threatened. "For many of every age, of every rank, and of both sexes, are being summoned before the tribunals or will be in the future. The contagion of this superstition has indeed affected not only the cities, but the village and country districts." Pliny has questioned the accused, and had two deaconesses put to the torture: he has found no crime whatever, "nothing but an evil, unrestrained superstition." This superstition, which is combined with a great deal of probity, the legate feels much inclined not to punish, either because he regards it as quite inoffensive, or because he thinks that it will be more

---

[1] Cf. C. CALLEWAERT's articles on the beginnings of the persecuting legislation in the "Revue d'hist. eccl." of Louvain, vol. II. (1901) and vol. III. (1902), in the "Revue des questions historiques," vol. LXXIV. (1903) and vol. LXXVI. (1904). The view by which I abide, and which is the same as that of Callewaert, I have already defended in the "Revue Biblique," vol. III. (1894), pp. 503-21. This is also the opinion of A. D'ALÈS, "Théologie de Tertullien" (Paris, 1905), pp. 381-8. A. Pieper, "Christentum, römisches Kaisertum und heidnisches Staat" (Münster, 1907). The opposite view (Mommsen, Le Blant, Boissier) is adopted by HARNACK, art. "Christenverfolgungen" in HAUCK's "Realencyklopädie".

easily suppressed if severity is not used. What, then, we ask, obliges him to use severity if not some law forbidding to profess this superstition? [1]  In short we must recognize here, the traces of a legislation which forbids Christianity: " . . . Those who have been brought before me as Christians I asked whether they were Christians; a second and a third time, and with threats of punishment, I questioned those who confessed; I ordered those who were obstinate to be executed." Hence, to own to be a Christian is to own to a capital crime: this Pliny goes on to state still more distinctly.

He feels concerned about the rigorous character of the measure he has to apply. He does not know "whether any allowance is to be made for age, or whether the treatment of the weaker should not differ from that of the stronger; whether pardon is to be granted in case of repentance, or whether he who has once been a Christian should gain nothing by having ceased to be one; whether the name itself without the proof of crimes, or the crimes inseparably connected with the name, are to be punished". [2]

---

[1] PLINY, "Epistul." x. 96. The authenticity of the text is beyond dispute. HARNACK, "Chronologie," vol. I, p. 256.

[2] The Christians accused by Pliny allege in their defence that their misdemeanour or their mistake is a mere offence of unlawful association : " . . . quod essent soliti stato die ante lucem convenire carmenque Christo quasi deo dicere secum invicem, seque sacramento non in scelus aliquod obstringere, sed ne furta, ne latrocinia, ne adulteria committerent, ne fidem fallerent, ne depositum appellati abnegarent : quibus peractis morem sibi discedendi fuisse, rursusque coeundi ad capiendum cibum, promiscuum tamen et innoxium ; quod ipsum facere desisse post edictum meum, quo secundum mandata tua hetaerias esse vetueram ". Observe that the Christians confess they are bound by an oath (this is the classical meaning of the term used by Pliny), an oath like that by which soldiers were bound to military service. Thus do they understand it themselves (2 Tim. II. 4 ; IGNAT. "Polycarp." 6). Later on TERTULLIAN, "Martyr." 3, says : " Vocati sumus ad militiam Dei vivi iam tunc cum in sacramenti verba respondimus ". So conscious are the Christians of being an association that, as soon as the edict against the *hetaeriae* is published, the less courageous turn their back on Christianity. Again it may be noticed that the oath by which Christians are bound obliges them to abstain from those sins which in Tertullian's age were called mortal. Also we may remark that the Christian worship is essentially social : *convenire, carmen dicere secum invicem, coeundi ad cibum.* That *cibus* is the Eucharist.

Hence the law condemns the name itself: the only question that arises is as to whether the law aims at the name apart from any crime, or at the crimes that are imputed to the name; and if this question arises, it is simply because as yet the law makes no distinction.

Pliny hesitates to apply so simple a law, just as under the French Directory (1795-99) some officials hesitated at times to apply the laws of the Convention (1792-95) against those priests who had refused to accept, under oath, the Civil Constitution of the Clergy. Yet Pliny does apply the law. "Those who denied that they were or had been Christians, ought, I thought, to be dismissed when they repeated after me a prayer to the gods and made supplication with incense and wine to your image—which I had ordered to be brought in for the purpose, together with the statues of the gods—and when besides they cursed Christus, not one of which things, they say, those who are really Christians can be compelled to do". This is a mere test and a way of administering the oath to the accused who are examined: they are to be considered guilty not of having refused to offer incense and wine to the statues of the gods and of the Emperor, but of being Christians, since any one who cannot be prevailed upon to perform those idolatrous practices shows by that very fact that he is a Christian. The legate is bent, not on making the Christians pay to the Emperor and to the gods the worship due to them, but on making them give up Christianity. "It seems possible," he says, "to stay the infection of this superstition and apply to it a remedy. It is already reported that the temples, which had been almost deserted, have begun to be frequented again, that the sacred rites, which had been neglected for a long time, have begun to be restored, and that the flesh of the victims, for which till now there was scarcely a purchaser, is sold. From which one may readily judge what a number of men can be reclaimed, if repentance is permitted." Pliny would willingly do his best to prevent the evil, instead of punishing it with severity: an existing law forbids him to tolerate it. He will endeavour indeed to bring back by means of kindness those who are undecided; but at the same time he will subdue the stubborn by the application of the law.[1]

This is what Trajan answers: "You have followed the right course, my Secundus, in conducting the cases of those who were accused before you as Christians, for no general rule can be laid down. They ought not to be sought out (*Conquirendi non sunt*); if they are brought before you and convicted they ought to be punished; provided that he who denies that he is a Christian and proves this by making supplication to our gods, however much he may have been under suspicion in the past, secures pardon on repentance." By this rescript Trajan does not make the law: he merely comments upon it. "*Conquirendi non sunt*," the Emperor says: this is the mitigation he introduces into the existing legislation. "*Puniendi sunt, si deferantur et arguantur*": this is the purport of the legislation itself. Christianity is tolerated, as seventeen centuries later, during the French revolution, the ministry of the "refractory" priests was to be tolerated; but, in case of a denunciation, the law, to which appeal is made, must of necessity punish. Such is, in the hands of Trajan, the deadly inheritance of the Neronian legislation.[2]

It is, then, to Nero that we must ascribe the commencement of the legislation against Christianity. Some critics do not regard this as certain. "There must . . . have been [before Trajan] a definite moment when the supreme authority in such matters decided that to be a Christian was a penal offence. At what time did this occur? It is very difficult to ascertain. Before Trajan, two persecutions are generally supposed to have taken place, that of Nero and that of

[1] The idea of crimes connected with the name, which originated in the most atrocious slanders regarding the Christian worship (infanticide, anthropophagy, incest) was destined to continue for many years. ORIGEN speaks of some of his pagan contemporaries, who, in their abhorrence for the bad reputation of Christians, made it a point of self-respect not to address any one of them ("Contra Celsum," VI. 27).

[2] See the earliest commentary on Trajan's rescript, in TERTULL. "Apolog." 2. Compare CLEMENT of ALEX. "Stromat." VI. 18 (P.G. V. IX. col. 400 c): τὴν ἡμετέραν διδασκαλίαν ἔκτοτε σὺν καὶ τῇ πρώτῃ καταγγελίᾳ κωλύουσιν ὁμοῦ βασιλεῖς καὶ τύραννοι κ.τ.λ. : "Our religion, on its very first proclamation, was prohibited both by kings and tyrants".

Domitian.   But the details recorded of these persecutions—
the martyrdom of Roman Christians falsely charged with the
conflagration in 64, and the death of a certain number of
men of high rank, whom Domitian put out of the way
as atheists—are isolated occurrences easily accounted for
quite apart from any official prohibition of Christianity,
and may have taken place before the existence of any pro-
scriptive law.   They do not therefore throw much light on
the question." [1]   We shall not then infer anything either
from these facts, or from the vague and uncertainly dated
text found in the *Prima Petri* (IV. 15).   But the following
is a more conclusive argument.

The recollection of the Christians for many years after
the event was that Nero had intended not only to do away
with the Apostles Peter and Paul and punish severely the
faithful of Rome, but to annihilate Christianity altogether
by making its profession a capital crime.   This recollection
is recorded by Sulpitius Severus and by Orosius,[2] and still
more clearly by Tertullian.   Twice this last writer recalls
that Nero condemned the Christian name: "*Principe
Augusto hoc nomen ortum est.   Tiberio disciplina eius
inluxit.   Sub Nerone damnatio invaluit. . . . Quales simus
damnator ipse demonstravit. . . . Et tamen permansit
erasis omnibus hoc solum institutum neronianum.*"[3]   And
under Tertullian's pen the word *institutum* means law.
At all events, it is a question of a lasting and prohibitive
measure: *damnatio permansit.*   In another text, Tertullian
reminds his reader that it is Nero who enacted the law that
forbids Christianity: "*Consulite commentarios vestros.   Illic
reperietis primum Neronem in hanc sectam cum maxime
Romae orientem caesariano gladio ferocisse.   Sed tali de-
dicatore damnationis nostrae etiam gloriamur.*"[4]   The

---

[1] DUCHESNE, "Histoire ancienne de l'Eglise," vol. I. p. 106.

[2] SULP. SEV. "Chron." II. 28.   OROS. "Hist." VII. 7.   The same
recollection is also found in the "Ascensio Isaiae," IV. 2-3 (ed. R. H.
CHARLES, London, 1900, pp. 24-6); but this passage does not belong to the
primitive text of this apocryphal writing, so we had better not use it.
SCHÜRER, vol. III. p. 282.

[3] TERTULL.   "Ad Nation." I. 7.

[4] TERTULL. "Apolog." 5.   In "Scorpiace," 15, he takes up the same
thought : " Et si fidem commentarii voluerit haereticus, instrumenta im-

word *commentarii* designates the imperial archives.[1]   In other places, he speaks more simply of the *Vitae Caesarum*, probably those composed by Suetonius.   Even granting that there is some rhetorical exaggeration in these references, it is beyond doubt that Tertullian alludes here to a bloody and legal persecution, emanating from the Emperor's authority.   The same fact is still more distinctly affirmed by another document, in fact the oldest document in our possession, that of Suetonius.

Suetonius who wrote in the year 120; Suetonius who is not one of those historians who, like Tacitus, are also psychologists and tragedians, rich in divinations and artistic devices, but one who records events with the artless accuracy and realism of a table of contents; Suetonius who frequently seems to take special pains to mention the important decisions of Emperors, magistrates, and the Senate, in enumerations that are like titles of laws filed one after the other and are probably borrowed literally from the "*Acta diurna populi*"; Suetonius does not connect the proceedings undertaken against Christians with the fire of the year 64.   Moreover he relates that the Christians were condemned to die, "because they followed a new and vicious superstition," a statement which is clearly not a mere literary divination, but tells of a particular kind of legal offence.   This statement is found in one of those enumerations of laws so frequent in Suetonius.   The law it presupposes is not referred to as a proof of Nero's cruelty, but as one of the few beneficial laws enacted by that prince, rigorous or new laws which are a credit to his rule.   They are such as tend to suppress abuses or to preserve public morality: laws against luxury, against taverns, against Christians, against coachmen, against actors, against forgers. . . . This amounts to an assertion that a special law placed Christianity under the ban:—

"*Multa sub eo [Nerone] et animadversa severe et coercita nec minus instituta : adhibitus sumptibus modus ; publicae caenae ad sportulas redactae ; interdictum ne quid in*

perii loquentur, ut lapides Ierusalem.   Vitas Caesarum legimus: orientem fidem Romae primus Nero cruentavit."

[1] FABIA, pp. 321-6.   These archives were kept secret.

*popinis cocti praeter legumina aut holera veniret, cum antea nullum non obsonii genus proponeretur ; adflicti suppliciis christiani, genus hominum superstitionis novae ac malefica ; vetiti quadrigariorum lusus, quibus inveterata licentia passim vagantibus fallere ac furari per iocum jus erat ; pantomimorum factiones cum ipsis simul relegatae ; adversus falsarios. . . ."* [1]

This being said, we may now conclude as follows :—

From the events of the year 64 it is evident that Christianity is at this time publicly recognized as distinct from Judaism, and that it has not only ceased to be protected by the laws which still protect Judaism—*"sub umbraculo insignissimae religionis, certe licitae"* [2]—but comes also under a legal prohibition aimed directly at it, and enacted by Nero. This prohibitive legislation determined, we may say, the civil status of Christianity.

## III.

Since, even as early as the first Christian generation, Christianity separated itself from Judaism, it could no longer depend on unity of race as a foundation for its own unity ; nor could it establish its unity on the observance of a Law which, in the eyes of Christians, had come to an end. Is it destined, then, to be made up of a widely-dispersed and uncertain multitude of recruits held together by no common bond, like the class of proselytes known as "those who feared God". If so, Christianity would have been but as the dust, as incapable of perpetuity as the work of those missionary philosophers who, like the Cynics, were prolific in all the Greek cities and in Rome. [3]

The result would have been similar, had the Christianity of the first generation been a "spiritual" movement, such as Montanism was to be later.

It is well known that there was, in the earliest Christian

---

[1] Sueton. "Nero," 16.          [2] Tertull. "Apologet." 21.

[3] See Origen, "Contra Cels." III. 50, where both Origen and Celsus mention those propagandists whom one could meet in every public square. On the philosophical propagandism among the people, cf. Wendland, p. 39 and foll.

communities, an extraordinary and exceptionally abundant outpouring of "charisms" (this is the term used by St. Paul), charisms due to an inspiration which was at times truly supernatural, at other times supernatural only in appearance. They are met with in many pages of the Acts: the Spirit gives commands; the Spirit foretells the future; the Spirit manifests itself in visions, dreams, ecstasies, prayers, and songs; the Spirit diffuses itself in gifts that are strange, even at times disordered and inexplicable, as the gift of tongues, for instance. Looking back on the past, the author of the Epistle to the Hebrews pictured to himself the early preaching of Christianity, as based indeed on the testimony of those who had heard the Lord, but also on the co-operation of "God bearing them witness by signs and wonders, and divers miracles, and distributions of the Holy Ghost according to His own will".[1]

However, a fact equally unquestionable is that Christianity was constituted in such a way that of itself it reacted against the excessive sway of those charisms.[2] St. Paul, who undoubtedly believed in the co-operation of the Spirit with his apostolic work, and in the real action of the Spirit in charisms, does not look upon these manifestations of the Spirit as supreme and exempt from all supervision; on the contrary, he holds them to be subordinated to two principles: first the received and authentic faith, and then the edification of the community. "But though we, or an angel from heaven, preach a gospel to you besides that which we have preached to you, let him be anathema" (Gal. i. 8).[3] "Wherefore I give you to understand, that no

[1] Heb. ii. 3, 4. On the charisms of the Apostolic age, the reader may consult with profit F. PRAT, "Théologie de Saint Paul" (Paris, 1908), pp. 182-4. As to the historical distinction between the charism and the ministry, in the first century, cf. H. BRUDERS, "Die Verfassung der Kirche bis zum Jahre 175 nach Chr." (Mainz, 1904), pp. 62-103.

[2] Cf. H. GUNKEL, "Die Wirkungen des heiligen Geistes" (Göttingen, 1899), pp. 66-71, and HARNACK, "Mission," vol. i. pp. 172-178.—The charism which plays a predominant part during the first two Christian generations, is that of prophecy. But the more important that part becomes, the more manifest also becomes the authority by which it is ruled and overshadowed.

[3] In classical Greek, the word ἀνάθημα signifies an offering dedicated to a god, to a temple. Later on—and then it was written ἀνάθεμα—it

man speaking by the spirit of God, saith Anathema to Jesus "
(1 Cor. XII. 3).   Here we may recall the whole instruction of St. Paul to the Corinthians regarding the gifts of
the Spirit and the use to be made of them (1 Cor. XII. 1-
XIV. 40).   He exhorts the Christians of Corinth to aspire
after charisms, the gifts of the Spirit, " but especially that
of prophecy ".   He is afraid of the disordered character and
of the unintelligible manifestations of the " glossolalia," i.e.
the gift of tongues.   The prophet speaks to men, is understood by them, gives them edification, encouragement,
consolation, whilst the Christian who speaks by tongues is
understood by no one.   In his good sense, the Apostle feels
but little interested in those fruitless displays:—

XIV. 6. "But now, brethren, if I come to you, speaking with tongues,
what shall I profit you unless I speak to you either in revelation, or in
knowledge, or in prophecy, or in doctrine? 7. Even things without life
that give sound, whether pipe or harp, except they give a distinction of
sounds, how shall it be known what is piped or harped? 9. For if the
trumpet give an uncertain sound, who shall prepare himself to the battle?
. . . 10. However many kinds of tongues there may be in this world,
none of them consist of unintelligible sounds. . . . 14. For if I pray in
tongues, my spirit prayeth, but my understanding is without fruit. . . .
18. I thank my God I speak with tongues more than you all.  19. But in
the church I had rather speak five words with my understanding, that I
may instruct others also, than ten thousand words in tongues. . . .
23. If therefore the whole church come together into one place, and all
speak with tongues, and there come in unlearned or unbelieving persons,
will they not say that you are mad? . . . 26. How is it then, brethren?
When you come together, every one of you hath a psalm, or a doctrine,
or a revelation, or a tongue, or an interpretation, but let all things be
done to edification. . . . 37. If any seem to be a prophet, or spiritual,
let him know the things that I write to you, that they are the commandments of the Lord.'

In presence of the outpourings of the Spirit, the right
is proclaimed of an authority whose mission it is to preserve

signified in current Greek, especially in that used for inscriptions, what
is consecrated to the infernal gods, therefore what is under a curse. The
LXX uses the word to express the Hebrew *herem*, that which is cursed
and doomed to be suppressed or exterminated. In this way the word,
*anathema*, definitely acquired its historical meaning of cursed, rejected,
vowed to destruction. E. Buonaiuti, " Saggi di filologia e storia del
N. T." (Roma, 1910), pp. 105-108, and DEISSMANN, p. 60.

the received order and faith, the Lord's commands, the teaching of the Apostle, the edification of the Church: "God is not a God of disorder". All this is decisively affirmed long before the rise of Montanism.

*<br>* *

Christianity, then, was not a mere religion of extraordinary ways, nor was it exclusively a religion of charity. We must, indeed, attach a great importance to the social solidarity which it established among all its members. The love and aid which a Jew was sure to find in every jewry, Christianity assured to the Christian; and of all the words of the Gospel, few have come home more forcibly to the Christian heart than the *logion*: "I was hungry, and you gave me to eat: I was thirsty, and you gave me to drink: I was a stranger, and you took me in: naked, and you covered me: sick, and you visited me: I was in prison, and you came to me" (Matt. xxv. 35-6). Nothing in Christianity impressed the pagans more than the love of Christians for one another; and it has been justly remarked that the tendency towards association has not been in the history of Christianity a fortuitous occurrence but an essential element, for from the very start Christianity has been a brotherhood.[1]

From Judaism it inherited a religious esteem for almsgiving. The history of Tabitha in the Acts (ix. 36-43) seems a Christian replica of the history of Tobias and a commentary on the words: *Eleemosyna a morte liberat* (Tob. iv. 11, xii. 9). In this spirit of alms-giving, there is not even a shadow of communism, since it is desirable that every Christian should have something to give that he may have the merit, the spiritual profit and the joy, of giving (Acts xx. 33-5).

Alms-giving, which by its own innate law must extend first of all to fellow-Christians (Gal. vi. 10), is practised in

[1] 1 Thess. iv. 9-10; Rom. xii. 10-13. The *communism* of the early Christians, concerning which so much has been written, never existed in the Gentile, nor even in the Jewish Christian communities : alms-giving always remained free, and property personal. HARNACK, " Mission," vol. I. p. 131, note, and E. VON DOBSCHÜTZ, " Probleme des apostolischen Zeitalters " (Leipzig, 1904), p. 39.

two ways: by hospitality (φιλοξενία), which consists in wel-
coming a travelling brother,[1] and readiness to join in generous contributions for common purposes (κοινωνία). By
means of a regular organization of alms-giving, help is given
to the poor members of the local community, and also to
missionaries. The expenses of religious propaganda are
met in the same way. Even remote communities receive
aid in their times of distress. Every Christian community
seems to have a common chest, to which each one of the
faithful brings every Sunday the offering he is able to make
(1 Cor. XVI. 1, 2). For instance, the community of Philippi
in Macedonia, can keep for the use of St. Paul, then in
Rome, a sort of current account from which he can draw
according to his needs (Philip. IV. 15-16). Such is the duty
of rich communities: "Be instant in prayer," writes St.
Paul, "contributing to the necessities of the saints, ever
anxious to give hospitality."[2] The Christians of Jerusalem
who are extremely poor are helped by voluntary collections
made for them in all the wealthy communities of the Gentile
world.[3]

Between the various communities there is a constant
exchange of guests, of missionaries, of aids, of counsels of
edification, and of affectionate control. The following
words of Harnack, which refer directly to the data supplied
by the Ignatian Epistles, are equally true of Christianity as
manifested in the Pauline Epistles: "What a continuity
of intercourse there is between the churches! What oneness of soul! What brotherly solicitude! Financial support retires into the background here. The foreground of
the picture is filled by proofs of that personal solidarity by
means of which whole churches are bound together . . .
aid one another, console and strengthen one another, and
share their sorrows and their joys. Here we come upon a
whole world of solidarity and mutual love."[4]

[1] Rom. XVI. 1-2, 23.
[2] Rom. XII. 13. Cf. Heb. XIII. 2-3, 16 ; 1 Pet. IV. 8-9.
[3] Rom. XV. 25-8 ; 2 Cor. VIII. 1-IX. 15 ; Gal. II. 10 ; Acts XI. 27-30.
At Jerusalem, wealth was in the hands of the Sadducees, and Christianity
made its recruits chiefly from among the poorest classes.
[4] HARNACK, "Mission," vol. I. p. 165 and ff.

Most certainly, early Christianity was all that, and by it was able to win many souls; but Christians were brothers because of their faith, and there is no brotherhood save in the fellowship of the same faith; hence this brotherhood is an application, not a principle. Indeed, no one would ever think of recognizing in mere altruism the generating principle of the new religion and of its unity.

\*\*\*

Must we seek that principle in the stable community-organization which Christianity assumed from the beginning? The more fully historians came to know of the organization of the pagan *collegia,* the more did they incline to look upon each Christian community as an association founded after the collegiate model.[1] Would not such an assimilation help to account for the formation of Christianity into a Church?

This hypothesis has lost prestige in proportion as the ascertainable facts have been more carefully studied, for it has become evident that Christianity was a religion, not of colleges, but of cities.[2] As early as the first generation, wherever it is established, for instance in large cities like Antioch and Rome, it forms neither separate synagogues like those of the Jews of Rome, nor autonomous colleges, like the pagan *collegia:* its followers have for their meeting-place the house of such or such a Christian. All the Christians of the city, however large it may be, make up but one and the same confraternity or ἐκκλησία which is called after the city. Whilst the worship of Mithra grows in the way of chapels or confraternities, which divide into separate confraternities when the number of the worshippers of the god increases, the law of Christianity on the contrary—a law that holds, long before the principle of the monarchical episcopate reveals itself as everywhere in vigour—is that there is but one church in each city, and that no church in any part of the world is isolated from the other churches.

---

[1] HATCH, "The Organization of the Early Christian Churches" (London, 1888), pp. 26 and foll.

[2] HARNACK, "Mission," vol. II. p. 278. R. KNOPF, "Nachapostolicher Zeitalter " (Tübingen, 1905), p. 61.

This twofold fact cannot be accounted for by the social organization of the *collegia*.

We must observe too that Christianity detached itself from the jewries, and the jewries had a community-organization which was not at all like the organization of *collegia*: the former existed in virtue of a legal status different from the legal status of the latter.[1] Had it been necessary for the Christian communities to seek recognition as *collegia* they would have been too late, and their legalization would have been impossible.

The question has arisen as regards the legal status of ecclesiastical property in the third century: at that time, churches possessed cemeteries and places of worship—a proprietorship acknowledged certainly as early as the time of Alexander Severus (A.D. 222-35), perhaps even as early as the end of the second century. "The common people were allowed to associate, in order to provide for themselves decent burial: these associations were allowed to collect monthly subscriptions, to hold property, and to have religious meetings; they were represented by an *actor*, or syndic, an official authorized to act in their name. Inscriptions prove that these clubs abounded throughout the empire. Why should not the Christian societies have been admitted to these privileges?"[2] De Rossi endeavoured to explain by such an adaptation of Christianity to the legislation regarding *collegia funeraticia*, the character of ecclesiastical property during the third century. However, this theory of De Rossi's has not been generally accepted, even for the third century when the legislation concerning the *collegia* had become more lenient. For how could Christianity, which was a religion, have concealed itself under the fictitious name of small funeral *collegia*? Who could have been deceived by the device? How could it have been possible for the Christian worship, with its meetings held every Sunday and often during the week, to be protected by a legislation which allowed the colleges to meet only once a month?

[1] JOSEPHUS, "Antiq." XIV. 10, 8: Cæsar forbids the colleges called also θίασοι, and allows the synagogues.

[2] DUCHESNE, "Histoire Ancienne," vol. I. pp. 383-4. Cf. GIRARD, "Textes de droit romain" (Paris, 1895), pp. 775-9.

How could Christians, who were admitted to communion in any church they visited, have complied with a legislation which forbade any one to belong to more than one such college?"[1]

The theory is still less probable for the first two centuries, for then the legislation for the *collegia* was extremely severe, treating the formation of a *collegium illicitum* as a crime,[2] and recognizing as lawful only a college sanctioned by the Emperor or the Senate.[3]   Did any Christian community ever ask this authorization?   It is hard to see how it could have done so, since Christianity was precluded from the possibility of being authorized as a college, by the very fact that it was prohibited as a religion, *religio illicita*.

[1] MARCIAN, "Institution." lib. III. ("Digest." lib. XLVII. tit. XXII. fr. 1): " Mandatis principalibus praecipitur praesidibus provinciarum, ne patiantur esse collegia sodalicia, neve milites collegia in castris habeant. Sed permittitur tenuioribus stipem menstruam conferre, dum tamen semel in mense coeant, ne sub praetextu huiusmodi illicitum collegium coeat.   Quod non tantum in Urbe, sed et in Italia et in provinciis locum habere divus quoque Severus rescripsit.   Sed religionis causa coire non prohibentur, dum tamen per hoc non fiat contra senatus consultum, quo illicita collegia arcentur.   Non licet autem amplius quam unum collegium licitum habere, ut est constitutum et a divis fratribus : et si quis in duobus fuerit, rescriptum est eligere eum oportere in quo magis esse velit . . ." (O. LENEL, "Iuris consultorum reliquiae," v. I. (Leipzig, 1889), p. 194).

[2] ULPIAN, "De officio proconsul." lib. VI. ("Digest." lib. XLVII. tit. XXII. fr. 2): "Quisquis illicitum collegium usurpaverit, ea poena tenetur, qua tenentur qui hominibus armatis loca publica vel templa occupasse iudicati sunt" (LENEL, v. II. p. 972).

[3] GAIUS, "Edictum provinciale," lib. III. ("Digest." lib III. tit. IV. fr. 1): " Neque societas neque collegium neque huiusmodi corpus passim omnibus habere conceditur : nam et legibus et senatus consultis et principalibus constitutionibus ea res coercetur.   Paucis admodum in causis concessa sunt huiusmodi corpora : ut ecce vectigalium publicorum sociis permissum est corpus habere, vel aurifodinarum, vel argentifodinarum et salinarum.   Item collegia Romae certa sunt, quorum corpus senatus consultis atque constitutionibus principalibus confirmatum est, veluti pistorum et quorundam aliorum, et naviculariorum, qui et in provinciis sunt.   Quibus autem permissum est corpus habere collegii societatis sive cuiusque alterius eorum nomine, proprium est ad exemplum rei publicae habere res communes, arcam communem et actorem sive syndicum, per quem tamquam in re publica, quod communiter agi fierique oporteat, agatur fiat. . . ." (LENEL, v. I. p. 194).—Cf. SUETON. "Caes." 42 : "Cuncta collegia praeter antiquitus constituta distraxit." "Aug." 32 : " Collegia praeter antiqua et legitima dissolvit."

3 *

Hence we may conclude that a Christian community was not a college, and that Christianity was not a federation of colleges. Christianity was in the Roman sense of the word a *religio*. But it was of the essence of such a *religio* to be a social bond uniting its members. Using the word *corpus* which was the legal term to designate an association, Tertullian writes, about the year 200: "*Corpus sumus de conscientia religionis, et disciplinae unitate, et spei foedere*".[1]

The divine originality of Christianity consists in the fact that it inaugurated in the world—not a charismatic or prophetic movement, still less a movement of eschatological suspense and anxiety—not a brotherhood, with reciprocity of aid and affection, superior to any exclusivism due to diversity of race—but, in Tertullian's appropriate words, a religious revelation, a rule of conduct, a covenant of hopes: all this held and lived in common by the "faithful," the "brethren," the "elect" of each church and of all the churches. At its rise this *corpus* had no legal existence; when the law began to notice it, it was to proscribe it as a capital crime. Yet it did not then dissolve: it resisted and kept united, in spite of all efforts to the contrary. *This* is the Catholic phenomenon, the true principle of which we have to discover.

---

[1] "Apologet." 39. Compare ORIGEN, "Contra Celsum," I. 1: Celsus charges the Christians with forming secret and unlawful associations: for, he says, associations which are conformable to the law are public: those which are kept secret are such as the law proscribes: συνθήκας κρύβδην πρὸς ἀλλήλους ποιουμένων χριστιανῶν παρὰ τὰ νενομισμένα, ὅτι τῶν συνθηκῶν αἱ μέν εἰσι φανεραί, ὅσαι κατὰ νόμους γίγνονται, αἱ δὲ ἀφανεῖς, ὅσαι παρὰ τὰ νενομισμένα συντελοῦνται. Celsus wrote about the year 180. In the "Octavius" of Minutius Felix, Christianity is denounced by the opponent as a *factio illicita*, a *profana coniuratio*, an *eruenda et execranda consensio* ("Octav." 8-9). We find always the idea of association and of conspiracy.

# CHAPTER II.

## THE INFANT CHURCH.

### I.

THE word ἀπόστολος belongs to classical Greek, where, taken as a substantive, it means a messenger, *missus*.[1] The word is found only once in the LXX (1 Kings XIV. 6). On the contrary, it is used frequently in the New Testament.[2] This already suggests the distinctly Christian character of the Apostolate as an institution.

Judaism had indeed its apostles ; but it would be a mistake to identify them, as regards their functions, with those known to primitive Christianity. The Jewish ἀποστολή is a late institution, unknown both to Josephus and to the ancient rabbinical sources. It seems to have arisen after the destruction of the Temple, and in connexion with that Jewish patriarchate which, at Iabneh, served for many years as a centre of national and religious life for Judaism.[3] We are told by Eusebius of Cæsarea that the Jews were wont to call ἀπόστολοι the messengers they sent out to carry to those addressed the circular letters of their authorities, i.e.—in this case—of the patriarchate of Iabneh ; of course, this attestation refers only to the time of Eusebius.[4] However, Eusebius affirms, in the same passage, that he has

---

[1] G. DITTENBERGER, "Sylloge inscriptionum graecarum " (Leipzig, 1901), vol. III. p. 170, index, at the word ἀπόστολος.

[2] LIGHTFOOT, "Galat." (1887), p. 94, remarks that the word ἀπόστολος is found in the New Testament seventy-nine times, of which sixty-eight are in St. Paul and in St. Luke.

[3] SCHÜRER, vol. III. p. 77.

[4] EUSEB. "In Is." XVIII. 1. A similar attestation is found in St. Epiph. "Haer." XXX. 4, 11 ; in the Theodosian code, XVI. 8, 14 ; in St. Jerome, "In Gal." I. 1.

found "in the writings of the ancients," that at the beginning of Christianity " the priests and ancients of the people of the Jews, who dwelt in Jerusalem, drew up and despatched letters to the Jews throughout every country, slandering the doctrine of Christ as a new-fangled heresy which was hostile to God. . . . Their ἀπόστολοι, conveying letters written on papyrus, spread themselves over the earth misrepresenting what was said of our Saviour."[1]  This statement, taken from "the writings of the ancients," seems to be borrowed by Eusebius from St. Justin, who, in the "Dialogue with the Jew Trypho" alludes three times to the "chosen men sent from Jerusalem to all countries, to say that a godless heresy, termed the Christian, had lately sprung up," and also to the "chosen men commissioned and sent throughout the whole world to announce that an atheistical heresy in opposition to the Law had been spread by one Jesus, a deceiver from Galilee, whose body, after He had been crucified, His disciples stole by night from the tomb in which He was laid . . . and they now deceive mankind, saying that He has risen from the dead, and ascended into Heaven."[2]  Justin's statement is, apparently, a supposition suggested by the narrative of the action taken by the chief priests and the Pharisees to urge Pilate to guard Jesus' tomb;[3] hence it has not the value of a fact.

It is beyond question, however, that the Judaism contemporaneous with the Gospel and with the earliest preaching of Christianity had also a kind of apostles.  Jerusalem communicated with the jewries of the Dispersion by means of letters and messengers.  On his arrival at Rome as a prisoner, St. Paul calls together the chief men of the Jews to justify himself before them.  They answer him in these words: "We neither received letters concerning thee from Judæa, neither did any of the brethren that came hither, relate or speak any evil of thee.  But we desire to hear of thee what thou thinkest: for as concerning this sect, we know that it is gainsayed everywhere" (Acts XXVIII. 21-2).  We must suppose, then, that the Jews might have received some official letter denouncing Paul to them.  The custom of the

[1] EUSEB. *l.c.*    [2] JUSTIN, "Dialog." XVII. and CVIII. 2.
[3] Matt. XXVII. 62-6.

Jews in such cases was well known to Paul, who formerly had gone to the High Priest and asked him for letters to the synagogues of Damascus. " Saul as yet breathing out threatenings and slaughter against the disciples of the Lord, went to the high priest, and asked of him letters to Damascus, to the synagogues: that if he found any men and women of this way, he might bring them bound to Jerusalem." [1] Saul had asked and obtained a mission from the Jerusalem authorities; he was, then, a kind of delegate commissioned by the High Priest, and was, in this sense, a Jewish ἀπόστολος. However, in relating the incident the author of Acts does not use the word ἀπόστολος; and, granting that at certain epochs similar missions were often entrusted by the Jerusalem authorities to Jews who were thus sent to some of the jewries of the Dispersion, we must not forget that these missions were only temporary and occasional.

Hence, dissenting from Harnack,[2] we believe that the apostolate of the first Christian generation was not an institution borrowed from Judaism. Let us try then to fix with more precision what this first Christian generation meant by the name.

*<sub>*</sub>*

In the first place, the name has a general meaning, in which it signifies simply a "messenger". The Philippians have sent help to St. Paul by the hands of Epaphroditus: St. Paul sends Epaphroditus back to Philippi, the bearer of the Epistle to the Philippians: "I have thought it necessary to send to you Epaphroditus, my brother and fellow-labourer and fellow-soldier, but your apostle and minister to my wants" (Phil. II. 25).

Paul writes to the Corinthians that he sends them Titus, and with Titus two other brethren: "Titus is my companion and fellow-labourer towards you; as to (the two others) our brethren, they are apostles of the churches" (2 Cor. VIII. 23). In these two instances, the word apostle

---

[1] Acts IX. 1-2. The text implies that there are several synagogues at Damascus. Cf. XXII. 5, XXVI. 9-12.

[2] " Mission," vol. I. pp. 274-277.

seems to have only the meaning of messenger, or of servant.[1] With that meaning in his mind, St. John puts on the Saviour's lips these words: "The servant is not greater than his lord; nor an ἀπόστολος greater than he that sent him" (John XIII. 16).

In the second place, the word apostle, whilst still remaining a common name, gradually tends towards its historical meaning, through the expression "apostle of Jesus Christ," an expression of which St. Paul is fond. It is the title with which he accompanies his name at the beginning of most of his Epistles: "Paul, an apostle of Jesus Christ, called by the will of God" (1 Cor. I. 1); "Paul, an apostle of Christ Jesus, by the will of God" (2 Cor. I. 1; Eph. I. 1). So too in the Pastoral Epistles. On the other hand, when Paul places in the subscription of some epistle, together with his own name, the names of some of his co-workers, he is careful not to give them a title which is not theirs. He writes at the beginning of the Epistle to the Philippians: "Paul and Timothy, the servants of Christ Jesus" (Phil. I. 1); to the Colossians: "Paul, an apostle of Christ Jesus, by the will of God, and Timothy [his] brother" (Col. I. 1); to the Thessalonians: "Paul and Sylvanus and Timothy" only (1 and 2 Thess. I. 1); to the Corinthians: "Paul, an apostle of Christ Jesus, by the will of God, and Timothy [his] brother" (2 Cor. I. 1). Unlike the appellation "servant of Christ," the appellation "apostle of Christ" does not signify a moral quality, but an exceptional mission.

However, Paul does not claim for himself alone this quality of Christ's apostle: he recognizes it in others, "the other Apostles," among whom he reckons "the brethren of the Lord and Cephas" and also Barnabas (1 Cor. IX. 6-7). On the contrary, Timothy is nowhere called an Apostle; nor is Apollos, nor—although the contrary has been maintained —Sylvanus. As to Andronicus and Junias (Rom. XVI. 7), there is some doubt: "Salute Andronicus and Junias, my

[1] See Acts XV. 22-3, in which Barsabas and Silas are thus despatched to Antioch by the church of Jerusalem. See also their letter (vv. 23-9). The case of Tychicus is exactly the same, in Eph. VI. 21-2. Cf. SCHÜRER, vol. III. p. 77.

kinsmen and fellow-prisoners, who are of note among the Apostles (ἐπίσημοι ἐν τοῖς ἀποστόλοις), who also were in Christ before me ". We are inclined to believe, with Lightfoot and Harnack,[1] that Andronicus and Junias, who had been converted before Paul, and were consequently of the number of the earliest Christians, missionaries to the Dispersion who had been imprisoned for a while—where we cannot determine—as St. Paul had been many a time (2 Cor. XI. 23) were of the number of the Apostles, rather than "of note in the eyes of the Apostles".

From this some have inferred that, for St. Paul, the number of the Apostles may have been quite large: an inference which St. Paul himself insinuates. "God indeed," he writes to the Corinthians, "hath set some in the church, first apostles, secondly prophets, thirdly doctors, then those who have the gift of miracles, the graces of healing, of helping, of governing, of speaking divers tongues. Are all apostles? Are all prophets? Are all doctors? Are all workers of miracles?" (1 Cor. XII. 28-30). It is Christ, he says elsewhere, who has "made some apostles, and some prophets, and other some evangelists and other some pastors and doctors, for the perfecting of the saints, for the edifying of the body of Christ" (Eph. IV. 11-12).

Let us accept the hypothesis that there were many apostles, as there were many prophets and teachers and thaumaturgi, during the earliest Christian generation.[2] Does it follow that the apostolate is a mere charism, an individual gift of the Spirit? Such, we are told, is St. Paul's conception of the apostolate, but, if such is the case, in what does an apostle differ from a prophet? Whence comes to the apostle that constant pre-eminence which St. Paul ascribes

---

[1] LIGHTFOOT, "Galatians," p. 96. HARNACK, "Mission," vol. I. p. 269. It is true that the question whether Junias is the name of a man or of a woman, may be raised. SANDAY—HEADLAM, "Romans" (1895), p. 242. ZAHN, "Einleitung in das N. T." vol. I. (Leipzig, 1906), p. 297.

[2] Cf. ORIGEN, "In Num. homil. XXVII." 11 : "Visus, inquit [Paulus], est illis undecim, deinde apparuit et omnibus apostolis. In quo ostendit esse et alios apostolos, exceptis illis duodecim." He speaks similarly in Comment. in Rom. X. 21, as regards Andronicus and Junias. In IRENÆUS ("Haer." II. 21, 1) and in TERTULLIAN ("Marcion." IV. 24), the seventy disciples are called "apostles".

to him in the hierarchy described in the passages we have just quoted ?  Some recent critics have spoken of what they call "a Pauline apostolate," an immediate personal call, proceeding from God, assigning a special missionary field and bestowing spiritual autonomy within that field :[1] but there is nothing to justify such a notion in the Epistles of St. Paul.  Moreover, even supposing this definition to be grounded on history, why did not this apostolate endure? Why did no one inherit such a spiritual office, since prophets, and prophetesses too, had successors, at least for a while?  And how can we help supposing that the pre-eminence of the apostolate, which no one inherited, was due to a circumstance of fact which could not recur?

*⁎*

This St. Paul can teach us better than any one else ; for he had to defend his apostolic character against stubborn and bitter adversaries, who pursued him almost wherever he went—at Antioch, in Galatia, especially at Corinth, to contest his claim to the name and quality of apostle.  From this fact alone we may gather how great was the importance attached to this name and quality.

Those who made it their business thus to harass St. Paul are emissaries who have come from Judæa ; they are emissaries, i.e. undoubtedly ἀπόστολοι—in the sense we described above when we spoke of the ἀπόστολοι τῶν ἐκκλησιῶν— that is, emissaries accredited by some letter of the " Saints " who resided there, in Judæa (2 Cor. III. 1).  Paul looks upon them as apostles who have received their mission from men (Gal. I. 1) whereas he, Paul, does not hold his mission from men.  Hence the name, false apostles, which he gives them.  " Such are false apostles, deceitful workmen, disguising themselves as the apostles of Christ.  And no wonder : for even Satan himself disguiseth himself as an angel of light.  Therefore it is no great thing if his ministers (διάκονοι αυτοῦ) be disguised as the ministers of justice: whose end shall be according to their works " (2 Cor. XI. 13-15).

But these emissaries claim to speak in the name of real

[1] H. MONNIER, " La notion de l'apostolat, des origines à Irénée " (Paris, 1903), p. 35.

Apostles, those who are at Jerusalem, and Paul, accused of usurping the apostolate, thus defends himself.

(1 Cor. xv.) "1. Now I make known unto you, brethren, the gospel which I preached to you, which also you have received, and wherein you stand ; 2. By which also you are saved, if you hold fast after what manner I preached unto you. . . . 3. For I delivered unto you first of all, which I also received : how that Christ died for our sins according to the Scriptures : 4. And that he was buried, and that he rose again the third day according to the scriptures : 5. And that he was seen by Cephas ; and after that by the twelve. 6. Then was he seen by more than five hundred brethren at once : of whom the greater part remain until this present, and some are fallen asleep. 7. After that he was seen by James, then by all the apostles. 8. And last of all he was seen also by me, as by one born out of due time. 9. For I am the least of the apostles, who am not worthy to be called an apostle, because I persecuted the church of God. 10. But by the grace of God, I am what I am ; and his grace in me hath not been void, but I have laboured more abundantly than all they : yet not I, but the grace of God with me."

Since an apostle is above all a missionary of the Gospel, St. Paul proves the authenticity of his apostolate first by the authenticity of the Gospel he has preached : he has taught what he had learnt. The authenticity of his apostolate is proved next by the help God has given him. For certainly Paul is, in every way, the least of the Apostles, and in his humility he insists strongly on this, the better to bring out the efficacy of the grace that has worked through him: a Christian community, like that of Corinth, which he has founded and in which God has sanctioned his work by the outpouring of His graces, becomes an empirical justification of the apostle's apostolate. "Do we need (as some do) epistles of commendation to you, or from you? You are our epistle, written in our hearts, which is known and read by all men: You are an epistle of Christ, written through our ministry not with ink, but with the spirit of the living God " (2 Cor. III. 1-3).

In the third place, the authenticity of Paul's apostolate is proved by the fact of his having seen the Lord. The Apostle attaches an exceptional importance to this fact, for it constitutes a prerogative he shares in common with those Apostles with whom his enemies contrast him, those Apostles who are at Jerusalem. "I think that I am in nothing less than the great apostles " (XI. 5). What! the Apostles of

Jerusalem claim to be, or are considered, Apostles after whom there can be none other (ὑπερλίαν ἀπόστολοι)! "They are Hebrews: so am I. They are Israelites: so am I. They are the seed of Abraham: so am I. They are the ministers of Christ: (I speak as one less wise), I am more" (XI. 22-3). Then Paul enumerates all the trials of his apostolate in the Gentile world, and concludes: "I have no way come short of them that are above measure apostles: although I be nothing" (XII. 11). Elsewhere taking up the defence of Barnabas as well as his own, he writes: "Have we not the right to take with us a sister, as well as the rest of the apostles, and the brethren of the Lord, and Cephas?" (1 Cor. IX. 5). Again (id. 1-3), in his own name: "Am not I free? Am not I an Apostle? Have not I seen JESUS our Lord? Are not you my work in the Lord? And if unto others I be not an apostle, but yet to you I am. For you are the seal of my apostleship in the Lord. My defence with them that reproach me in this." Here Paul comes back to the proof he has already given: the faithful he has converted are a proof that he is an apostle; however, this is only an accessory argument, since he recalls in the first place that he has seen the Lord: "Am not I an apostle? Have not I seen Christ Jesus?" [1]

However, this eloquent self-defence of St. Paul is chiefly an answer to the charges of his opponents; so far it does not touch the fundamental point, namely, what constitutes an apostle. Neither the purity of his doctrine, nor the activity and fruitfulness of his preaching, however miraculous it may be, suffice to make his apostolate an office of a higher order, distinct in itself, for instance, from the office of Timothy or of Apollos. Likewise to have seen Jesus is not the exclusive privilege of the Apostles, since the risen Lord appeared "on a single occasion to more than five hundred brethren,

---

[1] Since Paul draws an argument from his having seen Christ, we may infer that his opponents urged that the genuine Apostles had seen Christ, nay, had lived with Him. Thus the following words of the Epistle to the Galatians (II. 6) may be accounted for: "But of them who seemed to be something (what they were some time, it is nothing to me, God accepteth not the person of man) . . ." WEIZSÄCKER, "Das apostolische Zeitalter," p. 52. LIGHTFOOT, "Galat." p. 108.

of whom the greater part remain until this present," but whom Paul nowhere calls apostles.

In fact, "an apostle of Christ," in the sense in which Paul claims the quality for himself, signifies "a messenger of Christ, one sent by Christ," just as "an apostle of the Churches" signifies "one who is sent by the Churches". Paul speaks of the ἀπόστολοι Χριστοῦ (2 Cor. XI. 13), as he does of the ἀπόστολοι τῶν ἐκκλησιῶν (id. VIII. 23). Since in order to be accredited the apostles of the churches have a letter from the church that sends them, the ἀπόστολος Χριστοῦ could be accredited only by a letter from Christ; but, as that condition cannot be fulfilled, recourse is had to something equivalent, and this is why Paul can say to the Corinthians : "You are my epistle from Christ". To be sent by Christ implies that one has seen Christ, not in the third heaven, if one should be rapt thither, but upon earth, and just as the witnesses of His resurrection saw Him. This is why St. Paul is the last of the Apostles, being the last who saw the Lord. After Paul there will be no other apostle. Finally, and above all, to be sent by Christ implies that one has received upon earth a mission from Christ in person; this is the real root of the apostolate. Paul can proclaim himself "an apostle, not of men, neither by man, but by Jesus Christ, and God the Father, who raised him from the dead" (Gal. I. 1), solely because only those are Christ's apostles who are chosen and sent by Christ: "It pleased God, who separated me from my mother's womb, and called me by his grace, to reveal his Son in me, that I might preach him among the Gentiles ;" and forthwith Paul started for Arabia: "Immediately I condescended not to flesh and blood. Neither went I to Jerusalem to the apostles who were before me" (id. 16-17). Paul received his mission directly from God through Jesus Christ : "By whom we have received grace and apostleship for obedience to the faith in all nations for his name".[1] It is in this full sense that Paul is an apostle: not a mere apostle, but "an

---

[1] Rom. I. 5: δι' οὗ ἐλάβομεν χάριν καὶ ἀποστολήν. Rom. I. 1: κλητὸς ἀπόστολος. In 2 Cor. v. 20, Paul calls himself Christ's legate: ὑπὲρ Χριστοῦ πρεσβεύομεν (Cf. Eph. VI. 20). In the east, the Emperor's legate was called πρεσβευτής. DEISSMANN, p. 273.

apostle of Christ," personally called and sent by Christ in person.[1]

\* \*
\*

This first conclusion is now made good: Paul is the last of the Apostles, because he is the last to whom the risen Christ showed Himself: of all the other Apostles Paul can say they were Apostles before him. He is "the one born out of due time"; still he belongs to the same family as the others (1 Cor. XV. 8).

Another conclusion which must be looked upon as certain is that St. Paul is convinced he has received from God the mission to be the Apostle of the Gentile world, whilst the other Apostles, the Apostles before him, are sent to the circumcised. This is proved most clearly from the well-known passage of the epistle to the Galatians (II. 1-14).

For fourteen years Paul has preached among the pagans, in Syria and in Cilicia: during all that time he has remained "unknown to the churches of Judæa, which are in Christ" (I. 22). Acting upon a revelation, he goes to Jerusalem, there to explain the Gospel he preaches to the pagans, that he may be able to give an assurance that there are not two Gospels, and that the purity of his Gospel evinces the authenticity of his apostolate. For this object it was quite important that he should meet the Apostles of the circumcision and confer with them. This Gospel, he writes, "I conferred with those who seemed to be something".[2] Had they disowned Paul, a deadly blow would have been dealt to his apostolate, and for those last fourteen years he would have "run in vain" (II. 2): which plainly shows that the apostolate is not a charism that finds in itself its own justification. "But," Paul goes on, "to me they that seemed to be something added nothing. Contrariwise, when they

[1] Acts XXII. 21, XXVI. 16-18.

[2] Gal. II. 2: τοῖς δοκοῦσιν. Cf. Gal. II. 9, οἱ δοκοῦντες στῦλοι εἶναι. These men of note, these pillars, are Peter, James and John. This designation alludes to the exceptional authority ascribed to them by the Judaizers. PRAT, p. 227. There is not even a shadow of depreciation in his way of speaking. LIGHTFOOT, in loc., quotes the historian Herodian (2nd century): τῆς συγκλήτου βουλῆς τοὺς δοκοῦντας καὶ ἡλικίᾳ σεμνοτάτους, the members of the Senate, who were *held in esteem*, and were the most venerable for their age.

had seen that to me was committed the gospel of the uncircumcision, as to Peter was that of the circumcision: (for
he who had made Peter the apostle of the circumcision made
me also the apostle of the Gentiles). And when they had
recognized the grace that was given to me, James and
Cephas and John, who seemed to be pillars, gave to me and
Barnabas the right hands of fellowship: that we should go
unto the Gentiles, and they unto the circumcision."[1]

Hence, as St. Paul sees it, on one side is the apostolate
to the heathen, entrusted to him and Barnabas; on the other,
is the apostolate to the circumcised, entrusted to the Apostles
who have preceded him in the missionary field. Here he
gives us names: and first of all, James, Peter and John, who
are considered pillars among those prominent men. Peter
is an apostle: this quality St. Paul has just ascribed to him.[2]
James also is an apostle, according to the testimony of St.
Paul who, speaking of his first visit to Jerusalem, which took
place three years after his conversion and fourteen years
before that mentioned above, writes as follows: " I went to
Jerusalem to see Cephas, and I tarried with him fifteen days.
But other of the apostles I saw none; saving James the
brother of the Lord."[3] The expression used by St. Paul
makes it quite certain that James is one of the Apostles.
Let us bear in mind that this James, called " the brother of
the Lord," is not the son of Zebedee and brother of St.
John. Nor perhaps is he the James, son of Alphæus,[4] who,
together with the son of Zebedee, is of the number of the
Twelve, chosen by Jesus. At all events, at the time the
two visits were made by Paul to Jerusalem, this James is,

[1] Gal. II. 8-9. Cf. HARNACK, "Die Apostelgeschichte" (Leipzig,
1908), p. 15.

[2] Gal. II. 8. Peter is always called Cephas by Paul (Gal. II. 14;
1 Cor. I. 12, III. 22, IX. 6; xv. 5) except in Gal. II. 7-8. As to the
" pillars " see 1 Tim. III. 15 and Apoc. III. 12. Cf. " I Clem." v. 2,
where Peter and Paul are called οἱ μέγιστοι καὶ δικαιότατοι στύλοι. Cf.
FUNK's note, " Patres apostolici," Vol. I² (Tübingen, 1901), p. 105.

[3] Gal. I. 18-19.

[4] This is a disputed point. TILLEMONT, " Hist. eccl." vol. I. p. 618-
21. DOM CHAPMAN, " The Brethren of the Lord," in the " Journal of
Theological Studies," vol. VII. (1906), p. 422. M. MEINERTZ, " Der
Jacobusbrief und sein Verfasser " (Freiburg, 1905), p. 5.

like Peter, a person of the first rank, and owes his preeminence to the fact that after His resurrection Jesus appeared to him individually, as He did to Peter—as we know from St. Paul's testimony in the enumeration of the apparitions: "After that, he was seen by James, then by all the apostles" (1 Cor. xv. 7).

However, the number of apostles is so far undetermined. In all the Pauline Epistles, there is but one passage in which St. Paul speaks of the Twelve: "He was seen by Cephas, and after that by the twelve" (1 Cor. xv. 5). This passage, the critical value of which there is no reason to call in doubt, would suffice to prove that, for St. Paul, "the Twelve" is a number consecrated by the current tradition, the more so that, strictly speaking, Paul ought to have said here "the Eleven," instead of "the Twelve": in fact, the Vulgate has translated here δώδεκα by *undecim*.

In St. John's Gospel the Twelve are referred to as forming the group of disciples of Jesus who are most faithfully attached to Him. St. John does not tell us of their collective calling and choice, nor give their twelve names: indeed, he never gives them the name of apostles.[1] Still, St. John testifies that Jesus chose them: "Have not I chosen you twelve? and one of you is a devil. Now he meant Judas Iscariot, the son of Simon: for this same was about to betray him, he who was one of the twelve" (John vi. 70-1). Again he mentions St. Thomas: "Now Thomas, one of the twelve, who is called Didymus, was not with them when Jesus came" (xx. 24). It is not expressly stated that at the last supper Jesus had the Twelve near Him; but Peter, Thomas, Philip, Jude, Judas and the beloved disciple are mentioned as being present. Besides, the discourse after the supper is unquestionably a kind of investiture and glorification of the Twelve—"You have not chosen me: but I have chosen

---

[1] In Apoc. xxi. 14, mention is made of the city and of its wall with twelve foundations, on which the "twelve names of the twelve apostles of the Lamb" are inscribed. Cf. also Apoc. xviii. 20, where the Saints, the Apostles and the Prophets are reckoned among the blessed inhabitants of Heaven. In Apoc. ii. 2, the church of Ephesus is congratulated on having "tried them who say they are apostles". St. John does not seem to have had in his mind other Apostles than the Twelve. In the Johannine Epistles, the Apostles are not mentioned at all.

you ; and have appointed you, that you should go, and should bring forth fruit, and your fruit should remain ". Then, addressing His Father He says : " While I was with them, I kept them in thy name. Those whom Thou gavest me have I kept : and none of them is lost, but the son of perdition " (XVII. 12). " As Thou hast sent Me (ἀπέστειλας) into the world, I also have sent (ἀπέστειλα) them into the world " (XVII. 18).

According to some, this discourse refers, not to the Twelve, but to the disciples in the broader sense of the word, and is addressed to all the believers of subsequent ages ; and the conclusion is drawn that the idea of an Apostolic College is altogether foreign to the fourth Gospel. We believe, on the contrary, that all the features we have just noticed refer directly to the Twelve, the Twelve whom Jesus chose, whom He established, among whom Judas alone was unfaithful, whom He Himself sent in His name into the world. The idea of apostolate (the term itself all but appears) is here substantially the same as in St. Paul, with the difference, however, that it applies, apparently, only to the Twelve. As to the believers, they are in the background, and appear only under the shadow of the Twelve, whose converts they are: " Not for them only do I pray, but for them also who through their word shall believe in me " (XVII. 20).

In St. Mark's Gospel, the Twelve alone are mentioned. The Twelve are called Apostles only once, on their return from the mission entrusted to them by Jesus during the Galilean ministry : " Then he called the twelve, and began to send (ἀποστέλλειν) them two and two . . ." (VI. 7). They come back to the Master: " The apostles (ἀπόστολοι) returning to Jesus, related to Him all things that they had done and taught " (VI. 30). However, it seems possible that in this passage—the only one of its kind—the word ἀπόστολος has no other meaning than that of the verb ἀποστέλλειν. In St. Matthew's Gospel, mention is made only of the Twelve, the " twelve disciples ".

It is conceded that this constant agreement of the testimonies which speak of the Twelve, makes it certain that Jesus Himself really chose twelve disciples, in view of the

4

preaching of the Gospel, even as early as the Galilean ministry.[1]   But it is claimed that the idea of the apostolate underwent a process of transformation, in three successive stages: a primitive idea, a Pauline idea, and a Catholic idea. This view deserves a careful examination.

*<br>\* \*

It is certain that Jesus chose twelve of His disciples and associated them by a very special tie with His person and work.   They are His witnesses, and this is why, on the day of judgment, they, the Twelve, are to sit on twelve seats, and judge the twelve tribes of Israel (Matt. xix. 28), to which they will have announced the Gospel of Christ.   Is there a real connexion between that number—twelve—of the disciples who were especially chosen, and the number of the tribes, as though Jesus had wished to restrict to Israel the new missionary work?   This is a question to be considered later on: we need only say here, that at the beginning a special importance was attached to the number twelve, an importance which afterwards passed out of notice.

It is a fact, that in the first days of Christianity, twelve is a number which the eleven are anxious to preserve. Of the disciples who have accompanied the Twelve all the time the Lord Jesus lived with them, from His baptism at the hands of John to His ascension into heaven, one is to be chosen, to be " a witness of His resurrection " (Acts i. 21-2). By these words the Twelve are defined: they are the witnesses of the resurrection of Jesus, after having been the companions of His public ministry.   However, the definition is not yet complete.   One feature remains to be added.   The Twelve have been chosen by the Saviour Himself.   Is the twelfth, who is to be elected instead of Judas, to be the choice of the Saviour also?   The narrative of the Acts gives us the answer: " They presented two, Joseph, called Barsabas, who was surnamed Justus, and Matthias.   And praying they said: Thou, Lord, who knowest the hearts of all men, shew whether of these two Thou hast chosen, to take the place of the ministry and apostleship, from which Judas

[1] WEIZSÄCKER, p. 584.   P. WERNLE, "Die Anfänge unserer Religion" (Tübingen, 1901), p. 71.   HARNACK, " Mission," vol. i. p. 268.   LOISY, " Évangiles synoptiques " (Ceffonds, 1907), vol. i. p. 208-9.

hath by transgression fallen, that he might go to his own place. And they gave them lots, and the lot fell upon Matthias, and he was numbered with the eleven apostles." [1] Matthias received no imposition of hands : he is chosen by Jesus Himself, whose choice is held to be manifested by the drawing of lots.

An exceptional authority remained in the hands of the Twelve, who abode at Jerusalem, in the beginning at least and for several years—twelve years, later tradition will say. Weizsäcker, who has studied their position with great care and minuteness, observes, first, that the Twelve seem to have exercised the right of supervision not only over the Jerusalem community, but over all the communities in general, and secondly that the Twelve appear, not as a college or as a corporation, but as individuals.[2]

At the same time, missionaries go out from the company of the Twelve to announce the Gospel to the world. The seven elected to help the Twelve (Acts v. 1-6) are Hellenist Jews, and no longer " Hebrews," like the Twelve : Stephen, one of the seven, dies before becoming a missionary, but Philip does become one, and is called " an evangelist ".[3] As to Barnabas and Paul, who are " Hebrews," they will be called Apostles, and will be missionaries. Paul's apostolate was certainly called in question by Judaizers who found some support at Jerusalem : yet, the same men did not question the apostolate of Barnabas : they questioned Paul's right to the quality of an Apostle, yet did not reproach him for not being one of the Twelve. Hence they conceived the idea of the apostolate just as he did himself, since the dispute did not turn on the idea itself, but on the right of

---

[1] Acts I. 23-6 : ἀνάδειξον ὃν ἐξελέξω . . . λαβεῖν τὸν τόπον τῆς διακονίας ταύτης καὶ ἀποστολῆς. Notice the use of the word τόπος. Compare that of the word χάρις in Gal. II. 9. As to the meaning of the word διακονία, see below, p. 99.

[2] WEIZSÄCKER, p. 585.

[3] Later on, the term "evangelist" was applied to the authors of the Gospels. But, in its original meaning, it designated a missionary who was not an Apostle. See Eph. IV. 11, and 2 Tim. IV. 5. This word is found neither in the " Didachè," nor in the Apostolic Fathers. In the second century, however, Pantænus, who had preached in the Indies, is still called "an evangelist". EUSEB. "H. E." v. 10, 2 and 3.

St. Paul to claim it for himself. We conclude, then, that the apostolate of the Twelve is not opposed to the apostolate of Paul, as an antithesis of which the two terms exclude each other. There are the Apostles, "all the apostles" (1 Cor. XV. 7), who receive their mission from the risen Christ, and of these Paul is the last: there are also the Twelve (1 Cor. XV. 5), who are of the number of "all the apostles," but who were the subjects of a previous choice made by Jesus during His ministry, and for a purpose which was at first co-ordinated exclusively with that ministry.

What is called the "Catholic" idea of the apostolate resulted, according to the scholars already mentioned, from the oblivion into which the memory of all apostles other than the Twelve eventually fell, these latter coming to be looked upon as exclusively the founders of the Church. It is true that at a very early date, the Twelve only are spoken of: the Apocalypse, for instance, reckons only "the twelve apostles of the Lamb" (XXI. 14). The title chosen by the Didachè is: "The Lord's teaching through the twelve Apostles to the Nations". The expression "the twelve Apostles" is a synthetic expression rather than a strict enumeration: writers speak of "the Twelve," without on that account excluding from the apostolate Paul and Barnabas,[1] and regardless of the fact that the "Twelve" were actually fourteen. Again, in the same sense it was possible to say that the Twelve had preached the Gospel to all nations, which was true to some extent only; but by a simplification that is not unprecedented, and still less untruthful, the Twelve have been credited with a work of preaching which has in fact been the collective work of apostles whose number was perhaps far greater. We may remember the calling of the seventy-two disciples, in St. Luke (X. 1-17).

*<br>* *

At all events, whether we think of the Twelve, as they must have been thought of in some primitive circles of Judaizing tendency, with some sort of implicit reference to

---

[1] BARNAB. "Epistula," v. 9 and VIII. 3.

the twelve tribes;[1] or of the "Apostles of Christ," as St. Paul preferred to say, with reference to "all the apostles," the Twelve included; or of the "Twelve Apostles," as Christians said·later on, by way of synthesis, we find ourselves face to face, in early Christianity, with a rallying-centre, a principle of unity and authority,[2] a principle laid down by Jesus Himself.

Visible communities can be ruled only by a living authority: a written or traditional law is sure to give rise to controversies, discords, separations.[3]

In these first years of Christianity, when everything is oral, the "apostles of Christ" are, as it were, the authentic word, the word which justifies faith: the teaching of Jesus, and therefore His person, have for guarantee the testimony of the apostle. Even though the Christians of Corinth might have "ten thousand instructors in Christ," they have but one Apostle, who has begotten them in Jesus Christ through the Gospel (1 Cor. IV. 15). Timothy will go to Corinth to remind the Corinthians of the way in which Paul "teaches in every church" (id. 17). "If any seem to be a prophet or rich in spiritual gifts, let him know the things that I write to you, that they are the commandments of the Lord" (1 Cor. XIV. 37). "If I come again, I will not spare, since you seek a proof that Christ speaketh in me."[4] Does this look like a religion of private judgment?

The Apostles have, during their lifetime and whilst founding the Churches, an authority which, in so far as they attest the word of the Lord, can be best compared with the authority of Holy Writ; an authority which in so far

---

[1] "Evangel. Ebionit." (NESTLE, "N.T. Supplem." p. 175). HENNECKE, "Neutestamentliche Apokryphen" (1904), p. 27.

[2] WEIZSÄCKER, pp. 588-90, 597 brings out this view most clearly, whilst HARNACK, on the contrary, "Dogmengeschichte," vol. I. p. 94, sets it aside. F. LOOFS, "Leitfaden zum Studium der Dogmengeschichte" (Halle, 1906), pp. 72, 78, deals more fairly with the question.

[3] HARNACK, "Dogmengeschichte," vol. I. p. 380 : "A living community cannot be ruled by an oral tradition and written word, but only by persons ; for the letter will always separate and split up ". Harnack, who makes this concession for the time of St. Cyprian, ought a fortiori to make it for the first Christian generation, when the N.T. was still in fieri.

[4] 2 Cor. XIII. 2-3. Cf. 1 Cor. v. 4-5.

as it attaches to the counsels or lights they give on their own inspiration, can be likened to that of the Lord by Whom they are sent. "If any man seem to be contentious, we have no such custom, nor the churches of God" (1 Cor. XI. 16). In expressing himself thus, St. Paul gives consistency to a principle of authority which is evidently received in all the Christian communities, even in those of which he has not been the first Apostle—the Church of Rome, for instance (Rom. VI. 17). There resides in the hands of the Apostles an authority without which the genesis of the New Testament cannot be accounted for;[1] and which alone explains the idea of deposit of faith, of rule of faith, of tradition, of magisterium, of hierarchy.

Judging merely from what we have seen so far, do we not recognize, in the texts and facts of the Apostolic age, the historical part played by the apostolate, a part which, under the influence of a subconscious prejudice, most contemporary critics seem to agree in minimizing? These allow, with M. Sohm,[2] that the Christian community-organization is what they call a primitive creation of the Christian spirit, yet contend that the formation of this community-system had its centre in every local Church, in the episcopate, first plural soon monarchical, which imparted a constitution to every Christian community. These statutory and juridical forms of the first Christian communities are, however, in their eyes, merely exterior and disciplinary: they control the conduct and government of the community, they are super-imposed, as it were, from without, they have a political character in the broad sense, or, to speak more simply, a practical character. The plural episcopate thus represented becomes a kind of spontaneous association for worship! On the other hand, faith and teaching—so we are told—were founded on the charism, on the gift of the Spirit, and are

---

[1] This is well shown by JÜLICHER, "Einleitung in das N.T." (Leipzig, 1894), pp. 283-6.

[2] "Kirchenrecht," pp. 4-15. Likewise HATCH, "Organization," pp. 32, foll. HARNACK, "Mission," vol. I. p. 376, says far more truly: "Any estimate of the origin of the Church's organization must be based upon the Apostles and their missionary labours". And yet, some fifteen lines below, the same historian denounces what he calls "the magical conception of the apostolate".

in no way connected with administration, until the day when, charisms having ceased, the function of teaching becomes identified with that of ruling and both are placed in the h ɩnds of the bishop. All this historical reconstruction might have some verisimilitude, were it not for the fact that the earliest Christian generation was *both* taught and ruled by the apostolate.

## II.

The Jews were the sons of Abraham; of all nations, they were the nation chosen by God, they were the elect and holy race, the Lord's inheritance. The Lord had done for Israel what He had done for no other people: with her He had made a covenant; to her He had given a holy Law; in her behalf He had wrought many wonders through the course of ages. Now Christianity takes the place of Israel, and, in the order of faith, it too has become a people, "a chosen generation, a kingly priesthood, a holy nation, a people purchased by God".[1] There is, by God's choice, the substitution of one people for another; and the historical novelty consists in the formation of this new people, whose unity is both visible like that of Judaism, and at the same time spiritual, unlike that of carnal Judaism.

Here we discern, in its native state, no longer the principle of authority which we have recognized in the apostolate, but the idea and the reality of a society, which is at once visible and invisible, taking the place of the idea and the reality of a people interrelated by flesh and blood.

In its beginnings Christianity did not separate from Judaism *ex abrupto*. The Christianity preached to the Jews could hardly escape being Jewish in observance and in spirit, because of the tenacity of the Jewish faith, and of its religious attachment to the Law: the greatest peril to which the Gospel was exposed was the risk of being reabsorbed by Judaism. But Divine Providence averted this. We remember how, after the death of St. Stephen, because of the persecution raised against them, the disciples dispersed, and how the Gospel was thus carried into

---

[1] 1 Pet. ɪɪ. 9 : an allusion to Exod. xɪx. 5-6.

Phœnicia, Cyprus, and Antioch: the disciples "spoke the word to none, but to the Jews only" (Acts XI. 19). However, some were found—and these were of Cyrene and of Cyprus —who, "when they were come to Antioch, spoke also to the Greeks, preaching the Lord Jesus. And the hand of the Lord was with them, and a great number believing was converted to the Lord". Barnabas was sent from Jerusalem to Antioch that he might work in the new missionary field, where he was joined, towards the year 42, by Paul who came from Tarsus: "they conversed there in the church a whole year; and they taught a great multitude, so that at Antioch the disciples were first named Christians".[1]

This name did not originate with the faithful themselves, who called one another only "disciples" or "brethren". It is really remarkable that, for a long time, they did not adopt the name "Christians": it is only found twice in the New Testament, and in both passages it is put on the lips of pagans who of course do not share in the belief of the faithful.[2] The name was coined by the Greeks, to designate a class of people who, evidently, could be styled Jews no longer, and it indicates the special feature in these non-Jews, which was known to be the most characteristic of their sect, their faith in Christ, their faith in Jesus recognized as the Messias.

We must also observe in this passage of the Acts that,

---

[1] Acts XI. 20-6. The Jews had at first called the disciples of Jesus "Nazarenes," "Galileans," and perhaps too, the "poor" (Ebionim), a name suggested by some words of Jesus. Epictetus and the Emperor Julian use the term "Galileans". Even as late as the fourth century, the Jews made use of the term Nazarenes. Jesus gave the name of "disciples" to His followers, and it is most strange that that name was strictly applied only to the immediate disciples of Jesus. The three appellatives adopted by the Christians were "saints," "brethren" and "church". HARNACK, "Mission," vol. I. p. 334-339.

[2] 1 Pet. IV. 16 and Acts XXVI. 28, besides Acts XI. 26. We may recall the texts of Tacitus and of Pliny. St. Ignatius of Antioch was the first Christian author who used the word χριστιανός, and he was the first author who ever used the word χριστιανισμός. The word χριστιανός is of Latin origin: cf. ἡρωδιανοί (Mark III. 6) and καισαριανοί (DEISSMANN, p. 276). HARNACK, "Mission," vol. I. p. 345, note 1, suggests that the word χριστιανός was probably coined by the Roman magistrates of Antioch. At all events, the Jews would not have called the faithful χριστιανοί i.e. "followers of the Messias".

when those disciples of Cyprus and Cyrene had preached the Lord Jesus to the Greeks of Antioch, and the number of the Greeks who turn to the Lord had become great, the rumour of these events comes "to the ears of the church which was at Jerusalem," and from Jerusalem, Barnabas is sent to Antioch. Thus the church of Jerusalem does not intend to leave to itself and without an apostle the new and unexpected community. Barnabas, an apostle of the church of Jerusalem, takes Paul with him, and introduces him to the Antiochene mission.

In another passage of the Acts (XIII. 1-2), we find a list of those who seem to have been then the pillars of that Christian community of Antioch: first Barnabas; Paul, the last; between them, a Simeon, a Manahen, two Jewish names; and a Christian of Cyrene, named Lucius. The success of their common missionary-work tends to expand. Hence Barnabas is to depart, with Paul for his companion: first they are to go to Cyprus, then they are to bring the Gospel to Antioch of Pisidia, to Iconium, Lystra, and Derbe. After this apostolic expedition, which lasts four or five years (about 45 to 49), Barnabas and Paul return to Antioch, where "having assembled the church, they relate what great things God had done for them, and how He had opened the door of faith to the Gentiles. And they abide no small time with the disciples at Antioch" (Acts XI. v. 26-7).

The sending of Barnabas and Paul to Cyprus, Lycaonia, and Pisidia, as well as their missionary work in those places, was assuredly prompted and inspired by the same principle that gave birth to the Christian community of Antioch: that is, the admittance of the uncircumcised to the faith and—to speak still more accurately—to the faith unaccompanied by any observance of the Jewish Law. On this principle of preaching the Gospel to the Greeks Barnabas and Paul agree. It is not likely that the Church of Jerusalem, of which Barnabas was the apostle, did not know what the "Gospel" of Paul was; nor is it possible that, on such an essential point, there was disagreement between Barnabas and Paul. Hence the Christianity of the uncircumcised did not expand more or less surreptitiously, but with the knowledge of the Church of Jerusalem, and with its encouragement,[1] and through the agency of one of its own apostles, Barnabas. These inferences the sequel of events will confirm.

Suddenly there was a crisis. Some, "coming down from Judea," arrived at Antioch, and, like Eleazar in the story of the king of Adiabene, began to say to these Greeks who had become Christians: "Except you be circumcised according to the Law of Moses, you cannot be saved" (Acts xv. 2). Great indeed must have been the authority of those men "coming from Judea," who appealed more or less legitimately to the "pillars" of Jerusalem; for their unexpected declarations deeply disturbed the Christian community of Antioch, nor did all the credit of Barnabas and Paul suffice to counter-balance their influence. "When Paul and Barnabas had no small contest with them, it was determined that Paul and Barnabas, and certain others of their side, should go up to the apostles and elders to Jerusalem, about this question" (Acts xv. 2). It was indeed a most solemn and momentous question, for it was no less than that of deciding if Christianity was to become a mere extension of Judaism, a proselytizing movement ending in circumcision, or the rise of a new people?

Paul and Barnabas left for Jerusalem, accompanied by Titus: this was probably about the year 50, some twenty years after the Saviour's Passion.[2]

St. Paul has recorded these incidents in the Epistle to the Galatians. He was induced by a revelation, he says, to go up to Jerusalem, there to explain to those of Jerusalem the Gospel he was preaching to the Gentiles. We may see in these words a sign that Paul joined of his own accord Barnabas and those who were sent to Jerusalem by the Antiochian community: he intended to defend his Gospel himself. Does faith in Christ suffice to justify of itself

[1] Cf. Gal. i. 21-4. The antimontanistic writer, Apollonius (about 197), relates that the Saviour had told the Apostles to wait twelve years before leaving Jerusalem. EUSEB. "H. E." v. 18, 14. The same episode was also found in the Κήρυγμα Πέτρου, from which Apollonius may have borrowed his narrative. DOBSCHÜTZ, "Das Kerygma Petri" (Leipzig, 1893), p. 22.

[2] Acts xv. 4-29. Cf. Gal. ii. 2-10. For the discussion of the various problems that relate to the "council of Jerusalem" see PRAT, pp. 69-80.

alone, without the observance of the Law? This was the whole question. And, Paul goes on, "Titus, who went with me, being a Greek, was not compelled to be circumcised. And this because of false brethren unawares brought in, who came in privately to spy our liberty, which we have in CHRIST JESUS, that they might bring us into servitude. To whom we yielded not by subjection, no not for an hour, that the truth of the gospel might continue with you" (Gal. II. 3-5).

The minority, whom Paul styles "false brethren" is an anonymous group, which appears here for the first time in the history of the infant Church. In reality it belongs to Jerusalem; but the influence of its members is far-reaching, since it caused a crisis in Antioch, and later on rendered necessary St. Paul's Epistle to the Galatians. Paul calls these people "false brethren, brought in unawares"; and thereby casts a ray of light on the history of the Church of Jerusalem, a history otherwise so obscure from the time of Herod Agrippa's persecution, when Peter is thrown into prison and James beheaded (Acts XII. 1-24). Apparently since then some members had been added to the Jerusalem community who formed in its bosom a new element, members who had come from Pharisaism and remained strongly attached to the Law. They are diametrically opposed to St. Paul, who, likewise a convert from Pharisaism, preaches the abrogation of the Law through faith. That he styles them false brethren should cause no wonder: in his eyes, they have come into the Church, to spy her out and betray her; they have taken the best means they could devise to check and suppress the preaching of the Gospel to the Gentiles, by their appeal to the mother Church, that of Jerusalem. "It is manifest that the men of this party had only just joined the Church. It is impossible that they can have belonged to it at any time during the period in which the Jewish Churches looked with satisfaction on Paul's work in Syria, Cyprus and Cilicia. And it is also manifest that they joined with the fixed intention never, even as Christians, to abandon any part of the Law. The character of the mother Church was thus completely changed."[1]

[1] WEIZSÄCKER, p. 154.

But the "pillars," that is James, Peter, and John, to whom Paul has privately explained his Gospel, "they who are held to be something," as he says of them, decided that nothing should be imposed on the uncircumcised converts. The Zealots of the Jewish party would have been content with the circumcision of Titus: not even that single concession is made to them, out of respect for the principle upheld by Paul. "We did not consent to yield to them, no not for an hour."[1]    James, Cephas, and John "gave Barnabas and me the right hands of fellowship, that we should go unto the Gentiles, and they unto the circumcision" (Gal. II. 9).

These last words reveal a dualism destined to last for many years, on one side the *ecclesia ex Judæis* and on the other the *ecclesia ex gentibus.*   However, we cannot include in the former that anonymous minority which had vainly endeavoured, at Jerusalem, to force on the Gentile converts circumcision and, along with it, the whole Law.   This latter element is of Pharisaic origin[2] and spirit; it will continue in the mother Church for a while, then disappear, either by returning to Judaism or merging in the Judæo-Christian churches.   On the other hand, the true *ecclesia ex Judæis* consists of Christians of Jewish race, who after embracing Christianity continue to observe the Law, but without imposing it on the pagans who submit to the Gospel, or ceasing on that account to maintain friendly relations with them.   This is the sentiment expressed and upheld by St. James in the narrative of the Acts.[3] James advocates a compromise, which consists in getting the uncircumcised Christians to accept the obligations imposed in Leviticus on the foreigners who have settled in Israel: namely to abstain from things offered to idols, from what is strangled, from blood, from fornication. This compromise has for its purpose to solve the practical

[1] Gal. II. 5 : οἷς οὐδὲ πρὸς ὥραν εἴξαμεν τῇ ὑποταγῇ.  This *we* designates Paul and Barnabas.   For the justification of the reading οἷς οὐδὲ (two words that are missing in the so-called Western texts), see LIGHTFOOT'S note in "Galat." *in loco.* and ZAHN, "Der Brief des Paulus an die Galater ausgelegt " (Leipzig, 1905), p. 88.

[2] Acts xv. 5.                    [3] Acts xv. 12-21.

difficulty of bringing together into one and the same Christian community both those who are Jews and those who are not Jews, Jews who believe in the enduring character of the Law, and non-Jews who believe that the Law has been abrogated. That it was a real difficulty was soon to be revealed only too clearly by the conflict between Peter and Paul at Antioch.[1] The *ecclesia ex gentibus*, on the contrary, was formed of non-Jewish Christians, in whose estimation the Law had come to an end, as may an institution which, although truly divine, is, by the divine intention itself, meant to last only for a time. Man is justified by faith in Jesus Christ, not by the observances or works of the Law. Hence, in Jesus "neither circumcision availeth anything, nor uncircumcision, but to be a new creature is everything. Peace and mercy upon all who shall follow this rule, and upon the Israel of God."[2] This which is the argument of the Epistle Paul sent to the Galatians some six or seven years later, was, long before that Epistle, one of the fundamental principles of St. Paul's Gospel.

However, we must not call this "Paulinism," for the principle involved was held by St. Peter as well as by St. Paul.

As a matter of fact, Peter went to Antioch, and there "before that some came from James, he did eat with the [converted] Gentiles: but when they were come, he withdrew and separated himself, fearing them who were of the circumcision. . . ."

The schism was there.[3] " As to me," Paul says, "when I saw that they walked not uprightly unto the truth of the gospel, I said to Cephas before them all: If thou, being a Jew, livest after the manner of the Gentiles, and not as the Jews do, how dost thou compel the Gentiles to live as do

[1] The reader may observe that the decree of the " Council of Jerusalem " (Acts xv. 23-9) regarding forbidden food has left no trace at all either in ecclesiastical customs or in ecclesiastical writings, as though it had never been applied. At some time or other the text itself was altered that it might be harmonized with ecclesiastical practice. G. RESCH, " Das Aposteldekret" (Leipzig, 1905), p. 151 and foll. H. COPPIETERS, " Le décret des apôtres " (Revue biblique, 1907), p. 55 foll.

[2] Gal. VI. 15, 16. Cf. 1 Cor. VII. 19.

[3] WEIZSÄCKER, p. 159.

the Jews? We "—i.e. Peter and Paul and likewise Barnabas, and " the other Jews," converted at Antioch—" we by nature are Jews, and not sinners from among the Gentiles.        But knowing that man is not justified by the works of the law, but by the faith of JESUS CHRIST; we also believe in CHRIST JESUS, that we may be justified by the faith of Christ, and not by the works of the law." [1]        Hence, according to Paul's testimony, Peter is prepared to live after the fashion of the Gentiles, and to give up the obligations of the Law: a Jew by birth, he professes, like Paul, that faith in Christ suffices for justification.        Paul reminds him of it, so as to convince him that his present conduct is simply a contradiction; and although no word is said to that effect in Paul's narrative, we cannot doubt that Peter came back immediately to " the truth of the Gospel".

The principle which Paul calls " the truth of the Gospel," not of *his* Gospel, but of the Gospel in itself: the principle that man is justified by faith in Christ, and that the observances and works of the Law henceforth count for nothing —is one which, as was acknowledged quite plainly by the " Council " of Jerusalem, applies to the Gentile converts; but it applies equally well to the converts from Judaism, and in this respect the Council of Jerusalem implied more than it expressed.[2]        Paul is determined that this truth of the Gospel shall be fully brought out so that there may be neither speculative equivocation nor practical hesitation. Theoretically, Peter agrees with Paul; practically, he becomes inconsistent by hesitating to give up the observance of the Law: " *Conversationis fuit vitium, non praedicationis,*"

---

[1] Gal. II. 12-16.  PRAT, p. 229: " With all ancient ecclesiastical writers and many modern interpreters we admit that the whole passage [vv. 15-21] belongs to the discourse addressed by St. Paul to St. Peter before the faithful of Antioch.  The beginning (*Nos natura Judaei*, etc.) is certainly addressed to St. Peter, not to the Galatians: and there is no reason, no indication whatever, that justifies us in maintaining that the interlocutors change in what follows."  Besides, I believe that the passage *Nos natura Judaei*, etc. is addressed not only to Peter, but likewise to the Jewish converts of Antioch, designated in vv. 13-14 : " To his (Cephas) dissimulation the rest of the Jews consented, so that Barnabas also was led by them into that dissimulation.  But when I saw that *they* walked not uprightly unto the truth of the Gospel, I said to Cephas before them all. . . ."

[2] WEIZSÄCKER, p. 163.

says Tertullian of Peter's conduct.[1] A self-contradiction, we should say; a piece of hypocrisy, says St. Paul, somewhat angrily,[2] in terms that recall the severe words of Jesus against the Pharisees; a fault on the part of Peter, on the part of the Jews of Antioch who follow his example, and likewise on the part of Barnabas; a fault prompted by the fear of "those of the circumcision". This amounts to saying that so far the Jewish converts of Antioch had practised a Christianity that was openly and completely free from any Jewish observance.

"They of the circumcision" who have just overawed Peter, will go still further and declare that in giving up the works of the Law, and associating freely with the Gentiles, a Jew like Paul is "a sinner from among the Gentiles, a prevaricator". And Paul is glad to see them so confidently push their arguments to the logical conclusion. Therefore one must choose, says Paul: either the Law, or Christ, for Christ suffices. "I live, now not I; but Christ liveth in me. And that I live now in the flesh, I live in the faith of the Son of God, who loved me, and delivered himself for me. . . . If justice be by the Law, then Christ died in vain" (Gal. II. 20-21). He who uses this language is not a Greek converted to the Gospel, but a convert from Pharisaism; it is Paul, and what he says here, he says in Peter's name too. The discourse which Paul addresses here to Peter is not a thesis which he proves from the Bible, but an appeal to the latter's religion: an appeal which reveals the deepest motives of the faith of the two great Apostles, the faith which from the time of their first interview bound them together for ever. "Paul was a Jew by birth as well as Peter. Both were convinced that they belonged to the privileged people of God, and were separated from the Gentiles by the Law which regarded them as just and the Gentiles as sinners. And yet both had come to believe that

---

[1] "De Praescr." 23.

[2] Gal. II. 13 : συνυπεκρίθησαν αὐτῷ [Peter] καὶ οἱ λοιποὶ Ἰουδαῖοι [the Antiochian Jews], ὥστε καὶ Βαρνάβας συναπήχθη αὐτῶν τῇ ὑποκρίσει. We may recall that the word "hypocrite" is used in the Gospel, to designate the Pharisees, Matt. VI. 2, 5, 16, etc. ; Luke, VI. 42 and X. 11, 56. Cf. "Didachè," VIII. 1 and 2.

their Law did not justify them before God, and that there was only one way to justification, namely, faith in Christ, which faith freed them from the obligation of the Law." Faith, then, takes the place of the Law, and establishes a vital union between all those in whom, through faith, Christ is living.    Peter's practical hesitation at Antioch raises the question of the unity of the Church : Paul's decision solves the question in the sense of a unity, based not on condescension or political sagacity, but directly and solely on faith in Christ and His supernatural life in us.[1]

\*\*\*

Christianity does not spread like the philosophy of a school nor like a " wisdom" after the fashion in which Judaism recruited its proselytes among the Greeks.[2]    Undoubtedly it is a theodicy and a code of ethics : it proclaims the unity of God and repudiates idolatry altogether.    The day is gone by for dumb idols (1 Cor. XII. 2) and for a polytheism which is after all mere atheism (1 Thess. IV. 5).    But Christianity is above all a " catechesis " that takes the form of articles of faith and of precepts of authority.

"We know that an idol is nothing in the world, and that there is no God, but one.    For although there be many that are called gods, yet to us there is but one God, the Father" (1 Cor. VIII. 4-6), "the living and true God " (1 Thess. I. 9).    Likewise pagan corruption must come to an end: "Do not err: neither fornicators, nor idolaters, nor adulterers, nor the effeminate, nor liers with mankind, nor thieves, nor covetous, nor drunkards, nor railers, nor extortioners shall possess the kingdom of God. And such some of you were: but you are washed, but you are sanctified, but you are justified in the name of our Lord JESUS CHRIST, and the Spirit of our God " (1 Cor. VI. 9-11).    These are so many principles of theodicy and of ethics, which, in our logic, are the premises of faith ; but a missionary like Paul, even when preaching in a city like

---

[1] WEIZSÄCKER, p. 160-1, who demonstrates very well the community of faith between the two great Apostles.

[2] This does not mean of course that St. Paul's Epistles do not contain the fundamental principles of theodicy and of ethics.    Rom. I. 20-32 ; II. 14-16.

Corinth, does not think of proving them first by means of reason, nor are his converts reluctant to receive them merely on his word. Paul teaches what he has learned ; and what he tells them his converts must preserve just as they have been taught. The idea of the deposit of faith is active here.

"Now I make known unto you, brethren, the gospel which I preached to you, which also you have received, and wherein you stand ; by which also you are saved, if you hold it fast after what manner I preached it unto you" (1 Cor. xv. 1, 2). The whole of that Gospel may be reduced, in a sense, to one dogmatic fact: " Before all I delivered unto you that which I also received: how that Christ died for our sins according to the scriptures ". Jesus is the Messias, His death is our redemption : this had been announced by the Jewish Scriptures. But Christ, who was dead, also "rose again the third day according to the scriptures, and he was seen by Cephas, and after that by the Twelve. . . . Last of all, he was seen also by me " (*id.* 4-7). The Scriptures which announced Christ are our first motive of credibility. The testimony of the Apostles who saw the risen Christ is another motive.[1] "For both the Jews require signs, and the Greeks seek after wisdom. But we preach Christ crucified, unto the Jews indeed a stumbling-block, and unto the Gentiles, foolishness, but unto them that are called, both Jews and Greeks, Christ the power of God and the wisdom of God " (1 Cor. i. 22-4).

"*If then any be in Christ he is a new creature. The old things are passed away, behold all things are made new. But all things are of God, who hath reconciled us to himself by Christ, and hath given to us the ministry of reconciliation. For God indeed was in Christ reconciling the world to himself, not imputing to men their sins, and putting on our lips the word of reconciliation. For Christ therefore we are ambassadors, God as it were exhorting by us*" (2 Cor. v. 17-20).

---

[1] There is a third motive of credibility, viz. the miracles with which the preaching of the Gospel is accompanied, and the most sensible of these miracles is the outpouring of the Holy Spirit on those who are converted. Cf. Rom. xv. 18-19 ; Gal. iii. 5 ; 1 Thess. i. 5.

Reduced to the affirmation of these supernatural realities, the Gospel is a mystery accepted on God's authority. "We were approved by God that the gospel should be committed to us. . . . We preached among you the gospel of God. . . . We also give thanks to God without ceasing, because that when you had received of us the word of God which we taught you, you received it not as the word of men, but (as it is indeed) the word of God."[1] The Apostle is the missionary and still more the warrant for the divine authority of the Gospel. "How shall they believe him, of whom they have not heard? And how shall they hear without a preacher? And how shall they preach unless they be sent?"[2]

The Gospel is a divine message to which the faithful give their assent by an act which is an act of obedience:[3] every thought must submit to the yoke of Christ, and the Apostle will unhesitatingly punish all disobedience. "Thanks be to God," says Paul to the Romans, "that, after being the servants of sin, you have obeyed from the heart unto that form of doctrine, which has been delivered to you".[4] The Romans had not been evangelized by Paul personally; nevertheless Paul is most sure of the identity of the Gospel they have received with the Gospel he preaches.

The Gospel is both the preaching of what Christ is, and the preaching of the word of Christ: "Faith then cometh by hearing, and hearing by the word of Christ."[5] Paul knows but the "testimony of God," i.e. Jesus and Him crucified.[6] The object of faith is just as definite as the

---

[1] 1 Thess. II. 4, 9, 13. Cf. 2 Cor. II. 17; Rom. I. 9.

[2] Rom. x. 14, 15: Πῶς ἀκούσωσιν χωρὶς κηρύσσοντος, πῶς δὲ κηρύξωσιν ἐὰν μὴ ἀποσταλῶσιν; Notice the words κήρυγμα and ἀποστολή. Cf. Rom. I. 5: ἀποστολὴν εἰς ὑπακοὴν πίστεως, the apostolate to bring about the obedience of faith.

[3] 2 Cor. x. 6, 7: αἰχμαλωτίζοντες πᾶν νόημα εἰς τὴν ὑπακοὴν τοῦ Χριστοῦ.

[4] Rom. VI. 17: ὑπηκούσατε ἐκ καρδίας εἰς ὃν παρεδόθητε τύπον διδαχῆς. (Cf. Col. II. 7: βεβαιούμενοι τῇ πίστει καθὼς ἐδιδάχθητε). Notice the terms παράδοσις and διδαχή.

[5] Rom. x. 17: ἡ πίστις ἐξ ἀκοῆς, ἡ δὲ ἀκοὴ διὰ ῥήματος Χριστοῦ. (We must read Χριστοῦ and not θεοῦ). Cf. 1 Pet. I. 25: τὸ ῥῆμα [τοῦ κυρίου] τὸ εὐαγγελισθὲν εἰς ὑμᾶς.

[6] 1 Cor. II. 1-2. JÜLICHER, "Einleitung," pp. 279-80.

Divine authority on which it rests, and the Apostolic authority by which it is announced.

\* \*
\*

The Gospel does not require a merely subjective and speculative assent, faith must pass into action. When Paul says to the pagan converts at Corinth : Such sinners you used to be, but " you are washed, you are sanctified, you are justified in the name of our Lord Jesus Christ, and the Spirit of our God (1 Cor. VI. 11), the word ἀπελούσασθε reminds us of the baptism administered in the name of Christ and accompanied with the outpouring of the Spirit.[1] Some more precise indications are found elsewhere. Paul has been told of the disputes that divide the Church of Corinth : some claim they belong to Paul, others to Apollos, others to Cephas, others to Christ. Why these parties ? " Is Christ divided ? Was Paul then crucified for you ? Or were you baptized in the name of Paul ? I give God thanks that I baptized none of you but Crispus and Caius, lest any should say that you were baptized in my name."[2] Baptism is not a symbolical ablution or a legal cleansing : it confers on the faithful a new and lasting state : " As many of you as have been baptized in Christ have put on Christ. There is neither Jew nor Greek ; there is neither bond nor free ; there is neither male nor female ; for you are all one in Christ Jesus."[3]

As the Jewish communities meet on the Sabbath-day for the synagogue services, so also the Christian communities meet together : every week there is a special day set apart for those meetings (1 Cor. XVI. 2). A meeting—probably that same weekly meeting—has for its purpose the celebration of the Eucharist, the blessing of the chalice and the breaking of the bread (1 Cor. X. 16). They speak of

[1] Cf. 2 Cor. I. 22. It is interesting to compare this passage with Heb. VI. 1-2, and note the successive actions that are there enumerated : in the first place moral conversion, then faith in God, then the " doctrine of baptisms," the imposition of hands, the resurrection of the dead, and the last judgment. As to the meaning of verse 2, cf. WESTCOTT, " Hebrews " (1892), p. 145.

[2] 1 Cor. I. 13-15. Cf. 1 Cor. IV. 1.

[3] Gal. III. 27-9. Cf. 1 Cor. XII. 13.

gathering together to eat, i.e. to eat the meal of the Lord.[1]
This common celebration of the Eucharist is the centre of
the new religious life; it is the sensible expression of its
unity: communion in Christ's body, communion in His
blood: " As there is but one bread, we being many are one
body, all that partake of one bread ".[2]

This common worship is accompanied by a kind of
common sharing of souls. This we have already seen in
the case of the charisms, one of the criteria of which is the
good they bring to the community, and the edification they
give. The faithful are welded together by this new
solidarity which consists in separating themselves morally
from the pagan world by which they are surrounded; a
solidarity which requires them also to cease to hold communion with any brother who does not comply with the
duties of a Christian life. If you had to flee from fornicators and from idolaters, " you must needs go out of
this world," says Paul to the Corinthians (1 Cor. v. 10).
But you must part from any one bearing the name of
Christian, who " is a fornicator, or covetous, or a server of
idols, or a railer, or a drunkard, or an extortioner: with
such an one do not so much as eat ". As to those who
are not Christians, you may abstain from judging their conduct: " What have I to do to judge them that are without?
Do not you judge them that are within? For them that
are without, God will judge. Put away the evil one from
among yourselves."[3]

The faithful constitute then a society apart; they live
together in habitual contact, like members of one family,
so that Paul can write to those of Corinth: "I fear lest
perhaps when I come, I shall not find you such as I would

---

[1] 1 Cor. XI. 33 and XI. 20.

[2] 1 Cor. X. 17.  E. von DOBSCHÜTZ, "Die urchristlichen Gemeinden"
(Leipzig, 1902), p. 20.

[3] 1 Cor. v. 11-13.  Cf. 2 Thess. III. 6, where the command is given
to separate from any brother who lives irregularly and "not according
to the instructions received from us " (μὴ κατὰ τὴν παράδοσιν ἣν παρελάβοσαν
παρ' ἡμῶν).  The παράδοσις they have received from Paul holds good for
the Thessalonians: "If any man obey not our word by this epistle, note
that man, and do not keep company with him, that he may be ashamed "
(id. 14).

. . . lest perhaps contentions, rivalries, animosities, dissensions, detractions, whisperings, swellings, troubles be among you" (2 Cor. xii. 20).  If disputes regarding their temporal welfare arise among them, Paul entreats them earnestly to come to a friendly settlement by themselves, and not to have recourse to the pagan magistrates (1 Cor. vi. 1-6).  The faithful watch and protect one another. They supervise one another, even as regards what is served at table, we might say ; since even in those domestic details a Christian must carefully abstain from scandalizing his brethren.  "Let not then your good be evil spoken of. . . . Let us follow after the things that are of peace ; and keep the things that are of edification one towards another. Destroy not the work of God for meat" (Rom. xiv. 15-20). As they watch one another, so also they admonish one another.  "I myself also," says St. Paul to the Romans, "am assured of you . . . that you are able to admonish one another (νουθετεῖν)" (Rom. xv. 14).  Fraternal correction becomes an element of anarchy unless some authority intervenes to keep it within proper bounds ; and that authority is vested in others, besides the Apostle himself : "We beseech you, brethren, to consider those who labour among you, and are over you in the Lord, and admonish you ; that you esteem them more abundantly in charity for their work's sake."[1]

*
*  *

Among the jewries, the word συναγωγή designates the assembling together of the Jews, and thence, in a broader sense, the local community and the place where its. members assemble.[2]  Christians have no special buildings for their religious meetings, they assemble where they can, as the guests of this or of that Christian who can place a large hall at their disposal.  Neither do they use the word προσευχή or the word συναγωγή to designate the place where they worship ; they use the word ἐκκλησία.  This last word happens to belong both to the terminology of the LXX

[1] 1 Thess. v. 12-13 : ἐρωτῶμεν δὲ ὑμᾶς, ἀδελφοί, εἰδέναι τοὺς κοπιῶντας ἐν ὑμῖν καὶ προϊσταμένους ὑμῶν ἐν κυρίῳ καὶ νουθετοῦντας ὑμᾶς.  Cf. 2 Thess. iii. 14-15.

[2] SCHÜRER, vol. ii. p. 432.

which uses it as equivalent to συναγωγή, and to the most classical Greek, in which it designates the plenary deliberative assembly of all the free citizens of a city. A popular assembly, like that of the people of Ephesus in a theatre, is an ἐκκλησία; i.e. a *meeting*, a *convocation*.[1] But this meeting is truly an expression of unity: "You come together into one place" for the Eucharist, says St. Paul;[2] and in the same sense: "When the whole church comes together into one place".[3] In many passages St. Paul calls the faithful gathered together by the name ἐκκλησία: the prophet who prophesies is a source of edification for the church, that is, the faithful who are present (1 Cor. XIV. 4); the Christian who speaks in unintelligible tongues holds an inferior rank, as compared with the Apostle who only says five words to the faithful who are present, that is, to the church (XIV. 19); when the church assembles in the same place, if all the faithful speak in tongues, the unconverted Gentile "who comes in" will look upon them as out of their senses (XIV. 23). Women must remain silent in the meetings of the faithful, that is, in the churches (XIV. 34); for it is unbecoming for a woman to speak in such a meeting, that is in the church (XIV. 35).

Taken in a wider sense, the word ἐκκλησία comes to designate, not only the actual meeting together, but the people who habitually meet together in some particular place. Paul, writing from Ephesus to the Corinthians, says: "Aquila and Priscilla salute you much in the Lord, with the church (ἐκκλησία) that is in their house" (1 Cor. XVI. 19). Likewise, in the Epistle to the Romans, he says: "Salute

---

[1] Acts XIX. 32, 39, 41. DITTENBERGER, "Sylloge," vol. III. pp. 140-7, the index at the word ἐκκλησία. GLOTZ, art. "Ekklesia" in DAREMBERG's dictionary. SOHM, "Kirchenrecht," p. 16 and foll. HARNACK, "Lukas der Arzt" (Leipzig, 1906), pp. 25-6.

[2] 1 Cor. XI. 20: συνερχομένων ὑμῶν εἰς τὸ αὐτό.

[3] 1 Cor. XIV. 23: ἐὰν συνέλθῃ ἡ ἐκκλησία ὅλη ἐπὶ τὸ αὐτό . . . The Church, then, is above all a concrete and localized thing, not a transcendent and heavenly entity. HARNACK, "Mission," vol. I. p. 343, grants that the term ἐκκλησία was not invented by Paul, but by the Palestinian communities: Paul found it already in use. The Latin-speaking Christians will adopt it, without translating it. DEISSMANN, pp. 76-7.

Priscilla and Aquila . . . and the ἐκκλησία which is in their house " (Rom. XVI. 5).[1]

In a still wider sense, the word ἐκκλησία is used later on to designate the whole number of the faithful of one and the same city, as may be judged from the inscriptions of the Pauline Epistles. " Paul . . . to the church of the Thessalonians, in God the Father, and in the Lord Jesus Christ " (1 Thess. I. 1). " Paul . . . to the church of the Thessalonians in God our Father, and the Lord Jesus Christ " (2 Thess. I. 1). " Paul . . . to the church of God that is at Corinth " (1 Cor. I. 1). " Paul . . . to the church of God that is at Corinth, with all the saints that are in all Achaia " (2 Cor. I. 1). Paul does not speak of the church of Achaia. The church being a local community, St. Paul speaks of churches, in the plural, to designate several distinct communities. Nowhere are we told of the churches of Corinth or of the churches of Thessalonica. On the other hand, the Epistle to the Galatians is addressed to " the churches of Galatia " (Gal. I. 2). In the same Epistle, mention is made of the " churches of Judæa, that are in Christ " (Gal. I. 22). In the two Epistles to the Corinthians, the Apostle speaks of the " churches of Galatia " (1 Cor. XVI. 1) ; of the " churches of Asia " (*id.* 19), of the " churches of Macedonia " (2 Cor. VIII. 2). He speaks also, in the same sense, of " churches " in the plural, without designating the provinces. He says to the Corinthians : " What is there that you have had less than the other churches ? " (2 Cor. XII. 13). " Shall I recall too my daily cares, the solicitude for all the churches ? " (XI. 28) ; and to the Romans : " Salute Priscilla and Aquila . . . to whom not I only give thanks, but also all the churches of the Gentiles " (Rom. XVI. 3-4). " All the churches of Christ salute you " (Rom. XVI. 16).

Nor should we look for another meaning in the expression Church of God used elsewhere by St. Paul: " Brethren," he writes to the Thessalonians, " you are become followers of the churches of God which are in Judæa,

---

[1] Cf. " Acta S. Iustini martyris," 2 : " Quaesivit praefectus, quem in locum Christiani convenirent. Cui respondit Iustinus, eo unumquemque convenire quo vellet ac posset. An, inquit, existimas omnes nos in eumdem locum convenire solitos ? Minime res ita se habet."

in Christ Jesus: for you also have suffered the same things from your own countrymen, even as they have from the Jews " (1 Thess. II. 14). Again to the Thessalonians : "We ourselves glory in you in the churches of God " (2 Thess. I. 4) ; and, to the Corinthians: "If any man seem to be contentious, we have no such custom, nor the churches of God " (1 Cor. XI. 16). In all these passages the expression "church of God " is equivalent to the single word church. Thus St. Paul writes in the inscription of the first Epistle to the Corinthians: ". . . to the church of God that is at Corinth" (1 Cor. I. 1). There is in this expression, together with the idea of belonging to God, a certain shade of nobility and sanctity, which recalls the intensive use of the divine name in Hebrew, where a thing is called " of God," because it is eminent in its own kind.

The word Church has so far a merely local and empirical meaning; and it is easy to prove that this meaning is either the primary meaning or at least the first of all derivative meanings; and that the word is not, as some would have it, before all a title of honour, not to say an oratorical expression, chosen by the first Christian generation to designate, not the local community, but the whole number of the faithful dispersed all over the world, the invisible Church. We believe, on the contrary, that the Christian language proceeded rather from the concrete to the abstract, and that the word Church, after designating, like the word synagogue, a local reality, came to express another reality, another unity, which faith perceived with perfect consciousness; and this other meaning of the word Church is met with in the great Pauline epistles.

Paul says to the Galatians: "You have heard of my conversation in time past in the Jews' religion: how that beyond measure I persecuted the Church of God, and wasted it " (Gal. I. 13) ; to the Corinthians: "I am not worthy to be called an apostle, because I persecuted the Church of God " (1 Cor. XV. 9). When using this language, he has in view not a local church, the church of Jerusalem or that of Damascus, but the Church in the abstract, that which will be called later on the ",Christian name ". However, in the eyes of St. Paul, this abstraction is also a living reality, which his faith shows to be just as living as Israel or the Greek world. He writes to the Corinthians: "Be without offence to the Jews or to the Gentiles, or to the Church of God " (1 Cor. x. 32). The Church of God is the new people which has been created in Jesus Christ: "Neither circumcision availeth any thing, nor uncircumcision, but to be a new creature. And whosoever shall follow this *canon*, peace on them, and mercy, and upon the Israel of God "[1] by contrast with Israel according to the flesh.

We have now discovered the unity of unities, the foundation of that world-wide unity: namely in this that justification is both individual and collective: that through baptism we are grafted on the same tree.[2] This is why "we being many, are one body in Christ, and each and all members of one another ".[3]

As the body is one and has several members, and as all the members of the body, in spite of their number, form but one body, so it is with Christ ; for we were all baptized into one spirit, to form but one body, whether we be Jews or Gentiles, slaves or freemen, and all we have drunk of the same spirit . . . You are the body of Christ and his members.[4] The local Church is indeed the body of Christ ; still, all the churches are not so many bodies of Christ, for Christ is one and undivided: and therefore all the churches

---

[1] Gal. vi. 16. The word κανών here appears for the first time in Christian terminology : it belongs to the LXX (Judith xiii. 6 and Job xxxviii. 5) where it has the classical meaning of staff, then of metre, or measure. In 2 Cor. x. 13, it has still the sense of metre. In Gal. vi. 16, it signifies imperative rule, and thus we come to the meaning sanctioned by Christian terminology. Cf. T. ZAHN, "Grundriss der Geschichte des N.T. Kanons " (Leipzig, 1901), pp. 1-7.

[2] Rom. vi. 5 : σύμφυτοι γεγόναμεν. Paul takes up again this comparison and develops it in the quasi-parable of the wild olive-tree grafted on the cultivated olive-tree in Rom. xi. 17-24.

[3] Rom. xii. 5: οἱ πολλοὶ ἓν σῶμά ἐσμεν ἐν Χριστῷ, τὸ δὲ καθ' εἷς ἀλλήλων μέλη. Cf. 1 Cor. i. 9 : ἐκλήθητε εἰς κοινωνίαν τοῦ υἱοῦ αὐτοῦ Ἰησοῦ Χριστοῦ, τοῦ κυρίου ἡμῶν. Gal. iii. 28 : πάντες ὑμεῖς εἷς ἐστε ἐν Χριστῷ Ἰησοῦ.

[4] 1 Cor. xii. 12-13 : καθάπερ τὸ σῶμα ἕν ἐστιν καὶ μέλη πολλὰ ἔχει, πάντα δὲ τὰ μέλη τοῦ σώματος, πολλὰ ὄντα μν ἐστιν σῶμα, οὕτως καὶ ὁ Χριστός. Then comes what may be called the parable of the members and of the body, applied to the distribution of the charisms, and ending (v. 27) with the affirmation : ὑμεῖς δέ ἐστε σῶμα Χριστοῦ καὶ μέλη ἐκ μέρους.

under heaven are grafted on Christ and are one because He is one.

*<sub>*</sub>*

Harnack has called the attention of scholars to this primitive conception, namely that the Christians as Christians are conscious of being a *tertium genus*, a new race, a race apart.[1] Is not this conception already found in the great Pauline Epistles? For Paul, as for any convinced Pharisee, mankind is divided into two races, the Jews and the Greeks, and to Greeks are assimilated those whom the Greeks call Barbarians. Now Paul affirms that "there is no distinction between the Jew and the Greek: for the same Lord is over all, rich unto all that call upon him," and that every one who invokes Him shall be saved (Rom. x. 12). The privilege bestowed upon Israel on account of her race and of her Law is proclaimed to have come to an end: "the faith in the truth" and "the sanctification of the spirit," procured by "the preaching of the Gospel" (2 Thess. ii. 13) constitute a people, "the seed of Abraham,"[2] which is no longer Greek or Jewish and is most plainly distinct both from the Jews and from the Greeks.[3] A problem now arises, which is a stumbling-block for some, the problem of the reprobation of the Jews.[4] Separated from the Jews because they reject the Jewish Law, from the Greeks because they reject the heathen gods, the Christians form dispersed communities, that have been founded by the Apostles, and are bound together through

---

[1] This point is urged especially in the Κήρυγμα Πέτρου (CLEM. "Stromat." vi. 5 ; DOBSCHÜTZ, "Kerygma Petri,' p. 21) : τὰ γὰρ ἑλλήνων καὶ ἰουδαίων παλαιά, ὑμεῖς δὲ οἱ καινῶς αὐτὸν τρίτῳ γένει σεβόμενοι Χριστιανοί. Cf. also ARISTID. "Apolog." 2 (ed. ROBINSON, p. 100) and TERTULL. "Scorp." 10, "Ad Nation." 1, 8. HARNACK, "Mission," vol. i. p. 232, shows that the expression *tertium genus* was first a sarcastic insult cast at the Christians by the pagans. The Christians took it up and accepted it as a characteristic designation of the new people which they were. For them the word γένος expressed an aspect of the Church of God.

[2] Gal. iii. 29.

[3] Cf. 1 Cor. x. 32, already quoted: "Be without offence to the Jews and to the Gentiles, and to the Church of God".

[4] That is the problem taken up by St. Paul in Rom. ix.-xi.

a spiritual and visible union. They claim for their dispersed members the name of "Church of God," long before accepting the name of Christians given them by the Greeks.

## EXCURSUS A.

### *The Church in the Gospel. Value of Matt. XVI. 18-19.*

Nowadays scholars are willing to grant that the notion of a Church—the "master-piece in the Catholic system," indeed " Catholicism itself "—is in germ in the first Christian communities. In the previous pages, we trust to have shown the well-founded character of this assertion, and even of a less restricted assertion. But once this historical fact has been granted, the same scholars go on to say that, " If the founder of the Christian religion deemed belief in the Gospel and life in accordance with it to be compatible with membership of the synagogue and observance of the Jewish Law, the same could not have been incompatible with membership of the Catholic Church ".[1] Thus to formulate the question, is to put it badly, for Catholicism is not the Law, the Synagogue, and Pharisaism : Jesus may disown all that past, and yet not disown, *ipso facto*, and in anticipation, the Church, unless indeed the Gospel is a kind of elusive essence, as is claimed by some contemporary idealists ; or a kind of gross eschatology, as is claimed by others. Hence the question before us is whether the idea of the Church belongs to the Gospel of Jesus or is foreign to it.

\* \*
\*

Jesus, we are told, preached the near coming of the Kingdom of God ; His conception of it was purely apocalyptic : how then could He have come to conceive of a religious society constituted so as to abide? The notion of an earthly society, that would be neither the Kingdom of God, nor the people of Israel, but would take the place of both, is outside the perspective of Jesus, who ever preached only the Kingdom, and its imminent catastrophic advent. Hence He determined nothing and said nothing about an earthly institution destined to replace the Jewish dispensation.

[1] HARNACK, "Dogmengeschichte," vol. I. p. 306.

" Men could speak of the Church, only after the Church had come into existence, i.e. after the Jewish people, as a whole, had refused to listen to the Apostolic preaching, and the Christian groups had become more and more strongly and definitely organized outside the religious organization of Israel. . . . Instead of the expected kingdom, the Church came, and the idea of the Church was substituted by the force of events for the idea of the kingdom." [1]

In the first place, then, we are confronted with a critical systematization of the teaching of Jesus, and in this systematization no room is left for the idea of the Church. But, first of all, this systematization is itself far from certain. As a matter of fact, we must deny that the idea of the kingdom was exclusively apocalyptic. I know full well that in doing so we oppose what is considered in some quarters, an intangible dogma: nevertheless, we prefer to abide by the view of those who look upon the Gospel idea of the kingdom as something other than an apocalyptic idea, and as I have written a whole book in defence of this view, I may be excused from reopening the discussion here. [2]

In the second place the idea of the kingdom, as supplied by the Gospel, is distinct from the idea of the Church. For Jesus Himself, and in accordance with His own statements, the evangelical preaching of the Kingdom has not the gift of conquering all those to whom it is addressed: there are some who reject it, by reason of their unbelief; there are others who are not worthy of it; there are dogs, to whom we must not give what is holy, swine before whom we must not cast pearls, "your pearls,' lest perhaps they trample them under their feet, and, turning upon you, they tear you" (Matt. VII. 6). There are houses and cities against which the disciples are told to shake off the dust from their sandals, because those houses and cities have not received them (Mark VI. 11). There are hearers who understand the message of Jesus, and others who do not: " To you it is

---

[1] A. LOISY, " Les Evangiles Synoptiques," vol. II. p. 9. Cf. W. SANDAY, "The Life of Christ in recent Research" (Oxford, 1907), pp. 76-89.

[2] Cf. my " Enseignement de Jésus " (Paris, 1905).

given to know the mystery of the Kingdom of God: but to them that are without, all things are parables" (Mark IV. 11). Therefore even here below those who know the Kingdom are distinguished from those who are outside.

Those who know the Kingdom form, round Jesus, a group that is very small in the beginning. Jesus looks upon His followers as a flock, of which He is the Shepherd: and what a small flock it is! "Fear not, little flock, for it hath pleased your Father to give you the Kingdom" (Luke XII. 32). The figure of the flock recalls that of the chickens gathered under the wings of the hen (Luke XIII. 34). This latter comparison is quite in the manner of the parables of Jesus, and bears on its very face the surest signs of authenticity. Jesus announces beforehand that His passion will scandalize His disciples, and disperse the sheep of the flock whose shepherd He is. "I will strike the shepherd, and the sheep shall be dispersed" (Mark XIV. 27), He says, applying to Himself a word of the prophet Zacharias, the flock is distinct from the Kingdom.

But the flock seems to be the beginning of a Church. The Gospel has never been a bodiless spirit: its first followers were visible and made up a group. Even granting that Catholic historians may at times be suspected of discovering too early the first outlines of ecclesiology, are not Protestant historians, like Harnack, open to the charge of a constant tendency to postpone the time when they actually appear? Harnack is willing to concede that the earliest Christian community, that which was formed at Jerusalem, was a " community of brothers " for a " common worship of God;" but in all that he sees only " a mysterious shadow of the heavenly Church ":[1] why does he disjoin the fact of this common brotherhood and religion from the idea of the Church save because he desires, almost in spite of himself, to preserve the Protestant dogma of the Church's invisibility? Elsewhere,[2] the same historian notes the formation of a society, but only outside "the inner circle of the Apostles, the band of twelve whom Jesus had gathered around Him ". Why does he separate this formed and visible

---

[1] " Das Wesen des Christentums " (1908), p. 132.
[2] *Ibid.* p. 96. Cf. " Mission," vol. I. p. 32.

society from the group of the Twelve, when it is most certain that the Twelve were the centre around which it was formed ? We are told that Jesus alone was the Master, and the disciples alone the disciples, and that Jesus had not founded the group of the Twelve as a " union for the service of God ". But this is mere quibbling, for, in fact, the Twelve who are disciples of the Master, are distinguished from the other disciples, and are already a " union " so truly that, immediately after the departure of the Master, all the disciples rally around them, as a centre, unhesitatingly and unquestioningly. Harnack acknowledges that this " was the germ from which all subsequent developments sprang". But did not that " germ " exist before it began to germinate ?

Loisy has seen the realities of the case more distinctly than Harnack.   The infant "society" at its birth is to be identified with the Twelve and the faithful disciples. To whatever minimum some may reduce it, it remains a group and a group distinct from the world by which it is encompassed.   It is a "circumscribed group, perfectly re-cognizable, a very centralized, even a hierarchical fraternity. Jesus is the centre and the chief, the incontestable authority.   Around Him the disciples are not a confused mass; the Saviour has distinguished among them the Twelve, and has associated these, directly and effectively, with His own ministry; even among the Twelve there is one who stands first, not only by the priority of his conversion or the ardour of his zeal, but by a kind of designation by the Master, accepted by the apostolic community. . . . It was an actual situation, apparently created by the missionary journeys of the Galilean ministry, but also evidently received and ratified by Jesus some time before the Passion. . . . The Church was born and endured through the development of an organization of which the outline is traced in the Gospel." [1]

Whilst Harnack dissociates the Church from the Gospel, Loisy replaces the Church in the Gospel, but connects the fact of the Church with the idea of the eschatological Kingdom.   "Jesus," he writes, "provided for the diffusion of the Gospel for the time then present."   But why does

[1] " L'Evangile et l'Eglise " (1902), p. 90 and foll.

Loisy add: "He thus prepared the Kingdom to come. Neither the society round Him, nor the Kingdom, was an invisible, impalpable reality, a society of souls, but a society of men who were the bearers of the Gospel, and were to become the Kingdom"? Loisy assumes the imminent and catastrophic advent of the Kingdom, and therefore looks upon the society of the disciples gathered by Jesus around His person as an "inauguration of the Kingdom," which is soon to appear in all its glory. This, he thinks, was a tragic illusion of the Galilean prophet. The announced Kingdom did not come; but the society of the disciples to whom it had been announced, and who continued for many years to expect it, was perpetuated through this very expectation. The society of expectant disciples was the Church. We on the contrary who deny that the Kingdom preached by Jesus was to be realized forthwith and under apocalyptic forms, we who hold that the very complex notion of the Kingdom implies above all, as regards mankind here below, an inner and spiritual advent, and a glorious advent only in the next life, combine together— without confusing them—the idea of the Church and the idea of the inner advent. No one will venture to say that in the words: "Fear not, little flock, for it hath pleased your Father to give you the kingdom," the flock and the Kingdom are but one and the same reality. To this faithful flock the kingdom of the Father is promised in heaven; here below, this faithful flock is the group of souls that have obtained the precious stone of the interior kingdom; but here below, this flock is also a visible collectivity, although one can never be sure that there is an equation in it between the number of those who are seen, and the number of those who are justified by God.

* * *

When we have dismissed the hypothesis of those critics who maintain that Jesus thought the end of the world at hand, we can easily deal with their further difficulty that Jesus could not foresee the Church, since He foresaw no future for anything in this world. Let us note, however, the many corrections, required by the facts themselves, which are called for by such a broad assertion.

Conversion, as well as salvation, is doubtless personal, but perseverance is collective: "Follow me" is a call addressed by Jesus many a time and to many a disciple,[1] and that the disciples follow Jesus, is granted by those whose views we are now discussing; but they refuse to see in this any other social bond than attachment to the person of the Master. Why, then, is it that, after the Master is gone, the social bond continues to subsist?

The intention of the Saviour as regards the lasting, spiritual, and visible bond that was to hold together His disciples after He had gone back to His Father, is defined in some Gospel texts, which—as was to be expected—are most fiercely called in question. Let us note the texts of the fourth Gospel in which the Saviour commands His disciples to serve one another, after the example He sets them by washing their feet (John XIII. 14-16, 34-5); or again the comparison He draws between the vine and the branches, as an analogy to the life the Master shares with His disciples (XV. 5-7); the parable of the Good Shepherd (X. 14-16); the prayer after the last supper, especially the passage where Jesus begs that His disciples may be one (XVII. 6-26). The historical character of the Johannine texts is, we know, rejected as a whole; but is this a reason for setting them aside altogether and passing by even the analogy between the texts we have just recalled and the ecclesiology of the great Pauline Epistles? The writers from whose opinion we differ are willing to grant that the fourth Gospel is full of echoes of the Synoptics: why not then take into account the words ascribed to Jesus: "Simon, son of John . . . feed my lambs . . . feed my sheep" (XXI. 15-17)? Commenting on this passage, Loisy has observed that the designation of the Apostle by his full name, "Simon, son of John," marked the solemn character of the scene and recalled the apostrophe: "Blessed art thou, Simon, son of Jona," in St. Matthew's Gospel (XVI. 17). He observes, too, that in contents as well as in form, this passage is parallel to the "Thou art Peter" of St. Matthew

---

[1] Matt. VIII. 22, XVI. 24, XIX. 21; Mark, II. 14, X. 21; Luke v. 27; John XII. 26, XXI. 22. Cf. Matt. VIII. 19, XIX. 28; Luke IX. 57, 61, etc.

(XVI. 18), and to the "Confirm thy brethren" of St. Luke (XXII. 32). "We have here," he says, "three echoes of the same tradition, equally faithful as to its substance".[1] In all sincerity, I must confess that such a distinction between substance and (I suppose) accidents is not very satisfactory in the present case. But had this distinction a basis (*dato, non concesso*), we should have here a new attestation of a synoptic tradition favourable to the conception of the flock led by its shepherd, a conception which, as we have already seen, is the conception of ecclesiology.

The synoptic gospels must be assigned to an earlier date than the Gospel of St. John, and this includes St. Matthew. In my opinion this last-mentioned Gospel was written about the year 70. But however that may be, and even if the critics pronounce so early a date to be inadmissible, the features they recognize in this Gospel remain to be accounted for. "The horizon of Matthew," says Harnack, "is that of Palestine, and this gospel is the work of the Palestinian Church which it exhibits as emancipated from the law, and in friendship with the Gentiles. Most probably it is the work of the Hellenistic part of the original Christian community, and was intended for the Jews of the Dispersion, described in Acts VI., who lived at Jerusalem and in due course formed themselves into little circles in and around the original Christian community. . . . That the Gospel of St. Matthew speedily forced the two other synoptic gospels into the background, even in the Gentile Church, is a well-known fact." Harnack seeks for the reason of this fact and finds that it is because the Gospel of St. Matthew is a powerful vindication of Christianity against the objections of the Jews, because it has an interest in the teaching of Jesus for its own sake, and in general because it instructs and proves, and all through keeps the Church (*Gemeinde*) well in the fore-

---

[1] A. LOISY, "Le quatrième Evangile" (Paris, 1903), p. 941. Loisy does not indeed look upon chapter XXI. as authentic; he regards it as a supplement, the style of which imitates skilfully that of the fourth Gospel. Its unknown redactor, he says, had to take into account "the Roman tradition and the feeling that Peter's primacy continued in the Church of Rome" (p. 943). See the answer to this objection in A. JÜLICHER, "Einleitung" (1894), p. 245 and foll. CALMES, "Evang. selon saint Jean" (Paris, 1904), pp. 466-73.

ground.   This is in truth a characteristic feature of Matthew, and Harnack estimates it aright when he notes that the Gospel of Matthew is impersonal, and was compiled to be a sort of Church-book (*Gemeindebuch*) and is in many respects the "first liturgical book of the Christian Church, in the first place of the Church of Palestine".[1]   Thus in Harnack's judgment the Gospel of St. Matthew belonged to the earliest Christian community at Jerusalem, and was in some sort its Church-book.

To these inferences Jülicher, who dates this Gospel at about the year 100, adds others still more interesting inasmuch as in our opinion they hold good quite independently of the question of date.   Jülicher writes of the author of our Gospel: "He has written a Catholic Gospel, and its truly Catholic temper has gained for it the first place among the Gospels".   It is he who makes the Christ say "Baptize them . . . and teach them to observe all that I have commanded you".   "In his eyes the community, that is, the Church, forms the highest disciplinary authority, as the administrator of the heavenly gifts of grace, and it is already determined who is to rule and make laws within its jurisdiction; according to his principles primitive Catholicism is already determined in its fundamental features."[2]   These observations are very instructive when one reflects that this truly Catholic Gospel was the Church-book of the Hellenistic party in the original Christian community at Jerusalem.

And to their inferences Jülicher adds further confirmation, when he says of this Gospel: "Its standpoint is not that of Paul, or that of Peter, or that of James, but that of the Church, whose building he alone triumphantly predicts in xvi. 18".   This Gospel has exercised an extraordinary influence on the Church, because it is the work of a time "when the partition walls between the Brethren in Judæa and the Brethren without had finally fallen in, and because it is the work of a man who, whilst as a writer he attained the standard set in Matthew xiii. 52, bore in himself the spirit of the growing Universal Church, and knew how to

[1] A. HARNACK, "Lukas der Arzt" (Leipzig, 1906), pp. 118-20.
[2] JÜLICHER, "Einleitung," p. 265.

write, without succumbing to party spirit, a Catholic Gospel, that is to say, one intended and fitted for all classes of believers ".

It was necessary to cite these estimates of the character of St. Matthew's Gospel, in order that we might with Harnack demonstrate its Palestinian character and with Jülicher its simultaneous "Catholic" character; as also to show that a passage like that on the building of the Church (XVI. 18) is entirely in keeping with the fundamental tendency of this Gospel.

We must, moreover, further cite Wellhausen who says: "It is commonly and justly noted as distinctive of Matthew that he shows special interest in the ἐκκλησία, which he alone brings forward, and that in two places. Indeed, it is not only in those two places where he calls it by its accepted name, that he refers to it, for he has the reality itself in mind in all his parables concerning the Kingdom of Heaven. The Church is in his eyes the seed-plot on earth which attaches to the Kingdom of Heaven. It has, in the strict Catholic sense, worthy and unworthy members; the sifting and parting of which God allows to be delayed until the day of the Last Judgment, when the Kingdom of Heaven will pass from its preliminary to its definitive phase. A member who has been drawn away from the community (by seducers, ψευδοπροφῆται, σκάνδαλα) must not be allowed to depart uncared for, but must be won back by every means possible; only when all friendly representation has failed of their effect, must recourse be had to excommunication (XVIII. 10-17). The heads of the organization are the Teachers, and before all others Peter. As administrator of the Kingdom of Heaven, that is, of the community, he bears the keys, the *insignia* of the master of the house. He has also another power, which is not in essential connexion with the power of the keys, the power to bind and loose; that is, the power to determine what shall be forbidden or permitted, what shall count or not, and likewise the teaching authority, which, it is true, has to do with practical, not theoretical matters." [1]

[1] J. WELLHAUSEN, " Einleitung in die drei ersten Evangelien " (Berlin, 1909), p. 70.

We may come now to the most famous of all these texts.
"Thou art Peter: and upon this rock I will build my church,
and the gates of hell shall not prevail against it. And I
will give to thee the keys of the kingdom of heaven.
And whatsoever thou shalt bind upon earth, it shall be
bound also in heaven: and whatsoever thou shalt loose on
earth, it shall be loosed also in heaven" (Matt. XVI. 18-19).
Against this text it is urged that it is not found in the
parallel passages of Mark and Luke, and this cannot be
denied ; that it belongs therefore neither to the tradition represented by Mark, where Mark is reproduced by Matthew
and Luke, nor to those *logia* unused by Mark, which were
used by Matthew and Luke, and this is possible. But
neither of these two observations can justify the supposition
that this particular *logion* " *Thou art Peter* (Rock)," the only
one of its kind, is less authentic than any other similarly
isolated *logion*, to be found either in St. Matthew or in
St. Luke.[1]

---

[1] RESCH, " Aussercanonische Paralleltexte zu den Evangelien,"
vol. I. (Leipzig, 1893), p. 185, admits the authenticity of Matt. XVI. 17,
which is found in St. Justin ("Dial." c. 4), and to which he thinks
St. Paul alludes in Gal. I. 16-17. He thinks these words of the Saviour
to St. Peter ("Beatus es, Simon Bariona") belong to the primitive
Gospel ("Urevangelium"); that v. 19b ("Quaecumque ligaveris") is a
doublet of Matt. XVIII. 18 ; and that v. 19a ("Tibi dabo claves . . . ") is
authentic, but addressed, not to Peter only, but to all the Apostles. We
need not remark that these two judgments are mere conjectures. There
remains v. 18. M. RESCH is sure that it was lacking in the primitive
form of Matthew's Gospel : another pure conjecture, for there is in the
MSS. no trace whatever of any hesitancy. M. RESCH is sure that v. 18,
as we have it now, was unknown all through the second century, and
that it is not quoted, for instance, by Irenæus, or by Clement of
Alexandria (this may be disputed, as regards Irenæus). We grant
that this silence is worth careful notice, but it is no more conclusive
than any other argument *ex silentio*. Again M. RESCH is sure that the
earliest explicit quotation of this text that we know of, is found in
Tertullian ("De pudicit." 22) and in Origen (ap. EUSEB. "H. E." VI. 25,
8. Also "In Exod. hom. v." 4). But this shows that the text already belonged to the tradition of both Latin and Greek MSS. The alleged trace
of the text in the "Homil. Clementinae" is doubtful ("Epist. Clem. ad
Jacob." and "Homil. XVII." 19). Even if it were not, no conclusion
could be drawn, since the "Hom. Clem." and the "Recogn." are both
now dated from the fourth century.

This declaration of Jesus to His Apostle is made towards the end of the Galilean ministry; the place where it is made was in the country of Cæsarea Philippi, where the Master is then alone with His disciples.  As they go along, Jesus asks them: " Whom do men say that I am? "  They answer that some look upon Him as John the Baptist, others as Elias, others as one of the prophets.  " And you? " Jesus asks. Peter answers: " Thou art the Christ," to which Jesus replies: " Blessed art thou, Simon Bar-Jona, because flesh and blood hath not revealed it to thee, but My Father who is in heaven.  And I say to thee that thou art Peter. . . ."  We may observe that here St. Matthew gives the Apostle's name in its Aramaic form: *Simon Bariona* ($\Sigma i\mu\omega\nu\ Ba\rho\iota\omega\nu\hat{a}$), Simon, son of Jona or Jonas.  When it has to recall the same expression, the fourth Gospel uses a Graecized form $\Sigma i\mu\omega\nu$ '$I\omega\acute{a}\nu\omega\nu$ (John XXI. 15, 16, 17).  We must not fail to notice in this second reading a mark of St. Matthew's priority, and of the primitive character of the oral tradition which he used.[1]

The Father has revealed to Simon that Jesus is the Messias.  " And I say to thee, . . ." continues Jesus, contrasting His own words with what the Father has revealed directly to Peter, " And I say to thee, that thou art Peter; and upon this rock I will build . . . "  Jesus plays upon the Aramaic name Peter, but the play disappears both in Greek and in Latin: an excellent proof that the word was originally spoken in Aramaic, which was Jesus's mother-tongue: " Thou art *Kepha* and upon this *kepha* I will build . . .".[2]  Jesus says: " Thou art Peter [Rock] ($\sigma\grave{v}\ \epsilon\hat{\iota}$

[1] J. WELLHAUSEN, " Das Evangelium Matthaei " (Berlin, 1904), p. 83 : " Jona is Jona and no abbreviation of Johanan, and Matthew is in the right, not only against the Hebrew Gospel, a late compilation, but also against the fourth Gospel ".

[2] Recall John I. 42 : " Thou art Simon, the son of Jona : thou shalt be called Cephas (which is interpreted Peter) ".  Cf. J. HART, " Cephas and Christ," in the " Journal of Theol. Studies," vol. IX. (1907), p. 32 : " The actual word *Cepha* is not common in the oldest Targums in the sense of Rock.  But the Targum of Onkelos employs it in a very prominent and important passage as the equivalent of the *Sela* or Rock, from which Moses drew water for the children of Israel. . . . On the other hand, *Cepha* is used of a precious stone in the Targum of Proverbs, and this sense of stone seems to predominate in Palestinian Aramaic."

$Πέτρος$) and I will build upon this rock" (καὶ ἐπὶ ταύτῃ τῇ
πέτρᾳ οἰκοδομήσω) : Jesus points to this rock, it is present,
it can be seen: this rock cannot then be understood as referring to Christ, still less to the faith of Peter.[1] "Upon
this rock I will build . . ." might be a reminiscence of
Isaias (XXVIII. 16): "Behold I have laid a stone in the
foundations of Sion, a tried stone, a corner stone, a precious
stone, a stone firmly set . . . ". Again in Isaias (LI. 1),
Abraham is likened to the rock out of which Israel has been
hewn. A still more exact analogy might be found in the
short parable, recorded by St. Matthew (VII. 24-7) and St.
Luke (VI. 48-9), of the man who built his house upon a
rock, whom Jesus contrasts with the other man who built
his house upon the sand. A flood came, and the house
built upon the sand was carried away by the waters, whilst
the other remained unshaken, because it was founded upon
a rock. Here, as in the declaration of Jesus to Simon, the
rock is called πέτρα.

   "*Upon this rock I will build my Church,*" says Jesus:
in this passage, three words can give rise to a plausible objection, one which has become classical among contemporary
Protestant critics. They claim that the notion of the
ἐκκλησία is a Pauline creation; and they remind us that
St. Paul speaks, not of the ἐκκλησία τοῦ χριστοῦ, but of the
ἐκκλησία τοῦ θεοῦ. The expression *to build* applied to an
ἐκκλησία, is also a Pauline expression.[2] Hence the *logion*
ascribed to Jesus by St. Matthew bears the stamp of an
origin many years after the preaching of the Gospel.

   This objection is far from decisive: for, in the first
place, the word itself, ἐκκλησία, is not a Pauline creation,
since ἐκκλησία is also found in the LXX, where like the synonymous word συναγωγή it designates the assembly of the
Jews of one locality.[3] The *ecclesiastes* is one who addresses

---

   [1] These two interpretations have their history, which is summed up
by J. TURMEL, "Hist. de la théol. posit." vol. II. (Paris, 1906), pp.
152-71.
   [2] 1 Cor. III. 10-17 ; Eph. II. 19-22.
   [3] Moreover the word ἐκκλησία is found once again in St. Matthew :
"If thy brother shall offend against thee, go and rebuke him between
thee and him alone. . . . And if he will not hear thee, take with thee
one or two more. . . . And if he will not hear them, tell the church.

a Jewish assembly of that time. In Stephen's discourse (Acts VII. 38), the word ἐκκλησία is taken in the meaning of the LXX and is used to designate the people of Israel gathered around Moses in the wilderness. It is used likewise by the author of the Epistle to the Hebrews, to signify the assembly of the just of Israel in the heavenly Jerusalem (Heb. XII. 23).[1] To build an ἐκκλησία may be a bold image which St. Paul developed and brought into common use. But, in the *logion* of St. Matthew, it is couched in a most simple form and is introduced naturally by the context: a rock is chosen to build upon, nothing can prevail against what is built on that rock. We are still far from St. Paul's developments about the "upbuilding," and this is rather a mark of archaism. There remains another difficulty: that Christ says *My Church*, an expression which has no analogy in the New Testament. I confess that I should feel more disturbed if some analogies were found there; for if this *logion* were of recent origin, should we not find in it something of the language of the Pauline Epistles and of the Acts? Since the expression ἐκκλησία τοῦ θεοῦ was alone used[2] at the time when St. Matthew's Gospel was

And if he will not hear the church, let him be to thee as a heathen and publican" (Matt. XVIII. 15-17). In this text the word ἐκκλησία does not necessarily designate the Christian community: the progression clearly marked in that *logion*—first one, then two, finally all—shows quite clearly that the idea in view is of number alone. Hence ἐκκλησία designates here the collection of the people of one and the same city, according to the meaning in which this word is taken in the Psalms. Ps. XXI. 23, 26, XXXIV. 18, XXXIX. 10, CVI. 32, etc.

[1] WELLHAUSEN notes (p. 84) that the word ἐκκλησία was borrowed by the Christians from the Jews, and that the Aramaic word corresponding to it designates the Jewish as well as the Christian community: "The Aramaic primitive word *k'nischta* designates the Jewish as well as the Christian community". This remark (as against Schürer, Sohm, and the whole Protestant school) is of the greatest importance. Wellhausen adds that the Christians of Palestine used indiscriminately the word *k'nischta* to designate either the synagogue or the Church; the word *edta* is not Palestinian, but Syriac. "The Syrians say *edta* for the Christians, and *k'nuschta* for the Jews. But with them too the distinction is not ancient." If that is the case, the verbal opposition between the word ἐκκλησία and the word συναγωγή is not strictly primitive and the idea alone counts.

[2] Cf. however, Rom. XVI. 16.

drawn up, why was Christ made to say here, τὴν ἐκκλησίαν μου? It may assist us to answer if we compare the expression "my Church" with this other passage recorded by St. Matthew only: "All things are delivered to me by my Father. . . . Come to me, all you that labour. . . . Take up my yoke upon you, and learn of me . . . . For my yoke is sweet and my burden light."[1] We may compare also this other passage likewise recorded only by St. Matthew (XVIII. 20): "Where there are two or three gathered together in my name, there I am in the midst of them," and also this given both by St. Matthew and St. Luke: "Jerusalem, Jerusalem . . . how often would I have gathered together thy children".[2] Jesus is the one who calls,[3] who gathers, who wishes that all should come to Him and be with Him, who imposes a yoke similar indeed to that of the Law, but far more light and easy. He is also the one who can destroy God's temple and rebuild it three days after. Are not these so many analogues to the expression: " I will build my Church "?[4]

A still more specious objection urged against us is the following. Not only its form, it is said, but the spirit which animates this *logion*, is of a much later date than the preaching of Jesus. It appears to be the earliest testimony to the pretensions of the Roman Church to the hegemony of all the churches, an anticipation of the state of things which came

---

[1] Matt. XI. 27-30. The Son of Man speaks of His kingdom which is God's kingdom, and that precisely in St. Matthew (XIII. 41 and XVI. 28), a remark made by WELLHAUSEN, p. 84.

[2] Matt. XXIII. 37 (ἐπισυναγαγεῖν), Luke, XIII. 34 (ἐπισυνάξαι). Compare the net that gathers in (συναγαγούσῃ) all kind of fishes (Matt. XIII. 47). Matt. XII. 30: ὁ μὴ συνάγων μετ᾽ ἐμοῦ. We may notice that συνάγειν has the same root as σύναξις and συναγωγή.

[3] Cf. Mark II. 17; Matt. IX. 13; Luke IV. 16; Matt. XXII. 9. HOLTZMANN, "Neut. Theologie," vol. I. p. 211, likens ἔκκλητοι to ἐκκλησία. Cf. Matt. XXII. 14: πολλοί εἰσιν κλητοί.

[4] The verbal boldness with which St. Paul speaks of building up the Church, can be more naturally accounted for if he is alluding to some Word of Jesus, that was known to the faithful. HORT, "The Christian Ecclesia" (London, 1897), p. 9. J. WORDSWORTH, "Unity and Fellowship" (London, 1910), p. 76.

to be realized in the Church, and co-eval with that realization.[1]

Is not this a case of proving too much and so proving nothing? Holtzmann and Loisy place the composition of the Gospel according to St. Matthew about the year 100 : can they find, at that date, even a single expression analogous to what they call the Roman hegemony? If they could it would be no difficulty for us theologians, who believe in the Divine right of the Roman primacy; but it is a most serious difficulty for those critics who do not believe in that Divine right. To them we may justly say that the Flavian age is altogether too early for the state of things which you think occasioned the composition of that *logion*, and those critics are more consistent who maintain that it was interpolated into St. Matthew towards the end of the second century, at the time of Pope Victor, it may be, if not later. Then, on the supposition of Holtzmann and Loisy that the composition of the Gospel according to St. Matthew synchronized with the " work of building the Church," how account for the fact that this work has left in the final redaction of that Gospel so few and such faint traces of itself? If that redaction belonged really to the epoch of Clement of Rome and of Ignatius, should we not find in it some echo of the language of these two great leaders? Should we discover in the Gospel according to St. Matthew no other infiltration of the ecclesiastical spirit and of the Roman tendency than this declaration of the Saviour to Peter?

" *Upon this rock I will build my Church, and the gates of hell [Hades] shall not prevail against it.*" Hell is the abode of Satan the enemy of God, of Satan the tempter of Jesus in the wilderness, of Satan who makes Judas into a son of perdition. Paul heard Jesus say: "I send thee to the Gentiles to open their eyes, that they may be converted from darkness to light, and from the power of Satan to God" (Acts XXVI. 18). "The God of peace will speedily crush Satan under your feet," says St. Paul to the Romans (XVI. 20), and Jesus in St. Luke (XXII. 31) says to Peter:

---

[1] LOISY, " Evang. synopt." vol. II. p. 10. HOLTZMANN, " Neut. Theologie," vol. I. p. 210. J. WEISS, " Schriften des N.T." (Göttingen, 1907), vol. I. p. 344.

" Simon, Simon, behold Satan hath desired to have you that he may sift you as wheat ". However, the " gates of Hades " do not signify exclusively Satan and his power: they signify also death. (1 Sap. xvi. 13 ; 3 Mac. v. 51. Cf. Job xxxviii. 17 ; Ps. ix. 3, cvii. 18.) A promise of immortality is made here to the Church : the gates of Hades shall never close upon her, as they do upon the dead, of whom the prophet Jonas said : " The bars of the earth have shut me up for ever " (Jonas ii. 7).

Peter is the foundation stone, but here is another image of his function; Christ will give him the keys of the Kingdom of Heaven. This image of the keys may be understood in the sense that Peter is to be the one who opens to the Church the gates of the Kingdom, whilst the gates of Hades are powerless against her. The distinction between the Kingdom and the Church is here affirmed again. The keys signify the power of the chief steward : Isaias makes Yahweh address Eliacim in these words : " I will lay the key of the house of David upon his shoulder : and he shall open, and none shall shut : and he shall shut, and none shall open ".[1] Peter has authority over the Kingdom : he can receive Cornelius into it, as well as give over to Satan Ananias and Sapphira. Peter opens and closes the entrance to the kingdom of heaven, he is its steward here below.[2]

Jesus adds : " *Whatsoever thou shalt bind upon earth, it shall be bound also in heaven. . . .*" These words, to bind and to loose, belong to the rabbinical language, in which

---

[1] Isa. xxii. 22. Cf. Apoc. iii. 7-8, where it is Jesus who carries the key of David. Compare Apoc. i. 18 : " I am the first, and the last, and alive, and was dead, and behold I am living for ever and ever, and have the keys of death and of Hades." Cf. Apoc. xx. 13, 14, and Heb. ii. 14. KAUTZSCH, " Die Pseudepigraphen," p. 455. In the Apocalypse of Baruch xi. 1, the archangel Michael is the key-bearer to the Kingdom of Heaven. G. DALMAN, "Die Worte Jesu," vol. i. (Leipzig, 1898), p. 176. He who has the keys is not the janitor but the majordomo who is put over all that belongs to the king.

[2] The keys are given to Peter. The interpretation according to which they are given to the Church, has also a history (see TURMEL, "op. cit." pp. 177-85), but no critical value. DALMAN, p. 177. "Thus Peter has, Matt. xvi. 19, the keys of the heavenly kingdom, and in his character of key-bearer is invested with full powers as the steward of God on earth."

they mean respectively to forbid and to allow, in the sense in which a rabbi either forbids or allows an action, according as it is, in his eyes, in harmony with the Law or against it; in the sense in which we read in the Mishna that the rigorist Shammai binds and the more accommodating Hillel looses.[1] Jesus had denounced the Pharisees who "bind heavy burdens" to the shoulders of those who listen to them (Matt. XXIII. 2-4), whilst He, on the contrary, so often loosed His disciples from these Pharisaic rigours. That power to bind and to loose, which was exercised by Jesus, is given to Peter, and in Heaven God will sanction his decisions. The same thought is also found in another declaration of Jesus, which is addressed this time not to Peter, but to all the disciples together: "Amen I say to you, whatsoever you shall bind upon earth, shall be bound also in heaven; and whatsoever you shall loose upon earth shall be loosed also in heaven" (Matt. XVIII. 18). However the power to bind and to loose designates not only a function discharged by casuists in the interpretation of a written law: it implies also a legislative and judicial power, and an authority to remit sins.

The text of Christ's declaration to Peter makes one solid whole: Peter is he who binds and looses, as Jesus binds and looses, as the Apostles bind and loose; he is the foundation, as Jesus is, and as the Apostles are also; but besides all that, he holds the primacy, and he alone is the one who has the keys of the kingdom, since he alone is the chief steward.[2]

These are figures, but they are figures which the history of the days that immediately follow the Saviour's passion

---

[1] DALMAN, p. 175-176.

[2] Faithful to his theory of anticipation, LOISY writes as follows ("Evang. synopt." vol. II. p. 13): "It is not without reason that the Catholic tradition has based on this text the dogma of the Roman primacy. The consciousness of that primacy inspires throughout the development of Matthew, which has in view not only the historical person of Simon, but also the traditional succession of Simon Peter." We should remember LOISY's point of view. The same theory is in J. WEISS, vol. I. p. 345. P. WERNLE, "Die Quellen des Lebens Jesu" (Halle, 1904), p. 75: "The Catholics have been entirely justified in coining the word Roman-Catholic".

exhibit as passing into realities: the shepherd has been
stricken, the sheep have taken to flight, then suddenly they
gather together again; and gather around Peter, who first
saw the risen Christ.[1] It is not because Peter is called
Cephas that he becomes the rock on which rest the disciples
now rallied and strengthened, those disciples once so anxious
to know who was the first and the greatest among them?
If Peter is the rock and the chief steward, it is because of a
previously established economy, which alone can have laid
that foundation of authority and of union.

* * *

We have not yet finished with the difficulties raised by
present-day critics against the " ecclesiastical thesis ".   Harnack, who deserves credit for refusing to look upon the
message of Jesus as strictly eschatological, does not grant,
however, that He foresaw the calling of the Gentiles or spoke
of anything more than the salvation of Israel.   The love of
God and of men which was at the heart of the Gospel, was,
he contends, so intense and living that it impelled the
Apostles to undertake the conquest of the world, though
about this their Master had been altogether silent.[2]

Any one who has made up his mind to defend this
portion must set aside the testimony of the fourth Gospel,
which is thoroughly saturated with universalism.[3]   The
Word came into the world which He had made; He came
consequently unto His own, and men did not receive Him,
but to all those who did receive Him He gave the power to
become sons of God (John i. 10-12).   The incarnation of
the Word has for its end the adoption of mankind by God.
St. Paul was not more universalist when he said that God

---

[1] The decisive part Peter plays soon after the Passion, in rallying the
disciples and in bringing into existence the first of all the churches, the
mother church, is luminously demonstrated by WEIZSÄCKER, p. 12 and foll.
" Peter was unquestionably the first man in the Primitive Church ".   At
the time of his first visit to Jerusalem, Paul cared very little about seeing any one but Peter.   " The importance of Peter had been already
recognized by the Master Himself, by whom he had already been
distinguished beyond all his companions."

[2] HARNACK, " Mission," vol. i. p. 31 and foll.   See on this point
M. MEINERTZ, " Jesus und die Heidenmission " (Münster, 1908).

[3] See especially John i. 29, x. 16, xii. 20.

was in Christ and in Him reconciled "the world" unto Himself (2 Cor. v. 19). The critics of whom we are speaking dismiss also the testimony of St. Matthew: "Going therefore teach ye all nations" (XXVIII. 19), and that of St. Mark: "Go ye into the whole world and preach the Gospel to every creature" (XVI. 15), as well as that of St. Luke, in whose Gospel the risen Christ commands that "penance and the remission of sins be preached in his name unto all nations, beginning at Jerusalem" (XXIV. 47). This grand act of opening the Gentile world to the apostleship of His disciples, which is imputed to Jesus in the New Testament, expressed, we are told, the faith of the second Christian generation, "the faith estimating, some fifty years after the Saviour's death, the development of the Gospel work".[1]

The Gospels themselves are invoked to prove that Jesus had only Israel in mind. At the head of the commands given by Jesus to His missionaries, Matthew places this: "Go ye not into the way of the Gentiles, and into the cities of the Samaritans enter ye not: but go ye rather to the lost sheep of the house of Israel" (Matt. x. 5); and a few lines below: "When they shall persecute you in one city, flee into another. Amen, I say to you, you shall not finish all the cities of Israel, till the Son of Man come" (x. 23); and elsewhere: "You shall sit on twelve seats, judging the twelve tribes of Israel" (XIX. 28). Harnack infers from these texts that the evangelization of the Gentiles is beyond the horizon of Jesus. There are other texts, however, that suggest a contrary inference. In St. Matthew, Jesus foretells to His disciples that they shall be "hated by all nations" (XXIV. 9), and that "this Gospel of the kingdom shall be preached in the whole world, for a testimony to all nations" (XXIV. 14). In St. Mark, He speaks in a similar tone: "You shall stand before governors and kings for my sake, for a testimony unto them". But "first," before the advent of the Son of Man, "the Gospel must be preached to all nations" (Mark XIII. 9-10). In St. Mark also, Jesus praises the woman who at Bethany poured over His feet a vessel of perfume. "Amen I say to you, wheresoever this Gospel shall be preached in

---

[1] Loisy, "Evang. Synop." vol. II. pp. 775-6. Meinertz, p. 111 and foll.

the whole world, that also which she hath done, shall be told for a memorial of her" (XIV. 9).

In this conflict of texts that are thus pitted one against the other, is it not wiser to seek a broader basis for the judgment we have to pass?

A sure element of solution is given us by the narrative of the cure of the centurion's son at Capharnaum. This centurion is not a Jew, since he is a soldier. But Jesus grants his request, because of his faith which He admired: "I have not found so great faith in Israel" (Matt. VIII. 10; Luke VII. 9). St. Matthew adds: "And I say to you that many shall come from the east and the west, and shall sit down with Abraham and Isaac and Jacob in the Kingdom of Heaven" (VIII. 11). Why should not Jesus have spoken in that manner? Had not the Baptist said before: "Think not to say within yourselves, We have Abraham for our father. For I tell you that God is able of these stones to raise up children to Abraham" (Matt. III. 9). Similar affirmations in regard to the calling of the Gentiles to salvation may be found in every page of the prophets; the post-exilian Messianism is filled with them, alone they account for proselytism.[1] If Jesus is the Messias and knows He is the Messias, why, contrary to the Scriptures, should He have excluded the Gentiles?

Again, did Jesus, in the course of His preaching, find no occasion to proclaim Israel's obduracy? Like John the Baptist, did He not affirm, many a time, that the axe was laid to the root of the tree! Who then in default of Israel shall inherit the kingdom? Henceforth the preaching of the Gospel appears subject to no restriction; and such does it appear in the parable of the sower, in which the sower starts to sow, without asking himself whether the land is Jewish or not. "The good ground that received the seed, this is he that heareth the word and understandeth" (Matt. XIII. 23). In the parable of the cockles, "He that soweth the good seed is the Son of Man, and the field is the world" (Matt. XIII. 37).[2]

---

[1] HOLTZMANN, "Neut. Theologie," vol. I. p. 73. LAGRANGE, "Messianisme," pp. 268, 285. MEINERTZ, p. 17 and foll.

[2] As to the parables that may be understood of the Church, the reader may consult Dom G. DOLAN, "The Church in the Parables," in A. H. MATHEW's "Ecclesia or the Church of Christ" (London, 1906), pp. 1-19.

From these two observations we may infer that, in the Messianic plan of Jesus, the Gospel is not restricted to Israel, especially to that Israel which rebels against Him: Israel's privilege consists only in this that the Gospel message is brought to it first, according to the words of Jesus to the Cananæan woman : "Suffer first the children to be filled" (Mark VII. 27). The preaching of Jesus Himself is in fact confined to Galilee and to Jerusalem. He knows He has been sent to the lost sheep of the house of Israel (Matt. xv. 24) and to them only. This is why the sheep of Israel appear alone in the foreground of the Gospel. But this does not exclude a background, that of the Gentile world. The scruples which the Apostles will experience later on as to "passing over to the Gentiles" may be easily accounted for by the extreme boldness which such a step implies on the part of a Jew; but they are based on no word of the Master. On the contrary, even without having recourse to this or that parable, as to the parables of the wicked husbandman or of those who were invited to the wedding, or deducing from them that the Saviour had in view the rejection of Israel and the calling of the Gentiles, it suffices for us to affirm that the Gospel is not conditioned by any idea of race; every man is our neighbour; the disciples are the children of the Father who is in Heaven, and who "maketh His sun to rise upon the good and bad, and raineth upon the just and the unjust" (Matt. v. 45).

We conclude, then, that the message of Jesus is limited neither as regards time by the belief in the near advent of the end of all things, nor as regards mankind by the exclusion of the Gentiles. As to the notion of the Church, it is implied in the separation which Jesus marks so distinctly between those who follow Him and those who do not, the former becoming the flock of which He is the shepherd. The essential character of this flock is not that of an enthusiastic and individualistic Christianity without bond or rule ; this is rendered quite clear by the grant of powers made by the Saviour to His Apostles, and first of all to Peter, their leader.[1]

[1] In the "Zeitschrift für die neutestam. Wissenschaft," 1907, pp. 163-89, M. J. KREYENBÜHL has made strenuous attempts to prove that Matt. XVI. 17-19 is a reply made by the mother-Church of Jerusalem to the ac-

count they had received of the Antiochian conflict, as given in St. Paul's Epistle to the Galatians, Gal. II. 2-10.   The *Tu es Petrus*, thus understood, was the charter of the legitimacy of the mother-Church !   Peter represented the Church of Jerusalem and her rights against St. Paul's pretensions.   According to the same writer, the scene which is reported as having taken place at Cæsarea Philippi is not at all historical, though the narrative belongs to the collection of those *logia* which—as he thinks —formed the Gospel of the mother-Church.   This narrative began to spread abroad, probably soon after the date of the Epistle to the Galatians —hence after the year 50—but certainly before the destruction of Jerusalem in the year 70.   I should not have even mentioned this paradoxical view, which is not to be taken seriously, were it not the symptom of a reaction against the view—just as paradoxical—of M. Resch.

# CHAPTER III.

## THE INFANT CHURCH (CONTINUED).

WE have discovered in a number of texts anterior to St. Paul's captivity, the existence of a Christian community separated from Judaism and made up of converts, most of whom do not come from Judaism and have neither its culture nor its spirit. This Roman-Hellenic community of Christians is Catholicism already realized. Its characteristic features, which we have found clearly manifested in those sources, exhibit themselves, as we are about to see, with still greater precision and completeness in a series of testimonies which begin with the Epistles of St. Paul's captivity (57-62 A.D.), and come to a close with the Epistles of St. Ignatius of Antioch (about 110).

## I.

The distinction, clearly made in the first Epistle to the Thessalonians between the governing church and the church that is governed (1 Thess. v. 13) is marked in the Epistle to the Philippians with an unexpected precision. We read in the inscription of the Epistle: "Paul and Timothy, the servants of Jesus Christ, to all the saints in Christ Jesus, who are at Philippi, and to the bishops and deacons, grace and peace"[1]

For the first time there appears in the Christian litera-

---

[1] Phil. I: πᾶσιν τοῖς ἁγίοις . . . τοῖς οὖσιν ἐν Φιλίπποις σὺν ἐπισκόποις καὶ διακόνοις. The predicate ἅγιοι applied to the Christians is borrowed from the Old Testament, according to which Israel is a holy nation, and the Israelites are saints, because they belong to God (Exod. XIX. 6; Deut. VII. 6, etc.). Up to the middle of the second century the faithful call themselves ἅγιοι; later on this appellation is reserved to the Church. HARNACK, "Mission," vol. I. pp. 340. KATTENBUSCH, vol. II. p. 695.

ture the name of the office that succeeds to the office of the Apostolate; if the community of the saints of Philippi has its servants, διάκονοι,[1] it has especially its ἐπίσκοποι, a name which implies some primacy.[2] Saints, episcopi and deacons form, all together, one and the same ἐκκλησία (Philip. IV. 15). Paul entreats them to have but one mind, one love, one soul;[3] and to guard against the false apostles who would compel them to be circumcised,[4] for "we are the true circumcision, who in spirit serve God, and glory in Christ Jesus, not having confidence in the flesh" (III. 2-3). He encourages them to be without blame in the midst of a perverse and corrupt generation, where they shine as torches, since they "hold the word of life" (II. 15-16).

To judge only from the few texts at our disposal, we might say that the formation of the hierarchy shows itself at Philippi more advanced than elsewhere. But no local circumstance accounts for this development, which is soon to manifest itself the same everywhere.

The Epistle to the Colossians and that to the Ephesians show that the churches of Asia are organized like those of Macedonia and of Achaia.[5] The name "Church" serves to

---

[1] Rom. XVI. 1. Paul had already mentioned a deaconess at Cenchreæ, near Corinth. LIGHTFOOT, "Christian Ministry," pp. 16-17. Lightfoot shows (p. 14) that the function of the Christian διάκονος does not originate in that of the ḥazan or servant of the synagogue, but is an office altogether new. The ḥazan was the beadle of the synagogue, and also the schoolmaster who taught the children how to read. Cf. A. ROBINSON, art. "Deacon and Deaconess," in the "Encyc. Biblica".

[2] PRAT, pp. 488-94. Like the word ἐκκλησία, the word ἐπίσκοπος is common to Christian terminology and to the terminology of the Greek civil institutions. But the Christian office was not derived from its Greek analogue. Cf. (against Hatch and Harnack) A. ROBINSON, art. "Bishop" in the "Encyc. Biblica".

[3] Philip. II. 2 : τὸ αὐτὸ φρονῆτε, τὴν αὐτὴν ἀγάπην ἔχοντες, σύνψυχοι, τὸ ἓν φρονοῦντες.

[4] Philip. III. 2 : "Beware of dogs, beware of evil workers and of their mutilation". Cf. Gal. v. 12. We find in both Epistles the same adversaries of St. Paul, also the same tone in St. Paul's expressions : he retorts against them the insults they fling at Christians who, like all Gentiles, are for them mere dogs, i.e. an impure set of men (compare in Matt. xv. 22 and foll. the episode of the Cananæan woman).

[5] About the authenticity of these two Epistles, cf. T. K. ABBOTT, "Ephesians and Colossians" (Edinburgh and New York, 1897), introduction.

designate the assembly of the faithful of one and the same city, Laodicea for instance: " Salute the brethren who are at Laodicea," Paul writes to the Colossians, "and Nymphas, and the church that is in his house. When this epistle shall have been read with you, cause that it be read also in the church of Laodicea " (Col. IV. 15-16). Paul speaks of psalms and canticles which the faithful sing together; he wishes that the faithful of Colossæ should mutually teach and admonish one another;[1] he exhorts them to act with wisdom towards those who are outside the Church (οἱ ἔξω, IV. 5).

The Church of Colossæ has been evangelized, not by Paul, but by Epaphras, who has also devoted himself unsparingly to the churches of Laodicea and of Hierapolis (Col. IV. 13): Paul calls Epaphras the διάκονος τοῦ χριστοῦ, but here the word διάκονος signifies probably simply missionary.[2] The Colossians must abide in the faith they have received, in the faith as it has been taught them.[3] Let them beware lest any one lead them astray "by philosophy and vain deceit, according to the tradition of men, according to the elements of the world, and not according to Christ " (II. 8).

In this severe formula is comprised all that Paul deems the contrary of the truth according to Christ which he preaches and which Epaphras also preaches ; for he is sure he has regarding the Gospel the same ideas as Epaphras. The "elements of the world" are the popular errors of the Gentiles ; the "empty and deceitful philosophy" designates here some beginning of Gnosticism ; the " tradition of men " (παράδοσις τῶν ἀνθρώπων) means the teachers of this philosophy. It is easy to infer from these data that the errors against which St. Paul warns the Colossians belong to some Judæo-Greek syncretism, of an ascetical and specu-

---

[1] Col. III. 16 ; Eph. v. 19.

[2] Col. I. 7. Paul gives himself the title of διάκονος (Col. II. 23), and he gives it also to Tychicus (Eph. VI. 21).

[3] Col. II. 7 : ὡς παρελάβετε . . . καθὼς ἐδιδάχθητε. This is the notion of the παράδοσις, which is fundamental with St. Paul. Cf. Col. I. 7 (καθὼς ἐμάθετε ἀπὸ Επαφρᾶ). 1 Cor. XI. 2 (καθὼς παρέδωκα ὑμῖν τὰς παραδόσεις κατέχετε). 1 Thess. IV. 1 ; 1 Cor. XV. 1, 2, XI. 23 ; Gal. I. 9, 12 ; Phil. IV. 9,

lative kind.[1]  " If you be dead with Christ from the elements of this world, why do you subject yourselves to ordinances, as living in the world ? "   Some fasten upon you precepts of abstinence, which have indeed some appearance of wisdom, of humility, of contempt of the body, but they are in truth, " precepts and teachings of men ".[2]   The Gospel on the contrary is a precept and teaching of God.

It is in Christ you have believed, Paul says to the Ephesians, " after you had heard the word of truth, the gospel of your salvation : in whom also believing you were signed with the holy spirit of promise, who is the pledge of our inheritance " (Eph. I. 13).   We find always the same method : the preaching of the Gospel, the birth of faith in the faithful, baptism, the outpouring of the Holy Ghost. Through baptism, the faithful rise from the death of sin to a life which is the life of Christ.   The Gospel is the Gospel of salvation, since we are saved through faith (II. 8).   Formerly the faithful of Ephesus to whom Paul writes, and likewise all the faithful of Asia to whom his Epistle is addressed, " were called uncircumcision by that which is called circumcision "; for they were " aliens from the conversation of Israel '"; they were " without hope and without God ($ἄθεοι$) in this world."[3]   But now, they are " made nigh by the

---

[1] LIGHTFOOT, " Colossians," pp. 71-111, and PRAT, pp. 391-98, in their estimate of this first apparition of Gnosticism in the field of Christian propaganda, consider that Gnosticism was independent of Christianity and preceded it; it had attempted to build up Jewish syncretisms, before it attempted to do the same for Christianity.   W. BOUSSET, " Hauptprobleme der Gnosis " (Göttingen, 1907), pp. 5-7.

[2] Col. II. 20 : $εἰ ἀπεθάνετε σὺν Χριστῷ ἀπὸ τῶν στοιχείων τοῦ κόσμου,$ $τί ὡς ζῶντες κόσμῳ δογματίζεσθε ; . . . 22, κατὰ τὰ ἐντάλματα καὶ διδασκαλίας$ $τῶν ἀνθρώπων.$   F. CUMONT, " Les religions orientales dans le paganisme romain " (Paris, 1906), p. 248.   " All writers agree with Firmicus Maternus in acknowledging that heathens worshipped the *elements*.   This word meant not only the four simple substances whose opposition and various combinations produce the phenomena of the material world, but also the stars and, as a whole, the principles of all heavenly and earthly bodies." However, F. PRAT, p. 252, remarks that for St. Paul (Gal. IV. 3, 9 ; Col. II. 8, 20) the " elements of the world " signify elementary doctrines, like the alphabet ($στοιχεῖα$) which is taught to children.

[3] The word $ἄθεος$ is not found in the LXX and is found nowhere but here in the whole New Testament.   St. Paul means that the Gentiles,

blood of Jesus Christ," for Christ has overthrown the wall of separation that was raised between the circumcised and the uncircumcised : "He hath made both peoples one. . . . He makes the two in Himself into a new man. . . . He reconciles both to God in one body by the cross." The same peace is brought to the uncircumcised who were afar, and to the circumcised who were near : henceforth both have access to the Father "in one and the same Spirit". The uncircumcised are no longer strangers and pilgrims, but citizens of one and the same city, members of the house of God, " built upon the foundation of the apostles and prophets, JESUS CHRIST himself being the chief-corner stone : in whom all the building, being framed together, groweth up into an holy temple in the Lord, in whom you also are built together into an habitation of God in Spirit." [1]

This elaborate phrase reminds us of the words of Psalm cXVII. 22, about the stone rejected by the builders, which afterwards became the corner stone of the structure : an image preserved in a *logion* of Christ.[2] A building is being raised, of which Jesus is the corner stone, and the Apostles and Prophets of the Gospel, the foundation. The faithful are built on this foundation, ἐποικοδομηθέντες, they are bound together in the building συνοικοδομεῖσθε,[3] and the whole edifice is "a holy temple in the Lord," a dwelling of

who adore the " elements," do not know God. HARNACK, " Der Vorwurf des Atheismus " (1905), pp. 3-4.

[1] Eph. II. 11-22. The uncircumcised were excluded from τῆς πολιτείας τοῦ Ἰσραήλ, they were ξένοι as regards the people of God ; Christ has made τὰ ἀμφότερα ἕν ; Christ has created τοὺς δύο ἐν αὐτῷ εἰς ἕνα καινὸν ἄνθρωπον, a man made up of body and of spirit : he reconciles to God τοὺς ἀμφοτέρους ἐν ἑνὶ σώματι, which body is His own. Both have access to God, ἐν ἑνὶ πνεύματι. Henceforth there are no more ξένοι, no more πάροικοι, but only συνπολῖται. It should be noticed how the two notions, the notion of a visible city and that of a mystical body, penetrate each other. As to the right of citizenship and the foreigners dwelling in Greek cities, cf. CHAPOT, " Prov. d'Asie," p. 148 and foll.

[2] Mark. XII. 10 ; Matt. XXI. 42 ; Luke XX. 17. Cf. Acts IV. 11 and 1 Pet. II. 7.

[3] Cf. Heb. III. 6 : χριστὸς . . . οὗ οἶκος ἐσμεν ἡμεῖς. The author of the Epistle to the Hebrews means that henceforth the Christians are, to the exclusion of the Jews, the house of God, the people of God. For St. Paul, the new house of God is still being built : this is the meaning of the word οἰκοδομή, in contrast with οἶκος.

God in spirit. The image conveyed by the word οἰκοδομή which loses its peculiar force in the Latin word *aedificatio*, is very dear to St. Paul, who uses it in its full meaning: he writes to the Romans that the fact of his having preached the Gospel everywhere, from Jerusalem to Illyricum, without having ever visited them, is to be accounted for by his set purpose to preach the Gospel where the name of Christ had not been as yet invoked, "lest I should build upon another man's foundation" (Rom. xv. 20). Paul applies the image of οἰκοδομή not to the conversion or progress of each one of the faithful individually but to the collective building up or "edification," such as is the founding of a church, its instruction and correction, and still more to the growth of faith in the whole world.

A building, a city—these are imperfect analogies, since the Apostle wishes to portray the organic and living unity of a people whose members do not form a race joined together by ties of flesh and blood. Paul has in view the unity of the Spirit who lives in every Christian: nor does that content him, and he makes bold to conceive the unity as one of body, the faithful being only the members of the body, and the body being Christ Himself.[1] Through the faith they receive, and through baptism, circumcised and uncircumcised form together one single body, one and the same new man: Jews and Greeks become "members of the same body" (σύσσωμα, Eph. iii. 6).

This body, which is the Church, has Jesus Christ for its head.[2] Paul analyses the image he has thus conceived. He knows, and he has told the Colossians (Col. ii. 19), that the body receives from the head its normal increase by means of the bonds and joints through which it is united to the head. Writing to the Ephesians (Eph. iv. 15-6), he insists on this thought, that from the head the body receives its harmony,

---

[1] This image of the body of Christ, applied to the Church, had already been used by St. Paul. Rom. xii. 4-5 ; 1 Cor. xii. 12, 27.

[2] Eph. i. 22-3 : αὐτὸν ἔδωκεν κεφαλὴν ὑπὲρ πάντα τῇ ἐκκλησίᾳ, ἥτις ἐστὶν τὸ σῶμα αὐτοῦ, τὸ πλήρωμα τοῦ τὰ πάντα ἐν πᾶσιν πληρουμένου. For the meaning of this difficult text, see PRAT, p. 422. God gave Christ as the supreme head (ὑπὲρ πάντα) to the Church which is His body, the complement of Him who is fully completed in all His members.

its organic unity and energy, and its growth. Thus the faithful must grow up " in Him who is the head, even Christ ". And here is another point of view. The man and the woman united in wedlock are two in one flesh : but the husband is the head of the woman, and likewise " Christ is the head of the Church, whose Saviour He is ".[1] Thus the Church comes to be personified : she is, as it were, the spouse of Christ. " Christ loved the Church, and delivered himself up for it; that he might sanctify it, cleansing it by the laver of water in the word of life, that he might present it to himself a glorious church, not having spot or wrinkle, or any such thing, but that it should be holy and without blemish." [2] This Church, this mystical body, this mystical Christ, is not a being subsisting apart from the members of which it is made up : it is a number which increases day by day, unit by unit : hence the part of the Word and that of Baptism. Still, taken as a whole, this number is something that is one and organized ; something that is living and visible, like a spouse ; indeed, something that is sanctified and glorious and indefectible, like a holy and spotless spouse.

Unity and newness, and all this both mystical and tangible. " Lie not one to another : stripping yourselves of the old man with his deeds, and putting on the new, him who is renewed unto knowledge, according to the image of him that created him; where there is neither Gentile nor Jew, circumcision nor uncircumcision, Barbarian nor Scythian, bond nor free. But Christ is all, and in all." [3] Elsewhere Paul had

---

[1] Eph. v. 23 : ἀνήρ ἐστιν κεφαλὴ τῆς γυναικὸς ὡς καὶ ὁ Χριστὸς κεφαλὴ τῆς ἐκκλησίας, αὐτὸς σωτὴρ τοῦ σώματος·

[2] Eph. v. 25-7 : ἵνα αὐτὴν ἁγιάσῃ καθαρίσας τῷ λουτρῷ τοῦ ὕδατος ἐν ῥήματι . . . ἵνα ᾖ ἁγία καὶ ἄμωμος. The meaning of the word ῥήματι is rather obscure. Some commentators understand it of the baptismal formula. Many see in it an ꞏllusion to the preaching of the Gospel, by which faith is begotten in our souls. In support of this latter view, which we think preferable, see Rom. x. 17.

[3] The mention of the "Scythians" marks the belief which even at this early date obtained, that Christianity had already been preached everywhere. This is an important point, for it shows that the notion of Catholicity is very closely connected with the notion of Gospel, of κήρυγμα : the Gospel is for all mankind, and all mankind has already heard it. Col. I. 6 : τὸ εὐαγγέλιον τὸ παρὸν εἰς ὑμᾶς καθὼς καὶ ἐν παντὶ τῷ

already made a distinction between the interior and the exterior man: the former being renewed day after day, whilst
the latter falls away daily: to be a Scythian or a Greek or a
Jew, is something exterior: but one and the same inner character unites those separated, dissimilar, and hostile peoples:
it reconciles them and binds them all together. "Be careful to keep the unity of the Spirit in the bond of peace; one
body and one Spirit . . . one Lord, one faith, one baptism,
one God and father of all, who is above all, [working] through
all, [dwelling] in all," [1] i.e. all those who have been reconciled
to Him through Jesus Christ.

In his "History of Dogma," Harnack has these
words: "The mere fact that from nearly the beginning
of Christendom, its members reflected and speculated not
only about God and Christ, but also about the Church,
teaches us how profoundly the Christian consciousness was
convinced that the Christians were a new people, the people
of God". Harnack prefers, it is true, to postpone this
conscious recognition to the time of the Epistle of St.
Clement of Rome and of the Epistle of St. Polycarp of
Smyrna: but we have just learnt from St. Paul that, before
the year 60, i.e. before the dying out of the first Christian
generation, the Christians knew that they formed a body:
their "speculations" then concerning that Divine creation
which they believed the Church to be, had already forced
themselves upon them. "These speculations of the earliest
period of Gentile Christianity about Christ and the Church,
as inseparable correlative ideas, are of the greatest importance, for they have absolutely nothing Hellenic in them,
but rather are the outcome of the Apostolic tradition." [2]

The Church that is the object of those speculations, is
not the heavenly Church, nor merely the "mystical body".
Harnack is in error when, under the pretext that "on earth,
the members of the Church are dispers_d rather than united,"

κόσμῳ. *Id.* 23 : τὸ εὐαγγέλιον τὸ κηρυχθὲν ἐν πασῇ τῇ κτίσει τῇ ὑπὸ τὸν
οὐρανόν. The same thought is found in 1 Tim. III. 6, and still better in
Apoc. VII. 9.

[1] Eph. IV. 3-6. See the whole excellent chapter in PRAT, pp. 417-33,
"l'Eglise, corps mystique du Christ ".

[2] "Dogmengeschichte," vol. I. p. 144.

he affirms that the unity of the Church was not visible upon earth; and that it existed only in as far as it was to be one day effected "in the Kingdom of Christ".[1]

To these statements of Harnack's we may reply that the Jews of the Dispersion, even though dispersed, still belonged to one visible Israel. Do not the texts we have adduced show that the unity of the dispersed Christians is just as real as that of the Jews? If it is spiritual in its source which is faith, salvation, the Spirit, it is visible in its members, who are baptized with a visible baptism, grouped into visible communities, and communities united with one another so as to form one race (γένος), as manifest to the world as the Greek or the Jewish race. As to the heavenly Church, she is just as distinct from the visible Christian community, as the Jewish people was from the heavenly Jerusalem.

\*\*\*

Let us suspend for a while the study of the Pauline Epistles to make a study of the Didachè. This does not mean that, in our estimation, this document must be dated from about the year 60, although we believe, with Funk, that it certainly belongs to the last decades of the first Christian century. But it testifies to thoughts and institutions that are unquestionably primitive, and the general view it gives us is complete enough to explain and set in their proper place the fragmentary details we may gather later on.[2]

We shall be near the truth in supposing that the document in question draws its inspiration, at least in its ethical part, from that Jewish moralism of which the Epistle of St. James is so remarkable an echo—a spiritual condition very similar to that of the class of proselytes called φοβούμενοι τὸν θεόν. No mention is made of "wisdom," any more than in the Epistle of St. James; or of the "Law," but much of the

---

[1] As regards the heavenly Church or the heavenly Jerusalem, cf. "Apoc." xxi. 2 and SWETE's note, "Apoc." *in loc.* The Jews, although they were an earthly nation, expected nevertheless the heavenly Jerusalem: "IV Esdr." x. 27 ; "Apoc. Baruch," iv. 3 ; "Orac. Sibyll." v. 420, etc.

[2] BARDENHEWER, "Geschichte der altk. Litteratur," vol. i. (Freiburg, 1902), pp. 78-80. H. HEMMER, "Doctrine des apôtres" (Paris, 1907), pp. XXVI.-XXXV.

" fear of God ". The Christian must teach " the fear of God " to his children, from their infancy (Did. IV. 9). He must avoid giving orders with sharpness to his servants " who hope in the same God," lest, through ill-usage, he may turn them away from " fearing God " (IV. 10). These precepts, which are Jewish in spirit and in expression, may have been taken from a kind of ethical catechism used by the proselytes.

On this Jewish moralism is superimposed a Christianity that has none of that charismatic enthusiasm which, judging from a few texts, we might think was the predominant, and all-compelling feature of primitive Christian communities : on the contrary, this Christianity is made up entirely of distinct and peremptory precepts based on the word of the Lord : " Your prayers and alms and all your deeds so do, as ye have it in the Gospel of our Lord " (XV. 4). " Do thou in no wise forsake the commandments of the Lord ; but thou shalt keep what thou hast received, neither adding thereto nor taking away therefrom " (IV. 13). Individual inspiration—even should it come from the Holy Ghost—is subordinated to commands that have been handed down, received, and established, and are supreme. " Whosoever . . . cometh and teacheth you all these things that have been said here, receive him ; whoso teacheth a different and destructive doctrine, receive him not " (XI. 1-2). There was then a $\delta\iota\delta\alpha\chi\acute{\eta}$, a teaching, already determined and defined, a teaching which admitted of no opposition.[1]

Whilst the Epistle of St. James is addressed " to the twelve tribes which are in the Dispersion," the " Didachè " is addressed to the Gentiles. But this " Didachè " is the " Didachè " of the Lord, i.e. of Jesus Christ, and the twelve Apostles are entrusted with its announcement. The office assigned to the Apostles is that of announcing and attesting the doctrine of Him who alone teaches. The Twelve are considered no longer as sent to the twelve tribes : their message is for the $\check{\epsilon}\theta\nu\eta$ whom St. Paul had formerly reserved to himself, when leaving the circumcised to the care of the Twelve.

---

[1] DOBSCHÜTZ, p. 196 and foll., p. 205 and foll., draws the reader's attention to these " Catholicising " tendencies : it is true he assigns to the " Didachè "and to the Pastoral Epistles a later date than we do.

The centre of gravity of Christianity is thus displaced: nevertheless, the principle of authority remains the same.

Again, the "Didachè" bears witness to the fact that Christianity is not only an ethical rule and a religious faith, but also an organized worship: it has its stated fasts on Wednesdays and Fridays: "Let not your fasts be with the hypocrites; for they fast on Mondays and Thursdays" (VIII. 1), which amounts to saying, Do not fast on the same days as the Jews, and shows how deep was the separation between the Christians and the Jews. The "Didachè" continues in the same strain: "Neither pray as the hypocrites, but as the Lord commanded in His Gospel" (VIII. 2); then it gives the text of the Lord's Prayer, which Christians are expected to say three times a day. Elsewhere (VII. 1-4) the "Didachè" describes the rite of the baptism "into the name of the Father, and of the Son, and of the Holy Spirit". Further on (IX. 1-x. 7) it gives a description of the Eucharist in which those alone must be allowed to share "who have been baptized into the name of Jesus" (IX. 5). The Eucharist is celebrated in common, every Sunday (XIV. 1). It sets before us then a reserved and sacramental worship, in which no one is allowed to take part, save after an initiation which is also sacramental.

Moreover, some features stand out which were merely in-dicated in the Pauline Epistles of the Captivity. The chief of these is the local and settled hierarchy, in contrast with the itinerant missionaries: "Appoint, therefore, for your-selves, *episcopi* and deacons worthy of the Lord, men meek, and not lovers of money, sincere and proved; for they render to you the service of prophets and teachers".[1]

The community raises, by way of election, some of its members to the episcopate and to the diaconate. The

---

[1] "Didachè," xv. 1: Χειροτονήσατε οὖν ἑαυτοῖς ἐπισκόπους καὶ διακόνους ἀξίους τοῦ κυρίου . . . ὑμῖν γὰρ λειτουργοῦσι καὶ αὐτοὶ τὴν λειτουργίαν τῶν προφητῶν καὶ διδασκάλων.—The verb χειροτονεῖν is not synonymous with χεῖρας ἐπιτιθέναι, and means to choose with raised hands, to appoint by suffrage. The word λειτουργία has the indefinite meaning of service, *munus*: Philip. II. 25; Heb. VIII. 2; Rom. XIII. 6 and xv. 16. It denotes also the priestly service in the temple: Luke I. 23; Heb. VIII. 6, IX. 21. Regarding the civil offices of Greek cities, called also liturgies, cf. CHAPOT, "Province d'Asie," p. 265 and foll.

community elects: hence it is not a supernatural charism that designates and invests; nay, the community is not invited to take into account such extraordinary gifts of the Spirit, since the "Didachè" enjoins the faithful to prize chiefly the moral attainments of those they choose, their kindness, sincerity, disinterestedness: they must be δεδο-κιμασμένοι, i.e. men whose worth is vouched for by the judgment of all, as is observed in the election of the magistrates of Greek cities. The community elects those chosen, for itself (ἑαυτοῖς), for its local service, and not for a universal ministry. It chooses the *episcopi* and the deacons, first for the liturgical ministry previously described, the breaking of bread, celebrated on Sunday. The close connexion between that ministration and the election of *episcopi* and deacons is signified, as Funk justly remarked, by the conjunction οὖν which joins together the two developments.[1]

Before becoming a tradition that is maintained, Christianity is a "word" that is propagated. How invoke him in whom one does not as yet believe; and how believe in him of whom one has not as yet heard? "Remember your prelates, who have spoken the word of God to you," says the Epistle to the Hebrews[2]; and the "Didachè": "My child, him that speaketh to thee the word of God remember night and day; and thou shalt honour him as the Lord; for where the word of the Lord is uttered, there is the Lord" (IV. 1). Making its own these words of the "Didachè," the Epistle of Barnabas will say later on: "Thou shalt love, as the apple of thine eye, every one that speaketh to thee the word of the Lord".[3] When enumerating in the Epistle to the Ephesians the various offices God had given to the Church, St. Paul had already mentioned the Apostles,

---

[1] "Didachè," XI. 11, contains a rather obscure passage: "Every prophet proved true, doing [what he does] unto the mystery of the Church in the world (ποιῶν εἰς μυστήριον κοσμικὸν ἐκκλησίας), yet not teaching others to do what he himself doeth, shall not be judged by you, for it is for God to judge him: for so did also the ancient prophets". Scholars have framed many bewildering hypotheses as to the meaning of this cosmic mystery of the Church. H. WEINEL, "Die Wirkungen des Geistes und der Geister im nachapostolischen Zeitalter" (Freiburg, 1899), pp. 131-8. FUNK, "PP. apostol." v. 1, p. 28. HEMMER, p. XCVII.-XCIX.

[2] Heb. XIII. 7.　　　　[3] BARNAB. "Epistula," XIX. 9.

prophets, evangelists, and also the pastors and the teachers.[1] The "Didachè" witnesses to that sharing by the "pastors" in the doctrinal government of the Church: "Despise not" the *episcopi*, and the deacons, "for they are your honoured ones, like the prophets and teachers" (XV. 2).

According to Harnack, the preaching of the Lord's word is, in the "Didachè," the exclusive function of the itinerant missionaries (Apostles, prophets, and teachers): he recalls the indubitable fact that, unlike the *episcopi* and the deacons, these missionaries were not chosen by the local churches:[2] but perhaps he has failed to give its full value to the fact that, in the "Didachè," the local church is the judge of the credit to be given to these itinerant missionaries. We have already seen how St. Paul subordinated the charisms first to the received faith, and then to the edification of the community: an even stricter subordination is imposed by the "Didachè" on the ministry of these itinerant preachers. Whoever comes and teaches a doctrine that differs from the received faith, must not be listened to (XI. 2): "whoever comes:" he is, then, a missionary from the outside, and the community judges him from his words. The community has become a true and self-sufficing home: these missionaries must be welcomed, but only for a short while and when on their way. Apostles and prophets are received "as the Lord" (XI. 4); but if an apostle delays more than two days, "he is a false prophet" (XI. 5); and if, on leaving, he asks for money, "he is a false prophet" (XI. 6), for "not every one that speaketh in the spirit is a prophet, but only if he hold the ways of the Lord: therefore by their ways shall the false prophet and the real prophet be known" (XI. 8).

---

[1] Eph. IV. 11: ἔδωκεν τοὺς μὲν ἀποστόλους, τοὺς δὲ προφήτας, τοὺς δὲ εὐαγγελιστάς, τοὺς δὲ ποιμένας καὶ διδασκάλους. There is, in this text, a significant grouping. In the first place St. Paul puts the Apostles and the prophets (just as in Eph. II. 20, where the Apostles and prophets are called the foundations of the Church). In the second place, he places together pastors and teachers. Between the first and the second group come the "evangelists". Here, then, the teachers seem to be subject to the pastors. Pastors and teachers together make up the local hierarchy. Cf. 1 Pet. V. 2; 1 Tim. III. 2: δεῖ τὸν ἐπίσκοπον . . . διδακτικὸν [εἶναι]; Tit. I. 9.

[2] "Mission," vol. I. p. 280.

The "Didachè" insists on the marks by means of which true prophets will be distinguished from the false, as though each church were daily exposed to the danger of being over-reached and imposed upon, as in St. Jerome's time good Christians might be fleeced by the wayfaring monks, called *Remoboth*. The "Didachè" could not have affirmed more strongly the supremacy of the local church and of those who preside over it.

This, then, is the Christianity of the "Didachè"—a Christianity of community life and institutions, autonomous and authoritative—similar to the Christianity revealed to us by the documents of the first generation. The settled hierarchy is established everywhere, the wayfaring missionaries are subordinated to it, the great Apostles have disappeared, the prophets are about to disappear. Still those missionaries who for many years moved about from one church to the other,[1] were providential agents for the establishment of that unity which bound all the churches together, that unity the doctrinal character of which St. Paul had so forcibly expounded. Thus, though the "Didachè" is, on this subject of Christian unity, less explicit than St. Paul, with whose teaching it does not seem to have been at all acquainted, it has the same sense of unity. In its vocabulary, the word ἐκκλησία denotes the assembly of the faithful gathered for prayer (IV. 14), and also denotes the new people which the Gospel has brought forth into this world, and which shall be one day firmly established in God's kingdom as in its promised land. "Even as this broken bread was scattered over the hills, and was gathered together and became one, so let Thy Church be gathered together from the ends of the earth into Thy Kingdom."[2] "Remember, Lord, Thy Church, to deliver it from evil and make it perfect in Thy love, and to gather it from the four winds, to be sanctified in Thy Kingdom which Thou hast prepared for it."[3] The Christian

---

[1] HARNACK, "Mission," vol. I. pp. 286.

[2] Did. IX. 4 : συναχθήτω σου ἡ ἐκκλησία ἀπὸ τῶν περάτων τῆς γῆς.

[3] Did. X. 5 : σύναξον αὐτὴν ἀπὸ τῶν τεσσάρων ἀνέμων. Cf. the Jewish prayers for the return of the Jews of the Dispersion to Jerusalem. "Psalm. Salom." VIII. 34. These few words of the "Didachè" show how deeply those Christians realized the spread of Christianity all over the

community, now spread all over the world, shall be one day united in the kingdom of the Father: then and only then shall the unity be perfect; but even now, upon earth, Christians are penetrated by the deepest sense of that unity of unities.

*∗*
∗

Far better than the "Didachè," the first of the two Epistles that bear the name of St. Peter gives us approximately the date of its own origin, for it was written during a time of persecution which₁ may be identified with that undertaken by Nero.[1]

The Epistle is addressed to Christians who are not of Jewish birth (ii. 10) and who dwell dispersed amongst the Gentiles (ii. 12).[2] "Have your conversation good among the Gentiles: that, whereas they speak against you as evil-doers, they may by the good works, which they shall behold in you, glorify God in the day of visitation" (ii. 12). The will of God is that by their conduct the faithful should silence the foolish men who misjudge them (ii. 15). "Have a good conscience, that, whereas they speak evil of

world known to them, and this deep realization is met with in many other texts. Cf. HERMAS, "Simil." viii. 3 : "This great tree that casts its shadow over plains and mountains, and all the earth, is the law of God that was given to the whole world ($\delta o\theta\epsilon\grave{\iota}s$ $\epsilon\grave{\iota}s$ $\delta\lambda o\nu$ $\tau\grave{o}\nu$ $\kappa\acute{o}\sigma\mu o\nu$), and this law is the Son of God proclaimed to the ends of the earth " ($\kappa\eta\rho\upsilon\chi\theta\epsilon\grave{\iota}s$ $\epsilon\grave{\iota}s$ $\tau\grave{a}$ $\pi\acute{\epsilon}\rho a\tau a$ $\tau\hat{\eta}s$ $\gamma\hat{\eta}s$). The same thought is found in "Sim." ix. 17. Later on, St. Ignatius also speaks of the bishops who are established $\kappa a\tau\grave{a}$ $\tau\grave{a}$ $\pi\acute{\epsilon}\rho a\tau a$. The uncanonical ending of St. Mark's Gospel says that Jesus sent through the Apostles the message ($\kappa\acute{\eta}\rho\upsilon\gamma\mu a$) of salvation "from the East to the West " ($\grave{a}\pi\grave{o}$ $\grave{a}\nu a\tau o\lambda\hat{\eta}s$ $\kappa a\grave{\iota}$ $\check{a}\chi\rho\iota$ $\delta\acute{\upsilon}\sigma\epsilon\omega s$).

[1] Regarding the authenticity and date of St. Peter's first Epistle, cf. BIGG, " Epistles of St. Peter and St. Jude " (Edinburgh, 1901), pp. 1-87. Cf. HARNACK, " Chronologie," vol. i. pp. 454-5.

[2] The word $\grave{\epsilon}\kappa\kappa\lambda\eta\sigma\acute{\iota}a$ is not used in the address, which speaks of the elect of Jesus Christ, of the " Dispersion " in Pontus, Galatia, Cappadocia and Bithynia. To my knowledge, this is the only instance of the Christian use of the word " Dispersion ". The Epistle would seem to be afraid to draw the reader's attention to local churches. Likewise, in the subscription (v. 13), we read : " The elect that is in Babylon," instead of the Church of Rome. The "Prima Petri " does not use the word $\grave{\epsilon}\kappa\kappa\lambda\eta\sigma\acute{\iota}a$ even once. On the identity of Babylon with Rome see H. GUNKEL in J. WEISS, " Schriften des N.T." (Göttingen, 1908), vol. ii. p. 571.

you, they may be ashamed who falsely accuse your good conversation in Christ" (III. 16). It is precisely on account of their quality and name of Christians that the faithful are misjudged and slandered (IV. 16).

Their unity, then, is manifest, and this unity is the unity of their faith and of their brotherhood. "You have purified your souls in your obedience to the truth unto unfeigned love of the brethren, love then one another from the heart fervently, being begotten again, not of corruptible seed, but of incorruptible, through the word of God, which liveth and abideth for ever" (I. 22-3). The faithful are as new-born children (II. 2). Jesus is for them "the living stone," and they are themselves "as living stones, built up into a spiritual house".[1]

Many comparisons are used, which have for their purpose to describe the organic unity of Christians, but none describes it better than that of the chosen people. "For you are an elect race, a royal priesthood, a holy nation, a purchased people: that you may declare his virtues, who hath called you out of darkness into his marvellous light" (II. 9). In the midst of the unbelieving world and in contrast with blind Judaism, Christians have shared in the light: they are brothers, and therefore they form one family, one race; but it is a race of election, one freely chosen by God; they are a priestly and kingly *gens;* they are a holy ἔθνος; being converts from Gentilism, they are a new people of God.[2] They are a flock which was without a shepherd, and which has now come back to Him who is the shepherd and the "episcopus" of souls, i.e. to Christ.[3] When using these words, the Epistle has in view the faithful spread all over the world, not a special local community. God is

---

[1] 1 Pet. II. 4-5 : λίθοι ζῶντες οἰκοδομεῖσθε οἶκος πνευματικός.

[2] 1 Pet. II. 9 : ὑμεῖς δὲ γένος ἐκλεκτόν (Isa. XLIII. 20), βασίλειον ἱεράτευμα (Exod. XIX. 6), ἔθνος ἅγιον (ibid.). λαὸς εἰς περιποίησιν (Isa. XLIII. 21). In Exod. loc. cit. the people of Israel is called a people of priests, a title of honour and of grace ; and yet Israel has besides a special priesthood.

[3] 1 Pet. II. 25 : ἦτε γὰρ ὡς πρόβατα πλανώμενοι, ἀλλ' ἐπεστράφητε νῦν ἐπὶ τὸν ποιμένα καὶ ἐπίσκοπον τῶν ψυχῶν ὑμῶν. Cf. Ezech. XXXIV. 11, 12. Cf. "Oracula Sibyllina" the fragment cited by THEOPHILUS, "Ad Autolyc." II. 36 : οὐ τρέμετ' οὐδὲ φοβεῖσθε θεὸν τὸν ἐπίσκοπον ὑμῶν—ὕψιστον γνώστην πανεπόπτην μάρτυρα πάντων.

the shepherd: the name *episcopus*, given to Him, is a reminiscence of Ezekiel and also an allusion to the office of the *episcopus* in every church.

Like St. Paul in his great Epistles, the "Prima Petri" describes admirably both the newness and the unity of the Christian people; like St. Paul also, it does not forget the gifts of the Spirit who works in this new people. "As every man hath received grace, ministering the same one to another: as good stewards of the manifold grace of God" (IV. 10). As in St. Paul, the charism is granted by God for the welfare of the community. However the "Prima Petri" seems to look upon it as an office, we might say as a grace attached to a function. Charisms are distributed to those who announce the word of the Lord, and to those who serve. "If any man speak, let him speak as the *logia* of God" (*id.*) i.e. he who teaches must teach only what is from God, and not what is from man, or what comes from his own fancy. "If any man minister, let him minister as of the strength which God supplieth." We shall not force the terms of this antithesis, so as to see deacons in those who serve, and *episcopi* in those who speak; but on the other hand, we must at least grant that there are, in the local church, men filled with grace, whose mission it is to instruct that special Christian community and minister to its various needs.

Elsewhere the "Prima Petri" speaks more clearly on the same topic. "The elders therefore among you I exhort" (V. 1). Then it continues, in words which show that these presbyters are, by their office, the leaders of the community: "Feed the flock of God which is among you, taking care of it not by constraint, but willingly according to God: not for filthy lucre's sake, but voluntarily; neither as lording it over the clergy, but being made a pattern of the flock from the heart. And when the prince of pastors shall appear, you shall receive a never-fading crown of glory."[1] Here the fold is the local church, and has immediate pastors, who are called, in the Epistle, presbyters. Christ is their invisible leader and chief pastor (ἀρχιποίμην). They rule and ad-

---

[1] 1 Pet. v. 2-4: ποιμάνατε τὸ ἐν ὑμῖν ποίμνιον τοῦ θεοῦ, . . . τύποι γινόμενοι τοῦ ποιμνίου. Cf. Heb. XIII. 20. The expression ἀρχιποίμην is well known and denotes a leader of shepherds. DEISSMANN, p. 65.

minister: hence they may be tempted to be domineering, harsh, and self-seeking.

\* \*
\*

If we have put off till now the study of the Pastoral Epistles, it is not because we doubt their authenticity: we believe they are the work of St. Paul, and the various objections, some, not insignificant, raised against their Pauline origin especially on account of their style, do not seem to us decisive.[1] They belong to an horizon different from that of the great Epistles of Paul and from that of the Epistles of the captivity: they constitute by themselves an homogeneous, distinct, and late group; they are subsequent to all that we know, from other sources, of the Apostle's life and belong to the last days of his life; but they are his work.

Unlike the "Didachè," the Pastoral Epistles are not a didactic treatise on ecclesiastical life: they are completely or almost completely silent on several points, for instance on Christian worship. They dwell at length on some special features, as though their purpose were to emphasize some truth which it was opportune to emphasize at that particular time.

In the first place, Paul insists on the authoritative character of faith. "O Timothy, guard the deposit," "guard the good deposit,"[2] for the Gospel is a deposit which—from this definition itself—must suffer neither diminution nor addition. "Abide thou in those things which thou hast learned, and which have been committed to thee, knowing of whom thou hast learned them."[3] This refers to the doctrine the Apostle taught him: Paul does not hesitate to deem it just as sacred as "the holy Scriptures" which Timothy has known ever since his infancy (2 Tim. III. 15). "The things which thou hast heard of me before many witnesses, the same commend to faithful men, who shall be fit to teach others also"[4] (2 Tim. II. 2).

---

[1] See the discussion in F. PRAT, pp. 455-69.

[2] 1 Tim. VI. 20: τὴν παραθήκην φύλαξον. 2 Tim. I. 14: τὴν καλὴν παραθήκην φύλαξον διὰ πνεύματος ἁγίου τοῦ ἐνοικοῦντος ἐν ἡμῖν.

[3] 2 Tim. III. 14: μένε ἐν οἷς ἔμαθες καὶ ἐπιστώθης, εἰδὼς παρὰ τίνων ἔμαθες.

[4] Tit. III. 9-11: μωρὰς ζητήσεις καὶ γενεαλογίας καὶ ἔριν καὶ μάχας νομικάς (disputes about the Law) . . . αἱρετικὸν ἄνθρωπον μετὰ μίαν καὶ δευτέραν νουθεσίαν παραιτοῦ. The word αἵρεσις is found both in the LXX and in

In fact, the Church, to whose welfare Timothy devotes his efforts, is open to the danger of being invaded by false teachers, who are now so numerous: like those condemned by the Epistle to the Colossians, these errors savour of some Judæo-Greek syncretism, a kind of pre-Christian Gnosticism. "Avoid foolish questions, and genealogies, and contentions, and strivings about the law. For they are unprofitable and vain. A man that is a heretic, after the first and second admonition avoid; knowing that he that is such a one is subverted, and sinneth, being condemned by his own judgment ".[1] It is useless and unreasonable to argue with these mischief makers: they must be silenced.[2] Authority protects and defends the deposit of faith, by casting out of the Church

classical Greek : it means " choice," and by extension " an opinion freely chosen," and hence—in a sense which implies no depreciation—a " school," or a " party ". Thus the historian Josephus speaks of the Pharisees, the Sadducees, and the Essenes, as being three Jewish αἱρέσεις. " Antiquit." XIII. 5, 9. This is also the meaning of the word in St. Luke (Acts v. 17, xv. 5, xxiv. 5, 14, xxviii. 22). In St. Paul's Epistles, it signifies a culpable dissent, a schism (Gal. v. 20 ; 1 Cor. XI. 19). In this connexion JÜLICHER remarks (in his art. on " Heresy " in the " Encycl. Biblica ") that Christianity has so thoroughly adopted for her motto, " You are one in Christ Jesus," that henceforth any tendency towards individualism is looked upon with aversion, and heresy, which would be for a Greek philosopher a symptom of life, is for St. Paul a downright disorder. This is also the meaning of the word αἱρετικός in Tit. III. 10 which appears there for the first time and is found neither in the LXX nor in classical Greek. We must not fail to notice in this instance how the evolution of the meaning of the word implies the history of an institution.

[1] Tit. I. 10-11 : ματαιολόγοι καὶ φρεναπάται, μάλιστα οἱ ἐκ περιτομῆς, οὓς δεῖ ἐπιστομίζειν. Cf. 1 Tim. I. 3-4.

[2] 1 Tim. I. 19 : περὶ τὴν πίστιν ἐναυάγησαν. The Apostle designates by name two of them, Hymeneus and Alexander, whom he has " delivered up to Satan ". Cf. 1 Cor. v. 5. To deliver up to Satan means to expel from the Church of God : for to the Church of God the " synagogue of Satan " is opposed (cf. John VIII. 44, and especially Apoc. II. 9, 13, III. 9). The Jews also used at times to expel persons from their synagogues (Luke VI. 22 ; John IX. 22, XII. 42, XVI. 2). Satan's power over the present age is affirmed by the uncanonical ending of St. Mark, as given in FREER's MS. : the Apostles say to Jesus : " This world of wickedness and unbelief is under the control of Satan." Jesus answers : " The years of the power of Satan have come to a close." LAGRANGE, "Evangile selon Saint Marc " (Paris, 1911), p. 438.

those Christians who "have made shipwreck in the faith ". If any one teaches another doctrine,[1] if he does not adhere to the wholesome words of Our Lord Jesus Christ and to those lessons that are according to godliness, he is blind. "Speak thou the things that become sound doctrine ".[2] This wholesome teaching is in all cases "the doctrine of God our Saviour" (Tit. II. 10).

The Epistle to Titus denounces the perverse teachers, "disobedient and vain talkers" who are found especially among "them of the circumcision," and who by a crafty and deceitful propagandism "teach the things which they ought not ".[3] The Pastoral Epistles speak of the "circumcised" as the "Didachè" speaks of the "hypocrites"; they make no mention of false apostles or of false prophets, or of Christians speaking in the name of the Spirit: they refer only to teachers who betray the wholesome teaching.[4] This teaching is the teaching of Jesus Christ, and the authority for its preservation belongs to the Apostle who writes the Epistle, to the evangelist, his disciple, to whom the Epistle is addressed, and to trustworthy men trained and taught by the disciple. The Church, "the house of God," is the "pillar and ground of the truth ".[5]

Here then again we find, together with sound teaching, the hierarchy.

Like the "Didachè," the Pastoral Epistles show us the hierarchy of *episcopi* and deacons established. The Epistle to the Philippians had spoken of the Episcopate as of a plural episcopate ; the Epistle to Titus alludes to that

[1] 1 Tim. VI. 3 : εἴ τις ἑτεροδιδασκαλεῖ καὶ μὴ προσέρχεται ὑγιαίνουσιν λόγοις τοῖς τοῦ κυρίου καὶ τῇ κατ' εὐσέβειαν διδασκαλίᾳ. . . . On ἑτεροδιδασκαλεῖν, see 1 Tim. I. 3. Compare the whole Epistle of St. Jude.

[2] Tit. II. 1 : λάλει ἃ πρέπει τῇ ὑγιαινούσῃ διδασκαλίᾳ. Notice the persistence with which the *Pastoral* Epistles oppose the wholesome and saving doctrine to that which is corrupt: 2 Tim. II. 17 ; 1 Tim. VI. 4 ; Tit. I. 15.

[3] Tit. I. 11 : διδάσκοντές ἃ μὴ δεῖ.

[4] 2 Tim. IV. 3 : τῆς ὑγιαινούσης διδασκαλίας οὐκ ἀνέξονται, ἀλλὰ ἑαυτοῖς ἐπισωρεύσουσιν διδασκάλους.

[5] 1 Tim. III. 15 : ἐν οἴκῳ θεοῦ . . . ἥτις ἐστὶν ἐκκλησία θεοῦ ζῶντος, στῦλος καὶ ἑδραίωμα τῆς ἀληθείας. HOLTZMANN, "Neutestamentliche Theologie," vol. II. pp. 276-8, insists strongly on the "ecclesiasticism " of all these features.

plural government in the following words : " For this cause
I left thee in Crete, that thou shouldest set in order the
things that are wanting, and shouldest establish presbyters
in every city, as I have also appointed thee ".[1]   These presbyters are at the head of the local church, to govern and instruct it: " Let the presbyters that rule well be esteemed
worthy of double honour, especially they who labour in the
teaching of the word " (1 Tim. v. 17).

A word, which designates this stationary hierarchy, appears here for the first time, πρεσβυτέριον (1 Tim. iv. 14).
This college of presbyters is the depositary of a power
which can be likened to no other than that of Orders.   To
Timothy it is said : " Neglect not the grace [charism] that
is in thee, which was given thee by prophetic designation
with imposition of hands of the πρεσβυτέριον ".[2]   That prophecy intervened to point out Timothy to the Apostle and to
the presbyters,[3] is not to be wondered at.   As to the laying
on of hands, it is a gesture of blessing, borrowed from the
earliest history of Judaism.[4]   By charism, here, a spiritual

---

[1] Tit. i. 5.   Theodore of Mopsuestia, "In epistul. B. Pauli commentarii," ed. SWETE (1882), vol. ii. p. 121, recalls that at the beginning the office of presbyters and that of *episcopi* were one and the same,
and that the office which later on became the episcopate was then exercised in every province and for the whole province, by an "apostle," as
for instance, Titus in Crete, Timothy in Asia : the Apostle alone had the
right to ordain.   This theory of Theodore seems a mere exegetical hypothesis, framed for the purpose of accounting for the ministry of Timothy
and Titus ; it places between the missionary-staff and the local hierarchy,
a provincial hierarchy, all the churches of one province, Gaul, for instance,
being considered subject to one bishop.   On these words of Theodore,
Mgr. DUCHESNE, "Fastes épiscopaux de l'anc. Gaule," vol. i. (1894), p. 36
and foll., relies as accounting for the late formation of episcopal dioceses
in Gaul.   We believe with HARNACK, "Mission," vol. i. p. 376, that
Theodore's generalization as regarding the apostle-bishop of a province (in
contrast with a city) is a fancy, whatever the particular case of Gaul may be.

[2] 1 Tim. iv. 14 : μὴ ἀμέλει τοῦ ἔν σοι χαρίσματος ὅ ἐδόθη σοι διὰ τῆς
προφητείας μετὰ ἐπιθέσεως τῶν χειρῶν τοῦ πρεσβυτερίου.   The expression
ἐπίθεσις τῶν χειρῶν is found again in Heb. vi. 2.   See the note of WESTCOTT,
in loc.   The action of laying on hands, as signifying only an inde-
terminate blessing, is necessarily accompanied by some determining and
specifying word.

[3] This is the meaning suggested by 1 Tim. i. 18.   Cf. Acts xiii. 1-3.

[4] Cf. TERTULL. " De Baptismo, " 8 : " Manus imponitur per benedic-
tionem advocans et invitans Spiritum sanctum. . . . Sed est hoc quoque

gift, a πνεῦμα, is meant, but it is a gift that remains within the subject who has received it, and is conferred by the Apostle and the presbyters. Timothy on whom it has been conferred can in his turn confer it to others.[1]

Deacons are to be chosen for the purity and gravity of their lives, and for their disinterestedness; as we know already from the "Didachè," they must be tried before being chosen (δοκιμαζέσθωσαν πρῶτον). They must have shown that they ruled their children and their home well (1 Tim. III. 8-13). The *episcopus*—and we must notice that, whereas the Epistle speaks of deacons in the plural, it speaks of the *episcopus* in the singular—must be blameless and enjoy the respect even of those outside the fold (ἀπὸ τῶν ἔξωθεν); he must be hospitable and able to teach (*id.* 2); he must be free from the love of money; besides he must have given proof that he has governed his house properly and can command the obedience of his children, for "if a man know not how to rule his own house, how shall he have a care of the Church of God?"[2]

The Pastoral Epistles are the work of an Apostle of Christ, who, seeing his end approaching, confirms the institutions established in Churches like those of Crete and of Asia: the institutions now established have then been sanctioned by apostolic authority. The Apostle, as we have said, feels that his course is run (2 Tim. IV. 7): he gives his last instructions to his disciple whom he calls an evangelist (*ib.* 5); but, on his death, this disciple is to be replaced only by the *presbyterium* of every Church. Whatever may be the

de veteri sacramento quo nepotes suos ex Ioseph Ephraim et Manassem Iacob capitibus impositis et intermutatis manibus benedixerit." The same meaning is ascribed to the laying on of hands, as a gesture, by CLEMENT OF ALEX. "Paedagog." III. 11 ("P.G." vol. VIII. col. 637, B.); and by the Gnostic Isidore, quoted in "Stromat." III. 1 (Col. 1101).

[1] 1 Tim. V. 22: χεῖρας ταχέως μηδενὶ ἐπιτίθει. C. GORE, "The Ministry of the Christian Church" (London, 1889), p. 250, says: "It is only a very arbitrary criticism which can fail to see here . . . the permanent process of ordination with which we are familiar in later Church history, that conception of the bestowal in ordination of a special 'charisma,' which at once carries with it the idea of a 'permanent character,' and that distinction of clergy and laity which is involved in the possession of a definite spiritual grace and power by those who have been ordained."

[2] 1 Tim. III. 4-5. The same teaching is found in Tit. I. 5-9.

relation existing then between the *presbyterium* and the episcopate, and leaving aside liturgical functions, the episcopate is an office of temporal administration and of teaching. The Church has receipts and expenses (1 Tim. v. 16) : the *episcopus* must prove himself a good steward. Discipline must obtain in the Church : the *episcopus* must prove himself also a good educator. Above all, the deposit of the faith that has been received must be upheld and defended : the *episcopus* is expected to be an effective teacher who watches over his flock and carefully preserves the trust committed to him.[1]

\* \*
\*

The Johannine Apocalypse is the work of a prophet, to whom the God of the prophetic spirits has sent His angel, to show His servants what must come to pass shortly (XXII. 6). John has heard and seen, and the angel who has shown him all things says to him : "I am thy fellow-servant ($\sigma\acute{v}\nu\delta o\nu\lambda o\varsigma$) and the servant of thy brethren the prophets" (XXII. 9). However, judging from the tone of the rebukes and threats he feels able to address to the seven Churches, this prophet must stand in authority far above those prophets whom the "Didachè" has represented as journeying from one Church to the other, and depending on the judgment which each Church passed upon them.

The letter to the seven Churches attests the autonomy of each of those seven Churches. Such is the case, for instance, with the Church of Ephesus, which the prophet congratulates on hating "them that are evil" and on having tried "them who say they are apostles, and are not," for

---

[1] It is interesting to see how the critics who question the authenticity of the Pastoral Epistles, insist on those features in them which make up what HOLTZMANN calls "a moderately Catholic Paulinism" and "a sort of ecclesiasticism *in fieri*". Cf. VON SODEN, in the "Handcommentar" (Freiburg, 1891), vol. III. pp. 162-7. (VON SODEN dates the Pastoral Epistles from Domitian's age, about 81-96, at the earliest.) In concluding his analysis of the Pastoral Epistles, HOLTZMANN, "Neut. Theologie," vol. II. p. 280, finds in them the idea of tradition, the idea of a visible Church in which the good and the bad are mingled together, the idea of the Church as a teaching authority and intermediary between Christ and each of the faithful, and the Church considered as an object of faith : in a word " die ganze Katholicität *in nuce*" : It is not for us to contradict him.

the Church of Ephesus found them to be liars (II. 2). This reminds us of the rules laid down by the "Didachè". This Church hates the Nicolaites (II. 6), whereas the Church of Pergamus shows indulgence to those who hold the doctrine of Balaam (II. 14) and the doctrine of the Nicolaites (II. 15). As to the Church of Thyatira, she suffers the woman Jezabel, who claims to be a prophetess, to teach (II. 20): blessed are those of Thyatira, who do not share this doctrine, and have not known the depths of Satan (II. 24) as these false doctors are wont to say.[1]  The prophet says to the angel of the Church of Sardis: " Be watchful and strengthen those who remain . . . that are ready to die. . . . Have in mind in what manner thou hast received and heard; keep and do penance" (III. 2-3). Balaam and Jezabel are symbolical names that stand for errors similar to, if not identical with, those of the Nicolaites. Error has made its way into these inexperienced and impressionable communities: and error is a kind of fornication which the Son of God holds in ab-horrence and will chastise, " and all the churches shall know that I am he that searcheth the reins and hearts " (II. 23).

Perishing churches may be reformed by such extraordinary interventions of the Spirit, but an everyday government does not last in that way.  The Johannine Epistles follow, more closely than the Apocalyse, the principles and method of the Pastoral Epistles.  We find in them, together with the hatred of error, the affirmation of the primacy of the teach-ing received "from the beginning" (2 John 5); for "many seducers are gone out into the world, who confess not that Jesus Christ is come in the flesh: this is the seducer and the Antichrist " (ib. 7).  How can any one possess God, unless he abides by the doctrine of Christ?[2]  "If any man come to you, and bring not this doctrine, receive him not into the house, nor say to him, God speed you" (ib. 10). "As for you, let that which you have heard from the be-

---

[1] An allusion to some fanciful speculations of the Nicolaites.  Cf. 1 Cor. II. 10, in which the Spirit is said to search "the deep things of God," and IREN. " Haer." II. 21, 2, where we are told that some Gnostics endeavour to fathom "profunda Bythi '.

[2] 2 John 9: μένων ἐν τῇ διδαχῇ τοῦ Χριστοῦ.  On this HOLTZMANN writes: " Verse 9 is perfect evidence that the teaching of the Church was law to the author " (" Handcommentar," vol. IV. p. 242).

ginning, abide in you: if that abide in you which you have heard from the beginning, you also shall abide in the Son, and in the Father. . . . These things have I written to you, concerning them that seduce you" (1 John II. 24-6). The received doctrine is made up of Christ's commands: "He who saith that he knoweth him, and keepeth not his commandments, is a liar".[1] We found similar advice in the "Didachè". "Believe not every spirit, but try the spirits" to see "if they be of God, because many false prophets are gone out into the world" (*ib.* IV. 1).

The "Tertia Ioannis" testifies plainly to an authority which is exercised to protect the local Church against the spread of error. The Ancient ($\pi\rho\epsilon\sigma\beta\acute{\upsilon}\tau\epsilon\rho\sigma$), as the author of the "Tertia Ioannis" styles himself (and this is none other than St. John), tells a Christian named Gaius of the joy he experienced when some "brethren" came and gave testimony "in presence of the Church" (the Church in whose midst the Ancient dwells) to the charity Gaius has shown "to the brethren, and especially to the strangers". The Ancient encourages Gaius to continue to provide for the travelling expenses of these itinerants, "since they went out for the name, taking nothing of the heathen".[2] These are genuine missionaries sent by John the Apostle and by his Church. These missionaries, however, have not been everywhere so cordially received: from some Church, other than that of Gaius, they have been sent away. That Church has at its head a Christian named Diotrephes. The Ancient had previously written, not to Diotrephes, but to the local Church: Diotrephes who is fond of pre-eminence ($\acute{o}$ $\phi\iota\lambda\sigma\pi\rho\omega\tau\epsilon\acute{\upsilon}\omega\nu$ $\alpha\grave{\upsilon}\tau\hat{\omega}\nu$), answered in the name of the Church, refusing to receive the brethren recommended by the Ancient, forbidding any one of the faithful to receive them, and expelling them from the Church. "For this cause, if I come, I will bring to his remembrance his works which he doth, prating against us with wicked words."[3]

[1] 1 John II. 4: $\acute{o}$ $\lambda\acute{\epsilon}\gamma\omega\nu$ $\acute{o}\tau\iota$ $\acute{\epsilon}\gamma\nu\omega\kappa\alpha$ $\alpha\grave{\upsilon}\tau\acute{o}\nu$. These words seem to allude to some pseudo-apostles. Cf. Apoc. II. 2.

[2] 3 John 5, 6. The words $\acute{\upsilon}\pi\grave{\epsilon}\rho$ $\tau\sigma\hat{\upsilon}$ $\acute{o}\nu\acute{o}\mu\alpha\tau\sigma$ $\acute{\epsilon}\xi\hat{\eta}\lambda\theta\alpha\nu$ signify that these brethren travel for *the name*, i.e. for the name of Jesus. LAGRANGE, "Messianisme," p. 145, note 2.

[3] 3 John 9-12: $\acute{\epsilon}\gamma\rho\alpha\psi\acute{\alpha}$ $\tau\iota$ (rather than $\acute{\epsilon}\gamma\rho\alpha\psi\alpha$ $\acute{\alpha}\nu$) $\tau\hat{\eta}$ $\acute{\epsilon}\kappa\kappa\lambda\eta\sigma\acute{\iota}\alpha$ $\kappa.\tau.\lambda$,

We must not overemphasize the words: "Diotrephes doth not receive us," as though Diotrephes did not acknowledge the authority of the Ancient, and had broken with him ; since the Ancient proposes to come in person and to speak unsparingly to Diotrephes. Rather, we may suppose that, because of the intense opposition to itinerant begging propagandists, Diotrephes had not received even those itinerants who came recommended by a note from the Apostle : but Diotrephes doubtless had some right to speak in the name of the community. Ecclesiastical tradition loved to picture to itself the Apostle John surrounded by bishops he had placed in those Churches of which he was the founder.[1] Diotrephes is thus the first monarchical bishop whose name has come down to us, and the Protestant critics are very willing to set him against the Apostle : he stands for the hierarchy, the Apostle for the Spirit; the former will do away with the latter. . . . It would be more historical to ask oneself, not whether the pre-eminence of Diotrephes was the result of a usurpation, but whether his conduct was not that of a tactless person.

## II.

With St. Clement's Epistle we might bring to a close the study of the Apostolic ecclesiology, for this epistle is, in a sense, the term of the development of institutions and

---

[1] CLEM. OF ALEX. quoted by EUSEB. "H. E." III. 28, 6 (according to the "Quis dives salvetur," 42). Compare the statement of the Muratorianum : John wrote the fourth Gospel "cohortantibus condiscipulis et episcopis suis '; and still better Tertullian, "Adversus Marcionem," IV. 5 : "Habemus et Ioannis alumnas ecclesias. Nam etsi Apocalypsim eius Marcion respuit, ordo tamen episcoporum ad originem recensus, in Ioannem stabit auctorem". Tertullian seemingly thinks that the *ordo episcoporum* was inaugurated in Asia by the Apostle John. On the other hand, we know ("Exhort. castit.' 7) that he looked upon the distinction between the *plebs* and the *ordo* as a creation of the Church. As regards the difficult problem whether the angel of each of the seven Churches is its bishop, see SWETE, "Apocalypse," pp. 21-2, and LIGHTFOOT, "Christ. Ministry," p. 29. The last writer suggests an analogy between the "angels" of the Churches in the Apocalypse, and the "princes" in the prophecy of Daniel (x. 13, 20, 1).

ideas, to which the Apostolic documents cited bear witness;[1] it is besides the *epiphany* of the Roman primacy.

First of all, the notion of charism, which was so important some fifty years before, seems now to have vanished entirely and the word "charism" is about to assume a new meaning, that of the condition assigned by God to every man according to his social standing. Every Christian must be united with all his brethren by the bond of solidarity, and submit to his neighbour "according to the charism appointed to him" by God. What does this mean? He who is strong must strengthen him who is weak, and he who is weak must honour him who is strong. The rich must be generous, the poor must pray to God in behalf of the rich.[2] Hence strength is a charism, and so also is weakness: and likewise richness and poverty: as well as wisdom and humility and continence.

Secondly, we find no longer any trace of itinerant missionaries. The "Prima Clementis" speaks of prophets, it is true, but these are Elias, Eliseus and Ezekiel.[3] No mention is made of the word teacher (διδάσκαλος), nor of the word evangelist. The only Apostles are the great Apostles, like Peter and Paul.

The "Prima Clementis" does not merely re-echo the authoritative formulæ of St. Paul, of the "Didachè," of the "Prima Petri" and of the Johannine texts: from beginning to end, it proclaims unity through authority. As it was written to a Church that had fallen a prey to anarchy, we easily understand why it insists on the necessity of obedience: still, it insists upon obedience in such a way that unity through authority quickly appears to be the fundamental principle of its ecclesiology. The word "unanimity" (ὁμόνοια) comes often from the pen of St. Clement; so also do the words and images which convey the idea of discipline and of obedience.

---

[1] The inscription does not run in Clement's name: Ἡ ἐκκλησία τοῦ θεοῦ ἡ παροικοῦσα Ῥώμην τῇ ἐκκλησίᾳ τοῦ θεοῦ τῇ παροικούσῃ Κόρινθον. . . . One Church, one city, but this Church is a foreigner in this city. Regarding the meaning of the word πάροικος—a domiciled foreigner—cf. CHAPOT, p. 179, and in DITTENBERGER, "Sylloge," vol. III. p. 178, the index at the words πάροικοι and παροικέω.

[2] 1 Clem. xxxviii. 1-2.          [3] xvii. 1, xliii. 1.

Like the "Didachè," and the Apocalypse, Clement sees the Christian community spread through the whole world: as yet he does not know the word " catholic," but he *does* know that Paul preached righteousness to ὅλον τὸν κόσμον (V. 7) and that the elect are ἐν ὅλῳ τῷ κόσμῳ (LIX. 2).

The faithful are a people, an ἔθνος, which God has chosen to Himself in the midst of nations, a select share that God has taken, a holy portion He has reserved to Himself: hence let them perform the works of holiness and adhere closely to those to whom the grace is granted by God, let them " clothe themselves in unanimity ".[1] " Let our conscience then gather us together in unanimity in the same place, and let us cry unto God with one voice." [2] The Ignatian epistles will not insist more vigorously on the unity which must reign in the Christian community. The " Prima Clementis " likens ecclesiastical discipline to military discipline. "Let us mark the soldiers that are enlisted under our rulers, how exactly, how readily, how submissively, they execute the orders given them. All are not eparchs, or rulers of thousands, or rulers of hundreds, or rulers of fifties, and so forth: but each man in his own rank executeth the orders given by the king and his chief officers." [3] The " Prima Clementis " takes up a comparison we have seen already in St. Paul's Epistle to the Romans and in his first Epistle to the Corinthians: the faithful are

[1] xxix. 1-3, xxx. 3: ἐνδυσώμεθα τὴν ὁμόνοιαν.

[2] xxxiv. 7 : καὶ ἡμεῖς οὖν ἐν ὁμονοίᾳ ἐπὶ τὸ αὐτὸ συναχθέντες τῇ συνειδή- σει, ὡς ἑνὸς στόματος βοήσωμεν. This is an allusion to the liturgical chants and acclamations. The expression ἐπὶ τὸ αὐτὸ συναχθέντες, which we shall find again in St. Ignatius, had been already used by St. Paul ; the word συνειδήσει may be compared with the expression " conscientia religionis " of Tertullian.

[3] xxxvii. 2-3 : κατανοήσωμεν τοὺς στρατευομένους τοῖς ἡγουμένοις ἡμῶν . . . ἕκαστος ἐν τῷ ἰδίῳ τάγματι τὰ ἐπιτασσόμενα ὑπὸ τοῦ βασιλέως καὶ ἡγουμένων ἐπιτελεῖ. The chiliarchs, etc., are a reminiscence of Exod. xviii. 21. A "chiliarch" is like a tribune, a " hecatontarch," like a centurion. The Roman army had no grade corresponding to that of a "pentecontarch". An " eparch " is a civil " praefectus ". We find at an early date Christians using with special fondness those military comparisons. Cf. 2 Cor. x. 3-6 ; Eph. vi. 10-18 ; Phil. ii. 25. In the *Pastoral* Epistles, Christian life is represented as a period of military service, and the Christian as a soldier (1 Tim. i. 18 ; 2 Tim. ii. 3). St. Ignatius, and after him Tertullian and Cyprian, dwell on this comparison.

not only a people, an assembly, an army; they are a body,[1] which is the body of Christ: "Wherefore do we tear and rend asunder the members of Christ?" (XLVI. 7). The Church is also a flock: "Let the flock of Christ be at peace under the presbyters" who rule over it.[2] All these images are already familiar to us, but we have to see what definite and precise ideas they express.

Unity is procured by the religious training given by the presbyters to the faithful: the word παιδεία is almost as familiar to our author as ὁμόνοια. "Let us reverence our rulers," he writes, "let us honour our elders, let us instruct our young men in the lesson of the fear of God, let us form our women towards that which is good."[3] Here it is question only of moral training, but the same formation will apply to the mind and to the character, in order that ecclesiastical unity may be obtained. "Let us accept discipline, whereat no man ought to be vexed . . . the admonition (νουθέτησις) which we give one to another is good and useful" (LVI. 2). "Submit yourselves unto the presbyters, and receive discipline unto repentance. . . . Learn to submit yourselves. . . . It is better for you to be found little but of good repute in the flock of Christ, than to be had in exceeding honour and yet be cast out of the hope of Christ."[4] In other words: outside the fold no hope, outside the Church no salvation.

This discipline has for its matter the Lord's commands and the received faith. "Let the commandments and ordinances of the Lord be written on the tables of your heart" (II. 8). Woe to him who does not walk "in the ordinances of the commandments" of Christ.[5] Let us remember the "words of the Lord Jesus" and be "obedient to His hal-

---

[1] XXXVII. 5, XXXVIII. 1. We may recall what has been said above of the Latin word *corpus* as being the legal term for designating an association.

[2] LIV. 2. Cf. XVI. 1, XLIV. 3, LVII. 2.

[3] XXI. 6. The προηγούμενοι are the rulers of the church, the πρεσβύτεροι are the Christians who are advanced in age or of old standing, in contrast with the young, νεώτεροι.

[4] LVII. 1-2. Here again the πρεσβύτεροι are the elders, in contrast with the νεώτεροι. In this passage Clement follows 1 Pet. v. 5.

[5] III. 4: ἐν τοῖς νομίμοις τῶν προσταγμάτων αὐτοῦ.

lowed words ".[1]   He that hath love fulfils "the commandments of Christ "[2].   As true as God lives, and as the
Lord Jesus lives, and as the Holy Ghost lives, he who
fulfils humbly and perseveringly "the ordinances and commandments given by God" will be sure of a place among
those souls that are saved by Jesus Christ.[3]   When preaching union to the faithful of Corinth, the author of the
Epistle does not at all doubt that his admonitions will be
heard, because the Corinthians are men of good faith who
have pondered "the oracles of the teaching of God".[4]   The
words used to designate this teaching are as definite as
can be desired.   The Epistle does not speak of a "spirit,"
but of *logia*—a word which suggests the idea of precise and
without doubt written precepts.   Then, too, the idea of Holy
Writ is affirmed by the "Prima Clementis" in the most explicit terms: "You know," we read in the Epistle, "and you
know well, the sacred Scriptures and you have searched into
the *logia* of God".[5]   Whatever the contents of these sacred
Scriptures may be, whatever place the New Testament may
have in them, this is a law which will enable the presbyters
to judge rightly.   Then, conjointly, we have the word rule
itself (κανών) pronounced: and this word he does not apply
to Holy Writ exclusively, but to all that belongs to the received faith: "Let us forsake idle and vain thoughts; and
let us conform to the glorious and venerable canon which
has been handed down to us".[6]

The "Prima Clementis" does not need to apply this
principle of the *canon* to any doctrinal matter against
heretics.   It has to consider the hierarchical order, only inasmuch as it is the institution of Christ Himself.   "We ought
to do all things in order, whatever the master has commanded

---

[1] XIII. 1, 3.  Cf. XX. 1-10.

[2] XLIX. 1.  τὰ τοῦ Χριστοῦ παραγγέλματα.  Cf. L. 5.

[3] LVIII. 2: τὰ ὑπὸ τοῦ θεοῦ δεδομένα δικαιώματα καὶ προστάγματα.

[4] LXII. 3: τὰ λόγια τῆς παιδείας τοῦ θεοῦ.  Cf. Heb. XII. 6-9.

[5] LIII. 1: ἱερὰς γραφάς, λόγια τοῦ θεοῦ.  Cf. XLV. 2.

[6] VII. 2: ἔλθωμεν ἐπὶ τὸν εὐκλεῆ καὶ σεμνὸν τῆς παραδόσεως ἡμῶν κανόνα.
The word κανών which we had already found in 2 Cor. x. 13 and Gal.
VI. 16, reappears : here it signifies a binding rule, having authority.
Clement uses it in two other passages ; I. 3 (ἐν τῇ κανόνι τῆς ὑποταγῆς) and
XLI. 1.

us to perform at the appointed seasons."[1] This is an allusion to the Christian worship. Here, as in the " Didachè," the allusion to Christian worship brings up the thought of the Levitical worship. "Now the offerings and ministrations He commanded to be performed with care, not according to pleasure or in disorder, but at fixed times and seasons. And where and by whom He would have them performed, He Himself fixed by His supreme will." He has determined the function of the high-priest, the place assigned to the priests, and the offices of the Levites : there are prescriptions for the man of the people, the layman, i.e. for the Israelite who does not belong to the tribe of Levi and to the priestly family.[2] This is simple allegory, Levitism being the type of the order which, according to the " Prima Clementis," must prevail in the Christian liturgy. There is a dispute as to whether the high-priest (ἀρχιερεύς) typifies here the bishop, or whether he typifies Christ : this much is certain, that the priests (ἱερεῖς) typify the presbyters, and the Levites, the deacons. At all events, the Christian worship is in the hands of a hierarchy distinct from the people : there are clerics and there are laymen. "Let each one of us, brethren, keep to his own order . . . not transgressing the appointed rule of his office."[3]

We have already seen in the " Prima Clementis " a decidedly Roman image of that hierarchy : the Christians compared to an army serving under a certain number of officers, each soldier at his post and fulfilling, according to his grade, the commands of the basileus and of the officers. Here the basileus is Christ, and the officers (ἡγούμενοι) are the presbyters. We must note that the basileus gives orders, and

[1] XL. 1 : πάντα τάξει ποιεῖν ὀφείλομεν ὅσα ὁ δεσπότης ἐπιτελεῖν ἐκέλευσεν κατὰ καιροὺς τεταγμένους.

[2] XL. 2-5 : τῷ γὰρ ἀρχιερεῖ ἴδιαι λειτουργίαι δεδομέναι εἰσίν, καὶ τοῖς ἱερεῦσιν ἴδιος ὁ τόπος προστέτακται, καὶ λευίταις ἴδιαι διακονίαι ἐπίκεινται, ὁ λαϊκὸς ἄνθρωπος κ.τ.λ. As to the meaning of ἀρχιερεύς see LIGHTFOOT, " Clement," vol. II. p. 123. We should notice the use of the word τόπος. The word λαϊκός which is not found in the LXX, appears here for the first time in the ecclesiastical language.

[3] XLI. 1 : ἕκαστος ἡμῶν, ἀδελφοί, ἐν τῷ ἰδίῳ τάγματι, . . . μὴ παρεκβαίνων τὸν ὡρισμένον τῆς λειτουργίας αὐτοῦ κανόνα.

so also do the officers.[1]    Whence do the presbyters derive this right to command, and this authority which is added to the authority of the received precepts?    The "Prima Clementis" answers that Christ was sent by God, and the Apostles by Jesus Christ.    Tertullian will express the idea in no more striking terms a century later : "*Ecclesia ab apostolis, apostoli a Christo, Christus a Deo*".

In fact the "Prima Clementis" adds that, after receiving the instructions of the risen Saviour, the Apostles parted company to preach God's kingdom; they preached it in provinces and cities, where they established the "first-fruits," i.e. the first converts of those provinces and cities, in the functions of *episcopi* and deacons, to minister to those who were to join the Church later on (XLII. 1-4). Thus the hierarchy was based on the immediate authority of the Apostles.    When the "first-fruits," or first *episcopi* commissioned by the Apostles, in due course die, their office will be taken up and exercised by new *episcopi*, men who will command the esteem of all : for these new *episcopi* will have been invested with their office, if not by the Apostles themselves, at least by the *episcopi* chosen by the Apostles, the consent of the whole Church being required.[2]    In other words, unlike the magistracies of Greek cities, the episcopal

---

[1] XXXVII. 2 : τὰ ἐπιτασσόμενα ὑπὸ τοῦ βασίλως καὶ τῶν ἡγουμένων. These terms also express Clement's loyal fidelity to the Emperor and the magistrates.    In this respect the early Christian community had two sentiments : on one hand, the sentiment which is expressed in St. John's Apocalypse and looks upon the Empire as a manifestation of Antichrist ; on the other hand, the sentiment of loyalty, which impels to render to Cæsar the things that are Cæsar's.    Leaving aside the obscure text of 2 Thess. II. 6, 7, St. Paul expressed most decidedly the sentiment of loyalty, Rom. XIII. 1-7 and Tit. III. 1 ; likewise St. Peter, 1 Pet. II. 13-14, 17.    In return for this sentiment, the Christians, like the Jews, expect from the Empire nothing but justice and security : they dare not hope it to embrace the Gospel.

[2] XLIV. 2-3.    In these passages we may find an allusion to the collegiate episcopate, and also the manner of election.    Trustworthy men are chosen (δεδοκιμασμένοι).    They are invested by the Apostles, or, if the Apostles are dead, by the *episcopi* or presbyters instituted by the Apostles ; they are invested with the consent of the local Church. Τοὺς οὖν κατασταθέντας ὑπ᾽ ἐκείνων (the Apostles) ἢ μεταξὺ ὑφ᾽ ἑτέρων ἐλλογίμων ἀνδρῶν, συνευδοκησάσης τῆς ἐκκλησίας πάσης ; the local Church brings merely its consent to their investiture.

authority, together with the powers which constitute it, is not derived from the vote of the members of the assembly; it is not a power delegated by that assembly: it is an office, or λειτουργία which those invested with it pass on to their successors as an inheritance transmissible from hand to hand: in one word it is the *hierarchy*.

This is the principle in the name of which the "Prima Clementis" reproves the scandal given by the Church of Corinth. For as to the presbyters who fulfil blamelessly their function, "we consider that it is unjust to depose them" (XLIV. 3). It is indeed an abominable scandal, a scandal unworthy of Christianity, that in a Church as old and as firmly established as that of Corinth, a cabal should have been formed, for the sake of one or two personages, against the presbyters, or rulers of the Church (XLVII. 6). This rebellion is wicked and hateful: "It will be no light sin in us, if we turn out of their episcopal charge those who have offered the gifts blamelessly and holily".[1] These few words imply that, in case of a serious grievance, the community may deprive of the episcopal function one who has been invested with it. Apart from such cases, the office cannot be taken away, and is held for life (XLIV. 5-6).

The practical conclusion of the Epistle is that there were sent from Rome to Corinth "faithful and prudent men," men of mature age and well known, ever since their youth, for the gravity of their lives: "They shall be witnesses between you and us," in other words, they shall express to the Corinthians the sentiments of the Romans, and give them Clement's letter. "This we have done that you may know that we have had, and still have, every solicitude that you should be speedily at peace" (LXIII. 3-4). Whether the Roman Church had been asked by some Corinthians to intervene, the Epistle does not say; if the presbyters deprived of their office through the revolt of the Corinthians did, in fact, appeal to Rome, it may have been tactful on Clement's part not to mention it. If that did happen, we have here

---

[1] XLIV. 4 : ἁμαρτία οὐ μικρὰ ἡμῖν ἔσται, ἐὰν τοὺς ἀμέμπτως καὶ ὁσίως προσ-ενεγκόντας τὰ δῶρα, τῆς ἐπισκοπῆς ἀποβάλωμεν. Here again we find the priestly character of the episcopate affirmed and the episcopate included in the presbyterate, according to the meaning we have fixed elsewhere.

9

a most remarkable appeal to Rome, the first that history records.   But it may be that Rome was reliably informed by public rumour of the scandal which had arisen at Corinth, and that her intervention was spontaneous (XLVII. 7).   On this latter supposition, we realize the more distinctly how unprecedented is the intestine revolution that has taken place at Corinth, and also how Rome is already conscious " of possessing a supreme and exceptional authority," which she will not cease to claim in subsequent ages, and which, as early as this first intervention, is religiously obeyed by Corinth.[1]

Sohm, who has recognized the importance of the testimony which the Epistle of St. Clement of Rome bears to the history of Catholicism and of the Roman primacy, sees in it the manifesto of ecclesiastical law, of that famous " Kirchenrecht " which is, in his eyes, the framework of Catholicism.   The fundamental idea of Catholicism, he says, is that the visible Church governed by the bishops and by the Pope is identical with Christendom, i.e. the Church of Christ.   Why ?   Because Christendom has received from God Himself a definite legal constitution; in other words, because there is a divine law.   And this doctrine finds its first expression in St. Clement's Epistle to the Corinthians.   Before Clement there was nothing similar, so that one may justly say that Clement's letter put an end to the primitive condition of Christianity, and brought about " the most momentous accident in the whole evolution of the Church ".[2]

This view contains an important element of truth, in regard to which it describes accurately the teaching of the " Prima Clementis ".   Certainly, the " Prima Clementis " proclaims the divine right of the hierarchy founded by the Apostles; certainly, this divine law of the hierarchy is constitutive of Catholicism.   But did the " Prima Clementis " create thus entirely the divine right of the hierarchy on the occasion of the incident of Corinth, or was not the divine right already contained in the existing institutions and in the conception which all Christians had of those institu-

---

[1] DUCHESNE, " Eglises separées," p. 126.  We may remark too that the Apostle John, who was still living at Ephesus, did not intervene, although communications between Ephesus and Corinth were much more natural than between Corinth and Rome.

[2] SOHM, " Kirchenrecht," p. 160.

tions? Sohm claims that, till the time of Clement's Epistle, Christendom in its enthusiastic faith, knew no power save that of Love and of the Spirit:[1] but this is romancing! When he has to explain the intervention of Clement and of his legal mind in the midst of such a chaos, Sohm talks of the decrease of faith, of the necessity of regulating the eucharistic worship and the management of finance: "Practical considerations inspired the letter of Clement and brought about later on the triumph of his ideas". Catholicism is the fatal product of the decrease of faith and of the multiplication of sins: we have it on the authority of a Protestant professor.

## III.

The "Prima Clementis" is the expression of an ecclesiology that is more than merely Roman and legal. Great as the distance may be between the man of law and tradition who wrote the "Prima Clementis," and the emotional and mystical author of the Ignatian Epistles, it is not paradoxical to affirm that St. Clement of Rome and St. Ignatius of Antioch agree essentially in their conception of the Church.

A first feature common to both is this: St. Ignatius knows nothing of those itinerant missionaries who, prompted by the Spirit, were still going around from one Church to another, when the "Didachè" was composed. There is a constant correspondence going on between the Churches; and this mutual intercourse by means of letters and messengers is regulated and, we may say, official. For instance, Ignatius begs Polycarp, the Bishop of Smyrna, to assemble the faithful of Smyrna and choose a messenger to go to Antioch and tell the Christians of that city how grateful Ignatius is to the Smyrnians.[2] Again Ignatius asks

---

[1] SOHM, "Kirchenrecht," pp. 162-3. HARNACK, "Entstehung und Entwickelung der Kirchenverfassung und des Kirchenrechts in den zwei ersten Jahrhunderten" (Leipzig, 1910), pp. 121-86, has a pungent criticism of what elsewhere he calls Sohm's "Anabaptist thesis". Cf. also the criticism of Sohm's view by PAUL FOURNIER in the "Nouvelle Revue historique du droit," vol. XVIII. (1894), pp. 286-95.

[2] "Polyc." VII. 2: πρέπει συμβούλιον ἀγαγεῖν θεοπρεπέστατον καὶ χειροτονῆσαί τινα. The verb χειροτονεῖν always signifies to elect; and this is why Ignatius here calls the church συμβούλιον.

Polycarp to write to the neighbouring churches to entreat each of them to send, if possible, a messenger to convey to their destination Polycarp's letters to his bereaved flock. "I salute him who from Smyrna shall be appointed to go to Syria."[1]

The insistence of the " Prima Clementis " on the necessity of obedience to the established hierarchy on the part of the faithful might be accounted for by the state of anarchy into which the Corinthian Church had accidentally fallen. On the contrary, what imparts to this insistence its true significance, is the fact that the Ignatian Epistles repeat it, with a similar emphasis and when addressing all the Churches, in the manifest assumption that the principle is fundamental. The word ὁμόνοια is just as frequently used by Ignatius as by Clement; so also is the word ὑποτάσσειν in the same sense of submission and obedience. Everywhere we find a constituted hierarchy, with the bishop as supreme, a *presbyterium* of priests, and deacons.[2] "Let all the faithful respect the deacons as [they do] Jesus Christ," since Jesus Christ became willingly the servant of His own disciples; let them "respect the bishop as the image of the Father, and the priests as the council of God and the college of the Apostles: apart from these"—the bishop, the *presbyterium*, the deacons—"there is no Church".[3] Could the hierarchical idea of the Church be more strongly expressed?

Unlike Clement, Ignatius does not treat its Apostolic institution as the sole reason for the submission of the faithful to the hierarchy;[4] he desires that we should also see in it the divine authority it represents. Ignatius is a mystic in whose eyes the bishop is the grace of God, and the *presbyterium* the law of Jesus Christ; God is pre-emi-

---

[1] "Polyc." viii. 1-2. Cf. POLYCARP, "Philip." xiii., xiv.

[2] TIXERONT, "Hist. des dogmes" (Paris, 1905), vol. i. p. 140. DE GENOUILLAC, "L'Église chr. au temps de S. Ignace" (Paris, 1907), p. 137 and foll.

[3] "Trall." iii. 1 : χωρὶς τούτων ἐκκλησία οὐ καλεῖται. Cf. "Smyrn.' viii. 1. "Ad Polycarp." vi. 1. Cf. POLYCARP. "Philip.' v. 3.

[4] "Trall." vii. 1 : τοῦτο δὲ ἔσται ὑμῖν μὴ φυσιουμένοις καὶ οὖσιν ἀχωρίστοις Ἰησοῦ Χριστοῦ καὶ τοῦ ἐπισκόπου καὶ τῶν διαταγμάτων τῶν ἀποστόλων. LIGHTFOOT, "Ignatius" (1889), vol. ii. p. 169, finds in this passage a reference to the institution of episcopacy.

nently the bishop, the invisible bishop who manifests himself through and in the visible bishop.[1]  The faithful must submit to the bishop, as Jesus Christ submitted to His Father, and as the Apostles submitted to Christ, to the Father, and to the Spirit;[2] they must submit to the *presbyterium* as to Christ's Apostles.[3]  To describe that discipline, Ignatius uses the comparison already used by St. Clement, that of the military discipline: let there be no deserter among the faithful enlisted in the service of Christ.[4]  He also uses the comparison of the choral unison which we found in St. Clement: the *presbyterium* is attuned to the bishop like the strings of a lyre: the whole Church sings together and in unison, as a choir, forming but one voice.[5]  The faithful are united to their bishop by a bond which is not human but spiritual, the same bond as unites the Church to Jesus Christ, "that all things may be harmonious in unity".[6]  The faithful are the members of Christ.  Hence they should remain in "blameless unity, that they may also be partakers of God".[7]

The inscription of every one of the Ignatian Epistles bears testimony that the Church, the local and self-governing Church, is, in the eyes of Ignatius, a moral, predestined, sanctified thing, of which, prompted by his spirit of faith, he sings the praises in truly lyric tones.  The Church " which is in Ephesus " is " blessed through the greatness of God in all plenitude"; she is "predestined before all ages ".  The Church " which is at Magnesia, on the Meander," is " blessed through the grace of God the Father in Jesus our Saviour".  The Church " which is at Tralles of Asia " is " beloved of God," she is holy, chosen, worthy of God.  The Church " which is at Philadelphia of Asia " is established in the concord of God, she exults in the Saviour's passion and overflows with God's mercy that is in her.  The

---

[1] " Magn.' ii. and iii.; cf. " Polyc." inscr. and viii. 3, on the episcopate of God.

[2] " Magn." xiii. 2.            [3] " Trall." ii. 2.

[4] " Polycarp," vi. 2: ἀρέσκετε ᾧ στρατεύεσθε, ἀφ' οὗ τὰ ὀψώνια κομίσεσθε, μήτις ὑμῶν δεσέρτωρ εὑρεθῇ.  The reader will notice the Latinisms borrowed from military language.

[5] " Eph." iv.            [6] " Eph." v. 1.            [7] " Eph." iv. 2.

Church "which is at Smyrna of Asia" is full of grace, and beloved of God, and fertile in holiness.  Ignatius lyrically personifies each Church to impress vividly on the faithful that, if they wish to abide by the law given them by God, they must unceasingly adhere to their respective Churches, and therefore to their respective bishops, in constant fidelity.

Again, this personification proves how perceptible is this unity in every Church: could St. Ignatius speak as he does, were each city divided into dissenting and rival communities?  It proves also the mutual agreement among themselves of all these various Christian cities; could Ignatius write to all of them with this confidence, were he not sure that their sentiments were in harmony with his?  These Christian communities, it is true, are threatened with error: but what is so remarkable is that these errors, far from obtaining a lasting abode in the heart of the community, succeed only in separating from the community any one who embraces them.  Docetism, which reduces Christ to a divine phantom, is the error denounced by St. Ignatius as an actual danger: "Be ye deaf," he writes, " when any man speaketh to you of Jesus Christ as though He were not of the race of David or the Son of Mary, as though He had not truly eaten or drunk or suffered, as though He had not died or descended into hell, or been raised from the dead: the Christians who speak thus are unbelievers ($\check{\alpha}\pi\iota\sigma\tau o\iota$), and godless ($\check{\alpha}\theta\epsilon o\iota$) : avoid them ".[1]  The Christians of Ephesus are praised because they "all live according to truth, and no heresy hath a home among them ".[2]  "Truth " is to be understood here, it would seem, in the sense of the rule of faith.

A division, a heresy, is the contrary of the truth received by all.  Whoever strives to sow an "evil doctrine " is rejected, driven away as a mad dog that is beyond cure.[3]  The Philadelphians must beware of weeds which are not cultivated by Jesus Christ, which have not been planted by the Father.[4]  Whoever does not speak of Jesus Christ as the Church does, must be looked upon as dead: an allusion

---

[1] " Trall." ix.-x.   " Smyrn." iv.                    [2] " Eph." vi. 2.
[3] " Eph." vii. 1 and ix. 1.          [4] " Philad." iii. 1.   Cf. vi. 1-2.

perhaps to the custom of the philosophical schools of ancient Greece, in which the term "dead" was applied to those scholars who broke with the dogmas of their school.[1] . . . At all events the Churches which Ignatius has in view, effectively defend themselves against the inroads of Docetism: and this actual condition of things explains why adhesion to the visible Church is a guarantee that one is in possession of the truth.

As unity, however mystically it may be understood and preached, is not of self-evident necessity, St. Ignatius must broach a theory which can justify it. Here, as for the whole religion, faith has preceded theory, and theory—as it ever happens—has been made necessary by heresy. Ignatius writes to the Philadelphians as follows :—

" [VII.] Even though certain persons desired to deceive me after the flesh, yet the Spirit is not deceived, being from God : for it knows whence it comes and where it goes, and it searches out the hidden things. I cried out, when I was among you; I spake with a loud voice, with God's own voice, Give heed to the bishops and presbytery and deacons. Howbeit they suspected me of saying this because I knew beforehand of the schism of certain persons. But He in whom I am bound is my witness that I learned it not from flesh of man; it was the Spirit who spake in this wise; Do nothing without the bishop; keep your flesh as a temple of God; cherish union; shun divisions; be imitators of Jesus Christ, as He Himself also was of His Father.

" [VIII.] I did therefore my own part, as a man who is on the side of unity. Where there is division and anger, there God abides not. Now the Lord forgives all men when they repent, if repenting they return to the unity of God and to the communion of the bishop: I have faith in the grace of Jesus Christ, who shall strike off every fetter from us; and I entreat you, Do nothing in a spirit of factiousness, but in accordance with the teaching of Christ. For I heard certain persons saying, 'If I find not this doc-

---

[1] "Philad." VI. 1. Cf. the note of Funk on that passage. "PP. apostol." (1901), vol. I. p. 269, where he quotes Clement of Alexandria and Didymus.

trine of faith in the archives, in the Gospel,[1] I believe it not '. And when I said to them ' It is written,' they answered me, 'That is the question'. But as for me, my archives are Jesus Christ, the invisible archives are His Cross, His Death, His Resurrection, and faith through Him ; wherein I desire to be justified through your prayers."

Here we find St. Ignatius contending with Christians whose minds are being wrought on by heresy. Ignatius has repeated his maxim, which is always the same : Love unity, do nothing without the bishop. At Philadelphia the faithful did not think this was a principle, they saw in it a lesson given for the benefit of some who were then breaking with the bishop and with unity. Without doubt his warning was timely, but Ignatius was not thinking of that ; what he was saying at Philadelphia he had said everywhere. But, at Philadelphia, the faithful, who have been led away by Docetism, reason out their error and lay down this principle : Unless we find in the archives, i.e. in the Gospel, the article of faith on which we disagree, we shall not believe. By "archives" we must understand here, not the Old Testament, as Lightfoot thought, but simply, with Funk and Zahn, every collection of authentic documents, like those preserved in public archives : the collection appealed to by these controversialists is the Gospel. We believe, they say, only what is written.

Those few words of the Epistle to the Philadelphians indicate the antithesis between Holy Writ and the hierarchical authority, and even at an early date, heretics are found who appeal to what is written for the purpose of justifying themselves. Taken in itself, the appeal to Scripture could be no surprise for Ignatius, since he cannot but admit the authority of a Sacred Writing. Did he not say to the Magnesians: " Do your diligence that you be confirmed in the *maxims* of the Lord and of the Apostles ".[2] The word *maxims* is

---

[1] About the text of this passage see the note of FUNK, " PP. apostol." vol. I. p. 270. Concerning the ἀρχεῖα, i.e. the archives of Greek cities, CHAPOT, p. 245-8.

[2] " Magn." XIII. 1 : σπουδάζετε οὖν βεβαιωθῆναι ἐν τοῖς δόγμασιν τοῦ κυρίου καὶ τῶν ἀποστόλων. The word δόγμα signifies primarily any decision or decree that has force of law in a Greek city. See in DITTENBERGER,

not an appropriate translation of the Greek word δόγματα, which expresses the idea of a command or a decision emanating from an unquestioned authority, and, as such, obligatory. If the Lord and the Apostles have left to Christians "dogmas" of this kind, any writing that contains these "dogmas" is invested with an authority equal to that of the Lord and of the Apostles; this is the principle itself of the New Testament regarded as a canon.[1] Ignatius accepts the principle that we must believe what is written, and, addressing the Docetæ against whom he is arguing, he says to them : What is written testifies against you; to which the Docetæ reply : This is precisely the point. Here we are in a circle.

We should like to see St. Ignatius state more distinctly that Scripture is not self-sufficing and that the written faith is not the whole faith. He insinuates it when he writes : "For me, my archives are Jesus Christ . . . and faith through Him." The authoritative faith is that faith to which the Church as such gives testimony. . . . But the affirmation of Ignatius has not that distinctness with which Irenæus and Tertullian will speak later on.

To be complete, however, we must call attention to the importance attached by St. Ignatius to the authority of the Apostles. The "Prima Clementis" had already pointed to the Apostles as clothed with the power of Jesus for the establishment of the Church all over the world. As we have just seen, St. Ignatius places the "dogmas" of the Apostles on the same level with those of the Lord. He speaks of the Gospel as a real presence of Christ, and, in the same sentence, refers to the Apostles as the first *presbyterium* of the Church.[2] He likens the Apostles to the prophets of the

"Sylloge inscriptionum græcarum," vol. III. p. 173, the index at the word δόγμα. Naturally those δόγματα are preserved in the public archives of the city.

[1] Cf. "Philad." v. 1 : προσφυγὼν τῷ εὐαγγελίῳ . . . καὶ τοῖς ἀποστόλοις . . . καὶ, τοὺς προφήτας δὲ ἀγαπῶμεν κ.τ.λ., and LIGHTFOOT'S note *in loc.* : I cannot give here the explanations and remarks which would be required in a history of the formation of the canon of the New Testament. I have studied the conclusions of Zahn in an article in the "Revue Biblique," vol. XII. (1903), pp. 10-26, 226-33. For a criticism of Harnack's theory see W. SANDAY, "Inspiration" (London, 1893), pp. 1-69.

[2] "Philad." v. 1.

Old Covenant who also, in a certain way, announced the Gospel.[1] He places the authority of the Apostles far above that which he, a bishop and a martyr, may have: "I did not think myself competent for this, that being a prisoner I should order you as though I were an Apostle."[2] He excuses himself from writing to the Romans: "I do not enjoin you, as Peter and Paul did: they were Apostles".[3] The authority of the Apostles was evidently privileged and incommunicable, and it has not ceased to attach to the decisions that emanated from them, and the teachings given by them.

Thus unity is based on Divine right. Ignatius looks upon it as so manifestly the economy intended and actually established by God and by the Lord, that he adds nothing more for its justification. He sees unity realized in every Church, he sees it realized no less perfectly throughout the world in that unity which binds together all the Churches in one, through the unity of their faith. The Lord, in whom we believe "with immovable faith," was born of the Virgin Mary, baptized by John, nailed to the cross under Pontius Pilate, rose again "that He might set up a standard unto all the ages for His saints and faithful people, whether among Jews or among Gentiles, in the one body of His Church."[4] This standard is the cross. In the Church it is set up for ever, in order to gather Jews and pagans into

---

[1] "Philad." v. 2.

[2] "Trall." III. 3 : οὐκ . . . ὡς ἀπόστολος ὑμῖν διατάσσωμαι. (I summarize the text.) Compare Acts XVI. 4, and IGNATIUS himself, "Eph." III. 1 : οὐ διατάσσομαι ὑμῖν ὡς ὤν τι. The word διαταγή means a medical prescription, but also an imperial decision. DEISSMANN, pp. 56-7.

[3] "Rom." IV. 3 : οὐχ ὡς Πέτρος καὶ Παῦλος διατάσσομαι ὑμῖν, ἐκεῖνοι ἀπόστολοι, ἐγὼ κατάκριτος. Cf. "Eph." III. 1. Ignatius could not speak thus of St. Peter and St. Paul, unless these two Apostles were connected with the Roman Church by historical circumstances and had really given commands to the Romans.

[4] "Smyrn." I. 2 : ἵνα ἄρῃ σύσσημον εἰς τοὺς αἰῶνας διὰ τῆς ἀναστάσεως εἰς τοὺς ἁγίους καὶ πιστοὺς αὐτοῦ, εἴτε ἐν Ἰουδαίοις εἴτε ἐν ἔθνεσιν, ἐν ἑνὶ σώματι τῆς ἐκκλησίας αὐτοῦ. The Church is the Church of Jesus Christ: this may be an allusion to Matt. XVI. 18. It is a body : a thought borrowed from Col. I. 18 and Eph. II. 16, etc. Elsewhere ("Eph." XVII. 1) Ignatius explains that Christ was allegorically anointed with perfumes, to impart incorruptibility (ἀφθαρσία) to the Church.

one calling, which makes them—the faithful and the saints— one body. The same sentiment is expressed by Ignatius in his letter to the Christians of Smyrna. "Wheresoever the bishop shall appear," he writes, "there let the body [of the faithful] be; even as where Jesus Christ is, there is the Catholic Church."[1] In other words the bishop constitutes the unity of the local Church and Jesus Christ the unity of all the local Churches spread throughout the world, the unity of all the dispersed bishops. "For Jesus Christ," St. Ignatius writes to the Ephesians, " is the mind of the Father, even as the bishops that are settled in the farthest parts [of the world] are the mind of Jesus Christ."[2]

This is not the first time that we find in a Christian writer a sense of the actual unity of the Church in her geographical expansion, but for the first time in Christian literature, we find here the name "Catholic Church" pronounced.[3] Unlike the controversialists who will presently arise, Ignatius does not oppose the universal Church to the dissenting conventicles; his purpose is to contrast the local churches with

---

[1] "Smyrn." VIII. 2: ὅπου ἂν ᾖ Χριστὸς Ἰησοῦς, ἐκεῖ ἡ καθολικὴ ἐκκλησία. FUNK: " Revera ecclesiis singulis universa ecclesia opponitur, et ut episcopus illarum (visibile), sic Christus harum (invisibile) caput declaratur." LIGHTFOOT: "The bishop is the centre of each individual Church, as Jesus Christ is the centre of the universal Church."

[2] "Eph." III. 2: οἱ ἐπίσκοποι, οἱ κατὰ τὰ πέρατα ὁρισθέντες, ἐν Ἰησοῦ Χριστοῦ γνώμῃ εἰσίν. The geographical meaning of κατὰ τὰ πέρατα (cf. IGNAT. "Rom." VI. 1) is beyond dispute.

[3] The word καθολικός is met with neither in the LXX nor in the New Testament. It belongs to classical Greek, but there it seems used only in philosophical language to designate a universal proposition: thus we are told that Zeno the Stoic had written a treatise about Universals, καθολικά. We shall find the word used with the same meaning in Clement of Alexandria and in Origen. Quintilian writes: " Mihi semper moris fuit quam minime alligare me ad praecepta quae καθολικά vocitant, id est (ut dicamus quomodo possumus) universalia vel perpetualia ". " Inst. orat." II. 13, 14. The word καθολικός signifies *universal*, in expressions like "universal history," for instance in POLYBIUS, "Hist." VIII. 4, 11: τῆς καθολικῆς καὶ κοινῆς ἱστορίας. St. Justin applies it to the resurrection of the dead: ἡ καθολικὴ ἀνάστασις "Dial." 82; so also Theophilus of Antioch, "Autol." I. 13. In Philo, καθολικός signifies *general*, in contrast with *particular*, "Vita Mosis," II. 32 (ed. COHN, vol. IV. p. 212). Cf. LIGHTFOOT, "Ignatius," vol. II. p. 310, and KATTENBUSCH, "Apostol. Symbol." vol. II. pp. 920-2.

the universal Church. Yet he brings out distinctly the idea of that Church which despite the multiplicity of its parts is one, and gives her the name she will bear in history.[1]

A last point will complete the ecclesiology of Ignatius. Did he ascribe to the Church spread throughout the world, any one localized centre of attraction? Did it enter into his mind that the Church of Rome was vested with a primacy over the other churches? The passage in view of which these questions arise, is the address of his Epistle to the Romans. While the addresses of the other Epistles are marked by an emphasis which is to say the least, decidedly Asiatic, the address of the Epistle to the Romans has far more of this emphasis than any other. "Ignatius . . . (it reads) to the Church that hath found mercy in the bountifulness of the Father Most High and of Jesus Christ His only Son; to the Church that is beloved and enlightened through the will of Him who wills all things that are, according to the love of Jesus Christ, our God; [to the Church] also that presides in the place of the region of the Romans, worthy of God, worthy of honour, worthy of benediction, worthy of praise, worthy of being heard, worthy and chaste, and presiding over love, possessing the law of Christ, and bearing the Father's name, which Church I salute in the name of Jesus Christ. . . ."[2] This magnificent array of words is a primary witness that St. Ignatius pays more honour to the Church of Rome than to the other Churches to which he writes.

Some claim to find a still surer evidence of this pre-eminence of Rome in the fact that " she has the presidency

---

[1] It is noticeable how HARNACK ("Dogmengeschichte," vol. I[4], p. 406), SOHM ("Kirchenrecht," p. 197), and KATTENBUSCH (p. 922) strive to lessen the importance of this fact.

[2] "Rom." inscr. : . . . ἥτις καὶ προκάθηται ἐν τόπῳ χωρίου 'Ρωμαίων . . . , καὶ προκαθημένη τῆς ἀγάπης. Cf. FUNK's commentary in his edition, and his essay ("Der Primat der römischen Kirche nach Ignatius und Irenäus") in his "Kirchengeschichtliche Abhandlungen," vol. I. (Paderborn, 1897), pp. 2-12. A. HARNACK, "Das Zeugnis des Ignatius über das Ansehen der römischen Gemeinde," in the "Sitzungsberichte" of the Academy of Berlin, 1896, pp. 111-31. Dom CHAPMAN, "S. Ignace d'Antioche et l'Eglise romaine," in the "Revue bénédictine," vol. XIII. (1896), pp. 385-400.

in the place of the region of the Romans ". Funk grants
without difficulty that to say ἐν τόπῳ χωρίου 'Ρωμαίων for " at
Rome," is peculiar : but does not the style of Ignatius offer
many instances of such affectation? In case, then, Ignatius
meant to say simply, " at Rome," the verb προκάθηται will
be construed absolutely : the Church presides, and it presides at Rome.[1]

But what is the nature of this pre-eminence? According to Harnack, the expression προκαθημένη τῆς ἀγάπης gives
us the meaning of the enigma : the Roman Church is the
most charitable, generous, helpful of all the Churches, and
this is why she is called the " president of love ". Funk,
on the contrary, observes that προκαθημένη cannot be construed save with the name of a place or of a collectivity :
we read προκαθημένη τῆς ἀνατολῆς, and προκαθημένη τῆς
οἰκουμένης ; hence the word which here is joined to προκαθημένη, should designate, not a virtue, but a collectivity.
Now, in several passages, Ignatius uses the word ἀγάπη as
synonymous with ἐκκλησία :[2] he says " the love of the
Ephesians," for " the Church of Ephesus ". Since, then, a
local Church may be called ἀγάπη, why should not the same
word designate the universal Church ? So Funk contends.
His argument—I need not observe—establishes a possibility
rather than a conclusion; and he himself holds that the
pre-eminence of the Roman Church is affirmed less by the
expression προκαθημένη τῆς ἀγάπης than by the word προκάθηται.

With Funk, we may regard as certain that St. Ignatius
believed in that pre-eminence, confirmed as we are in
that view by other data of the Epistle of Ignatius to the
Romans. We have already noted the reverence with which
the Bishop of Antioch addresses the Church that has heard the

---

[1] Cf. IGNAT. " Magn." VI. 1 : προκαθημένου τοῦ ἐπισκόπου = the bishop
who presides. LIGHTFOOT recalls " Apostol. Constit." II. 26 : ὁ γὰρ ἐπίσκοπος προκαθεζέσθω ὑμῶν ὡς θεοῦ ἀξίᾳ τετιμημένος.

[2] " Trall." XIII. 1 : ἀγάπη Σμυρναίων καὶ Ἐφεσίων. " Rom." IX. 3 : ἡ
ἀγάπη τῶν ἐκκλησιῶν. " Philad." XI. 2 : ἡ ἀγάπη τῶν ἀδελφῶν τῶν ἐν
Τρωάδι. Cf. " Smyrn." XII. 1. Perhaps this special use of the word
ἀγάπη might be compared with that of the word ὁμόνοια, when designating
the confederation of several cities, as was the case in Asia, for instance.
CHAPOT, " Province d'Asie," p. 346.

Apostles Peter and Paul.[1]  In the inscription of the Epistle,
he praises the Christians of Rome for being faithful to all
that is commanded by Christ, and for being filled wholly
with the grace of God, and "clear from every foreign stain".[2]
He congratulates them on having "instructed others," and
he adds: "My desire is that those lessons may be held
firm which you teach and enjoin".[3]

Since the Romans have taught "others," those others
represent churches other than that of Rome: churches that
come to Rome to ask, or receive from ·Rome without asking,
the lessons of the Apostolic commands which Rome preserves
more safely than other churches.

Between the captivity of St. Paul and that of St. Ignatius,
the space of half a century intervenes, in the course of which
the essential features of ecclesiology have been revealed to us.

The preaching of the Gospel and the faith it creates
give birth to communities in the whole world.   Christian life

---

[1] "Rom." IV. 3.

[2] "Rom." inscr. ἀποδιϋλισμένοις (literally, *filtered*, Cf. "Philad." III. 1)
ἀπὸ παντὸς ἀλλοτρίου χρώματος. LIGHTFOOT, *in loc.* : "The χρῶμα refers to
the colouring matter which pollutes the purity of the water ".

[3] "Rom." III. 1 : ἄλλους ἐδιδάξατε, ἐγὼ δὲ θέλω ἵνα κἀκεῖνα βέβαια ᾖ ἃ
μαθητεύοντες ἐντέλλεσθε.  According to LIGHTFOOT and FUNK, this may be
an allusion to the " Prima Clementis ".  Cf. the εἰς τὰς ἔξω πόλεις of Hermas
("Vis." II. 4).   "She presides in the country of the Romans. . . .
Here there is no question of the bishops, but of the Church.  Over what
did the Roman Church preside ?  Was it merely over some other Churches,
or dioceses, within a limited area ?  Ignatius had no idea of a limitation
of that kind. . . . The most natural interpretation of such language is that
the Roman Church presides over all the Churches. . . . And be it observed
that Ignatius speaks with a thorough knowledge of the matter ; he knows
the past of the Church of Rome, he even makes allusion to some of her
attitudes and acts, the remembrance of which is lost : ' You have never
deceived any one ; you have taught others.  My desire is that all that is
prescribed by your teaching should remain uncontested.'  Of what teaching, of what prescriptions, is there question here ?  Does he mean the
'Prima Clementis' ?  Or the 'Shepherd of Hermas' ?  The simplest
thing is to admit that there were other acts and other documents, the
memory of which was fresh in the time of Ignatius, but which have since
perished and been forgotten.  In any case, the manner in which he speaks
of the authority of the Roman Church in matters of doctrine, and of the
prescriptions sent by her to other Churches, is well worthy of attention."
DUCHESNE, "Eglises separées," pp. 127-9.

is an intercommunion (κοινωνία) of souls, of belief, of worship. Everywhere the apostolate has been succeeded by a settled hierarchy the various degrees of which become gradually more and more defined, the whole being recognized as an institution of Divine right, invested with supernatural powers. The idea of the faith which is everywhere prevalent, is an authoritative conception, for faith is a command or a teaching of God, of the Lord, accepted on the testimony of the Apostles:[1] and is preserved as a deposit. Christians must shun empty talkers, seducers, and false prophets, useless and foolish questions, traditions of men, unauthorized observances: the false teacher and his products must be placed under the ban, he must be silenced, driven away: he is a heretic. There is but one Church for every city. The Churches are linked by the bond of solidarity. United together by means of constant intercourse, they are conscious of their unity in their dispersion, for they realize their conformity of faith, and the charity which prevails among them: since each of them is autonomous, their unity is a kind of confederacy, a confederacy which is daily expressed in facts. The primacy of Rome is affirmed. The faith, which is one, just as the Lord is one, gathers the dispersed faithful and their Churches into a still deeper unity, that of the supernatural life, which is common to all the faithful, in Christ and in the Spirit: the Church of Churches is mystically the body of Christ, of which the faithful are the individual members. There is circuminsession of the visible and of the invisible: where the bishop is, there the local Church is, and where the Catholic Church is, there Jesus Christ is.

## EXCURSUS B.

*A Critical Examination of Protestant Theories on the Formation of Catholicism.*

The "formation of Catholicism" is an historical problem that has been raised by criticism only in our own

---

[1] JÜLICHER, "Einleitung," p. 285, goes so far as to say that the words of Serapion, bishop of Antioch (about the year 200): "We accept Peter and the other Apostles as we do the Lord" (ἀποδεχόμεθα ὡς Χριστόν, EUSEB. "H. E." VI. 12, 3), might have been pronounced a hundred years earlier, for even then Christians embodied all truth in the Apostles.

times.[1]   The Catholic controversialists of the sixteenth and seventeenth centuries were satisfied with a demonstration of the marks of the Church, especially her apostolicity : in his " Symbolik " (1832) Moehler appeals to the fact of her immemorial possession, and the testimony she bears to herself.   Neander (1842) was, according to Ritschl, the first to introduce the historical method into the investigation of the origins of this " creation "—for such " Catholic Christianity " was in his eyes.   After Neander, the same problem was taken up by Baur (1853) in the palmy days of the Tübingen school.   Later on, and in a spirit of reaction against the Tübingen thesis, comes Ritschl himself, in the second edition of his " Entstehung der altkatholischen Kirche " (1857). The problem of the Church came into the foreground with this monograph of Ritschl's which, however, Harnack considers " really too narrow "; and it is dealt with as of prime importance in Harnack's " Dogmengeschichte " (1885). Meanwhile in his " Apostolisches Zeitalter " (1886) Weizsäcker ascribed to the first century the fundamental principles of the Church system, thereby reacting against the system of Harnack, which was still too narrow and mechanical. In his " Kirchenrecht," (1892) Sohm, whose special interest was in determining the origin and growth of ecclesiastical law, lent the weight of his authority to this reaction.   In his researches into the history of the Apostles' Creed (1894-1900) Kattenbusch contributes to restore the historical idea of tradition.   Lastly, we cannot omit to mention Zahn's works and controversies regarding the history of the Canon. We are here in presence of a phenomenon like that signalized by Harnack in his criticism of the sources, when he used the now famous formula : " We are moving back towards the tradition ".[2]

If it is true that in history, reality is often reached only by means of successive approximations, it may be that during the last fifty years critical scholars outside the Catholic

---

[1] Father Christian PESCH, "Praelectiones Dogmaticae," vol. I. (Freiburg, 1894), pp. 178-80, is, as far as I know, the first and only scholastic theologian who has mentioned and discussed the theories of Ritschl, Harnack and Hatch.

[2] " Chronologie," vol. I. p. x.

fold have gradually come nearer to a more comprehensive view, and one nearer to our traditional beliefs. However, even now, is there not too much of the spirit of system and —to say the word—of Protestant prejudice in their contentions? The best exposition of the views now current among Protestant historians, has been given in French by A. Sabatier: [1] to his work we shall have recourse, in the desire to present these views with as much objectivity as possible. We will reserve our criticisms till we have before us this system as a whole.

\* \*
\*

1. In the first place this school contends that the idea of a Church is foreign to the Gospel of Jesus.

2. In the earliest stage the Christian communities—for from the very beginning Christians grouped themselves in communities—are all characterized by the same faith in the near return of Christ, and the obsession of this firm truth keeps out all thought of a lasting establishment.

3. Living in this feverish expectation of the "parousia," the early Christian communities in that first hour of their existence need no discipline. "The individual gifts (charisms) apportioned by the Spirit to divers members of the community met all needs. The Spirit, acting in each believer, thus determines vocations, and portions out to one and another, according to their faculties or zeal, ministries and offices which appear to be only provisional." Hence, in the beginning all the members of the community are equal; then, a distinction is made among them, based on

---

[1] [This is also the opinion of Dom C. BUTLER : "In my judgment, the importance of Sabatier's book for Catholics lies in this, that it sets forth more powerfully and with more clear-cut precision than any other book known to me, the real difficulties and the fundamental problems in the domain of history which apologists of Catholicism have at the present to face" ("Hibbert Journal," April, 1906, p. 482). Sabatier's book has been translated into English, under the title "Religions of Authority," New York, 1904.—T.] Consult also HARNACK'S "Kirche und Staat bis zur Gründung der Staatkirche " in the book "Die christliche Religion " (Berlin, 1906), pp. 129-60, of the collection of HINNEBERG, " Die Cultur der Gegenwart". See also SCHMIEDEL, art. " Ministry " (1902) in CHEYNE'S " Encyclopædia Biblica," and the bibliography that accompanies the article.

the diversity of the gifts of the Spirit; later on, the charism becomes "a permanent ecclesiastical function". Under or side by side with the Apostles, prophets and teachers, "who hold their vocation directly from God alone, and who are essentially itinerants," every community chooses for itself presbyters or elders, *episcopi* and deacons: thus there arises, on lines parallel to "the nomad apostolate, a settled system of ecclesiastical functionaries, which is destined little by little to replace and absorb it." [1]

4. However, "the evolution of every organism is governed by a directing idea, which is, as it were, its ideal and hidden soul. This idea is no more wanting here than elsewhere." Sabatier does not say that this directing idea can be detected in the Judæo-Christian communities. He finds it only in the communities founded by St. Paul, which, he says, "had from the beginning a vivid consciousness of their spiritual unity," so that "above the particular and local Churches," there appears "the idea of the Church of God or of Christ, one and universal". This unity is in no way external or visible: it is a communion of souls, the mystical body of which the invisible Christ is the head. It is not founded on unity of government, or on a certain number of rites or even of dogmas: it is purely moral. The Church is the holy bride of Christ: she awaits her spouse who is soon to come down from Heaven. "This Pauline notion of the Church of Christ, like all the Apostle's theology, is essentially idealist and transcendent"; none the less we must "recognize here the great idea which was to preside over the evolution of the Christian communities, and culminate in the constitution of the Catholic Church".[2]

5. That the Pauline conception of the Church as Christ's mystical body had this influence on the genesis of Catholicism, must be accounted for by the success of St. Paul's missions in the territories of the Roman Empire, and by the ruin of Jerusalem in the year 70. From that moment, "the centre of gravity of the nascent Christianity was for ever displaced". After vainly attempting to impede

---

[1] SABATIER, pp. 60, 61. Cf. SOHM, pp. 22-8.
[2] SABATIER, pp. 61-3. Cf. SOHM, pp. 16-22. HARNACK, "Dogmeng." vol. I⁴, p. 98.

Christian missionary work among the pagans, the Judæo-Christian party which, in Sabatier's eyes, represents "primitive orthodoxy," declines and finally dies away. The mass of the new converts from paganism take up a middle position "between the theology of Paul which they were incapable of comprehending," and the severe demands of the Judaizers which they thoroughly disliked. "Thus was formed a sort of elementary and neutral doctrine, half Greek rational wisdom and half Israelite tradition:" such was the theology of the Apostolic Fathers, "the first basis of Catholic doctrine".[1]

6. These Græco-Roman Christian communities needed a centre around which they might group. Rome was there. "The capital of the Empire was marked in advance to become the capital of Christianity." This was a social fact which could not be disregarded. Hence "in the formation of the Catholic Church the genius of Rome exercised a decisive influence," for this genius, which is neither speculative nor mystical, is the genius of law and government.[2]

7. The Pauline conception of the Church as Christ's mystical body is, then, the idea which, when translated into facts, gives birth to Catholicism. This evolution can be noticed already in the Pastoral Epistles, which, we are told, mark the transition, in the first years of the second century, from the Apostolic communities in which charismatic inspiration was predominant to the Catholic Church which is about to appear. It is, indeed, about this time, in the beginning of the second century, that the name Catholic Church, "destined to so great a fortune," is uttered for the first time by St. Ignatius in his Epistle to the Smyrnians. As yet it is merely a "general expression," designating "the great Church," the whole community of the faithful, in opposition to the sects, heresies, and schools that swarm on all sides. This indefinite mass will become an organized and conscious society, only when two elements have been introduced into the dispersed and confused Christian community: a statutory rule of faith accepted by all the

---

[1] SABATIER, p. 68. Cf. HARNACK "Dogmeng.' vol. I⁴, pp. 239-48.

[2] SABATIER, p. 69. Cf. RENAN, "Lectures on the Influence of Rome on Christianity" (1880), especially the third and fourth lectures. HARNACK, "Kirche und Staat," p. 138. "Mission," vol. I. p. 398.

Churches as the expression of Apostolic tradition, and an episcopal government powerful enough to reduce the whole to unity. "The double crisis of Gnosticism and Montanism which broke out between A.D. 130 and 150, and lasted nearly a century, furnished both."[1]

This decisive crisis took place during the period 150-80, under the reigns of Antoninus and of Marcus Aurelius. "In the vat into which the whole vintage had been gathered a fermentation was going on, an intense ebullition, the rapid decomposition of the old elements and the slow recomposition of a new system: it was this which constituted the crisis out of which the Catholic theory of the Church issued."[2] Rome realized the danger to which the still shapeless Christianity of the second century was exposed, on the left from Gnosticism, which was an inroad of the Greek spirit of speculation into Christianity and an attempt to merge Christianity in the general philosophy of the time; and on the right from Montanism, which was a revival of the "prophetic spirit" with its charisms, its ethical rigorism, and its preaching of the approaching "parousia".

8. Rome warded off the danger from the left by accrediting a rule of faith, which she drew up "by adding a few clear and well-defined propositions to the formula of baptism ": it was thus the so-called Creed of the Apostles originated at Rome between the years 150 and 160, "the first and the venerable monument of Catholic orthodoxy," which the Roman Church was soon to pass on rapidly to the other Churches.[3]

9. The danger from the right lasted longer; in the end, however, the bishops got the better of the prophets and of the private inspiration of the faithful. The result of this victory was that henceforth the Holy Ghost must use as its authentic organ the hierarchy alone. Rome crowned the victory by creating the theory of Apostolic succession, which has become the foundation of the authority of the bishops.[4]

---

[1] SABATIER, p. 72. This is the leading contention of RITSCHL, "Entstehung," p. 271 and foll. HARNACK, "Kirche und Staat," p. 136, and for the development of these views "Dogmeng." vol. $I^4$, p. 337 and foll.

[2] SABATIER, p. 76.

[3] SABATIER, p. 79. HARNACK, "Dogmeng." vol. $I^4$, p. 354 and foll.

[4] SABATIER, p. 82. HARNACK, "Dogmeng." vol. $I^4$, p. 399 and foll.

\* \*
\*

We may now take up in succession the various points of this theory.

1. The contention that the idea of a Church is foreign to the Gospel of Jesus, and even irreconcilable with it, is held in Protestant circles to be certain and almost beyond dispute. We shall not waste time on this point, as we have already given our reasons for discovering in the teaching of Jesus the point where the Church comes in.

2. The critics in question suppose that the early Christian communities were not concerned to establish a lasting organization, their horizon being limited by their expectation of the near " parousia ".

Here we detect the inner and radical inconsistency of the theory which claims to reduce the teaching of Jesus to a strictly eschatological message, for had the message of Jesus been only that, it could not have lived. It could hardly have taken root save in a Jewish soil saturated with pharisaic and apocalyptic teachings; and certainly it could not have outlived the disappointment which must necessarily have accompanied the indefinite postponement of the " parousia ".

With far more historical sense, Renan wrote : " If founded upon a belief in the end of the world which the years as they rolled by must convince of error, the Galilean congregation could only have ended by breaking up into anarchy ".[1] If, then, this handful of Galileans did not sink into its eschatology as into a grave, it is because eschatology was not the sole object of their faith, or even an essential feature in it. Harnack had forestalled Sabatier's error, when he laid down as a principle that the Gospel was more than an apocalyptic message which had issued from the Old Testament, that it was " a new thing," namely " the creation of a universalist religion founded on that of the Old Testament,"[2] and founded, we will add, on the person of Christ.

If such was the horizon of the Gospel, can we say that the first Christian communities did not think of any lasting organization? How did the first of these communities

[1] " Marc Aurèle," p. 407.    [2] " Dogmeng." vol. 1⁴, p. 48.

begin to form other communities? Could it have formed others if it had not felt compelled to carry on an unlimited propagandism? Is not this propagation of the faith a first indication of the action of an apostolate, of that apostolate which Sabatier hardly mentions, but which was already the Church?

3. We are told that the Christian communities, in their earliest stage, hypnotized by their expectation of the " parousia," were subject to no action but that of the Spirit; that charisms seized on the first disciples, and the diversity of charisms gave rise to the first elements of organization.

Here again Renan's judgment is better. He writes: " Free prophecy, the charisms, the speaking with tongues, and individual inspiration—this was more than was necessary to reduce the whole movement to the proportions of an ephemeral dissenting-sect, such as one sees so much of in America and in England. Individual inspiration creates, but destroys at once what it has created. After liberty, rule is necessary." He continues: "The work of Jesus may be considered saved on the day on which it was admitted that the Church had a direct power—a power representing that of Jesus. The Church from that moment dominated the individual, and drove him if need were from her midst. Soon the Church, a body unstable and changing, was personified in the elders, the powers of the Church became the powers of a clergy, who were the dispensers of all graces, the intermediaries between God and the believer. Inspiration passes from the individual to the community. The Church has become everything in Christianity; one step more, and the bishop becomes everything in the Church." [1]

In these few lines Renan has well expressed the powerlessness of private inspiration to bring forth anything but anarchy. Starting from this psychological fact, we first ask Sabatier and Sohm: Why did not anarchy actually result? Then we ask Renan: Was it really only when the work of Jesus was jeopardized through the outpouring and contagious spread of charisms, that discipline arose to save His work? To unruly charisms, Renan opposes in each community the ancients or presbyters; but if their office did not come to

[1] " Marc Aurèle," p. 408.

these ancients and presbyters in virtue of some higher privilege, whence and how did they get the power they exercised over the charisms themselves?  Order could never have issued out of charismatic anarchy, had not some authority existed previously to the outpouring of the charisms—an authority which can only be that of the apostolate, continuing the authority of the Master.

To say that every permanent ecclesiastical function is a charism which fixed and imposed itself, seems a mere conjecture as gratuitous as it is improbable; for the earliest permanent ecclesiastical function which history records is that of presbyters and of ancients—to which no charism corresponds—and the same remark can be made of the *episcopi* and the deacons.  The traditional view which derives episcopacy, not from any transformation of unknown charisms, but from the powers of the apostolate, is much more plausible; and accounts far more easily for the fact that in all Christian communities episcopacy was set on the same foundations.  Is it not mocking us with words to tell us that this uniformity of development is explicable as " a case of the sport of general laws which rule social phenomena of this order "?[1]

4. Sabatier had no trouble to find in St. Paul the idea of the Church as the mystical body of Christ: and he claims it as the leading idea which guided the evolution of the various Christian communities and led it ultimately to Catholicism.  Sabatier, who has an eclectic method, may have borrowed this particular element in his theory from Sohm, in whose judgment the word ἐκκλησία was first used to designate Christendom in general, the new people of God made up of the Christians spread all over the

---

[1] We do not, however, intend to deny the influence exercised on the growth of the organization of Churches, (1) by the institutions which prevailed in jewries and which a religion, born in the midst of Judaism, could not ignore, (2) by the conditions of life and thought, which necessarily dominated the followers of a religion so essentially social as Christianity. Mgr. DUCHESNE, "Origines du culte" (1898), pp. 7-10, has assigned their proper share to these two historical elements.  On the contrary, HARNACK, "Kirche und Staat," p. 132, makes them too preponderant.  We must say the same of the supposed influence of municipal institutions ; these were never directly imitated by the churches, DUCHESNE, p. 12.

world; or he may have borrowed it from Harnack who sees
in the spiritual unity of Christians, separated from the Jewish
people and henceforth constituting the true Israel, an affirmation of faith that was present to the consciousness of
Christians, and was operative from the very beginning.[1]
Were this the case, the idea of the Church of God would not
be exclusively Pauline; it would attach to Christianity from
the very fact that, by separating itself from Judaism, it became denationalized.

We may here call attention to the embarrassment of
those critics who, adhering exclusively to the idea of an
invisible Church, strive to account for its formation. According to Sabatier, it is a Pauline creation; according to
Harnack, it is the necessary conclusion to which the Christian consciousness came in its search for an ideal unity that
could replace the racial unity of the people of God. Harnack's hypothesis seems very frail, for. one does not see why
it was necessary for the Gentile converts to substitute for
the racial unity of the people of God of which they had had
no experience, an ideal unity which nothing in them demanded. We should prefer to say with Sabatier that the
communities founded by St. Paul, being "children of the
same father," were bound together by "very close family
ties". But did they really owe these ties to the fact that
they had been founded by St. Paul? Had the Churches
never known any other missionary than St. Paul? Was he
a stranger to the Romans, whom he had not yet visited
when he wrote to them his Epistle? No, a bond did
truly unite the Pauline communities, but that bond did

---

[1] "Kirchenrecht," pp. 16-22 ; "Dogmeng." vol. I[4], pp. 51, 89. True,
Harnack declares later (p. 489) that "it was not theories that created the
empiric unity of the Chuiches, for theories were incapable of overcoming
the elementary causes of difference that could not fail to operate as soon
as Christianity became naturalized in the various provinces and towns of
the Empire". Hence he ascribes the unity of Christendom to the
"unity which the Empire possessed in Rome". To this must be added
the peculiar character of the Roman Church, which was at the same
time Greek and Latin, which was rich and zealous, and "displayed much
solicitude for all Christendom". All these causes contributed to "convert
the Christian communities into a real confederation under the primacy
of the Roman community",

not depend on St. Paul, who was not an Apostle to lend himself to ideas of this kind : " Is Christ divided ? Was Paul then crucified for you ? or were you baptized in the name of Paul?." (1 Cor. I. 13).

The faithful did not retain the name of "disciples," which had been borne by the sole disciples of the one Master : they took that of " brethren " (ἀδελφοί), which, as has been rightly pointed out by Weizsäcker, well expresses their consciousness of the bond that united all together in Jesus Christ.[1] The universality of the use of the name " brethren " witnesses to a fundamental article of faith, the faith in a new birth which made the Christian who had it not merely the citizen of a heavenly and future city, but the brother of existing brethren, and therefore the member of an earthly community which is primarily the local Church. Since the faithful were equally brethren, from whatever place they came, all these communities bore a name that was the same everywhere, ἐκκλησία, a name just as concrete as that of " synagogue," to which it was opposed. The conscious-ness of their fraternity and their continual social experience of it, however dispersed they might be, showed clearly to these " brethren " that their communities were united by a bond resembling that by which they were united individu-ally. The Churches of the various provinces were thought of in groups : Christians spoke of the Churches of Judæa, of Achaia, of Galatia, and thus came very naturally and gradually to conceive of a Church of all the Churches, the Church of all the " brethren " spread over the whole world. [2]

[1] WEIZSÄCKER, pp. 35-38 ; cf. HARNACK, " Mission," vol. I. pp. 336-47.

[2] In his " Mission," vol. I. p. 362 and foll., HARNACK, treating of the formation by communities and of its part in the spread of Christianity, reaches the same conclusion as ourselves. Christian preaching, he writes, " from the very outset worked through a community, and had for its aim to form a union of believers ". This union would have remained merely ideal, and would not have been easily effective, had it not been allied with a local organization. " Christianity from the first borrowed this organization from Judaism, from the synagogue ; the first Apostles and the brothers of Jesus laid the foundation. Designed to be essentially a brotherhood, and springing out of the synagogue, each Christian com-munity developed a local organization which was twice as strong as that of Judaism ". Later (p. 364) Harnack recalls the features of this community idea, so marked in the Pauline Epistles, and writes : " Paul's Epistles

Thus the "great idea" is not restricted to the Pauline missions; it lies at the very heart of all the communities that came into existence whether on Gentile or on Jewish soil.

5. The fall of Jerusalem, in the year 70, did not influence the Gentile communities, because Jerusalem had no important place in their faith. Nowhere in fact do we find any trace of emotion aroused in the souls of Christians by this great catastrophe.

The fall of Jerusalem could have influenced only that Judæo-Christianity whose emissaries had so often thwarted the preaching of St. Paul; but, before the year 70, even before the year 64, the separation of Christianity from Judaism had become an actual fact. This separation, which amounted to a sharp and final rupture, had been the end of Judæo-Christianity, in so far as it was a Jewish propagandism in the Gentile communities. It survived in the "Ebionite" or "Nazarene" communities, who were separated from the rest of the world by their religious tongue, as may be inferred from the " Gospel according to the Hebrews ". Nor can these Ebionites be said to represent "primitive orthodoxy," since they, who believed in Christ, practised circumcision : they were orthodox neither as Jews, nor as Christians. The part Baur ascribed to them in the genesis of Catholicism appears more and more unreal, a mere fancy excogitated to meet the requirements of an hyperhistorical speculation. "The question is whether this Jewish Christi-

---

prove how vigorously and unweariedly he taught these lessons, and it is perhaps the weightiest feature both in Christianity and in the work of Paul that, so far from being overpowered, the impulse towards association was most powerfully intensified by the individualism which here attained its zenith." Speaking of Clement and Ignatius (p. 366), "Never," he says, "has the absolute subordination of Christians to the local community been more peremptorily demanded, or the position of the local community itself more eloquently assigned, than in these primitive documents". Lastly, as regards the monarchical episcopate (p. 369), " Ignatius had already compared the position of the bishop in the local Church with that of God in the Church collective. . . . As the office grew to maturity, it seemed like an original creation; although it had only drawn to itself from all quarters the powers and the forms already existing". Except for a few details, all this fourth chapter of the third book witnesses to the Catholic idea of Christian origins.

anity as a whole, or in certain of its tendencies, was any factor at all in the development of Christianity into Catholicism. This question is to be answered in the negative, quite as much in view of the history of dogma as in view of the political history of the Church. From the standpoint of the universal history of Christianity, these Jewish Christian communities appear as atrophied organs which now and again, as objects of curiosity, engaged the attention of the main body of Christendom in the East, but could not exert any important influence on it, just because they were a purely national party." [1]

The fall of Jerusalem, then, did not displace the centre of gravity of Christianity, because Christianity was, even then, external to Judaism, and because, at the time of St. Paul's missions, Judæo-Christianity had been set aside in most of the Gentile communities. Can we say, however, that these Gentile communities adopted a neutral doctrine, partly Jewish, partly Greek, which was unable to assimilate St. Paul's theology? We recognize here the old antithesis of the Tübingen school, which was bent on opposing Judæo-Christianity to Paulinism, and on disengaging from this conflict a neutral element which was to be the doctrine of the future.

As a matter of fact, Gentile Christianity took its position as early as the first generation outside Judæo-Christian influence. Nor is the freedom of Gentile Christianity from all connexion with the Jewish people and its law due to St. Paul alone: whilst he did perhaps more than any one else to bring about this result, others, too, worked for it effectively. Christian communities just as free from Judaism as the Corinthian community—for instance, the community of Alexandria and that of Rome—did not have St. Paul for their founder. If, then, "Paulinism" means primarily the denationalization of Christianity, "Paulinism" is everywhere.

These Gentile Christians could not be converted, nor could they afterwards keep the faith, unless that faith were simple, and, as it were, rudimentary. This, St. Paul was not the last to realize: his catechesis is easily found, even

[1] HARNACK, "Dogmeng." vol. i[4], p. 313. Cf. HÖNNICKE, "Das Judenchristentum," p. 368, who holds the same opinion as Harnack.

in the most difficult epistles.[1]  In this catechesis, the
mystery of Jesus continues to hold a central place, and how
could it be otherwise?  On the other hand, this presentation
of the faith is something popular, neutral, Greek—it matters
not how you qualify it, but it is noteworthy that this element, far from being foreign to Paul's preaching, actually
belongs to it.  The author of the Epistle to the Hebrews,
who has some hard truths to explain to his readers, complains that they are slow to understand, and that he is still
obliged to give them only milk, as to children, instead of
the strong food of strong men (Heb. v. 11-13).  St. Paul
speaks in like manner to his converts at Corinth (1 Cor.
III. 1-2).

We may conclude that in this way a faith came to prevail, which was not a reaction against Judæo-Christianity,
or against Paulinism, but was the direct outcome of the
preaching of Christianity in the Gentile world, and is found
in no small measure in the Epistles of St. Paul himself.
True, this faith, like the Gospel itself, had its roots in the
tradition of Israel, and it meant to preserve the Old Testament.  The Greek mind influenced it by means of the
language which it lent to it.  However, we cannot, properly
speaking, call this a middle position, for it was truly a
common faith, a kind of Christian κοινὴ διάλεκτος, elementary and simplified, bound, like any doctrine which was to
spread, to adopt formulas that could be easily transported
from place to place in the minds of the hearers.  This theology, this " first basis of Catholic doctrine," the Apostolic
Fathers did not create, for it was substantially and from the
beginning the catechesis given to the Gentile converts: it
was the Christian faith presented in a missionary form.[2]

6.  Græco-Roman Christianity needed a centre.  Rome,
we are told, became the capital of Christendom, because she
was already the capital of the Empire ; then Rome stamped
Græco-Roman Christianity with the impress of her genius of
government.  Roman imperialism took the place of Jewish

---

[1] PRAT, pp. 81-3.   Cf. WEIZSÄCKER, vol. I. pp. 92-102 and 634-37.
who explains the chief topics of St. Paul's preaching to the Gentiles.
[2] See the similar remarks of HARNACK, " Mission," vol. I. pp. 319-
25 and " Lukas der Arzt, p. 101.

nationalism which had been set aside. This was a new factor in Catholicism, in the first and second centuries, for, in the third century, Rome would have no longer been able to exercise that influence. "That extraordinary city was at the culminating point of its grandeur; nothing allowed one to foresee the events which, in the third century, would cause it to degenerate and become nothing more than the capital of the West. Greek was at least as much spoken there as Latin, and the great future secession of the East could not be guessed." [1]

To this view of the part taken by Rome in the genesis of Catholicism, Renan was the first to ascribe historical importance. To the scandal of German Protestantism, it has been strongly advocated by Harnack.[2] It has been insisted on still more systematically by Sohm. We who believe in the providential character of this co-operation of Rome in the part to be played by the *Cathedra Petri*, shall not be so ungracious as to contest it; we take exception only to the terms of civil government used to describe it, and to the tendency to transform into a generative cause what is only a circumstance.

7. We may notice that Protestant critics have already, however much against their will, transported to the heart of the Apostolic age some of the factors in the "formation of Catholicism". This is a consequence of the retrogression which has gradually taken place, since the days of Baur, Ritschl and Renan, in the study of some questions closely connected with that of the "formation of Catholicism"— such as, above all others, the question of the origin of episcopacy, and also that of the authenticity of the Ignatian

[1] RENAN, "Marc Aurèle," p. 69.

[2] In his well-known Excursus "Catholic and Roman," "Dogmeng." vol. I[4], pp. 480-96. SOHM, p. 157 and foll. It must not be forgotten that the insistency with which these critics exalt Roman hegemony is but a new form of prejudice. Feeling the theory which explains Catholicism as a realization of the invisible Church to be insufficient, they have devised the complementary theory, which explains it as an imperialization of ecclesiastical life. Cf. two pages of far greater historical exactness in Mgr. DUCHESNE, "Hist. Anc.," vol. I. pp. 536-38, and the criticism of Harnack's Excursus by Dom CHAPMAN, "The Catholicity of the Church," in MATHEW, "Ecclesia," pp. 82-8.

Epistles.[1]  Were the authenticity of the Pastoral Epistles, still so much contested, generally admitted, as is the authenticity of the Ignatian Epistles, the displacing of the question would be still more perceptible, and the importance of what some critics are pleased to call the crisis of the second century would be very considerably diminished.

For this crisis, which is said to have occurred in the years 150-80, would not have the importance which, since Ritschl, a certain number of critics ascribe to it, except for the two results which are attributed to it : the formation of a statutory faith everywhere the same, and the formation of an episcopal government everywhere supreme.  But do these two institutions really issue from the reaction against Gnosticism and Montanism?

Harnack, who, in this particular case deserves credit for introducing into the doctrinal history of the first two centuries a sociological consideration which is new, and which enables him better to understand, from an historical point of view, the formation of Christianity into a Church, has not failed to recognize that, as early as the period 30-130, every Christian community has its unity secured by the existence of a collective worship, of collective funds, and of officers entrusted with worship, discipline, and charitable works. I fear indeed that he does not recognize in those early communities any other features than such as they have in

---

[1] One cannot help smiling over the long resistance made by Protestant critics to the claims to authenticity of the seven Ignatian Epistles.  In 1835, Baur thought they had been composed at Rome towards the middle of the second century by some forger, on behalf of episcopacy.  In 1850, and still later in 1857, Ritschl postponed their composition to the fourth century, and held to be authentic only the three Epistles to Polycarp, to the Ephesians, and to the Romans, in the Syriac version—an abbreviated and rather tame document, edited by Cureton in 1845.  As late as 1877, Renan regarded as authentic the Epistle to the Romans alone.  Finally, after dating them from the time of Hadrian or Antoninus, Harnack, who admits the authenticity of the seven Epistles, assigns them to their true period, the age of Trajan.  We may notice here the vicious circle : Renan deems the ecclesiology of the Ignatian Epistles too mature to belong to the beginning of the second century.  " All this," he says, " belongs, not to the beginning, but to the end of the second century." Compare with this systematic postponement LIGHTFOOT'S luminous remarks, " Christian Ministry," pp. 145-8.

common with the Evangelical communities of the kingdom of Prussia. At all events, after thus proclaiming the characteristic unity of every community, he signalizes what he calls "the beginnings · of interecclesiastical dispositions," which unite the widely dispersed communities by means of collections and letters, as well as of hospitality offered to travelling brethren; and which "secure in all important questions the solidarity of the evolution". And he adds : "A single centre of unity, such as Judaism had as long as the temple was standing, the earliest Christianity had not; but it did have several centres, among which at a very early date Rome was the most important.[1]

Hence, long before the year 150, long before the crisis caused by Gnosticism and Montanism, there existed an interecclesiastical bond, there existed influential rallying centres, there existed among the Churches a good understanding which "secured a common process of evolution in all important matters". Harnack assures us that, in the year 220, there existed a Church not merely ideal and spiritual, i.e. invisible, but one which from the Euphrates to Spain, was visibly constituted, forming a genuine political organism.[2] That is true, but it is not enough. If from the year 220 this historical reality is henceforth undeniable, how can one say that it is new? Is there no continuity between the state of things which is perfectly manifest in the year 220 (and as much might be said of the year 180), and the state of things revealed by the Ignatian Epistles and by the "Prima Clementis"? True, the characteristic features became gradually more and more pronounced, but if, during the second century, Gnosticism is driven out from the Churches; if it succeeds, wherever it appears, only in organizing itself into dissenting conventicles or into schools; if it is everywhere looked upon and treated as heresy, is not this a proof that the Churches are already constituted on the basis of a most solid faith under the rule of *episcopi* who justify their name by their vigilance, and are bound together by a solidarity which has already become a confederacy.[3]

---

[1] "Kirche und Staat," p. 136.   [2] *Ibid.* p. 141.
[3] See the Excursus in HARNACK'S " Mission," vol. i. pp. 373-97, " Ecclesiastical Organization and the Episcopate, from Pius to Constantine ".

Hence an attentive historical study discovers in the Christianity anterior to the so-called crisis of Gnosticism something other than an amorphous religion; the energies that were thought to have originated after the year 150, are seen to have been at work as early as the first three Christian generations; and far from appearing as the result of an anti-Gnostic reaction, they manifest themselves as forces which prevent Gnosticism from finding a home in the Churches.

8. There remains the assertion which ascribes to Rome the editing of "the Apostles' Creed". This symbol is certainly the baptismal symbol of the Roman Church. From its literary history we may infer that, at Rome, it is at least coeval with Irenæus, Marcion, and Justin, but everything leads us to believe that it is very much older. It is not correct to say that this Roman text was, in some way, imposed by Rome on all the Churches towards the end of the second century. In the time of Tertullian Christian Africa had this creed in common with Rome, but we cannot affirm the same of the Greek Churches, where the direct influence of the "Apostles' Creed" cannot be detected before the Council of Nicæa. It may be doubted whether, before this Council, the Oriental Churches had any liturgical formulary of their faith. The history of the Roman symbol may be summed up in these few propositions; and it suffices to show that this symbol did not play the dominating part ascribed to it by Sabatier.[1]

The author states and shows that "the tendency of early Christianity to form complete, independent communities, under episcopal government, was extremely strong" (p. 389). When a locality had no bishop, it was because the number of Christians was insignificant (p. 391). The hypothesis that, wherever during the third century there are found communities without a bishop, they represent a survival of the primitive organization, is not only improbable, but erroneous (p. 397).

[1] For a fuller historical exposition of this point, I take the liberty to refer the reader to my article "Apôtres (Symbole des)" in VACANT'S "Dictionnaire de théologie". KATTENBUSCH, "Das Apostolische Symbol, seine Entstehung . . . " (1894-1900), who has published what I believe to be the profoundest study of the history of the Roman symbol—a study which is not exempt, however, from many a foregone conclusion—has contributed to a very large extent to overthrow the classical Protestant theorem. Kattenbusch thinks that the Roman symbol (R) was composed at Rome about the year 100. In the West, as early as the second century, R was

If we look upon it as a "monument of Catholic orthodoxy," should we at any rate consider it to be the earliest manifestation and the oldest monument of that orthodoxy, a document composed under the influence of an arbitrary and pre-arranged eclecticism? The hypothesis is that previously the baptismal formula alone existed; that at the time of the anti-Gnostic crisis, a few clear and decisive articles were added to it, and that this short "Syllabus" of the second century defined the faith when threatened with dissolution.

To this hypothesis we can oppose the text itself of the "Symbol of the Apostles". As a matter of fact, it is difficult to find a document that has less the appearance of a series of anathemas, and conveys less the thought of doctrinal attack and defence: it shows no anti-Gnostic preoccupation whatever. Being so elementary in its tenor, how could it have sufficed to guard the faithful at large against the Gnostic errors! In reality, it merely sets forth the catechetical faith for the benefit of simple-minded Christians, to whom Gnosticism, a learned error, must have been altogether strange.

Again, was not the common faith of the Churches sufficiently self-conscious to define its own meaning in clear

received both at Rome and in the Churches of Gaul and Africa. As to the Churches of Greece (Corinth, Athens, Thessalonica), we know nothing, owing to the lack of documents ; the same may be said of the provinces of Pontus, Galatia, Cappadocia, and of Syria, Palestine and Egypt. Origen seems to know a symbol similar to R, perhaps R itself, but whether this symbol was received in Egypt we cannot say. All the Eastern symbols of the fourth century seem to come from Antioch ; it may be surmised that R appeared for the first time at Antioch, after the deposition of Paul of Samosata. In the province of Asia, R was known during the second half of the second century, perhaps owing to Polycarp (?). See the conclusions of Kattenbusch, vol. II. pp. 960-1 ; substantially similar are those of Harnack, art. "Apostolisches Symbolum" in HAUCK's "Realencyklopädie". However, we must distinguish the strictly so-called baptismal symbol from the *regula fidei* or κανὼν ἐκκλησιαστικός—so often appealed to by ecclesiastical writers, for instance Irenæus, Tertullian, Clement, Origen—which represents a more complete and detailed body of doctrines than the liturgical profession of faith. On this point, which is disputed among Protestant critics (Harnack, Zahn, Kattenbusch, Kunze), see LOOFS, pp. 131-2.

and precise articles, before the late epoch (150-60) in which we are told the " Symbol of the Apostles " was constituted ? The articles of this creed have nothing particularly Roman in them, nor do they imply any particular date.  They are found equivalently in the Apologists, like Justin and Aristides, and also in St. Ignatius.  They are found in a scattered state in the Christian literary remains of the Apostolic age.

Finally, if we merely wish to ascertain if the object of the faith is determined and traditional, and not amorphous or plastic, it suffices to reflect that faith is not presented in the primitive Christian literature as a gnosis which every Christian frames for himself, but as a διδαχή, a παράδοσις, a κάνων πίστεως, and other synonymous expressions.  Nothing is more alien to the Christianity of the early ages, than the idea that the believer remains autonomous in presence of the faith.[1]

9. After all that has just been said, it may be unnecessary to dwell on the share attributed to Montanism in the growth

[1] For the justification of this statement, it might suffice to refer to the appendix added by Harnack to HAHN's collection, " Bibliothek der Symbole und Glaubensregeln der alten Kirche," third edition (Breslau, 1897), pp. 364-90.

But it is opportune here to take notice of the theory according to which, from the beginning, the faith was presented in the shape of a kind of historical and moral summary : historical as in 1 Cor. XI. 23 and XV. 3, moral as in 1 Cor. XI. 2 ; a summary of which numerous traces are said to be discoverable in the New Testament.  This theory, which is a noteworthy advance towards the Catholic principle of tradition, has been proposed by WEIZSÀCKER, " Apost. Zeitalter," p. 594, who discovers what he ingeniously calls a " Christian Halacha," in Rom. VI. 17, XVI. 17 ; 2 Thess. II. 14 ; 1 Cor. IV. 17.  KATTENBUSCH ("Apost. Symb." vol. II. pp. 335-47, " the New Testament and the Symbol ") shares the same view, and cites (p. 345) one of the earliest articles of Harnack, written in the same sense.  Following in the same direction, Seeberg has endeavoured to reconstruct what he calls the catechism of primitive Christianity (" Der Katechismus der Urchristenheit," Leipzig, 1903).  In an essay of which I know only the title, Wernle had advanced the hypothesis that the lists of sins, so often found in the New Testament, proceed from a traditional formula (" Der Christ und die Sünde bei Paulus," 1897).  G. RESCH (" Aposteldekret," p. 92 and foll.), takes up Seeberg's hypothesis.  Evidently the Ritschlian thesis of a kind of doctrinal challenge, formed artificially during the second half of the second century, is being abandoned.

of Catholicism. Montanism is a late movement: it was only in the year 177 that it created any stir in Western Christendom; and, at this date, the authority of bishops was nowhere disputed. "The Church," says Renan, "was already too strongly constituted for the undisciplined habits of the visionaries of Phrygia to do her real harm."[1] As to the attitude of Rome, her resistance to Montanism, so far from being more ardent than that of other places, was singularly moderate and hesitating, so much so that the authorities there came very near to favouring the Phrygian prophets. To say that Rome saved the hierarchy is an affirmation which is groundless, and even improbable; to say that she crowned the victory, by creating the theory of Apostolic succession, is to forget that the theory of Apostolic succession had been formulated by the "Prima Clementis" some hundred years before.

[1] "Marc Aurèle," p. 225.

# CHAPTER IV.

## THE CATHOLICISM OF ST. IRENÆUS.

ABOUT the year 180, Irenæus is the dogmatist who brings to an end—so we are told in some modern histories of dogmas—the anti-gnostic and anti-montanist crisis; he is the first of the "old Catholic" Fathers; he is the author of the theory of such victorious principles as the authority of the rule of faith, the authority of the episcopal succession, the authority of the confederation of bishops: it is he who synthesizes Catholicism and imparts to it its definitive and "Roman" expression. . . . We hope to show how systematic and Protestant this presentation is. For us St. Irenæus is an excellent exponent of the theory of Catholicism; but there is hardly a single element of his theory that is not anterior to his time; and the principles on which he insists are those organic principles which, obscurely or explicitly, characterize Gentile Christianity from the very beginning.

If we study first the forerunners of Irenæus during the second century and then his contemporaries, we shall easily see that his principles are not of his own creation. We shall then endeavour to solve the problem which Harnack propounds as insoluble, namely, "To what extent were the principles of Irenæus new, to what extent were the rules he formulated already received in the Churches, and in which of them?"[1]

## I.

The Epistle to the Philippians, written by the Bishop of Smyrna, St. Polycarp, is the only one which has reached

[1] "Dogmeng." vol. 1⁴. p. 352. The reader may consult with profit J. DURELL, "The Historic Church: an Essay on the conception of the Christian Church and its Ministry in the Sub-Apostolic Age" (Cambridge, 1906).

us of those many Epistles[1] which according to St. Irenæus he wrote both to individual Christians and "to neighbouring Churches," to warn some, and strengthen others—a new index of the constant communications going on between the Churches during the second century.

Polycarp of Smyrna writes to the Philippians, i.e. to a Church of Macedonia. They have asked him to send them a letter: "You invited me," he can say to them; and he adds that neither he nor any one else can in any way pretend to equal the wisdom of St. Paul who brought them "the word of truth".[2] All that he can do, is to give advice to the faithful, deacons, and presbyters of Philippi.

These counsels recall those of the Pastoral Epistles, as well as those of the Ignatian Epistles: "You must," says Polycarp, "submit yourselves to the presbyters and deacons as to God and Christ" (V. 3). They must shun all vain and empty teaching and the common error: an allusion to heathenism, and perhaps—already—to Gnosticism. They must abide steadfast by the Lord's commands and by what the Lord has taught (II. 1-3). They must forsake any one who "will not confess the testimony of the Cross": words that refer certainly to the same Docetism as that opposed by St. Ignatius. "For every one who will not confess that Jesus Christ is come in the flesh, is an antichrist . . . and whosoever shall pervert the *logia* of the Lord to his own lusts, and say that there is neither resurrection nor judgment, that man is the first born of Satan."[3] Here we find what we had already found in St. Ignatius : heretics exploiting the Gospel records and interpreting them in the sense of their errors. "Wherefore, let us forsake the vain doing of the many and their false teachings, and turn unto the word which was delivered unto us from the beginning.[4]

---

[1] EUSEB. "H. E." v. 20, 8. Polycarp's Epistle to the Philippians was written not long after the death of St. Ignatius, which took place under Trajan, within the period 107-17.

[2] POLYCARP, "Philip." III. 1-2.

[3] "Philip." VII. 1. With these last words compare the fact recorded of the Apostle St. John by St. Irenæus, who got it from St. Polycarp, concerning the meeting of Cerinthus and St. John, "H. E." III. 28, 6.

[4] "Philip." VII. 2 : ἐπὶ τὸν ἐξ ἀρχῆς ἡμῖν παραδοθέντα λόγον ἐπιστρέψωμεν.

Let us . . . serve the Lord with fear and all reverence, as He Himself gave commandment, as did also the Apostles who preached the Gospel to us, and the prophets who proclaimed beforehand the coming of our Lord."[1]

The Bishop of Smyrna answers directly the argument urged against St. Ignatius by the Docetæ of Philadelphia. That appeal may be made to the Lord's *logia*, these great bishops are most willing to grant; but there must be no commentary, no dialectical explanation; the doctrine received from the first must be held. The faith which is the true faith and claims our assent is that preached by the Lord and by the Apostles, and announced by the prophets of Israel. Faith is based upon the "sacred Writings,"[2] i.e. upon the Old Testament, and the authentic teaching of the Lord and of the Apostles, such as it has been transmitted from the beginning.

Polycarp died on 23 February, 155; it cannot then be said that the rule of faith outlined in this Epistle even before the year 120—viz. the submission of the faithful to the presbyters in every Church, fidelity to the teaching imparted from the beginning by the Apostles who evangelized the Churches—was first propounded between the years 150 and 180, in the heat of the fight of the Churches against Gnosticism.

An incident told of St. Polycarp by St. Irenæus witnesses to the identity of the attitude of these two Bishops and the identity of their method. Writing to a Roman presbyter, Florinus, who has been seduced by the Gnosticism of Valentinus, St. Irenæus rebukes him for his errors:[3] "These opinions,[4] O Florinus, I speak with assurance, are not sound

---

[1] "Philip." VI. 3: καθὼς αὐτὸς ἐνετείλατο, καὶ οἱ εὐαγγελισάμενοι ἡμᾶς ἀπόστολοι, καὶ οἱ προφῆται κ.τ.λ.   Cf. IX. 1: Παύλῳ καὶ τοῖς λοιποῖς ἀποστόλοις.

[2] "Philip." XII. 1: καλῶς γεγυμνασμένοι ἐστὲ ἐν ταῖς ἱεραῖς γραφαῖς.

[3] IREN. *ap.* EUSEB. "H. E." v. 20, 4-7.

[4] δόγματα. Here the word δόγματα is taken in the sense of opinion, like the distinctive views or opinions of the various schools of philosophy. On the sense attached by the Greeks to the word "dogma" see E. HATCH, "The Influence of Greek Ideas and Usages upon the Christian Church" (London, 1890), p. 120. In classical Greek, the word δόγματα may be translated *placita philosophorum.* We may say it is synonymous with

in doctrine.  These opinions disagree with the Church, and lead to the greatest impiety those who accept them.  These opinions, not even the heretics outside of the Church have ever dared to express.  These opinions, the presbyters, who were before us, and who were companions of the Apostles, did not deliver to thee.

"For when I was a boy, in lower Asia, where you were conspicuous by reason of your employment at the court, I used to see you by the side of Polycarp,[1] endeavouring to gain his approbation.  I remember the events of that time more clearly than those of more recent years.  For what we learn in our boyhood grows with our minds, and becomes a part of them; so that I am able to describe the very place in which the blessed Polycarp sat as he discoursed, his gait, his physiognomy, his manner of life, his features, his discourses to those present, and the accounts which he gave of his intercourse with John and with the others who had seen the Lord.  And all that he heard from them concerning the Lord, and concerning His miracles and His teaching, having received them from eye-witnesses of the Word of life, Polycarp related in harmony with the Scriptures.

"These things, thanks to the mercy of God, I listened to attentively, noting them down, not on paper, but in my heart.  And continually, through God's grace, I recall them faithfully.  And I am able to bear witness before God that, if that blessed and apostolic presbyter had heard any such thing [as your doctrines], he would have cried out, and stopped his ears, and, as was his custom, would have exclaimed, O good God, unto what times hast thou kept me

---

αἵρεσις.  It means also a decree, an edict, enacted by the public authorities; and this meaning it has in the New Testament (Luke ii. 1; Acts xvii. 7).  It is synonymous with διάταγμα (Heb. xi. 23).  We find it thus understood by St. Paul (Eph. ii. 15; Col. ii. 14.  Cf. Acts xvi. 4).

[1] The words ἐν τῇ βασιλικῇ αὐλῇ present an enigma which as yet has not been explained.  Hadrian visited Asia in 122 and in 129, and L. Verus in 162.  We know of no other stay of any Emperor in Asia, and these dates hardly fit in with Polycarp's age.  Lightfoot suggests that it may be an allusion to the court of the proconsul of Asia.  This, about 136, was T. Aurelius Fulvus who later on became Emperor under the name of Antoninus Pius (LIGHTFOOT, "Ignatius," vol. i. p. 448).

that I should endure these things? And he would have fled from the place where he had heard such words."

The language of St. Irenæus is his own; but the language he ascribes to St. Polycarp is like it, in its apostolic candour. Polycarp would close his ears to the Gnostic novelties, because his faith had for its criterion the teaching given from the beginning by the Apostles and the others who had seen the Lord. Papias, a companion of Polycarp, will uphold the same criterion in the same terms. This appeal to the Apostles' authority was by no means a controversial expedient: it appertains to the faith of those venerable ancients, who can speak of the Apostles as old men speak of the by-gone generation which witnessed their own youth.

As regards the solidarity of the various Churches, St. Polycarp's Epistle to the Philippians gives an excellent testimony. Polycarp sends his Epistle to Philippi through a Christian named Crescens, who, after staying for a while at Smyrna, leaves for Macedonia with his sister; the Bishop of Smyrna recommends both to the kindness of the Church of Philippi.[1] This is a mere exercise of interecclesiastical hospitality; what follows is more significant. "I was exceedingly grieved about Valens, who was aforetime made a presbyter among you, because he so misunderstands the office which was given unto him. I warn you *therefore* that you refrain from covetousness, and that you be pure and faithful. Refrain from all evil. He who cannot govern himself in these things, how doth he instruct others?"[2]

The Bishop of Smyrna, then, has been told of the accusations brought by the Philippians against one of their presbyters (perhaps their bishop): he intervenes and reproves the culprit, as though he had authority to do so. The trials of a particular Church are known to distant Churches, and the Churches admonish one another in a brotherly spirit. May we not assume that what takes place in questions of conduct and of discipline occurs likewise in matters of faith?

[1] "Philip." XIV.

[2] *Id.* XI. 1-2. Polycarp says that Valens ἀγνοεῖ τὸν δοθέντα αὐτῷ τόπον. The word τόπος designates the rank in the hierarchy. LIGHTFOOT, "Ignatius," vol. II. p. 333.

Most assuredly, and the more so that in this regard universal attention is at its highest pitch: as much is said by the Pastoral Epistles and those of Ignatius. In confirmation, we can cite a passage from the Epistle of St. Irenæus to Pope Victor: the letter dates from the time of the Paschal controversy, i.e. from about the year 190, but it mentions a fact about St. Polycarp which must be assigned to the time when St. Anicetus presided over the Roman Church, that is, to the year 155 or a little before.

Polycarp came to Rome, Irenæus relates,[1] under Anicetus, and they had some little difficulties, but soon came to an understanding. On the subject of Easter, neither made any concession to the other, but they did not cease to live in peace. Anicetus was unable to persuade Polycarp to give up a custom which he held from John, the Lord's disciple, and from the other Apostles. Nor could Polycarp persuade Anicetus to discard what he called the tradition of the presbyters who had preceded him in the Roman Church.

So, the Bishop of Smyrna goes to Rome, at a time when the controversy with the Marcionites and the Valentinians is raging, as we learn from another passage;[2] the Bishop of Smyrna is welcomed as a brother, and to do him greater honour, the Bishop of Rome makes him celebrate the Eucharist in his stead; a fact that shows most plainly the intercommunion of the Churches. However, the Bishop of Smyrna and the Bishop of Rome are anxious to settle a few points on which they disagree; for solidarity is not merely mutual kindliness or the common breaking of the same eucharistic bread, it demands also community of faith and practice. Anicetus and Polycarp come to an understanding on certain contested points; distant as Smyrna is from Rome, the two Bishops wish that there should be between the two Churches a community of decisions. On the more important question of the date of Easter, they cannot agree, but let us note their respective motives; Polycarp appeals to the authority of the Apostles, and especially to that of St. John; Anicetus appeals to the tradition of the presbyters who have preceded him. In this instance Polycarp shows

[1] IREN. *ap.* EUSEB. "H. E." v. 24, 16.
[2] IREN. "Adv. haer." III. 3.

himself to be such as he had already manifested himself some thirty or forty years before, in his Epistle to the Philippians; his criterion of truth has remained the same. As to Anicetus, he has no other criterion than that of Polycarp, or rather Anicetus accepts the criterion of Polycarp and completes it by taking into account the continuity of the tradition of presbyters more ancient than himself—and this is to invoke the principle of Apostolic succession. Nor can it be said that this way of arguing was devised for the sake of the cause they had to defend against Gnosticism, since in the case before us, two bishops appeal to it, as to the only justification they can give each other of the special tradition of their respective Churches.

We cannot leave Smyrna without mentioning the Epistle of "the Church of God that sojourneth at Smyrna to the Church of God that sojourneth at Philomelium" in Phrygia, —which contains the narrative of the martyrdom of St. Polycarp. The copy addressed to the Christians of Philomelium is conveyed to them by a Christian named Marcion: they are asked to transmit the Epistle to the more distant brethren. Hence the Epistle will pass round from one Church to the other, and gradually the copies will increase in number and reach the farthest Churches. This is why we read in the inscription of the letter that it is addressed "to all the [Churches] of the holy and catholic Church, sojourning in every place".[1] This circulation of an Epistle coming from Smyrna proves that the "interecclesiastical confederacy" is a concrete reality.

This reality is designated by the word καθολική. St. Ignatius had first applied the term καθολική to the Church and given to it its concrete and geographical meaning. The compiler of the Epistle from the Smyrnians now writes, not in the inscription of the letter, but in the narrative itself: "When at length he brought his prayer to an end, after remembering all who at any time had lived near him, small and great, high and low, and all the (catholic) Church

---

[1] "Martyrium Polycarpi," inscr. (FUNK, " Patr. apost." i. 314): πασαῖς ταῖς κατὰ πάντα τόπον τῆς ἁγίας καὶ καθολικῆς ἐκκλησίας παροικίαις. We must bear in mind that the expression " Catholic Church," was used first by Ignatius writing to the Smyrnians.

[spread] throughout the world. . . ."[1]   The writer's aim is to show the worldwide embrace of the charity of the martyred Bishop: the Church for which he prays is not his Church of Smyrna, but the Church Catholic, inasmuch as it comprises the Churches scattered all over the world.

Funk maintains that the compiler of the Epistle of the Smyrnians knew also the secondary meaning of the term καθολική: "In the number of these elect was the glorious martyr Polycarp, who was an apostolic and prophetic teacher in our own times, a bishop of the Catholic Church which is in Smyrna."[2]   In this passage, καθολική is, Funk thinks, a term signifying orthodoxy, and for the first time in the texts of ancient Christian literature that have come down to us, the word has this meaning.[3]

*<sub>*</sub>*

According to the testimony of St. Irenæus, Papias was the familiar friend of St. Polycarp at Smyrna. Eusebius says he was Bishop of Hierapolis in Phrygia. Eusebius, who had his treatise in five books, entitled "Expositions of the Logia of the Lord," has preserved for us its title and a few too short quotations: the treatise, a refutation of Gnosticism, is referred by Funk to about the year 130.

The title itself reveals the author's method: having to

---

[1] "Martyr." VIII. 1: καὶ πάσης τῆς κατὰ τὴν οἰκουμένην καθολικῆς ἐκκλησίας. Also, XIX. 2: [Ἰησοῦν Χριστὸν] ποιμένα τῆς κατὰ τὴν οἰκουμένην καθολικῆς ἐκκλησίας.

[2] "Martyr." XVI. 2: διδάσκαλος ἀποστολικὸς καὶ προφητικὸς γενόμενος, ἐπίσκοπος τῆς ἐν Σμύρνῃ καθολικῆς ἐκκλησίας. On the strength of one Greek MS. and of the old Latin version, Lightfoot reads ἁγίας instead of καθολικῆς. We leave aside Harnack, who thinks that the word καθολική in the "Martyrium" is everywhere an interpolation. Kattenbusch is undecided. Zahn shares Funk's opinion and sees in the expression a touch of irony against the "ecclesiolæ hæreticorum". Besides, Lightfoot owns that the presence of the word καθολική as a qualification of orthodoxy, would not at all tell against the authenticity of the document, for at the time of Polycarp's martyrdom, there were heretical communities, for instance, those of the Basilidians, Valentinians, Marcionites, etc.; and Christians had to use an epithet as a sign of distinction. When it becomes opportune, each formula appears somewhere.

[3] The Passion of St. Pionius, of Smyrna, cannot be brought forward here, for St. Pionius was martyred, not in the time of Marcus Aurelius, but in the year 250.

refute Gnosticism, he takes for his basis the *logia* or sayings
of the Lord.   In this term we must not see an allusion to
the sources of the Synoptics, for these sources had long since
dried up; in the Churches, the fundamental authority is the
word of the Lord, and their endeavour is to understand it
aright, unlike the Gnostics who disfigure it, either by explain-
ing it in their own way, or by substituting for it apocryphal
sayings: their teaching is a novelty to which genuine Christians will oppose the teaching of the ancients, who have
known the Apostles and received from them the authentic
truth, that which was taught by Christ.

"I shall not hesitate, in order to guarantee the truth of
my own interpretations, to add to them whatsoever things I
have at any time learned carefully from the presbyters and
carefully remembered.   For I did not, like the multitude,
take pleasure in those that speak much, but in those that
teach the truth; not in those that relate strange commandments (ἀλλοτρίας ἐντολάς), but in those that deliver the
commandments given by the Lord to the faith, which springs
from the Truth itself.   If, then, any one came, who had
been a follower of the elders, I asked them what the elders
had said—what Andrew or what Peter said, or what Philip,
or Thomas said, or James, or John, or Matthew, or any other
of the disciples of the Lord, and what Aristion and the
presbyter John say. . . . I did not think that what was
to be gotten from books would profit me as much as what
came from a living voice." [1]

To the "babblers" Papias opposes the ancients who
teach what is true; he opposes to strange precepts those
which are authentic, those given to the faith by the Lord
Himself, and here the faith means the collective and traditional
faith.   To verify with greater security these authentic pre-

---

[1] PAP. *ap.* EUSEB. "H.E." III. 39, 3-4.   See a commentary on this
fragment in FUNK, "Patr. apostol." vol. I. p. 352.   With Funk I believe
that the word πρεσβύτεροι designates here the Apostles and disciples, such
as Aristion and the other John.   As regards the ἀλλοτρίαι ἐντολαί, compare the words of a presbyter quoted by St. Irenæus (III. 17, 4): ". . .
sicut quidam dixit superior nobis de omnibus qui quolibet modo depra-
vant quae sunt Dei et adulterant veritatem: In Dei lacte gypsum male
miscetur."   The "Muratorianum" says later on in the same sense: "Fel
cum melle misceri non congruit".

cepts, Christians must inquire about what was said by the Apostles, Andrew or Peter, Philip or Thomas, James or John, and by the disciples of the Apostles, such as Aristion and John the presbyter. What is contained in books, for instance in the books of Gnostics, does not at all compare with what has been said by the living voice of those primitive witnesses. Thus, Eusebius concludes, " Papias confesses that he received the words of the Apostles from those that followed them ". Again, Papias declares he has personally heard Aristion and John the presbyter. " He mentions them frequently by name, and gives their traditions (παραδόσεις) in his writings ".[1] The method followed by Papias is that which opposes tradition to gnosis, and justifies tradition by deriving it from the Apostles and from the Lord.

Unlike Polycarp and Papias, Hegesippus is not a bishop: Eusebius classes him with Justin as he is entitled to do by the fact that both Hegesippus and Justin were born in Palestine, and that Hegesippus, who was Justin's contemporary, sojourned in Rome at the time Justin taught there. Papias had gone to Jerusalem to inquire into the most authentic canon of the Old Testament : a like desire of investigation led Hegesippus from one Church to the other, and, according to the testimony of Eusebius,[2] he relates in the fifth book of his treatise, how he consulted many bishops until he reached Rome, and how he gathered from all of them the same teaching.

Acting thus, Hegesippus was doing what was required for the purpose of his treatise, which, as we know from Eusebius, was to find out " the true tradition of Apostolic doctrine ".[3]

Thus, Hegesippus arrives at Corinth, when Primus is

[1] EUSEB. ibid. 7. Cf. 14. In the Κήρυγμα Πέτρου, which dates from the age of Papias, the Apostle Peter is made to say : " Having learned holily and religiously what we entrust to you, you will observe it and offer up to God through Christ the new worship " : ὥστε καὶ ὑμεῖς ὁσίως καὶ δικαίως μανθάνοντες ἃ παραδίδομεν ὑμῖν, φυλάσσεσθε καινῶς τὸν θεὸν διὰ τοῦ Χριστοῦ σεβόμενοι (ed. DOBSCHÜTZ, p. 21).

[2] EUSEB. " H. E." IV. 22, 1 : δηλοῖ ὡς πλείστοις ἐπισκόποις συμμίξειν ἀποδημίαν στειλάμενος μεχρὶ Ῥώμης, καὶ ὡς ὅτι τὴν αὐτὴν παρὰ πάντων παρείληφεν διδασκαλίαν.

[3] EUSEB. IV. 8, 2 : τὴν ἀπλανῆ παράδοσιν τοῦ ἀποστολικοῦ κηρύγματος.

bishop of this city: during a somewhat prolonged stay he converses with the Bishop; he ascertains that the Church of Corinth is faithful to the sound doctrine; with the Corinthians he rejoices over the purity of their faith.[1] Hegesippus next passes from Corinth to Rome; there also he inquires about the faith, and in a few words he tells us his method: he does not content himself with ascertaining that the faith is pure, he takes pains to ascertain also that it comes down from the Apostles through a continuous and well-authenticated succession. This is why he said of the Corinthian Church that it "continued in the true faith until Primus," which does not mean that since Primus it had departed from the true faith, but, as we may conjecture, that he himself had been able to follow the succession from Primus back to Paul the Apostle. At Rome, Hegesippus writes, I verified the "succession down to Anicetus," i.e. by ascending from Anicetus to the Apostles; and, he adds, "in every succession, and in every city that is held which is preached by the law and the prophets and the Lord".[2]

We find then here a twofold criterion of the sound faith affirmed: that the faith is the same in all the Churches, and that it comes from the Apostles.

The Churches do not come together or deliberate to lay down a profession of faith that may be henceforth common to all; but men acting in their own name, travelling from one Church to the other, witness that, as a matter of fact, the faith is everywhere the same and that it is traceable back to the Apostles themselves, through a succession which can be everywhere ascertained. Hegesippus is no theorist as to the nature of catholicity and of apostolicity; he is a witness thereof, because catholicity and apostolicity were contained in the facts, before becoming arguments.

Hegesippus speaks of the Church of Jerusalem, where he applies himself to find out the διαδοχή: James the Just

---

[1] HEGESIPP. ap. EUSEB. IV. 22, 2: ἐπέμενεν ἡ ἐκκλησία ἡ Κορινθίων ἐν τῷ ὀρθῷ λόγῳ . . . and a few lines further: συνανεπάημεν ἐν τῷ ὀρθῷ λόγῳ.

[2] Ibid. 3: ἐν Ῥώμῃ διαδοχὴν ἐποιησάμην μέχρις Ἀνικήτου . . . ἐν ἑκάστῃ δὲ διαδοχῇ καὶ ἐν ἑκάστῃ πόλει οὕτως ἔχει ὡς ὁ νόμος κηρύσσει καὶ οἱ προφῆται καὶ ὁ κύριος. For the justification of the expression διαδοχὴν ἐποιησάμην see LIGHTFOOT, "Clement," vol. I. pp. 325-33.

is the first link, and after him Simeon, son of Clopas, is made bishop. But chafing at not having obtained the episcopal dignity, Thebutis begins to corrupt the people : a work of corruption that was derived from the seven Jewish sects[1] out of which arose the Christian sects, named the Simonians, the Cleobians, the Dositheans, the Menandrians and Marcianists and Carpocratians, Valentinians, Basilidians and Saturnilians which "introduced each privately and separately its own peculiar opinion. These were the false Christs, false Prophets, false Apostles, who divided the unity of the Church by corrupt doctrines against God and against His Christ."[2] This genealogy of the Gnosticism of the great Gnostics, Valentinus and Basilides, is very ingenious : it is clear that Hegesippus intends to compromise them by thus ascribing to them undesirable ancestors. This disreputable genealogy is to contrast with the sound διαδοχή, that which has for its ancestor the first authentic bishop, successor of the Apostles.

Another contrast : James was faithful to Christ's teaching so also, we may infer, was Simeon ; "then they called the Church a Virgin, for it was not yet corrupted by vain doctrine "[3] but as soon as men like Thebutis break with the διαδοχή there follows the corruption of the truth ; each goes his own way and thinks as he pleases : Christ, the Prophets, the Apostles, the three foundations of the faith, are henceforth shaken ; the unity of the Church no longer exists.

*∗*

A similar testimony is given by Abercius in the well-known inscription which he composed for his tomb and of which, by rare good fortune, we still possess both the text and the marble slab itself.[4] This text served as model for

---

[1] Hegesippus gives their names : Essenes, Galileans, Hemerobaptists, Masbotheans, Samaritans, Sadducees and Pharisees.

[2] *Ibid.* 5-6 : ἕκαστος ἰδίως καὶ ἑτεροίως ἰδίαν δόξαν παρεισηγάγοσαν. Ἀπὸ τούτων ψευδόχριστοι, ψευδοπροφῆται, ψευδαπόστολοι, οἵτινες ἐμέρισαν τὴν ἕνωσιν τῆς ἐκκλησίας. We may notice the expression, "The unity of the Church ".

[3] *Ibid.* 4 : ἐκάλουν τὴν ἐκκλησίαν παρθένον, οὔπω γὰρ ἔφθαρτο ἀκοαῖς ματαίαις.

[4] See our article " Abercius " in the " Dictionnaire de Théologie ".

a Christian inscription, found at Keleudræ in Phrygia, of which the original has likewise come down to us and is assigned to the year 216; from which scholars infer that the inscription of Abercius, composed at Hieropolis, in Phrygia, dates at the latest from the first years of the third century. The Bishop of Hieropolis, Abercius, was seventy-two years old when he had his inscription engraved; hence he must have been born about the year 130. He is a contemporary of Hegesippus, Melito, and Papias. "*I am,*" says Abercius, "*the disciple of a holy shepherd who feeds his sheep upon the hills and plains, and who has great eyes which see all.*" We may recall the Epistle of the Smyrnians, about the year 155, in which Jesus is called "the shepherd of the Catholic Church [spread] throughout the world"; and the "Shepherd" of Hermas, which speaks of the large tree that covers with its shade the whole earth, "plains and hills".[1]

Abercius continues: "*He taught me the faithful letters*" (γράμματα πιστά). Josephus often calls the Jewish Bible ἱερὰ γράμματα, and the same expression is frequently applied in the Pastoral Epistles to Holy Writ in general.[2] As to the word πιστός, it is distinctly Christian.

"*He it is,*" the inscription continues, he the pure shepherd, "*who sent me to Rome to see the sovereign queen, clad in a golden robe, and with golden shoes.*" Abercius, then, made the journey to Rome like Polycarp and Hegesippus, prompted as they were by the thought of his faith. For him Rome is the queen city: St. Justin had already spoken of the honours paid to Simon the Samaritan ἐν τῇ πόλει ὑμῶν βασιλίδι 'Ρώμῃ.[3] Rome's sovereignty shines

---

[1] Cf. "Oracula Sibyll." fragm. (éd. Geffcken, p. 228): παντοκράτωρ ἀόρατος ὁρώμενος αὐτὸς ἅπαντα. "Martyr. Polycarp." xix. 2. HERM. "Simil." viii. 3, 2.

[2] 2 Tim. iii. 15: ἀπὸ βρέφους ἱερὰ γράμματα οἶδας. The Imperial letters also were called ἱερὰ γράμματα. DEISSMANN, p. 274.

[3] JUSTIN, "I. Apolog." xxvi. 2. The expression ἐν τῇ βασιλίδι 'Ρώμῃ was commonly used. I notice it three times in the well-known inscription of Pozzuoli, which dates from the year 174 A.D.: BÖCKH, "C. I. G." n. 5853. Compare the text of the "Acta Pauli" (an Asia Minor text of about the year 180), on the Christian community of Rome, which outdoes in number all other communities and has no equal. HARNACK, "Analecta zur ältesten Geschichte des Christentums in Rom." (Leipzig, 1905), p. 6.

forth in her sumptuous dress: a golden robe and golden shoes.[1]

" *There I saw a people who had a gleaming seal.*" This people is the Christian people. The word σφραγίς, which we translate "seal" signifies literally the signet-ring that authenticates a signature, a letter.[2] By extension, it designates the mark put on goods or on beasts, by which they may be recognized.[3] During the second century, the Gnostic Theodotus writes in a fragment that has been preserved: " Irrational animals testify by the *sphragis* of their owner to whom they respectively belong, and it is by the testimony of the *sphragis* that the owner claims them ".[4] Figuratively taken, the *sphragis* is the baptism every Christian receives as an imprint by means of which the Divine Shepherd recognizes His sheep.

This baptized people Abercius has met with wherever he has gone, and he has observed everywhere that these same baptized men and women have in common with him the same faith and the same worship. " *There I saw a people who had a gleaming seal.*[5] *I also saw the plains of Syria and all the cities and Nisibis, beyond the Euphrates. Everywhere I found fellow-believers. I had Paul for* . . . (here one word has been lost). *Everywhere was faith my guide, and everywhere it gave me for food a fish from the spring, the great, the*

---

[1] ORIGEN, " Selecta in psalm. XLV." 10 : καὶ νῦν μὲν ἡ ἐκκλησία τοῦ θεοῦ διάχρυσα ἔχει ἱμάτια. It is disputed whether the queen spoken of by Abercius is Rome or the Roman Church. De Rossi, Duchesne, and Lightfoot think that the Roman Church is meant. DE ROSSI, " Inscriptiones," vol. II. p. XIX.

[2] As regards the σφραγίς thus understood, see the curious text of CLEMENT, " Paedagog." III. 11 (" P. G." vol. VIII. col. 633 A.).

[3] A commercial papyrus from Fayoum, of the end of the second century A.D., speaks of σφραγῖδα ἐπιβάλλειν ἑκάστῳ ὄνῳ, to mark all asses with a mark of property, that they may be recognized. A. DEISSMANN, " Neue Bibelstudien " (Marburg, 1897), p. 66.

[4] " Excerpta Theodot." 86 (" P. G. " vol. IX. p. 698). Cf. ORIGEN, " Comment. in Ioan." I. 2. Compare what is said by Celsus in ORIGEN, " Contra Celsum," VI. 27, περὶ τῆς καλουμένης παρὰ τοῖς ἐκκλησιαστικοῖς σφραγῖδος.

[5] In the " Acta Philippi," 144 (ed. BONNET, p. 86), the Apostle thus addresses Christ in a prayer : Ἔνδυσόν με τὴν φωτεινήν σου σφραγῖδα τὴν πάντοτε λάμπουσαν.

*pure, which a spotless virgin caught; she ever puts it before her friends to eat: she has also delicious wine, and she offers wine mixed with water together with bread. . . . Let every one who understands this pray for Abercius."* [1]

The faith of Abercius makes him welcome everywhere, for everywhere his faith is professed; and that faith gives him the right to be everywhere admitted to communion; faith and worship cannot be disjoined. We may recall Polycarp admitted to communion at Rome, like all the faithful of the Quartodeciman Churches who visit Rome. The fish is Jesus Christ, according to the well-known symbolism of the *ichthus.* As to the spotless virgin who has caught the Divine fish, Catholics agree in seeing in her the Virgin Mary, instead of the Church.[2] The union of all Christians throughout the whole world is the result of faith and of worship, which bind them one to another and make them all friends, initiated, and guests at a common meal. After their death, the prayers of those who remain accompany them beyond the grave.

\* \*
\*

We have not as yet taken Egypt into our inquiry, and except for the Epistle of Barnabas this country is altogether silent. The first author whose voice is heard in the second half of the second century is Pantænus, of whom Clement of Alexandria was the disciple: this makes him a contemporary of Justin and Hegesippus. He is in fact represented as an ancient who knew those who had seen the Apostles.[3]

[1] Ταῦτ' ὁ νοῶν εὔξαιτ' ὑπὲρ 'Αβερκίου πᾶς ὁ συνῳδός. The word συνῳδός is to be translated "concentor" or "he who sings with me": we might see here an allusion to the Christian worship; at least it is easy to recognize the prayer for the dead.

[2] Compare ARISTID. "Apolog." 15 (ed. ROBINSON, p. 110): οἱ χριστιανοὶ γενεαλογοῦνται ἀπὸ τοῦ κυρίου 'Ιησοῦ Χριστοῦ, οὗτος . . . ἐκ παρθένου ἁγίας γεννηθεὶς κ.τ.λ.

[3] PAMPHIL. ap. PHOT. "Cod." 118: Πάνταινον τῶν τε τοὺς ἀποστόλους ἑωρακότων ἀκροάσασθαι, οὐ μὴν ἀλλὰ καί τινων αὐτῶν ἐκείνων διακοῦσαι. We do not know what Apostles Pantænus may have met. However—and this confirms the attribution to Pantænus of the epilogue of the Epistle to Diognetus—we shall hear presently the author of that epilogue state that he is "a disciple of the Apostles". We may observe, however, that Clement of Alexandria gives the name Apostles to disciples of the Apostles: thus he calls Clement of Rome an Apostle. "Stromat." IV. 17 ("P. G." vol. VIII. col. 1312).

Clement set a very high value on having been a disciple of Pantænus and also of some others—ancients like the latter: one of whom he had met in Achaia, another in Southern Italy, a third in Cœle-Syria, a fourth in Palestine ; but to Clement, Pantænus was the dearest of all. "I found him concealed in Egypt," he says, "and having found him I sought for no other. This veritable Sicilian bee ran over the meadows and gathered from the flowers of Prophets and Apostles wherewith to form in the souls of his hearers, as in a sacred hive, pure combs not of honey but of knowledge and light." This brief indication betokens already the method Clement rejoiced to find used by those masters of old, but he insists : these ancients, he says, "preserved the true tradition of the blessed doctrine," that of the Saviour, and they "derived it directly from the holy Apostles Peter, James, John and Paul ".[1]

Has any writing of Pantænus come down to us ?

Anastasius Sinaita mentions four authors " old and prior to the Councils," who, he says, applied to Christ and to the Church the whole Hexaemeron. These four authors were Ammonius, Clement of Alexandria, Pantænus of Alexandria, and, the oldest of the four, Papias, Bishop of Hierapolis. In another passage, Anastasius relates that these interpreters "applied to the Church what is said of the paradise" in Genesis.[2]

Now the text of the Epistle to Diognetus ends with a fragment, which, according to all critics, does not make one whole with the Epistle, and is entirely foreign to it, both in substance and in style: Lightfoot has suggested it might be the work of Pantænus:[3] a tempting conjecture, on condition that one looks upon it as a mere conjecture. Those two

---

[1] CLEM. "Strom." I. 1 ("P. G." vol. VIII. col. 700): τὴν ἀληθῆ τῆς μακαρίας σώζοντες διδασκαλίας παράδοσιν, εὐθὺς ἀπὸ Πέτρου τε καὶ Ἰακώβου, Ἰωάννου τε καὶ Παύλου τῶν ἁγίων ἀποστόλων.

[2] ANASTAS. in "P. G.' vol. LXXXIX. pp. 860, 962. FUNK,"Patres Apost." I. 364. As regards Ammonius of Thmuis (third century), HARNACK, "Chronol." vol. II. p. 81.

[3] LIGHTFOOT, "Apostolic Fathers, Ep. to Diogn." (1891), p. 488. In the "Theolog. Quartalschrift," vol. LXXXVIII. (1906), p. 28-36, DI PAULI (after Bunsen, Dräseke, Bonwetsch) ascribes—wrongly, I think—the fragment to Hippolytus. Cf. HARNACK, op. cit. p. 232.

pages are written in a most affected, and even rhythmic style; and what Clement has just said of Pantænus and his admiration for him, leads one to think that the latter's style had not the rude simplicity of that of Papias. From quotations made by St. Irenæus, we have some verses of presbyters of the second century, which show that those early writers did not shrink from making use of prosodical forms.

"I do not speak of strange things, nor do I aim at anything inconsistent with right reason; but having been a disciple of the Apostles, I am become a teacher of the Gentiles." The unknown author addresses converts from paganism, and represents himself as a disciple of the Apostles, probably in contrast with the Gnostics, whose teachings are foreign and absurd. He is a διδάσκαλος, a word that recalls the Alexandrian διδασκαλεῖον, of which Pantænus was the first master, according to Eusebius.[1]  Our author continues: "I give faithfully what I have received (τὰ παραδοθέντα) to those that become disciples of the truth; for who that is rightly taught (ὀρθῶς διδαχθείς), and is becoming a friend to the Word, would not seek to know accurately the things which the Word taught directly to His Disciples?" Christian wisdom, then, consists in knowing that which has been taught by Christ Himself to His disciples, and has been faithfully transmitted from hand to hand by tradition. "The Father sent the Word, that He might manifest Himself to the world; and the Word, being despised by the (Jewish) people, was preached (κηρυχθείς) by the Apostles, and believed by the Gentiles. Through Him the Church is rich." The Gentile world has received from the Apostles the message destined for it; the Son is thus begotten in the hearts of the Saints, and the Church holds Him as a treasure. "The fear of the Law is chanted, the grace of the Prophets is known, the faith of the Gospels is established, the tradition of the Apostles is preserved, and the grace of the Church exults."[2]  Christ immanent in the

---

[1] EUSEB. "H. E." v. 10, 4.

[2] "Ep. ad Diogn." XI. 6 : εἶτα φόβος νόμου ᾄδεται καὶ προφητῶν χάρις γινώσκεται, καὶ εὐαγγελίων πίστις ἵδρυται, καὶ ἀποστόλων παράδοσις φυλάσσεται, καὶ ἐκκλησίας χάρις σκιρτᾷ. With the word ᾄδεται compare the word

Church is manifested therein through the Law, the Prophets, the Gospels, the Apostles, the Apostolic tradition.

The Gentiles who became converts have a share in this treasure. "You are made a paradise of delight, cause to spring up in yourselves a tree bearing all kinds of fruits. . . . For in this place the tree of knowledge and the tree of life have been planted; but it is not the tree of knowledge that destroys—it is disobedience that destroys. For what is written is not obscure, how God from the beginning planted the tree of knowledge and the tree of life in the midst of paradise, revealing through knowledge the way to life. . . ." The Gentiles are ushered into paradise and led to the two trees God has planted there; or still better those two trees are planted in them and bear fruits, "which the serpent cannot reach". Then follows a rather obscure statement, which refers perhaps to the Church: "Eve is not corrupted, but she is called a virgin ".[1] Christ is the new Adam, and the Church, his helpmate, is Eve, who remains for ever a virgin.

He whom Clement of Alexandria likened to a Sicilian bee may have expressed his thoughts in this poetic style, so full of Johannine and Pauline reminiscences; and, if these two pages are the work of Pantænus, we have in their resemblance to Clement's own writings a concrete piece of evidence of the mental affinity between master and disciple, and an explanation of Clement's admiration. In this passage, moreover, we should then find a confirmation of the statement of Anastasius Sinaita, that Pantænus applies to the Church what is said, in Genesis, of the earthly paradise.

The instruction in the form of a homily, which has been preserved under the name of " Second Epistle of Clement to the Corinthians," is neither an epistle, nor by Clement of Rome, but may be an instruction addressed to the Corinthians

συνῳδός in the inscription of Abercius. We find always the same insistence on singing, in connexion with the Church.

[1] *Id.* XII. 8 : οὐδὲ Εὔα φθείρεται, ἀλλὰ παρθένος πιστεύεται. Recall what Hegesippus says of the virginity of the Church.

and composed at Corinth. With Funk, we may date it at about the year 150.[1]

The author of the "Secunda Clementis" is not a controversialist; indefinite indeed are the anti-gnostic features which some scholars have thought to find in his work. He describes the Christian community he addresses, as subject to the authority of the presbyters (XVII. 3 and 5): a teaching and disciplinary authority. The written authority is that of the precepts of Jesus Christ (XVII. 3 and 6): these must be kept "that all [the faithful] having the same mind may be gathered together unto life" (XVII. 3). Elsewhere the author speaks of God's *logia*, which are for Christians the rule of conduct (XIII. 3). One becomes a Christian through Baptism—an imprint that must be kept spotless; for any one who does not preserve it, there is in store, a fire that shall never cease:[2] the community of the faithful is, thus, a community of the clean: a rigorist and encratistic inspiration animates the "Secunda Clementis" and connects it with the great ethical current of second century Christianity. "In doing the will of the Father, in keeping the flesh pure, and observing the commandments of the Lord, we shall receive life eternal (VIII. 4). If we do the will of God our Father, we shall be of the Church, which is first, which is spiritual, which was created before the sun and the moon."[3]

This thought has no affinity with the exegesis which applied to the Church what is said of the paradise in Genesis; it belongs to an order of speculation which we shall find

---

[1] This date and origin are conjectural. Against Harnack, who deems it a Roman production and even the work of Pope Soter (about 170), Bartlet inclines towards an Alexandrian origin, of about the year 140. "Zeitschrift für die neut. Wissenschaft," 1906, p. 123 and foll. HARNACK, "Chronol." vol. I. p. 448. FUNK, "Patr. Apostol." vol. I. p. lii.

[2] "2 Clem." VI. 9: ἐὰν μὴ τηρήσωμεν τὸ βάπτισμα ἁγνὸν καὶ ἀμίαντον. . . . VII. 6: τῶν μὴ τηρησάντων τὴν σφραγῖδα . . . VIII. 6: τηρήσατε τὴν σάρκα ἁγνὴν καὶ τὴν σφραγῖδα ἄσπιλον.

[3] XIV. 1: ἐσόμεθα ἐκ τῆς ἐκκλησίας τῆς πρώτης, τῆς πνευματικῆς, τῆς πρὸ ἡλίου καὶ σελήνης ἐκτισμένης. FUNK, loc. cit.: "Auctor potius ante quam post medium saeculum (II) se vixisse indicare videtur, quoniam quae c. XIV. de ecclesia spirituali leguntur, postquam Gnostici errores suos per totum orbem disperserunt, haud facile dici poterant."

again in Hermas, and which, in some Gnostics, ends in making the Church an æon; it affirms the pre-existence of the Church as a dogma similar to that of Christ's pre-existence. The Jews likewise speculated about the heavenly Jerusalem, that which the author of the Apocalypse beholds "coming down out of Heaven from God, having the glory of God" (XXI. 10-11). The idea of the pre-existence of the Church is dependent on these speculations about the heavenly Jerusalem.

The pneumatic Church, is the earliest in the sense that she has preceded the Jewish people: as is plainly stated elsewhere by the "Secunda Clementis," the opposition between the two is the same as between Sara and Agar.[1]

"Let us choose rather to be of the Church of Life, that we may be saved. For I do not suppose you are ignorant that the living Church is the body of Christ; for the Scripture saith, *God made man, male and female.* The male is Christ, and the female is the Church. And the books of the Prophets and the Apostles plainly declare that the Church is not of to-day, but hath been from the beginning: for she was spiritual, as our Jesus also was spiritual, but was manifested in these last days that she might save us. Now the Church, which is spiritual, was manifested in the flesh of Christ, thereby showing us that, if any of us guard her in the flesh and defile her not, he shall receive her again in the Holy Spirit: for this flesh is the antitype of the spirit. No man, therefore, when he hath defiled the antitype, shall receive the reality. Listen then, brethren; Guard ye the flesh, that you may partake of the spirit. But if we say that our flesh is the Church and the spirit of Christ, then he that hath soiled the flesh hath soiled the Church, and such an one, therefore, shall not partake of the spirit, which is Christ" (XIV. 1-5).

These mystical considerations are subordinate to the encratism of our author: the law of Christians consists in keeping their bodies spotless, in order not to lose the imprint of baptism, and to be able to obtain life everlasting. Through baptism and through the preservation of the bap-

---

[1] "II Clem." II. 1: στεῖρα ἦν ἡ ἐκκλησία ἡμῶν πρὸ τοῦ δοθῆναι αὐτῇ τέκνα, κ.τ.λ. Cf. JUSTIN, "Apolog." I. 53.

tismal imprint, Christians belong to the Church of life (ἐκκλησία τῆς ζωῆς), the living Church (ἐκκλησία ζῶσα), the same which St. Paul (Eph. i. 22-3) calls the body of Christ, the same which is united to Christ, as the husband to the wife, as we read also in St. Paul (Eph. v. 31-2), the same that was created pneumatic at the beginning of all things, the same that became manifest in Christ's flesh.

In these lofty reflections on the supernatural life, the Church is no longer anything visible and social: she is the life, she is the Spirit, she is Christ in so far as Christ is Spirit. Still she is distinct from Christ, just as the wife is distinct from the husband.

Let us leave this mysticism. Eusebius has had in his hands a collection of letters of Dionysius, who was bishop of Corinth when Soter was bishop of Rome (166-75), letters addressed to churches and called by Eusebius "Catholic epistles".[1] The expression "catholic" seems to be used here in the meaning it has when it designates the "Catholic Epistles" of the New Testament: it means that these Epistles are addressed to all the Churches, at the same time as to some particular Church. Eusebius mentions a letter to the Lacedæmonians, which is a "catechism of the orthodox faith and a treatise on peace and unity"; one to the Athenians, on the remissness of their faith; one to the Christians of Nicomedia, in which he strenuously opposes the heresy of Marcion, and defends "the canon of the truth"; one to "the Church that sojourns in Gortyna" and to the other communities of Crete, in which he forewarns them against any kind of intercourse with the heretics; one to "the Church that sojourns in Amastris, and to those in Pontus"; and one to the Christians of Cnosos. In the same collection was contained the answer of Pinytos, bishop of Cnosos, in which he begs Dionysius to write again to his Church, so grateful is it for the benefits derived from his first letter.

We can see from this by what relations the Churches were bound together; also how the monarchical episcopate was vigorous in every church; how gladly the bishops

---

[1] EUSEB. "H. E." iv. 23, 1: καθολικαῖς πρὸς τὰς ἐκκλησίας ἐπιστολαῖς. Cf. IGNAT. "Ad Polycarp." viii. 1.

helped and counselled one another, always bent on arousing everywhere an attachment to unity, to the sound faith, to the canon of truth, and to the hatred of heresy.

Eusebius knew also another Epistle of Dionysius, sent to the Romans or rather " to Soter, who was their bishop at that time ". In it the Roman Church is warmly praised for her boundless charity, that extends to all the churches.

" From the beginning," Dionysius writes to the Romans, " it has been your practice to do good to all the brethren in various ways, and to send succours (ἐφόδια) to the Churches in all the cities [of the earth].[1] In thus relieving the want of the needy, and making provision for the brethren in the mines by the gifts which you have sent from the beginning, you Romans, keep up the hereditary custom of the Romans, which your blessed Bishop Soter has not only maintained, but has added to, by furnishing an abundance of supplies to the saints, and encouraging the brethren from abroad with blessed words, as a loving father does with his children." [2]

The fame of the Roman charity dates "from the beginning," which refers to the time when St. Paul had already praised the Romans for their faith "spoken of in the whole world " (Rom. i. 7) and had experienced himself the heartiness of their welcome (Acts XXVIII. 15). This charity has not grown cold in the course of time: it is known to all the brethren, and has extended to all the Churches both through material helps and the kind reception which the Christians of all the Churches are assured of finding at Rome.

\* \*
\*

Like the unknown author of the " Secunda Clementis,"

---

[1] In Greek : ἐκκλησίαις πολλαῖς ταῖς κατὰ πᾶσαν πόλιν. The text may be amended. I follow the common reading. From the beginning there were in the Roman Church some of the faithful who belonged to the most aristocratic and wealthy families, and at times the amount of their wealth was very considerable. Regarding this peculiar feature of the Roman Church, see HARNACK, " Mission," vol. II. pp. 26-38.

[2] EUSEB. ibid. 10. This letter of Dionysius was an answer to a letter of Soter. The former alludes to the letter (now lost) of Soter : " To-day we have kept the Lord's holy day, in which we have read your epistle : . . . we shall continue to read it always as an admonition (νουθετεῖσθαι), together with the former epistle, which was written to us through Clement " (ibid. 11). An allusion to the " Prima Clementis ".

Hermas is not directly a controversial writer; but he knows that some hypocrites have done their best to spread among the faithful strange and foolish teachings, which he holds in abhorrence [1]  These hypocrites must be driven away; there is no place for them in the symbolic building, the Church, which is being built; they are the stones that are cast aside. "In this way, will the Church of God be purified . . . after it has rejected the wicked, and the hypocrites, and the blasphemers. . . . After these have been cast out, the Church of God will be one body, one mind, one spirit, one love: and then the Son of God will be exceeding glad, and will rejoice among them [the clean], because He has received His people pure ".[2]  Unity of thought, of faith, of love, is, then, the law of the Church. But whether that Church is the concrete Church here below or the unseen Church in Heaven, Hermas does not state.

He sees in a vision twelve mountains, the figure of men "who inhabit the whole world, and to whom the Son of God was preached by the Apostles". All the nations "that dwell under heaven," have, then, heard the message. The men "who have received the *sphragis* have one thought, one mind, one faith, one love ".[3]  These are of course the faithful who are still here below, subject to be tempted to sin and error. Hermas pays more attention to sin than to error: the Lord says to him: "Keep thy flesh pure and stainless, that the Spirit which inhabits it may bear witness to it, and it may be justified. . . . If you defile your flesh, you will also defile the Holy Spirit; if you defile the Spirit you will not live."[4]  This life begins for the Christian even in this world, and it continues "with the Saints of God" and His Angels in Heaven.[5]  The Church, the communion of the Saints, is, then, earthly and heavenly at the same time.

---

[1] HERM. "Sim. VIII." 6, 5 : ὑποκριταὶ διδαχὰς ξένας εἰσφέροντες . . . ταῖς διδαχαῖς ταῖς μωραῖς πείθοντες.

[2] "Sim. IX.' 18, 3-4 : ἀποβληθῆναι τοὺς πονηροὺς καὶ ὑποκριτὰς καὶ βλασφημούς . . .—ἔσται ἡ ἐκκλησία τοῦ θεοῦ ἐν σῶμα, μία φρόνησις, εἶς νοῦς, μία πίστις, μία ἀγάπη.

[3] "Sim. IX." 17, 4 : λαβόντες οὖν τὴν σφραγῖδα μίαν φρόνησιν ἔσχον καὶ ἕνα νοῦν, καὶ μία πίστις αὐτῶν ἐγένετο καὶ μία ἀγάπη.

[4] "Sim. v." 7, 1-2.          [5] "Vis. III." 8, 8.   "Sim." IX. 25, 2.

She is a creation in view of which God has created everything else.[1] A most handsome youth appears to Hermas and addresses him in these words: "Who do you think this aged woman is from whom you received the book? The Sibyl? No, it is the Church." "Why then is she an aged woman?" Hermas asks. "Because," the youth answers, "she was created first of all, and for her sake was the world made."[2]

Although she is that spiritual creation, the Church nevertheless is constituted in local and visible Churches, that are subject to rule. The aged woman, the image of the unseen Church, has given a book to Hermas that he may hand it over to the presbyters. Hermas has been commissioned to carry it to Clement—who in the mind of the author of the "Shepherd," is Clement of Rome—and then, Clement must send the book "to foreign cities".[3] Hermas will read it publicly in the city of Rome where he dwells "with the presbyters who preside over the church".[4]

These reflections on the Church spiritual are superadded then to the fact of the existence of the local churches, and, though they are probably connected with the teaching of the Epistle to the Ephesians, they occur so rarely that we can hardly say that they had any influence on the ecclesiastical organization.

We should have a far better expression of the thoughts of the Roman Church in the work of Justin, had this work been preserved entire, and especially had we still in our hands that "Syntagma adversus omnes hæreses," which we know only from its title. St. Irenæus quotes Justin against

---

[1] "Vis. I." 1-6.     [2] "Vis. II." 4, 1.     Cf. "Vis. III." 3, 5.

[3] Mgr. DUCHESNE, "Eglises Séparées," p. 130, remarks that, besides the writings that were rightly or wrongly called after some Apostle, the "Prima Clementis" and the "Shepherd," two Roman compositions, were the only works that had a place, during the second century, in the canon of some Churches.

[4] "Vis. II." 4 : πέμψει οὖν Κλήμης εἰς τὰς ἔξω πόλεις, σὺ δὲ ἀναγνώσῃ εἰς ταύτην τὴν πόλιν μετὰ τῶν πρεσβυτέρων τῶν προισταμένων τῆς ἐκκλησίας (cf. "Vis. III." 5). Hermas alludes elsewhere ("Vis. III." 9) with some slight tinge of criticism τοῖς προηγουμένοις τῆς ἐκκλησίας καὶ τοῖς πρωτοκαθεδρίταις. There are rivalries for the first place in the churches: "Sim." VIII. 7; "Vis. II." 4, III. 1. We must not forget that Hermas is a "prophet",

Marcion;[1] Tertullian quotes him, together with Irenæus and Miltiades, against Valentinus and the Valentinians: and he represents them all three as the contemporaries of those heresiarchs whom they fought in books written with vigour (*instructissimis voluminibus*): he declares that his greatest wish is to become their equal.[2] Scholars think that the authors of works against heresy, beginning with Irenæus and Tertullian, most probably knew and used many a time the " Syntagma " of St. Justin, which must have been the earliest sample of this kind of literature. Most probably too, Justin's criteria are the same with those which Irenæus will develop some twenty-five years later. As ground for these suppositions, we have the indications we can find in the two " Apologies " and in the "Dialogue with the Jew Trypho ".

Justin is an apologist, in the " Apologies " as well as in the " Dialogue "; there appears in him the dualism of the believer who affirms the articles of his faith, and the apologist who justifies them by means of reasons; for the truth of the articles of faith is such as can be perceived by reason.[3]

But when it is a question of establishing the foundations of the articles of his faith, Justin is in perfect accord with Polycarp, Papias, and Hegesippus—as Irenæus later on will be with him—in proclaiming as a principle that faith is a teaching received as an inheritance and faithfully transmitted: that it is a deposit. The plea of the presbyters of Smyrna opposing to the novelties of Noetus, the rule, " We declare what we have learned," is already found in Justin.[4]

Among many others, there are two terms that he uses with noticeable frequency: the word διδαχή and the word παράδοσις, the latter being the sequel and the guarantee of the former.[5]

Now the διδαχή is the teaching of the Prophets, of

---

[1] " Adv. hær." IV. 6, 4.    [2] " Adv. Valentinian." 5.

[3] JUSTIN, " Apolog. I." 23 : τὸ ἀληθὲς λέγομεν. Cf. 43 : ἀληθὲς ἀποφαινόμεθα . . . ὡς δείκνυσιν ὁ ἀληθὴς λόγος. Celsus will entitle his criticism of Christianity a *True Discourse*.

[4] " Apolog. I." 13 : ὡς ἐδιδάχθημεν λέγοντες . . . —14 : ταῦτα δεδιδάγμεθα καὶ διδάσκομεν. HIPPOLYT. " Contra haer. Noet." 1 (" P. G." vol. x. p. 805) : ταῦτα λέγομεν ἃ ἐμάθομεν. The condemnation of Noetus at Smyrna occurred about the year 180.

[5] " Apolog. I." 39,

Christ, and of the Apostles. "These teachings, which we have received from Christ and from the Prophets, His predecessors, are the only true teachings, as contrasted with the fables of the Greeks." [1] "The doctrine which we have received from the Apostles" has the same authority; [2] for it is by the Apostles that Christ's doctrine was preached to the Gentile world: "From Jerusalem there went out into the world twelve men in number, and they simple persons, and unskilled in speaking; but through the power of God they declared to every race of men that they were sent by Christ to teach all men the word of God".[3]

The conviction which we have noted in Abercius and in Hegesippus is again expressed here, the conviction that the διδαχή spread all over the world is everywhere identical with itself. On stepping from his baptismal bath, the newly baptized Christian is led "where those who are called brethren are assembled together"; prayers are offered up to God by all those who are present, for the assembly present, for the newly baptized brother, for "all others everywhere," i.e. for the "brethren" dispersed in the whole world and wherever they are, in order that to all Christians "who have learned the truth" God may grant that they keep what is prescribed to them.[4] The liturgy which opens with this prayer ends with the eucharist of which no one is allowed to partake "but he who believes in the truth of our doctrines, and has been baptised; and who so lives, as Christ has directed".[5]

In opposition to the truth which we have received from Christ through the Apostles and which we preserve with

---

[1] "Apolog. I." 23. Cf. 53: τοὺς ἀπὸ παντὸς ἔθνους ἀνθρώπους διὰ τῆς παρὰ τῶν ἀποστόλων αὐτοῦ διδαχῆς πεισθέντας.

[2] "Apolog. I." 61: καὶ λόγον παρὰ τῶν ἀποστόλων ἐμάθομεν τοῦτον.—66: ἐδιδάχθημεν, οἱ γὰρ ἀπόστολοι οὕτως παρέδωκαν.—67: τοῖς ἀποστόλοις ἐδίδαξε ταῦτα ἅπερ ὑμῖν ἀνεδώκαμεν.

[3] "Apolog. I." 23: ὁπόσα λέγομεν μαθόντες παρὰ τοῦ Χριστοῦ καὶ τῶν προελθόντων αὐτοῦ προφητῶν. "Apolog." II. 2: τὴν ἀπὸ τοῦ Χριστοῦ διδαχήν. "Dialog." CXIX. 6: τῇ φωνῇ τοῦ θεοῦ τῇ διά τε τῶν ἀποστόλων τοῦ Χριστοῦ λαληθείσῃ, πάλιν καὶ τῇ διὰ τῶν προφητῶν κηρυχθείσῃ.

[4] "Apolog. I." 65: κοινὰς εὐχὰς ὑπὲρ . . . ἄλλων πανταχοῦ πάντων . . . ὅπως καταξιωθῶμεν τὰ ἀληθῆ μαθόντες . . . καὶ φύλακες τῶν ἐντεταλμένων εὑρεθῆναι.

[5] "Apolog. I." 66: . . . ὡς ὁ Χριστὸς παρέδωκεν.

fidelity, error has multiplied, stirred up by the devils, ever since the day they saw that Christ "was believed in by every nation"; the devils have thus raised up Simon and Menander, both from Samaria, both of them magicians. Simon accompanied by a harlot, named Helen, came under Claudius to Rome, where a statue was erected to him as to a god. Menander took up his abode at Antioch, where some of his disciples are still to be found. Marcion, a native of Pontus, is still teaching: with the help of the devils, he has made his followers deny God, the creator of the world, and believe in a superior God. The heretics are called Christians, but for the same reason that all philosophers are called philosophers, in spite of the variety of the doctrines they profess.[1] Heresy—so we may infer from this description—can be recognized by its inspiration, which comes from the demons: hence come those impieties, those blasphemies and scandals, by which it is accompanied; it is preached by men who are well known, who have nothing at all of the mission of the Apostles, who are magicians like Simon and Menander, or sophists like Marcion. The heretics, disciples of these heresiarchs, bear the name of Christians: but, in contrast with the unity of faith of the genuine Christians, what characterizes the heretics is the diversity of their opinions; and in this they are like philosophers who follow but their own sense. "However," Justin concludes, "I have composed a treatise against all the heretics that have existed, which, if you wish to peruse it, I will present to you."[2]

[1] "Apolog. I." 26 : πάντες οἱ ἀπὸ τούτων ὁρμώμενοι χριστιανοὶ καλοῦν-ται, ὃν τρόπον καὶ οὐ κοίνων ὄντων δογμάτων τοῖς φιλοσόφοις τὸ ἐπικαλούμενον ὄνομα τῆς φιλοσοφίας κοινόν ἐστιν. The word *dogma* is still used here in its philosophical sense.

[2] "Apolog. I." 26. The same argument, drawn from the disagreement of heretics among themselves, is made use of by Rhodon, a native of Asia, who had come to Rome like Justin, and there became Tatian's disciple. Eusebius places Rhodon in the time of the Emperor Commodus (180-92). See the fragment in which Rhodon expresses his mind regarding these contradictions of the heretics, and particularly of Apelles and Marcion; EUSEB. "H. E." v. 13, 2-4. This argument used by apologists like Justin and Rhodon is the same that is used by apologists like Tatian against the pagan philosophers whose contradictions they denounce. M. Puech has shown that in this respect our apologists—whilst using them

In his two Apologies, addressed, as was said before, to the public at large—to the Prince, the Senate, and pagan public opinion—Justin appeals only to arguments resting on equity, on reason, or on fact : there was no motive for recalling then that Christianity formed an association within the Roman Empire ; even the word Church is not mentioned. The "Dialogue with Trypho the Jew," which is posterior to the first Apology and destined for Christian or Jewish readers, is more explicit.

When the prophet Malachy announces that everywhere, in the midst of all nations, a clean oblation is offered up to God, Justin shows to the Jew Trypho that in this passage Malachy foretold Gentile Christianity. For, he says, it is a fact that Judaism is not spread all over the world, from the rising of the sun down to its setting, and that there are still many peoples in whose midst no Jew has as yet taken up his abode, whilst "there is not any one race of men, barbarian or Greek, nay, of those who live in chariots, or without houses, or shepherds in tents, among whom prayers and eucharists are not celebrated in the name of the crucified Jesus ".[1]   Again, dealing with the prophecy of Michæas, that a time would come when the law would go forth from Jerusalem, and the word of the Lord would subdue the far distant nations, put an end to wars, and change swords into ploughshares, and when every man would sit in peace under his own vine, Justin shows that this time has actually come since the Apostles have carried the Gospel from Jerusalem to the Gentiles in the whole world; and that nothing, not even bloody persecution, is able to dismay the Christians. "The vine which is planted by Christ our God and Saviour is His people."[2]

The catholicity of the Christian faith (the word $\kappa\alpha\theta o\lambda\iota\kappa\acute{o}s$ has not this meaning in St. Justin) is geographical, concrete and conspicuous.[3]   Though thus dispersed,

---

for an opposite purpose—had undergone the influence of the pagan $\pi\rho o\tau\rho\epsilon\pi\tau\iota\kappa o\grave{\iota}$ $\lambda\acute{o}\gamma o\iota$, for instance of that of Posidonius.  PUECH, "Recherches sur le discours aux Grecs de Tatian " (Paris, 1903), p. 41.  On the contrary, the proof from tradition is distinctly ecclesiastical.

[1] "Dialog." CXVII. 5.                    [2] *Ibid.* CX. 4.
[3] Cf. "Dialogue," CXIX. 4.

Christianity possesses a unity which is just as real. " Those who believe in Christ are one soul, one synagogue, one church," this is why—in the text of the Psalm *Audi filia et vide, et inclina aurem tuam, et obliviscere populum tuum* —the word of God addresses as " His daughter, the Church that is born of and partakes of His name, for we are all called Christians." [1]  That Justin uses indiscriminately the words synagogue and church, need cause us no great surprise : for he is disputing with a Jew, and in speaking of the Christian people which in God's plan takes the place of the Jewish people, he intends to make use of general designations only : in the present discussion, " Church " has no other meaning than that given to the word by the LXX. But, at bottom, Justin has in view the Church, that which stands over against the Synagogue, and elsewhere he clearly asserts this opposition, saying that Jacob is the figure of Christ, inasmuch as Jacob served Laban for his two daughters and was deceived as regards the former. Lia is the figure of " your people and synagogue," Justin says to Trypho, " and Rachel is our Church ".[2]

But here an objection can be raised : Among those who bear the name of Christians, are there not many heretics ? Justin realized probably far more than Trypho, the bitterness of this scandal : men bold enough to " affirm themselves to be Christians and confess Jesus, who was crucified, to be both Lord and Christ," and at the same time " teaching not His doctrine, but such as proceeds from the spirits of error ".[3]  Justin appeals to the " true and pure teaching of Jesus Christ "; he recalls that the Saviour foretold what is taking place now : that false prophets will come in the clothing of sheep who inwardly are ravening wolves, pseudo-Christs, pseudo-apostles, seducers of the faithful.

Here we find again the trilogy of the Prophets, of Christ and of the Apostles, as the foundation of the pure and authen-

[1] " Dialog." LXIII. 5 : ὅτι τοῖς εἰς αὐτὸν πιστεύουσιν ὡς οὖσι μιᾷ ψυχῇ καὶ μιᾷ συναγωγῇ καὶ μιᾷ ἐκκλησίᾳ, ὁ λόγος τοῦ θεοῦ [εἴρηται] ὡς θυγατρὶ τῇ ἐκκλησίᾳ τῇ ἐξ αὐτοῦ ὀνόματος γενομένῃ καὶ μετασχούσῃ τοῦ ὀνόματος αὐτοῦ (χριστιανοὶ γὰρ πάντες καλούμεθα).

[2] *Ibid.* CXXXIV. 2 : Λεία μὲν ὁ λαὸς ὑμῶν καὶ ἡ συναγωγή, Ῥαχὴλ δὲ ἡ ἐκκλησία ἡμῶν.

[3] *Ibid.* XXXV. 2.

tic faith.    Outside this foundation, there is nothing but blasphemy and error.    "There both are and have been, many who have presented themselves in the name of Jesus, and taught men to speak and act atheistically and blasphemously, but they are known among us by the name of those by whom the doctrine and opinion peculiar to them was first taught. . . . Some are called Marcionites, some Valentinians, some Basilidians, and some Saturnilians; and others by other names, each deriving his name from the creator of his heresy, just as each of those who consider themselves philosophers . . . bears the name of the father of the philosophy he follows." [1]    This is the argument outlined already in the first Apology; [2] heresy is inspired by the devils and brings forth blasphemies; it originates with men who, like the philosophers, follow their own judgment, and therefore forfeit the right to be called Christians.

* *
*

To the preceding testimonies, which set before us the Church as seen from within, we may join that of the pagan Celsus, who, although he was an outsider, had made himself well acquainted with all that appertained to Christianity, because, as a philosopher and as a controversialist, he was anxious to speak with knowledge (a boast which he often made) of what he was opposing.

Celsus is a Greek, but most probably a Greek of Rome; and his book was written, probably, at Rome during the last years of the reign of Marcus Aurelius, between the years 177-80, in the period when Commodus shared the imperial dignity. [3]    Despite Origen's opinion that he is an Epicurean, we believe that Celsus is a Platonist: he is a religious pagan, as was possible for a man with Platonic tendencies, who, associating the established religion with his love of the Roman greatness, is anxious to preserve it, provided it be interpreted in an allegorical sense, according to a method not unlike that employed by the symbolo-fideism of our day. Religion of this sort does but render him the more hostile

---

[1] "Dialog." XXXV. 6.            [2] "Apolog." I. 26.
[3] Cf. NEUMANN, art. "Celsus" in HAUCK's "Realencyklopädie". Still we must not overlook FUNK's hesitations, "Die Zeit des *Wahren Wortes* von Celsus," in his "Kirch. Abhandl." vol. II. (1899), pp. 152-61,

to Christianity, which he undertakes to criticize thoroughly, in his "True Discourse".

In what pertains to Christianity he does not avoid a certain number of mistakes to which Origen, according to recognized tactics of war, does not fail to call due attention; yet he does show a wonderful erudition. He has travelled in Phœnicia, Palestine, Egypt. He quotes the Old Testament, the Book of Henoch, and the Sibylline oracles: he knows the four canonical Gospels, and also other texts from which "he draws against Jesus and against us objections he could not draw from our Gospels".[1] It is not proved that he was acquainted with the Acts of the Apostles; but he knows St. Paul's ideas, although it is uncertain whether he had read his Epistles. Celsus distinguishes between the authentic Gospel texts, and those which "certain Christian believers (like persons who in a fit of drunkenness mutilate themselves), have corrupted from their original integrity three times, four times, and even more, so that they might be able to answer objections": words that doubtless refer to the Marcionites.[2] That Celsus was acquainted with the work of St. Justin, we cannot affirm. On the other hand, he does know the "Dialogue"—now lost—"of Jason and Papiscus," which he says, "is rather pitiable and detestable than ridiculous".[3] He has perused many Marcionite and Gnostic writings. After having consulted such disparate sources of information, it is very strange that Celsus should have had a normal view of Christianity, one which really corresponds with Catholic institutions as they were towards the middle of the second century.

Celsus does not denounce Christianity primarily as a superstition contrary to the naturalism which he believes to be the truth, but as an unlawful association. Christians, he says, enter among themselves into secret agreements that are contrary to the laws, and these agreements, which constitute the mutual love of Christians, are made in view of the common danger, and are more binding than sacred oaths (i. 1). Their whole worship is secret, for in case they are denounced, death is their punishment (i. 3). Well and good,

---

[1] ORIGEN, " Contra Cels." II. 74.
[2] " Contra Cels." II. 27,        [3] Ibid. IV. 52.

were their doctrine reasonable; but they accept without any reason "dogmas" that are simply absurd. "Certain persons among them," Celsus writes, "who do not wish either to give or receive a reason for their belief, keep repeating: 'Do not examine, but believe!' and 'Your faith will save you!'" Celsus affirms that they say: "In this life wisdom is bad, but foolishness is a good thing".[1]

He knows well that among Christians there are found honourable, gentle and cultivated men—"capable of comprehending allegories," he says:[2] however, most Christians are simple and uneducated (I. 27). Of these simple people he draws a kind of sketch, in which, under his caricature of their characteristics, we detect a reality which we are not surprised to meet: the pathetic missionary spirit of those "workers in wool and leather, fullers, and persons of the most ignorant sort, who nevertheless are zealous in bringing women and children to their faith (III. 55). The instruction required by these lowly clients is furnished by presbyters who are hardly less ignorant than themselves, says Celsus.[3]

At the beginning of Christianity, Christians were few and had only one mind; but as they spread and became a multitude, they ceased to agree and branched off into many sects, "each wishing to have his own party" (III. 10). Those who separate from the "multitude" anathematize one

---

[1] "Contra Cels.' I. 9: φησὶ δέ τινας μηδὲ βουλομένους διδόναι ἢ λαμβάνειν λόγον περὶ ὧν πιστεύουσι, χρῆσθαι τῷ "μὴ ἐξέταζε ἀλλὰ πίστευσον," καὶ "ἡ πίστις σου σώσει σε" καί φησιν αὐτοὺς λέγειν "κακὸν ἡ ἐν τῷ κόσμῳ σοφία, ἀγαθὸν δὲ ἡ μωρία". Cf. ibid. 12.

[2] On allegory, especially among the Stoics, as a method of interpreting religious myths, cf. P. DECHARME, "La critique des traditions religieuses chez les Grecs" (Paris, 1904), p. 270 and foll.

[3] "Contra Cels." VI. 40. Cf. III. 72 and 77. As regards the spread of Christianity among the educated classes, see HARNACK, "Mission," vol. I. pp. 408-18. Catholicism opposed authority to criticism and to Gnostic speculation. A "philosopher" like Justin was rather an exception; and such a man had very little influence on the cultivated pagans of his time. Celsus does not know him at all. In spite of Origen and his disciples, Christianity found its opponent in "the ancient learning," and in what may be called the higher education of the old world. CUMONT, "Les religions orientales dans le paganisme romain," p. 324, thinks that until the end of the fifth century the higher education remained in the hands of the heathen.

another, and continue to have only the name in common, if it can be said that they have anything at all in common.[1] Celsus mentions successively the Simonians (the disciples of Simon Magus), the Carpocratians, whom he knows only by name, the Marcionites, whom, on the contrary, he seems to have met and questioned (v. 62). All these factions, he continues, fiercely tear one another.[2] In Phœnicia and Palestine, he has come across prophets and prophetesses, visionaries who are the forerunners of the Montanists.[3]

Did we pay attention only to these features, we might believe that Christianity was then in a state of universal disunion. But we must not forget that Celsus beheld it first united in a charity that seemed to him like a covenant of mutual defence, or that he himself has noted down that those sects were separate factions which had almost nothing in common. There are then two Christian bodies opposing each other, the one united—the other disunited; and it is in the same light that, somewhat later, St. Irenæus describes heresies. Even Celsus clearly realizes that the Christian body, that which has not gone off into schism, forms a visible unity, based on the unity of faith, between all the members of which there is perfect solidarity: he defines this unity by a striking epithet: "the great Church."[4]

\* \*
\*

If we now attempt to extract from the preceding analysis the leading ideas, we may say in the first place, that Christianity is regarded with insistence as a real and visible collectivity, spread like a race over the whole world (Hermas, Abercius, Justin); that, among all the dispersed groups or communities of which it is made up, there is cohesion and exchange, in other words an inter-ecclesiastical bond which is felt by all (Polycarp, the Smyrnians, Abercius, Dionysius of

---

[1] "Contra Cels." III. 12 : ὑπὸ πλήθους πάλιν διιστάμενοι.

[2] *Ibid.* v. 63 and 64.   [3] *Ibid.* VII. 9 and VIII. 45.

[4] *Ibid.* v. 59 : σαφῶς γε τῶν ἀπὸ μεγάλης ἐκκλησίας τοῦτο ὁμολογούντων κ.τ.λ. Here it is question of the faith regarding creation and the work of the six days, common to the Christians and to the Jews, probably in contrast with the Marcionites. Compare v. 61 : τί τοῦτο φέρει ἔγκλημα τοῖς ἀπὸ τῆς ἐκκλησίας, οὓς ἀπὸ τοῦ πλήθους ὠνόμασεν ὁ Κέλσος ; he opposes the great Church (τὸ πλῆθος) to the Ebionites.

Corinth, Celsus) ; that especially, in all that pertains to the faith, there exists an agreement which is likewise felt by all (Hegesippus, Abercius, Dionysius, Hermas, Justin, Celsus) ; so that at first sight the heretics appear as strangers (Papias, Pantænus, Hermas, Celsus).

This concord of the Churches in their faith results from the fact that the faith is regarded as a divine teaching, first received and then faithfully transmitted as a deposit : it is the Lord's teaching (Polycarp, Papias), or, more precisely, the teaching of the Lord, of the Prophets, of the Apostles (Polycarp, Papias, Hegesippus, Pantænus, Justin), a teaching propagated and vouched for by the Apostles (Polycarp, Papias, Hegesippus, Pantænus, Justin), received and handed down by the presbyters (Polycarp, Anicetus, Papias, Pantænus), the transmission of which has been made concrete in the succession of bishops (Hegesippus) to whom the faithful must submit (Polycarp, " Secunda Clementis," Dionysius, Hermas).

It is this unity of faith—Catholic faith, Apostolic faith— which they were wont to contrast with the heresies : but the unity lies far deeper, for it embraces the whole ecclesiastical life, liturgy and discipline, in subjection to the authority of the hierarchy (Polycarp, Hegesippus, Abercius, Dionysius, Hermas, Justin).

Rome is a centre in which the faith of all the faithful (Polycarp, Abercius, Hegesippus, Dionysius) is concerned.

The heretics can appeal only to the man after whom they have been called (Hegesippus, Justin) : their systems are unreasonable and contradict one another (Hegesippus, Pantænus, Justin, Celsus).

The idea of the unseen or pneumatic Church, pre-existing ever since the beginning of the world, is one that is developed only by the author of the " Secunda Clementis " and by Hermas.

## II.

St. Irenæus, a native of Asia, lived as a youth at Smyrna under the eyes of St. Polycarp, in the midst of the presbyters who, like Polycarp, have " conversed with St. John and the other witnesses of the Saviour " ; and he must have spent in Asia more than the years of his youth. Towards the year 155, he is in Rome, at the time when St. Justin is teaching there. When the persecution of Marcus Aurelius breaks out, the Church of Lyons, to whose *presbyterium* Irenæus belongs, sends him to Rome as the bearer of a letter from the confessors of Lyons to Pope Eleutherius. On his return from Rome, he is made Bishop of Lyons (177-8). It is at Lyons that Irenæus composes his great work in five books against the Gnostics: the first three books date from the time of Pope Eleutherius, probably from the period 180-9; the last two were composed during the time of Pope Victor (189-98). This great work is not a Περὶ ἐκκλησίας, the title of a book, now lost, by Melito, Bishop of Sardis; but, whilst refuting the Gnostic error, it expounds the theory of the Church and of her doctrinal function with such fullness and firmness that the third book is a veritable treatise on the Church, and the oldest in existence.[1]

\*\*\*

The first point we notice in the ecclesiology of Irenæus is the importance he ascribes to the diffusion of Christianity and to the unity of faith maintained in this dispersion. True, this point is not new; but under the pen of Irenæus it attains to the value of an argument, and no one before him had set it forth with such eloquence.

The Church, dispersed all over the world and reaching its utmost boundaries, has one and the same rule of faith, of which Irenæus mentions successively the various articles: one God, Father Almighty; one Jesus Christ, son of God, become man for our salvation; the Holy Ghost, which announced through the Prophets the designs of God; the incarnation, virginal conception, passion, resurrection and ascension of the well-beloved Jesus Christ our Lord, His future return for the restoration of all things and for the bodily resurrection of mankind.

[1] To the treatise " Adversus hæreses " we must add the small treatise in Armenian recently found, Εἰς ἐπίδειξιν τοῦ ἀποστολικοῦ κηρύγματος, and published in 1907 : K. TER MEKERTTSCHIAN and E. TER MINASSIANTZ, "Des heil. Irenäus Schrift zum Erweise der apostolischen Verkündigung (Leipzig, 1907). The " Demonstratio " (as we shall call it), is subsequent to the " Adv. hær." to which it refers the reader (ch. 99).

This is the rule or canon of the faith that is professed everywhere,[1] as though the Church, spread in the vast universe, dwelt in but one house. Each one of the faithful, on the day of baptism, binds himself to profess this faith;[2] and thus the Church has but one heart, one soul, one voice, one mouth. There are many languages, indeed, in the world, but the tradition is one. Churches have been founded in Germany, but their faith does not differ from ours; the same is to be said of the Churches in Spain and in Gaul, in the East and in Egypt, in Libya and in Judæa.[3] Just as the sun, God's creature, is the same for the whole universe, so too the preaching of the truth is the Light that shines everywhere and enlightens all those who are willing to know it. The most eloquent bishops—for the bishops are at the head of the Churches, "*praesunt ecclesiis*,"—can teach nothing else, nor can the least important among them lessen it in any way:[4] so is it in the Church which is established every-

---

[1] "Haer." I. 10, 1 : " Ecclesia enim per universum orbem usque ad fines terrae disseminata, et ab apostolis et a discipulis eorum accepit eam fidem quae est unum Deum, patrem omnipotentem. . . . " For the parallel passages in Irenæus, cf. HAHN, " Bibliothek der Symbole," pp. 6-8. Add " Demonstr." 6.

[2] "Haer." I. 9, 4 : " Regulam veritatis immobilem ($\kappa \alpha \nu \acute{o} \nu \alpha \ \tau \hat{\eta} s \ \dot{\alpha} \lambda \eta$-$\theta \epsilon \acute{\iota} \alpha s \ \dot{\alpha} \kappa \lambda \iota \nu \hat{\eta}$) . . . , quam per baptismum accepit [quisque]." Cf. III. 11, 1 ; 15, 1, and " Demonstr." 6. The expression *regula fidei* or $\kappa \alpha \nu \grave{\omega} \nu \ \tau \hat{\eta} s$ $\dot{\alpha} \lambda \eta \theta \epsilon \acute{\iota} \alpha s$ does not strictly and always designate the baptismal symbol, but the faith common to all the Churches, the tradition. For Irenæus, cf. the remarks of KATTENBUSCH, vol. II. p. 31 and foll. Cf. VOIGT, " Eine verschollene Urkunde des antimontanistischen Kampfes " (Leipzig, 1891), pp. 185-207.

[3] Irenæus does not use the word Judæa ; he says : $\alpha i \ \kappa \alpha \tau \grave{\alpha} \ \mu \acute{\epsilon} \sigma \alpha$ $\tau o \hat{v} \ \kappa \acute{o} \sigma \mu o v$. Christians thought that Judæa and Jerusalem were at the centre of the world.

[4] "Haer." I. 10, 2 : " Hanc praedicationem cum acceperit et hanc fidem, quemadmodum praediximus, Ecclesia, et quidem in universum mundum disseminata, diligenter custodit, quasi unam domum inhabitans, et similiter credit iis, videlicet quasi unam animam habens et unum cor, et consonanter haec praedicat et docet et tradit quasi unum possidens os. Nam etsi in mundo loquelae dissimiles sunt, sed tamen virtus traditionis una et eadem est. Et neque hae quae in GERMANIA sunt fundatae ecclesiae aliter credunt aut aliter tradunt, neque hae quae in HIBERIS sunt, neque hae quae in CELTIS, neque hae quae in ORIENTE, neque hae quae in ÆGYPTO, neque hae quae in LIBYA, neque hae quae in medio mundi constitutae : sed sicut sol, creatura Dei, in universo mundo unus et idem

where: "*Ea quae est in quoquo loco Ecclesia universa*".[1]
If the word "catholic" is missing both in the vocabulary of
Irenæus and in that of his Latin translator, he has the
thing.[2]

\* \*
\*

Unity and Catholicity are merely human facts, unless the
faith has its source in the teaching of the Prophets, of the
Lord, and of the Apostles. Irenæus sets in strong relief
this trilogy, so often pointed out by others before him.[3]   By
Prophets, he means also the .Law, "*legislationis ministratio*"; as to the Apostles, he distinguishes between their
preaching, which was oral, and their "dictatio," the testament which they dictated.   " Quoniam autem dictis nostris
consonat praedicatio apostolorum, et Domini magisterium, et
prophetarum annuntiatio, et apostolorum dictatio, et legislationis ministratio, unum eumdemque omnium Deum Patrem
fundantium. . . ."[4]

The only true and Vivifying faith is that which the
Church has received from the Apostles and now distributes

est, sic et lumen, praedicatio veritatis, ubique lucet et illuminat omnes
homines qui volunt ad cognitionem veritatis venire.   Et neque is qui
valde praevalet in sermone ex iis qui praesunt ecclesiis, alia quam haec
sunt dicet, . . . neque infirmus in dicendo deminorabit traditionem."—
See also "Haer." II. 31, 2, III. 4, 1, III. 11, 8, V. 20, 1-2 and "Demonstr." 98.

[1] "Haer." II. 31, 2.   Cf. "Demonstr." 98.

[2] HARNACK, "Dogmeng." vol. I. p. 371.   However, Irenæus writes
("Haer." III. 11, 8): ἐπειδὴ τέσσαρα κλίματα τοῦ κόσμου ἐν ᾧ ἐσμὲν εἰσί,
καὶ τέσσαρα καθολικὰ πνεύματα.   The Latin translator says : "Quatuor
*principales* spiritus ".

[3] "Haer." II. 2, 6 :  " Iam quidem ostendimus unum esse Deum : ex
ipsis autem apostolis et ex Domini sermonibus adhuc ostendemus.   Quale
enim est, prophetarum et Domini et apostolorum relinquentes nos voces,
attendere his [ = *haereticis*] nihil sani dicentibus ? " III. 9, 1 : " Ostenso
hoc igitur plane . . . neminem alterum . . . Deum, neque prophetas,
neque apostolos, neque Dominum Christum, confessum esse." III. 17, 4 :
" Spiritu . . . uno et eodem existente, sicut et ipse Dominus testatur,
et apostoli confitentur, et prophetae annuntiant."

[4] [II. 35, 4].   A favourite expression of Irenæus.   Cf. II. 30, 9 :
" Deus . . . quem et Lex annuntiat, quem prophetae praeconant, quem
Christus revelat, quem Apostoli tradunt, quem Ecclesia credit."   This
insistence in bringing together the Old and the New Testament is motived
apparently by his purpose of refuting Marcionism.

to her children; for the Lord has given His Gospel to His Apostles: "*Qui vos audit me audit, qui vos contemnit me contemnit et eum qui misit me*". Hence the mission of the Apostles as teachers cannot be questioned: from them we obtain the truth, i.e. the doctrine of the Son of God.[1]

In the case of the Gospels, one sees at once the importance Irenæus attaches to the fact that they were composed by the Apostles or by writers whose authority is vouched for by the Apostles. Matthew and John were Apostles: John composed his Gospel during his stay at Ephesus; Matthew wrote his Gospel in Hebrew, at the time when Peter and Paul "*Romae euangelizarent et fundarent Ecclesiam*". Mark was one of Peter's disciples, and his interpreter; he has put down in writing what Peter preached. Luke was of the number of Paul's companions, and he in like manner has written down the Gospel preached by Paul (III. 1, 1). This short literary history of the Gospel is a justification of their Apostolic authority.[2]

Irenæus, who like his contemporaries, has a pronounced taste for symbolism, finds a connexion between the four Gospels and the expansion of the Church over the whole world. As there are four winds of heaven, so there are four Gospels:[3] these four Gospels are the four pillars of the Church, which has for her foundation the spirit that inspired the Gospel; this Spirit breathes life into mankind by means of the Church.

The unwritten teaching of the Apostles has for its witness the teaching of the "presbyters," i.e. of the immediate

---

[1] "Haer." III. *praef.* : "Dominus omnium dedit apostolis suis potestatem euangelii, per quos et veritatem, hoc est Dei filii doctrinam, cognovimus." Cf. III. 1, 1, and "Demonstr." 41.

[2] This authentication of the four Gospels is not peculiar to Irenæus : it is found already in Papias, *ap.* EUSEB. "H. E." III. 39, 15-16, also in Clement of Alexandria, who did not know Irenæus. "Hypotyp." *ap.* EUSEB. "H. E." II. 15. Likewise, in the "Muratorianum". We have here, together with a valuable tradition, a thesis of apologetics.

[3] "Haer." III. 11, 8 : "Quoniam quatuor regiones mundi sunt in quo sumus, et quatuor principales spiritus, et disseminata est Ecclesia super omnem terram, columna autem et firmamentum Ecclesiae est euangelium et spiritus vitae, consequens est quatuor habere eam columnas, undique flantes incorruptibilitatem et vivificantes homines."

disciples of the Apostles.[1]   Thus, as to the question whether the ministry of Jesus lasted only one year, as is supposed by the Valentinian Ptolemy, we must believe the Gospel and the "presbyters," who tell us that Jesus was baptized when he was about 30 years old, and was still teaching at the age of about 50.   By πρεσβύτεροι or *seniores* Irenæus designates here the elders who have known St. John in Asia and who witness that such was truly on this point the teaching of the Apostle, the Lord's disciple.[2]   But the word "presbyters" has a wider meaning, for it designates also those who in the Church are the depositaries both of the living authority and of the doctrine inherited from the Apostles.

[IV. 32, 1.]   "Omnis sermo ei constabit, si et scripturas diligenter legerit apud eos qui in Ecclesia sunt presbyteri apud quos est apostolica doctrina, quemadmodum demonstravimus."

Any one, provided he be even slightly attentive, can behold in every Church the transmission of the Apostolic doctrine, authenticated by the actual bishops who date back from the Apostles through a continuous and ascertainable succession.

[III. 3, 1.]   "Traditionem itaque apostolorum in toto mundo manifestatam, in omni ecclesia adest respicere omnibus qui vera velint videre : et habemus annumerare eos qui ab apostolis instituti sunt episcopi, et successores eorum usque ad nos. . . ."

The Apostles are the "*dodecastylum firmamentum Ecclesiae*," a foundation laid by Christ Himself.[3]   It behoves us to adhere to their legitimate successors, who preserve their doctrine, and who have received together with the order of

---

[1] "Demonstr." 3 : "Der Glaube ist es nun, der dies in uns veranlasst, wie die Aeltesten, die Schüler der Apostel, uns überliefert haben ".

[2] "Haer." II. 22, 5 : ". . . Sicut euangelium et omnes seniores testantur, qui in Asia apud Ioannem discipulum Domini convenerunt, id ipsum tradidisse eis Ioannem.   Permansit autem cum eis [*Ioannes*] usque ad Traiani tempora.   Quidam autem eorum non solum Ioannem, sed et alios apostolos viderunt, et haec eadem ab ipsis audierunt, et testantur de huiusmodi relatione.   Quibus magis oportet credi ?   Utrumne his talibus, an Ptolemaeo, qui apostolos nunquam vidit, vestigium autem apostoli ne in somniis quidem assecutus est ? "

[3] "Haer." IV. 21, 3.

the presbyterate the secure charism of truth.[1]    There is no truth outside the teaching of the Apostles, no teaching of the Apostles outside Catholicism, no Catholicism outside the episcopal succession.

It would be too long to enumerate the episcopal lists of all the Churches, writes Irenæus ;[2] it will suffice to recall the list of a Church which is the greatest, most ancient and best known of all Churches, that founded by the two glorious Apostles, Peter and Paul, the Church of Rome.    For, after founding and organizing this Church, the Blessed Apostles left its government in the hands of Linus who was succeeded by Anacletus.    The third to receive the episcopate after the Apostles was Clement, who had seen the Apostles and conversed with them, who had heard the very sound of their preaching, and himself beheld their tradition.    After Clement came Evaristus, then Alexander, Sixtus, Telesphorus who died a martyr, Hyginus, Pius, Anicetus, and Soter ; the twelfth successor of the Apostles, Eleutherius, is now the

---

[1] "Haer." IV. 26, 2 : "Eis qui in Ecclesia sunt presbyteris obaudire oportet, his qui successionem habent ab apostolis, . . . qui cum episcopatus successione charisma veritatis certum . . . acceperunt ; reliquos vero qui absistunt a principali successione et quocunque loco colligunt, suspectos habere, vel quasi haereticos et malae sententiae, vel quasi scindentes et elatos et sibi placentes." *Ibid.* 4 : "Ab omnibus igitur talibus absistere oportet, adhaerere vero his qui et apostolorum, sicut praediximus, doctrinam custodiunt, et cum presbyterii ordine sermonem sanum. . . ." *Ibid.* 5 : "Ubi igitur charismata Domini posita sunt, ibi discere oportet veritatem, apud quos est ea quae ab apostolis Ecclesiae successio. . . ."

The remarkable expression "*charisma veritatis certum*" has a parallel in the preface of the "Philosophoumena" ("P. G." vol. XVI. p. 3020). Gnostic errors will be refuted by the Holy Spirit which is transmitted in the Church, which the Apostles first received, which they imparted to the faithful, and which we, their successors, possess together with their priesthood and their *magisterium*, since we are the guardians of the Church :
Ταῦτα δὲ ἕτερος οὐκ ἐλέγξει ἢ τὸ ἐν ἐκκλησίᾳ παραδοθὲν ἅγιον πνεῦμα, οὗ τυχόντες, πρότεροι οἱ ἀπόστολοι μετέδοσαν τοῖς ὀρθῶς πεπιστευκόσιν, ὧν ἡμεῖς διάδοχοι τυγχάνοντες τῆς τε αὐτῆς χάριτος μετέχοντες ἀρχιερατείας τε καὶ διδασκαλίας καὶ φρουροὶ τῆς ἐκκλησίας λελογισμένοι.

[2] "Haer." III. 3, 2-3.   Irenæus probably means to say that this was done elsewhere and by some one else, and we naturally think of Hegesippus.

Roman *episcopus*.[1] This succession is the channel through which the tradition of the Church and the message of truth have come down to us.

After this appeal to the testimony of the Roman Church, which he has some reason to know well and some reason to esteem more highly than any other Church, Irenæus cites the Church of Smyrna, where in his youth, he knew St. Polycarp, who had been taught by the Apostles and had conversed with the immediate witnesses of the Lord: Polycarp, he says, professed to teach what he held from the Apostles, as is witnessed by the Churches of Asia and by the bishops who have succeeded Polycarp in the see of Smyrna. What has been thus established concerning Rome and Smyrna may be generalized. We must conclude then that the Church has authority because she preserves the authentic heritage of the faith of the Apostles.

[III. 4, 1.] "Tantae igitur ostensiones cum sint, non oportet adhuc quaerere apud alios veritatem, quam facile est ab Ecclesia sumere, cum apostoli, quasi in depositorium dives, plenissime in eam contulerint omnia quae sint veritatis. . . . Et si de aliqua modica quaestione disceptatio esset, nonne oporteret in antiquissimas recurrere ecclesias, in quibus apostoli conversati sunt, et ab eis de praesenti quaestione sumere quod certum et re liquidum est?"

* * *

The Church is "the Church of God".[2] She is a body of which the Word is the head, as the Father is the head of

---

[1] Regarding the origin of this Roman chronology, see the note in DUCHESNE, "Histoire ancienne," t. I, p. 92. Even supposing that the Roman episcopal list was drawn up at Rome by Hegesippus, in the time of Anicetus, towards the year 160, and that for this point Irenæus depends on Hegesippus, this episcopal list is equally valuable. For a good discussion of Harnack's paradox about the late (under Anicetus?) establishment of the monarchical episcopate at Rome, cf. J. TURMEL, "Hist. du dogme de la papauté" (Paris, 1908) who concludes in the same sense as Mgr. DUCHESNE and H. BÖHMER, "Zur altrömischen Bischofsliste," in the "Zeitschrift für die neut. Wissenschaft, 1906," pp. 333-9. See also MICHIELS, "Origine de l'épiscopat," pp. 306-36 and Dom J. CHAPMAN, "La chronologie des premières listes épiscopales de Rome," in the "Revue bénédictine," XVIII. (1901), pp. 399-417, XIX. (1902), pp. 13-37 and 145-70.

[2] "Haer." I. 6, 3, and 13, 5.

Christ: the Holy Ghost is in each one of her members.[1] There is, then, between the Father, the Son, the Holy Ghost, and the faithful of the Church, such real and unseen communication that what St. Paul writes of the Church invisible is true of the Church visible. The Church visible is that through which we belong to the invisible Church, and we belong to the Church visible through our adhesion to the Apostolic teaching continued by the bishops of the Catholic world : "*Agnitio vera est apostolorum doctrina, et antiquus Ecclesiae status in universo mundo, et character corporis Christi, secundum successiones episcoporum, quibus illi [apostoli] eam quae in unoquoque loco est ecclesiam trdiderunt*".[2] The Catholic Church is something organic, τὸ ἀρχαῖον τῆς ἐκκλησίας σύστημα, and, thus it has the character of Christ's body. Schism is a sin which on the day of the last judgment the Holy Ghost will judge most severely : woe to any one who sacrifices unity ! woe to him who rends Christ's glorious body ! The Spirit will judge all those who are outside truth, i.e. outside the Church.[3]

The Spirit aids the Church. If the preaching of the latter is so constant, it is because the Spirit of God renews its youth, as an exquisite deposit preserved in a goodly vessel, and the Spirit of God keeps the vessel itself from becoming old.[4] The Spirit is the gift made by God to His Church, just as God imparted breath to Adam, His creature, in order that that breath might vivify his members.

---

[1] " Haer." v. 18, 2.

[2] *Ibid.* IV. 33, 8. In Greek : γνῶσις ἀληθὴς ἡ τῶν ἀποστόλων διδαχή, καὶ τὸ ἀρχαῖον τῆς ἐκκλησίας σύστημα κατὰ παντὸς τοῦ κόσμου. ORIGEN, " Contra Cels." III. 7 and 31, speaks in the same sense of the σύστασις of Christians. He admires their incredible organization : παραδόξως συστάντας χριστιανούς. *Id.* VIII. 47. SOHM ("Kirchenrecht," p. 202), translates σύστημα " die Körperschaft, die organisierte Gesamtheit der Ekklesia ". See his note on this text.

[3] " Haer." IV. 33, 7 : " [Spiritus Dei] iudicabit . . . eos qui schismata operantur, qui sunt inanes, non habentes Dei dilectionem suamque utilitatem potius considerantes quam unitatem Ecclesiae, et propter modicas ei quaslibet causas magnum et gloriosum corpus Christi conscindunt et dividunt et quantum in ipsis est interficiunt. . . . Iudicabit autem et omnes eos qui sunt extra veritatem, id est qui sunt extra Ecclesiam."

" Haer.," III. 24, 1.

" In ea[1] disposita est communicatio Christi, id est Spiritus sanctus, arrha incorruptelae et confirmatio fidei nostrae et scala ascensionis ad Deum. *In ecclesia enim*, inquit, *posuit Deus apostolos, prophetas, doctores* [1 Cor. xii. 28], et universam reliquam operationem Spiritus, cuius non sunt participes omnes qui non currunt ad Ecclesiam, sed semetipsos fraudant a vita per sententiam malam et operationem pessimam. Ubi enim Ecclesia ibi et Spiritus Dei, et ubi Spiritus Dei illic Ecclesia et omnis gratia: Spiritus autem veritas. Quapropter qui non participant eum, neque a mammillis matris nutriuntur in vitam, neque percipiunt de corpore Christi procedentem nitidissimum fontem ".[2]

What Christ gives us through the Church is the Holy Ghost, which is for us a pledge of incorruptibility, the confirmation of our faith, the ladder by which we ascend to God. Outside the Church, there can be no share in the Spirit; but where the Church is, there is also the Spirit of God. Where the Spirit of God is, there is the Church, and the Spirit is Truth.

In Irenæus, we find none of the apocalyptic views of Hermas or of the " Secunda Clementis ".[3] The Church is a number; she is a people; she is a church of churches, that is as visible as the pillar of salt into which Lot's wife was changed, and, notwithstanding all kinds of trials, remains incorruptible, the true salt of the earth, still better, a living statue whose limbs grow again after they have been lopped off.[4]

---

[1] The text reads *in eo*, (MASSUET). I read *in ea*, referring *ea* to the Church.

[2] " Haer. " iii. 24, 1. Cf. ii. 32, 4.

[3] Cf. " Demonstr." 26, and " Haer." iv. 8, i. and v. 20, 2. No pre-existence, only figures are affirmed.

[4] " Haer." v. 34, 3 : " Quoniam autem repromissiones non solum prophetis et patribus, sed ecclesiis ex gentibus coadunatis annuntiabuntur, quas et insulas nuncupat spiritus, et quod in medio turbulae sint constitutae, et tempestatem blasphemiarum sufferant, et salutaris portus periclitantibus existant, et refugium sunt eorum qui altitudinem *ament* et bythum id est profundum erroris conantur effugere." Instead of *ament*, we should like to read *amentiae*. This comparison of churches to islands that possess safe havens is also found in THEOPHILUS OF ANTIOCH " Ad Autolyc." ii. 14.

[IV. 31, 3.] "Et cum haec fierent, uxor remansit, in Sodomis, iam non caro corruptibilis, sed statua salis semper manens, et, per naturalia ea quae sunt consuetudinis hominis, ostendens quoniam et Ecclesia quae est sal terrae subrelicta est in confinio terrae patiens quae sunt humana; et, dum saepe auferuntur ab ea membra integra, perseverat statua salis, quod est firmamentum fidei, firmans et praemittens filios ad patrem ipsorum." [1]

Let us not pass without due attention over these few lines of uninviting Latin; and let us be grateful to one who, though born in Asia, was a citizen of Lyon, for discovering this expressive symbol of the stability, the miraculous and indefectible life of the Church.

*  *
*

A last element in which the ecclesiology of Irenæus agrees with that of his predecessors is in the place he assigns to the Roman Church.

As we have seen already, he gives her the name of "*maximae, et antiquissimae, et omnibus cognitae, a gloriosissimis duobus apostolis Petro et Paulo Romae fundatae et constitutae ecclesiae*".[2] The same thought he expresses in words that are still more emphatic and well known.[3]

[III. 3, 2.] "Ad hanc enim Ecclesiam propter potentiorem principalitatem necesse est omnem convenire ecclesiam, hoc est eos qui sunt undique fideles, in qua semper ab his qui sunt undique conservata est ea quae est ab apostolis traditio.

The original Greek text of this phrase is missing; so that we have here only a translation with the risk of its

[1] Irenæus is alluding to the Haggadic legend according to which the statue of Lot's wife had its periods like a living woman, and its members grew again after being broken.

[2] "Haer." III. 3, 2.

[3] Cf. FUNK, "Der Primat der röm. K. nach Ignatius und Irenäus," in his "Kircheng. Abhandlungen," vol. I. pp. 12-23. HARNACK, "Das Zeugniss des I. über das Ansehen der röm. K." in the "Sitzungsberichte" of the Berlin Academy, 1893, pp. 939-55. Dom CHAPMAN, "Le témoignage de S. I. en faveur de la primauté romaine," "Revue bénédictine," vol. XII. (1895), pp. 49-64. Dom MORIN, "Une erreur de copiste dans le texte d'Irénée sur l'église romaine," "Revue bénéd," vol. xxv. (1908), pp. 515-20.

being more or less inexact in its renderings, a risk not lessened by the fact that this Latin translation is quite old, dating perhaps from the time of Tertullian.[1]

*Ad hanc ecclesiam necesse est omnem convenire ecclesiam.* The necessity of which St. Irenæus speaks is that of a logical conclusion.[2] He does not mean that every Church must agree with the Roman Church merely in the sense that every Church, in as far as it preserves the Apostolic tradition intact, will agree *ipso facto* with the Roman Church; for, by this interpretation, we take all the strength out of such a strong expression as *convenire ad*, which suggests the idea of an active step taken to find the truth.[3]

*Omnem ecclesiam, hoc est eos qui sunt undique fideles.*

The expression *hoc est* ushers in an explanatory periphrasis, and we naturally expect that Irenæus should pronounce the word " catholic ": but strange as that omission may appear, the word " catholic,"—as has been already noted —is not found in the terminology of Irenæus. The faithful will come to Rome from every place, *undique*, an allusion to the Christians who, from all the Churches of the world, direct their steps towards Rome, like Polycarp, Abercius, Irenæus himself, and so many others during the second century.[4]

*Omnem ecclesiam . . . in qua.* Every Church will agree with the Roman Church, every Church in which. . . . Harnack, Mgr. Duchesne and Funk think that *in qua* refers, not to the Roman Church, as has been long thought, but to the

---

[1] H. JORDAN, " Das Alter der lat. Uebers. des Hauptwerkes des Ir." (Leipzig, 1908), p. 60, ascribes it to the latter part of the fourth century.

[2] Compare " Haer." v. 20, 1 : " Necessitatem ergo habent praedicti haeretici," and v. 30, 1 : ἔπειτα . . . ἐμπέσειν ἀνάγκη.

[3] HARNACK, " Dogmeng." vol. I⁴, p. 488, after observing that Polycarp deemed it most important to agree with Anicetus, and for that purpose made his journey to Rome ; adds : " It was not Anicetus who came to Polycarp, but Polycarp to Anicetus. This is also the meaning we attach to *convenire ad* (συντρέχειν). We may recall III. 4, 1 : " Si de aliqua modica quaestione disceptatio esset, nonne *oporteret* in antiquissimas *recurrere ecclesias*, in quibus apostoli conversati sunt ? "

[4] About these pilgrims of the second century, like St. Justin, Rhodon, Tatian, Irenæus, Abercius, Polycarp, Hegesippus, Tertullian, etc., cf. C. P. CASPARI, " Quellen zur Geschichte des Taufsymbols," vol. III. (Christiania, 1875), pp. 336-48, and HARNACK, " Mission," vol. I. pp. 311-12.

Churches other than that of Rome.   It seems to me that Dom Morin's correction authorises us to understand *in qua* as referring to the Roman Church.[1]

*In qua semper ab his qui [sunt undique] conservata est ea quae est ab apostolis traditio.*   Dom Morin has luminously shown that *sunt undique* is due to a copyist's error: these two words have been substituted for other words that designated the leaders of the Churches (*praesunt ecclesiis?*) or rather the presbyters who have presided at Rome (*præsident*).

*Propter potentiorem principalitatem.*   The adjective used in the comparative implies that the *principalitas* is an attribute that belongs, not exclusively, but pre-eminently to the Roman Church.   What is, then, this *principalitas* which other Churches possess?   We must carefully abstain from ascribing to the word a meaning that would not be in keeping with the argument of St. Irenæus.   Hence we shall not translate it by πρωτεία because that word does not take with it any comparative;[2] nor by ἡγεμονία because that is a term which Irenæus uses always in a genealogical sense;[3] nor by πλήρωμα, which the translator of Irenæus renders at times by *principalitas*, but which, properly speaking, designates the Gnostic pleroma.[4]   Some have suggested the word αὐθεντία, in this sense that the Roman Church is more authentic than any other Apostolic Church, since it was founded by the two glorious Apostles, Peter and Paul.   To this origin she owes her ἱκανωτέραν αὐθεντίαν, which requires that all Churches shall go to her and take their pattern from her.[5]

At all events, the authority which Irenæus sees in the

---

[1] Compare " Haer." III. 3, 1 : " Traditionem apostolorum in toto mundo manifestatam, in omni ecclesia adest respicere ".   Here we have again the expression *omnis ecclesia*, synonymous with *unaquaeque ecclesia*.

[2] " Haer." IV. 38, 3 : " Principalitatem habet in omnibus Deus quoniam et solus infectus et prior omnium " (πρωτεύει ἐν πᾶσιν ὁ θεός).

[3] Thus, Adam is the head of mankind, he is the " principalis plasmatio ".   " Haer." V. 14, 1 and 2.   Likewise III. 11, 8 : " Primum animal principale " (πρῶτον ζῶον ἡγεμονικόν).

[4] " Haer." IV. 35, 2 and 4.   Cf. I. 26, 1, and 31, 1.

[5] The word αὐθεντία signifies also power, domination, and in 1 Tim. II. 12, αὐθεντεῖν is used in that remarkable sense.   Cf. DEISSMANN, " Licht vom Osten," p. 56.

Catholic Church as such, and inasmuch as she is the safe depositary of the tradition that goes back to the Apostles, he sees still more manifestly in the Roman Church. He has said: " *Oportet confugere ad Ecclesiam,*" meaning the Church which is "*in universo mundo,*" and which preserves "*firmam ab apostolis traditionem*".[1] He says in like words: "*Necesse est ad hanc ecclesiam* [*romanam*] *convenire omnem ecclesiam*". "It would be difficult," Mgr. Duchesne writes, "to meet with a clearer assertion, (1) of unity of doctrine in the universal Church, (2) of the unique importance of the Church of Rome, as witness, guardian and organ of the Apostolic tradition, (3) of her superior pre-eminence over the whole of Christianity."[2]

*
* *

The Church being for Irenæus the institution, of historical fact and divine right, which we have just described, heresy is at once characterized. The Church did not organize and, as it were, arm herself, by way of reaction against Gnosticism. It is much more in keeping with facts to say that Gnosticism was a formation incompatible with the Church, which sprang from a reaction against the Church.

Indeed, if we set aside the popular and extravagant forms[3] it assumed here and there, Gnosticism is, historically, an attempt on the part of intellectual Christians, some of them of an exceptional vigour of mind, to assert their right to speculate, to systematize, and to dogmatize, in the proper sense of that word, after the fashion of the pagan schools of philosophy. It is easy to realize that such a claim offends against the very notion of the faith received as a deposit, and the Gnostics themselves declare emphatically that it is so. The teaching of the Church, they say, is for the *simpliciores* only, to which Irenæus replies that, whilst that is perfectly true, yet it is far better for any one to be simple and unlearned, provided he be near God through charity,

---

[1] " Haer." v. 20, 2.        [2] " Eglises Séparées," p. 119.

[3] In connexion with the Ophians (or Ophites), ORIGEN, " Contra Cels." VI. 28, charges Celsus with taking for a Christian sect an aggregation of people who had nothing at all in common with Christianity (cf. CLEMENT, "Stromat." III. 2).

than to know much and blaspheme God as do the Gnostics.[1] We have then before us the antithesis of two methods, one secular, the other ecclesiastical, and we find in Gnosticism a criticism of Catholicism.

The Valentinians feel pity for the adherents of the Church: they treat the Catholics as common people and " ecclesiastics "; and yet they do their best to seduce those *simpliciores*, by clothing their ideas in ecclesiastical language, " *nostrum tractatum*," says Irenæus, for there is such a language. If difficulties are raised against their tenets, if any one dares to contradict their statements, they resume their supercilious demeanour and declare that Catholics do not understand the truth, that they have received none of the higher seeds of the " Mother," and are mere *psychics*.[2] The Gnostics are the perfect, the seeds of election: the Catholics are illiterate and ignorant. To the psychics [3] belongs the naked faith; to the perfect, the perfect Gnosis.[4]

[1] " Haer." II. 26, 1: " Melius est ergo et utilius idiotas et parum scientes existere, et per charitatem proximum fieri Deo, quam putare multum scire et multa expertos in suum Deum blasphemos inveniri ".

[2] " Haer." III. 15, 2: " Hi enim [qui a Valentino sunt] ad multitu-dinem—propter eos qui sunt ab Ecclesia, quos communes ecclesiasticos ipsi dicunt—inferunt sermones per quos capiunt simpliciores et alliciunt eos, simulantes nostrum tractatum. . . . Et si aliquis quidem ex his qui audiunt eos quaerat solutiones vel contradicat eis, hunc quasi non capien-tem veritatem, et non habentem de superioribus a matre sua semen affir-mantes, in totum nihil dicunt ei, mediarum partium dicentes esse illum, hoc est psychicorum." Notice the word *communes* (κοινοί) taken as synonymous with καθολικοί. Cf. KATTENBUSCH, vol. II. p. 924.

[3] The adjective " psychic " is taken from St. Paul, 1 Cor. II. 14. In Jude 19, it is applied to the man who is not spiritual: ψυχικοὶ πνεῦμα μὴ ἔχοντες. The distinction was common in Greek Judaism. Cf. FRIEDLÄNDER, " Synagoge und Kirche," p. 74.

[4] " Haer." I. 6, 4: " Nos quidem, qui per timorem Dei timemus etiam usque in mentibus nostris et sermonibus peccare, arguunt quasi idiotas et nihil scientes, semetipsos extollunt, perfectos vocantes et semina electionis." *Ibid.* 2: " Erudiuntur psychica (id est animalia) psychici (id est animales) homines, qui per operationem et fidem nudam firmantur, et non perfectam agnitionem [=γνῶσιν] habent. Esse autem hos nos, qui sumus ab Ecclesia, dicunt." In confirmation of these words of Irenæus, see the same distinction between psychics and pneumatics in Heracleon cited by ORIGEN, " Comment. in Ioann." XIII. 16 and 50; it was known also to CELSUS, " Contra Cels." v. 61.

On the contrary, judged from the Catholic standpoint, the Gnostics are like Greek sophists, ever seeking after novelties.[1] Among them, there is no standard of truth, and, as each one makes his own doctrine for himself, they resemble the pagan schools of philosophy: "*Et contraria sibimet dogmata statuentes, sicut et gentilium philosophorum quaestiones*".[2] If this method is to be adopted, man will continue seeking, ever seeking, and never finding, since he has discarded of his own accord the true "*inventionis disciplina*".[3] Doctrinal inconstancy is the lot of Gnostics: they are sophists doomed for ever to variations of every sort, tossed about by the waves of their errors, having no rock whereon to rest their edifice, nothing but moving sand.[4] Irenæus already outlines the history of variations.

When reminded of the authority of Holy Writ, they find Holy Writ at fault in one way or another. Its text is uncertain, or the book quoted against them does not belong to the true canon, or Scripture contradicts Scripture, or in fine no one who is ignorant of the tradition can find out the truth. We have here an echo of the controversies stirred up by the Gnostic leaders as to the text and the canon, especially in the field of exegesis where they were so prolific; above all we have here a proof that a certain number of Gnostics came to acknowledge the principle that the letter is not self-sufficing, and that oral tradition does complete it and must do so.[5] But, whereas Catholics, when speaking of tradition, know well that there is but one tradition, viz. that of which the presbyters impersonally

---

[1] "Haer." I. 11, 5.    Cf. I. 18, 1, II. 17, 10, IV. 2, 2, v. 20, 2.

[2] *Ibid.* II. 27, 1.              [3] *Ibid.* 27, 2.    Cf. I. 21 ; 5, 31, 3.

[4] *Ibid.* III. 24, 2 : " Alienati a veritate, digne in omni volutantur errore, fluctuati ab eo, aliter atque aliter per tempora de eisdem sentientes, et nunquam sententiam stabilitam habentes, sophistae verborum magis volentes esse quam discipuli veritatis. Non enim sunt fundati super unam petram, sed super arenam habentem in seipsa lapides multos." Cf. II. 17, 10. The words " fundati super *unam* petram " may have been a reminiscence of Matt. XVI. 18.

[5] "Haer." III. 2, 1 : "Cum enim ex Scripturis arguuntur, in accusationem convertuntur ipsarum Scripturarum, quasi non recte habeant, neque sint ex auctoritate, et quia varie sint dictae, et quia non possit ex his inveniri veritas ab his qui nesciant traditionem. Non enim per litteras traditam illam, sed per vivam vocem ". Cf. I. 8, 1.

preserve the deposit, every heretic presents his own fancies under the cover of the tradition to which he appeals; and truth can no longer be recognized, if to-day we must recognize its presence in the system of Cerinthus, to-morrow in that of Valentinus, next in that of Basilides or of Marcion, all of which contradict one another.[1]   For can we imagine a truth that varies?

The Gnostics answer that these variations are stages on the way towards the definitive truth, which was neither possessed by the Apostles nor taught by the Lord.   Hence no appeal should be made to the tradition that goes back to the Apostles and is authoritatively preserved in the Churches through the succession of bishops or presbyters; for a Gnostic, after he has found the pure truth and reached the mystery that as yet had remained concealed, is more enlightened than the presbyters, or even than ·the Apostles themselves.[2]

This infatuated individualism, this reliance on human gnosis, this pretension to knowledge greater than that of the Apostles, is, from the ecclesiastical standpoint, ludicrous presumption.[3]   Irenæus feels the more justified in denouncing it, because he can oppose to the variations of the Gnostics the perpetuity and unity of the faith of the Church, as a sign of truth.[4]   Moreover, by its sophistical method, by its

---

[1] "Haer." III. 2, 1.   Cf. III. 16, 9, and 16, 4.   We have already noticed this argument in St. Justin, and noted with Puech that it was borrowed from the Greek schools of philosophy.

[2] "Haer." III. 2, 2 : "Cum autem ad eam iterum traditionem quae est ab apostolis, quae per successionem presbyterorum in ecclesiis custoditur, provocamus eos, adversantur traditioni, dicentes se non solum presbyteris, sed etiam apostolis existentes sapientiores, sinceram invenisse veritatem . . . et indubitate et intaminate et sincere absconditum scire mysterium. . . . Evenit itaque neque scripturis iam, neque traditioni consentire eos."

[3] See " Haer." III. 15, 2, in which the sarcastic remarks of Irenæus prelude Tertullian's irony.

[4] " Haer." III. 12, 7 : "Imperfectus igitur secundum hos [= haereticos] Petrus, imperfecti autem et reliqui apostoli, et oportebit eos reviviscentes horum fieri discipulos ut et ipsi perfecti fiant.   Sed hoc quidem ridiculum est.   Arguuntur vero isti [= haeretici], non quidem apostolorum, sed suae malae sententiae esse discipuli.   Propter hoc autem et variae sententiae sunt uniuscuiusque eorum recipientis errorem quemadmodum capiebat.

unrestrained criticism of the preaching of the Prophets, of
the teaching of the Lord, and of the tradition of the Apostles,
by its constant manipulation of the Scriptures, and its utter
disregard for the deposit preserved by the presbyters, Gnosticism proclaims itself an emancipation of the mind, an intellectual secularization.[1]  It prompts its followers to have
recourse to the religious wisdom of Homer, and, after the
heathen fashion, to crown the images of Jesus, Pythagoras,
Plato, and Aristotle.[2]  Harnack declares rightly that, taking
it as a whole, Gnosticism is "Greek society under a Christian
name".[3]  Still more precisely, is it a form of Christianity
which indulges in all the syncreticisms against which
Catholicism guards itself.

At the same time, and because the Church is from the
beginning a close union of souls and of churches in one and
the same authoritative faith, Gnosticism, by the very fact of
pretending to revise the faith, places itself beyond the pale
of the established unity.  Once the bond is broken, heresy
ceases to be able ever to bring about a lasting unity; it can
but found schools.  "There can be no doubt that the Gnostic
propaganda was seriously hindered by that inability to organize and govern Churches which is characteristic of all
philosophic systems of religion.  The Gnostic organization
of schools and mysteries was not able to contend with the

Ecclesia vero per universum mundum ab apostolis firmum habens initium,
in una et eadem de Deo et de filio eius perseverat sententia."  Cf. III. 12,
12 and I. 13, 6.

[1] "Haer." IV. 1, 1 : "Manifeste falsa ostenduntur ea quae dicunt
circumventores et perversissimi sophistae, . . . et perversi grammatici,
. . . doctrinam quidem Christi praetermittentes, et a semetipsis autem falsa
divinantes, adversus universam Dei dispositionem argumentantur."  Cf.
II. 14.

[2] "Haer." I. 9, 4.  Cf. IV. 33, 3 : "Accusabit autem eos Homerus
proprius ipsorum propheta, a quo eruditi talia invenerunt."  See the
curious passage, I. 25, 6, in which Irenæus upbraids the Gnostics—those
of the school of Carpocrates—for having portraits of Jesus, which they
say, were made by Pilate (dicentis formam Christi factam a Pilato,
illo in tempore quo fuit Jesus cum hominibus) : these portraits they
crown : "Et has coronant, et proponunt eas cum imaginibus mundi
philosophorum, videlicet cum imagine Pythagorae et Platonis et Aristotelis
et reliquorum, et reliquam observationem circa eas similiter ut gentes
faciunt."

[3] "Dogmeng." vol. I⁴, p. 250, note.  LOOFS, "Leitfaden," p. 105.

episcopal organization of the Catholic communities".[1] Wherever it appears, Gnosticism is a seceder: it detaches itself of its own accord. Hence we must say, not that the Church organizes herself to ward off Gnosticism, but rather that the Church is so constituted that Gnosticism cannot originate or abide freely and openly within her pale.

In fact, if we set aside the Marcionites, who, alone among the heretics of that period, possessed for many years Churches of their own, the Gnostics thought only of having disciples. Resuming an argument formerly used by Hegesippus and by St. Justin, Irenæus draws up the genealogy, the διαδοχή, of the heretics. This argument was doubtless the counterpart of that which Catholics drew from the διαδοχή, or the Apostolic succession of the bishops, and it was not without a touch of irony that orthodox writers connected the heretics with Simon Magus.[2] Nevertheless these genealogical lists of heretics—setting aside the legendary elements they contain—show how anxious the Gnostics were to appeal to some master, prompted however to this by a sentiment that was in no way ecclesiastical, but had come from the schools of sophists.[3]

As to the Church, the Gnostics not only depart from it, they also disfigure the idea of it. For them, the Church is an æon. The first principle discernible in the pleroma is the couple of Abyss and Silence, which brings forth the couple of Intelligence and Truth, which brings forth that of the Word and of Life, a third couple which in its turn brings forth that of Man and of the Church. From this ogdoad proceed the other æons, and at last Jesus, who alone will manifest Himself outside the invisible pleroma.[4] For some Gnostics, it is true, Adam is an image of the æon Man, and likewise the visible Church is an image of the æon Church:[5] for others,

---

[1] HARNACK, *Ibid.* p. 278.   SOHM affirms on the contrary that the heretics are Christianity not yet catholicized and represent the "old style" in face of Catholicism then in the period of its formation. "Kirchenrecht," p. 188-90.   Always the same a priori assumption.

[2] " Haer." I. 27, 4.          [3] CLEMENT, "Stromat." I. 14.

[4] " Haer." I. 1, 1-2.   Cf. 11, 1, and also " Philosophoumena," VI. 30, 43, 46, 51, 53, x. 13.

[5] " Haer." I. 5, 6 : ἐκκλησίαν εἶναι λέγουσιν ἀντίτυπον τῆς ἄνω ἐκκλησίας. ORIGEN, "Comment. in Ioan." x. 21 (" P. G." vol. XIV. p. 376), mentions

the union of the Father, the Son, and the Christ (the last is the son of the Father and of the Son) is the true and holy Church ;[1] for others, the æon Church is the archetype of the Virgin, the mother of Jesus, by the operation of the *Virtus altissimi*, which is the æon Man joined in the pleroma with the æon Church.

\* \*
\*

So much for the fanciful speculations of the Gnostics. We must now come back to Irenæus who looks upon Christendom as a Church of churches spread all over the immense world, but united together by one and the same faith.

This faith is based upon the Old Testament, the Lord, and the Apostles; the authenticity of the actual faith is guaranteed by the fact that the presbyters received it from the Apostles, and the bishops then living from the presbyters whom they have replaced through a succession that can be ascertained everywhere. The bishops possess the heritage of revealed truth.

The Church of churches is the Body of Christ. Wherever the visible and hierarchical Church is, there is the Spirit of God. The Church assisted by the Spirit is indefectible.

The Church of Rome, the most illustrious of all, is that by which all others must be ruled, on account of her *potentior principalitas*.

Heresy is illegitimate, because of its origin, its sophistical method, its variations, and its feebleness.

Irenæus's conception of Catholicism may be summed up in these leading ideas; but, as we have shown, this con-

---

Heracleon's view about the resurrection which is to take place in three days : the resurrection of matter on the first day, the psychic resurrection of the second day, the pneumatic resurrection on the third. The third day is that of the resurrection of the Church. This resurrection is preparing. Cf. *id.* XIII. 11 and 50. St. Hippolytus speaks of a three-fold Church imagined by some Gnostics (Naassenians) : the angelic, the psychic, and the material Church. " Philosophoum." v. 6. Cf. " Excerpt. Theodot." 21, 42, 56-9.

[1] " Haer." I. 30, 2 : " Esse autem hanc et veram et sanctam Ecclesiam ". Cf. *ibid.* 15, 3. Regarding the æon Church, cf. TERTULL. " Adv. Valentinianos," 25, 28, 39 ; " Praescr." 33 ; ORIGEN, "Contra Cels." VI. 34, 35. " Excerpt. Theodot." 13, 17, 26, 33, 40, 41.

ception of Catholicism does not date from Irenæus, nor is the institution thus described the product of the reaction of Christianity against Gnosticism.

## III.

It remains for us to group around the name of Irenæus certain facts that will show that Catholicism is to be found, not merely in the books of certain controversialists, but chiefly in the life of the Christian community. Of these facts, the first is Montanism.

We must begin by remarking that Montanism is a movement which was localized in Phrygia; it was an illuminist movement: the Paraclete speaks in the new prophets, Montanus, Prisca and Maximilla, and announces the end of the world; the heavenly Jerusalem is shortly to appear in the clouds, and come down to Phrygia, in a plain near Pepuza. Large crowds of Christians, both in Phrygia and in Asia, come eagerly to Pepuza, to hear the Paraclete. The memory of those prophecies will continue for many years to agitate the land of Phrygia: even in the time of St. Epiphanius, there were still some "Cataphrygians," and a local worship, of a most eccentric kind, which, every year, brought to Pepuza many pilgrims.

We must observe in the second place that, in so far as it is a kind of prophetic reawakening, Montanism is not an unexpected phenomenon. The belief in the persistency of prophetical charisms within the Church was in no way illegitimate: Christians were on their guard against false prophets, it is true, but they believed in prophets, and were convinced that true prophets were able to speak under the genuine inspiration of the Divine Spirit.[1] The "extraordinary ways" have always been part of God's action in His Church.

[1] See in H. WEINEL, "Die Wirkungen des Geistes und der Geister" (Freiburg, 1899), p. 71 and foll., an attempt at classifying the operations ascribed to the Spirit, during the post-apostolic age and during the second century. This work has at least the merit of showing the continuance of the action of the Spirit and of the "extraordinary ways" in the Christian community, before the rise of Montanism. The subject deserves to be taken up.

Hermas was, in his way, a prophet; he relates the allegorical visions he beholds, and the words he hears from the Lord and from the Angels. In one of his visions, he sees men sitting on a bench, and one man alone sitting on a chair: the former are some of the faithful; the latter is a pseudo-prophet, who has no share in the power of the Divine Spirit, a magician filled with the spirit of the devil. Now this pseudo-prophet is not, as one might be tempted to think, a Gnostic teacher: he is a wandering Christian, an alms-collector, a half-witted impostor.[1] Nevertheless he deceives the good souls whom the " Didachê " had already warned against these suspicious mendicants : " How, then, Lord," Hermas asks, " will a man know how to distinguish the true prophet from the false prophet? " The Lord answers : " You will recognize the man who has the Divine Spirit by his conduct ". The genuine prophet does not answer when he is questioned; he speaks when God wills it. When he who has the spirit of God comes into the assembly of the just who have the faith of the Spirit of God, and when all pray the Lord together, then it is that the angel of the prophetic Spirit that stands by him fills this man, who then speaks to the assembly of the brethren according as the Lord wills.[2] Hermas writes before the rise of Montanism in Phrygia, and therefore cannot allude here to the Montanist prophets.

[1] " Mandat. XI." 1-4. Compare Celsus in " Contra Celsum," VII. 9.

[2] *Ibid.* 7-9. These last words of the " Shepherd " have been found in one of the " Oxyrhynchus Papyri " (Part I, London, 1898) of GRENFELL and HUNT, accompanied with the following remark : Τὸ γὰρ προφητικὸν πνεῦμα τὸ σωματεῖόν ἐστιν τῆς προφητικῆς τάξεως, ὅ ἐστιν τὸ σῶμα τῆς σαρκὸς Ἰησοῦ Χριστοῦ, τὸ μιγὲν τῇ ἀνθρωπότητι διὰ Μαρίας. The προφητικὴ τάξις or *ordo propheticus* is the human body of Jesus Christ ; the prophetic Spirit is the σωματεῖον or essence of the προφητικὴ τάξις. Harnack considers this papyrus to be a remnant of a book or prophecy (of Melito ?) and the προφητικὴ τάξις to be a kind of *ordo propheticus* distinct from what St. Cyprian calls *ordo sacerdotalis*. See " Sitzungsberichte " of the Berlin Academy, 1898, pp. 516-20, and DE LABRIOLLE " La polémique antimontaniste," in " Revue d'hist. et de litt. relig." 1906, pp. 104-5. From this it would follow that the Pneumatics or Spirituals, are the true body of Christ. Later on we shall find in Origen an echo of this teaching, which shows how Christians even then were uncertain as to the relations between the Church and the Spirit.

St. Justin speaks of prophetic charisms as of a Divine gift which is continued in the Church, at a time when for long past the Jews have ceased to have any prophets.[1]

On the authority of a venerable presbyter whom he does not name, St. Irenæus denounces as false prophets those who are bold and unrestrained. Evidently Irenæus judges prophecy just as Hermas did, and his criterion is the same, viz. chiefly moral.[2] "We hear many brethren in the Church, who possess prophetic gifts, and who through the Spirit of God speak all kinds of languages, and bring to light for the general benefit the hidden things of men, and declare the mysteries of God."[3] These, he goes on to say, are called by the Apostle "spiritual men," for "they partake of the Spirit, the Spirit alone, and are not moved by the fraud of the flesh".[4] Irenæus speaks as though these prophets were his contemporaries.[5]

Bishops, then, were not uneasy at the continuation of prophetical charisms. As in the time of St. Paul, a prophet was judged first by his holiness of life, and then—but just as much—by his submission to the hierarchy. Recall the respect shown by Hermas for the Roman presbyters. It was no novelty the Montanists proclaimed when they said: "There must be charisms in the Church, and these must be received".[6] The novelty of the Montanists lay in their claiming to impose their own peculiar revelations as a supple-

---

[1] "Dialog." LXXXII. 1.          [2] "Haer." I. 13, 3-4.          [3] *Ibid.* v. 6, 1.

[4] *Ibid.* cf. PSEUDO-CLEMENT, "De virginit." I. 11. GAIUS quoted by EUSEB. "H. E." III. 28, 2, and 31, 4.

[5] For an instance of this, see what Irenæus says of the confessor Attalus and of his revelations, in the letter of the Lyonnese martyrs. St. Ignatius too has supernatural revelations. The Alexandrian Apelles, one of Marcion's disciples at Rome, publishes a book containing the φανερώσεις, i.e. the visions of a Roman prophetess, called Philumena. "Philosophoumena," x. 20. At the time of Pope Callistus, the Syrian Alcibiades circulates at Rome the so-called book of Elchasaï, which seems to be a sort of counterpart of the "Shepherd" of Hermas, and claims to be a revelation that was given in the third year of Trajan (an. 100). "Philosophoumena," IX. 13.

[6] EPIPH. "Haer." XLVIII. 2. In this chapter (XLVIII. 1-13) Epiphanius draws his information from a Roman document, of the time of Pope Callistus, and according to some (VOIGT, ROLFFS), the work of St. Hippolytus.

ment to the deposit of faith, and in their striving to obtain
credit for them by means of suspicious ecstasies and con-
vulsions.

The author referred to as the *Anonymous Antimon-
tanist* of Eusebius (an author who wrote about the years
192-3) describes the raptures of Montanus in these terms:
"Agitated by the spirits suddenly he became as one possessed and seized with a false ecstasy, and in his transports
took to uttering inarticulate sounds and strange words, and
to prophesy in a manner contrary to the constant custom
of the Church handed down by tradition from the beginning.
. . . The devil stirred up besides two women, and filled
them with the spirit of lies, so that they talked unintelligibly,
irrationally, and extravagantly, like the person already
mentioned."[1] By these transports, in which the so-called
prophet lost consciousness and spoke as though he were the
Spirit itself,[2] the Phrygian fanatics tended far more to dis-
credit every kind of prophetic charism, than to obtain credit
for their own prophecy. The way of the Spirit as it had
been "handed down by tradition from the beginning" was
not recognizable in those phenomena.

Hence from the very beginning Montanism was regarded with too much suspicion by the good sense of most of
the faithful, for it to be capable of creating a general crisis
motived by the antagonism between prophecy and hierarchy.[3]

We know of no synods of bishops held in Asia, for the
purpose of pronouncing on Montanism. All that we know
is that Serapion, who was Bishop of Antioch from about the

[1] Euseb. "H. E." v. 16, 7-9. Renan, "Marc Aurèle," p. 212:
"There was mixed with it also an orgiastic or corybantic element, peculiar
to the country, and entirely foreign to the orderly methods of ecclesiastical
prophecy, which were already subject to a tradition." One cannot without a smile find this same writer saying a little before "Mediocrity
founded authority. Catholicism began. . . . This was the first victory
of the Episcopate, and perhaps the most important, for it was obtained
over a sincere piety".

[2] See the oracles quoted by Epiphan. xlviii. 4.

[3] Euseb. "H. E." v. 16, 17, quotes an oracle of Maximilla, which
attests perhaps a spontaneous reaction brought on by her prophetism:
"I am driven away from the sheep like a wolf. I am not a wolf. I am
word and spirit and power."

year 190 to about the year 211, declares that "the new prophecy is rejected by all the brotherhood throughout the world"; [1] and that in confirmation of his words, he quotes a writing against the Montanists, composed by Apollinaris, Bishop of Hierapolis in Phrygia, and some letters of different bishops, two of whom belong to Thracia.

All Christendom arrayed itself silently against Montanism, in a reaction which was spontaneous and in which charity lost nothing.   Witness the letter of the Lyonnese "to the brethren throughout Asia and Phrygia, who hold the same faith," in the year 177.   "It was at the time," says Eusebius, "when the followers of Montanus, Alcibiades, and Theodotus in Phrygia were first giving circulation to their opinions on prophecy [2] . . . and as dissension arose concerning them, the brethren in Gaul expressed their own prudent and most orthodox judgment" in the form of several letters sent by the martyrs who were still in prison, "to the brethren throughout Asia and Phrygia, and also to Eleutherius, who was then Bishop of Rome, to procure the peace of the Churches".[3]

From the fact that Eusebius, who had read these letters, calls the judgment they passed on Montanism a "prudent and most orthodox judgment," we may infer that it fully agreed with the opinion that prevailed at Rome and in all Christendom.   The decision that had to be taken was complex : the principle of the supernatural working of the Spirit had to be safe-guarded ; but it had also to be properly defined.

Christians turned their eyes towards Rome.   Is it not to Rome, asks Harnack, that Irenæus addresses the expression of his views about the "new prophecy"?   And is it not to Rome that Praxeas comes from Asia, to lodge a protest against the representations of Irenæus? [4]   Again we must

[1] EUSEB. "H. E." v. 19, 2 : παρὰ πάσῃ τῇ ἐν κόσμῳ ἀδελφότητι.

[2] APOLLONIUS, the anti-Montanist writer, quoted by EUSEBIUS ("H. E." v. 18, 5) relates that a Montanist martyr, Themiso, "dared in imitation of the Apostle to write a certain Catholic Epistle," in which he "blasphemed against the Lord and the Apostles and the Holy Church" (καθολικήν τινα συνταξάμενος ἐπιστολήν).

[3] EUSEB. "H. E." v. 3, 4.

[4] HARNACK, "Dogmeng." vol. I⁴, p. 489.  BONWETSCH, art. "Montanismus," in HAUCK's "Realencykl." p. 425.

observe with Harnack, it was not Roman Montanists who were here concerned, but the Montanists of Phrygia and Asia who were soliciting recognition for their own persons and the principle of the " new prophecy " : to the judgment of Rome, then, they must have attached an exceptionally great importance, since they were so anxious to win over to their side her *potentior principalitas.*

*\* \**

When we come to Tertullian, we shall see Rome decide on the question of the prophecy; but before leaving Irenæus we have still to speak of another fact that throws much light on his ecclesiology, the fact of the Easter controversy.

Churches disputed among themselves as to the proper time for celebrating the feast of Easter. The Churches of the province of Asia, proconsular Asia, kept it, like the Jews, on the fourteenth of the first Jewish month, i.e. on the fourteenth of Nisan, on whatever day of the week that date might fall; at Rome, on the contrary, and in most other places, it was kept always on the Sunday following the fourteenth of Nisan. For the Asiatics, the feast of Easter marked the anniversary of Christ's death ; for the others, the anniversary of His resurrection.

The disagreement was very conspicuous, and the solidarity between the various Churches was such a daily reality that the religious authorities were necessarily anxious to do away with this disagreement. As we have seen, Polycarp, the Bishop of Smyrna, went to Rome to come to an understanding with Pope Anicetus; but Anicetus did not yield to the Asiatics, nor did Polycarp adopt the Roman custom. Even after this, however, essential agreement continued to subsist between the disputants. In the year 167, the Easter question having arisen at Laodicea, on what precise occasion we do not know, Apollinaris, Bishop of Hieraoplis, and Melito, Bishop of Sardis, intervened for the purpose of defending the Asiatic or Quartodeciman custom ; whence we may infer that the Church of Laodicea had been asked to give it up.[1] About the year 191, Pope Victor, whether of his own accord, or at the request of some Church, directly intervened in Asia.

[1] Laodicea of Phrygia, Sardis and Hierapolis belong to the province of Asia.

He wrote to the Bishop of Ephesus, asking him to assemble the Asiatic bishops, in order that they might settle the Easter controversy and adopt the universal custom. Polycrates wrote back a refusal based on considerations which are easily recognizable as the counterpart of those probably appealed to by the Bishop of Rome. Rome had doubtless made appeal to the Apostolic tradition, and to the Apostles Peter and Paul, whose tombs were in her territory, and to presbyters like Clement: to this Ephesus replied:[1] "It is we, who are faithful to tradition, neither adding nor taking away from it. For in Asia these great bases are resting in peace. . . ."[2] Among them are Philip, one of the twelve Apostles, who is buried at Hierapolis, and his two aged virgin daughters, and another daughter, who lived in the Holy Spirit, and now rests at Ephesus; and, moreover, John, who was both a martyr and a teacher (διδάσκαλος), who reclined upon the bosom of the Lord, and being a priest wore the πέταλον:[3] who is buried at Ephesus. And there is Polycarp in Smyrna, who was a bishop and a martyr; and Thraseas, bishop and martyr of Eumenia, who is buried at Smyrna. Why need I mention the bishop and martyr Sagaris who is buried at Laodicea, or the blessed Papirius, or Melito, the holy eunuch, who lived altogether in the Holy Spirit,[4] who lies in Sardis? . . . All these kept the Passover on the fourteenth day, according to the Gospel, making no innovation, but following the rule of faith.[5] And I also, Polycrates, the least of you all, do according to the tradition of my relatives, some of whom have been my

---

[1] EUSEB. "H. E." v. 24, 1-8.

[2] In Greek : μεγάλα στοιχεῖα. We have already met this word (above, p. 102) which signifies "elements". It might be better translated here by "lights" or "stars".

[3] The πέταλον (LXX) is the golden plate worn by Aaron on the forehead : Exod. XXVIII. 32, XXIX. 6 ; Lev. VIII. 9. In his translation of Eusebius, Rufinus writes ". . . fuit summus sacerdos et pontificale πέταλον gessit".

[4] In Greek : τὸν ἐν ἁγίῳ πνεύματι πάντα πολιτευσάμενον. The reader will remark that Melito, who, unlike Polycarp, Thraseas and Sagaris, is not a martyr, is praised for his continence and as a "spiritual".

[5] In Greek : κατὰ τὸ εὐαγγέλιον, μηδὲν παρεκβαίνοντες, ἀλλὰ κατὰ τὸν κανόνα τῆς πίστεως ἀκολουθοῦντες.

224 PRIMITIVE CATHOLICISM

masters; for seven of my relatives were bishops; and I am the eighth. . . .

I, therefore, brethren,[1] who have lived sixty-five years in the Lord, and have met with the brethren throughout the world,[2] and have gone through the whole of Holy Scripture, shall not lose my head, for I am not affrighted by terrifying words. For those greater than I have said: " We ought to obey God rather than man.[3] I could mention the bishops who were present, whom I summoned at your desire, whose names, should I write them, would constitute a great multitude. And they, notwithstanding my littleness, gave their adhesion to the letter, knowing that I do not bear my gray hairs in vain, but have always governed my life by the Lord Jesus."

The Bishop of Ephesus and the Asiatic Bishops, then, in meeting at Ephesus, complied with the demand of the Bishop of Rome. There is in the words of the Bishop of Ephesus nothing to suggest that such meetings were a usual occurrence; the contrary rather is implied: Polycrates makes excuses for gathering the Bishops of Asia around his humble person, by saying that Rome desired that they should be assembled. Had the Asiatic Churches been accustomed for a long while to meet in a synod, and to form a confederacy after the type of the κοινὸν 'Ασίας,[4] Polycrates would not have used such timid language. And then, Polycrates seems to ask, are these meetings called for? The tradition is faithfully preserved, free both from addition and from diminution; Christians believe and live in harmony with the Gospel, without making any innovations, but following scrupulously what the presbyters, the immediate disciples of the Apostles, taught and practised—they live "according to the rule of faith," for

---

[1] We have not the address of the epistle. Eusebius only says that it is sent " to Victor and to the Church of the Romans ".

[2] In Greek : συμβεβληκὼς τοῖς ἀπὸ τῆς οἰκουμένης ἀδελφοῖς. Compare the inscription of Abercius and the " eos qui sunt undique fideles " of Irenæus.

[3] Acts v. 29.

[4] V. CHAPOT, " La province d'Asie," pp. 529-32, and DE GENOUILLAC, pp. 43-6, have well shown (against MONCEAUX) that there is no real analogy between the solidarity of the Churches, even those of the same province, and the κοινά or leagues of Asiatic or Syrian cities.

Christianity is no uncertain and changing religion, it is a canon and a canon that is the same everywhere : this Polycrates knows well, for, the Christian faith being spread all over the earth, he has been in relation with the brethren of the whole world.

The argument of Polycrates is the same as that of Irenæus. It is that used by Polycarp before Pope Anicetus : viz. the argument of Apostolic tradition, authenticating the faith actually held. Unfortunately, there is, in the present case, a conflict between two customs both of which are authenticated by an Apostolic tradition. Which of the two will be victorious?

Threats do not suffice to frighten me, the Bishop of Ephesus says. From this we may infer that he has been called upon to give up the Asiatic custom ; and as it seems quite clear that Rome alone intervened—since it is Rome alone that Ephesus answers and resists—we see the authority Rome exercises in this conflict. Renan has said rather appropriately in reference to this case : " The Papacy was born and well born ".

About the same time, Pope Victor wrote to all the Churches. Whether this step was taken by Rome before her intervention at Ephesus or after the latter's reply, cannot be clearly made out from the narrative of Eusebius. Eusebius found in the official records the letters by which the bishops, after meeting together in synods, declare the ecclesiastical faith that connected the feast of Easter with Sunday.[1] If the synod of the Asiatic Bishops was held at Ephesus on Pope Victor's demand, we may suppose that the other synods were held in compliance with a similar demand, especially if they were to deal with the subject on which the Bishops of

[1] In their synodal epistle, the Bishops of Palestine declare they write, so as to be in no wise responsible for the error of those who think wrongly, and they affirm that the practice of the Sunday celebration of Easter is a " tradition which has come to them in succession from the Apostles " (ἐκ διαδοχῆς τῶν ἀποστόλων παράδοσις). At the same time, they beg those addressed to send a copy of their epistle to all the Churches : τῆς ἐπιστολῆς ἡμῶν πειράθητε κατὰ πᾶσαν ἐκκλησίαν ἀντίγραφα διαπέμψασθαι. We may remember the words of Irenæus : " Necesse est omnem convenire ecclesiam." Rome appears here as the acknowledged centre of inter-ecclesiastical relations : and this is attested by the Bishops of Palestine.

Asia had been asked to deliberate, the Sunday celebration of Easter. Rome on this occasion gives an order to all the bishops of the Christian world, and the order is complied with everywhere.

Eusebius mentions the synodal letter of the bishops of the province of Pontus (around Amastris); that of the Churches of Osroene (around Edessa); that of the Churches of Gaul (around Lyons); that of the Bishop of Corinth; that of the synod of Palestine (Jerusalem, Cæsarea, Tyre . . . ); but he mentions neither Antioch nor Alexandria. The synodal epistle of Palestine tells us that the Bishops of Palestine observe Easter on Sunday, after the example of Alexandria, which every year makes the date of the celebration known to them by means of a letter.[1]  At no other time has cohesion appeared so fully.   Catholicity too was born, and well born.

His position strengthened by this cohesion and also by the universal acknowledgment of the genuineness and authority of the Sunday custom, Pope Victor thought it necessary to take a still bolder step: viz. that of doing away with non-conformism, by separating from the Church all the Asiatic Churches.[2]  Probably he had previously threatened the Bishop of Ephesus with this measure as within the range of possibility: now that the latter resisted, Victor passed from warning to actual deed.   He wrote to all the Churches, declaring that the brethren of Asia without exception were outside the pale of Catholic communion.[3]

[1] EUSEB. "H. E." v. 25.

[2] *Ibid.* 24, 9: Βίκτωρ . . . στηλιτεύει γε διὰ γραμμάτων, ἀκοινωνήτους πάντας ἄρδην τοὺς ἐκεῖσε ἀνακηρύττων ἀδελφούς. The verb στηλιτεύω, to write down on a stele, designates the public act of proscription.

[3] HARNACK, "Dogmeng." vol. i[4], p. 489, remarks that it is a question, not merely of the communion of the Roman Church, but of the communion of the Catholic Church.   In fact, how could we account for the remonstrances of Irenæus and of the other great bishops, were this the case of a rupture between Rome only and Christian Asia?  Pope Victor acted about the year 190, just as Pope Stephen did some sixty years later: this Eusebius clearly realized (v. 24, 9): Victor, he says, attempts to separate at once all the Churches of Asia from the common unity (τῆς κοινῆς ἑνώσεως), and by letters declares them cut off (ἀκοινωνήτους).  He attempts (πειρᾶται): which means that he asks all the Churches to associate themselves to the excommunication he pronounces.

As Eusebius relates, this measure did not please all the bishops, from which we may reasonably conjecture that it did please some of them, and obtain their approval. But there were also found other bishops who took exception to the severity of the Bishop of Rome and reminded him of peace, union, and charity; there were most emphatic protests of which Eusebius saw the text itself. When we come to the third century, we shall find that, then too, such remonstrances were admissible in the Christian community. Irenæus sent to Victor a letter, of which a celebrated fragment has been preserved by Eusebius: in this document the Bishop of Lyons represents to the Bishop of Rome that the observance of the Easter solemnity on Sunday is not a custom of such importance that refusal to conform to it should be regarded as a reason sufficient to justify expelling any one body of Christians. He adds that Victor's predecessors had taken this view of the matter, judging that " both those who observed and those who did not, were in agreement with the whole Church ".[1] Irenæus wrote in the same sense to most of the bishops, and ultimately won universal assent. Rome had gained her point on the question of principle, and did not insist on her disciplinary measure.

But how remarkable it is that, about the year 190, the Bishop of Rome should excommunicate, in a kind of peremptory edict, the Churches of the provinces of Asia, Churches Apostolic and venerable, with the Bishop of Ephesus for their spokesman! The Bishop of Rome condemns their observance of Easter as a usage that is against the Canon of the Apostolic faith, and he cuts them off, not from the Roman, but from the Catholic communion. He is conscious, then, that such a sentence on his part is legitimate. Iren-

---

[1] " H. E." v. 24, 18 : πάσης τῆς ἐκκλησίας εἰρήνην ἐχόντων καὶ τῶν τηρούντων καὶ τῶν μὴ τηρούντων. Here again Irenæus does not use the word " catholic ". On the other hand, we find it used with remarkable insistence in the Canon of Muratori, a Roman document of the period 190-200. " Una per omnem orbem terrae ecclesia diffusa esse dinoscitur . . . " The " Pastoral Epistles " " in honorem ecclesiae catholicae, in ordinationem ecclesiasticae disciplinae, sanctificatae sunt ". A certain epistle, wrongly ascribed to Paul, and actually composed by the Marcionites, " in catholicam ecclesiam recipi non potest ". Jude and 1-2 John, " in catholica habentur ". ZAHN, " Grundriss," pp. 75-9.

æus protests against the excommunication of the Asiatics, it is true, but he does not dream of questioning Victor's power to pronounce this excommunication.   "What term are we to use if we are forbidden to designate as 'Head of the Church' one who is the depositary of such authority?"[1]

*  *
*

In this exposition, we have not gone beyond the age of Irenæus: nor do we need to go beyond it, or follow the development of Christianity down to the second half of the third century, merely to prove that—within the boundaries of the Empire, and apart from any Judæo-Christian communities that may still exist here and there—"Christianity has an undivided history".[2]   It is acknowledged that it has reached by this time a form of government common to all the Churches, and to that solidarity between all the Churches which is, we are told, "Catholicism as we conceive of it to-day".

Yet those who make this acknowledgment assume towards us, Catholics of to-day, a triumphant attitude, and exclaim: What you look upon as the providential development of principles essentially inherent in Christianity, is only a secularizing of Christianity, its adaptation to the life of the Empire, a Christian imperialism: "Roman," politically understood, is truly synonymous with "Catholic," and the best proof of this is furnished by the fact that, about the year 190, the Roman Church had definitively acquired all the elements that are fundamental in Catholicism.   Has she not her rule of faith—the Apostles' Creed?   Has she not a definite and settled canon of the New Testament?   Has she not, the first of all the Churches, drawn up the list of her bishops, reaching back to the Apostles?   Do not the dispersed Churches communicate with one another through the medium of Rome?   And has not the Church of Rome become the rule for all the Churches, precisely because she is at Rome?

This imperialist conception of Catholicism would be very specious, were it not open to an objection the gravity of

---

[1] DUCHESNE, "Eglises Séparées," p. 144.
[2] HARNACK, "Dogmeng." vol. I[4], p. 480.

which Harnack has not concealed, viz.: that the development effected by the Roman Church within herself took place simultaneously in the Churches of all the provinces: in some provinces reaching its term sooner than at Rome; in others, later.

Moreover, even as early as the time of the Easter controversy, there are Churches beyond the boundaries of the Empire, in the Kingdom of Edessa; and, the King of Edessa being a Christian, Christianity is there for the first time in history a State religion. And yet, what is said of the Churches that are in Gaul is said also of the Churches that are in Osroene. Though they are Syriac in language, they hold epistolary relations with the Bishop of Rome, they place in his hands the official attestation of their Easter custom, which is the same as that followed in Palestine, in Syria, and at Rome. The Syriac Catholicism of the kingdom of Edessa proves that Catholicism is not mere " Roman-ism " (*romanitas*).[1]

To the hypothesis of the rise of Catholicism at the

---

[1] EUSEB. "H. E." v. 23, 3. BURKITT, "Early Christianity outside the Roman Empire" (Cambridge, 1899), p. 11. The kingdom of Edessa was not made a part of the Roman province of Mesopotamia till the year 216. HARNACK, "Mission," vol. II. p. 119, contends that the primitive Christianity of Edessa is represented historically by Tatian, "the Assyrian," and Bardesanes, of whom neither was "Catholic," but rather, "measured by the doctrinal standards of the Catholic confederation, both were mild heretics". It is only at the beginning of the third century—we are told—that the Church of Edessa accepted Catholic Christianity, by receiving from Serapion, Bishop of Antioch, (190-211), a Bishop, named Palut, who thus became the first Catholic Bishop of Edessa, but not its first Bishop. To this we may reply that Tatian is more of a Greek, and that the theatre of his literary activity was first Rome, and then Antioch (BARDENHEWER, vol. I. p. 245). Edessa and Syriac Christianity are indebted to him for the " Diatessaron," which Catholics received without reluctance (HARNACK, loc. cit.). As to Bardesanes, we cannot set aside the testimony of EUSEBIUS (" H. E." IV. 30), who represents him as a Valentinian who had retracted his erroneous views, and as a controversialist who opposed Marcionism and the other heresies. Eusebius relates also that the writings of Bardesanes were translated into Greek. In the eyes of Eusebius Bardesanes does not seem to have been more of a heretic than Origen, and this was doubtless the common impression until the time of St. Ephrem and St. Epiphanius. Besides, neither Bardesanes, nor Tatian held the episcopal dignity in Osroene.—Cf. TIXERONT, " Les Origines de l'Eglise d'Edesse " (Paris, 1888), pp. 9-19.

centre of the Empire and of its expansion through the whole Empire by way of conquest, we oppose then the fact that the constitutive elements of Catholicism are found everywhere throughout Christendom, and that, in proportion as historical examination can observe it, their development is everywhere spontaneous, not forced on from without. The only recorded case of compulsion is that of Pope Victor's endeavour to force conformity on the Asiatic Churches in the observance of Easter, and, as a matter of fact, the Churches of Asia did not at the time yield to the constraint, although gradually and silently they came over to the Catholic practice.

This is the illuminating phenomenon: the symbol of faith, the episcopate, the canon of the New Testament, the Roman primacy—institutions which are represented as so many *coups d'état* secretly perpetrated by the Roman Church —appear to the historian as principles laid down from the first and developing with the continuity and harmony characteristic of the growth of an organism, which, once it is created, grows and expands according to its law.

## EXCURSUS C.

### Marcionism and Catholicism.

" The Syrian charlatans ceased not to propagate their oriental Gnosticism, with its strangely-named æons and the Semitic glitter of its magic. In Alexandria subtle spirits tricked out these absurdities in philosophic garb to suit the local taste. But neither achieved more than the foundation of some lodges of initiates of higher or lower degree. Meantime, a man arose who set himself to extract from this jargon a few simple notions in harmony with those of ordinary men, as the basis for a religion which should be Christian, of course, but new, anti-Jewish, and dualist; and should no longer find expression in secret confraternities, but in a Church. This man was Marcion." [1]

Marcion was born at Sinope, a port on the Black Sea. He was the son of a bishop and possessed a hand-

---

[1] DUCHESNE, " Histoire Ancienne," t. I, p. 182.

some fortune. According to a narrative, borrowed probably from St. Hippolytus, he was excommunicated at Sinope for seducing a young girl. "*Marcion, ponticus genere, episcopi filius, propter stuprum cuiusdam virginis ab ecclesiae communicatione abiectus.*"[1] Mgr. Duchesne remarks on this that neither St. Irenæus, nor Tertullian, neither of whom was very tender towards Marcion, seems to be aware of this imputation, which, therefore, is hardly probable. We may conjecture then that the story is a kind of anticipation of Marcion's heresy? The virgin defiled by Marcion was the *Ecclesia virgo*.

On leaving Sinope, Marcion went to Rome: he was one of those many Christians whom Rome drew to herself, because she was a unique centre, alike for the upholders of the tradition and for agitators.

It is not very probable that on his way to Rome he passed through the city of Smyrna, and that it was at this time that he had the interview with Polycarp recorded by St. Irenæus: when Marcion asked the venerable old Bishop if he recognized him, and Polycarp is reported to have replied: "I recognize the first-born of Satan".[2] Marcion would have been, already, were the story true of that time, an open heretic, and it would be hard to understand his receiving at Rome the kind welcome we are told he did. We cannot suppose that Rome was either unacquainted with the feelings of the Church of Smyrna or—which is still more improbable—was incautious as regards errors that filled Polycarp with indignation. It is more probable that Marcion and Polycarp met at Rome, towards the years 154-5, when the latter came to visit Anicetus.

Marcion arrived at Rome at the time when Valentinus also was there; both, Tertullian affirms, were as yet Catholics: "*Constat illos . . . in Catholicae primo doctrinam credidisse apud ecclesiam romanensem, sub episcopatu Eleutherii benedicti, donec ob inquietam semper [eorum] curiositatem, qua fratres quoque vitiabant, semel et iterum eiecti.*"[3] Marcion professed then the teaching of the

---

[1] (PSEUDO) TERTULLIAN, "Praesc." 51. EPIPHAN. "Haer." XLII. 1.

[2] IREN. "Haer." III. 3.

[3] TERTULL. "Praescr." 30. Together with the "Muratorianum" quoted above (p. 227), this text of Tertullian is the oldest witness we

"Catholica" and he belonged to that "Catholica" in the ranks of the Roman Church. He even presented the Roman Church with a sum of 200,000 sesterces, which it gave back to him on the day he was excommunicated.[1] Later on Tertullian will emphasize the fact that Marcion was at first, and in the strictest sense, a Catholic, the better to show that he changed when becoming a heretic: "*Marcion Deum quem invenerat extincto lumine fidei suae amisit: non negabunt discipuli eius primam illius fidem nobiscum fuisse, ipsius litteris testibus*":[2] words which allude to a written profession of faith, given by Marcion in the form of a letter to the authorities of the Roman Church, which from the first probably was somewhat uneasy about the purity of his faith.

Marcion broke with the Roman Church in the year 144. This rupture must be understood of a sentence of excommunication pronounced by the Roman Church, and even, it seems, of a double sentence: one by which he was called upon to recant his errors ; the other, by which he was cast out "*in perpetuum discidium*": the same procedure was pursued in Rome, at the same time, against Valentinus.[3] From this we may infer that, in the year 144, the authorities of the Roman Church were not taken unawares in presence of such doctrinal errors as those of Valentinus and Marcion, and that, to suppress these errors, they had not to resort to an hitherto unused procedure.

The novelty of Marcionism, when once it was cast out from the Catholic Church, lay in its constituting itself in churches: the Donatists in the fourth century, and the Novatians in the third, will follow the same policy: the

---

have to the use of the word *Catholica* as a substantive synonymous with *Ecclesia catholica*. This use does not appear among the Greeks ; among the Latins it ceases after the seventh century. It has been found 240 times in the works of St. Augustine, who opposes the "Catholica" to the "pars Donati," the Donatist schism (cf. Dom ROTTMANNER, "Catholica," in the "Revue bénédictine," 1900, pp. 1-9).

[1] TERTULL. "Praescr." 30.   Two hundred thousand sesterces are equivalent to about $8000 or $10,000 (£1600 or £2000).

[2] "Adv. Marcion." I. 1.

[3] "Praescr." 30.   As to the date, "Adv. Marcion." I. 19, and KRÜGER, art. "Marcion," p. 268, in HAUCK's "Realencykl."

Marcionites were the first to adopt it. In this they differ from the Gnostic schools :[1] the Valentinians, for instance, are characterised by Tertullian as a "*frequentissimum plane collegium inter haereticos*".[2] Tertullian writes *collegium*. In another passage, he speaks of heretics in the following remarkable terms, every one of which expresses, by way of contrast, a special attribute of the Church: "*Plerique nec ecclesias habent, sine matre, sine sede, orbi fide, extorres, sine lare vagantur;*"[3] but this description does not apply to the Marcionites : "*Faciunt favos et vespae, faciunt ecclesias et Marcionitae,*" says Tertullian.[4]

It is most interesting to observe that Marcionism starts from Rome as from a centre of propagandism, and that, less than half a century later, it has spread through the whole Empire, so great evidently were at that time the facilities for such an expansion of ideas and of sects : the " great Church " must have been most closely united and most solidly founded, to remain stable in the midst of that quicksand. In fact, less than ten years after the rupture between Marcion and the Roman Church, St. Justin in his first Apology (in the year 150 or very soon after) says : " A certain Marcion, of Pontus, is even now teaching his disciples to believe in another God

---

[1] Clement of Al. cites a "homily ' of Valentinus, "Stromat." IV. 13 ("P. G." vol. VIII. p. 1296) and VI. 6 (vol. IX. p. 276). In the latter quotation, Valentinus speaks of "the Church of God," which he calls "the people of the Beloved, the people loved [of Christ] and loving Him ". The homily was entitled Περὶ φίλων, " On Friends ". The word φίλοι was often used to designate the members of the same philosophical school : Valentinus probably took it in that sense. HARNACK, " Mission," vol. I. p. 354.

[2] "Adv. Valent." 1. See St. Ambrose's Letter XL, 16, on the affair of Callinicum (in Osroene), where some monks, molested by the Valentinians of the place, burned, in the year 388, the sanctuary of the sect.

[3] "Praescr." 42.

[4] "Adv. Marcion." IV. 5 : "Habet plane et illud [Euangelium] ecclesias, sed suas, tam posteras quam adulteras . . . Marcione scilicet conditore vel aliquo de Marcionis examine. Faciunt favos," etc. Clement is perhaps alluding to the Marcionites, in a passage where he reproves the heretics who reject the prophecies of the Old Testament from "their Church," just as naughty children drive away their teacher. " Stromat." VII. 16 ("P. G." vol. IX. p. 537 A.).

greater than the Creator. He, with the assistance of the devils, has persuaded many persons of every nation to blaspheme and deny God, the Creator of this universe. . . . Many believe this man to be the only one who possesses the truth, and deride us."[1] Towards the end of the second century, in almost all the provinces we find the leaders of Christian thought engaged in fighting Marcionism: witness St. Irenæus at Lyons, Tertullian at Carthage, the *Muratorianum*, Hippolytus and Rhodon at Rome, Clement at Alexandria, Theophilus at Antioch, Bardesanes at Edessa, Dionysius at Corinth, Philip of Gortyna in Crete. At the close of the fourth century, St. Epiphanius speaks of Marcionism as still existing at Rome and in Italy, in Egypt and in Palestine, in Arabia and in Syria, in Cyprus, in the Thebaid, in Persia, and elsewhere: during the fifth century Theodoret mentions some villages in his diocese of Cyrus that are composed exclusively of Marcionites.[2]

In common with Montanism, Novatianism, as well as Donatism, Marcionism claims to be a Church more exacting than the " great Church ". As early as the end of the second century, it claims to have more martyrs than the great Church.[3] For Marcion, continency is an absolutely necessary condition for Christian life and salvation, baptism is only for those who renounce matrimony.[4] Hence baptism commits to a life of continency any one who receives it, unless it be deferred to the approach of death. The Marcionites must abstain from meat: fish and vegetables only shall be their food, "*sanctior cibus*".[5] The word *sanctitas* expresses the obligatory state of a Christian, in the system of Marcion, "*sanctissimus magister*," as Tertullian styles him ironically.[6] In short Marcionism takes the course common

---

[1] "Apol." i. 26.  [2] HARNACK, " Mission," vol. ii. p. 265.
[3] EUSEB. " H. E." v. 16, 21. The testimony is taken from the work of the anonymous anti-Montanist, who wrote about the years 192-3. For the Montanists also claimed to have more martyrs than any other religious organization, and they saw in it "a sure evidence of the power of the prophetic spirit," which they claimed for their sect. This is a primitive form of the argument drawn from the constancy of the martyrs.
[4] TERTULL. "Adv. Marcion." i. 29, and iv. 11.
[5] " Adv. Marcion." i. 14.  [6] *Ibid.* i. 28, 29 and *passim*.

to all forms of Puritanism by pretending to be a reaction against the laxity of the Church, and to surpass it in moral value.

Marcion is not an enthusiast, a "pneumatic," or, strictly speaking, a Gnostic; he is a reformer who sets himself the task of dispassionately reforming the existing Church in her morals, as we have just seen, and in her faith, as we are about to see.

His method consists in clinging to St. Paul's teaching, which he sets against the teaching of the other Apostles. Thus he attacks the authority of the Twelve, whom he considers to be prevaricators and dissemblers, condemned by St. Paul himself.[1]  But to repudiate the authority of the Apostles (other than Paul) is to undermine the historical and dogmatic foundation of the great Church, and this Marcion probably realizes; the Apostles are for him judaizers whom he rejects.    Tertullian arrays against Marcion the faith and the institutions that still endure in the Churches founded by Paul, in the Church of Rome founded both by Peter and Paul, in the Churches founded by John, from which Marcion has himself taken something, since the *ordo episcoporum* was inaugurated by John: now all those Churches, says Tertullian, are unanimous against Marcion: "*Dico apud illas, nec solas iam apostolicas, sed apud universas quae illis de societate sacramenti confoederantur. . . .*"[2]   The paradoxical thought of isolating Paul from Peter and from the other Apostles is peculiar to Marcion, and on him rests the responsibility for the innovation.

This exclusive and violent Paulinism leads Marcion to a kind of Christianity which has for its base the rejection of the Old Testament.   But for any one to speak of the Old Testament is to imply that there is a New Testament. Marcion makes the latter consist of the Gospel of St. Luke (though mutilated and revised), of the Pauline Epistles (except the Pastoral Epistles), and of his own work on the contradictions between the New and the Old Testament, entitled "Antitheses".   This book "*proprium et principale opus est Marcionis nec poterunt negare discipuli eius, quod in summo*

---

[1] "Adv. Marcion." IV. 3.   Cf. "Praescr." 22 and 32.
[2] "Adv. Marcion." IV. 5.

*instrumento habent, quo denique initiantur et indurantur in hanc haeresim* ".[1]  The Marcionites have but one testament (*instrumentum*).  They use Marcion's " Antitheses " as a book of initiation.  Here again Marcion innovates : first, in repudiating the Jewish Bible which had always been received in the Church without dispute ; and secondly, in placing his " Antitheses " on the same footing as one of the Gospels and as the Pauline Epistles.  Some scholars would have us believe that the drawing up a canon of the New Testament was also an innovation, and that, before Marcion, the great Church had no such canon : I have shown elsewhere that this supposition is improbable.[2]  Tertullian had already said as much when he affirmed that by framing a canon of his own, Marcion had set himself up for the censor and reformer of the ecclesiastical canon already received : " *Utique non potuisset [Marcion] arguere nisi quod invenerat.*"[3]

Just as the Marcionites have an *instrumentum*, i.e. authoritative Scriptures, so they have a rule of faith.  We have already noted that they have Baptism, the Eucharist, and episcopacy ;[4] and that Marcion's work is the book *quo initiantur*.  Marcion's theodicy consists in opposing the God of the Old Testament to the God of the New, the Creator to the Father, and in introducing what Tertullian calls " *ex diversitate sententiarum utriusque testamenti diversitatem deorum* ".  In Marcion's Christology, Christ is represented as the manifestation of the good God : " *Immo, inquiunt Marcionitae, Deus noster . . . per semetipsum revelatus est in Christo Iesu . . . Anno XV Tiberii, Christus*

---

[1] " Adv. Marcion." I. 19.

[2] " Revue biblique," vol. XII. (1903), pp. 25-6, after ZAHN, " Grundriss,' pp. 27-9.

[3] " Adv. Marcion.' IV. 4 : " Itaque dum emendat, utrumque confirmat ; et nostrum anterius, id emendans quod invenit ; et id posterius, quod de nostri emendatione constituens suum et novum fecit ".  Cf. " Praescr." 30 : " Si Marcion Novum Testamentum a Vetere separavit, posterior est eo quod separavit, quia separare non posset nisi quod unitum fuit. Unitum ergo antequam separaretur, postea separatum, posteriorem ostendit separatorem ".

[4] Must we apply to the Marcionites what Tertullian says in " Praescr." 41, about the disorder that prevails in heretical churches ? As to episcopacy among the Valentinians, cf. " Philosophoumena," VI. 41.

*Iesus de caelo manare dignatus est, Spiritus salutaris* ". No conception, no birth, no infancy : Christ comes down from Heaven suddenly, as He will return thither. Docetism is the true doctrine ; and yet redemption by the cross is equally real. But what is all this save a correction of the ecclesiastical rule of faith ? "*Aiunt enim [Marcionitae] Marcionem non tam innovasse regulam . . . quam retro adulteratam recurasse.*" [1] Tertullian does not fail to remind Marcion that he began by giving up the Catholic truth which he used to hold, as is proved from the letter sent to Rome by Marcion himself : "*Quid nunc si negaverint Marcionitae primam apud nos fidem eius, adversus epistulam quoque ipsius ?* " [2]

Let us recall now, the converging developments by which the Ritschlian school explains the formation of Catholic Christianity—a definition of Christianity held for Apostolic ; a baptismal formulary of faith, accepted as a rule of faith, likewise regarded as Apostolic ; a collection of Apostolic writings, placed on the same level as the Old Testament ; a monarchical episcopate, everywhere instituted and proclaimed to be Apostolic, bishops regarded as the successors of the Apostles—all these data are found in Marcionism.

The conclusion to be drawn from those well-ascertained facts is that Marcionism is a Catholicism without a hall-mark.[3]

Catholicism was not formed in opposition to Marcionism, it existed before Marcionism, with the characteristic elements we have just mentioned ; after seceding from it, Marcionism could not make any stand at all nor endure, without framing for itself a *regula fidei*, a canon, a monarchical episcopate, all based on the authority of an Apostle ;

---

[1] " Adv. Marcion." I. 19-20.   [2] *Ibid.* IV. 4.

[3] A "reformed " Catholicism, Harnack would say, but he has realized this feature of Marcionism, a feature which, once admitted, becomes for the Ritschlian theory an unanswerable difficulty. " Dogmeng." vol. I⁴, p. 305 : " That Marcion was conscious of being a reformer, and that he was recognized to be such in his Church is still not understood, although it is clearly involved in the nature of his enterprise and the facts connected with it ". Again (*ibid.* p. 340) : " In the formation of the Marcionite Church, we have . . . the attempt to create a close œcumenical communion, based solely on religion. The Marcionite Church therefore had a founder, the Catholic Church has none."

namely, Paul. Moreover, as Marcionism had to face this crushing objection, that, from time immemorial, the great Church had rested on another faith, it had to extol Marcion, and even equal him with St. Paul, naming after him the Christianity which he had reformed, and giving him a throne in Heaven at the left hand of God.[1] Truly, we have in Marcionism " the attempt to create a close œcumenical communion ": but why is this attempt dated, and why is it called after Marcion, whilst Catholicism has no date, and bears no one's name?

EXCURSUS D.

*The End of Judæo-Christianity.*

To be complete, a sketch of the historical development of the "great Church" must tell what became of Jewish Christianity, of Judæo-Christianity, as it is called.

It has been rightly observed that Judæo-Christianity is a most inappropriate term, if it is meant to imply that the Christianity of the Gentiles had nothing in common with Judaism: for first it kept the Old Testament, and secondly, though it declared itself freed from the Law by the Gospel, it claimed not less confidently to be the true Israel, the heir of all the promises, a true Israel from which the Jews were by no means excluded, provided they believed in Christ Jesus. To oppose Judæo-Christianity to Catholicism is therefore an historical absurdity; a point which has been very distinctly brought out by the discovery of the " Didachè ". The term, Judæo-Christianity, strictly speaking, applies only to those Christians, born in Judaism, who looked upon the Law as still binding, and who therefore found themselves engaged in an irreconcilable conflict not only with St. Paul, but with all Christianity.[2]

---

[1] This was actually done : " Alii enim aiunt, hoc quod scriptum est, sedere a dextris salvatoris et sinistris, de Paulo et de Marcione dici, quod Paulus sedet a dextris, Marcion sedet a sinistris ". ORIGEN, "In Luc. Homil." xxv. In the "Praef. arab. ad Concil. Nic.," we read that the Marcionites call Marcion "principem apostolorum". KRUEGER, p. 273.

[2] HARNACK, "Dogmeng." vol. I[4], p. 310. Cf. HÖNNICKE, "Judenchristentum," pp. 367-77.

Although these Jewish Christians belong to the earliest Christian community, and the mother-church, yet, far from representing the oldest orthodoxy, they represent the oldest error, and far from having ever exercised over the formation of Catholicism that decisive influence which Baur ascribed to them, they were gradually isolated by Catholicism, and reduced to insignificance.

St. Paul speaks to the Thessalonians of the "Churches of Judæa," testifying that they have suffered at the hands of those Jews who put to death the Lord Jesus, and "who forbid us to speak to the Gentiles that they may be saved" (1 Thess. II. 14-16). The Acts of the Apostles tell us of Christian communities in Galilee, in Samaria, and on the coast. Those "Churches of Judæa," praised by St. Paul and persecuted by the Jews, were not of the same spirit as the Judæo-Christians who opposed the Apostle. Hence, even as early as the Apostolic age, two elements are combating each other in the "Churches of Judæa"—one judaizing, the other universalistic.

The fact has been often recalled that, when interpreting the number of the elect of Israel, as given by the Apocalypse (VII. 4), Origen sets aside the idea that those 144,000 elect may represent the Judæo-Christians; to him that number seems altogether too high. "Origen wrote after two centuries of Christianity, and hence his estimate would cover five or six generations. He cannot then have thought the Judæo-Christians very numerous."[1] This would be a very small number of Christians for the country that had seen the rise of the Gospel, had we not reasons for supposing that the "Churches of Judæa," which did not come to an end in the disasters of the Jewish wars, had become hellenized, long before the time of Origen.

Eusebius has preserved a list of the former Bishops of Jerusalem who he says succeeded one another until the revolt of the Jews in the year 132. "The first two," Mgr. Duchesne writes, "are James and Simeon, who bring us down to A.D. 107; the remaining thirteen Bishops have therefore to be got into twenty-five years. This is a large

[1] DUCHESNE, "Hist. anc." t. I, p. 127. Origen's text is found in his "Comment. in Ioan." I. 1.

number. But if we accept the list and the time-limits given by Eusebius, the natural explanation is that the list includes the Bishops, not only of Pella [where the Church of Jerusalem had taken refuge, in the year 70], but of some other colonies from the primitive Church of Jerusalem." [1]

Hegesippus, who lived at the same time as Irenæus, relates that, under Simeon's episcopate, the Church of Jerusalem was preyed upon by heresies, which were started by a certain Thebutis, "because he was not made bishop".[2] This Thebutis brings us back to the time of St. Ignatius of Antioch: at Pella as at Antioch, the episcopate, the monarchical episcopate, was in existence at that time.

About the year 190, at the time of the Easter controversy, the Bishops of Palestine meet in a synod, at Pope Victor's request: their synodal answer witnesses to the fact that they do not follow the Quartodeciman practice, but the Sunday practice which was received at Rome and everywhere else except in Asia. This Palestinian synod is presided over by Theophilus, Bishop of Cæsarea, and by Narcissus, Bishop of Jerusalem, and attended—as we know from Eusebius—by Cassius, Bishop of Tyre, and Clarus, Bishop of Ptolemais. None of these names are Jewish. In their letter to Victor, the Palestinian Bishops state that they are in relation with the Church of Alexandria, for every year they concert with her as to the determination of the date of Easter. And they ask that their letter may be communicated by Rome to all Christendom, κατὰ πᾶσαν ἐκκλησίαν.[3] Hence, at the close of the second century, the "Churches of Judæa," as well as those of Gaul, are in close union with the "Catholica". This conclusion can be confirmed by other and more ancient facts.

[1] DUCHESNE, op. cit. p. 120. HARNACK, "Mission," vol. I. p. 387. HÖNNICKE, pp. 106-7. As to the part played in those Churches by members of the family of Jesus, cf. DUCHESNE, ibid. and KNOPF, "Nachapost. Zeitalter,' pp. 25-8. In this part, nothing reminds us of a Califate.

[2] HEGESIP. ap. EUSEB. "H. E." IV. 22, 5.

[3] EUSEB. "H. E." V. 23, 25. The same historian, ibid. IV. 11, 2, tells us, in connexion with a fact belonging to the years 212-3, of the bishops of the churches in the neighbourhood of Jerusalem (HARNACK, "Mission," vol. II. p. 85) being convened for the election of the Bishop of Jerusalem.

At Pella was born Aristo, who, between the years 135-175, wrote the famous "Dialogue of Jason and Papiscus," after the manner of Justin's "Dialogue with the Jew Trypho". In Aristo's dialogue, as in that of Justin, a Jew disputes with a Christian about Christianity and finally surrenders to his arguments. Was Aristo a Judæo-Christian, as Harnack thinks, or a Greek-Christian, as Zahn would have it? We cannot say. That he wrote his "Dialogue" at Pella, is likewise uncertain. At all events, the "Dialogue" was read everywhere in Greek: Celsus attacks it with violence; Origen, who upholds it against the criticisms of Celsus, praises it without any restriction, which he would not have done had the dialogue disagreed with his faith.[1]

Hegesippus, writes Mgr. Duchesne, "was himself a Judæo-Christian. This was the impression of Eusebius, who had read all he wrote; and it is confirmed by his use of the Gospel of the Hebrews, by his language which abounds in Hebrew words, and by his familiarity with the history of the Church of Jerusalem." But if he was by birth a Judæo-Christian or even a Jew, Hegesippus had become a thorough Catholic: "he did not feel out of his element among the Corinthian or Roman Christians. He investigated their episcopal successions, and the way by which they preserved primitive traditions. According to him, all their customs were in accordance with what the Law, the Prophets and the Lord had taught." If to this, we add his utter dislike for the heretics who "divided the unity of the Church,"[2] we must confess that his are not the sentiments of a dissident.

Were there truly Judæo-Christians dissenting from the "great Church"? Yes, and in two ways.

There remained groups of Christians, who were Jews by birth and Jews by circumcision; and these groups were unable to subsist, save by admitting into their ranks only such as were circumcised. As we learn from St. Justin who

---

[1] ORIGEN, "Contra. Cels." IV. 52. BARDENHEWER, vol. I. p. 187.

[2] HEGESIP. *apud* EUSEB. "H. E." IV. 22, 5 : ἐμέρισαν τὴν ἕνωσιν τῆς ἐκκλησίας.

had good opportunities of knowing them,[1] they lived after the Jewish fashion.    Their propaganda amounted to nothing among the Jews, or among the Gentiles either.    These groups soon found themselves reduced to members who were exclusively " Hebrews " and whom both their legalism and their language kept apart from other men.    By the force of circumstances, it came to pass that, as they were strangers to all that was written in Greek, they were familiar only with the Aramæan Gospel, which they had used from time immemorial, the " Gospel of the Hebrews," as it was called among the Greeks : a Gospel more or less independent of the Synoptics, and adapted to the tradition peculiar to these " Hebrews ".    Unlike the groups that bear the name of Cerinthus and Carpocrates, these " Hebrew " Christians did not form a heresy, but a remnant.    Their communities became more and more isolated both from Christianity and from Judaism, and they passed into obscurity and disappeared in the beginning of the fifth century.[2]

There existed, during the fourth century, another form of Judæo-Christianity, not confined to some " Hebrew " villages of Palestine, but widely spread.    It is found at Alexandria, for instance, and also at Rome.    It was for this class of Judæo-Christians that the Gospel of the Hebrews was translated into Greek; it may be too that the Greek *Logia*,

---

[1] JUSTIN, " Dialog." XLVII. 2-5.  It is recorded of Septimius Severus that, on his way through Palestine in the year 202, he took measures against the Jews and against the Christians.  SPARTIAN.  " Sever." **17** : " In itinere Palaestinis plurima iura fundavit : Iudaeos fieri sub gravi poena vetuit, idem etiam de christianis sanxit ".  As far as I know, it has not as yet been observed that the said edict is directed against circumcision as well among the Christians as among the Jews.  If this is so, it must have had specially in view the Judæo-Christian community of Palestine, since, among the Christians, the practice of circumcision was confined to Judæo-Christians.

[2] EPIPHAN.  " Haer." XXIX. **7,** and the other texts brought together by HARNACK, " Mission," vol. II. p. 81 and foll.  St. Jerome, " Epistulæ " LXXXIX. speaks of them as an heretical sect opposed to orthodox Judaism : " Inter Iudaeos haeresis est quae dicitur Minaeorum et a Pharisaeis nunc usque damnatur. . . ."  But it may be that here St. Jerome was misled by the anathema against heretics, *Minim*, contained in the daily prayer of the Jews, the Shmone Esre.  LAGRANGE, " Messianisme," p. 294.  HÖNNICKE, p. 386.

found within these last years in Egypt belonged to it. Symmachus, who in the time of Marcus Aurelius (161-180) translated into Greek the Hebrew books of the Old Testament, was a native of Samaria and a Judæo-Christian. He published a commentary on the "Gospel of the Hebrews," in which he endeavoured to justify the features in that Gospel which are distinctly judaizing.[1] This Judæo-Christianity is a reaction against Marcionism: we know that its adherents rejected all that came from St. Paul. On the other hand, it accepted several apocryphal writings, the titles of some of which we know—for instance the "Gospel of the Twelve Apostles,"[2] and those Πέτρου κηρύγματα, to which St. Peter's Epistle to St. James, found at the beginning of the "Clementine Homilies," formed the preface.[3] The details contained in this epistle, as we shall see presently, are very interesting.

The Apostle Peter, who is regarded as the Prince of the Apostles, knowing that he is soon to die, sends to James,

---

[1] EUSEB. "H. E." VI. 17. BARDENHEWER, vol. I. p. 349.

[2] ORIGEN, "In Luc. homil. I."

[3] The Clementine apocryphal writings are no longer credited with having exercised the influence ascribed to them in the palmy days of Baur and of the Tübingen school. In his "Die Pseudoclementinen Homilien und Rekognitionen" (Leipzig, 1904), H. WAITZ arrives at the conclusion, that the document on which the "Homilies" and the "Recognitions" are based is inspired with a "syncretist, though catholic" tendency, and connected with Rome: together with the Epistle of Clement which forms its preface, it was composed between the years 220 and 230. It has various sources, notably the Κηρύγματα Πέτρου and the Πράξεις Πέτρου. These Κηρύγματα Πέτρου (which are quite distinct from the Κήρυγμα Πέτρου) are a revised edition, made about the end of the second century or beginning of the third, of some older Judæo-Christian Κηρύγματα Πέτρου, savouring of Gnosticism, to which Peter's letter to James belongs: these latter were probably composed at Cæsaraea soon after the year 135 in Judæo-Christian surroundings. The "Homilies" and "Recognitions," in their actual state, are subsequent to the Council of Nicæa, though previous to the year 400. Mgr. DUCHESNE, "The Early History of the Church," pp. 95-6, accepts the conclusions of Waitz, and believes that in "Recogn." and "Hom." there are traces of the Lucianist or Arian school. Dom CHAPMAN, "On the Date of the Clementines," in the "Zeitschrift für die Neutestamentliche Wissenschaft," 1908, pp. 21-34, even thinks that the document which is at the basis of the "Recogn." and of the "Hom." was composed about the year 330, in Palestine or in Syria.

" bishop of the Holy Church," the book of his Κηρύγματα, i.e. of his teachings.   Peter recommends James to make the book of the Κηρύγματα known only to men whose worthiness has been tried, just as Moses " gave his chair to the seventy " elders he had chosen.   This policy of Moses has had for its result, that the Jews have unanimously kept " the canon of the [Divine] monarchy and of the life [according to the Law]," and that even now they have no other thoughts than those sanctioned by Holy Writ,   They are educated in accordance with the canon transmitted to them:[1] they allow no one to teach before he has learned how to use the Scriptures; for them there is but one God, one law, one hope.   So must it be with us.

Hence James is to give Peter's Κηρύγματα as Moses gave his own Κηρύγματα to the seventy: otherwise, the teaching will degenerate into mere opinions.   " This I know not in my quality as a prophet, but I see already this evil beginning to sprout."   For some Gentiles have already rejected my teaching, which is in keeping with the Law, whilst others strive by means of interpretation so to alter it " as to destroy the Law ".   God forbid! for such a thing were to act against God who gave us His Law by Moses, and against Our Lord who proclaims that the heavens and the earth shall pass away, but that one jot or one tittle shall in no wise fall from the Law.   But if, while I am still alive, they dare thus to make me say what I did not say, what will it be after I am gone ?

Let James—Peter insists for the last time—give the Κηρύγματα only to trustworthy men, able to keep the Law faithfully, able to transmit everywhere the canon of truth,[2] doing their best to explain everything according to our tradition,[3] not according to their ignorance or their own devisings.

This epistle shows the importance attached by Judæo-Christians to the Apostles, above all to Peter.   Peter stands for Moses, as James for Aaron.   Just as Moses chose seventy elders from whom the " tradition of the ancients "

[1] κατὰ τὸν παραδοθέντα αὐτοῖς κανόνα.
[2] πανταχῆ τὸν τῆς ἀληθείας κανόνα παραδῶσιν.
[3] πρὸς τὴν παράδοσιν ἡμῶν.

originates, so also James will entrust the teaching of Peter to reliable men who will establish the tradition of the Apostles, and that tradition will preserve the canon of truth. Woe to those who shall be bold enough to reject the Law, and to explain in a different sense the teaching of the Apostles! ˌJames, who is a bishop of the holy Church, must be on the watch.

The severe expressions contained in this epistle of St. Peter to St. James, whether they are aimed at Marcion or at St. Paul, proceed from a conception of the canon of truth, of the authority of the Apostolic tradition, of the part of episcopacy and of the presbyters, which, whilst striving to shield itself behind Moses and the ancients, coincides with the " Catholic " conception.

# CHAPTER V.

## THE CASE OF CLEMENT OF ALEXANDRIA.

"It is very remarkable," writes Harnack, "that the theory of the bishop's power to determine the truth of ecclesiastical Christianity is completely unknown to Clement of Alexandria. We have not the slightest evidence that he had any conception of a hierarchical antiheretical Church; he seldom mentions the ecclesiastical offices (still less the bishops), who do not belong to his conception of the Church. . . . On the other hand, according to Clement, the true Gnostic has an office like that of the Apostles. . . . Clement could not have expressed himself in this way if the office of bishop had at that time been as much esteemed in the Alexandrian Church of which he was a presbyter, as it was at Rome and in the other Churches of the West. According to Clement, the Gnostic as a teacher, has the same importance as a bishop in the West. . . . Origen, has fundamentally the same conception as Clement. But numerous passages in his works, and above all his own history, show that in his day the episcopate had become stronger in Alexandria also, and claimed the same attributes and rights as in the West. . . . Clement represents an earlier stage, whereas by Origen's time the transformation has been completed. Wherever this happened, the theory that the monarchical episcopate was based on Apostolic institution was the natural result." [1]

Clement of Alexandria is a contemporary of Irenæus and of Tertullian. Like many other Greek Christians of the

[1] "Dogmeng." vol. 1⁴, p. 403. LOOFS, "Leitfaden," p. 167, adopts the theory of Harnack. For a less absolute judgment, cf. HORT and MAYOR, "Clement of Alexandria, Miscellanies, Book VII" (London, 1902), pp. xxii-xlvii (against HARNACK and HATCH).

second century, he has travelled a great deal : he has visited Italy, Greece, the East, Palestine; he settles down for a while, probably about the year 180, at Alexandria, and there he resides until the year 202 or 203, when he retires perhaps to Jerusalem.   Hence, Clement's ecclesiology does not represent that of Alexandria and of the Alexandrians only, and his testimony—if it be what Harnack claims it is—would also express the mind of Greek Christendom; and yet we have seen that the latter, with Dionysius of Corinth and Hegesippus, held the common view.

But Harnack's judgment in the present instance seems to us more marked by tendency than any other : Clement, we venture to say, is both an orthodox Gnostic and an orthodox traditionalist, and, once this dualism is admitted, it becomes easy to discover in his traditional orthodoxy the very same characteristics as we have found in that of Irenæus ; only we must first extract them from the intolerable diffuseness of his writings which have been preserved, and from the scanty information that can be obtained regarding those of them which have been lost.

\*  \*
\*

Clement's " Hypotyposes," a work as important as his " Stromata," was a doctrinal exposition based on the Scriptures of the Old and the New Testament, including besides, as Eusebius tells us, some books the canonicity of which is disputed, such as the Epistle of Jude, the Epistle of Barnabas, the " other Catholic Epistles," the Apocalypse of Peter and the Epistle to the Hebrews which Clement ascribes to St. Paul.   The " Hypotyposes " contained, it is thought, a defence of the canon of the New Testament : in which Clement strove to prove the Apostolic authenticity of the Epistle to the Hebrews,[1] and gave an account of the origin of the second Gospel which connected it through Mark with the Apostle Peter who sanctioned that Gospel with his Apostolic authority, "for reading in the Churches".[2] Eusebius observes that Papias uses the same argument.

[1] EUSEB. " H. E.," VI. 14, 1.
[2] *Ibid.* II. 15, 2.   After these declarations, we fail to understand how some critics can suggest that Clement was unacquainted with the canon of the New Testament (in the sense of Irenæus, Tertullian, and the

Clement states that he has these reminiscences concerning the origin of the New Testament from "the tradition of the presbyters of old," and in giving his authority for what he relates concerning the Epistle to the Hebrews he uses the formula so dear to Irenæus: "as the blessed presbyter used to say".[1]   Here we have an indication of Clement's method in these matters of tradition, and of the reverence he pays to the sayings of the presbyters.   According to Eusebius, Clement says in his work Περὶ τοῦ πάσχα that he has been constrained by his hearers to write down the traditions gathered from the ancient presbyters, among whom he reckons Melito, Irenæus, and some others.[2]   Later on, Alexander of Jerusalem will give Clement himself the title of "blessed presbyter".[3]

At the request of Alexander of Jerusalem, Clement composed a work, of which the title alone has been preserved: Κανὼν ἐκκλησιαστικὸς ἢ πρὸς ἰουδαΐζοντας.   This might seem to be a treatise against the Quartodecimans, but Clement had already written a treatise about the Passover, Jerusalem had accepted the principle of keeping that feast on Sunday, and the Easter-controversy was over when Alexander had Clement with him at Jerusalem : so many reasons for believing that the treatise in question was not directed against the Quartodecimans.   It was directed then against the Judæo-Christians; and from this it may be inferred that the "ecclesiastical canon " which it defends is the ecclesias-

" Muratorianum "), and that not until the time of Origen did Alexandria reach the point which Rome had reached some forty years before.   The discussion (Zahn, Harnack) on the canon of the New Testament as accepted by Clement, is summed up by BARDENHEWER, vol. II. pp. 59-61. Cf. ZAHN, "Grundriss," pp. 41-4.   The demonstration would be more conclusive if the hypothesis of Dom Chapman, who suggests we should look upon the " Muratorianum " as a fragment of the " Hypotyposes," were accepted.   CHAPMAN, "L'auteur du canon Muratorien," in the "Revue bénédictine," 1904, pp. 240-64.   But, to my mind, that view is not probable.

[1] EUSEB. VI. 14, 4.

[2] Ibid. VI. 13, 9 : ἃς ἔτυχε παρὰ τῶν ἀρχαίων πρεσβυτέρων ἀκηκοὼς παραδόσεις.

[3] Ibid. VI. 11, 6.   The sayings ascribed to the presbyters by Irenæus and by others have been collected by various scholars, particularly by FUNK, "Patres Apostol." vol. II. pp. 301-14.

tical rule and standard of faith, as demanding, not a literal, but a spiritual interpretation of the Sacred Writings.[1] The expression itself, "ecclesiastical canon," already reveals an idea of the Church which connects Clement with all the presbyters we know of.

Besides, the idea of ecclesiastical rule or canon is familiar to Clement. Some heretics refuse to make use of wine in the eucharist, and "take for the offering bread and water, contrary to the canon of the Church".[2] Hence, as regards the Sacraments, the canon of the Church must be followed, and heretics are condemned by the very fact that they transgress this canon. Clement then recognizes the antithesis between the canon and heresy. Elsewhere he writes: "We must never, as do those who embrace the heresies, do violence to the truth or defraud the canon of the Church".[3]

What is this ecclesiastical canon? It is, answers Clement, "the concord and harmony of the Law and the Prophets [on the one side], and of the Testament delivered in accordance with the presence of the Lord";[4] in other words, to use the well-known trilogy, it is the harmony of the Prophets, the Lord and the Apostles: perhaps an allusion to the contradictions denounced by Marcion. "Liars, then, are . . . those who, by forsaking the fundamental doctrines reject the Lord, as far as in them lies, and corrupt the true teaching of the Lord; who discuss and teach the Scriptures in a manner unworthy of God and of the Lord: for the deposit we have to render to God, according to the

---

[1] KATTENBUSCH, vol. II. p. 176.

[2] "Stromat." I. 10 (Migne, "P. G." vol. VIII. p. 813): μὴ κατὰ τὸν κανόνα τῆς ἐκκλησίας.

[3] "Stromat." VII. 16 (IX. 545): οὐ χρή ποτε, καθάπερ οἱ τὰς αἱρέσεις μετιόντες ποιοῦσι, μοιχεύειν τὴν ἀλήθειαν οὐδὲ μὴν κλέπτειν τὸν κανόνα τῆς ἐκκλησίας. We may recall the rigorous character of the penitential discipline against fornication and "defrauding". On the fundamental purpose of the κανὼν ἐκκλησιαστικός or κανὼν τῆς ἐκκλησίας in Clement's writings, cf. KATTENBUSCH, vol. II. pp. 110-29.

[4] "Stromat." VI. 15 (IX. 349 A): κανὼν δὲ ἐκκλησιαστικὸς ἡ συνῳδία καὶ ἡ συμφωνία νόμου τε καὶ προφητῶν τῇ κατὰ τὴν τοῦ κυρίου παρουσίαν παραδιδομένῃ διαθήκῃ. See also "Stromat." VI. 11 (309 C), in which the "ecclesiastical symphony" is described as the accord of the Prophets, the Apostles and the Gospel.

teaching of the Lord by His Apostles, is the understanding and practice of the religious tradition."[1] Preach on the housetops," the Saviour said: i.e. "explain the Scriptures according to the canon of the truth".[2] Still more accurately: "[He who wishes to be saved] must believe . ... the disciples of God, and trust in God, in the Prophets, the Gospels, the Apostolic words".[3] The "canon of the truth" is the same as "the canon of the tradition" or the "canon of the Church'": it is a fixed and exclusive doctrine, and not merely the symbol used in the baptismal liturgy, which is only a catechetical formula and summary of that teaching.

Clement comments as follows on the narrative of the vessel of perfume poured on the Saviour's feet:—

"*This may be a symbol of the Lord's teaching, and of His passion. For the feet anointed with that fragrant ointment signify the divine instruction which travels gloriously to the ends of the earth. . . . And if I seem not to insist too much, the feet of the Lord which were anointed with this myrrh are the Apostles who have, according to the prophecy of the fragrant unction, received the Holy Ghost. The Apostles, therefore, who travelled over the world and preached the Gospel, are, allegorically, the feet of the Lord."*[4]

The preaching of the Gospel to the whole world is then the work of the Apostles.[5] Prophecy was full of "gnosis,"

---

[1] "Stromat." vi. 15 (843 B): Ψευσταί . . . οἱ εἰς τὰ κυριώτατα παραπίπτοντες . . . ἀποστεροῦντες δὲ τοῦ κυρίου τὴν ἀληθῆ διδασκαλίαν . . . Παραθήκη . . . ἡ κατὰ τὴν τοῦ κυρίου διδασκαλίαν διὰ τῶν ἀποστόλων αὐτοῦ, τῆς θεοσεβοῦς παραδόσεως σύνεσις.

[2] *Ibid.* (C): κατὰ τὸν τῆς ἀληθείας κανόνα διασαφοῦντες τὰς γραφάς, "Stromat.' i. 1 (viii. 704 C): κατὰ τὸν τῆς παραδόσεως κανόνα.

[3] "Quis div. salv." 42 (ix. 652 A): προφητείαις, εὐαγγελίοις, λόγοις ἀποστολικοῖς.

[4] "Stromat." ii. 8 (viii. 465). Cf. "Stromat." vii. 12 (lx. 501 C). The Holy Ghost bestowed on the Apostles, continues to work in the Church. If the "Excerpta ex scriptis Theodoti" are extracts made by Clement intermingled with his remarks, we may consult "Excerpt." 24 (ix. 672), where the author affirms the presence and working of the Spirit in the Church, of that same Spirit which worked through the Prophets of the Old Testament. Compare "Eclog. prophet." 23 (ix. 708).

[5] Clement quotes often the Κήρυγμα Πέτρου, an apocryphal work which, according to some critics, was composed in Egypt in the first

of that "gnosis," which was revealed through the Lord to the Apostles, "James, Peter, John, Paul,"[1] and which has reached us from the Apostles, handed down unwritten, by a succession limited to a few individuals.[2]  In these obscure words, Clement designates the teaching of presbyters like Melito and Irenæus, or better still of Pantænus and the others spoken of at the beginning of the "Stromata".  "They preserved," he writes, "the tradition of the blessed doctrine [of Christ], received directly from the holy Apostles, Peter, James, John and Paul."[3]

The teaching of the presbyters derives its authority from the apostles who have left it as an inheritance that has come down to us by succession (κατὰ διαδοχάς).  We must grant that in this passage it is not, strictly speaking, the succession of the bishops in general which is referred to ; for, unlike Melito and Irenæus, neither Pantænus nor Clement himself is a bishop.  But Clement justifies the teaching of the presbyters—whom he does not distinguish from the

quarter of the second century.  Now this Κήρυγμα had already insisted on the fundamental part played by the Apostles : it gave the instructions of the Saviour concerning the preaching of the Gospel ; the Apostles were told to preach it to Israel first, and to devote twelve years to that work : after these twelve years, they were to turn to the Gentile world. "Stromat." vi. 5.  Clement may have taken from the same source what he says of the preaching of the Apostles, of all the Apostles, in Limbo. *Ibid.* 6 (ix. 268 A).  At all events it is from this source he borrowed the discourse of the risen Saviour to the Twelve. *Ibid.* (269 C).  These texts may be found in DOBSCHÜTZ, "Kerygma Petri," pp. 22-3.

[1] "Stromat." vi. 8 (ix. 289 C).

[2] *Ibid.* 7 (284 A) : ἡ γνῶσις δὲ αὐτή, ἡ κατὰ διαδοχὰς εἰς ὀλίγους καὶ τῶν ἀποστόλων ἀγράφως παραδοθεῖσα, κατελήλυθεν.  Cf. "Excerpt. Theodot." 66 (ix. 689), and "Eclog. prophet." 59 (728).

[3] "Stromat." i. 1 (viii. 700) : τὴν ἀληθῆ τῆς μακαρίας σώζοντες διδασκαλίας παράδοσιν, εὐθὺς ἀπὸ Πέτρου κ.τ.λ.  As to Peter's primacy over the other Apostles, we may recall what Clement writes in the VIIIth book of his "Hypotyposes" : "Christ is said to have baptized Peter alone ; and Peter, Andrew ; and Andrew, James and John ; and they, the rest." "P. G." vol. ix. col. 745 C (taken from the "Spiritual Meadow").  Elsewhere Clement calls Peter "the chosen, the pre-eminent, the first of the disciples (ὁ πρῶτος τῶν μαθητῶν), for whom alone, along with Himself, the Saviour paid tribute.'  "Quis div. salv." 21.  In the book of "Hypotyposes," Clement thinks he knows that the Cephas St. Paul withstood to the face was not the Apostle Peter, but one of the seventy disciples.  EUSEB. "H. E." i. 12, 2.

bishops—by the same consideration as Irenæus, Hegesippus, Papias, and Polycarp employed to justify the teaching of the bishops and the faith of the churches.[1]

The Episcopate, which is distinct from the Apostolate, dates back from the Apostles: "Peter and James and John, after the ascension of our Saviour, even though preferred by our Lord, strove not after honour, but chose James the Just, to be Bishop of Jerusalem."[2] Alluding to a phrase in the Pastoral Epistles (1 Tim. III. 4, 5), Clement writes: "Bishops, says [St. Paul], must be appointed, who know, after [ruling] their own house, how to rule the whole Church;"[3] for the Church is both ruling and ruled. On one side is the people.[4] On the other are the pastors of this people, the "heads of the Churches," including under this name of heads both bishops and priests: "We who preside over the Churches are shepherds after the image of the good Shepherd, and you are the sheep."[5]

*"Such an one is truly a presbyter of the Church, and a true minister (deacon) of the will of God, if he do and teach what is the Lord's: and he is deemed righteous not as being elected by men or because he is a presbyter, but is enrolled in the presbyterate because he is righteous. And even if here upon earth he be not honoured with the chief seat, he will sit on the four-and-twenty thrones, judging the people, as John says in the Apocalypse. . . . For the order [which we see here below] in the Church, of bishops, priests, deacons, is, in my opinion, an imitation of the angelic glory, and of that economy which, the Scriptures say, awaits those who, following the footsteps of the Apostles, have lived in perfection of righteousness according to the Gospel. For these taken up in*

---

[1] As to the "presbyters" in Clement (cf. "Eclog. prophet." 27 (IX. 712) and 56 (724).

[2] Quoted from the sixth both of the "Hypotyposes," by EUSEB. "H. E." II. 1, 3.

[3] "Stromat." III. 12 (VII. 1180 A) : τοῦ ἰδίου οἴκου καὶ τῆς ἐκκλησίας ἁπάσης προΐστασθαι. Cf. ibid. 18 (1212 B).

[4] Ibid. I. 1 (VIII. 692 B). Cf. "Stromat." III. 12 (VIII. 1189 C) : πρεσβύτερος, διάκονος, λαϊκός.

[5] "Pædagog." I. 6 (VIII. 293 D) : εἴτε ποιμένες ἐσμὲν οἱ τῶν ἐκκλησιῶν προηγούμενοι, κατ᾽ εἰκόνα τοῦ ἀγαθοῦ ποιμένος, τὰ δὲ πρόβατα ἡμεῖς (so STAEHLIN). SYLBURG suggests that we should read ὑμεῖς.

*the clouds, the Apostle writes, will first minister as deacons, then be classed in the presbyterate, by promotion of glory (for glory differs from glory), till they grow into a perfect man.*"[1]

The absence of distinction which Clement apparently leaves between the priests and the bishop is most worthy of notice: the *presbyterium* is an honour, a glory to which they are raised together:[2] the bishop is the presbyter to whom the πρωτοκαθεδρία has been granted. Elsewhere, however, the distinction between the various degrees of the hierarchy is clearly stated. "Innumerable commands . . . are written in the Holy Bible," says Clement,[3] "appertaining to chosen persons, some to presbyters, some to bishops, some to deacons, others to widows."

In the beautiful story of St. John, found at the end of the "Quis dives salvetur," the Apostle is represented as visiting a Church near Ephesus, which he had probably founded. At the head of that Church there is one, and only one "episcopus" to whom the Apostle entrusts the youth he has brought to the faith. The bishop instructs the young man and finally baptizes him. After the new Christian has been perverted and has gone away, John arrives and asks what has become of him: "O bishop, restore to us the deposit which I and the Saviour committed to thee in the presence of the Church over which thou dost preside" (τῆς ἐκκλησίας ἧς προκαθέζῃ). All the Churches in Clement's time were certainly organized after the model of that Johannine Church.

Baptism imparts the forgiveness of sins and the knowledge of God. The catechesis is the foundation of faith.[4]

---

[1] "Stromat." VI. 13 (IX. 238) : . . . οὐχ ὑπ' ἀνθρώπων χειροτονούμενος, οὐδ' ὅτι πρεσβύτερος, δίκαιος νομιζόμενος, ἀλλ' ὅτι δίκαιος ἐν πρεσβυτερίῳ καταλεγόμενος · κἂν ἐνταῦθα ἐπὶ γῆς πρωτοκαθεδρίᾳ μὴ τιμηθῇ κ.τ.λ.—αἱ ἐνταῦθα κατὰ τὴν ἐκκλησίαν προκοπαὶ ἐπισκόπων, πρεσβυτέρων, διακόνων, μιμήματα ἀγγελικῆς δόξης κ.τ.λ.

[2] *Ibid.* VII. 1 (IX. 405 A), has the same absence of distinction.

[3] "Pædagog." III. 12 (VIII. 677 A) : ὑποθῆκαι εἰς πρόσωπα ἐκλεκτὰ διατείνουσαι, . . . αἱ μὲν πρεσβυτέροις, αἱ δὲ ἐπισκόποις, αἱ δὲ διακόνοις, ἄλλαι χήραις, περὶ ὧν ἄλλος ἂν εἴη λέγειν καιρός.

[4] *Ibid.* I. 6 (VIII. 296 A) : ἡ πίστις εἰς θεμέλιον ἐκ κατηχήσεως συνεστραμμένη. Cf. " Eclog. prophet." 28 (IX. 713) : οὐκ ἔστι πιστεῦσαι ἄνευ κατηχήσεως.

Faith is trained by Baptism and by the Holy Ghost. The grace of Baptism makes a man entirely different from what he was before being baptized.[1] Baptism conferred by the heretics is not a true, a legitimate baptism: its waters are like those of a river that loses itself in the sea, together with all those who give up the solid ground of truth.[2] Hence Baptism is truly a new birth, and there is no legitimate birth outside the Church, which alone possesses, together with the truth, the Holy Spirit. Clement designates the authentic Christians by this title: " those of the Church ".[3] There are martyrs only for them and among them. The elect are to be found only within the bosom of the Church.[4] God's will is creative, and we call it the cosmos: but it wills also the salvation of men, and as such it is called the Church.[5]

\* \*
\*

The word Church designates the local Church, properly speaking the synaxis, i.e. the gathering of the faithful: *ecclesia* is used in this sense, just as is the word *agora*.[6] The word Church serves also to designate the number of the elect received into Heaven: "Yea, O Instructor [and Divine Shepherd], lead us [as Thy flock] to Thy holy mountain the Church, which towers aloft, which is above the clouds, which touches heaven."[7] This " heavenly Church," which is unseen and above the earth, is the most real of all things;[8] it contrasts with the Church upon earth just as a reality contrasts with its image; in this case the image, the shadow, is the visible Church, the Church that is here below.[9]

[1] "Pædagog." I. 6 (VIII. 285).

[2] "Stromat." I. 19 (VIII. 813 A) : τὸ βάπτισμα τὸ αἱρετικὸν οὐκ οἰκεῖον καὶ γνήσιον ὕδωρ.—ὁ παρεκτραπεὶς ἐκ τῆς κατ' ἀλήθειαν ἑδραιότητος. (These words recall 1 Tim. III. 15.)

[3] *Ibid.* IV. 9 (VIII. 1284 B) and 12 (1293 B).

[4] "Pædagog." II. 10 (VIII. 529 B).

[5] *Ibid.* I. 6 (VIII. 281 B) : ὡς τὸ θέλημα αὐτοῦ ἔργον ἐστι, καὶ τοῦτο κόσμος ὀνομάζεται, οὕτω καὶ τὸ βούλημα αὐτοῦ ἀνθρώπων ἐστὶ σωτηρία, καὶ τοῦτο ἐκκλησία κέκληται.

[6] *Ibid.* II. 10 (VIII. 512 B) and III. 11 (657, A).

[7] *Ibid.* I. 9 (VIII. 352 A).        [8] *Ibid.* II. 1 (VIII. 382 A).

[9] "Stromat." IV. 8 (VIII. 1277 B) : εἰκὼν τῆς οὐρανίου ἐκκλησίας ἡ ἐπίγειος.

More universal than any philosophy, the word of the Divine Master " was diffused through the whole world, gaining over both Greeks and barbarians, in every people and town, bringing in here an entire city, there whole houses, . . . and not a few of the philosophers themselves ".[1] Does not Clement seem to have in his mind St. Ignatius of Antioch, when he writes : " The altar that is with us here, the terrestrial one, is the congregation of those who devote themselves to prayer, having as it were one common voice and one mind. . . . The Church truly draws but one breath ".[2] Universality and unity : these are the two aspects under which Clement considers the earthly Church ; hence he often uses this expression : "the whole Church ". In the state of marriage, the husband is the crown of the wife. " And the crown of the whole Church is Christ."[3]

This Church, one and universal, hierarchical and apostolic both in origin and teaching, is for Clement the living and triumphant antithesis of heresy. Clement quotes from the Epistle to the Ephesians the text in which St. Paul expresses his sincere wish that the faithful should not be like children carried to and fro by surging waves, tossed to and fro by every wind of doctrine.

"[Paul] says these things for the edification of the body of Christ who is the head [of the body] and the spouse [of the Church], the only one perfect in righteousness : and as for us, we are the children, guarding ourselves against the blasts of heresies that are filled with infatuation ; not putting our trust in those who teach us otherwise than our fathers [did], and being made perfect, when we are the Church, with Christ for the head ".[4]

---

[1] " Stromat." vi. 18 (ix. 400 B).

[2] Ibid. vii. 6 (ix. 444) : ἔστι τὸ παρ' ἡμῖν θυσιαστήριον ἐνταῦθα τὸ ἐπίγειον τὸ ἄθροισμα τῶν ταῖς εὐχαῖς ἀνακειμένων, μίαν ὥσπερ ἔχον φωνὴν τὴν κοινὴν καὶ μίαν γνώμην.—Ἡ σύμπνοια δὲ ἐπὶ τῆς ἐκκλησίας λέγεται κυρίως.

[3] " Pædagog.' ii. 8 (vii. 480 B) : τῆς συμπάσης ἐκκλησίας στέφανος ὁ Χριστός. " Stromat." iii. 11 (1173 B) : εἴτε ὁ καθ' ἕκαστον ἡμῶν, εἴτε καὶ ἀθρόα ἡ ἐκκλησία. Ib. iv. 8 (1272 A) : πᾶσα ἡ ἐκκλησία.

[4] Ibid. i. 5 (viii. 269 C) : ἐσμὲν ἐκκλησία. Clement states that we are perfect, in the order of gnosis, when we are the Church, for there is no other perfect gnosis than the " ecclesiastical gnosis ".

Elsewhere, commenting on a text of Proverbs, he writes as follows :—

"*He who relies on falsehoods feeds the winds and pursues winged birds* [Prov. IX. 12]. *I do not think that the Logos says this of philosophy . . . but against the heresies. For it is added : He forsakes the ways of his own vineyard, and loses himself in the tracks of his own lands. Such are [the heresies] which desert the Church that is from the beginning.*" [1]

In another place, he speaks as follows of the Church regarded as the spouse of God :—

"*. . . The wife, i.e. the Church. She must be pure from all the inner thoughts that are contrary to the truth, and from all the outer thoughts that assail it. I mean the followers of heresies, who would fain persuade her to become adulterous and be unfaithful to her only spouse, God Almighty. The serpent deceived Eve, Eve who was called life : we at least must not transgress the commands, by allowing ourselves to be deceived by the active perfidy of heresies.*" [2]

Again he writes from a more philosophical point of view :—

"*Now, since there are three states of the soul—ignorance, opinion, knowledge—those who are in ignorance are the nations, those in knowledge the true Church, and those in opinion the heretics. . . .*

"*We have learned that pleasure, which is attributed to the nations, is one thing; and wrath, which is supreme among the heretical sects, is another; and joy, which is characteristic of the Church, another; and delight, which is to be assigned to the true Gnostic, another.*" [3]

Therefore, when compared with heresies, the Church is the lawful, the chaste, the faithful spouse : heresies assail her from the outside. The Church is the truth: heresies are the opinion that changes like the wind.

---

[1] "Stromat." I. 19 (VIII. 812 C) : τὰς αἱρέσεις ἐπιρραπίζει . . . αὗται δέ εἰσιν αἱ τὴν ἐξ ἀρχῆς ἀπολείπουσαι ἐκκλησίαν.

[2] *Ibid.* III. 12 (VIII. 1180 B) : τῶν τε ἔξωθεν πειραζόντων, τουτέστι τῶν τὰς αἱρέσεις μετιόντων.

[3] *Ibid.* VII. 16 (IX. 540) : οἱ ἐν τῇ ἐπιστήμῃ ἡ ἐκκλησία ἡ ἀληθής, οἱ δὲ ἐν οἰήσει οἱ κατὰ τὰς αἱρέσεις.

" *Is the demonstration needed?   It is necessary to come
to the questions [raised by heretics], and to demonstrate
from the Scriptures themselves how the heresies failed, and
how in the truth alone and in the ancient Church is both the
most exact gnosis and the truly best ' heresy' (i.e. choice).* . . .

" *We know that heresies are necessarily so called because
they are opposed to the truth; from which truth the sophists
(for such are the heretics) have, to the misfortune of men,
taken certain elements and mingled them with inventions and
artifices of their own; and having done this they glory in
being a school rather than a Church.*" [1]

Clement's method becomes more explicit: the Church
represents knowledge (ἐπιστήμη), as opposed to mere opinion.
Clement strives to show it by means of a discussion, in which
he is willing to take the same ground as his opponents:
and so prove to them that the most accurate gnosis is the
traditional teaching, and that of all " heresies " the one we
should " choose " is orthodoxy.   Clement's attitude is novel
and bold: but these concessions made to heresy, and, after
all, to the ever-recurring demands of controversy, are a mere
tactical expedient, which detracts in no degree from the
rightful claims of the " old Church," presided over by the
presbyters, to possess the deposit of the revealed faith.

We insist purposely on the anti-heretical character of
Clement's ecclesiology, for the Protestant authors of histories
of dogma take delight in denying it that character.   In their
eyes, Tertullian and Irenæus are Catholics, because they require an external standard of faith, and their Christianity is
essentially a system of doctrinal enactments; but Clement
is a Protestant, or at least—for those who hesitate to use
this term—a mystic: " Clement's Christianity is the Spirit,
which inspires him, guides him, and mostly determines his
choice of the various elements which he borrows from
Philosophy." [2]   Thus is found at Alexandria, towards the
year 200, the " religion of the Spirit " and Liberal Pro-

---

[1] " Stromat." VII. 15 (IX. 528): ἐν μόνῃ τῇ ἀληθείᾳ καὶ τῇ ἀρχαίᾳ
ἐκκλησίᾳ ἥ τε ἀκριβεστάτη γνῶσις καὶ ἡ τῷ ὄντι ἀρίστη γνῶσις · αὐχοῦσι
προΐστασθαι διατριβῆς μᾶλλον ἢ ἐκκλησίας.

[2] E. DE FAYE, " Clément d'Alexandrie " (Paris, 1898), p. 298 and foll.
The same view is taken by C. BIGG, " The Christian Platonists of
Alexandria " (Oxford, 1886), especially p. 101.

testantism, in contrast with Catholicism which, about the same time, triumphantly prevails at Carthage, Rome and Lyons.

This theory disturbs the equilibrium of Clement's doctrine. For him, revelation and philosophy are co-ordinated under three terms : the first is philosophy, whose mission it is to purify the soul, to elevate it morally, thus to prepare it for the reception of faith ; the second is faith itself ; the third is gnosis, that gnosis which truth builds up on the foundation of faith.[1]  This distinction is of the greatest importance.  What motive have we for saying that Clement discards the central term, faith, for the profit of the two others ?  For that Clement receives that faith in no other way than Tertullian and Irenæus, we have already shown, and we shall prove it still more conclusively.

" *Those who attack grave questions will inevitably fall into grave errors unless they receive from the Truth itself the rule of the truth.  Such people, in consequence of falling away from the right path, err in many points ; as you might expect from their not having the criterion by which to judge what is true and what false. . . .*

" *As if a man should, like those drugged by Circe, become an animal, so, he, who has spurned the ecclesiastical tradition, and embraced the opinions of heretical men, has ceased to be a man of God and to remain faithful to the Lord. . . . For we have, as the source of doctrine, the Lord, who by the Prophets, the Gospel, and the blessed Apostles, 'in diverse manners and sundry times'* [Heb. i. 1] *leads us from the beginning of the gnosis to the end.  But if one should suppose that another principle was required, then no longer could the principle be truly kept sound. . . . The Scripture and voice of the Lord, such is our criterion in the discovery of the things [of gnosis]. . . . The principle is above all discussion.*"[2]

---

[1] " Stromat." VII. 3 (IX. 424 C) : φιλοσοφία ἡ ἑλληνικὴ οἷον προκαθαίρει καὶ προεθίτει τὴν ψυχὴν εἰς παραδοχὴν πίστεως, ἐφ᾽ ᾗ τὴν γνῶσιν ἐποικοδομεῖ ἡ ἀλήθεια.  On this co-ordination of faith and of gnosis with philosophy, cf. BARDENHEWER, vol. II. pp. 56-8.

[2] *Ibid.* VII. 16 (IX. 532).  In view of these texts, HARNACK (" Dogmeng," I[4], 413) grants that " the empirical conception of the

Clement does not speak here of philosophical pro-pædeutics: he speaks of the faith, and of the gnosis that is built on the faith. Now, as that gnosis is also claimed by the heretics, what is the difference between the heretical and the ecclesiastical gnosis? The heretics have no respect for the canon of truth, they have no criterion of truth, because they repudiate the ecclesiastical tradition (παράδοσις ἐκκλησιασ-τική). What is meant by this tradition? It is the πίστις, which here Clement calls ἀρχή: it is the teaching of the Prophets, of the Gospel, of the Apostles; or again, it is the Scripture and voice of the Lord. Faith, or revelation is, then, the starting-point of reflexion, of speculation, in a word of the gnosis, which is our work, our contribution, our in-vention (εὕρεσις). In this work of discovery, Greek philo-sophy may have a legitimate place and function;[1] far from being for the Christian a cause of the loss of his faith, it will strengthen his faith: " We shall not be torn away by it from the roots of our faith . . . but rather, if we may so say, we shall find in it a fuller protection and a kind of exercise which furnishes a demonstration of our faith ".[2] Still, we must not forget that, for Clement, this exegetical and theological superstructure rests on the faith contained in the ecclesiasti-cal tradition. Christ's teaching is truly the only and neces-sary foundation,[3] and no other gnosis than that which Clement calls ἐκκλησιαστικὴ γνῶσις can be accepted.[4]

" *For us, then, he alone is a gnostic, who has grown old*

Church, which regards her as the institution in possession of the true doctrine, was . . . completely adopted by Clement ": " but," he adds, " Clement employed it simply in polemics and not in positive teach-ings ". I hope to show that this is not a true account of Clement's thought.

[1] " Stromat. ' I. 1 (VIII. 705) and 20\(816-7).

[2] *Ibid.* I. 2 (VIII. 709 B): συγγυμνασίαν τινὰ πίστεως ἀποδεικ-τικήν.

[3] Cf. " Cohort. ad Gent." 11 (VIII. 228 and foll.).

[4] " Stromat." VII. 16 (IX. 544 A). How can Harnack say (*loc. cit.*) that Clement ascribes to his own gnosis a value independent of the Catholic Church? The same erroneous view is found in LOOFS (op. cit. p. 171), who draws attention to the contrast between " the inner freedom of the personal Christianity " of Clement, and the great ecclesiasticism (" Kirchlichkeit ") of Origen, his disciple.

*in [the study of] the Sacred Scriptures, maintaining the apostolic and ecclesiastic rectitude of doctrines."* [1]

Can we wish for a declaration that could be more in keeping with the thought of Irenæus and could reassure us better as to the nature of Clement's " gnosticism "? Still we will cite another. The heretics, Clement writes, make a wrong use of the Divine discourses of Holy Writ, and thus neither enter into the kingdom of Heaven nor let others reach the truth.

*" Not having the key of entrance, but a false and (as the common phrase expresses it) counterfeit key, they do not enter in as we enter in, by drawing aside the curtain,[2] that is, the tradition of the Lord, but by making an opening in the side, piercing clandestinely through the wall of the Church, and stepping over the truth, they constitute themselves the mystagogues of the souls of the impious.*

*" For that the human assemblies which they hold are posterior to the Catholic Church,[3] requires not many words to show. The teaching of Our Lord during His presence [upon earth], beginning with Augustus and Tiberius, was completed in the middle of the reign of Tiberius [14-37]: the teaching of the Apostles of the Lord, embracing the ministry of Paul, ends under Nero [54-68]. It was at the earliest in the times of Hadrian [117-138], that those who invented the heresies arose, and they continued to the time of Antoninus the elder [138-161], as for instance, did Basilides, though he claims for his master Glaucias, a pretended interpreter of Peter, as [those heretics] boast; likewise too Valentinus, who, they allege, was a disciple of Theodas, a self-styled pupil of Paul; so also Marcion . . .* [4]

---

[1] " Stromat." VII. 16 : τὴν ἀποστολικὴν καὶ ἐκκλησιαστικὴν σῴζων ὀρθοτομίαν τῶν δογμάτων.

[2] διὰ τῆς τοῦ κυρίου παραδόσεως εἴσιμεν.

[3] ὅτι μεταγενεστέρας τῆς καθολικῆς ἐκκλησίας τὰς ἀνθρωπίνας συνηλύσεις πεποιήκασιν.

[4] Three lines follow on the text of which editors do not agree. Hort and Mayor substitute "Mark" for "Marcion," and propose to read : " Mark the evangelist was more ancient than Glaucias and Theudas, so-called disciples of the Apostles. He was more ancient even than Simon, who most assuredly heard Peter." This Simon (Magus) was the first heretic.

"*Such being the case, it is evident that these later heresies and [with still greater reason] those subsequent to them in time, are novelties and corruptions as compared with the eldest and truest Church.*[1]

"*From what has been said, it is my opinion that the true Church, that which is really ancient, is one, and that in it those who are truly just .are enrolled ; since for the very reason that God is one, and the Lord one, that which is in the highest degree venerable is lauded because it is single, imitating in this its source which is one. The Church then is associated to the nature of unity which they [i.e. the heretics] strive to divide into many heresies.*[2]

"*Therefore, in substance, in idea, in principle, in pre-eminence, we say that the ancient and catholic Church*[3] *is alone, in the unity of the one faith, which is according to the Testaments. . . . The preeminence of the Church, as well as the principle of its constitution, is in this oneness,*[4] *and it surpasses all things else, and has nothing like or equal to itself.*

"*As to the heresies, some bear a person's name, as those which are called after Valentinus, after Marcion, after Basilides although they boast of possessing the teaching of Matthias;*[5] *for as the teaching of all the Apostles was one, so also the tradition [of that teaching] is one. Some take their designation 'from a place, as the Peratici ; some, 'from a race, as the Phrygians; some, 'from a virtue, as the Encratites ; and some, 'from their peculiar dogmas, as the Docetae. . . .*"[6]

The opposition between the Church and the heresies

---

[1] τῆς προγενεστάτης καὶ ἀληθεστάτης ἐκκλησίας.

[2] The Greek text is as follows : φανερὸν οἶμαι γεγενῆσθαι, μίαν εἶναι τὴν ἀληθῆ ἐκκλησίαν, τὴν τῷ ὄντι ἀρχαίαν · . . . Τὸ ἄκρως τίμιον κατὰ τὴν μόνωσιν ἐπαινεῖται, μίμημα ὂν ἀρχῆς τῆς μιᾶς · Τῇ γοῦν τοῦ ἑνὸς φύσει συγκληροῦται ἐκκλησία ἡ μία, ἣν εἰς πολλὰς κατατέμνειν βιάζονται αἱρέσεις.

[3] μόνην εἶναι φαμὲν τὴν ἀρχαίαν καὶ καθολικὴν ἐκκλησίαν.

[4] ἡ ἐξοχὴ τῆς ἐκκλησίας, καθάπερ ἡ ἀρχὴ τῆς συστάσεως, κατὰ τὴν μονάδα ἐστί.

[5] Clement alludes to the Παραδόσεις, wrongly ascribed to St. Matthias. This apocryphal writing, which dates from the first quarter of the second century and was held in great esteem by the school of Basilides, is often quoted by Clement. PREUSCHEN, " Antilegomena," pp. 13, 15.

[6] "Stromat." VII. 17. HORT and MAYOR, pp. 188-90.

can hardly be more strongly emphasized. Against the many heresies that strive to oppose her, the Church stands one,[1] because of her very constitution, her principle, her origin, the idea of her divine founder. Against the heresies, all of recent formation, the Church stands, the first-born, ancient, true, worthy of respect, holy, to whom alone the just belong, as to her alone belongs the teaching of the Apostles, of all the Apostles, in an authentic tradition. One, holy, apostolic, she is besides catholic : this last word, which is missing in Irenæus, is actually uttered by Clement.[2] She is also, we may add, the Mother Church.

"*O mysterious wonder ! One is the Father of the universe, one the Spirit Who is everywhere, and one is the only virgin mother. I love to call the Church by this name, . . . pure as a virgin, loving as a mother.*"[3]

Utterances of mystical enthusiasm are these, it is true, like those of St. Ignatius of Antioch ; but they have an object as directly perceptible as the heresies, since their purpose is to proclaim more emphatically the contrast between the unity of the Church, on one hand, and the multiplicity of heresies, on the other. We readily grant that, unlike Irenæus, Clement does not dwell on the bonds that bind together all the members of this large body ; still it remains beyond dispute that the Catholic Church, as conceived and described by Clement, possesses a rule of faith, a standard of liturgy, a canon of the Scriptures, a common tradition. Again if in this empiric Catholicism, episcopacy is not as clearly brought forward as it is in the writings of Irenæus, it is well for us to remember that no more stress is placed on the various churches, those single units whose total sum makes up empiric Catholicism. Yet, they do exist, as so many individuals, and their individual unity has for its guar-

---

[1] The reader will find a remarkable development of this idea of the unity of the Church in " Pædagog." I. 4 (VIII. 260) and in " Stromat." III. 11 (VIII. 1172). Hence it is not possible to share Harnack's view, " Dogmeng." vol. I[4], p. 412, and say that Clement changes his conception of the Church, beginning with chapter 15 of "Stromat." VII. The " Stromata " (about 208-11) was the latest work of Clement.

[2] KATTENBUSCH, vol. II. p. 926, does his utmost to explain the word καθολική in the sense of τοῦ θεοῦ.

[3] " Paedagog." I. 6 (VIII. 300 B).

antee the monarchical episcopate which, like the churches themselves, owes its origin to the Apostles. Abundant as may be the share assigned, in those of Clement's works that have reached us, to philosophical propædeutics, on one hand, and to ecclesiastical gnosis, on the other, the framework of the faith is the same for him as for Irenæus ; his Church is both hierarchical and anti-heretical.

Perhaps, after the perusal of the previous pages, some may hesitate to say with Mr. Bigg: "No echo of the strife which was raging at his time for the triumph of the hierarchy penetrated the tranquil seclusion in which Clement lectured and composed. He reflects with calm fidelity the image of the bygone times in which he had himself been reared. His heart is with the republic; he is the Samuel of the new monarchy."[1]

[1] BIGG, "Christian Platonists," pp. 100-1. For a more complete description of the episcopal régime at the time of Clement, we might refer to what is known, especially through EUSEBIUS, "H. E." VI. 12, of Serapion, who was Bishop of Antioch between the years 190 and 211. We might also recall two most striking incidents related by Hippolytus in the "Comment. on Daniel," XVIII. and XIX. ("Hippolytus Werke," vol. I. 1, pp. 230-4). These facts, the first of which refers to a Bishop of Syria, the second, to a Bishop of Pontus, show that in each Church the bishop was everything, and that, if he had a rather limited measure of common-sense, he could draw all his Church after him into such extravagances as those described by Hippolytus. The "Commentary on Daniel" was written in the year 204, and therefore dates exactly from Clement's epoch.

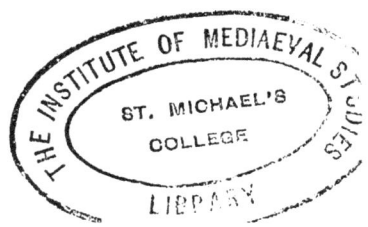

# CHAPTER VI.

## TERTULLIAN'S VARIATIONS.

To Tertullian, a Carthaginian by birth, Eusebius gives the title of "Roman," and most rightly so, for the great African is just as much a "Roman" as Irenæus. Born about the year 160, he was in his maturity when he embraced Christianity (about the year 195). He became at once a priest of Carthage. An apologist after the manner of Justin and Irenæus, he was for a short while the spokesman both of Latin and of Greek Christendom, for he writes both Latin and Greek; he is, with a brilliancy of his own, *eristicus et ardens vir*,[1] tradition personified.[2] Then he passes over to the party of the "new prophecy," rebels against Rome, and ends his days in isolation and obscurity.

Had Tertullian died before embracing the Montanist error, his ecclesiology would hardly differ from that of Irenæus, whose important treatise "Contra Haereses" he certainly knew and turned to account. But Tertullian did not remain a Catholic: he attempted to harmonize the principle of the rule of faith based on tradition, with the principle of individual prophetical inspiration. His Catholicism, in his best days, confirms the notion of Catholicism presented to us by Irenæus; his semi-Montanism and his open Montanism confirm the same notion, but by way of contrast.

This we shall see by studying, first, the "De Praescriptione haereticorum" (composed about the year 200).

## I.

Since Christianity consists in unity through conformity to a rule of faith, no wonder that the existence of "non-con-

---

[1] The words are from St. Jerome, "Epistul." LXXXIV. 2.

[2] On this point (against Harnack), cf. BARDENHEWER, vol. II. pp. 340 and 362.

formists " becomes a scandal : " *Plerique hoc ipso scandali-zantur quod tantum haereses valeant* ". They are too many and too important. They succeed in winning to their errors some of the faithful who were known to be prudent and approved : here a bishop, there a deacon, elsewhere a doctor, even a martyr.[1] Tertullian grants the facts, but desires that no one should be moved by them. For we must not judge the faith, he says, by the persons who betray it : the wind carries off the chaff ; the corn that remains is the purer for it. Was not the Lord Himself abandoned and betrayed ? And St. Paul ? Did not the Lord foretell that there would arise false prophets, false apostles, antichrists ? Did not the Apostle Paul warn us against heresies ? Let no one, therefore, be troubled by this flood of heresies, since they have been announced beforehand.[2]

Then, Tertullian goes to the heart of his inquisition : he criticises the heresy which he is opposing, i.e. learned Gnosticism, and brings against it the reproach already brought against it by Irenæus and Clement of Alexandria : viz. that it is a mere web of secular sophistry.[3] The Gnostic errors, "*natae de ingenio sapientiae saecularis*," are a rash interpretation of the Divine Nature and of the In-carnation. They draw their inspiration from philosophy : Valentinus borrowed from the Platonists, Marcion from the Stoics and Epicureans. Heretics and philosophers discuss the same topics : the origin of evil, the origin of man, the

---

[1] "Praescr." 3 : "Quid ergo, si episcopus, si diaconus, si vidua, si virgo, si doctor, si etiam martyr lapsus a regula fuerit, ideo haereses veri-tatem videbuntur obtinere ? "

[2] *Ibid.* 1-6.

[3] The same argument will later on be taken up by St. Hippolytus, quoted by Euseb. "H. E." v. 28. The view that the various Gnostic errors are borrowings from Greek philosophy, is driven home by the "Philosophoumena" (particularly in the VIIth book), according to which Basilides was perverted by Aristotle, Valentinus by Plato and Pythagoras, Marcion by Empedocles, and so too the other leaders of Gnosticism. Tertullian and Hippolytus meant to react, in this way, against the in-dulgent attitude which the Greek apologists who had preceded them, and perhaps, too, the Hellenistic Jews, had adopted towards the Greek wisdom.

origin of God.   Their method, the method of them all, is
that of Aristotle, that " miserable Aristotle ".[1]

Of what avail is all this philosophy?   Against its seduc-
tions St. Paul has forewarned us; and the Apostle knew
well this human wisdom " *affectatricem et interpolatricem
veritatis*," he had seen it at work at Athens.[2]   We have
nothing in common with it.

"*Viderint qui stoicum et platonicum et dialecticum
christianismum protulerunt.   Nobis curiositate opus non
est, post Christum Iesum ; nec inquisitione, post evangelium.
Cum credimus, nihil desideramus ultra credere : hoc enim
prius credimus, non esse quod ultra credere debeamus.*"[3]

Irenæus does not think differently, when, as against the
Gnostics who aim at perfect knowledge and despise the
simple-mindedness of the " Psychics," he stands for simple
faith and affirms its claims.   A typical African, Tertullian
presents this thought in an absolute and somewhat aggres-
sive form.   He thinks it quite useless on the part of some
to bring against him the words of the Gospel: " Seek and
ye shall find," for no one seeks, unless he has not already

---

[1] " Praescr." 7 : " Miserum Aristotelem, qui illis dialecticam instituit,
artificem struendi et destruendi, versipellem in sententiis, coactam in coni-
ecturis, duram in argumentis, operariam contentionum, molestam etiam
sibi ipsi, omnia retractantem, ne quid omnino tractaverit ! . . . Quid
ergo Athenis et Hierosolymis ?   Quid Academiae et Ecclesiae ?   Quid
haereticis et christianis ? "   Compare the interesting Greek fragment of
the Περὶ ἐκκλησίας, ascribed to Anthimus, Bishop of Nicomedia ( + 302) discovered and published by G. MERCATI, " Note di letteratura biblica e cris-
tiana antica " (Rome, 1901), pp. 95-8.   This fragment reminds us far more
of Irenæus and of Tertullian than of Origen.   It begins as follows : " As
there is one God, one Son of God, one Holy Ghost, so also God created one
man, one cosmos only, and there is one Catholic and Apostolic Church, and
one baptism for the whole cosmos.   Μία τοίνυν καθολικὴ καὶ ἀποστολικὴ ἐκκλησία ἔστι καθ' ὅλης οἰκουμένης, which continues to preserve to this day the
faith she received from the Apostles.   She is called Catholic, because she is
spread all over the world. . . .   But heresies have received [their teaching]
neither from the Apostles, nor from the disciples of the Apostles, nor
from the bishops, successors of the Apostles, . . . nor are they established
everywhere, nor are their churches called Catholic."   Then the author
shows that those heresies originated with the Sadducees, or Simon, etc.,
and all the heresiarchs borrowed their doctrines from the philosophers,
especially from Plato, Aristotle and Hermes Trismegistus.

[2] Cf. " De Anima," 3.                    [3] " Praescr." 7.

found; and we who have found the faith, have but one thing left: viz. to preserve it. Even supposing we had still something to seek after, should we apply for information to the heretics, in whose systems everything is either foreign or opposed to "our truth," our *regula fidei?*[1] Tertullian gives in his own style the articles of this *regula fidei*, the baptismal symbol received at Carthage.[2] This, he continues, was the rule established by Christ, a rule that raises no questions save those which are put forth by heretics and form the very essence of their heresy. Let us leave this rule intact, and preserve its order and wording. Or, if you find in it anything equivocal or obscure, consult some one in the Church, who is learned and experienced, so that he may seek with you the light you need. But to remain in ignorance is still better.[3]

However heretics may and actually do object that, after all, the *regula fidei* is not everything, since there are also the Scriptures, that are sources of faith; and so, they base their disputes on the Scriptures. But, replies Tertullian, this is precisely what we must not allow them to do: first, because the Apostle Paul forbids us to have any discussion with heretics; secondly, because, with the heretics of to-day, no one knows what Scriptures they accept, what text they read, what interpretation they give: you will gain nothing at all from discussion, and the faithful, whom you intend to enlighten by disputing before them with the heretics, will go away more uncertain than before. It is most unprofitable to discuss the contents of the Scriptures, "*in quibus aut nulla, aut incerta victoria est, aut par incertae*". One question only must be asked: to whom does the deposit of faith belong, to whom does the deposit of the Scriptures belong?[4]

[1] "Praescr." 12: "Nemo inde instrui potest, unde destruitur : nemo ab eo illuminatur a quo contenebratur. Quaeramus ergo in nostro, et a nostris, et de nostro, idque dumtaxat quod salva regula fidei potest in quaestionem devenire ".

[2] *Ibid.* 13. Concerning the value of this text, as representing the symbol of Carthage, cf. D'ALÈS, "Théologie de Tertullien " (Paris, 1905), pp. 256-7, and K. ADAM, "Der Kirchenbegriff Tertullians " (Paderborn, 1907), pp. 38-40.

[3] *Ibid.* 14. Cf. "De Anima," 2.　　　　　[4] *Ibid.* 15-19.

The answer to the question thus put must be an answer of *fact;* for it is of no importance to have proved first what Jesus is in relation to God. This alone is of importance : that, when here below, Jesus taught; that, among His disciples, He chose twelve men, whom He destined to be the teachers of nations and whom He sent to the nations, to instruct them, and baptize them in the name of the Father, the Son and the Holy Ghost. These Apostles preached the faith of Jesus first in Judæa, where they also founded Churches; then they went to the nations, and preached to them the same doctrine and founded Churches in every city; later on, from these Churches established by the Apostles the other Churches received the germ of faith and the seed of doctrine ; and this is also done every day by the Churches that are being founded in our midst : and therefore they too are called Apostolic, because they are the offspring of the Apostolic Churches. So, there is a first Church founded by the Apostles, from which all others have sprung.[1]

Here Tertullian does but develop the argument of apostolic succession, as he found it in the works of Irenæus : what the Apostles preached, they held from Christ ; and our Churches are Apostolic in their origin. In other words : the

---

[1] " Praescr." 20 : " Apostoli . . . primo per Iudaeam contestata fide in Iesum Christum et ecclesiis institutis, dehinc in orbem profecti, eamdem doctrinam eiusdem fidei nationibus promulgaverunt, et proinde ecclesias apud unamquamque civitatem condiderunt, a quibus traducem fidei et semina doctrinae ceterae exinde ecclesiae mutuatae sunt et cotidie mutuantur ut ecclesiae fiant, ac per hoc et ipsae apostolicae deputantur ut soboles apostolicarum ecclesiarum. Omne genus ad originem suam censeatur necesse est. Itaque tot ac tantae ecclesiae, una est illa ab apostolis prima ex qua omnes. Sic omnes prima et apostolicae, dum una omnes probant unitatem, dum est illis communicatio pacis, et appellatio fraternitatis, et contesseratio hospitalitatis. Quae iura non alia ratio regit quam eiusdem sacramenti una traditio. " Praescr." 21 : " Constat omnem doctrinam quae cum illis ecclesiis apostolicis, matricibus et originalibus fidei, conspiret veritati deputandam, id sine dubio tenentem quod ecclesiae ab apostolis, apostoli a Christo, Christus a Deo accepit; omnem vero doctrinam de mendacio praeiudicandam, quae sapiat contra veritatem ecclesiarum et apostolorum et Christi et Dei ".

Churches, being Apostolic, bear witness to the Apostles, just as the Apostles bear witness to Christ.[1]

Tertullian has to answer the difficulties which the heretics (in this case, the Marcionites) are wont to urge against this familiar argument. Two hypotheses can be made: according to the first, the Apostles did not know everything, and hence in Scripture and by means of Scripture, we may reach depths which they failed to fathom; according to the second, they did not teach everybody all that they knew, and consequently there may be an esoteric tradition, more profound than the tradition of the Apostolic Churches.

Tertullian accepts neither hypothesis. How could we ever believe that Christ concealed anything pertaining to the faith from those He was constituting the teachers of mankind? For instance, how could Peter, who was to be the corner-stone of the Church, have been ignorant of anything in the domain of faith?[2] Again, the hypothesis of a secret teaching which the Apostles entrusted only to a few privileged persons, is just as improbable. Nor can it be said, either, that the Churches may have misunderstood what was taught them by the Apostles.[3]

Tertullian is not loth to grant that particular Churches may fall into error and need correction: St. Paul styled the Galatians foolish, and the Corinthians carnal. Yet, St. Paul praised the faith and knowledge of other Churches, that are now in perfect harmony with those he formerly corrected:

[1] In the " De Virg. vel." 2, Tertullian, when a Montanist, will say : " Sed eas ego ecclesias proposui, quas et ipsi apostoli vel apostolici viri condiderunt, et puto ante quosdam ". Tertullian writes thus against some Catholics who, like him, were appealing to the authority of the Churches founded by Apostles : he recalls that he had invoked this authority before they did : an allusion to the passage of the " De Praesc." we have just quoted. We may look upon these " quosdam," as certain Roman clerics, as is suggested by HARNACK, "Dogmeng." vol. i[4], p. 490, 161, and E. ROLFFS, " Urkunden aus dem antimontanistischen Kampfe des Abendlandes " (Leipzig, 1895), p. 44.

[2] " Praescr." 22 : " Latuit aliquid Petrum aedificandae Ecclesiae petram dictum, claves regni caelorum consecutum, et solvendi et alligandi in caelis et in terris potestatem ? "

[3] *Ibid.* 27.

"*Hodie cum illis correptis unius institutionis iura mis-cent*".[1]  Shall we say that all the Churches have erred? Shall we suppose that the Holy Ghost, whom Christ was to send as the teacher of truth, had no regard for any Church, and that He, the Vicar of Christ, failed in His duty and left the Churches to think and believe whatever they pleased, and otherwise than He Himself was preaching by the Apostles?[2]

Unanimity of belief, combined with faith in the guidance of the Holy Ghost, is, then, a first proof of the authenticity of tradition.[3]

This tradition is more ancient than any heresy whatever.[4]  This tradition was in possession long before men spoke of Marcion the Stoic, or of Valentinus the Platonist.[5] Apelles is even more recent, since Marcion was his master. Nigidius, Hermogenes, and a host of others are still living. As is self-evident, merely from a chronological point of view, that comes from the Lord and is true which is older in tradition, whereas what appeared later is strange and false.[6]

The priority of the ecclesiastical tradition is vouched for by the fact that the Apostolic Churches prove they truly come down from the Apostles: Smyrna claims Polycarp who was put there by John, Rome claims Clement who was put there by Peter; so also for the other Churches.[7]  Let the heretics

---

[1] "Praescr." 27.

[2] *Ibid.* 28: Nullam [ecclesiam] respexerit Spiritus sanctus, uti eam in veritatem deduceret ["Ioan." xiv. 26], ad hoc missus a Christo, ad hoc postulatus de patre, ut esset doctor veritatis ["Ioan." xv. 26].  Neglexerit officium Dei villicus, Christi vicarius, sinens ecclesias aliter interim intellegere, aliter credere, quam ipse per apostolos praedicabat."

[3] *Ibid.* 28: "Nullus inter multos eventus unus est exitus: variasse debuerat error doctrinae ecclesiarum.  Ceterum quod apud multos unum invenitur, non est erratum, sed traditum."

[4] *Ibid.* 29.

[5] *Ibid.* 30.  The same considerations are urged in the "Adv. Marcion." i. 19.  And we have seen the same argument developed by Clement of Alexandria.

[6] *Ibid.* 31: "Ita ex ipso ordine manifestatur id esse dominicum et verum, quod sit prius traditum; id autem extraneum et falsum, quod sit posterius immissum".

[7] *Ibid.* 32: "Edant ergo [haeretici] origines ecclesiarum suarum, evolvant ordinem episcoporum suorum ita per successiones ab initio de-

show such a διαδοχή if they can! If, however, apostolic ancestors must at any cost be found for them, they are to be found in the fomenters of errors, condemned by the Apostles themselves: the Sadducees, Ebion, Simon, the Nicolaites: this is the genealogy of heresies and of their adulterous doctrines.[1] If they are bent on crushing us, let them bring forward against us the proof we bring forward against them, let them show that our Catholic faith is a heresy. But this, they cannot do, for it is a fact that we have our priority; that we have been in occupation since the Apostles, and, that far from condemning us, the Apostles confirm us in our property. "Posterior nostra res non est, immo omnibus prior est: hoc erit testimonium veritatis ubique occupantis principatum. Ab apostolis utique non damnatur, immo defenditur: hoc erit indicium proprietatis."[2]

Tertullian concludes as follows:—

"Si haec ita se habent ut veritas nobis adiudicetur quicumque in ea regula incedimus quam Ecclesia ab apostolis, apostoli a Christo, Christus a Deo tradidit, constat ratio propositi nostri definientis non esse admittendos haereticos ad ineundam de scripturis provocationem."[3]

The "De Praescriptione" closes with a few thoughts that are disconnected with the argument we have been using, but deserve notice, because they recall the similar thoughts which we have found in Irenæus. Heretics, says Tertullian, have no other inspiration than that of Satan. The lack of ecclesiastical discipline, which prevails among them, is beyond belief; a like disorder prevails in their preaching. They are not unwilling to associate with astrologers, philosophers . . . and charlatans. How severely God will deal, on the day of judgment, with these adulterers! "*Quid dicent qui illam*

currentem, ut primus ille episcopus aliquem ex apostolis vel apostolicis viris qui tamen cum apostolis perseveraverit, habuerit auctorem et antecessorem. Hoc enim modo ecclesiae apostolicae census suos deferunt . . ." Compare chapter 36, in which Tertullian comes back to this apostolicity of the great Churches, especially of the Roman Church; we shall quote it later. The same thoughts are found in "Adv. Marc." I. 21, III., IV. 5.

[1] "Praescr." 33-4.     [2] *Ibid.* 35.     [3] *Ibid.* 37.

*stupraverint adulterio haeretico virginem traditam a Christo?"* [1]

\* \*
\*

To estimate aright the argument we have been analyzing, we must first determine how far it depends on the juridical theory of prescription.

Prescription, as described in our modern legal codes, is but one kind of prescription in general, as the latter is understood in the language of Roman Law. For, by prescription, the Romans meant any mode of procedure resorted to by one of the parties for stopping at once the opponent's action, and duly recorded by the prætor in the formula that was delivered to the judges: briefly, prescription was any plea of exception. There can be, of course, various pleas of exception : as regards ownership, for instance, a plea of exception may consist in invoking actual occupancy as a title that bars any action to recover, after the lapse of a certain number of years : this is called *praescriptio longi temporis.* [2] Prescription thus based on occupancy, is an exception which appears comparatively late; Gaius is unacquainted with it; we find it mentioned for the first time in a rescript of 29 December, 199 A.D. ; and the first law that makes it of general observance is enacted by Theodosius II in the year 424. [3] It is hardly probable that Tertullian applied to theological questions a device of legal procedure, which, towards the year 200, was so new and so little known ; he used the juridical term, *praescriptio*, most probably, in its oldest meaning, to designate an argument disputing the presuppositions of the main point, interposed to make the discussion of the latter nugatory.

---

[1] "Praescr." 41-4. We do not need to say that chaps. 43-53 are no part of Tertullian's work, and are not found in the best MSS., for instance in the "Codex Agobardinus" (Paris. lat. 1622). They form a "Libellus adversus omnes haereticos" or descriptive catalogue of heresies, which dates probably from the first half of the third century.

[2] DE SAVIGNY, "Traité de droit romain" (French transl., Paris, 1846), vol. v. p. 284 and foll. ; F. GIRARD, "Manuel élémentaire de droit romain," fourth edit. (Paris, 1906), p. 299 ; P. MONCEAUX, "Hist. litt. de l'Afrique chrét." vol. I. (Paris, 1901), p. 304.

[3] SAVIGNY, p. 293. See the rescript of Severus and Caracalla, dated 29 December, 199, in GIRARD, "Textes de Droit romain," p. 187. P. DE LABRIOLLE, "L'Argument de Prescription," in "Revue d'Hist. et de Littr. relig." vol. XI. (1906), p. 431.

In fact, if we read attentively the "De Praescriptione haereticorum," we easily perceive that Tertullian's argument on the previous question is just the argument from tradition. In reality—to quote Monceaux' appropriate remark—"his proof is the proof from tradition, to which the defenders of Catholicism have always appealed. The Greek controversialists of the second century had already fought Gnostic speculations in the name of the teaching of the Apostles, regularly handed down from generation to generation, and kept intact in the one doctrine of the Church. But here, as in all his apologetic works, Tertullian strengthens the method by the rigour of his argumentation, and extends considerably its bearing, by applying to the controversy the procedure of jurisprudence."[1] I may be allowed to change slightly the last words of Monceaux' sentence : Tertullian has a logical rigour of argumentation which neither Irenæus nor any one else possessed before him: and augments not its significance but its force by giving it an appearance of novelty through the application to controversy of the language of the forum.[2]

Let us reconstitute Tertullian's argument. The authentic faith is that which is contained in the *regula fidei* common to all the churches: hence this rule of faith must be preferred to any opposite contention which the heretics may claim to justify either by Scripture or by philosophy.

This Tertullian proves first by means of a principle we have already met with in Irenæus, the authentic tradition is that which does not vary. This principle he expresses in epigrammatic form: "*Quod apud multos unum invenitur, non est erratum, sed traditum*". Tertullian does not lay stress on perpetuity in time, he appeals to the subsisting unanimity only, and, as he is opposing living heretics, he does not speak precisely of unanimity, but of a faith common to many, "*apud multos unum*". Later on, Vincent of Lerins will not preserve, in his over-rigid canon, the shades of meaning so carefully respected here by Tertullian. Secondly, Tertullian invokes another argument in proof of the agreement of the actual teaching of the churches with the

---

[1] MONCEAUX, vol. I. p. 331 ; DE LABRIOLLE, "Tertullien, De Praescr." (Paris, 1907), p. xxv.
[2] See especially "Praescr." 73.

teaching of the Apostles : the aid of the Holy Spirit was promised by the Saviour to the disciples who believed in Him, until the end of the ages : if all the churches had erred, what had become of that aid ?[1]  Thirdly—and this is strictly the argument of the Apostolic succession, the one which Irenæus has so fully developed—Tertullian appeals to the fact that all the great Churches are Apostolic in their origin, and therefore the tradition common to those Churches is also Apostolic. On this theme Tertullian writes an eloquent page, which manifestly draws its inspiration from the work of St. Irenæus.[2]

Tertullian then does not appeal to the *praescriptio longi temporis*.[3] He uses, it is true, the following expressions which have been misunderstood : "*Mea est possessio, olim possideo*"; but he does not appeal to this actual and ancient possession, as entitling him to dismiss the claims of heretics ; for he adds immediately : "*Habeo origines firmas, ab ipsis auctoribus quorum fuit res : ego sum haeres apostolorum. Sicut caverunt testamento suo, sicut fidei commiserunt, sicut adiuraverunt, ita teneo*".[4]  The property is proved to

---

[1] ADAM, "Kirchenbegriff," p. 34, distinguishes, as we do, the three proofs of Tertullian : the first and the third rest on facts, the second rests on a doctrine of faith, I mean, the aid of the Holy Ghost : a proof touched upon already by Irenæus (III. 24, 1).  Later on Novatian also will intist on the aid given to the Church by the Spirit ("De Trinitate," 29) : "Unus et idem Spiritus qui in prophetis et apostolis, nisi quoniam ibi ad momentum, hic semper. . . . Hic est qui ipsorum [ = discipulorum] animos mentesque firmavit, qui euangelica sacramenta distinxit, qui in ipsis illuminator rerum divinarum fuit. . . . Hic est qui prophetas in ecclesia constituit, magistros erudit, linguas dirigit, virtutes et sanitates facit . . . quaeque alia sunt charismatum dona componit et digerit. . . . Hic est qui operatur ex aquis secundam nativitatem, semen quoddam divini generis. . . . Hic est qui . . . sectas repellit, regulam veritatis expedit, haereticos revincit, improbos foras expuit, euangelia custodit. . . . In hoc Spiritu positus nemo . . . alia et sacrilega decreta constituit. . . . [Hic] ecclesiam incorruptam et inviolatam perpetuæ virginitatis sanctitate custodit."

[2] "Praescr." 36 ; IREN. III. 3.

[3] Nor does he make such an appeal in the other books where he "prescribes" against heretics.  Those texts are given by DE LABRIOLLE in the article quoted, pp. 425-7.  "Adv. Marc." I, 1, 9, 21, 22 ; III, 1, 3, IV. 4, 5, 10, 38, v. 19 ; "Adv. Hermog." 1 ; "Adv. Praxean," 2 ; "De Carne Christi," 2.

[4] "Praescr." 37.  Cf. "Scorpiace," 9 : "haereditarii discipuli et apostolici seminis frutices".

be legitimately in the hands of its actual occupant by the very titles which prescription if unsupported would have to supply : for the occupant affirms that he holds his property on the title of inheritance and he produces the will : he shows that there is a legacy, and thus gives a full and direct proof of his right of property, a proof which a *praescriptio longi temporis* would have rendered unnecessary.

Thus presented, the argument from tradition demonstrates the legitimacy of the inherited faith : any doctrine contrary to that *regula fidei* is rightly condemned by the bare fact that it arose later than the doctrine that is Apostolic. We have thus against heresy a *praescriptio novitatis* which is a corollary of the positive and direct authentication of the Apostolic faith, already given.[1] The controversialists of the seventeenth century, who held in such honour the argument from prescription—as it is generally called—can claim Tertullian as their forerunner, inasmuch as he opposed to the heretics this *praescriptio novitatis*.[2]

However, he realized that the authentication of the *regula fidei* by the tradition is a general proof that does not dispense from a careful study of the various circumstances and details : as also that the *praescriptio novitatis* dismisses at once the claims of heretics, but does not dispense with the necessity of solving their objections. This Tertullian wisely and frankly acknowledges at the close of the " De Praescriptione," where he sums up his whole argument thus : " *Sed nunc quidem generaliter actum est a nobis adversus omnes haereses* ". He has shown how, in the name of the *praescriptio novitatis* —a corollary of the thesis on the apostolicity of the rule of faith—we must refuse to dispute with heretics about the Scriptures ; but he adds presently : If God in His grace permit, " *etiam specialiter quibusdam respondebimus* ".[3] Irenæus followed the same method. Like him, Tertullian will make a thorough criticism of Marcionism, and write against

---

[1] Against Tertullian, after he became a Montanist, Catholics will urge precisely that prescription of novelty : " Novitatem igitur abiectant . . ." " De Jejunio," 1. The treatise "De Jejunio " was composed after the year 213.

[2] PESCH, " Prael. dogm." vol. I. p. 246 ; BARDENHEWER, vol. II. p. 360.

[3] " Praescr." 44.

Hermogenes, against the followers of Apelles and Valentinus, against Praxeas.   Truth is that which is *a primordio ;* heresy is that which is recent;  hence without undertaking any further detailed examination, " *sine retractatu doctrinarum,*" we reject heresy straight off.   However, this method, when applied to religious questions, and when applied exclusively and always to those questions, tends to inspire a legitimate distrust.[1]   Although the novelty of a doctrine suffices to judge it, yet, if we wish effectively to forewarn the minds of men against its surprises, and to avoid the appearance of condemning it without adequate knowledge, we must examine it in detail.[2]

The " De Praescriptione haereticorum " has the merit of setting in the clearest light the truth that the Church is above all a society whose teaching is authoritative and whose authority is apostolic.

On this point Tertullian is absolutely at one with Irenæus and Clement of Alexandria.   But with what force and incisiveness he can express his thoughts!   He sets before us the Apostles journeying through the world, and announcing to the nations the same doctrine of the same faith :  " *In orbem profecti, eamdem doctrinam eiusdem fidei nationibus promulgaverunt*".   In each city a Church is founded ; but all these Churches are knit together by the bond of their common Apostolic origin.   Hence their abiding unity : however numerous they are, however great, " they all bear witness to their unity by their peaceful inter-communion, their sense of brotherhood, their interchange of hospitality— rights which no other law sustains save the one tradition of the self-same faith." [3]

But neglecting the polemical standpoint, which for tactical reasons Tertullian assumes in the " De Praescriptione," let us study his conception of the living teaching authority :

[1] " Adv. Marcion." I. 1.

[2] " Adv. Praxean," 2 : " . . . id esse verum quodcunque primum, id esse adulterum quodcunque posterius.  Sed salva ista praescriptione, ubique tamen propter instructionem et munitionem quorundam dandus est etiam retractatibus locus, vel ne videatur unaquaeque perversitas non examinata, sed praeiudicata damnari."

[3] " Praescr." 20.

"Go through the Apostolic Churches, in which the very seats of the Apostles, at this very day, preside in their place. . . . Art thou near Achaia? Thou hast Corinth. If thou art not far from Macedonia, thou hast Philippi, thou hast Thessalonica. If thou canst travel in Asia, thou hast Ephesus. But if thou art near to Italy, thou hast Rome, where we also have an authority close at hand. Happy Church on which the Apostles poured out all their doctrine, together with their blood: where Peter had a like passion with the Lord; where Paul was crowned with a death like that of John [the Baptist]; where the Apostle John was plunged into boiling oil, and suffered nothing! . . . Let us see what she [Rome] has learned, what taught, what she has certified in common with the Churches of Africa. She acknowledges one only God, the Creator of the universe; Christ Jesus the Son of God the Creator, born of the Virgin Mary; the resurrection of the flesh. She joins the Law and the Prophets with the Gospels and thence drinks in her faith. That faith she seals with the water, clothes with the Holy Spirit, feeds with the Eucharist; she exhorts to martyrdom; and she receives no one save in accordance with this rule: "*adversus hanc institutionem neminem recipit*".[1] Speaking of all the Churches, Tertullian had already said: "*Unius institutionis iura miscent*".[2]

Baptism is the Sacrament through which we become Christians: we are fishes after the pattern of Jesus, our

---

[1] "Praescr." 36. This is the well-known passage: "Si Italiae adiaces, habes Romam unde nobis quoque auctoritas praesto est. Ista quam felix ecclesia, cui totam doctrinam apostoli cum sanguine suo profuderunt, ubi Petrus passioni dominicae adaequatur, ubi Paulus Ioannis exitu coronatur. . . . Videamus quid didicerit, quid docuerit, quid cum africanis quoque ecclesiis contestetur." Compare "Adv. Marcion." iv. 5, where Tertullian speaks of the Romans to whom "euangelium et Petrus et Paulus sanguine quoque suo signatum reliquerunt." D'ALÈS, "Tertullien," p. 216: "Tertullian did not speak as plainly [as Irenæus] of the nature of the prerogatives vested in the see of Rome. However, he emphasizes the primacy of Peter. He speaks of Peter as the foundation of the Church, the depositary of the keys of the kingdom of Heaven, and as the one to whom has been awarded full power to bind and to loose. . . . [The Church of Rome] is the mother of the African Churches; she appears as the centre of unity by her doctrine and action."

[2] "Praescr." 27.

symbolical $IX\Theta\Upsilon\Sigma$, and, like fishes, we are born in water.[1] Baptism is conferred by means of a formula the few words of which when pronounced suffice to work the stupendous miracle of regeneration.[2] These few words consist in the invocation of the Father, of the Son, and of the Holy Ghost ("De Bapt." 6). Tertullian affirms that the formula of Baptism implies by logical connexion the mention of the Church: ". . . *Necessario adicitur Ecclesiae mentio, quoniam ubi tres, id est Pater et Filius et Spiritus sanctus, ibi Ecclesia, quae trium corpus est*" (*ibid.*). He has said elsewhere that to invoke the Father, in the Lord's prayer, is to invoke also the Son, and not to forget the Mother: "*Ne mater quidem Ecclesia praeteritur: si quidem in Filio et Patre mater recognoscitur, de qua constat et patris et filii nomen*".[3] According to Tertullian, one is baptized implicitly *in Ecclesiam.*

After the immersion, the new Christian is anointed: "*Egressi de lavacro perungimur*" ("De Bapt." 7). He then receives the imposition of hands; and at the same time the Holy Ghost, earnestly entreated to come down, descends on the body which has been cleansed and blessed (8). After this rite, he is admitted to pray with those who now are his brethren. Tertullian sets before our eyes the newly baptized coming out of baptism and praying for the first time in the Church: ". . . *primas manus apud Matrem cum fratribus aperitis*" (20). Outside the Church there is no baptism; for there is but one Baptism, just as there is but one Church, and one Christ. Heretics have not the same Christ as we have, nor the same baptism. How could there be two Christs, or two baptisms? "*[Baptismum] cum rite non habeant, sine dubio non habent.*"[4] In their counter-

---

[1] "De Baptismo," 1.

[2] *Ibid.* 2: "homo in aquam demissus et inter pauca verba tinctus".

[3] *Ibid.* 6. See LUPTON's note, "Tertull. De Bapt." (Cambridge, 1908), p. 19. "De Orat." 2.—On the Church as our mother, see "Adv. Marcion." II. 4, III. 24, IV. 11, V. 4; "De Bapt." 20; "De Monog." 6 and 7; "Ad Mart." 1.—On the Church as associated with the three Persons of the Trinity, see HIPPOLYT. "Contra Noet." 18. On this point, at least with Tertullian, a strange and somewhat obscure conception prevailed.

[4] *Ibid.* 15: "Sed de isto plenius iam nobis in graeco digestum est". This is an allusion to the Greek edition of the "De Baptismo" previously issued by Tertullian.

feit and weak faith, heretics baptize "*in iudicium*," whilst, in their genuine faith, true Christians baptize "*in salutem*" (10). "Dandi quidem habet ius summus sacerdos, qui est episcopus. Dehinc presbyteri et diaconi, non tamen sine episcopi auctoritate, propter Ecclesiae honorem. Quo salvo, salva pax est. Alioquin etiam laicis ius est. . . . Sed quanto magis laicis disciplina verecundiae et modestiae incumbit, cum ea maioribus competat, ne sibi assumant dicatum episcopis officium. Episcopatus aemulatio schismatum mater est" ("De Baptismo," 17).

The Church is a hierarchical society: the laity are subordinate to the deacons and to the priests; and these, to the bishop: all—the laity as well as the *minores*, i.e. deacons and priests—must respect the bishop.[1] Only on these conditions can peace and unity be preserved. Woe to the priests who usurp the episcopal office, for these rivalries give rise to deplorable schisms. The bishop is vested with the sovereignty of authority and order: he may be rightly called a "*summus sacerdos*": a title given formerly only to the Jewish High Priest at Jerusalem. The first bishops were established by the Apostles.[2] In each Church, none are promoted to the "*ordo ecclesiasticus*"[3] without receiving the testimony of all: "*Praesident probati quique seniores, honorem istum non pretio, sed testimonio adepti: neque enim pretio ulla res Dei constat*".[4] If convicted of a grave fault, a presbyter may be deposed.[5] Presbyters alone—to the exclusion of laymen—may exercise, in union with the bishop, the "*sacerdotalia munera*":[6] viz. teach, baptize and cele-

---

[1] Cf. "De Praescr." 42 : "[Haeretici] nec suis praesidibus reverentiam noverunt. . . . Schisma est unitas ipsis."

[2] "De Praescr." 32. Cf. "De Fuga," 13 ; "Adv. Marcion." IV. 5.

[3] I find the expression *ordo ecclesiasticus* in the "De idolol." 7. True, in this passage, Tertullian, still Catholic, expresses his indignation at the fact that Christians not thoroughly converted are received among the clergy: "Adleguntur in ordinem ecclesiasticum artifices idolorum !"

[4] "Apol." 39.

[5] "De Bapt." 17 : "Sciant in Asia presbyterum, . . . convictum atque confessum, . . . loco decessisse". Cf. "Ad Uxor." I. 7.

[6] "Praescr." 41.

brate the Eucharist.[1]    The presbyters, the bishop being with
them, are the intercessors to whom the penitent goes, kneel-
ing before them as a suppliant soliciting forgiveness.[2]    To the
bishop belongs the right of pardoning those penitents whose
sins can be remitted.[3]    If the sinner's offence is so great that
it requires expulsion from the Church, the sentence is given
by the bishop after mature examination : " *Nam et iudicatur
magno cum pondere, . . . si quis ita deliquerit ut a communicatione orationis et conventus et omnis sancti com-
mercii relegetur* ".[4]

Heresies necessarily cut themselves off from this community of life and doctrine; they are the bitter wild olive-
tree that springs from the kernel of the olive; or again, the
barren and useless wild fig-tree, that springs from the seed
of the fig: though they spring from our stock, they are not
of our family,[5] and we must break with them, just as we
do with public sinners.[6]    " *Haeretici nullum habent consortium nostrae disciplinae, quos extraneos utique testatur
ipsa ademptio communicationis* ".[7]    The right to teach,
which belongs to the bishop and to his presbyterium, involves,
as its complement, the right to condemn error and proscribe
the heretic.

These, then, are the ideas of Tertullian, the Catholic.
Yet the same impetuous dialectician, who has so forcibly in-

---

[1] " Virg. vel." 9 : " Non permittitur mulieri in ecclesia loqui [1 Cor.
XIV. 34], sed nec docere, nec tinguere, nec offerre, nec ullius virilis muneris
nedum sacerdotalis officii sortem sibi vindicare ".

[2] De Paenit." 9 : ". . . presbyteris advolvi et caris Dei adgeniculari ".
Cf. " De Pudicit." 13.    This attitude of suppliants had given rise to a
peculiar calumny, of which some use may be made for the history of the
penitential discipline.    HARNACK, " Mission," vol. I. p. 410.

[3] "De Pudicit." 18 : ". . . levioribus delictis, veniam ab episcopo
consequi poterit ".    The sins that are not *leviora* are enumerated by
Tertullian, whilst still a Catholic, in " De Idololatria," 1 ; "De Bapt." 4 ;
" Apolog." 2 and 11 : " De Spectac." 3 and 20.    Cf. D'ALÈS, "Tertullien,"
pp. 272-5.

[4] " Apol." 39.    To pronounce excommunication is " in praesidentis
officio ".    " De Pudicit." XIV. 16.

[5] " Praescr." 36.

[6] " De Jejun." 1 : ". . . dum quaque ex parte anathema audiamus,
qui aliter adnuntiamus ".

[7] " De Bapt." 15.

sisted that the mark of Catholicism is above all "*eiusdem sacramenti una traditio*," came to plead on behalf of private inspiration and individual charisms.

## II.

The work " De Virginibus velandis " was composed between the years 208 and 211, when Tertullian had not yet broken with the Church. The occasion that gave rise to this short treatise is in appearance insignificant, but the fundamental issue it raises is identical with that raised in the Paschal controversy. Between two Biblical interpretations, tradition decides ; but in case two traditions conflict, how is the question to be settled ? We must choose, he says, between two customs. According to one custom, virgins have to wear a veil ; according to the other, they are not obliged to wear it : the former custom prevails in many Churches of Greece, and the latter, in the Churches founded by the Apostles or their immediate disciples. We cannot say that this latter custom is " foreign " since those are not " foreigners with whom we are in the communion of peace and brotherhood " : their faith is our faith : we are all but one and the same Church.[1]

We must not forget that there is custom and custom. A custom may arise from ignorance or from simple-mindedness, then obtain recognition through the duration of time (*per successionem*), and afterwards be unlawfully arrayed against truth. Christ said : " I am the truth ". He did not say : " I am the custom ". The rule of faith, alone, can neither change nor be improved.[2] Whilst on the one hand, this rule of faith must be kept as inviolable as a law, on the other hand, all that pertains to discipline and Christian life

---

[1] " De Virgin. veland." 2 : ". . . non extraneorum, cum quibus scilicet communicamus ius pacis et nomen fraternitatis. Una nobis et illis fides unus Deus, idem Christus, eadem lavacri sacramenta. Semel dixerim, una Ecclesia sumus." Cf. " Praescr." 20. The Church founded by the Apostles which Tertullian has in mind, is surely the Roman Church.

[2] *Ibid.* 1 : " Haeresim non tam novitas quam veritas revincit : quodcumque adversus veritatem sapit, hoc erit haeresis, etiam vetus consuetudo". We are rather far from the " praescriptio novitatis ".

admits of corrections and innovations, inasmuch as it is the mission of Divine grace to labour for the progress of souls to the end of time;[1] for, just as Satan is constantly working and daily adding to the mass of wickedness, so too the work of God never stops, or ceases to advance, the more so that the Lord has sent the Paraclete, in order that He might enlighten human infirmity which could not comprehend all at once, and in order that the same Paraclete, being Christ's vicar, might gradually perfect discipline.[2]   Hence, Tertullian acknowledges, side by side with the intangible faith, an unceasing action of the Spirit.

"Quae est ergo Paracleti administratio nisi haec, quod disciplina dirigitur, quod Scripturae revelantur, quod intellectus reformatur, quod ad meliora proficitur?" ("De Virgin. vel." 1)

These expressions contain certain obscurities which we must clear up.   The work of the Holy Ghost here referred to, is not that which He did before the coming of Christ, but that which He does now when, being sent by the glorified Christ, He supplies His place in the Church.   By this Holy Spirit, Christian life is daily ruled and reformed: for has not Tertullian just told us that all pertaining to discipline may be corrected and improved?   By the Spirit the mind, too, may be enlightened and corrected, as well as the conduct.   By the Spirit also, through an action intermediate between these two, "*Scripturæ revelantur*," Scriptures (manifestly such as are new and inspired), are revealed.[3] Hence revelation is not as yet concluded, it still continues, daily growing richer as a tree which daily expands.   But revelation continues within the sphere of discipline and of Christian life, not in that of belief, since the rule of faith

---

[1] "De Virgin. veland." 1: "Hac lege fidei manente, cetera iam disciplinae et conversationis admittunt novitatem correctionis, operante scilicet et proficiente usque in finem gratia Dei".

[2] *Ibid.* : ". . . cum propterea Paracletum miserit Dominus, ut quoniam humana mediocritas omnia semel capere non poterat, paulatim dirigeretur et ordinaretur et ad perfectum perduceretur disciplina ab illo vicario Domini Spiritu sancto".

[3] "Quae est ergo Paracleti administratio nisi haec, quod disciplina dirigitur, quod Scripturae revelantur, quod intellectus reformatur, quod ad meliora proficitur?"   Cf. "De Monogam." 4.

remains such as it was established by Christ. Hence we can say that righteousness was first rudimentary; then the Law and the Prophets brought it to a sort of childhood; the Gospel to youth; and the Paraclete brings it to maturity.

"Nunc per Paracletum componitur in maturitatem: hic erit solus a Christo magister et dicendùs et verendus. Non enim ab se loquitur, sed quae mandantur a Christo. Hic solus antecessor, quia solus post Christum. Hunc qui receperunt, veritatem consuetudini anteponunt. Hunc qui audierunt usque nunc, non olim, prophetantem, virgines contegunt." [1]

In this question of discipline—viz. whether or not young women have to be veiled—Tertullian opposes to the custom of the Apostolic Churches the truth revealed by the new prophets, through the Spirit, who does not speak of Himself, but announces what Christ gives Him to announce (John XVI. 13), and is also the only Master whom Christ gives us to recognize and revere.

In the "De Anima" (208-211), we have the description of a scene of prophetism, that takes place at Carthage, in the open Church and before the clergy. A Christian lady of the city, the recipient of the charisms of revelation, passes into this extraordinary state, generally on Sundays whilst the liturgical synaxis is going on: she converses then with the angels, nay, at times, with the Lord Himself; she sees or hears mysteries. The matter of her visions relates to the liturgy: lessons, psalmody, homilies, prayers. One day, Tertullian relates, he and others had discoursed about the soul, whilst this Christian woman was rapt in spirit. When the synaxis was over and the people had been dismissed, she was asked what she had seen "*Nam et diligentissime digeruntur, ut etiam probentur,*" [2]—and she answered that

---

[1] "De Virgin. vel." 1. The expression "*hic solus antecessor*" alludes to the fact that Catholics bring forward the authority of the presbyters and bishops of old: "*Tempora et antecessores opponunt*" ("De Virg. vel." 2). "Sed nec inter consuetudines dispicere voluerunt illi sanctissimi antecessores" (*ibid.* 3). Tertullian has become entirely averse to any mention of the traditional *magisterium*: his chief thought is now of the Spirit, and the Spirit alone.

[2] The prophetic texts quoted by Tertullian may be found in D'ALÈS, "Tertullien," p. 452.

she had seen a soul in bodily shape. Tertullian has no doubt whatever that this is a supernatural revelation fully guaranteed.[1]

This revelation regarding the nature of the soul proves that the Paraclete cannot limit His action to discipline alone, and that, notwithstanding Tertullian's previous assertions, it extends even to matters of doctrine, as had already been sufficiently suggested by the visions of Perpetua and Saturus, which are preserved in the "Passio" of St. Perpetua and of St. Felicitas, which dates from the year 203. In this way will be formed a new variety of Gnosticism, claiming to be inspired by the Paraclete: "He [the Holy Ghost] has accordingly now dispersed all the equivocations of the past, and the pretended parables, by a full and clear explanation of all the mysteries, through the new prophecy, which descends in copious streams from the Paraclete."[2]

So speaks Tertullian, during the years 208-211.

The Church had disowned the energumens, Montanus and his two prophetesses: but a decision has yet to be taken concerning prophetism itself, and its claim to be a continuation of revelation. It seems that this question remained long unanswered. Certainly, even before the year 213, Tertullian speaks with harshness of those Christians who do not accept the new prophecy: he calls them *psychici*,[3] whilst he calls *spiritales*, those who acknowledge the charism of the Spirit—in allusion to the text of St. Paul, who affirms that the carnal man does not receive what is from the Spirit of God. In the year 211, in the "De Corona," he adopts an insulting tone: he maintains that his opponents

---

[1] "De Anima,' 9.

[2] "De Resurr. carnis," 63. The text of the "Passio" of St. Perpetua and St. Felicitas may be found in MIGNE, "P. L." vol. III. pp. 13-60, and in ROBINSON, "The Passion of St. Perpetua." (Cambridge, 1891). The original text is the Latin, but its author is not Tertullian. At the time of the martyrdom of St. Perpetua and her companions, there is evidently, in the Christian community of Carthage, an intense outburst of the spirit of vision and revelation; but we cannot say that Montanism strictly so called had a share in this extraordinary phenomenon.

[3] "Adv. Marcion." IV. 22 (about the year 207-208). "Adv. Praxean," 1: "Et nos quidem postea agnitio Paracleti et defensio disiunxit a psychicis".

are retrograding towards apostasy. "Clearly nothing remains but that those should refuse martyrdom also, who have rejected the prophecies of the same Holy Spirit" that makes martyrs.[1] Hence we cannot say that the formal condemnation of the prophecies must have taken place at the beginning of the year 213, between the composition of the treatise "Ad Scapulam" and that of the treatise "De Fuga": this condemnation is a well-ascertained fact, but except that it occurred about the year 210, no precise date can be given.

St. Jerome wrote that Tertullian had been goaded into Montanism by the harsh proceedings of the Roman ecclesiastics: "*Invidia et contumeliis clericorum Romanae ecclesiœ ad Montani dogma delapsus*".[2] Although when speaking of the Roman ecclesiastics Jerome is always under suspicion of not being impartial, he can hardly have made this statement without some ground, and it may have been suggested by the reading of Tertullian's now lost treatise "De Extasi," written after the year 213. Were that so, it would furnish a proof that the new prophecy was condemned by the Roman Church.

As a matter of fact, the Roman authorities had been on their guard for a long time against the new prophets, an attitude in which they were in perfect agreement with the tradition. If Pope Eleutherius hesitated for a moment to repudiate the prophecies of Montanus, Priscilla and Maximilla, when reminded of the sentiments of the Roman bishops, his predecessors, he determined to issue his condemnation.[3] The "Muratorianum" forbids the "Shepherd" of Hermas to be read at the public readings of the Church, because he cannot be reckoned among the Prophets, whose number is complete, " . . . *neque inter prophetas*

---

[1] "De Corona," 1.

[2] "De Viris inl." 59. The reader may remember that Hippolytus, a Roman ecclesiastic, composed a Περὶ χαρισμάτων ἀποστολικὴ παράδοσις. It is believed that in the "De Monogamia," Tertullian opposes St. Hippolytus. ROLFFS, "Urkunden," p. 69.

[3] TERTULL. "Adv. Praxean," 1: " . . . praedecessorum eius auctoritates defendendo". We have already seen (p. 283) the importance that was attached to the "antecessores". By *auctoritates*, decisions, documents may be meant.

*completos numero, neque inter apostolos*".[1]   These words
suggest that the " prophetical" question was no longer as to
the character of the prophecies of Montanus and others, but
as to whether or not the Biblical Canon was closed.   About
the year 200, the Churches felt they could not hesitate to
give an affirmative answer; and probably there came from
Rome a solemn judgment, of which we have an echo in the
" Muratorianum": private revelations—such as those contained in the " Shepherd " of Hermas, which was held in
great esteem in Rome—might preserve their private value,
but Scripture alone was canonical.   The severe measures of
the Roman Church against the new prophecy so dear to
Tertullian, were doubtless adopted by the other Churches,
particularly in Africa: thus we may account for the insulting allusions to the hierarchy which Tertullian will henceforth allow himself to make.

\* \*
\*

Is it lawful to flee in the time of persecution, he asks
in the " De Fuga ".   For the " spiritual," this question
raises no difficulty whatever: he does not flee.   Nor does
it trouble the Catholics, either : they flee, so cold and frivol-
ous is their faith !   Their leaders can teach them only how
to retreat : " Their leaders themselves—I mean the very
deacons, and presbyters, and bishops—take to flight ".[2]   Do
you feel any scruples ?   " So much the worse for you, if,
by not accepting the Paraclete, the guide to all truth, you
have become embarrassed in regard to other questions." [3]
You have thrust aside the Paraclete, and received instead a
most worldly spirit: " Apparently, the Apostles founded
and with so much foresight organized the episcopate, that

[1] ZAHN, " Grundriss," p. 78.   Compare " Philosophoumena," VIII.
19.

[2] " De Fuga," 11 : " Sed cum ipsi auctores, id est ipsi diaconi, presbyteri et episcopi fugiunt, quomodo laicus intellegere poterit. . . .  Cf.
" De Corona," 1 : " Novi et pastores eorum, in pace leones, in praelio
cervos ".

[3] *Ibid.* 1 : ". . . Paracletum non recipiendo deductorem omnis veritatis ".   Cf. 14 : " Paracletus necessarius deductor omnium veritatum
. . . quem qui non receperunt," etc.  " De Jejun." 10 : " Paracleto
duce universae veritatis ".

bishops might be able to enjoy in security the revenues of their kingdom under pretext of administering it".[1]

The very violence of these attacks attests the strength of the episcopal authority. Henceforth the bishops gather together in councils, at least in Greek-speaking countries, to deliberate in common about the interests of the Church at large.[2] As we shall see presently, the African bishops will not delay to do likewise. The whole ecclesiastical discipline, and even more so the teaching and safe-keeping of the doctrine, is in the hands of the bishops.[3] Because the bishops have not accepted the " new prophecy," Tertullian will not forgive them. The " Psychics," he writes, strive to set bounds to the divine action itself: " *Palos terminales figitis Deo* ".[4] He sees in the episcopal authority both a restraining power, against which he rebels, and a relaxing power, which provokes his indignation. The Apostle forbids bishops to enter into a second marriage, and behold among the Psychics, bishops take another wife: " *Quot et digami praesident apud vos, insultantes utique apostolo!* " The Holy Ghost had clearly foreseen that one day bishops would exclaim: " *Omnia licent episcopis* ".[5]

These last words prepare us for the outbursts which

[1] " De Fuga," 13 : " Hanc episcopatui formam Apostoli providentius condiderunt, ut regno suo securi frui possent sub obtentu procurandi."

[2] " De Jejun." 13 : " Aguntur per Graecias illa certis in locis concilia ex universis ecclesiis per quae et altiora quaeque in commune tractantur, et ipsa repraesentatio totius nominis christiani magna veneratione celebratur ".

[3] Witness the excommunication pronounced against Theodotus by Pope Victor, and known to us through the testimony of St. Hippolytus, in Euseb. " H. E." v. 28, 9 : ἀφορισθέντος τῆς κοινωνίας ὑπὸ Βίκτορος τοῦ τότε ἐπισκόπου. Cf. "Philosophoum." vii. 25.

[4] " De Jejun." 11. Rolffs, " Urkunden," pp. 42-9, surmises that in the " De Jejunio," Tertullian is answering a written work, perhaps a kind of edict, that emanated from the Roman Church and had been issued by Pope Callistus. This document condemned the fasts and abstinences imposed by the rigorists of the time, whether Marcionites or Montanists. In pp. 31-5, Rolffs attempts to reconstruct the document from the allusions of the " De Jejunio ". We may note this Roman declaration : " constituta sunt sollemnia huic fidei [ieiunia] scripturis vel more maiorum, nihilque observationis amplius adiciendum ob illicitum innovationis " [" De Jejun." 13]. Compare Pope Stephen's " Nihil innovetur ".

[5] " De Monog." 12. Cf. " De Pudicit." i. 15.

brought Tertullian's career to a close, the "De Pudicitia" (between the years 217-222). The circumstances under which that pamphlet was published are so well known that we need not record them here. It is enough to say that it is aimed directly at the Roman Bishop, Pope Callistus. In order the better to proclaim the primacy of the Spirit, Tertullian assails the most Apostolic of all Churches, that to which he had paid, like Irenæus, so glorious a tribute. "I hear that an edict has been brought to the knowledge of the faithful and a peremptory one too. The 'Pontifex Maximus' —otherwise called the bishop of bishops—proclaims : 'I remit, to such as have done penance, the sins both of adultery and of fornication'. . . . And where shall this act of liberality be posted up? On the gates of the abodes of evil? No ; in the Church itself this edict is read, in the Church itself it is pronounced ; and the Church is a virgin ! Far, far from Christ's spouse be such a proclamation ! She, the true, the chaste, the holy, must keep even her ears free from pollution. She has none to whom she can promise such pardons ; she will not promise them." [1] The Spouse of Christ is summoned, so to speak, by Tertullian to choose between the rigorism of the new prophecy and the laxism proclaimed by the bishop of bishops.[2]

---

[1] "De Pudicit." i. 6-9.

[2] Without wishing to return to an historical problem which has been treated elsewhere ("Etudes d'Hist. et de Théolog. posit. Ière Série," fifth edit., 1907, p. 327 and foll.), we may repeat that this rigorism is not a Montanist innovation. At the time of Callistus, and even against Callistus himself, the same rigorism is defended at Rome, by Hippolytus, as a discipline not open to discussion. See the passage of the "Philosophoumena," vi. 41, relative to the sacrament of redemption ($\dot{\alpha}\pi o\lambda\acute{\upsilon}\tau\rho\omega\sigma\iota\varsigma$), by which the heretics deceive the simple in persuading them "that, even after they have been baptized, they may receive again the forgiveness" of their sins. See ibid. ix. 15, the formula of the so-called Elchasaïte baptism brought to Rome by the Syrian Alcibiades, at the time of Callistus or shortly after, and what Hippolytus tells us (ibid. 13) of that baptism which it was contended could be administered to Christians, already baptized, who had sinned. To this testimony of Hippolytus we may add that of Clement of Alexandria, "Stromat." ii. 13, commenting upon the work of Hermas. On Irenæus, as expressing the same view, cf. H. KOCH, "Die Sündenvergebung bei Irenäus " in the "Zeitschrift für die neut. Wissenschaft," 1908, pp. 35-46.

The episcopal authority, that of Rome, is then directly attacked by Tertullian. The act promulgated by that authority he calls an edict, to assimilate it ironically with the act of a secular magistrate, i.e. of the praetor in previous times, of the Emperor, now.[1]   Then to give a new point to his irony, Tertullian calls the Roman decision an "*edictum peremptorium*," one of those fundamental judgments which close a trial and put an end to all controversy.[2]   The indulgent step taken by Callistus he styles "*liberalitas*," a word commonly used to signify an imperial favour: "*Liberalitas praestantissimorum imperatorum . . .*" he writes in another passage.[3]   He pushes his irony so far as to imagine that the edict, in regular form, begins with this declaration : "*Pontifex maximus, quod est episcopus episcoporum, edicit. . . .*"   It is thus that imperial edicts were worded in the first person, in contrast with the laws which ran in the third person of the imperative.[4]   Tertullian calls the Bishop of Rome *Pontifex maximus*—a title which was then a pagan title and remained so until the reign of Gratian, in the fourth century.[5]   In a word, Tertullian strives, with insolent sarcasm, to impart to the decision of the Bishop of Rome, a secular and even an imperial tone and character.

It may be asked what could the decision of a bishop who is not the Bishop of Carthage matter to this Carthaginian priest?   But it is this which makes Tertullian's pamphlet the more significant.   For if he is so stirred by the edict of the Bishop of Rome, is not this a proof that such an edict

---

[1] TERTULL. "De Bapt." 11 : "Imperator proposuit edictum ".   See E. ROLFFS, "Das Indulgenz-Edict des röm. Bischofs Kallist " (Leipzig, 1893), p. 20 ; DE LABRIOLLE, "Tertullien, De Paenitentia " (Paris, 1906), pp. xxii-xxiii.

[2] "Digest." v. 1, 70 : "Quod inde hoc nomen sumpsit quod perimeret disceptationem, hoc est ultra non pateretur adversarium tergiversari ".

[3] "De Corona,' 1.

[4] GIRARD, "Textes," p. 173 : "Ti. Claudius Caesar Augustus Germanicus pontifex maximus . . . dicit. . . ."   Cf. DEISSMANN, p. 49. Tertullian's tone inclines us to think that the formula " *Ego et moechiae* " etc. is not given in its authentic terms.

[5] See TERTULL. "De Monog." 17 : "Pontifex Maximus et Flaminica. . . ." ; BOUCHÉ-LECLERCQ, art. "Pontifices," p. 578, in the "Diction. des Antiq." of DAREMBERG and SAGLIO.

is of a nature to make itself felt in all the Churches? The "*potentior principalitas*" enters as a factor into the settlement of an important question: one may even gather that the Bishop of Rome has asserted the right and acted on it. Tertullian calls him "*episcopus episcoporum*,"[1] either because the Bishop of Rome had taken this title, which is doubtful, or, which is more probable, because the wording of his edict alluded to the primacy of his see.

Tertullian's invectives are directed against the Roman primacy: Gallicanism was born in Africa! They are also, and even more, directed against the whole episcopal hierarchy. Or rather, Tertullian makes a distinction between what he calls discipline and what he calls power: discipline is something external, like politics, whilst power is something supernatural. "What is power? It is the Spirit, and the Spirit is God. Callistus claims the power of forgiving sins: well and good, if those sins were sins committed

---

[1] D'ALÈS, "Tertullien," p. 217, thinks that Callistus did not assume the title, *episcopus episcoporum.*—In the "De Pudic." XIII. 7, Tertullian calls Callistus "benedictus Papa"; but at that time the appellation *papa* was given to bishops, and expressed the filial deference of those who used it. The earliest indication found at Rome of its being applied to the Bishop of Rome is an inscription which dates from the time of Pope Marcellinus (+ 304): "Cubiculum . . . iussu p[a]p[ae] sui Marcellini diaconus iste Severus fecit. . . ." DE ROSSI, "Inscriptiones Christ. Urbis Romae," vol. I. p. cxv. Until then, no Bishop of Rome is addressed as *papa*, and yet we have many letters sent to the bishops of Rome. We may be referred to the letter of the martyrs of Lyons to Eleutherius, whom they style πάτερ Ἐλεύθερε (EUSEB. "H. E." v. 4, 2). But it is true also that, in writing to St. Cyprian, the Roman clergy calls him pope (*inter* CYPRIANI, "Epistul." xxx. inscr. and 16, xxxi., xxxvi.); and so do the Carthaginian confessors of the faith ("Epistul." xxiii.). The Roman clergy writes to that of Carthage: "Didicimus secessisse benedictum papatem Cyprianum . . ." ("Epistul." viii. 1). St. Augustine is often addressed as *papa* by his correspondents. St. Jerome gives this title to such bishops as St. Epiphanius, John of Jerusalem, Theophilus of Alexandria, St. Athanasius, Chromatius of Aquileia, but also to the Bishops of Rome, Anastasius and Damasus for instance. As early as the time of St. Cyprian, the Bishop of Alexandria is called pope, as likewise the Bishop of Carthage (see EUSEB. "H. E." VII. 7, 4: τοῦ μακαρίου πάπα ἡμῶν Ἡρακλᾶ, in a letter of his successor, Dionysius). Cf. BENSON, pp. 29-31, DEISSMANN, pp. 138 and 150, and BUONAIUTI, "Saggi di filologia e storia" (Roma, 1910), pp. 237-45.

against Callistus; but how can Callistus forgive sins committed against God? If the Apostles remitted such sins, they did it, not in virtue of discipline, but in virtue of their power" (*ex potestate*).

"Exhibe igitur et nunc mihi, apostolice, prophetica exempla et agnoscam divinitatem, et vindica tibi delictorum eiusmodi remittendorum potestatem. Quod si disciplinae solius officia sortitus es, nec imperio praesidere, sed ministerio, quis aut quantus es indulgere?"[1]

Is not the bishop, then, the heir of the supernatural powers granted by God to the prophets and to the Apostles? Not at all, replies Tertullian: his only business is to see that discipline be observed. But, says Callistus, the Church has the power (*potestas*) of forgiving sins. Certainly, answers Tertullian, and our new prophecy proclaims that power. " De tua nunc sententia quaero, unde hoc ius ecclesiae usurpes. Si quia dixerit Petro Dominus: *Super hanc petram aedificabo ecclesiam meam, tibi dabo claves regni caelestis,* vel *Quaecunque alligaveris vel solveris in terra erunt alligata vel soluta in caelis,* idcirco praesumis et ad te derivasse solvendi et alligandi potestatem, id est ad omnem ecclesiam Petri propinquam?*[2] Qualis es, evertens atque commutans manifestam Domini intentionem personaliter hoc Petro conferentem?"[3]

How can Callistus be bold enough to claim for himself the power of the Church? Is it because of the words said to Peter? By what right does Callistus misinterpret the plain intention of the Saviour, who, when He addressed

---

[1] "De Pudicitia," XXI. 5-6. We have seen elsewhere the title ἀποστολικός applied to the immediate disciples of the Apostles, to St. Polycarp for instance (EUSEB. "H. E." III. 36, 10).

[2] From this we may infer that, in order to justify his claim to the power of the keys, Pope Callistus appealed to Matt. XVI. 18-19, "the first instance of the kind recorded in history," as Harnack observes ("Dogmeng." vol. I[4], p. 492). Granted, but Tertullian does not question the fact that the Church is founded on St. Peter, he concedes that point: " *Omnis ecclesia Petri propinqua,*" words to be translated: "Every church is connected with Peter" instead of: "Every church which is connected with Peter," as de Labriolle takes it. Tertullian refuses to admit that the power of keys passed over to any church, as such.

[3] "De Pudicit." XXI. 9-10.

Peter, manifestly meant to grant him a privilege that was
to be personal and for him only? " I will give to *thee* the
keys," not to the Church. The keys are the symbol of St.
Peter's Apostolic ministry,[1] as recorded in the book of the
Acts.

What, then, is the power granted by Christ to the
Church, to every Church?

" Quid nunc et ad Ecclesiam, et quidem tuam, psychice ?
Secundum enim Petri personam spiritalibus potestas ista
conveniet : aut apostolo aut prophetae.   Nam et ipsa Ecclesia proprie et principaliter ipse est Spiritus, in quo est
trinitas unius divinitatis, Pater et Filius et Spiritus sanctus.   Illam ecclesiam congregat, quam Dominus in tribus
posuit.   Atque ita exinde etiam numerus omnis, qui in hanc
fidem conspiraverint, ecclesia ab auctore et consecratore cen-
setur.   Et ideo Ecclesia quidem delicta donabit, sed Ecclesia
Spiritus per spiritalem hominem, non Ecclesia numerus
episcoporum.[2]

Christ conferred on Peter and the Apostles the power
of forgiving sins, when He gave them the Holy Ghost :
" Receive ye the Holy Ghost.   Whose sins you shall forgive. . . ."   Hence that *potestas* belongs to any one who
has received the Holy Ghost, it belongs to all the *Spirituals*,
i.e. to the Apostles, and after them, to the prophets.   It
belongs also, and equally well, to the Church, since (a reminiscence of Irenæus) where the Church is, there is also
the Spirit ; but the ministers of the Spirit are the Spirituals
only, and not those who are merely invested with such or
such a disciplinary function, like bishops.[3]

We grant that " exceptional historical importance attaches to " these statements of Tertullian ;[4] but we cannot

[1] " De Pudicit." xxi. 11-15.          [2] *Ibid.* 16-17.

[3] If this is the case, the distinction between the laity and the hierarchy is of merely ecclesiastical origin : as a matter of fact, Tertullian will
boldly declare, later on, that the priesthood belongs to all, and that, in
the absence of a priest, a layman can validly celebrate the Eucharist, just
as well as he does Baptism.   Cf. " De Exhort. Castit." 7 ; " De Monog."
7 and 12 ; " De Pudic." 21.   It may be remembered that Tertullian,
speaking of the heretics, had once said, with indignation : " Laicis sacerdotalia munera iniungunt ! "   " Praescr." 41.

[4] HARNACK, " Dogmeng." vol. 1[4], p. 403.

see in them, as some would have us do, a proof of the evolution of the episcopate in Tertullian's age, and of audacious pretensions set up by the Bishop of Rome.    It is Tertullian who is the revolutionary.

For, in the first place, he reduces episcopacy to a mere function of discipline, of police.    In the second place—and this he does even in his Catholic works—he extols the rule of faith, as though it could be preserved without the help of a *magisterium* : unlike Irenæus who insisted on the Apostolic *magisterium* and on the charism of truth entrusted to bishops, Tertullian comes, ultimately, to proclaim the Paraclete as " *solus a Christo magister et dicendus et verendus*"; and this substitution is a novelty, since—as we have seen all through the history of the early Church, even at its very beginning—the *teaching* function of presbyters and of bishops was essentially connected with their office.    In the third place, Tertullian distinguishes in the Church an *imperium* and a *ministerium* : bishops are servants, the *imperium* belongs to the Spirit, so that, the Spirit governing the Church, the episcopate has hardly any place left for it in the Church— which is surely a paradox.    In the fourth place, Tertullian denies to the episcopate any *potestas* inherited from the Apostles : in his eyes, any *potestas* is a spiritual gift of the Paraclete.    This is another paradox in view of the affirmations of the " Pastoral Epistles," the " Didachè," and the letters of Clement of Rome and St. Ignatius on the powers of Order, which are also essential to the hierarchy.    Fifthly, Tertullian will not admit that a Church is realized, so to speak, in its bishop : for him the bishop does not make the unity of his Church, the Spirit alone makes the Church : " *non Ecclesia numerus episcoporum* " : another paradox for those who bear in mind how often the opposite is affirmed in the texts anterior to Tertullian.[1]

---

[1] HARNACK, loc. cit., in his endeavour to prove that the episcopal prestige grew exceedingly during the first third of the third century, refers us to the edict of persecution of Maximinus in 235, directed not against all Christians indiscriminately, but only against bishops, as alone answerable for the new religion (EUSEB. " H. E." vi. 28).    Harnack forgets the bishops who suffered during the second century—St. Ignatius and St. Polycarp for instance ; he forgets that scene of Polycarp's martyrdom, when the heathen populace of Smyrna ask for Polycarp by name

It is very easy, indeed, to choose between Callistus and Tertullian: Callistus introduces no new notion of the Church, when he proclaims the notion of an ecclesiastical hierarchy, in which each bishop is the head of his own Church, and the Church is the *numerus episcoporum*. Novelty is on the side of Tertullian who, to find a place for the "new prophecy" in the long-established and traditional ecclesiastical system, overturns it all, and demands that the "spirituals" shall take precedence of the clergy, and the Spirit alone be permitted to speak and rule. Tertullian's contemporaries must certainly have looked upon this chimera as preposterous.

("Martyr. Polyc." 3) and that other scene, when, on seeing Polycarp in chains, the same populace exclaim: "This is the teacher of Asia, the father of the Christians, the overthrower of our gods, he who has been teaching many not to sacrifice, or to worship the gods". The prestige of the Bishop of Smyrna, in the year 155, seems to be just as great as that of the Bishop of Carthage a century later.

# CHAPTER VII.

## ORIGEN AND GREEK ORTHODOXY.

WHEN, from Christians like Irenæus and Tertullian, we come to Origen, we feel ourselves in a different atmosphere. We are witnessing the growth of Hellenic culture in Christianity.

Clement had opened out the way upon which Origen now enters with such distinction. "Greek philosophy," says Origen, has its falsehoods, and also some elements of truth " not to be lightly esteemed ": St. Paul had already " seen a certain grandeur in the words of the world's wisdom ".[1] On the other band, the Word of Jesus has spread all over the inhabited world ; it has conquered kings and leaders of armies, archons of cities, soldiers and citizens: no obstacle has been able to check its advance, for it is the word of God, more powerful than all its opponents, more powerful than Greeks and barbarians : it has converted to the religion that is according to God thousands and thousands of souls. It is no wonder that, among all these converts, the simple and uneducated should exceed in number the learned. But from this to infer—as Celsus does—that a doctrine within the reach of every human soul is a doctrine fit only for the simple, and that just because of its simplicity it is not capable of being justified by reason, is to insult it gratuitously.[2]

---

[1] ORIGEN, "Contra Celsum," praef. i. 5 ("P. G." vol. xi. col. 648).

[2] *Ibid.* i. 27 ("P. G." xi. 712) : . . . οἴεται εἶναι ἰδιωτικὴν καὶ διὰ τὸ ἰδιωτικὸν καὶ οὐδαμῶς ἐν λόγοις δυνατόν, ἰδιωτῶν μόνων κρατήσασαν. Irenæus had already noted that this was one of the charges brought by the Gnostic leaders against the Church. Clement of Alexandria mentions it also as a reproach addressed to Christianity by the sophists of his time. "Stromata," i. 3 ("P. G." viii. 712). Evidently it was a common thing in the cultivated circles of the time to jeer at the intellectual shortcomings of the Christians ;

The proof of this is in the fact that, if any one comes to us from the Greek " dogmas " and schools of learning, he perceives not only that our faith is true, but also—which is still better—that it is susceptible of a " Greek demonstration ". " It must be said, however," Origen adds immediately, " that our faith has a demonstration of its own, more divine than any established by Greek dialectics " : viz. a demonstration by means of prophecies and miracles.[1] Dialectics will cure learned men of their errors. Hence we say to no one, not even to the simple : " ' See that none of you lay hold of knowledge ' ; nor do we say that ' knowledge is an evil ' ; nor are we mad enough to say that ' knowledge causes men to lose their sanity of mind '. We would not even say that any one ever perished through wisdom ; we give instruction, but we never say : ' Believe me,' but : ' Believe the God of all things, and believe Jesus the giver of instruction concerning Him '." [2]

This is indeed a new language—absolutely new, and bold in its novelty. Origen is not afraid to speak of science and dialectics and philosophy, even of *gnosis*—and let us not forget that Greek philosophy was the encyclopædia of the time for all schools and scholars indiscriminately. Origen, self-taught, eclectic, claims for Christianity the right to make use of this intellectual storehouse for its own benefit. He writes : " All that the sons [disciples] of the philosophers are wont to say about geometry and music, grammar, rhetoric and astronomy, as natural attendants on philosophy, we say about philosophy itself, in its relation to Christianity."[3]

(τὸ βάρβαρον ἐν παιδείᾳ, are the words of Clement). Cf. "Stromat." II. 2 ("P. G." VIII. 940).

[1] " Contra Cels." I. 2 (XI. 656): λεκτέον ὅτι ἐστί τις οἰκεία ἀπόδειξις τοῦ λόγου, θειοτέρα παρὰ τὴν ἀπὸ διαλεκτικῆς ἑλληνικήν. Origen speaks of a Christian ἀπὸ ἑλληνικῶν δογμάτων καὶ γυμνασίων ἐλθών.

[2] *Ibid.* III. 75 (XI. 1020): οὐ λέγομεν, ὁρᾶτε μὴ ποτέ τις ὑμῶν ἐπιστήμης ἐπιλάβηται, οὐδὲ φάσκομεν ὅτι κακόν ἐστιν ἐπιστήμη οὐδὲ μεμήναμεν ἵν' εἴπωμεν ὅτι γνῶσις σφάλλει τοὺς ἀνθρώπους κ.τ.λ. Cf. *ibid.* 47 and 48 (XI. 981). The same is said by CLEMENT, "Stromat." VI. 10 (IX. 301).

[3] " Epistula ad Gregor." 1 (XI. 88). The same idea is in CLEMENT, "Stromata," I. 2. At Rome, on the contrary, the former attitude still prevails about the same time. We must remember how Hippolytus (EUSEB. " H. E." V. 28), like Tertullian, is shocked that some should admire Aristotle and use the syllogism.

The inspiration manifested in these thoughts reminds us of that which gave birth to the Jewish Alexandrian literature, and to the movement of Hellenistic-Jewish thought to which Philo belongs. Still, we must be careful not to overlook the deep-rooted and firm tradition in the midst of which this new spirit makes its appearance. It has been said that " if all appearances are not deceptive, the Alexandrian Church . . . was, up to the time of Septimius Severus, pursuing a path of development which, left to itself, would *not* have led to Catholicism, but, in the most favourable circumstances, to a parallel form ".[1]   Unfortunately, history records little about the Church of Alexandria in the first two centuries ; but, as soon as it does record something, through the writings of Clement and Origen, we see Catholicism established at Alexandria on the same foundations as elsewhere : why then maintain that this Alexandrian Catholicism was something new,[2] something that began only in the first half of the

---

[1] HARNACK, "Dogmeng." vol. 1[4], p. 481.

[2] HARNACK, *ibid.*, quotes but one fact in support of his supposition. EUSEBIUS ("H. E." vi. 2, 13-14) relates that Origen, who happened to be in very poor circumstances, was given hospitality by a lady of rank in Alexandria, who " lodged and entertained in her house, besides Origen, then a young man, a famous heretic". The latter, whose name was Paul, came from Antioch.   Harnack, whom we have just quoted, continues as follows : " The lectures on doctrine delivered by this heretic and the conventicles over which he presided were attended by a μύριον πλῆθος οὐ μόνον αἱρετικῶν ἀλλὰ καὶ ἡμετέρων [a large crowd, not only of heretics, but of our own people also].   This is a valuable piece of information which reveals to us a state of things in Alexandria that would have been impossible in Rome at the same period."   No, we may reply, this piece of information attests merely the well-known levity of the "respectable people " of Alexandria, who were attracted by the eloquence of this heretic. As to the question of orthodoxy, we see, from the sequel of the narrative, that it existed at Alexandria just as at Rome.   In point of fact—to quote the words of Eusebius—" Origen could never be induced to join with him [Paul] in prayer ; for, although then a boy, he held the rule of the Church (οὐδὲ πώποτε προὐτράπη κατὰ τὴν εὐχὴν αὐτῷ συστῆναι, φυλάττων ἐξέτι παιδὸς κανόνα ἐκκλησίας), and abominated, as he somewhere expresses it, heretical teachings (βελυττόμενός τε, ὡς αὐτῷ ῥήματί φησί που αὐτός, τὰς τῶν αἱρέσεων διδασκαλίας).   This detail of Origen's childhood (he was born about the year 182) shows that, before the end of the second century, the genuine Christians of Alexandria would suffer no compromise in what belongs to the ecclesiastical rule of faith.   See the similar declarations of Dionysius, Bishop of Alexandria, EUSEB. "H. E." vii. 7.

third century? Let us not separate the Hellenic spirit of our Alexandrian doctors from their Catholicism and from what gives them their fitting place in the κοινὴ ἕνωσις, in that ecclesiastical unity of which we shall find all the distinctive features in the works of Origen.

\*\*\*

As a matter of fact, in the eyes of Origen, the Church is not a school open to all, and thus differs from the schools of philosophy where " the philosophers discuss in public and do not pick and choose their hearers, but he who likes stands and listens." Far from it! For the Christians try, as far as possible, " the souls of those who wish to become their hearers ": they previously instruct them in private, and only when they deem them sufficiently prepared do they bring them into their assembly (εἰς τὸ κοινόν), although even then they distinguish between the true disciples and those who have not yet received the sign of purification: for it is thus that Origen, speaking to Celsus, designates baptism.[1] Among the Christians there are special officers whose duty it is to make inquiries into the conduct of applicants for initiation, to set aside men of irregular lives, and to make the good still better. " The practice of the Christians is the same with those [of their brethren] who sin, especially with the unchaste: they exclude them from their assembly."[2] The Pythagoreans erect cenotaphs to those who have given up their philosophy, because they treat them as dead; " but the Christians lament as dead those who have been vanquished by impurity or any other sin, because they are lost and dead to God; but (if they manifest a true conversion) they receive them back as risen from the dead, though after a longer probation than in the case of those who are admitted for the first time; yet never do they admit to any charge or authority in the Church of God those who, after once professing the Gospel, have lapsed and fallen."[3]

This does not mean, however, that the Church consists

---

[1] " Contra Cels." III. 51 (XI. 988): τὸ σύμβολον τοῦ ἀποκεκαθάρθαι.

[2] Ibid.: οὓς ἀπελαύνουσι τοῦ κοίνου.

[3] Ibid.: εἰς οὐδεμίαν ἀρχὴν καὶ προστασίαν τῆς λεγομένης ἐκκλησίας τοῦ θεοῦ καταλέγοντες. . . . On the holiness of the Church, see " De Orat." 20 (XI. 477).

of saints only. The Church is a treasure-house that contains vessels of mercy and vessels of wrath, a granary where straw and wheat are gathered in together, a net that brings to the surface fishes that must be cast aside and fishes that are excellent.[1] The Christian community as a whole has become exceedingly lukewarm, nor must we judge it from the increasing number of its crowds. Where are the martyrs of old? Formerly, when returning from the cemeteries whither we had taken the bodies of our martyrs, " from the whole assembly no lament arose ". Catechumens were instructed by the sight itself of the sufferings of the martyrs or of the death of the confessors. " Few indeed were the faithful then, but they were truly faithful." Now that we are so many, the word of Jesus is proved to be true, which says : " Many are called, few are chosen ".[2] Many who are indifferent are now found in our midst, mingled with the sinners. The faithful no longer come punctually to the liturgical synaxes : hardly do they come even on feast days, and when they do come, it is not so much to hear the word, as for the sake of diversion, and of the spectacle.[3]

The ecclesiastical *ordo* comprises three degrees :[4] the deacons, the priests, the bishop. While the obligation of each towards the Church is grave, the bishop's obligation

[1] " In Ierem. Homil." xx. 3 (xiii. 536).

[2] *Ibid.* iv. 3 (xiii. 289). As to the wonderful multiplication of Christians as early as the end of the second century, see the sarcastic comment of Celsus, in " Contra Celsum," iv. 23 (xi. 1060).

[3] " In Genes. Homil." x. 1 (xii. 215) : " Vix festis diebus ad ecclesiam proceditis, et hoc non tam desiderio verbi, quam studio solemnitatis et publicae quodammodo remissionis obtentu. Quid igitur ego faciam, cui dispensatio verbi credita est ? "

[4] In this study of Greek ecclesiology during the first half of the third century, I shall not use the so-called Canons of Hippolytus or the document designated generally by German scholars the " Aegyptische Kirchenordnung." Most critics believe with Funk (against Achelis and Harnack) that these two documents depend on the " Apostolic Constitutions," which must belong to about the year 400. Nor shall I appeal, either, to the " Didascalia apostolorum," although it may be ascribed very probably to the third century, probably to the second half of the third century. (Whether it comes from Antioch or from Jerusalem, is uncertain.)

is graver than that of any other, and he will be held accountable by the "Saviour of the whole Church ".[1] The bishop has sovereignty over both the priests and the faithful.[2] He must be severe, and woe to his sheep, if he is over lenient towards sinners, if he is afraid of what they may say, if he hesitates to rebuke them, and, if need be, to banish them from the Church.

"Dum uni parcunt, universae ecclesiae moliuntur interitum. Quae ista bonitas? quae ista misericordia est, uni parcere et omnes in discrimen adducere? Polluitur enim ex uno peccatore populus. Sicut ex una ove morbida grex universus inficitur, sic etiam uno vel fornicante, vel aliud quodcumque sceleris committente, plebs universa polluitur. Et ideo observemus nos invicem et uniuscuiusque conversatio nota sit, maxime sacerdotibus et ministris. Nec putent se recte dicere: Quid hoc ad me spectat si alius male agit? . . . Tale ergo est quod [dicunt] ii qui ecclesiis praesunt, non cogitantes quia unum corpus sumus omnes qui credimus, unum deum habentes qui nos in unitate constringit et continet, Christum, cuius corporis tu qui ecclesiae praesides oculus es, propterea utique ut omnia circumspicias, omnia circumlustres, etiam ventura praevideas. Pastor es, vides oviculas Domini ignaras periculi ferri ad praecipitia et per praerupta pendere, non occurris? non revocas? non saltem voce cohibes et correptionis clamore deterres?"[3]

The Church, then, is a tangible unity: she is a body of which the bishop is the eye, and the right hand: he is ἐπίσκοπος that he may watch, he is a pastor, he must be zealous and vigilant especially as regards sinners. This is the counterpart to the diatribes of Tertullian, the Montanist.

There is for the sinner a hard and toilsome penance, in which he waters his couch with his tears and is not ashamed to make his sin known to the bishop.[4] After the manner of

---

[1] "De Orat." 28 (xi. 524): . . . ὀφειλή, καὶ ἑτέρα διακόνου, καὶ ἄλλη πρεσβυτέρου, καὶ ἐπισκόπου δὲ ὀφειλὴ βαρυτάτη ἐστὶν ἀπαιτουμένη ὑπὸ τοῦ τῆς ὅλης ἐκκλησίας σωτῆρος (ita KOETSCHAU).

[2] "In Ierem. Homil." xi. 3 (xiii. 369): ὁ τὴν πάντων ἡμῶν ἐγκεχειρισμένος ἀρχὴν αὐτὴν τὴν ἐκκλησιαστικήν.

[3] "In Ies. Nave Homil." vii. 6 (xii. 862).

[4] "In Levit. Homil." ii. 4 (xii. 448): ". . . Non erubescit sacerdoti Domini indicare peccatum suum ".

the high priest of old, as prescribed in Leviticus, it belongs to the bishop to offer up to God the sacrifice of propitiation for the sin.[1] He has the power to exclude the sinner from the Church : "*Si quis nostrum peccaverit abiectus est, etiamsi non abiciatur ab episcopo, sive quod lateat, sive quod interdum ad gratiam iudicetur, eiectus est tamen ipsa conscientia peccati*".[2] In allusion to the words in which St. Paul declares that he delivers over to Satan the incestuous Christian of Corinth, Origen observes that the Apostles are not the only ones who have this power, since a like punishment can be inflicted "*per eos qui ecclesiae praesident et potestatem habent non solum solvendi, sed et ligandi.*"[3] For "*in ecclesiis Christi consuetudo tenuit talis, ut qui manifesti sunt in magnis delictis eiciantur ab oratione communi*".[4]

The mission of every Christian is, indeed, to bring all mankind to the kingdom of God ; but this is preeminently the mission of the bishops, priests and deacons: "*Maxime hoc faciunt qui videntur in ecclesia clariores, quales sunt episcopi, presbyteri, diaconi,*" and this duty they fulfil, by leading a life of virtue. Evil-living pastors, mercenaries, turn away from the kingdom those who were advancing towards it, particularly when they excommunicate unjustly, through jealousy or anger, members who are at times much better than they, and who can oppose only patience to these tyrannical deeds.[5]

[1] "In Levit. Homil." v. 4 (454): "Discant sacerdotes Domini qui ecclesiis praesunt quia pars eis data est cum his quorum delicta repropitiaverint". Cf. *ibid.* vi. 12 (464-5).

[2] *Ibid.* xii. 6 (542). Cf. xiv. 2 (553): "Peccavit aliquis fidelium : iste etiamsi nondum abiciatur per episcopi sententiam, iam tamen per ipsum peccatum quod admisit eiectus est; et quamvis intret ecclesiam tamen eiectus est, et foris est, segregatus a consortio et unanimitate fidelium. Cf. *ibid.* 3 (556): "Interdum fit ut aliquis non recto iudicio eorum qui praesunt ecclesiae depellatur, et foras mittatur." Cf. "In Ierem. Homil." vii. 3. (xiii. 333) ; *ibid.* xii. 5 (385).

[3] "In Judic. Homil." ii. 5 (xii. 961).

[4] "In Matt. Comment. ser." 89 (xiii. 1740). Cf. "In Levit. Homil." xiv. 2 (xii. 553).

[5] *Ibid.* 14 (xiii. 1620): ". . . maxime quando . . . non propter peccata quae faciunt excommunicant quosdam, sed propter aliquem zelum et contentionem . . . , vincentes sua patientia et longanimitate tyrannides eorum."

Let bishops be on their guard not to misuse their discretionary authority of cutting off a Christian from communion, depriving him of the bread and of the chalice, excluding him from the house of God which is the Church,[1] and banishing him from the Church his fatherland.[2]

The bishop has the administration of charity; he is the innkeeper to whom the good Samaritan gives two pence, that the wounded man whom he has picked up on the way may have all the necessary care.[3] Whoever is called to the episcopate "*non ad principatum vocatur, sed ad servitutem totius ecclesiae*".[4] Woe to him if, prompted by the love of riches, he takes for himself the gifts offered to God,[5] and the money contributed by the faithful for the needs of the poor, and the support of the clergy.[6]

Origen shows us the seat apart of the bishop and of his priests, and below them the deacons standing, ready

---

[1] "Comment. in Ioan." XXVIII. 4 (XIV. 688) : οὐ παντὶ καθήκει μὴ χρῆσθαι τῷ ἄρτῳ καὶ μὴ πίνειν ἐκ τοῦ ποτηρίου, καὶ μὴ πόρρω εἶναι τοῦ οἴκου θεοῦ καὶ τῆς ἐκκλησίας.

[2] "In Psalm. XXXVII. Homil." I. 6 (XII. 1380) : "Iste si decidat de patria sua, id est de ecclesia, in insulam quamdam atque in horrentes scopulos quae peccati sedes est propellatur".

[3] "Comment. in Rom." IX. 31 (XIV. 1231): ". . . stabulario . . . qui ecclesiae praeest".

[4] "In Is. Homil." VI. 1 (XIII. 239).

[5] "Comment. in Rom." II. 11 (XIV. 897) : "Quod si, ut nonnunquam fieri solet, munera oblata Deo et stipem in usus pauperum datam, ad roppria lucra converterit. . . ." Concerning the charitable services rendered by the Church see "Comment. in Rom." IX. 2 (XIV. 1212). "Comment. in Matt." XI. 9 (XIII. 932) : τὸ τῆς ἐκκλησίας γλωσσόκομον. "In Levit. Homil." IV. 6 (XII. 431) : "Vota et munera quae in ecclesiis Dei ad usus sanctorum, et ministerium sacerdotum, vel quae ob necessitatem pauperum, a devotis et religiosis mentibus offeruntur". By *vota* we must understand here what the faithful vow to give to the Church, as is explained in "Homil." XI. 1 (*ibid.* 531). Clement of Alexandria intimates that some became Christians, because once in the ranks of the Christian community they were sure to be safe from destitution, Christianity being a powerful charitable institution. "Stromat." I. 1 ("P. G." vol. VIII. col. 693 A.).

[6] "In Num. Homil." XI. 2 (XII. 644). To the bishop also belongs the administration of the ecclesiastical property, which then consisted of the Christian cemeteries. Cf. "Philosophoumena," IX. 12 ("P. G." XVI. 3383).

to minister at the divine service.[1] We are seated higher
than you, it is true — says Origen to his hearers — and
some of the faithful aim at reaching the same degree, but
do not believe that it suffices to belong to the clergy to be
saved : many even among the priests lose their own souls,
and many of the laity will be happier ; for what truly matters,
is not to have one's seat in the *presbyterium*, but to live
worthy of that station.[2]

The prince (ὁ ἡγούμενος), for " this name, I believe, should
be given to him who in the Churches is called bishop " ; the
prince must be the servant of servants, according to the
command left us by the Word of God. On the contrary,
we so act " that at times we exceed in pride the wicked
princes of the nations, and we all but surround ourselves,
like kings, with bodyguards. We are formidable, inaccessible,
especially to the poor. When some one comes to us and
makes a request, we are more haughty than are the most
cruel tyrants and princes towards their supplicants. This
can be seen in many famous Churches, chiefly in those of
the largest cities." [3]

Those who prove themselves unworthy of ecclesiastical
dignities, can certainly be deprived of them. A Church is
like a city, which can strike the name of a decurion off the
roll of its Curia, just as it can condemn to exile such or such

[1] " In Cantic." II. (XIII. 107) : " Vidit et sedem puerorum eius. Ecclesiasticum puto ordinem dicit, qui in episcopatus vel presbyterii sedibus
habetur. Vidit et ordinationes sive stationes ministrorum eius. Diacon-
orum, ut mihi videtur, ordinem memorat astantium divino ministerio."

[2] " In Ierem. Homil." XI. 3 : δοκοῦμεν εἶναι ἀπὸ κλήρου τινὸς προκα-
θεζόμενοι ὑμῶν. . . . Τὸ ὠφελοῦν οὐκ αὐτὸ τὸ καθέζεσθαι ἐν πρεσβυτερίῳ
ἐστίν, ἀλλὰ τὸ βιοῦν ἀξίως τοῦ τόπου. . . . Πλεῖον ἐγὼ ἀπαιτοῦμαι παρὰ τὸν
διάκονον, πλεῖον ὁ διάκονος παρὰ τὸν λαικόν. As to the meaning of the
word τόπος, cf. ap. EUSEB. " H. E." VI. 11, 3, the letter of Alexander,
Bishop of Jerusalem, to the Christians of Arsinoë.

[3] " Comment. in Matt." XVI. 8 (XIII. 1393). Cf. " In Matt. Comment."
ser. 61 (XIII. 1695). In these words, which are particularly harsh, some
have seen an acrimonious allusion to the Roman Church : a view which,
it is almost unnecessary to say, has not failed to obtain the full approval
of the Old Catholics, of Langen for instance. The bishops of Alexandria
and the bishops of Antioch might lay themselves open, just as well, to
similar criticisms ; consider, for instance, the formal charges of pride made
against Paul of Samosata.

of its citizens : " *Infamia est a populo Dei et ecclesia separari :
dedecus est in ecclesia surgere de consessu presbyterii, proiici
de diaconatus gradu* ".[1]

The people have the right to assist at the election of
their bishop, for they should convince themselves on that day,
that the most learned and holy candidate is chosen.[2]  We
know, from other sources, that the neighbouring bishops
take part in the election of a new bishop.[3]

Between the *ordo*, which consists of the bishop, priests
and deacons on the one hand, and of the people, which consists of the faithful ($\pi\iota\sigma\tau oi$) and the catechumens on the
other, Origen does not mention any clerics as intermediaries.[4]
He speaks of virgins and of abstinents,[5] and gives us to understand that virginity and asceticism are a profession.[6]  He
speaks of widows, and also of virgins, as dedicated to the
service of the Church, like the priests, the deacons, and
the bishop.[7]  Origen protests against a protracted stay in
the ranks of the catechumens,[8] for, in truth, whoever is
born again through divine baptism is introduced into Paradise, i.e. into the Church.[9]

Whenever he is led to speak of the clergy of his age,
Origen is extremely severe.  A pessimistic preacher, he does
not fear to denounce the faults of the clergy even before
the assembly of the faithful.  He compares them to the
Pharisees who love to be called Rabbis and claim the first

---

[1] " In Ezech. Homil." x. 1 (xiii. 740) : " Poteris intellegere quod
dicitur, si consideraveris quae cotidie in civitatibus fiunt. Inhonoratio
civi est de patria sua exulare, et infamia decurioni eradi de albo
curiae. . . ."

[2] " In Levit. Homil." vi. 3 (xii. 469) : " Requiritur in ordinando
sacerdote et praesentia populi. . . . Ille eligitur ad sacerdotium, et hoc
adstante populo ".

[3] EUSEB. " H. E." vi. 11, 2, where the bishops whose dioceses are
near Jerusalem choose a coadjutor for the aged Bishop of Jerusalem,
Narcissus.

[4] " In Ierem. Homil." xiv. 4.

[5] " Comment. in Rom." i. 2 (xiv. 841).  Cf. ix. 1 (1205).

[6] " Contra Celsum," v. 49 (xi. 1257).

[7] " Comment. in Rom." viii. 10 (1189).

[8] " In Jes. Nave Homil." ix. 9 (xiii. 878).  Cf. " Comment. in Rom."
i. 13 (xiv. 900).  " In Luc. Homil." vii. (xii. 1819).

[9] " In Genes. Selecta " (xii. 100).

seats. Avaricious and hypocritical men intrigue to become deacons; when they have become deacons, they fight among themselves to get the first seats, those of the priests; and when they are priests, they cabal to be made bishops. How far they are from the manners of the early Church, " *caelestes primitivorum ecclesias!* " [1] Then the arrogance of their relatives becomes simply unbearable, for great is their pride if they should have for father or grandfather one " who has been honoured in the Church with the precedency of the episcopal throne, or with the dignity of the presbyterate, or of the diaconate ". [2] In the temple of Jerusalem, which is also the Church, sellers are always to be found, " who have need of Jesus to scourge them and overturn their tables ". [3] The worst Temple-vendors are those bishops and priests who, on election days, sell the Churches to men that are unworthy. [4]

These ecclesiastical elections seem to be a stone of scandal to Origen : he thinks of the Apostles, who, for the choice of Matthias, leave the whole matter in the hands of God, by prayer and by the drawing of lots; and yet they are the Apostles, " *qui utique multo sapientiores erant quam ii qui nunc episcopos vel presbyteros vel diaconos ordinant* ". [5] Even Moses did not take upon himself to appoint his successor ; and still he had sons and nephews : a striking example for the *ecclesiarum principes*, which should deter them from appointing in their wills their relatives for their successors and making the ecclesiastical dignity an inheritance ; a striking example for the people also, who often think they may intervene in the appointment of the bishop, by their repeated outcries—outcries that are dictated by venality or by passion. [6]

---

[1] " In Matt. Comment." ser. 11 (XIII. 1616).

[2] " Comment. in Matt." xv. 26 (XIII. 1329) : ἐπὰν τύχῃ πατράσιν ἐπαυγεῖν καὶ προγόνοις προεδρίας ἠξιωμένοις ἐν τῇ ἐκκλησίᾳ ἐπισκοπικοῦ θρόνου ἢ πρεσβυτερίου τιμῆς ἢ διακονίας εἰς τὸν λαὸν τοῦ θεοῦ.

[3] " Comment. in Ioan." x. 16 (XIV. 348). Cf. for the same comparison in " Comment. in Matt." xvi. 22 (XIII. 1448). As to the expulsion of scandalous bishops, see " In Exod. Homil." x. 4 (XII. 373).

[4] " Comment. in Matt." xvi. 22 (XIII. 1452) : οἱ τὰς πρωτοκαθεδρίας πεπιστευμένοι τοῦ λαοῦ ἐπίσκοποι καὶ πρεσβύτεροι, καὶ ὡσπερεὶ ἀποδιδόμενοι ὅλας ἐκκλησίας οἷς οὐ χρὴ καὶ καθιστάντες οὓς οὐ δεῖ ἄρχοντας.

[5] " In Ies. Nave Homil." xxiii. 2 (XII. 935).

[6] " In Num. Homil. " xxii. 4 (XII. 744) : " Discant Ecclesiae principes successores sibi non eos qui consanguinitate generis iuncti sunt, nec qui

Do we not see, in some Churches, piety treated as an article of trade, and the Gospel, as a means of getting rich? If Jesus wept over Jerusalem, how much greater reason will He have to weep over the Church, the house of prayer, which luxury and lucre have made a den of thieves—" and would to God that it were not the leaders of the people who have done it!"[1]

Origen's severity towards the clergy finds its explanation in the high idea he has of their eminent and divinely appointed function.     For, if the Church is an edifice, the bishops and priests are its roof, made of cedar and cypress: but cypresses are hardy and sweet-smelling trees, and cedars are incorruptible and sweet-smelling also: a symbol of the virtue and knowledge which priests and bishops should possess.[2]     If men demand of the clergy that it should judge itself first, it is because it has a mission to judge the people: "Thinkest thou . . . that thou shalt escape the judgment of God?" says St. Paul, not to the princes of this earth, nor to the kings of this world, but to the leaders and princes of the Churches, i.e. to bishops, priests, and deacons; to these he says that they must not think they will escape the judgment of God, if they do themselves what they judge and condemn others for doing."[3]     Othoniel was made judge over Israel because the Holy Spirit was with him and because he judged Israel through the Holy Spirit: "*Sunt ergo omnium hodie ecclesiarum quae sunt sub caelo quamplurimi iudices, quibus iudicium non solum rerum gestarum datum est sed et animarum : verum nescio si qui tales Ecclesiae iudices sunt quos dignos faciet Deus*

carnis propinquitate sociantur, testamento signare, neque haereditarium tradere Ecclesiae principatum".

[1] " Comment. in Matt." xvi. 21 (xiii. 1445).

[2] " In Cantic. lib." iii. (xiii. 149).   Cf. " In Genes. Homil." xvii. 6 (xiii. 259).

[3] " Comment. in Rom." ii. 2 (xiv. 873) : " Ecclesiarum rectoribus et principibus loquitur, his videlicet qui iudicant eos qui intus sunt, id est episcopis vel presbyteris et diaconibus . . . si ea committant ipsi de quibus alios iudicant et condemnant.   " In Ezech. hom." v. 4 : " Quid mihi prodest quia prior sedeo in cathedra resupinus, honorem maioris accipio, nec possum habere dignitate mea opera condigna ?"

*Spiritu sancto repleri.*" [1]   Let the Pontiff follow the example of Moses and Aaron, and not leave the Lord's tabernacle.   Let the Pontiff meditate on Holy Scripture and instruct the people.   Let him teach what he has learned from God, and received from the Holy Ghost.[2]

Origen—we may notice—asks that the bishops may be worthy to be filled with the Holy Ghost.   Here we come to a very special point of doctrine, to which Origen returns several times.   The Churches are too wealthy and ecclesiastical dignities too greedily sought after, for hypocrisy not to be constantly on the increase :—

" Sunt quidam et martyrii simulatores ; quidam autem episcopatus, vel presbyteratus, vel diaconatus, vel ecclesiasticae scientiae et doctrinae, tantum personas et ostentationem virtutum habentes, vere autem sunt inimici earumdem virtutum quas simulant." [3]

We can just understand how there can be fictitious martyrs ; but how can true bishops simulate the episcopate, true priests, the priesthood, and true deacons, the diaconate ? They merely play a part, Origen tells us, they dislike the virtues they simulate : is it because their unworthiness might deprive them of the powers of their order ?

Elsewhere, when speaking of the power of sanctification, attached to " the word of God and prayer," Origen uses the following expressions, that remind us of the sacramental liturgy :—

" *Sanctificantur per verbum Dei et orationem* [1 Tim.

---

[1] " In Iudic. Homil." iii. 3 (xii. 964).   Cf. " Oracula Sibyllina," ii. 264-7.

[2] " In Levit. Homil." vii. 2 (xii. 478).   The points just noted may be compared with the following affirmations of HARNACK : "The hierarchy has still no significance in Clement's ecclesiology.   Origen entirely agrees with Clement on this point.   He also starts with the theory that the Church is essentially a heavenly Communion and a holy communion of believers, and he keeps this idea constantly before him.   Again, like Clement, he cannot, when opposing heretics, refrain from identifying the Catholic Church, in so far as it is the Church of the true doctrine, with this invisible Church.   But, also like Clement, he is far from having a hierarchical [conception of the Church].   " Dogmeng." vol. i⁴, p. 414. See also BIGG, " Christian Platonists," p. 213.

[3] " In Matt. Comment." ser. 24 (xiii. 1629).

II. 5]. . . . Per orationem autem non cuiuscunque sanctificantur, sed eorum qui *levant puras manus sine ira et disceptatione* [1 Tim. IV. 8].[1]

Does this mean—we ask again—that the impurity of the hands and hearts of priests and bishops renders ineffectual the Sacraments they administer? Cannot the Donatists claim Origen as one of their forerunners?[2] Before answering this question, we had better read with care his commentary on the *Tibi dabo claves regni caelorum.*

This promise was made to Peter, "and to every one who is Peter ".[3] " He is worthy to receive the keys . . . who is so fortified against the gates of Hades that they do not prevail against him," that he " may open these gates to those who have been conquered by them ". The Lord " gives to those who are not conquered by the gates of Hades as many keys as there are virtues ".

"*But as those who claim the dignity of the episcopate*[4] *base their claim like Peter on these words, so as to say that they have received the keys of the kingdom of heaven from the Saviour, and that things bound by them, that is to say, condemned by them, are also bound in heaven, and that those which have obtained remission from them are also loosed in heaven*[5]—*we must say that they speak truly if they do the deeds on account of which it was said to Peter:* " *Thou art Peter*"; *and if they are such that upon them the Church is built by Christ, and to them with good reason this word can be referred. For the gates of Hades ought not to prevail against him who wishes to bind or to loose. But if he is bound himself with the bonds of his sins, to no purpose does he bind or loose.*"[6]

Does not this amount to saying that, if the bishop is a

[1] " Comment. in Rom." IX. 42 (XIV. 1249).

[2] HUET, " Origeniana," qu. XIV. (XVII. 1075).

[3] " Comment. in Matt." XII. 14 (XII. 1012) : λέλεκται τῷ Πέτρῳ καὶ παντὶ Πέτρῳ κ.τ.λ.

[4] *Ibid.* (1013) : οἱ τὸν τόπον τῆς ἐπισκοπῆς ἐκδικοῦντες.

[5] *Ibid.* : τὰ ὑπ' αὐτῶν ἄφεσιν εἰληφότα. The word ἄφεσιν implies that it is a question of sins.

[6] *Ibid.* : εἰ δὲ σειραῖς τῶν ἁμαρτημάτων αὐτοῦ ἔσφιγκται μάτην καὶ δεσμεῖ καὶ λύει.

sinner, he cannot exercise effectually as regards sinners the power of the keys?[1]

\*\*\*

The Church possesses the right faith.[2] The heretics bear the name of Christians, and boast of imparting a doctrine of which they say the men of the Church are ignorant (*quae latere ab ecclesiasticis dicunt*): but really they are thieves and adulterers—thieves who steal the vessels of the temple, adulterers who defile with their errors the chaste dogmas of the Church (*casta et honesta Ecclesiae dogmata*).[3] We strive to understand Holy Writ, not like Basilides, whom we abandon to his ungodliness, but "*secundum pietatem ecclesiastici dogmatis*".[4] We perform the baptismal liturgy "*secundum typum ecclesiis traditum*".[5] We think "*secundum doctrinam ecclesiasticam*".[6] The true prophets of Christ are the teachers who "*ecclesiastice docent verbum*".[7] Elsewhere Origen speaks of the κήρυγμα ἐκκλησιαστικόν.[8] He says of the articles of faith: "*Est et illud definitum in*

---

[1] See in "De Orat." 28 (XI. 528), another confirmation of this inference. He alone can forgive the sins committed against God, who is "inspired by Jesus like the Apostles" (ἐμπνευσθεὶς ὑπὸ τοῦ Ἰησοῦ ὡς οἱ ἀπόστολοι—an allusion to "Joan." xx. 23 : *Accipite Spiritum sanctum, quorum remiseritis*, etc.), and proves by his works that he has received the Holy Ghost, and has become spiritual (ὡς χωρήσας τὸ πνεῦμα τὸ ἅγιον καὶ γενόμενος πνευματικός). The power to forgive sins committed against God belongs "to the Apostles and to the pontiffs, similar to the Apostles, according to the pattern of the great Pontiff"—an allusion to Heb. v. 1. Then follows the well-known passage where Origen is astonished that some bishops claim the right to remit sins of idolatry, fornication and adultery. Cf. "In Psalm." XXXVII. "Homil." I. 1 (XII. 1369 and 1371).

[2] "Comment. in Rom." I. 19 (XIV. 870).

[3] *Ibid.* II. 11 (898). The same thought is found in CLEMENT, "Stromat." VII. 16, quoted above. We must take into account the gravity of theft and adultery as estimated by the penitential discipline of those days.

[4] *Ibid.* V. 1 (1015). KATTENBUSCH, vol. II. pp. 134 and foll. on the place of the *regula fidei* in Origen.

[5] *Ibid.* V. 8 (1038). Cf. "In Epistul. ad Tit." fragm. (1300) : "ecclesiastica regula". "Comment. in Ioan." XIII. 16 (XIV. 421): κανὼν τῆς ἐκκλησίας. KATTENBUSCH, vol. II. p. 143.

[6] "In Matt. Comment." ser. 137 (XIII. 1787).

[7] *Ibid.* 47 (1669).        [8] "Periarchon," III. 1, 1 (XI. 249).

*ecclesiastica praedicatione . . ."* [1] This *praedicatio*, this κήρυγμα, is the teaching which, through the succession of the bishops by whom it is preserved, comes down from the Apostles. Of this official teaching Origen gives the following definition which is at the beginning of the " Periarchon " but which we might think was taken from Irenæus: " Cum multi sint qui se putant sentire quae Christi sunt, et nonnulli eorum diversa a prioribus sentiant—servetur ecclesiastica praedicatio per successionis ordinem ab apostolis tradita et usque ad praesens in ecclesiis permanens. Illa sola credenda est veritas quae in nullo ab ecclesiastica et apostolica discordat traditione." [2]

Of each of the articles, on which the *praedicatio ecclesiastica* is plainly affirmative, one may say: " . . . *de quo totius Ecclesiae una sententia est.*" [3] Of a dogma, such as that of the resurrection of the body, Origen declares that it is τὸ βούλημα τῆς ἐκκλησίας τοῦ Χριστοῦ, [4] inasmuch as it is like a law or a decree of the βουλή of a large city. The unity of faith makes the unity of Christendom, of that people *"qui in sacramentis Christi confoederatus est".* [5]

In all the expressions we have accentuated, the Church appears as the depositary of revealed truth: ecclesiastical

---

[1] " Periarchon," I. 1, 5 (118). The same expressions occur in nn. 6 and 7.

[2] *Ibid.* I. 1, 2 (XI. 116). Cf. *ibid.* II. 11, 3 (345): " . . . secundum apostolorum sensum ". " In Genes. Homil." I. 6 (XII. 151): " Christus . . . ex cuius lumine illuminata Ecclesia, ipsa etiam lux mundi efficitur . . . Christus quidem lux est apostolorum, apostoli vero lux mundi, ipsi enim sunt . . . vera Ecclesia." " Selecta in psalm." CXXVI. (XII. 1641): τὸν οἶκον τοῦ θεοῦ, ὄντα ἐκκλησίαν αὐτοῦ, οἱ οἰκοδομοῦντες ἀπόστολοι Χριστοῦ καὶ οἱ τεταγμένοι ὑπ' αὐτοῦ διδάσκαλοι, οὐ μάτην ἐκοπίασαν . . . Καὶ ἄλλως δὲ οἶκον οἰκοδομοῦσιν οὐ μετὰ κυρίου οἱ ἑτερόδοξοι, τὴν ἐκκλησίαν πονηρευομένων . . . Ὁμοίως καὶ Ἰουδαῖοι. We may notice in this last text an anticlimax dear to Origen : the ecclesiastic, the heterodox, the Jew.

[3] *Ibid.* 1, 8 (119). Cf. *ibid.* 7, 1 (171): " . . . secundum dogma nostrum id est Ecclesiae fidem." " In Genes. Homil." III. 2 (XII. 176): " Alienum hoc est ab Ecclesiae fide." " In Levit. Homil." XV. 2 (XII. 560): " . . . fidei, quae muro ecclesiastici et apostolici dogmatis cincta est ". " In Num. Homil." XXV. 4 (XII. 768): " Quis non animetur pugnare pro Ecclesia et resistere adversum inimicos veritatis, eos scilicet qui dogmata Ecclesiae oppugnare docent ? "

[4] " Contra Cels." V. 22 (XI. 1216).

[5] " In Num. Homil." XVI. 9 (XII. 701).

preaching is synonymous with authentic faith, and the actual ecclesiastical preaching finds its justification in the fact that it is the tradition of the Apostles, transmitted in a direct line as an inheritance. This is also the theory of Irenæus, and even of the Greek writers of the second century, prior to Irenæus.[1]

The canon of the Scriptures is that which the Church guarantees. Thus, whilst the heresies have so many Gospels, the Church has four Gospels only. Origen knows indeed the "Gospel according to the Egyptians," a "Gospel of the Twelve Apostles," a "Gospel according to St. Thomas," a "Gospel according to St. Matthias," and the gospel which Basilides was bold enough to compose and to which he gave his own name. But there are only four approved Gospels: *"quatuor tantum euangelia sunt probata, e quibus sub persona Domini et Salvatoris nostri proferenda sunt dogmata."* Of all the gospels that are in circulation, *"nihil aliud probamus, nisi quod Ecclesia".*[2]

Holy Scripture, is contained both in the Old and in the New Testament, and comes to an end with the books of the Apostles, after which there is no more Scripture. To the canon now closed the Church adds nothing, not even a prophecy, but in this heretics do not imitate her: *"Sola Ecclesia neque subtrahit . . . neque addit quasi prophetiam*

---

[1] "The theory that the bishops are successors of the Apostles, and possess an apostolic office, may be considered a Western one which was very slowly and gradually adopted in the East. . . . It is very important to note that the theory of the bishop's office in determining the truth of ecclesiastical Christianity is completely unknown to Clement of Alexandria. . . . Origen in the main still held the same view as his predecessor. But numerous passages of his works and above all his own history show that in his day the episcopate had become very strong in Alexandria also, and had begun to claim the same attributes and rights as in the West. . . . Clement represents an earlier stage, whereas by Origen's time the revolution has been completed." HARNACK, "Dogmeng." vol. I[4], p. 403. We can now judge how far the facts agree with these statements.

[2] "In Luc. Homil.' I. (XIII. 1803). Cf. "In Matt. Comment." ser. 28 (1638): " . . . ecclesiarum canonem non requirentes ". On the well-defined character of Origen's Biblical Canon, see BARDENHEWER, vol. II. p. 122 (against KOETSCHAU).

*aliud aliquid* ".[1]     These words contain an allusion to Montanism,[2] and are similar in tone to those of the " Muratorianum " on the same subject.

The Scriptures, on condition they are explained, not in the materiality of their literal sense, but in their spiritual sense, are not composed of human words, written as they have been for Jesus Christ through the inspiration of the Holy Ghost and at the command of the Father : they have been given and entrusted to us in order to confirm those who observe " the standard of the heavenly Church of Jesus Christ according to the succession of the Apostles ".[3]

The elements of faith are comprised in the baptismal symbol.[4]     The words of Deuteronomy *Aegyptius tertia generatione intrabit in ecclesiam Dei* (Deut. XXIII. 8) must be understood of the Christian who believes in the Trinity : " *Credo propter fidem Patris et Filii et Spiritus sancti, in quam credit omnis qui sociatur Ecclesiae Dei, tertiam generationem mystice dictam*".[5]     The cords that uphold the veil of the tabernacle represent the same baptismal faith : " *Funis enim triplex non rumpitur, quae est Trinitatis fides, ex qua dependet et per quam sustinetur omnis Ecclesia*".[6]     On several occasions Origen speaks so precisely of the baptismal symbol, that we can recognize its structure and reconstitute the tenor of the symbol to which he is

---

[1] " In Mat. Comment." ser. 47 (XIII. 1668). Cf. *ibid.* 28 (1637) : " Nemo uti debet ad confirmationem dogmatum libris qui sunt extra canonizatas scripturas ". *Ibid.* 46 (1667) : " Canonicas scripturas in quibus omnis christianus consentit et credit '.

[2] See how severely Origen judges Montanism, " In Mat. Comment." ser. 28 (1637), and " In Epist. ad Philem." fragm. (XIV. 1306).

[3] " Periarchon," IV. 9 (360) : τοῦ κανόνος τῆς Ἰησοῦ Χριστοῦ κατὰ διαδοχὴν τῶν ἀποστόλων οὐρανίου ἐκκλησίας. The adjective οὐράνιος must be understood here in the sense of divine, and not as the antithesis of earthly, ἐπίγειος.

[4] As to the existence of a baptismal symbol at Alexandria, see the testimony of Dionysius of Alexandria in EUSEB. " H. E." VII. 8 ; where the Bishop upbraids Novatian for denying the profession of faith that is made before Baptism. Τὸ λουτρὸν τὸ ἅγιον καὶ τήν τε πρὸ αὐτοῦ πίστιν καὶ ὁμολογίαν. The symbol of Origen is given in HAHN, " Symbole," pp. 11-13.

[5] " In Levit. Homil." v. 3 (XII. 452).

[6] " In Exod. Homil." IX. 3 (XII. 365).

alluding. At the same time he shows how the articles which compose it suffice to condemn the heretics of his time.[1]

God has provided his Church with a living magisterium, which not only teaches the ecclesiastical canon of faith, but also strives to fathom it and to go beyond it. "Let us observe," says Origen, "that the holy Apostles delivered themselves with the utmost clearness on those articles which they believed to be necessary to every one, even when preaching the faith of Christ to those who seemed somewhat dull in understanding the things of God; leaving, however, the deep-laid causes to be explored by those who had received from the Holy Spirit the excellent gifts of speech, of wisdom, and of knowledge : while on other subjects they merely stated the fact that things were so, keeping silence as to the cause and manner or origin of their being; in order that the more zealous lovers of study and wisdom, might in times to come have a subject on which to exercise their talents, with profit." [2] Origen thus lays down the principle of the distinction of the two domains—that of revelation, and that of theology understood in the scholastic sense. He distinguishes with no less precision the domain of rational philosophy, the investigation of which logically precedes the Christian's study of the Scriptures,[3] and the domain of mystery which in its sublimer regions exceeds the capacity of every created intelligence.[4]

These distinctions made, Origen does not suffer opponents like Celsus to charge Christianity with being the religion of the ignorant. And were it so, he adds, "I shall answer that I endeavour to improve [and enlighten the ignorant] to the best of my ability, although I do not admit that the Christian community consists only of them. For I seek in preference those who are clever and acute, who are able to comprehend the meaning of the hard sayings, and to see clearly into the obscurities of the Law, and Prophecies, and Gospels.[5]

[1] " Comment. in Ioan." xxxii. 9 (xiv. 784).

[2] " Periarchon," i. 3 (xi. 116).

[3] *Ibid.* i. 3, 1 (147).          [4] *Ibid.* ii. 6, 2 (211).

[5] " Contra Cels." iii. 74 (xi. 1016).   Cf. iii. 52-3 (989) and vi. 1 (1289).

Contrary to what Celsus affirms, there is nothing hidden or secret in the ecclesiastical teaching: from the very beginning we teach those who come to us to despise idols, and we lead them on to worship God, the only Creator; then, by means of the prophecies, we show them that He who had been foretold actually came, according to the testimony of the Gospels and of the Apostolic writings.[1]  The people are initiated into the baptismal rudiments, but such knowledge is not imparted to those who do not belong to the Church. At the summit of the ladder, there are the truths reserved to God : these are above our senses, and surpass our understanding ; we had better say nothing of them rather than express them inaccurately.  Between these two degrees, " *sunt et alia Ecclesiae dogmata ad quae possunt pervenire etiam levitae, sed inferiora sunt ab his quae sacerdotibus adire concessum est* ".[2]  Strictly speaking, this distinction is forced ; yet it agrees well with Origen's idea of doctrine and its distribution.  A part of the doctrine is for the simple and the multitude ; another part is for the enlightened, the perfect, the saints, the disciples to whom Jesus disclosed the meaning of His parables.[3]

\* \*
\*

The disciples come to the Divine Master and ask Him explanations ; we must do likewise : if we have a question to propose, let us go to one of those teachers God has established in the Church.[4]

The office of doctors in the Church—an office which is " the ministry " of the ecclesiastical word—is that on which Origen most insists.  The doctor must not only aim at correcting the morals of the Christian people, he must also deal out, as it were, the science of Christianity, pour out the consolation of the Scriptures, explain the mysteries, and attain

---

[1] " Contra Cels." III. 15 (940).

[2] " In Levit. Homil." v. 3 (XII. 452).

[3] *Ibid.* v. 6 (441).  BIGG, pp. 141 and foll., shows how much is exclusively Alexandrian and hardly Christian in this theory of a knowledge more sublime, and drawn from the use of allegory, side by side with the knowledge possessed by ordinary believers.

[4] " Comment. in Matt." XIII. 45 (XIII. 1132) : τινι τῶν ὑπὸ τοῦ θεοῦ τεταγμένων ἐν τῇ ἐκκλησίᾳ διδασκάλων.

to a more penetrating knowledge.[1] The function of teaching the catechumens belongs to the *doctor ecclesiae*.[2] The bishop in his Church is preeminently this *doctor ecclesiae*, but the priests also share in his office : Origen, for instance, presents himself as a *doctor ecclesiae*.[3] We should note the precise meaning of the expression and also the special stress Origen lays on it : the *doctor ecclesiæ* is not he who teaches in the Church, but he who teaches the Church.[4]

Holy Scripture can be compared to the loaves which Jesus multiplied when breaking them. Doctors, like Origen, break a few loaves only, and multitudes are satiated : but these loaves must be broken, i.e. the letter of Holy Scripture must be discussed minutely. Let every one follow the doctors' example :—

"Tenta ergo et tu, o auditor, habere proprium puteum et proprium fontem, ut et tu, cum apprehenderis librum Scripturarum, incipias etiam ex proprio sensu proferre aliquem intellectum, et, secundum ea quae in ecclesia didicisti, tenta et tu bibere de fonte ingenii tui. Est intra te natura aquae vivae, sunt venae perennes, et irrigua fluenta rationabilis sensus, si modo non sint terra et ruderibus oppleta."[5]

No one, before Origen, had urged his fellow-Christians, with such noble earnestness, to the acquisition of culture, to intellectual effort, to the spread of knowledge within the Church ; but he always subordinated this expansion of intellectual inquiry to the control of the *praedicatio ecclesiastica*. The Passover was not eaten by those who did not belong to Israel : unless they were circumcised, the slaves whom a Jew had bought, or who were born in his house, could not share in the family Passover. These prescriptions are to be understood allegorically of our different kinds of

---

[1] "In Exod. Homil." xiii. 4 (xii. 392). "Comment. in Rom." iii. 2 (xiv. 929).

[2] "Comment. in Rom." ii. 11 (xiv. 897) : ". . . eo usque pervenit ut etiam dux et doctor ecclesiae sit ad illuminandos eos qui in scientia caeci sunt et instruendos parvulos in Christo". This refers to the bishop.

[3] "In Ezech. Homil." ii. 2 (xiii. 682): "Nec quia adversum me aliqua dicuntur, qui videor doctor esse ecclesiae, debeo tacere."

[4] "Comment. in Rom." ix. 2 (xiv. 1209): "in verbo Dei ecclesiam docentibus adesse gratiam. . . ." *Ibid.* x. 7 (1262) : "ecclesias docere ".

[5] "In Gen. Homil." xii. 5 (xii. 229).

knowledge : one kind is born, so to speak, in our house, and is the fruit of our own minds ; the other has been acquired and has come from the outside: both must be circumcised, for no stranger has a right to the Passover; and by a stranger must be understood any one who professes a strange dogma.[1]

No one has spoken of Greek culture in more glowing terms than Origen ; but how he contrasts it with the truth concealed in the God-inspired Scriptures !  The ingot of gold which the Hebrew Achan seizes for himself, against Josue's command, in the sack of Jericho, is an appropriate symbol of the artful resources of philosophers and orators, and of the "*perversa dogmata*" to which they can so successfully impart a seductive appearance.  If you steal away this ingot of gold and hide it under your tent, " *si introduxeris in cor tuum ea quae ab eis asseruntur, pollues omnem Ecclesiam Domini.  Hoc fecit infelix Valentinus, et Basilides, hoc fecit et Marcion haereticus : furati sunt isti linguas aureas de Iericho, et philosophorum nobis non rectas in ecclesias introducere conati sunt sectas, et polluere omnem Ecclesiam Domini.*"[2]

Since the Church possesses the true faith, one word suffices to give heretics their right name : they are the ἑτερόδοξοι, those who think differently from the Church. Origen has a predilection for this expressive term, which, in his vocabulary, is opposed to ἐκκλησιαστικός.[3]

Every day the heretics are busy in attacking the ecclesiastical faith, "*inquirentes quomodo dogmata veritatis infringant ;*" they devote to this task all the keenness of their minds and all their learning, "*perspicaces et argumentosi sunt in falsa scientia*".  Such is Marcion, such Basilides,

---

[1] " Selecta in Exod." (XII. 285).

[2] " In Ies. Nave Homil." VII. 7 (XII. 863).  A similar reflection is found in St. Hippolytus, " Philosophoumena," preface of Book I.

[3] " In Luc. Homil." XVI. (XIII. 1841) :  " Ego vero quia opto esse ecclesiasticus, et non ab haeresiarcha aliquo sed a Christi vocabulo nuncupari [christianus] ".  Cf. " In Matt. Comment." ser. 33 (XIII. 1643) : "Utinam soli qui extra Ecclesiam sunt seducerentur. . . . Nunc autem ipsi qui profitentur se ecclesiasticos esse de necessariis quibusque capitulis falluntur et seducuntur." Cf. " Contra Cels." VI. 37 (XI. 1353) : οἱ ἀπὸ τῆς ἐκκλησίας.

such Valentinus, " *vel ceteri auctores pravorum dogmatum* ".[1]
Except Marcion, none of them founded any Church ; they left
only schools after them, " *schola Valentini et Basilidis* ".[2]
Whereas the Church is the house of God, built up by the
" *ecclesiastici qui in Ecclesia sunt magistri*," the schools
of heretics are simply abodes of evil : " *Haeretici aedificant
lupanar in omni via, ut puta magister de officina Valentini,
magister de coetu Basilidis, magister de tabernaculo Marcionis* ".[3] Very noticeable is the sarcastic force of these
last words, which remind us of Tertullian's utterances.

Whenever, says Origen, the heretics propose a discussion concerning the canonical Scriptures, those which are
unanimously received by every Christian, we may examine their varied assertions : " *Sed nos illis credere non debemus, nec exire a prima et ecclesiastica traditione, nec aliter
credere nisi quemadmodum per successionem Ecclesiae Dei
tradiderunt nobis* ".[4] Such is the tradition, which dates
from the very beginning, and which the Churches have
preserved, authenticating it by the succession of their respective bishops. Moreover, this tradition is the same
everywhere : " *Veritas enim similis est fulguri egredienti ab
Oriente, et apparenti usque ad Occidentem, qualis est veritas
Ecclesiae Dei : ab ea enim sola sonus in omnem terram
exivit* ".[5] To what heresy can this criterion apply ? To the
teaching of Marcion, to the " *traditiones Valentini*," to the
*longa fabulositas* of Basilides, or to Apelles who contradicts
St Paul ?[6]

---

[1] " Comment. in Rom." viii. 8 (xiv. 1181). " In Levit. Homil." iv.
5 (xii. 438).

[2] *Ibid.* viii. 11 (xiv. 1191). Cf. " Periarchon," ii. 5 (xi. 220).

[3] " In Ezech. Homil.' viii. 2 (xiii. 730). The Latin translation is
by St. Jerome. In other passages Origen expresses himself just as
vigorously on the same subject. " Periarchon," ii. 9, 6 (xi. 230) ; *ibid.*
10, 2 (*ibid.* 234).

[4] " In Matt. Comment." ser. 46 (xiii. 1667). [5] *Ibid.*

[6] *Ibid.* Cf. " In Levit. Homil.' vii. 4 (xii. 484) : " . . . christianis
quibus apostolicorum dictorum chara esse debet auctoritas. Si quis vero
arrogantia tumidus apostolica dicta contemnit aut spernit, ipse viderit.
Mihi autem, sicut Deo et Domino nostro Iesu Christo, ita et apostolis eius
adhaerere bonum est, et ex divinis scripturis secundum ipsorum traditionem
intellegentiam capere ". See the most complete description of the heresies
denounced by Origen, of " In Epistul. ad Tit." (xiv. 1903).

Hence the teaching of heretics can be compared most appropriately to counterfeit money :—

"Ego puto quod Valentini sermo humana pecunia est et reproba, et Marcionis et Basilidis pecunia humana est et reproba, et omnium haereticorum sermo non est probata pecunia, nec dominicam integre in se habet figuram, sed adulteram, quae, ut ita dicam, extra monetam ita figurata est quia extra Ecclesiam composita est." [1]

A general prescription does not suffice ; the ecclesiastical teacher must face error, as it is in itself, take its own ground, use against it its own arguments and refute it by its own methods. "Under the pretence of higher wisdom, the heterodox assail the holy Church of God [2] and multiply works in which they offer explanations of the Evangelical and Apostolic precepts ; if we keep silence and do not oppose to them the saving and true doctrines, these teachers will get hold of souls, who hunger after the food which preserves, but go after food that is forbidden, and is, in fact, unclean and abominable. It appears to me, therefore, to be necessary that one who is able to defend, without altering it in any way, the doctrine of the Church, and to refute those dealers in knowledge falsely so-called (ψευδώνυμον γνῶσιν) should take his stand against heretics and their lies, and oppose to them the sublimity of the Evangelical message (τὸ ὕψος τοῦ εὐαγγελικοῦ κηρύγματος), the harmonious

---

[1] "In Psalm." xxxvi ; "Homil." iii. 11 (xii. 1347). Origen uses another comparison, "Comment. in Rom." x. 5 (xiv. 1256) : "Sicut piratae solent in mari in locis vadosis occultisque scopulis, per obscurum noctis lumen accendere, quo navigantes sub spe confugiendi ad portum salutis, ad naufragia perditionis invitent : ita et istud lumen falsae sapientiae vel falsae fidei [haereticorum] a principibus mundi et spiritibus aeris huius accenditur, non per quod evadant, sed per quod pereant homines mundi huius fluctus et vitae pelagus navigantes". The translation of this passage is by Rufinus. Elsewhere Origen compares heresies to the gates of hell that shall not prevail against the Church : ἕκαστος τῶν ἑτεροδόξων καὶ γεννησάντων ψευδώνυμόν τινα γνῶσιν, ᾠκοδόμησεν ᾅδου πύλην, ἄλλην μὲν Μαρκίων, καὶ Βασιλίδης ἄλλην, καὶ Οὐαλεντῖνος ἄλλην. "Comment. in Matt." xii. 12 (xiii. 1008).

[2] "Comment. in Ioan." ii. (xiv. 196) : νῦν δὲ προφάσει γνώσεως ἐπανισταμένων τῶν ἑτεροδόξων τῇ ἁγίᾳ τοῦ θεοῦ ἐκκλησίᾳ κ.τ.λ. Note in passing the expression, "the holy Church ".

plentitude of the doctrines, common to the Old and New Testament." [1]

Will the *magisterium* of the *doctores ecclesiae* suffice to guard the Church against the onsets of heresy? Is truth always so evident, that it forces conviction, and that every controversy comes to an end? Here Origen's optimism and his ingenuous confidence in his methods betrays itself.

" Qui scripturam legit et aliter quam scripta est accipit, Scripturam mendaciter videt. Qui vero audit Scripturam ut se veritatis intellectus habet et sic eam interpretatur, videt veritatem." [2]

These two axioms are very candid. How much more cautious is the distrust felt by Irenæus and Tertullian! And Origen himself adds immediately:—

" Audi haereticos, quomodo traditiones apostolorum habere se dicant. Audi falsos magistros, quomodo affirmant doctrinam suam Domini esse doctrinam, sensum suum congruere sensui prophetarum, et dicunt: *Haec dicit Dominus.*" [3]

What does this mean, except that those whom Origen treats here as heretics and false teachers appeal in vindication of their teaching to the criterion of Irenæus—to the agreement of their teaching with the Apostolic tradition, the authority of the Prophets, the Lord and the Apostles? A *doctor ecclesiae* may be found to show these false teachers that they are in error: but who will prove that he himself is not mistaken?

" Orate pro nobis ut sermones nostri non sint falsi. Licet quidam homines ignorantia iudicii eos asserant falsos, Dominus non dicat, et recte nobiscum agetur. Si vero, mille hominum eos dixerint veros, iudicio porro Dei fuerint falsi, quid mihi proderit? Dicunt et Marcionitae magistri sui veros esse sermones; dicunt et Valentini robustissimam

---

[1] " Comment. in Ioan." l.c. Compare " Periarchon," II. 3 (XI. 201): " Sed quoniam solent interdum huius haeresis assertores per deceptiosa quaedam sophismata simpliciorum quorumque corda decipere, absurdum non puto si etiam ea quae in assertionibus suis proferre solent, proponentes subreptionem eorum ac mendacia, confutemus ".

[2] " In Ezech. Homil." II. 5 (XIII. 686).

[3] *Ibid.* Cf. " Homil.' VII. 4 (*ibid.* 730).

sectam [1] qui fabularum eius commenta suscipiunt. Quae utilitas, quia plurimi Ecclesiae haeretica pravitate decepti in eorum conspiravere sententiam? Hoc est quod quaeritur, ut Dominus sermonum meorum testis assistat, ut ipse comprobet quae dicuntur sanctarum testimonio Scripturarum." [2]

Origen appeals to an authoritative judgment of God, which he identifies with the testimony of Scripture : always the same circle. Yet Origen knows well, that when doubt is so wide-spread, the decisive pronouncement in the last resort belongs to authority—in this case to the authority of bishops. This he does not say with all desirable explicitness ; but he does say it, nevertheless : witness, for instance, his comment on the Biblical passage that refers to the censers of Core, Dathan and Abiron—censers which Moses had beaten into plates and fastened to the altar of holocausts, after the death of the three rebels. See how he expresses himself :—

" Si apud homines hodie iudicaretur haec causa, et apud ecclesiarum principes haberetur examen de iis, verbi causa, qui diversa ab ecclesiis docentes divinae vindictae pertulerint ultionem, nonne iudicarent ut si quid locuti sunt, si· quid docuerunt, si quid etiam scriptum reliquerunt, universa pariter cum ipsorum cineribus deperirent ? Sed non sunt iudicia Dei sicut iudicia nostra." [3]

Take the case of a Christian who teaches heterodox doctrines both by preaching and by writing : he is condemned, and by whom ? By God Himself, for here Origen speaks expressly of the "*divinae vindictae ultio*" of the "*iudicia Dei*," just as he had spoken before of the same "*iudicium Dei*". This divine judgment precedes the examination made by the leaders of the Churches, and directs their decision ; it has motived it : they determine and apply the divine teaching of the Scriptures. The brass-censers of Core, Dathan, and Abiron typify Holy Scripture ; this is why Moses fastens them to the altar of holocausts, as God's property. But to the heretics belongs the fire burning in the censers, i.e. the interpretations that disagree with

---

[1] The text of this Latin translation—the work of St. Jerome—is too elliptical not to be faulty.

[2] "In Ezech. Homil." II. 5.      [3] "In Num. Homil." IX. 1 (XII. 624).

the thoughts of God and are against the truth—an incense which the Lord rejects.

" Et ideo forma ecclesiarum sacerdotibus datur, ut, si quando tale aliquid fuerit exortum, ea quidem quae a veritate aliena sunt ab Ecclesia Dei penitus abstrudantur." [1]

To the bishops then it belongs to guard Scripture against the erroneous meanings which the heretics, such as Marcion, Basilides, and their fellows, strive to put upon it: to eliminate error is in itself progress made towards truth.

" Si doctrina ecclesiastica simplex esset, et nullis intrinsecus haereticorum dogmatum assertionibus cingeretur, non poterat tam clara et tam examinata videri fides nostra. Sed idcirco doctrinam catholicam contradicentium obsidet oppugnatio, ut fides nostra non otio torpescat, sed exercitiis elimetur." [2]

The theory of the development of dogma, as understood by Bossuet, is outlined in these few profound and accurate words. Yet we must not forget Origen's purpose: he wishes here to show that the supervision of this dogmatic work is a part of the office of the bishops, which is typified by the pontificate of Moses. The Churches are ruled by the bishops in what pertains to conduct and discipline ; [3] by them also are they governed in what pertains to doctrine.[4]

---

[1] " In Num. Homil." IX. 1 (XII. 624), " forma " has here the sense of norm.

[2] *Ibid.* This Latin translation is due to Rufinus. I should like to be sure that the word *catholicam* comes from Origen, who uses generally the word *ecclesiasticam*. At all events, the thought expressed here by Origen was familiar to the school of Alexandria. Cf. CLEMENT, " Stromat." I. 2 (VIII. 709 B.).

[3] There is a strict analogy between the practical and the intellectual order, between conduct and belief, as was observed by Origen himself. " In Matt. Comment." ser. 33 (XIII. 1644) : " Malum est invenire aliquem secundum mores vitae errantem, multo autem peius arbitror esse in dogmatibus aberrare et non secundum verissimam regulam Scripturarum sentire. Quoniam si in peccatis mortalibus puniendi sumus, amplius propter dogmata falsa peccantes." Cf. " In Psalm xxxvii. Homil." I. 1 (XII. 371) : " Necesse est eum qui peccat argui. . . . Nos qui episcopi arguentis iracundiam ferre non possumus. . . ."

[4] Cf. " In Num. Homil." XII. 2 (XII. 660). Speaking of the Apostles, whom he calls kings, Origen writes : " Si reges a regendo dicuntur, omnes utique qui ecclesias Dei regunt reges merito appellabuntur, multo autem

This divine right of bishops is daily exercised : witness the case of Origen himself, and that of his contemporary Beryllus, Bishop of Bostra.[1]   Councils of bishops are, in the time of Origen, a definitely and firmly established institution both in Egypt and in the East.   Tertullian had already mentioned the "*concilia ex universis ecclesiis*" which were wont to be held "*per Graecias*," i.e. in the Greek-speaking countries.[2]

* * *

In the course of the preceding pages, it will have been noticed that Origen constantly and with a certain insistence uses the expression "the Churches".   We in our turn must insist on this peculiar expression.

Origen looks upon Christendom chiefly as a number of scattered Churches.   In order to conquer the wickedness of the evil spirits, God planned that, all over the inhabited world, Churches should be founded, which should contrast, by the pure lives of their members, with what Origen calls the "churches of superstition, intemperance and wickedness".   The Churches of God, taught by Christ, when compared with the neighbouring churches of pagans, shine truly like stars in the world.[3]   The interesting feature of this text is that the term "Church" is applied by Origen to pagan cities.   No doubt Origen remembered that the word ἐκκλησία has in Greek an exclusively political meaning and designates the deliberative assembly of the citizens of a city, like

rectius illi qui et illos ipsos dictis atque scriptis suis regunt a quibus reguntur ecclesiae."

[1] HEFELE, "Hist. des Conciles" (Farnborough edit.), vol. I. pp. 156-64.

[2] TERTULL. "De Ieiun." 13.   Cf. FIRMILIAN, *inter* CYPRIANI, "Epistul." LXXV. 4 : "Qua ex causa necessario apud nos fit ut per singulos annos seniores et praepositi in unum conveniamus ad disponenda ea quae curae nostrae commissa sunt, ut si qua graviora sunt communi consilio dirigantur."   HARNACK, "Geschichte des altchrist litt.," in "Ueberlieferung," pp. 797-800.

[3] "Contra Cels." III. 29 (XI. 957) : . . . ἐποίησε πανταχοῦ τῆς οἰκουμένης . . . γενέσθαι πανταχοῦ ἐκκλησίας ἀντιπολιτευομένας ἐκκλησίαις δεισιδαιμόνων καὶ ἀκολάστων καὶ ἀδίκων.   Τοιαῦτα γὰρ τὰ πανταχοῦ πολιτευόμενα ἐν ταῖς ἐκκλησίαις τῶν πόλεων πλήθη.   Αἱ δὲ τοῦ θεοῦ Χριστῷ μαθητευθεῖσαι ἐκκλησίαι, συνεξεταζόμεναι ταῖς ὧν παροικοῦσι δήμων ἐκκλησίαις, ὡς φωστῆρές εἰσιν ἐν τῷ κόσμῳ.

Ephesus, for instance; but, did he not also conceive of a Christian Church as formed after the type of a city?

The Church of God, which is at Athens, he says, is meek and stable, whereas the ἐκκλησία of the Athenians is turbulent, and is not at all to be compared with the Church of God in that city. We may say the same thing of the Church of God at Corinth and of the assembly of the Corinthian people or *demos;* and also of the Church of God at Alexandria and of the assembly of the Alexandrian *demos.* Let us admire Him, he continues, who not only conceived the design, but also was able to secure in all places the establishment of Churches of God side by side with the Churches of the people in each city.[1]

In like manner also, if you compare the council or βουλή of the Church of God with the βουλή in any city, you will find among the councillors of the Church some who are worthy to administer the city of God,[2] whilst nowhere do the councillors of cities justify by their virtues the authority they enjoy over their fellow-citizens. Compare for yourself the archon of each Church with the archon of the city, and you will notice that our archons in the Church of God, imperfect as they may be at times, are far superior in their moral worth.[3] In all this, Origen develops the analogy between the Church and the city: the *presbyterium* becomes a council; the bishop, an archon; the local Church, a "city of God," a "nation according to God".[4]

The whole world is thus filled with Churches.[5]

---

[1] "Contra Cels.' III. 30 (957).

[2] *Ibid.* : τίνες τῆς ἐκκλησίας βουλευταὶ ἄξιοί εἰσιν, εἴ τις ἐστὶν ἐν τῷ παντὶ πόλις τοῦ θεοῦ, ἐν ἐκείνῃ πολιτεύεσθαι.—Note in passing the expression "city of God". It is an expression which is found already in the "Shepherd" of Hermas ("Sim." I.), but there it designates Heaven in contrast with the earth.

[3] *Ibid.* (960) : ἄρχοντα ἐκκλησίας ἑκάστης πόλεως ἄρχοντι τῶν ἐν τῇ πόλει συγκριτέον κ.τ.λ.

[4] *Ibid.* VIII. 75 (XI. 1629) : ἡμεῖς ἐν ἑκάστῃ ἄλλο σύστημα πατρίδος κτισθὲν λόγῳ θεοῦ ἐπιστάμενοι. . . . Further on : εἰ καλῶς ἄρχουσιν οἱ ἄρχοντες ἐν τῇ ἐκκλησίᾳ, τῆς κατὰ θεὸν πατρίδος, λέγω δὲ τῆς ἐκκλησίας, λεγόμενοι προστάται κ.τ.λ.

[5] "Selecta in Psalm." XXXII. 8 (XI. 1305) : πᾶσα ἡ γῆ Χριστοῦ ἐκκλησίαις πεπλήρωτο. "In Cantic. Lib." II. (XIII. 110) : "Ecclesiae innumerae sunt quae per orbem terrae diffusae sunt". "In Ezech. Homil." IV. 1

The Churches spread through the whole world form a mystic unity: they are, in Origen's crude words, "the entire body of the synagogues of the Church;"[1] likewise he speaks of those who "inhabit the ecumenicity of the Church of God".[2] He also says more felicitously that "the Church is the cosmos of the cosmos".[3] Taking up a thought dear to St. Paul, Origen speaks of the Church as the body of Christ: "The holy Scriptures declare the whole Church of God to be the body of Christ, animated by the Son of God".[4]

Thus understood, the Church is like a house—a house to which we may apply allegorically the command of Moses regarding the Pasch: "*In una domo comedetur*". In this respect, Origen contrasts the Church with the Synagogue.[5] One must not seek to eat the word of God both in the Church and in the synagogue of the Jews, nor may one partake of it both in the Church and in the synagogue of the heretics. "Realize, then, that the Church is the only house: never eat the Paschal lamb outside the Church." The precept of Moses in its allegorical meaning is for you:

(IV. 698): "Quando terra Britanniae ante adventum Christi in unius Dei consensit religionem? Quando terra Maurorum? Quando totus semel orbis? Nunc vero propter ecclesias quae mundi limites tenent, universa terra cum laetitia clamat ad Dominum."—On the diffusion of Christianity all over the world, Origen is less positive in another text. "In Matt. Comment." ser. 39 (XIII. 1655). In this passage, he states that as yet the Gospel has not been brought to the Ethiopians, or to India, Britain, Germany, or among the Dacians, the Sarmatians and the Scythians.

[1] "Comment. in Matt." XIII. 24 (XIII. 1157).

[2] "Selecta in Psalm." XXXII. 8 (XII. 1305). The adjective "catholic," applied to the Church, is found, as far as I know, chiefly in the Latin translations of Origen, and there it does not seem to have been necessarily taken from the original. Origen uses the word καθολικός to designate what is general or universal; a universal proposition is catholic; God's benefits also are catholic, i.e. universal.

[3] "Comment. in Ioan." VI. 38 (XIV. 301).

[4] "Contra Cels." VI. 48 (XI. 1378): σῶμα Χριστοῦ φασιν εἶναι οἱ θεῖοι λόγοι, ὑπὸ τοῦ υἱοῦ τοῦ θεοῦ ψυχούμενον, τὴν πᾶσαν τοῦ θεοῦ ἐκκλησίαν. Cf. ibid. 79 (1417).

[5] "In Genes. Homil.' XII. 3 (XII. 226). "In Exod. Homil." II. 4 (ibid. 309). "In Cantic. Homil." II. 3 (XIII. 49). "In Ierem. Homil." IX. 3 (ibid. 352).

" *Non efferetis e domo de carnibus foras* ". The ecclesiastical word must not be carried outside the Church : " I mean it must not be carried into the synagogue of the Jews or of the heretics ".[1]

Elsewhere Origen compares the Church to the ark of Noe : as there was but one ark, this allegory must be understood of the universal Church.[2]   When He foretold that He would rebuild the temple in three days, the Saviour had in mind His real and historical body; but He thought also of His mystical body which is the Church and which he will raise up on the last day with all the Saints who compose it.[3] There is one Church upon earth, and there is one Church in Heaven.[4]   The Church upon earth rules the world.[5]

The Church is the spouse spoken of in the Canticle: " *Ego Ecclesia, ego sponsa, ego sine macula, plurimarum custos sum posita vinearum*," [6] and the bridegroom replies to her : " *Tanto melior es omnibus filiabus, tu sponsa, tu ecclesiastica anima, omnibus animabus quae non sunt ecclesiasticae* ".[7]   Strengthened by the grace of Him who was crucified for her, the Church is a virgin and virgins are her glory : " *Ecclesia Christi . . . virgo sponsa Christi castis et pudicis virginibus floret* ".[8]   She is also a mother, the mother of all the children whom she brings forth to Christ : " *Utinam essetis gaudium matris Ecclesiae* ".[9]   This personification of the Church upon earth, is an expression of her unity.

Can the unity of the universal Church be inferred from

[1] " In Genes. Homil. cit."   Cf.   " Select. in Psalm." cxviii. 85 (1602).

[2] " In Genes. Homil." ii. 3-6 (167 and foll.).

[3] " Comment. in Ioan." x. 20 (xiv. 372).

[4] " In Num. Homil." iii. 3 (xii. 596).

[5] " Selecta in Psalm." xxix. (xii. 1296).   The Church is the Lord's mountain.   Τούτῳ τῷ ὄρει κράτος ἀπὸ τοῦ Πατρὸς ἐν τῇ εὐδοκίᾳ αὐτοῦ ἐστι βεβαίως δοθὲν, κρατεῖ δὲ ἡ ἐκκλησία βασιλεύουσα τῶν λοιπῶν ἐπὶ γῆς καὶ Χριστῷ συμβασιλεύουσα.

[6] " In Cantic. Homil." i. 7 (xiii. 45).   Cf. "In. Cantic." Lib. iv. (*ibid.* 187) : " Possunt diversae ecclesiae quae per orbem terrae habentur vites dici florentes vel vineae."

[7] " In Cantic. Homil. cit." 10 (46).

[8] " In Genes. Homil." iii. 6 (xii. 181).   Cf. " Homil." xvii. 2 (254).

[9] *Ibid.* " Homil." x. 1 (215).

the promise made by the Saviour to St. Peter? Origen understands this promise literally: "Peter is the one on whom is built the Church of Christ, against which the gates of Hell shall not prevail".[1] And elsewhere: "*Vide magno illi Ecclesiae fundamento et petrae solidissimae super quam Christus fundavit Ecclesiam, quid dicatur a Domino: Modicae fidei quare dubitasti?*"[2] Above the other Apostles Peter enjoys prerogatives that are given by the Saviour Himself, and place between him and his colleagues a difference of excellence.[3] We should like to see Origen giving some firmer indication of the dogmatic and juridical meaning of this primacy, something more definite regarding its perpetuity, a perpetuity which was so sensibly felt, as we shall see, in the events of his time. But if, unlike Irenæus, Origen is not an exponent of the doctrine of the primacy, must he be deemed an exponent of the doctrine of the equality of Churches? A passage in his commentary on St. Matthew has been thought to favour this supposition.

If the light which the Heavenly Father has bestowed upon our hearts prompts us to say to Christ: "Thou art Christ, the Son of the living God," if we say so, not influenced at all by flesh and blood, we too may become what Peter was, to whom Christ said: "Blessed art thou; "[4] and to us also Christ may say: "Thou art Peter, and upon this rock I will build my Church". For every disciple of Christ is a rock, and upon every such rock is built the ecclesiastical teaching and the life in accordance with it; whoever has this teaching and this life realized in him, has the Church built by God also realized in him.

Continuing his commentary, Origen answers an objection which he foresees might be raised: "If you suppose," he says, "that upon this one Peter alone the whole Church is built by God, what will you say about John the son of thunder or about each one of the Apostles?"[5]

---

[1] "Comment. in Ioan." xv. 3 (xiv. 188).

[2] "In Exod. Homil." v. 4 (xii. 329).

[3] "Comment. in Matt." xiii. 31 (xiii. 1180).

[4] *Ibid.* xii. 10 (xiii. 997).

[5] *Ibid.* 11 (*ibid.* 1000): εἰ δὲ ἐπὶ τὸν ἕνα ἐκεῖνον Πέτρον νομίζεις ὑπὸ τοῦ θεοῦ οἰκοδομεῖσθαι τὴν πᾶσαν ἐκκλησίαν μόνον. . . . Notice the precision

Some have surmised that in this, and in a few other texts, Origen was aiming a silent, though real blow at the Roman Church and her policy of capturing the ecclesiastical primacy, which, we are told, she was slowly pursuing,[1] I do not believe that such a thought is in any way in Origen's mind; he seems rather to be occupied exclusively with the moral application he can make of the text "Thou art Peter". This moral application requires that the promise be in no way personal to the Apostle Peter; hence he forces the text in this direction. "Shall we dare to say," he exclaims, "that against Peter alone the gates of Hades shall not prevail, but that they shall prevail against the other Apostles and the perfect?" No indeed! But Origen notices neither the sophism into which he actually falls, nor the violence he does to the literal meaning of his text. To be Peter is to be one of those living stones on which the Church is built: "All bear the surname of 'rock' who are the imitators of Christ".[2] It is a striking example of the freedom with which Origen sacrifices the literal meaning of Holy Scripture.

What may be said, as we have seen, of the episcopal authority, must be said of the Roman primacy also: it is found chiefly in the facts: it is a fact that Origen, who in his youth had visited many Churches, deems it an honour to have visited the Roman Church, "desiring, as he himself says, to see the very ancient Church of the Romans,"[3] which he did in the time of Pope Zephyrinus (about the year 210). It is a fact also, that having drawn upon himself, at Alexandria, the anger and jealousy of Demetrius, the Bishop, the latter forbade him to teach and deposed him from the priesthood; causing this sentence to be passed on him by the Bishops of Egypt, assembled at Alexandria, and then

of Origen's words : That Peter, who has just answered Jesus and whom Jesus is actually addressing. As to the prerogatives of John and of the other Apostles, compare the text of St. Cyprian, "Hoc erant ceteri apostoli," etc., to be given later on (p. 368).

[1] HARNACK, "Dogmeng." vol. I⁴, p. 490.

[2] Loc. cit. : παρώνυμοι πέτρας πάντες οἱ μιμηταὶ Χριστοῦ.

[3] Quoted by EUSEB. "H. E." VI. 14, 10 : εὐξάμενος τὴν ἀρχαιοτάτην Ῥωμαίων ἐκκλησίαν ἰδεῖν. Cf. "Contra Cels." VI. 24 (XI. 1328), where Origen alludes to his foreign travels.

publishing it to all the Bishops of Christendom:[1] Demetrius obtains the adhesion of the bishops he approached, except those of Palestine, Arabia, Phenicia and Achaia; but the adhesion he receives from Rome is especially mentioned. Again, it is a fact that, to defend his orthodoxy, Origen sends letters to most of the bishops, among whom Eusebius cites first the Bishop of Rome, Fabian[2]: which makes Harnack say that "in Origen's case, the voice of Rome seems to have been of special importance." If we pass beyond the time of Origen and come to the affair of Paul of Samosata, the sentence of deposition pronounced against the latter by the council that had assembled at Antioch, is notified to the bishops of "the whole Catholic Church under heaven," and, as Harnack observes again, the Roman bishop Dionysius is mentioned first in the address.[3] Lastly, it is a fact, and one far more significant, that the Bishop of Alexandria himself, Dionysius, is denounced to his namesake, Dionysius, Bishop of Rome, as having expressed himself faultily on the Trinity: a council at Rome deliberates on the matter, and the Bishop of Rome sends to Alexandria in his name and in that of the council, a letter in which, whilst mentioning no one in particular, he condemns the Modalistic errors and conjointly Subordinationism. At the same time (in a special letter), the Bishop of Rome invites Dionysius of Alexandria, to explain his meaning: which the latter does by sending to Rome an Apology in four books.[4] In reference to this,

---

[1] EUSEB. "H. E." VI. 8, 4 : τοῖς ἀνὰ τὴν οἰκουμένην ἐπισκόποις καταγράφειν. Cf. ibid. 23, 4.

[2] Ibid. 36, 4.

[3] "Dogmeng." vol. I[4], p. 493, according to EUSEB. "H. E." VII. 30, 2 : Διονυσίῳ (Rome) καὶ Μαξίμῳ (Alexandria) καὶ τῆς κατὰ τὴν οἰκουμένην πᾶσι συλλειτουργοῖς ἡμῶν ἐπισκόποις καὶ πρεσβυτέροις καί διακόνοις καὶ πάσῃ τῇ ὑπὸ τὸν οὐρανὸν καθολικῇ ἐκκλησίᾳ. The episode belongs to the year 267 or 268. To understand why Rome and Alexandria are mentioned in the address drawn up at Antioch, one must remember that Rome and Alexandria were looked upon by the Greeks at the time of the Empire as the two metropolitan cities of the world.

[4] ATHANAS. "De Sent. Dionys." 5. In his "Epistula ad Antiochenos" (JAFFÉ, 186), Pope Julius rebukes the Eusebians, for having judged St. Athanasius, Bishop of Alexandria, before consulting the Bishop of Rome as is customary : this is an allusion to the precedent of Dionysius, in the third century.

Harnack observes that this procedure, the denunciation to Rome, the judgment of Rome, the intervention of Rome at Alexandria, the justification of Alexandria at Rome, gives rise to no objection at Alexandria, where Christians evidently regard the Roman Church as primarily charged with the duty of watching over " the strict observance of the conditions of the general ecclesiastical confederation," [1] or still better—as we might say—of watching over the preservation of the Catholic faith.

\* \*
\*

Origen is above all a teacher; and attaches the chief value to Christian doctrine, the unanimous acceptance of which is, in his eyes, well secured by the defeat of the Gnostics, by the solidity of the rule of ecclesiastical faith, by the security he finds in his theological method. Such a conception was good for the Greeks, whose fondness for exegesis and dialectics led them to believe that exegesis and dialectics suffice to secure the unity of the Church. Do we not find in the one-sidedness of this conception the germ, as it were, of the future of Greek Christendom, with its controversies, its councils, its schism that obstinately continues to assume the title of orthodoxy?

Again, Origen failed to study ecclesiology in itself. The Church is not in the number of the subjects of which he speaks *ex professo* in the " Periarchon ". There he treats of the divine unity, of the last things, even of tradition and of

---

[1] HARNACK, loc. cit. We may note, with the same writer, that Rome was by no means unconcerned with the life of the Churches in this part of the *orbis romanus*. Dionysius of Alexandria speaks of the material help contributed many a time by the Church of Rome to the Churches of Syria and of Arabia. EUSEB. " H. E." VII. 5, 2. We may recall too that, when Paul of Samosata, after his deposition, had tried to maintain his ground at Antioch, the Emperor Aurelian, who is approached by the Antiochians—the first instance of an appeal to the imperial intervention to settle an ecclesiastical dispute—rules that the legitimate bishop is the one who is acknowledged by the bishops of Italy, and the bishop of Rome. EUSEB. " H. E." VII. 30, 19. The fact is the more significant because Rome had not intervened in the procedure against Paul of Samosata, and the sentence of deposition had been given only by the bishops of Asia Minor and of Syria, who had assembled at Antioch. Did Paul, after his condemnation, appeal to Rome, or was Aurelian's decision suggested to him by the orthodox of Antioch?

the rule of faith, but not of the Church: a strange omission, which was to persist in Greek dogmatics—for instance, in the " Catechetical Discourse " of St. Gregory of Nyssa, and especially in the work of St. John Damascene—an omission which was to be reproduced in scholastic theology.

But before parting with Origen, let us note in his writings an intuition of another order. The Church is one all over the world, and they only are Christians, who " belong to the Church which takes its name from Christ ".[1] Now, between Judaism and Christianity there is this far-reaching difference that the former had a Law which was suited to the Jews and to the Jews only, and which, therefore, could not be universal; the latter, on the contrary, has received a new legislation, which can adapt itself to human life wherever it is led.[2] Even where Christians refuse to enter the army, what civic spirit is superior to theirs! By their moral worth they are the good citizens; they serve the prince by their prayers. Separated from pagans by their faith, they contribute to the public welfare by their righteousness and the asceticism they profess.[3] What would happen, if all Romans embraced Christianity? Origen asks himself this question which Celsus had first asked in sarcasm. Origen is enchanted at the vision of peace and unanimity it presents: no more wars, no more enemies, since God can protect His people. Does He not put an end to persecutions, when it pleases Him to do so? Through the conversion of the Romans, God would establish His kingdom upon earth, the Church would become the kingdom of God substituted for the Roman Empire and identified with

---

[1] " Contra. Cels." VIII. 16 (XI. 1540).

[2] *Ibid.* IV. 22 (1060): νόμους καινοὺς καὶ ἁρμόζοντας τῇ πανταχοῦ καθεστώσῃ πολιτείᾳ.

[3] *Ibid.* VIII. 79 (1628): συμπονοῦμεν τοῖς κοινοῖς πράγμασιν κ.τ.λ. The whole page is worth reading.—This idea is not new, for it was an apologetic theme touched upon by Justin (" Apol." I. 12) and developed by Melito (EUSEB. " H. E." IV. 26) in a remarkable page of his Apology addressed to Marcus Aurelius. On the contrary, Tertullian, under the influence of Stoicism, regarded the State as something Christians had better not take into account: " Nulla magis res nobis aliena quam publica: unam omnium rempublicam agnoscimus, mundum." " Apolog." 38.

mankind, she would be the " city of God ". Before falling from the lips of St. Augustine, these words fall from the lips of Origen : the idea belongs to Plato, to Philo, and to the Stoics, just as much as to Origen himself ; but in expressing it as a hope, as a myth, Origen has an intuition in advance of his time, of the policy of Theodosius and the union between the Church and the Empire.

# CHAPTER VIII.

## ST. CYPRIAN AND ROME.

CYPRIAN was martyred on 14 September, 258. He had been made Bishop of Carthage in the year 248 or 249. He was involved, during his episcopate, which lasted hardly ten years, in important ecclesiastical controversies, for the history of which we have many documents: thanks to Cyprian and to the disputes of his time, much light is thrown on ecclesiology.

Two preliminary observations must be made if we would avoid misconceiving the part played by Cyprian in the history of the treatise on the Church.

In the first place, he is both a brilliant Latin writer, and a bishop in the noblest sense of the term. His " genius " is not that of an original theorist: it is easy to see that the ideas he develops are borrowed from the Catholic works of Tertullian;[1] and certainly there must be some truth in the legend that every day he caused the works of Tertullian to be brought to him, saying: " *Da magistrum* ". It is true that he does not once mention Tertullian; and this shows that the ideas he takes from him, from Tertullian as a Catholic, are the received ideas in Africa in the first half of the third century.

In the second place, Cyprian is not—as he has been represented at times—a man of one idea. The idea of the Church and of her unity does not explain all his work. In this respect Möhler is wrong in comparing him with St. Ignatius of Antioch. He is still less—in spite of what O. Ritschl suggests—a vacillating publicist who had no other doctrine than that which was imposed on him from day to

[1] This is noticed by St. Jerome, " Epistulae," LXXXIV. 2 : " Cyprianus Tertulliano magistro utitur, ut eius scripta probant ".

day by his ecclesiastical policy. But it must be granted that having, like Bossuet fourteen centuries later, to contend with the equivocation inherent in episcopalianism, he died before he could entirely free himself from its entanglements.

Let us try first to ascertain from St. Cyprian what were the leading features of the hierarchical system in his time.

## I.

The first and most conspicuous feature that we find is that the Church is constituted like a city. The faithful form a collectivity which bears the old Roman name of *plebs* : the deacon Pontius gives the name of *plebeius* to Cyprian, before his elevation to the presbyterate.[1] The term *ordo* or *clerus* is complementary to the term *plebs*.[2]

The *ordo* in the Church is made up of the bishop, the priests, and the deacons. In the *plebs*, there is no distinction of ranks : the Edict of Valerian, which opens the persecution of 257, commands the magistrates to prosecute the bishops, the priests and the deacons, and then to despoil of their goods those Christians who are *senatores, egregii viri, equites romani* ;[3] these civil distinctions have not entered into the ecclesiastical language.

When Cyprian writes to a Church, he addresses the bishop alone : *Cyprianus Cornelio fratri, Cyprianus Iubaiano fratri.* If the see is vacant, he writes to the clergy : *Cyprianus presbyteris et diaconis Romae consistentibus.* When he happens to be separated from his Church, and

---

[1] PONT. " Vita Cypriani ' (HARTEL, vol. III. p. xc and foll.) 3. Cf. " Epistulae," LI. 1 : " Clerus et plebs, fraternitas omnis ".

[2] CYPRIAN, " Epistulae," LIX. 19 : ". . . florentissimo illic [at Rome] clero tecum [the Pope] praesidenti et sanctissimae atque amplissimae plebi. . . ." The terms *ordo* and *plebs* belong to the language of Tertullian " Monog." 11 and 12 ; " Exhort castit." 7. Compare " Epistulae," XL., in which Cyprian notifies to his clergy and to his people at Carthage that the priest Numidicus henceforth " adscribatur presbyterorum carthaginiensium numero et nobiscum sedeat in clero " and that he will " in consessus nostri honore florere ". Cf. " Epistulae," LIX. 18 ; ". . . in cleri nostri sacrum venerandumque congestum ".

[3] " Epistulae," LXXX. 1.

in flight, Cyprian writes: *Cyprianus presbyteris et diaconis et plebi universae.* If he addresses exclusively either his clergy or his people: *Cyprianus presbyteris et diaconis* or *Cyprianus plebi universae*, respectively.

Although there is an *ordo* in every Church, there is also everywhere a monarchical episcopate. Episcopacy is the " *Sacerdotii sublime fastigium* " ; the bishop is, in his Church, the supreme *sacerdos*, as well as the supreme *judex ;* and he is *sacerdos* and *judex* in Christ's place and stead.[1] Go to the assembly of the faithful, and there only two personalities at first appear to you: the bishop and the people.[2]

Generally no one is elected bishop, unless he has gone through the different grades of the hierarchy and the different offices of the Church.[3] The election of the bishop does not take place without the suffrage of the faithful of the Church that is to be provided for, and without the votes of the clergy.[4] The bishops take part in the election, on them it depends, and from them it receives its validity.[5] By

---

[1] "Epistulae," LIX. 5 : "Unus in ecclesia ad tempus sacerdos et ad tempus iudex vice Christi cogitatur ". Tertullian treated the bishop as "summus sacerdos " (" De Bapt." 17) ; Cyprian says " *unus sacerdos* ". It may be that, by this shade of thought, Cyprian means to reprove the theory of Tertullian—when a Montanist—as to the priesthood of the laity.

[2] *Ibid.* LVIII. 4 : "Collectam fraternitatem, tractantes episcopos ".

[3] *Ibid.* LV. 8 : "Non iste [Cornelius] ad episcopatum subito pervenit, sed per omnia ecclesiastica officia promotus, et in divinis administrationibus Dominum saepe promeritus, ad sacerdotii sublime fastigium cunctis religionis gradibus ascendit ".

[4] *Ibid :* "Factus est Cornelius episcopus . . . de clericorum paene omnium testimonio, de plebis quae tunc adfuit suffragio." The biographer of Alexander Severus writes in the Augustan history as follows : "Ubi aliquos voluisset . . . rectores provinciis dare . . . nomina eorum proponebat, hortans populum ut, si quis quid haberet criminis, probaret manifestis rebus ; si non probasset, subiret poenam capitis ; dicebatque grave esse, cum id Christiani et Iudaei facerent in praedicandis sacerdotibus qui ordinandi sunt, non fieri in provinciarum rectoribus, quibus et fortunae hominum committerentur et capita." "Alexand. Sev." 45.—It is not at all certain that the members of the Jewish sanhedrim were thus elected, but the assertion is true of the *sacerdotes* among Christians—i.e. of the bishops—and, in fact, of the whole Christian *ordo*.

[5] *Ibid. :* "Et factus est episcopus a plurimis collegis nostris qui tunc in urbe Roma aderant. '—When defending his own election before

the bishops, we must understand the bishops of the province, and not all of them, but those only who can come, in most cases those who are nearest. Such is the Apostolic rule followed from time immemorial in Africa and in all—or to speak more correctly—in almost all the provinces.[1]

When the election is over, the bishops who are present lay their hands upon the candidate, to "confer upon him the episcopate".[2] The bishops are the successors of the Apostles. The words spoken by Christ to His Apostles : "*Qui vos audit me audit*," are true of the bishops, for they were said for the legitimate bishops, "*qui apostolis vicaria ordinatione succedunt*".[3]

Pope Cornelius against the charges of Felicissimus, Cyprian recalls that his election was made "post populi suffragium, post coepiscoporum consensum " ; but he says also : "post divinum iudicium ". "Epistulae," LIX. 5. Cyprian does not conceive of any one being made a bishop, without the divine judgment. He often recurred to this orthodox idea of the faith which confirms the divine right of every bishop.

[1] "Epistulae," LXVII. 5 : "Diligenter de traditione divina et apostolica observatione servandum est et tenendum, quod apud nos quoque et fere per provincias universas tenetur, ut ad ordinationes rite celebrandas ad eam plebem cui praepositus ordinatur episcopi eiusdem provinciae proximi quique conveniant, et episcopus deligatur plebe praesente, quae singulorum vitam plenissime novit."—The restriction *fere per provincias universas* may refer to the very exceptional case of Alexandria. We see at Rome Pope Cornelius himself assign bishops to three churches of Italy whose former bishops had been deposed. EUSEB. "H. E." VI. 43, 10.

[2] Cf. the letter of Cornelius (EUSEB. loc. cit.) in which he relates how Novatian, after bringing to Rome under false pretences three poor Italian bishops, "rustics," constrained them to lay their hands upon him. This was done at the tenth hour (four P.M.) and the unfortunate bishops were drunk : Μετὰ βίας ἠνάγκασεν εἰκονικῇ τινι καὶ ματαίᾳ χειρεπιθεσίᾳ ἐπισκοπὴν αὐτῷ δοῦναι. It may be inferred from this that, even then, three bishops had to be present for an episcopal consecration. Notice the expression : χειρεπιθεσίᾳ ἐπισκοπὴν δοῦναι : the bishops give through the imposition of hands the episcopate they possess themselves. Notice, too, that the three heretical bishops are represented by Cornelius as having performed an invalid ordination (ματαίᾳ).

[3] *Ibid.* LXVI. 4. Cf. "Sententiae episcoporum," 79 (HARTEL, I. 459): "Manifesta est sententia Domini nostri Iesu Christi apostolos suos mittentis et ipsis solis potestatem a patre sibi datam permittentis, quibus nos successimus eadem potestate Ecclesiam Domini gubernantes et credentium fidem baptizantes." (Sententia of Clarus, bishop of Mascula). In this document the bishops of Africa affirm that they possess that divine *potestas* which was denied to them by Tertullian, when a Montanist.

The priests are somewhat like mute personages, who follow the bishop and second him, but have no history of their own, except when they rebel, which they do at times, as did Novatus at Carthage and Novatian at Rome.[1] The deacons are more prominent, and stand more apart; but they hold an inferior rank which demands of them subordination: St. Cyprian urges them to remember that the Lord Himself chose the Apostles, i.e. the bishops, whilst the deacons were instituted by the Apostles, to be the ministers of the Apostles and of the Church.[2]

The priests have for their office to offer up the Holy Sacrifice where the bishop himself does not celebrate.[3]

When away from Carthage, Cyprian expects that his priests, and his deacons also, will fulfil the office which he, their bishop, is unable to fulfil. "*Officium meum vestra diligentia repraesentet.*"[4] This delegation of the episcopal office is confined to the celebration of the Holy Mysteries, to Baptism and the reconciliation of sinners *in extremis*, to preaching and almsgiving. A function which ordinarily devolves on the priests is that of teaching the catechumens: the priests who perform this duty are called *presbyteri doctores* or *doctores audientium*, the *audientes* being the cate-

---

[1] "Epistulae," xvi. 1 : ". . . quando aliqui de presbyteris, nec euangelii nec loci sui memores, sed neque . . . nunc sibi praepositum episcopum cogitantes, quod nunquam omnino sub antecessoribus factum est, cum contumelia et contemptu praepositi, totum sibi vindicent ! "—The priests are called by the bishop his *compresbyteri* :—an appellation which recalls the time when the *episcopus* was the first among the presbyters. But likewise the bishop calls other bishops *compresbyteri*. These two archaic expressions are worthy of notice.

[2] *Ibid.* iii. 3 : "Meminisse diaconi debent quoniam apostolos, id est episcopos et praepositos, Dominus elegit, diaconos autem post ascensum Domini in caelos apostoli sibi constituerunt episcopatus sui et ecclesiae ministros."—Cyprian confounds the institution of the bishops with that of the Apostles : a confusion which is also met with in Theodore of Mopsuestia, and in Theodoret. LIGHTFOOT, " Christian Ministry," p. 23.

[3] *Ibid.* xvi. 4 : " Interim prohibeantur offerre ". Cf. " Epistulae," lxi. 3 : ". . . cum episcopo presbyteri sacerdotali honore coniuncti ". The idea of priesthood is connected with that of sacrifice (*offerre*). Tertullian, when a Catholic, expressed both ideas with force (ADAM, p. 96-102), and in this respect Cyprian is no innovator.

[4] *Ibid.* xii. 1. Cf. v. 1 : " Fungemini illic et vestris partibus et meis, ut nihil vel ad disciplinam, vel ad diligentiam desit ".

chumens.[1]  Pontius relates that Cyprian was taught the true religion and converted by the priest Cæcilian;[2] besides, he tells us that Cyprian himself, when he was a priest, was charitable towards the widows; that whoever needed light found it through him; that whoever was weak found in him a support; and that whoever sought the help of a strong hand could rely upon his. The rhetoric of these expressions may be poor but under them we can read that the priestly ministrations embrace the service of widows, the service of the catechesis, and probably also the service of penitence, that is of the penitence of individual and private persons.[3]

From a letter of Pope Cornelius to the Bishop of Antioch, Fabius, we learn that in the year 251 the Roman Church had forty-six priests, seven deacons, seven sub-deacons, forty-two acolytes, fifty-two exorcists, lectors or ostiarii, taken all together, and that it supported more than fifteen hundred widows and destitute persons.[4] The people were innumerable, says Cornelius. We do not know how many ecclesiastics there were in Carthage at the time of Cyprian. We do know, however, that, besides the priests and the deacons, the Carthaginian Church has also, like the Church of Rome, subdeacons (*hypodiaconi*),[5] acolytes (*acolythi*),[6] exorcists,[7] and lectors. No mention is made of ostiarii or porters. No one of these clerics is raised to his office without the approval of the clergy and of the people.

---

[1] " Epistulae," xxix. and xviii. 2. See also lxxiii. 3. Tertullian, when a Catholic, had said that the bishops, priests, and deacons alone have the right to teach : " Nisi episcopi iam, aut presbyteri aut diaconi, vocantur discentes ". " De Bapt." 17.

[2] " Vita Cypriani," 4.

[3] *Ibid.* 3 : " Domus eius patuit cuicumque venienti : nulla vidua revocata sinu vacuo, nullus indigens lumine non illo comite directus est, nullus debilis gressu non illo baculo vectus est, nullus nudus auxilio de potentioris manu non illo tutore protectus est ". But we must not overstrain these expressions.

[4] Euseb. " H. E." vi. 43, 11-12. Renan, " Marc Aurèle," p. 451, estimates that the Christians of Rome must have been from thirty to forty thousand in number.

[5] " Epistulae," xxix., xxxiv. 4, lxxviii., lxxix. etc.

[6] *Ibid.* vii., xxxiv. 4, xlv. 4, xlix. 3, etc.

[7] *Ibid.* xxiii. The exorcists have for their function to exorcise, before baptism, those who are possessed. See " Epistulae," lxix. 15.

As regards the lectorate, one should read the thirty-eighth letter of Cyprian, a beautiful and expressive letter, in which he tells the clergy and the *plebs* of Carthage—from whom he is still exiled—of his having raised to the lectorate the young martyr Aurelius. Cyprian begins by excusing himself for not having taken beforehand the advice of his clergy or asked the assent of his people.[1] But had not Aurelius the divine suffrage of his martyrdom? Aurelius is a mere youth : worthy as he is on account of his courage to be promoted to some higher rank of the clergy, he shall start in the lectorate.

". . . Interim placuit ut ab officio lectionis incipiat, quia et nihil magis congruit voci quae Deum gloriosa praedicatione confessa est quam celebrandis divinis lectionibus personare, post verba sublimia quae Christi martyrium prolocuta sunt euangelium Christi legere unde martyres fiunt, ad pulpitum post catastam venire. . . . Hunc igitur a me et a collegis qui praesentes aderant ordinatum sciatis." [2]

Aurelius, then, who, as a martyr, went to the *catasta*, i.e. the rack, will come, as a lector, to the *pulpitum*, i.e. to the desk. He will read in the liturgical meetings the Gospel, the divine words. The lectores are once called by Cyprian " *lectores doctorum audientium* " : a title which implies that they are attached to the priests who teach the catechumens.[3]

The members of the clergy being vowed to the service of things divine and spiritual, owe their service to the Church, to the altar, and to prayer; hence they are forbidden to accept functions which are purely secular and civil.[4]

---

[1] " Epistulae," xxxviii. 1 : " In ordinationibus clericis, solemus vos ante consulere et mores ac merita singulorum communi consilio ponderare."

[2] *Ibid.* 2. Compare the thirty-ninth Letter.

[3] *Ibid.* xxix. : " . . . Quando . . . cum presbyteris doctoribus lectores diligenter probaremus, Optatum inter lectores doctorum audientium constituimus." O. RITSCHL, " Cyprian von Karthago " (Göttingen, 1885), p. 233. The theory which represents the "lectores" as the last " prophets " hardly deserves any mention.

[4] We may infer that the temptation to undertake such functions was great for the bishops in those ages, and that often in their anxiety to provide for a poor Church they were drawn into the world of business.

Geminius Victor, Bishop of Furni, near Carthage, appointed in his will the priest Geminius Faustinus administrator of the goods he had left at his death; but Cyprian intervened with the reminder that no cleric can be named a guardian or executor. He justifies this prohibition by the condition in which the tribe of Levi had been placed by the Old Law : as they were bound to the service of the Temple, the members of this tribe were to live on the tithes given to them by the other tribes which owned the land : all which, he says, "was done by the authority of God who would not allow the Levites to be drawn off in any way from His service". The decree forbidding ecclesiastics to be guardians or executors was enacted by the bishops previously to Cyprian's election (*episcopi antecessores nostri censuerunt*) with the sanction that any one who, in his will, failed to observe it, should not be entitled, after his death, to have the Holy Sacrifice offered up for his soul, or his name pronounced in the memento of the Mass. Since, then, the Bishop Geminius Victor has not complied with the rule laid down by the bishops (*formam nuper in concilio a sacerdotibus datam*), Cyprian forbids the Holy Sacrifice to be offered up for him, or his name to be mentioned in the prayers of the Church, "*ut sacerdotum decretum religiose ac necessarie factum servetur a nobis:*" bishops ought to be the first to obey episcopal decisions.[1]

This thirty-ninth Letter supplies us with interesting details concerning the remuneration of the clergy by the Church. Celerinus, who has been made a lector by St. Cyprian, is, like Aurelius, a martyr: although both are only lectors, Cyprian has conferred on them what he calls the "*presbyterii honorem*," which means that, even though they are not priests, they are to sit in the *consessus*, i.e. on the bench of the priests, and participate in the same distributions (*sportulae*) as the priests, and share the monthly allowances (*divisiones*)

CYPRIAN, "De lapsis,' 6 : "Episcopi plurimi quos et hortamento esse oportet ceteris et exemplo, divina procuratione contempta, procuratores regum saecularium fieri, derelicta cathedra, plebe deserta, per alienas provincias oberrantes, negotiationis quaestuosae nundinas aucupari, esurientibus in ecclesia fratribus habere argentum largiter velle, fundos insidiosis fraudibus rapere, usuris multiplicantibus foenus augere."

[1] "Epistulae," I. 1-2.

in equal quantities: ". . . ut et sportulis idem cum pres-byteris honorentur, ut divisiones mensurnas aequatis quan-titatibus partiantur, sessuri nobiscum." [1]

The subordination of the *plebs* to the *ordo* is not such as to exclude the laity from all share in the government of the local Church. And, in what pertains to the welfare of the community, this right of the laity is upheld with a scrupulous deference both by Cyprian and by Pope Cornelius. Thus, for instance, in the eyes of Cyprian the reconciliation of the *lapsi*, who had fallen during the persecution of Decius, is a matter on which the whole Church should be consulted, according to the rule that questions of common interest relating to the government of the Church must be exa-mined by all in common.[2] Even supposing that this rule was not everywhere observed, we know at least that Cyprian resolved to follow it, when he became Bishop of Carthage. In matters which concern the whole Church, Cyprian is unwilling to pronounce sentence until he has first taken the advice of his clergy—i.e. of the priests and deacons, and obtained the assent of the *plebs*.[3]

As we have seen, the *plebs* also takes part in the election of the bishop—a real part, but one which tends to become chiefly negative : the *plebs* might oppose the choice which, probably is most often made without its participation ; but this suffices to make it responsible for the actual choice and enables Cyprian to say that the *plebs* holds "*potestatem vel eligendi dignos sacerdotes vel indignos recusandi* ".[4]

---

[1] "Epistulae," xxxix. 5. Compare "Epistulae," xli. 2 : ". . . ut cum ecclesia matre remanerent et stipendia eius episcopo dispensante percipe-rent ". The *sportulae* were certainly the shares in the offerings in kind made by the faithful. Eusebius, " H. E." v. 28, 10, relates that the heretical bishop Natalios received 150 denarii a month for his salary. Cf. Tertull. " De Ieiunio," 13 : " Episcopi universae plebi mandare ieiunia adsolent, non dico de industria stipium conferendarum, ut vestrae cap-turae est. . . ."

[2] " Epistulae," xiv. 1.

[3] *Ibid.* Cf. " Epistulae,' xxxiv. 4. Sohm, p. 234, draws attention to the shade of difference between *consilium* and *consensus* : the bishop asks the priests their *consilium*, and the people its *consensus*. " The *plebs* says only, Aye."

[4] *Ibid.* lxvii. 3. Cf. xlix. 1. See in the " Passio Montani," 24 (" Acta Sanctorum Februarii," vol. iii. p. 446), the speech of the martyr

The Church continues to be what she was from the beginning: a social brotherhood, securing its members from misery and neglect. Cyprian bids Eucratius, the Bishop of a small Church (that of Thenae, it seems) not to allow a comedian—who had become a convert—to continue to give lessons for the stage; if the poor fellow gives as an excuse that his profession is, for him, the only way to get a living, the Bishop may place him among those Christians who receive their maintenance from the Church; and, if the Church of Thenae cannot afford to feed all its poor, the Bishop of Thenae may send the comedian to Carthage, where he will be fed and clothed.[1] At the very height of the Decian persecution, Cyprian, absent from Carthage, writes to his clergy, priests and deacons, and begs them not to discontinue the aids they are wont to grant to the widows, the sick, all the poor, and also to indigent travellers. Cyprian has left a certain sum of money in the hands of one of his priests, and, fearing that this amount is already exhausted, he sends another sum, by an acolyte.[2] Some Churches of Numidia have suffered from the inroads of the Berbers; a great many Christians have been taken prisoners. The Numidian bishops appeal to the charity of the Church of Carthage, for means to redeem the captives. We still possess the letter in which Cyprian thanks the Bishops of these sorely-tried Churches for having given him the opportunity to help them in their distress: a collection has been made at Carthage among the clergy and faithful; consequently, Cyprian sends to the Bishops of Numidia a sum

Flavianus, suggesting to the faithful that they should choose the priest Lucianus to replace Cyprian who has just departed from this life.

[1] " Epistulae," ii. 2 : " Quod si illic ecclesia non sufficit ut laboranti- bus praestet alimenta, poterit se ad nos transferre, et hic quod sibi ad victum atque ad vestitum necessarium fuerit accipere ".

[2] *Ibid.* vii. 1 : " Viduarum et infirmorum et omnium pauperum curam peto diligenter habeatis. Sed et peregrinis si qui indigentes fuerint sumptus suggeratis de quantitate mea propria quam apud Rogati- anum compresbyterum nostrum dimisi. Quae quantitas ne forte iam universa erogata sit, misi eidem per Naricum acoluthum aliam portionem, ut largius et promptius circa laborantes fiat operatio." He gives similar instructions in " Epistulæ," v. 1. Likewise in " Epistulae," xiii. 6 (in the variant reading of the " Codex remensis ").

of money that reaches quite 100,000 sesterces,[1] and he gives the names of the donors, that they may be remembered in the prayers of the Churches they have assisted.

The brotherly union of the members of the Church continues even in death. The faithful are buried together in the same cemeteries. It is for a Christian an act of impiety to accept the posthumous hospitality of a pagan sepulchre, and to be willing to sleep in the midst of dead who did not profess the Christian faith.[2]

* * *

Membership of the Church of Carthage (and the same is true of all Churches) may be forfeited, for the bishop, the head and the foundation of the Church, may break off relations with a member when he judges it necessary : the ancient city exiled, the bishop excommunicates, and it is he who grants ecclesiastical communion.   Here the word communion must be understood in its most comprehensive meaning, for it implies, together with the participation in the Sacred Mysteries, the fact of belonging to the Christian community —to its spiritual brotherhood and to its material solidarity.[3] When excommunicating Felicissimus, Cyprian confines himself to these words : " *Abstentum se a nobis sciat* " ; and he

---

[1] " Epistulae," LXII. 4 : " Misimus autem sestertia centum milia nummorum, quae istic in ecclesia cui de Domini indulgentia praesumus cleri et plebis apud nos consistentis collatione collecta sunt, quae vos illic pro vestra diligentia dispensabitis ".   100,000 sesterces amount to about 4000 or 5000 dollars or £800 or £1000.

[2] *Ibid.* LXVII. 6 : " Martialis praeter gentilium turpia et lutulenta convivia in collegio diu frequentata, et filios in eodem collegio exterarum gentium more apud profana sepulcra depositos et alienigenis consepultos . . . "   Martialis is the Spanish Bishop of whom we shall speak later (p. 375).

[3] *Ibid.* LV. 24 : " Quisque ille est et qualiscumque est, christianus non est qui in Christi ecclesia non est.   Iactet se licet et philosophiam vel eloquentiam suam superbis vocibus praedicet, qui nec fraternam caritatem nec ecclesiasticam unitatem tenuit, etiam quod prius fuerat amisit." Cyprian speaks here of Novatian, a declared heretic.   To those who are excommunicated he applies in all its rigour the saying : " Outside the Church no salvation : " " Superbi et contumaces *necantur*, dum de ecclesia eiciuntur : neque enim vivere foris possunt, cum domus Dei una sit et nemini salus esse nisi in ecclesia possit."   " Epistulae," IV. 4.   This fourth epistle was written previously to the Novatian crisis.

adds that such will be also the punishment of any one who joins Felicissimus : " *Quisque se conspirationi et factioni eius adiunxerit sciat se in ecclesia nobiscum communicaturum non esse* ".[1] There is still extant, in Cyprian's correspondence, the sort of official document by which the priests of Carthage announce the excommunication of Felicissimus and of six of his followers.[2] The excommunication is preceded by an inquiry, which is conducted by the bishop and his *presbyterium* : the sentence given by the bishop is notified to the people.[3]

The reconciliation of the excommunicated is a public act, of which we find a moving description in the letter sent to Cyprian by Pope Cornelius. The case was that of a priest, Maximus, and two Roman confessors, Urbanus and Sidonius, who abandon the schism of Novatian and come back to the Catholic Church. Cornelius has them first questioned by some priests, in order to test their sincerity. A report is made to Cornelius, who orders that the *presbyterium* be convoked. Five bishops from elsewhere, then present in Rome, take part as by right in the deliberation of the *presbyterium*. This deliberation seems to take place privately, and each one of the consultors gives his opinion, which is immediately put down in writing. Then the three culprits are brought before the *presbyterium* : together with them come many of the faithful to plead in their behalf. Maximus, Urbanus and Sidonius begin to speak : they recant their error and protest that, in their hearts, they have never ceased to be attached to the true Church : " *Cor nostrum*

---

[1] "Epistulae," XLI. 2. Cf. XLIII. 7 : "Si quis . . . in Felicissimi et satellitum eius partes concesserit et se haereticae factioni coniunxerit, sciat se postea ad ecclesiam redire et cum episcopis et plebe Christi communicare non posse."

[2] *Ibid.* XLII. : " Abstinuimus a communicatione Felicissimum et Augendum, item Repostum de extorribus et Irenem Rutilorum et Paulam sarcinatricem. . . . Item abstinuimus Sophronium et ipsum de extorribus Soliassum budinarium."

[3] *Ibid.* XLI. 2 : "[Felicissimus] abstentum se a nobis sciat, quando ad fraudes eius et rapinas quas dilucida veritate cognovimus, adulterii etiam crimen accedit, quod fratres nostri graves viri deprehendisse se nuntiaverunt." The letter is sent by Cyprian, not to his people, but to his priests. Compare TERTULL. "Apologet." 39 : "Iudicatur magno cum pondere . . . Praesident probati quique seniores."

*semper in ecclesia ;fuit,"* and that there ought to be only one bishop in the Catholic Church, *unum episcopum in Catholica esse debere"*. Then Cornelius pronounces the restoration of the priest Maximus to his priestly dignity, and that of the two confessors to their place in the Church, *" cum ingenti populi suffragio "*.[1]    We have here the full formalities of a judgment.

This procedure is not, strictly speaking, the same as that applied to penitents, although there is a great similarity between the two.   The sins committed after baptism, can be forgiven, through the mercy of God: God, who conferred innocence upon us in baptism, did not intend to bind us by precept to an innocence beyond our reach; He permits us to expiate our faults by almsgiving.[2]    However, there are some especially grievous sins that cannot be thus expiated privately: such are adultery, apostasy, and homicide.[3]    The *lapsi*, for instance, will be obliged to atone for their apostasy by penance, and to perform their penance before the whole Church.    Only then will they be allowed to receive the imposition of the hands of the bishop in sign of peace and reconciliation; after which they may approach Holy Communion.[4]    Here then we have again a previous trial, a public penance, and a public sentence of reconciliation.

---

[1] " Epistulæ," xlix. 1-3 : " Omni actu ad me perlato placuit contrahi presbyterium.   Adfuerant etiam episcopi quinque, qui et eo die praesentes fuerunt. . . . Sententias nostras placuit in notitiam perferri, quas et subiectas leges.   His ita gestis in presbyterium venerunt Maximus, Urbanus, Sidonius et plerique fratres qui eis se adiunxerant, summis precibus desiderantes ut . . . Quorum voluntate cognita magnus fraternitatis concursus factus. . . . Quapropter iussimus . . ." Compare the procedure of the judgment by which St. Cyprian is condemned to death by the proconsul : " Acta proconsularia," 3-4 (Hartel, vol. iii. p. cxii).

[2] " De Opere et Eleem." 11 and 14.

[3] " De Bono patientiae," 14 : "Adulterium, fraus, homicidium mortale crimen est." In the time of St. Cyprian, the ecclesiastical discipline, which had become more lenient as regards the sins of lust and the sin of apostasy, was still unbending as regards murder.   See Cyprian, "De dominica oratione," 24 : "Qui fratrem suum odit homicida est, nec ad regnum pervenit aut cum Deo vivit homicida. . . . Quale delictum est quod nec baptismo sanguinis potest ablui, quale crimen est quod martyrio non potest expiari ! "

[4] " De Lapsis," 16 : No *lapsus* must be admitted to Communion " . . . ante expiata delicta, ante exomologesim factam criminis, ante

The bishop reconciles others, but he himself cannot be reconciled; if he has to do penance, he must resign the episcopate and henceforth cannot rise above lay communion.[1]

The custom of assembling in council the bishops of the same region is already ancient. Cyprian tells us of a bishop of Lambesa, Privatus, who "*ante multos ,fere annos*" was condemned for many grievous faults by the judgment of ninety bishops.[2] Later on we shall see Cyprian invoke the decision given by a council of Carthage, about the year 220, which was attended by seventy-one bishops belonging to two provinces—proconsular Africa and Numidia.[3] By provinces, we must understand imperial provinces, for at this time ecclesiastical provinces are not yet in existence.[4] At the Council of Carthage in the year 256, there are present eighty-seven bishops from three provinces

purgatam conscientiam sacrificio et manu sacerdotis, ante offensam placatam indignantis Domini et minantis". On the share of the people in the judgment of the reconciliation of the *lapsi*, see "Epistulae," LIX. 15, and LXIV. 1.

[1] "Epistulae," LV. 11, LXV. 2, LXVII. 6, LXXII. 2. Cf. EUSEB. "H. E." VI. 43, 10 (letter of Cornelius).

[2] *Ibid.* LIX. 10. Still, the expression "ante multos annos" cannot designate a very remote epoch. Privatus appeals to the council of Carthage of the year 252. The sentence by which he had been deposed had been sanctioned by Pope Fabian (236-50), when Donatus († 249), Cyprian's predecessor, was Bishop of Carthage. BENSON, "Cyprian" (London, 1897), p. 227.

[3] *Ibid.* LXXIII. 1. We learn from the letter of Pope Cornelius to Fabius that the Council of Rome, which condemns Novatian, is attended by sixty Italian bishops, and by "a great many more presbyters and deacons". EUSEB. "H. E." VI. 43, 2.

[4] *Ibid.* XLVIII. 3. Cf. DUCHESNE, "Origines du culte chrét," p. 13 and foll. "Hist. anc.'" vol. I. pp. 526-7 : "Nowhere, before Diocletian, certainly not in the West, is there in the grouping of churches the least indication of a desire to reproduce the lines of the imperial provinces. The·Bishop of Carthage, or at least his Council, presides over all the African provinces—the Pro-consular, Numidian and Mauritanian [both Caesariensis and Tingitana]. Italy depends entirely on the See of Rome ; the See of Alexandria is the ecclesiastical centre for both Egypt and Cyrenaica, although in civil affairs these countries had separate administrators. Here, the connexions between the churches had nothing to do with the connexions of the civil administration, but arose solely out of the circumstances of their evangelization,' which again depended on geographical conditions."

—proconsular Africa, Numidia and Mauritania.   An official record of the sessions of these assemblies is drawn up: the *sententiae episcoporum* [1] of the Council of the year 256 are the oldest Latin specimen we have of such acts.

The decrees passed by a council are regarded as authoritative: the bishops themselves are not above the laws they have made in council.   As we have seen, Cyprian recalled this principle, when the will of Geminius Victor, Bishop of Furni, came before him.   The Council of Africa, presided over by Cyprian, cites the same principle against Therapius, Bishop of Bulla, who, by reconciling one of his priests before submitting him to a sufficiently long penance, had not complied with the rule laid down by the Council of the year 251 : " *Quae res nos satis movit, recessum esse a decreti nostri auctoritate* ".[2]

The bishops, then, are amenable to a council and can be deposed by it, as was the case with Privatus of Lambesa. The Council of Africa meets at Carthage generally twice a year, in the spring and in the autumn.   Laymen take no part in councils.

Cyprian, who frequently and emphatically proclaims that all bishops are equal, none the less exercises a real primacy, not only over proconsular Africa, but also over all Christian Africa, as far as the shores of the Atlantic.   The Council of Africa assembles at Carthage, and he truly presides over it.   Even outside its sessions he has authority to act in its name and carry out its decrees; he speaks in its name to the Bishops of Africa and to those of foreign lands.[3]

For, beyond the boundaries of Africa, there is the *orbis*. The relations, by means both of messengers and of letters, which unite Carthage with Rome and Rome with Carthage, show the profound solidarity which binds the two Churches together: they hold themselves bound to observe the same rules of conduct and to maintain a like discipline.   This is a thought prompted by charity, and likewise by their sense of duty.   Cyprian writes to the Roman clergy: " *Et dilectio*

---

[1] HARTEL, vol. I. p. 435 and foll.

[2] " Epistulae," LXIV. 1.   Cf. *ibid.* 2.

[3] MONCEAUX, vol. II. p. 13.   RITSCHL, p. 228.   HARNACK, " Mission," vol. I. pp. 394-5,

*communis et ratio exposcit, nihil conscientiae vestrae sub-
trahere de his quae apud nos geruntur ut sit nobis circa
utilitatem ecclesiasticae administrationis commune consilium* ".[1] The clergy of Rome (the see was then vacant
and Cornelius had not yet been elected) answers in terms of
higher import: " *Omnes enim nos decet pro corpore totius
Ecclesiae, cuius per varias quasque provincias membra
digesta sunt, excubare* ".[2]

A bishop, like that of Rome, on being elected, never
fails to announce his election to a see like that of Carthage.
This is not a recent custom, and Cyprian refers to it, as a
rule that is generally observed. When he begs Cornelius to
send him the testimony of the bishops who took part in his
election to the see of Rome, he protests that he does not forget
the established custom: " *Non veteres mores obliti novum
aliquid quaerebamus, nam satis erat utite episcopum factis
litteris nuntiares* ".[3] Another of St. Cyprian's letters intimates that the election of Cornelius has been notified to
all the bishops of the Christian world, and that all have
recognized it.[4]

As soon as the affair of Felicissimus breaks out at
Carthage, Cyprian takes care to send to Pope Cornelius
all the documents that refer to it, and begs the Pope
to let the clergy and faithful of Rome read the letter
which he, Cyprian, has written on the subject to the clergy
and faithful of Carthage—in order that every one may be

---

[1] " Epistulae," xxxv.

[2] *Ibid.* xxxvi. 4. The case referred to is that of Privatus, of
Lambesis. By " omnes nos " the Roman clergy mean the heads of the
Churches. See " Epistulae," viii. 3, a letter of the Roman clergy, during
the vacancy of the see, to the clergy of Carthage, Cyprian having then
fled : " Salutant vos fratres qui sunt in vinculis (notice the importance of
confessors) et presbyteri et tota ecclesia, quae et ipsa cum summa sollicitu-
dine excubat pro omnibus qui invocant nomen Domini." The solicitude
with which the clergy of Rome watches over all the Churches, must not
be overlooked.

[3] *Ibid.* xlv. 3.

[4] *Ibid.* lv. 8 : " . . . coepiscoporum testimonio quorum numerus
universus per totum mundum concordi unanimitate consensit ". We
recall the words of Tertullian, then a Montanist: " Non Ecclesia
numerus episcoporum ". " De Pudicit." xxi.

well acquainted with the whole affair, "*ut tam istic quam illic circa omnia per nos fraternitas instruatur*".[1] Cyprian receives and communicates to his Church the letter in which Cornelius announces his election : he has received at the same time a memorial (*librum*) sent by Novatian's party, which is a formal requisition against Cornelius. Cyprian does not communicate this libel to his Church, but asks Cornelius for information which will enable him to refute it. He informs by letters all the African bishops of the legitimacy of the election of Cornelius, in order—as he himself writes to Cornelius—"*ut te universi collegae nostri et communicationem tuam id est catholicae ecclesiae unitatem pariter et caritatem probarent firmiter ac tenerent*".[2]

On his part, Cornelius complains that the followers of Novatian have appealed to all the churches;"[3] and he informs the churches—we know that he does so for that of Carthage—of the incidents and vicissitudes of the schism.[4] Would that such accounts were always simple and true ! But there are already in the Church informers and mischief-makers : witness the letter in which Cyprian complains that some have spoken at Rome of the conduct of the Bishop of Carthage "without due sincerity and fidelity ".[5]

All the Churches being dispersed over the world, but bound together through their bishops, there is but one Church, as there is but one episcopate : the unity of the episcopate manifests the unity of the Church. It is a unity that is everywhere cemented, "*connexam et ubique conjunctam Catholicae ecclesiae unitatem*".[6] "For us," writes Cyprian

---

[1] " Epistulae," XLV. 4.　　　　[2] *Ibid.* XLVIII. 3.

[3] *Ibid.* XLIX. 1 : " . . . quod per omnes ecclesias litterae calumniis et maledictis plenae eorum nomine frequentes missae fuissent, et paene omnes ecclesias perturbassent ". Cf. " Epistulae," LV. 5 : " . . . quae litterae per totum mundum missae sunt et in notitiam ecclesiis omnibus et universis fratribus perlatae ".

[4] *Ibid.* L.

[5] *Ibid.* XX. 1 : " Quoniam comperi, fratres carissimi, minus simpliciter et minus fideliter vobis renuntiari quae hic a nobis et gesta sunt et geruntur. . . ."

[6] *Ibid.* IV. 24 : " Cum sit a Christo una Ecclesia per totum mundum in multa membra divisa, item episcopatus unus episcoporum multo-

to Pope Cornelius, " the Church is one, we have but one soul and this concord is indivisible: *Nam cum nobis et ecclesia una sit, et mens iuncta, et individua concordia* ".[1] One and the same faith, one and the same tradition is observed by the dispersed bishops: " . . . *episcopos plurimos ecclesiis dominicis in toto mundo divina dignatione praepositos euangelicae veritatis ac dominicae traditionis tenere rationem, nec ab eo quod Christus magister et praecepit et gessit humana et novella institutione decedere* ".[2]

This—we are told—is truly the hierarchical idea of the Church, and this idea is wrought out by St. Cyprian! The Catholicism of Irenæus and of Tertullian rested on a doctrinal basis, that of Cyprian rests on a hierarchical basis. But we are constrained to recognize that the hierarchical idea of the Church is found already in Irenæus and Tertullian, and that, in the East, in the first half of the third century, it is already embodied in the facts.[3] Decidedly Cyprian cannot be claimed as the originator of the hierarchical idea.

What had still to be made clear in Cyprian's time, was neither the apostolicity of the faith common to all the Churches, nor the divine right of the episcopate, nor even the unity, so conspicuous to all, of the universal episcopate. But, at a critical moment, when this unity was about to be menaced from within, it was necessary to familiarize the Christian people with the inner law of their nature, to explain how the Holy Ghost co-operates in its preservation, and how the see of Peter is not only the source, but also the perpetual guarantee of its endurance; in a word, it was necessary to formulate the divine constitution of Catholicism.

The glory of such a demonstration all but fell to Cyprian's treatise " De Unitate ecclesiae ".

rum concordi numerositate diffusus. . . ." Observe the words : *concors numerositas.*

[1] " Epistulæ," LX. 1.     [2] *Ibid.* LXIII. 1.
[3] HARNACK, " Dogmeng." vol. I⁴, p. 416.   Cf. LOOFS, p. 204.

## II.

Cyprian had ruled the Church of Carthage for about a year when the persecution of Decius broke out, in the autumn of the year 249. The bishop left Carthage and found a safe place of refuge, from whence he remained in daily intercourse with his Church, whose chief trial was caused not so much by the number of her martyrs, as by the number of her children who fell away—the *lapsi*.[1] In the height of the persecution, at the time when the number of apostasies was multiplying, Cyprian, still in his shelter, was asked by four priests of Carthage to authorize them to reconcile the *lapsi*, without previous penance, solely on the presentation of a letter from some martyr or confessor of the faith. This request raised the question whether an apostate could be reconciled to the Church. It seems clear that Cyprian and his clergy inclined unanimously towards indulgence in this respect, but the request raised the less-expected question whether a martyr could, by pleading in behalf of one who had lapsed, exempt him from the expiatory exercises of penance and, in effect, declare him absolved from his sin, leaving to the priests merely to ratify this absolution by admitting him to communion. The martyrs were thus assuming a power reserved to the bishop, and Cyprian refused to grant the request of the four Carthaginian priests, declaring that he intended to postpone the study of the case until his return, when he could consult with his clergy and people.[2]

But some priests—probably those who had written to St. Cyprian—ignored Cyprian's decision, and did not hesitate to admit the *lapsi* to communion, without delay, without penance, on the mere sight of a letter from a martyr.[3] Those of the clergy who remained faithful in this time of confusion,

---

[1] See "Études d'hist. et de théol. positive, 1ère série," pp. 111 and foll., "La crise novatienne".

[2] "Epistulae," xiv. 4. This pretension on the part of the martyrs is explained by the prevalent belief that the Holy Ghost granted a special help to the martyrs; the Holy Ghost was in them. The pretension of the Carthaginian martyrs is in line with Origen's theory of the power of the "spirituals".

[3] *Ibid.* xv. 1.

begged Cyprian to interfere. The latter thought best to give a provisional answer: those *lapsi* who had received from some martyr a letter of intercession, might be reconciled by the priests, but only if they were in danger of death: otherwise, they must await the return of Cyprian.[1]

The Bishop of Carthage communicated his decision to many bishops, his colleagues, who answered that his feeling was theirs, and that it was in conformity with the Catholic faith,[2] which, placed in the hands of the bishops the power to reconcile as well as the power to baptize. The See of Rome was vacant, since the death of Pope Fabian, on 20 January, 250. The clergy, who administered the Church, were inclined to rigorism and blamed Cyprian for what was called " his flight," but they agreed with him that it was better to take no decision on the subject until peace was restored.[3] They had written a letter in this sense to the bishops of Sicily; and they had come to an agreement with other bishops, some from near at hand, some from far off regions: " . . . *cum quibusdam episcopis vicinis nobis et adpropinquantibus et quos ex aliis provinciis longe positis persecutionis istius ardor eiecerat, ante constitutionem episcopi nihil innovandum putavimus* ".[4] There also, then, only such of the *lapsi* as were in danger of death might be reconciled; the others must wait in suspense.

Cyprian does not allow his priests to take any decision without him; the priests of Rome declare their unwillingness to take any decision, as long as no bishop presides over them: is not this a strong affirmation of the bishop's right, both at Carthage and at Rome? The Novatian crisis, we are told, led St. Cyprian to define the Church as a community ruled by its bishop, whereas until then he had conceived it to be a *consortium* of the bishop, the clergy and the laity.[5] But from these declarations, Roman and African, which

---

[1] "Epistulae," xix. 2.  [2] *Ibid.* xxv.
[3] *Ibid.* xxx. 5.  [4] *Ibid.* 8.
[5] HARNACK, " Dogmeng." vol. I[4], p. 417. In this passage Harnack contends that the texts in which Cyprian regards the Church as " constituta in episcopo et in clero et in omnibus credentibus " date from an earlier period, and represent " the old idea on the subject ". On the contrary Cyprian writes in " Epistulae," xxxiii. 1: " . . . quando ecclesia

are previous to the appearance of Novatian, we see that the Church is constituted hierarchically, and that the supreme power is truly in the hands of the bishop. Of the institutions that are then in existence Rome affirms already her "*Nihil innovandum*".

The bishop is the foundation of his Church: such is the leading idea of the thirty-third letter of St. Cyprian—a first draft of the "De Unitate". The *lapsi* who have dared to send me a letter in the name of the Church, "*ecclesiae nomine*," are indeed bold, he says. Perhaps they would like to be taken for the Church, "*ecclesiam se volunt esse*". . . . But a choice must be made between the bishop whose will is that the *lapsi* should wait, and those *lapsi* who defy the bishop's authority: on whom, then, is the Church founded?

"Dominus noster, cuius praecepta metuere et servare debemus, episcopi honorem et ecclesiae suae rationem disponens in euangelio loquitur et dicit Petro: *Ego tibi dico quia tu es Petrus, et super istam petram aedificabo ecclesiam meam, et portae inferorum non vincent eam, et tibi dabo claves regni caelorum, et quae ligaveris super terram erunt ligata et in caelis, et quaecumque solveris super terram erunt soluta et in caelis.* Inde per temporum et successionum vices episcoporum ordinatio et ecclesiae ratio decurrit ut ecclesia super episcopos constituatur et omnis actus ecclesiae per eosdem praepositos gubernetur." [1]

Cyprian vindicates, in the name of the Gospel, the bishop's dignity (*honor*): the Church is founded on the bishops, each Church is ruled by its bishop, and this divine constitution rests on the words of Christ to St. Peter. The words *Tu es Petrus* established the episcopacy, since the power instituted in Peter's person has passed on to the bishops, as

in episcopo et clero et in omnibus stantibus sit constituta, absit . . . ut ecclesia esse dicatur lapsorum numerus ". He means that the Church is made up of the bishops, the clergy and the faithful who have not fallen away, in contrast with the *lapsi*, who pretend to lay down the law. But he does not mean that the Church is built upon the faithful as well as upon the bishops and the clergy: neither before Cyprian's time nor in his writings was there any question about the subordination of the *plebs* to the *ordo*, within the unity of each Church. It is enough to recall Origen.

[1] " Epistulae," xxxiii. 1. Cf. lxvi. 8.

an inheritance, "*per successionum vices*". In virtue of this inherited power, the bishop presides over the whole activity of his Church. Therefore, no one can be a minister of reconciliation without his approval and against his will.

These declarations of principle did not suffice to restore order and bring back to their duty the rebellious priests. Cyprian felt compelled to threaten the recalcitrants with exclusion from his communion.[1]

Apparently these threats did not produce the result Cyprian expected, for a short time after, he had to excommunicate the prime mover in the rebellion of the *lapsi*, Felicissimus. From Cyprian's forty-first Letter we learn that Felicissimus was accused of misappropriating funds and was suspected of adultery: these charges were apparently to be investigated after Cyprian's return, in the presence of the council of Carthage.[2] But the notorious scandal was the revolt of Felicissimus against Cyprian: Felicissimus had on his side a certain number of the faithful (*portionem plebis*); and strong in their support, the more so that he was pleading their cause, he had done his utmost to thwart the endeavours of the priests whom Cyprian had appointed to bring back the *lapsi* to the path of duty, declaring that those who obeyed Cyprian's commands would by that very fact break with him—Felicissimus: "*secum in morte non communicarent*".[3] In his folly, Felicissimus went so far as to excommunicate without hope of forgiveness those who abandoned his party and submitted to Cyprian.[4]

In acting as he did, Felicissimus, it is true, betrayed the

---

[1] "Epistulae,' xxxiv. 3 : "Interea si quis immoderatus et praeceps sive de nostris presbyteris vel diaconis sive de peregrinis ausus fuerit ante sententiam nostram communicare cum lapsis, a communicatione nostra arceatur, apud omnes nos causam dicturus temeritatis suae, quando in unum permittente Domino convenerimus."

[2] *Ibid.* xli. 2 : "Quae omnia cognoscemus, quando in unum cum collegis pluribus permittente Domino convenerimus".

[3] *Ibid.* 1.

[4] *Ibid.* 2 : "... accipiat sententiam quam prior dixit, ut abstentum se a nobis sciat". Although separated at this time from his clergy and his people, Cyprian pronounces the excommunication of Felicissimus in words which affirm the principle of episcopal supremacy. However, Cyprian does not pronounce excommunication without hope of forgiveness.

nature of his ulterior designs.   The election of Cyprian to the
See of Carthage had not been made without opposition ; and
the opponents sided with Felicissimus.    Cyprian could
boldly denounce in this rebellion what he calls the " *antiqua
illa contra episcopatum meum venena,*" and " *veterem contra
nos impugnationem* ".[1]    But he does not waste time on these
designs of Felicissimus and of the few Carthaginian priests
who belong to his party ; he desires to have the case limited
to the question of the *lapsi* and to the indisputable principle
that dominates the whole controversy ; to reconcile the *lapsi*
without demanding penance of them, is to oppose the Gospel; it is "*ecclesiae pudicitiam corrumpere et veritatem
euangelicam violare* ".[2]    Then, what kind of reconciliation
can be given by priests who are outside the Church ?    Here
Cyprian comes to another argument which we shall meet
again in the " De Unitate," viz. that outside the Church
there is neither sacrifice, nor priesthood, nor reconciliation.[3]

The faction of the *lapsi* hoped for the support of Rome
and especially of the bishop who must soon be elected.   One
of the rebellious priests of Carthage was despatched to Rome
to work for the election of a Pope who would break with
Cyprian and acknowledge the rival whom the party of
Felicissimus was doubtless preparing to set up against him.[4]
Their intrigues failed.   The election of the Roman Bishop
took place towards the middle of March, and the priest
Cornelius, who had nothing to do with these quarrels, was
chosen.   The Roman faction, which this choice disconcerted, first murmured, then passed to deeds, and, notwithstanding the legitimacy of the election of Cornelius,
elected his unfortunate competitor, the Roman priest Novatian.

St. Cyprian could not hesitate : the election of Cornelius

[1] " Epistulae," XLIII. 1.                     [2] *Ibid.* 4.

[3] *Ibid.* 5 : "Pacem nunc offerunt qui ipsi non habent pacem, nec
ecclesiam lapsos reducere et revocare permittunt qui de ecclesia recesser-
unt.   Deus unus est, et Christus unus et una ecclesia, et cathedra una
super Petrum Domini voce fundata.   Aliud altare constitui, aut sacerdotium novum fieri, praeter unum altare et unum sacerdotium non
potest ".

[4] DUCHESNE, " Hist. anc.," vol. I. pp. 407-8.

was recognized as legitimate, and that of Novatian as having been made in spite of and against the legitimate Church, "*contra ecclesiam catholicam;*"[1] and, as some emissaries from Novatian were trying to make partisans among the Christians of Carthage, Cyprian broke off communion with them and immediately reported the fact to Pope Cornelius. At the same time, two African bishops were sent to Rome to aid in destroying the schism and bringing back the Romans who were making it, to the unity of the Church which at Rome was alone Catholic, "*ut ad catholicae ecclesiae unitatem scissi corporis membra componerent*".[2] Cyprian deemed it his duty to work with all his might for the restoration of unity at Rome. He writes to Cornelius:—

"Hoc enim vel maxime, frater, et laboramus et laborare debemus ut unitatem a Domino et per apostolos nobis successoribus traditam quantum possumus obtinere curemus, et quod in nobis est balabundas et errantes oves, quas quorumdam pervicax factio et haeretica temptatio a matre secernit, in ecclesia colligamus."[3]

When writing thus on the subject of the Roman schism, St. Cyprian was repeating the arguments he had formerly employed when dealing with the faction of Felicissimus at Carthage. Unity must above all prevail in every Church, because Christ desired unity, and unity is an inheritance transmitted by the Apostles to the bishops, their successors. We shall meet with these arguments again in the "De Unitate".

Besides writing to Pope Cornelius, Cyprian writes to the confessors who form Novatian's party at Rome a letter in which he praises the courage they exhibited in the time of persecution, and recognizes the sincerity of the scruples which led them to believe that the *lapsi* ought not to be reconciled; but he reminds them that attachment to the unity of their Church is also a duty, and that they are inexcusable for having set up a bishop against the legitimate bishop. By thus acting, they have run counter to the order established by God, to the law of the Gospel, "*contra institutionis catholicae unitatem*": in consenting to have a bishop

---

[1] "Epistulae," XLIV. 1.    [2] *Ibid.* XLV. 1.    [3] *Ibid.* 3.

other than the one already recognized, they have consented to have a church other than *the* Church, and such conduct is sacrilegious and unlawful.[1] Cornelius having announced to Cyprian the return of some of the confessors to the legitimate Church, the latter replies expressing his joy that they should "*unitatis ac veritatis domicilium repetisse*," and break off with the "*proditores fidei et ecclesiae catholicae impugnatores*".[2] Some of the Christians of Carthage whom those "*proditores fidei*" had won over, also come back to the true Church. The light has entered all hearts, "*et ecclesia catholica una esse nec scindi nec dividi posse monstrata est*".[3]

When the persecution came to an end, Cyprian called the Council of Carthage, in May 251. The Council had first to judge Felicissimus. It is probable that Cyprian took no part in this judgment, in which he was the accuser: the sentence was passed by his colleagues, who transmitted it immediately to Pope Cornelius.[4] The priests who were at the head of the faction of the Carthaginian *lapsi* were condemned, as well as Felicissimus, whom they had made their deacon,[5] a fact which shows their desire to organize themselves into a separate church. Moreover Novatus, the most compromised of all the priests of the party of Carthaginian

---

[1] "Epistulae," XLVI. 1 : ". . . contra institutionis catholicae unitatem alium episcopum fieri consensisse, id est, quod nec fas est nec licet fieri, ecclesiam alteram institui."

[2] *Ibid.* LI. 1.

[3] *Ibid.* 2. We must, however, clear up a point which might be misinterpreted. The unity insisted on by Cyprian is the unity in each church. The term "ecclesia catholica" refers, here, not to the whole Church, but to each particular church. Cornelius writes to Fabius (EUSEB. "H. E." VI. 43, 11): ἕνα ἐπίσκοπον δεῖ εἶναι ἐν καθολικῇ ἐκκλησίᾳ. Assuredly Cornelius did not mean to tell the Bishop of Antioch that there can be but one bishop in the whole catholic world. The Roman confessors who submit to Cornelius ("Epistulae," XLIX. 2) say : "Nos Cornelium episcopum sanctissimae catholicae ecclesiae electum a Deo scimus . . . nec ignoramus unum episcopum in catholica esse debere." See for the same use of the term "Epistulae," XLV. 1. Hence the meaning of the word "catholic" is determined by the extension of the word "church". This observation is very important.

[4] *Ibid.* XLV. 4. Regarding Cyprian's absence from the trial of Felicissimus, cf. BENSON, pp. 132-3.

[5] *Ibid.* LII. 2.

*lapsi*, anticipating the condemnation which they saw was inevitable, had gone to Rome, and had there been one of the instigators of Novatian's election.[1] At Carthage, then, even before the Council had condemned the schismatical faction, the cause of unity had triumphed.

The treatise " De Unitate ecclesiae " was published at this precise juncture, when, after the restoration of order at Carthage, the case of Novatian had yet to be settled at Rome. The supposition has been made that the treatise " De Unitate " was read in the Council of Carthage, in May, 251 ; this has been inferred from the following words of St. Cyprian : " *Quam unitatem tenere firmiter et vindicare debemus, maxime episcopi qui in ecclesia praesidemus* ".[2] The hypothesis is plausible, on condition that we do not exclude from this first hearing of the " De Unitate " either the clergy or the people of Carthage.[3] At all events the " De Unitate " was not concerned with the case of Felicissimus, on which Cyprian had fully expressed his mind before the Council met and in deciding which he had taken no part during the Council, as we have already seen. But we have also seen that emissaries from Novatian had done their utmost at Carthage to recruit adherents for their cause ; that Cyprian had excommunicated them and had sent to Rome two African bishops, to aid Cornelius in reducing the schism of Novatian : it is not surprising, then, that he should have wished to render further aid by composing a treatise on the principles of Church unity as held at Carthage ; such a book would enlighten the Carthaginians if they needed enlightenment ; it would be still more appreciated by the Romans, for whom especially it was written.

\* \*
\*

[1] " Epistulae," LII. 2 : " Idem est Novatus, qui apud nos primum discordiae incendium seminavit, qui quosdam istic ex fratribus ab episcopo segregavit. . . . Ipse est qui Felicissimum satellitem suum diaconum nec permittente me . . . constituit ". Novatus goes to Rome, and " quoniam pro magnitudine sua debeat Carthaginem Roma praecedere, illic maiora et graviora commisit : qui istic adversus ecclesiam diaconum fecerat, illic episcopum fecit ".

[2] " De Unit." 5. BENSON, p. 181.

[3] " Epistulae," LIV. 4 : ". . . libellis quos hic nuper legeram ". That letter, sent to Maximus and to the Roman confessors who had given up Novatian's schism, is, as it were, the dedication of the " De Unitate ".

Let us now examine the argument of the " De Unitate ecclesiae ".

The duty of every Christian is to defend himself against the ever-changing wiles of the devil. Formerly, the enemy made use of idolatry to seduce men : now that the idols are given up, their temples abandoned, and the Christians are increasing in number, he has recourse to a new device and, under the cover of the Christian name, seeks to seduce unwary Christians, by fomenting schisms and heresies. What can we oppose to this artifice of the devil? A fundamental principle, that of ecclesiastical unity (" Unit." 1-3).

For those who defer to the teaching of the Divine Master it is easy to establish this principle.

" Loquitur Dominus ad Petrum : *Ego tibi dico,* inquit, *quia tu es Petrus et super istam petram aedificabo ecclesiam meam, et portae inferorum non vincent eam. Dabo tibi claves regni caelorum : et quae ligaveris super terram erunt ligata et in caelis, et quaecumque solveris super terram erunt soluta et in caelis.*" Super unum ecclesiam aedificat (" Unit." 4).

Thus the Lord has built His Church upon one sole Apostle. Does this mean that this Apostle enjoys a privilege which the other Apostles have not received? No indeed, Cyprian somewhat hastily answers, since after His resurrection, Christ gives to all His Apostles the same powers, " *apostolis omnibus parem potestatem,*" when He sends them as He was sent by His Father, and gives them the Holy Ghost with the power of forgiving sins (John xx. 21). However numerous the Apostles, however numerous the bishops who have succeeded them, unity begets unity.

" . . . tamen ut unitatem manifestaret, unitatis eiusdem originem ab uno incipientem sua auctoritate disposuit. Hoc erant utique et ceteri apostoli quod fuit Petrus, pari consortio praediti et honoris et potestatis, sed exordium ab unitate proficiscitur, ut ecclesia Christi una monstretur " (" Unit." 4).

Hence, in the eyes of Cyprian, Christ's words to Peter mean only that each church is one, since the first of all the churches, that founded by Christ on Peter, is one.[1]

---

[1] Cyprian frequently returns to the same contention, that Christ founds the Church on Peter, and every church reproduces this primordial

As a fact, the Church has spread all over the world, without loss of unity, even as a tree whose boughs are many, and as a river that diffuses its waters: do not break a branch from the tree, for once broken it can live no longer; do not separate the stream from its source, for it will dry up. The episcopate is òne, all the bishops hold it severally and conjointly: "*Episcopatus unus est, cuius a singulis in solidum pars tenetur*" ("Unit." 5).

The Church is the spouse of Christ, a chaste spouse, having but one home and one chamber: whoever is not with her, is with an adulteress. Such a one is a bastard who has not God for his father, since he has not the Church for his mother. "*Habere non potest Deum patrem qui ecclesiam non habet matrem.*" The Church is the ark of Noe outside which all perish. Whoever is not with Christ is against Him: he who does not gather with Christ, scatters, and therefore "*Qui alibi praeter ecclesiam colligit Christi ecclesiam spargit*" ("Unit." 6). St. Cyprian accumulates the figures which seem to him apt to inculcate this unity. The seamless coat of Christ is for him a new "*unitatis sacramentum*" ("Unit." 7). So too is the privilege granted by Josue to the house of Rahab and the command to eat the paschal lamb "*in una domo*". The word of Christ "*unus grex et unus pastor*" (John x. 16) affords a further argument to the same effect ("Unit." 8).

Whoever separates himself from the Church forfeits all the blessings of which she is the source. In their fruitless usurpations, they make themselves bishops, but they are not

unity. "Epistulae," LIX. 7 and 14, LXVI. 8, LXXI. 3, LXXII. 7. Cf. BENSON, pp. 197-9. Speaking of St. Peter, and alluding to the fact that he was married, Tertullian had already said : "Petrum solum invenio maritum, propter socrum : monogamum praesumo, per Ecclesiam, quae super illum aedificata omnem gradum ordinis sui de monogamis erat collocatura". "De Monog." 8. This is a Montanistic treatise. Tertullian interprets the *Super hanc petram aedificabo*, as referring to the Apostle Peter : the Church is built upon Peter, retrospectively. The close connexion between the interpretation of Cyprian and that of Tertullian will be noticed. D'ALÈS, "Tertullien," p. 216. Regarding the various meanings given by the Fathers to the *Tu es Petrus*, see LAUNOI, "Opera omnia," vol. v. (1731), pp. 99-124 (letter of 1661) ; but we must bear in mind Launoi's Gallican and quasi-anarchistic spirit.

bishops: "*Nemine episcopatum dante episcopi sibi nomen adsumunt*" ("Unit." 10). The baptism conferred outside the Church is no baptism: "*Non abluuntur illic homines sed potius sordidantur, nec purgantur delicta, sed immo cumulantur*" ("Unit." 11). Let not seceders think they can defend themselves by means of texts; let them not say that, in the words of Christ, wherever two or three are gathered together in His name, He is with them. When He spoke thus, Christ was referring exclusively to His faithful followers and to His Church: "*Dominus de ecclesia sua loquitur et ad hos qui sunt in ecclesia loquitur*" ("Unit." 12). On the contrary, to these unworthy Christians who leave the Church, He said that when any one comes to pray he must cast aside all resentment against his neighbour; now, what kind of prayer, what kind of sacrifice can such enemies of brotherly peace offer up? "*Quae sacrificia celebrare se credunt aemuli sacerdotum? Secum esse Christum cum collecti fuerint opinantur, qui extra Christi ecclesiam colliguntur?*" ("Unit." 13). Not even by martyrdom can their lack of brotherly charity be expiated: "*Inexpiabilis et gravis culpa discordiae nec passione purgatur: esse martyr non potest qui in ecclesia non est*" ("Unit." 14).

St. Cyprian concentrates all his aversion for seceders into the following passage:—

"Aversandus est talis atque fugiendus quisque fuerit ab ecclesia separatus. Perversus est huiusmodi et peccat et est a semetipso damnatus. An esse sibi cum Christo videtur qui adversum sacerdotes Christi facit, qui se a cleri eius et plebis societate secernit? Arma ille contra ecclesiam portat, contra Dei dispositionem repugnat. Hostis altaris, adversus sacrificium Christi rebellis, pro fide perfidus, pro religione sacrilegus, inobsequens servus, filius impius, frater inimicus, contemptis episcopis et Dei sacerdotibus derelictis, constituere audet aliud altare, precem alteram inlicitis vocibus facere, dominicae hostiae veritatem per falsa sacrificia profanare, nec scire quoniam qui contra ordinationem Dei nititur ob temeritatis audaciam divina animadversione punitur ("Unit." 17).

The abettors of schisms, who must be compared to Core, Dathan and Abiron, can offer no excuse; they are still more blameworthy if they are men who, in the time of persecution, were courageous confessors ("Unit." 18-22). Hence the faithful must leave these culprits to their fate: "*Unus Deus est, et Christus unus, et una ecclesia eius, et fides una, et plebs una in solidam corporis unitatem concordiae glutino copulata: scindi unitas non potest, nec corpus unum discidio compaginis separari*" ("Unit." 23).

The allusion to the confessors who have done their duty during the persecution does not of course refer to the party of the Carthaginian *lapsi;* it refers to the Roman confessors, such as Maximus, Urbanus, Sidonius, Macarius, who have come back to the lawful Church, and it is, besides, a dexterous and honourable invitation extended to the other confessors, who, influenced by their rigorism, still adhere to Novatian. It is easy to recognize Novatian and the rigorist priests by whom he is surrounded, in those "*ministros iustitiae*" who preach "*desperationem sub obtentu spei*" ("Unit." 3).

Of all the arguments marshalled by Cyprian, there is not one which does not directly aim at Novatian as the chief abettor of schism: "*nemine episcopatum dante episcopi sibi nomen adsumunt*".[1] The controversial and occasional character of the "De Unitate" may help to excuse the weakness of some of its reasonings, which are more oratorical than conclusive. But when we have set aside considerations of this nature, we find that Cyprian bases the unity of the Church on two foundations.

The first is Christ's address to St. Peter.

The second is that the blessings imparted by Christ, especially baptism, the priesthood and the altar, belong to the legitimate Church and to no other. The principle laid down here by St. Cyprian will give rise later to the baptismal controversy, and we shall then have occasion to examine it more thoroughly. For the present we need only note that in the "De Unitate" this principle is strongly insisted on. Whoever is outside the Church is condemned by the words of the Saviour: "*Qui non mecum colligit spargit*" (Matt. XII. 30). Outside the Church, no baptism: "*Non abluuntur*

---

[1] "De Unit." 10 ; BENSON, p. 181. TILLEMONT, vol. IV. p. 105, had already surmised that Cyprian had in view Novatian, and not Felicissimus.

*illic homines*"; outside the Church, no sacrifice: "*Falsa sacrificia*"; outside the Church, no episcopate: "*Episcopi nomen*"; we may add: outside the Church, no martyrs.

The words of Christ to Peter furnish an argument which St. Cyprian has used in letters written before the "De Unitate". We have found it in the thirty-third Letter, sent to the *lapsi* of Carthage: where Cyprian finds in the words of Christ to St. Peter the institution of the episcopal dignity and the principle itself of the Church,[1] for the Church rests on the bishops. We have found it in the forty-third Letter, directed to all the faithful of Carthage: where Cyprian finds in the same words of Christ to St. Peter the affirmation that there is but one *cathedra* in each Church. We have found it in the forty-fifth Letter, addressed to Pope Cornelius: where Cyprian speaks of the unity that comes from Christ and comes from Christ to the bishops through the Apostles whose successors they are.[2]

---

[1] "Epistulae," XXXIII. 1: "Dominus noster, cuius praecepta metuere et servare debemus, episcopi honorem et ecclesiae suae rationem disponens in euangelio loquitur et dicit Petro. . . ." Cyprian dwells much on this point, perhaps because he means to refute Tertullian's theory regarding the merely ecclesiastical origin of the hierarchy (" Exhort. castit." 7).

[2] The author of the " De Aleatoribus " will later on take up the same argument. These are the words in which he, a bishop, speaks of his dignity: "Quoniam in nobis divina et paterna pietas apostolatus ducatum contulit, et vicariam Domini sedem caelesti dignatione ordinavit, et originem authentici apostolatus super quem Christus fundavit ecclesiam in superiore nostro portamus, accepta simul potestate solvendi ac ligandi et curatione peccata dimittendi . . ." "De Aleat." 1 (HARTEL, vol. III. p. 93). To us bishops God has entrusted the "leadership of the apostolate"; we hold the "vicarious seat of the Lord," i.e. we sit in the Church in the Lord's stead; "we bear in our ancestor," the Apostle Peter, the origin of the authentic apostolate; on this apostolate Christ has built His Church; together with Peter we have received the power to bind and to loose, the charge to remit sins. . . . Taken by itself, this text might seem to apply only to a Bishop of Rome. But it must be taken together with other passages of the same treatise, in which the author shows that he is an ordinary bishop, and then with some texts of Cyprian on the same subject. For Cyprian, Peter was the founder of the Roman Church, but Peter was first of the Apostles, in whose person Christ had formally founded that Church from which all other churches are genealogically derived. The unknown African bishop to whom we owe the "De Aleatoribus" was an imitator of Cyprian's style, and took from him this interpretation of the words of Christ to St. Peter. MONCEAUX, vol. II.

The interpretation which St. Cyprian applies to the text *Tu es Petrus* is based on the principle that what prevails in the Church of to-day has its reason and its law in what Christ laid down. We may compare the application of this principle Cyprian is about to make here with the application he makes of it elsewhere to the Eucharist: let us come back, he says in this latter case, "to the root and origin of the tradition of the Lord," and what Christ did, let us do with fidelity.[1] When Christ built His Church, He established it on one man, on Peter, "*super unum aedificat ecclesiam*": hence *a pari* every church is built upon one only.

We need not observe that St. Cyprian misunderstands the bearing of the text, *Tu es Petrus:* he deprives the words of Jesus of nearly all their real and historical meaning.[2] The Saviour is made to institute, not a primacy special to Peter over the whole Church, but the episcopal monarchy in each Church.

Are we to attribute this unnatural interpretation to an error of Cyprian regarding the nature of the Church? If all the Apostles received the same powers as Peter, if all the Apostles are equal, and Peter is without privilege, all the bishops are equal, and the see of Peter is without privilege. Has not the Bishop of Rome " the right to preside in a more effective manner over the Catholic unity," of which Peter was the starting-point, " to maintain it and to secure it by means of a sovereign intervention in the questions of faith

p. 115 : "If we read at the beginning of the ' De Aleat.' that its author is the vicar of the Lord, that he is the heir of the authentic apostolate on which Christ has built the Church, that he has the power to bind and to loose, and the mission to forgive sins, this means merely that he is a bishop. Cyprian and his African colleagues did not speak otherwise of their own functions." This is in reply to Harnack, who ascribes the "De Aleat." to Pope Victor, see BARDENHEWER, "Geschichte," vol. II. p. 447.

[1] "Epistulae," LXIII. 1 : ". . . ad radicem atque originem traditionis dominicae revertatur. . . . Quando aliquid Deo inspirante et mandante praecipitur, necesse est domino servus fidelis obtemperet." Cf. "Epistulae," LXXIII. 2 : "Nos autem qui ecclesiae unius caput et radicem tenemus. . . ." *Ibid.* 7 : "Petro primum Dominus, super quem aedificavit ecclesiam et unde unitatis originem instituit et ostendit. . . ."

[2] J. DELAROCHELLE [?], "L'idée de l'Eglise dans saint Cyprian," "Revue d'hist. et de litt. relig." vol. I. (1896), p. 528.

and discipline that may arise ?" No, "no more than any other bishop, at least if we keep to the absolute and theoretical point of view taken by Cyprian. . . . There is a universal episcopate, which comprises all the bishops; there is no universal bishop. Each bishop is really a centre of the Church, and the intercommunion of all the bishops makes the unity of the whole. . . . Of the bishops, the Bishop of Rome is the one who holds in his hands, so to speak, the threads of the universal communion; but he has nothing to do save to hold them; it is beyond his province to determine by himself the conditions of a communion of which he is not the head but the official representative. Christian unity has for its intimate cause the Holy Ghost, and for its external guarantee the obligation, binding upon all, not to abandon, not to divide, not to trouble the Church of Christ ".[1]

It may be said with more fairness that the treatise " De Unitate ecclesiae "—a controversial work written for a special occasion—does not set forth a system of the universal Church, in other words, of Catholicism: it is concerned exclusively with this thesis that in every Church there is room for but one bishop. The title of the treatise by no means comprises all that the identical title of Bossuet's sermon comprises. If it is true, as St. Fulgentius testifies, that Cyprian's treatise was sometimes entitled " De Simplicitate praelatorum," [2] this latter title, which is less authentic and less extensive, expressed much better the special point of view to which Cyprian confined himself.

When we view his treatise in this perspective we understand why he devotes his attention exclusively to the oneness of the *cathedra* in each church, and insists on it to such an extent as to seem to forget that the bishop, in each particular Church, is dependent on Catholicism as a whole: Cyprian and all the Christians were so clearly reminded of this by the traditional facts, by the institutions contemporary

---

[1] J. DELAROCHELLE, p. 531. HARNACK takes the same view in "Dogmeng." vol. i⁴, p. 418; MONCEAUX, vol. ii. p. 338; LIGHTFOOT, " Christian Ministry," p. 95 ; TURMEL, " Hist. du dogme de la papauté, vol. i. pp. 113 and 134.

[2] HARTEL, vol. i. p. 209.

with Cyprian himself, by the ecclesiastical customs, that he could afford to pass it over without mention. What would the councils, then in universal usage, have meant, if the bishop was amenable to God alone? Even supposing that Cyprian had purposely set aside the traditional Roman fact, can we say that he abstained with like deliberation from speaking of councils? No: Cyprian simply makes a strained application of the text *Tu es Petrus* to the one point he has in mind; and this is not the only case in which he sinned by one-sidedness.

As a demonstration of the necessity of unity in each church Cyprian's treatise was a success: he gained his point against Novatian, and gained it for all time. What a usurping bishop, and what an antipope, were in the eyes of faith, he showed in terms so striking that the principle of unity can nevermore be called in question; but the principle of unity applies to the universal Church just as well as to particular churches. As Bossuet has expressed it in a striking epigram, " unity is the guardian of unity " ; the unity of the chair of Peter safeguards both in doctrine and in discipline the unity of the whole episcopate. In the " De Unitate Ecclesiae " Cyprian did not reflect on this higher unity; and because he confined his attention to each bishop in each Church, he was led to lose sight of the guidance of the Holy Ghost promised to all. Catholic unity thus took on the appearance of a political confederacy, dependent on the ever unstable good will and the ever fallible freedom of individuals.[1]

---

[1] "These statements (of Cyprian), which savour of episcopalianism, are surprising, as coming from a man so much in love with unity, who so well realized the conditions of good government. They may be explained, not only by the heat of polemics, but also by the influence of Tertullian, whom St. Cyprian had much studied, and by the fact that he paid far more attention to the unity of each particular church, of which the bishop is the centre, than to the unity of the universal Church." TIXERONT, " Hist. des dogmes," vol. I. p. 387. We find the same judgment in D'ALÈS, " Question baptismale," pp. 40-41 : " Cyprian held by every fibre of his soul to the unity of the Church. . . . But of this [universal] unity, and of the prerogatives of St. Peter's successor, he had a rather unsettled idea. He conceives the episcopal power as an undivided mass in which every bishop shares according to his needs. . . . After showing that the Church is one flock, which is fed jointly by all the pastors, he does not think of defining the conditions of this unity, and he

So true is it that all the elements of the constitution of Catholicism hold together !

## EXCURSUS E.

### *The Two Editions of the "De Unitate ecclesiae".*

The " De Unitate ecclesiae " gives rise to a last problem—the problem of the well-known interpolation, which has been so long denounced as a hateful papistical forgery, and quite recently " as a Papal aggression upon history and literature ".[1]

This interpolation did not appear in the text of the *princeps* edition (Rome, 1471), nor in that of the subsequent editions. It appeared for the first time in the edition of Paul Manutius (Rome, 1563). It remained in the subsequent editions of James de Pamèle (Antwerp, 1568), of Rigault (1648), and of Dom Maran (Paris, 1726). On the other hand, the Anglican edition (Oxford, 1682) eliminated it with joy. A critical text was at last furnished by the edition of G. de Hartel (Vienna, 1868). But at the same time it was discovered that unfortunately the falsification perpetrated by the Papists did not originate with the printed edition but could be traced far back in the history of the MSS.

First, a family of MSS.—which we will designate by the

---

relies, for its actual realization, on the spontaneous agreement of all the individual wills in view of the common task, rather than on the central action of a strong government."

[1] BENSON, p. 219. The dispute has been wonderfully cleared up by DOM CHAPMAN, " Les interpolations dans le traité de S. Cyprien sur l'unite de l'Eglise," " Revue Bénédictine," v. xix. (1902), and v. xx. (1903). According to Harnack, Dom Chapman has proved indisputably that the interpolation contains nothing that is not Cyprianic, that it is specifically Cyprianic, that it is directed against Novatian, that it cannot be ascribed to an intellectual circle other than that of Cyprian. " Theologische Literaturzeitung," 1903, pp. 262-3. G. Krüger ("Theolog. Literaturzeitung," 1909, p. 413) writes : " Richtig ist, dass von Fälschung nicht mehr reden darf ". The objections raised by M. TURMEL, " Hist. du dogme de la papauté," vol. I. p. 109, proceed from an insufficient study of the question. For a continuation of the discussion see H. KOCH, " Cyprian und der Römische Primat " (Leipzig, 1910), pp. 158-69, and Dom Chapman's criticism of Koch (Professor Hugo Koch on S. Cyprian) in " Revue Bénédictine," Oct. 1910, pp. 447-64.

letter *C*—had combined the genuinè text and the interpolation: the archetypal MS. of that family is a MS. of the tenth century.[1]  A second group (*B*) of MSS. did not contain the interpolation, and this is the text adopted by Hartel as the genuine text: the MSS. on which it is based date back with the " Seguierianus " to the sixth or seventh century.[2]  A third group of MSS. (*A*) places the interpolation and the genuine text one after the other: the MSS. of this group are primarily represented by a Munich MS. of the ninth century, and a Troyes MS. of the eighth or ninth century.[3]

The following is the text *C :* we italicize the words taken from the text *A* :—

"*Et eidem post resurrectionem suam dicit : Pasce oves meas.*  Super *illum* unum aedificat ecclesiam *suam, et illi pascendas mandat oves suas.*  Et quamvis apostolis omnibus post resurrectionem suam parem potestatem tribuat et dicat: Sicut misit me Pater, et ego mitto vos, accipite Spiritum sanctum: si cui remiseritis peccata remittentur illi: si cui tenueritis tenebuntur, tamen ut unitatem manifestaret *unam cathedram constituit, et* unitatis eiusdem originem ab uno incipientem sua auctoritate disposuit.  Hoc erant utique et cæteri apostoli quod fuit et Petrus, pari consortio praediti et honoris et potestatis, sed exordium ab unitate proficiscitur, *et primatus Petro datur, ut una ecclesia Christi et cathedra una monstretur.  Et pastores sunt omnes, et grex unus ostenditur, qui et apostolis omnibus unanimi consensione pascatur ;* ut Ecclesia Christi una monstretur, quam unam Ecclesiam etiam in cantico canticorum Spiritus sanctus ex persona domini designat et dicit ; una est columba mea, perfecta mea, una est matri suae, electa genitrici suae. Hanc Ecclesiae unitatem qui non tenet, tenere se fidem credit?  Qui Ecclesiae renititur et resistit, *qui cathedram Petri super quam fundata est ecclesia deserit,* in ecclesia se esse confidit ? "

[1] The MS. Vossius is the MS. Lat. (in 8vo) 7 of the Leyden University Library.

[2] The MS. Séguier is the MS. Lat. 10592 of the Paris National Library.

[3] Munich 208 and Troyes 581.

This is the text printed by Paul Manutius at Rome. The words in italics, writes Benson, are "from the pen of one who held the cardinal doctrine of the Roman See," and the introduction of those words into the text has altogether misrepresented the thought of Cyprian. However, let us continue our inquiry.

We now give in a parallel the text *B* and the text *A* :—

| A | B |
|---|---|
| Et eidem post resurrectionem dicit : Pasce oves meas. | |
| Super illum aedificat ecclesiam et illi pascendas oves mandat. | Super unum aedificat ecclesiam. |
| Et quamvis apostolis omnibus parem tribuat potestatem | Et quamvis apostolis omnibus post resurrectionem suam parem potestatem tribuat et dicat : Sicut misit me Pater, et ego mitto vos. Accipite Spiritum sanctum : si cuius remiseritis peccata, remittentur illi : si cuius tenueritis tenebuntur, tamen ut unitatem manifestaret |
| unam tamen cathedram constituit, | |
| et unitatis originem atque rationem sua auctoritate disposuit. | unitatis eiusdem originem ab uno incipientem sua auctoritate disposuit. |
| Hoc erant utique et ceteri quod fuit Petrus, | Hoc erant utique et ceteri apostoli quod fuit Petrus, pari consortio praediti et honoris et potestatis, sed exordium ab unitate proficiscitur |
| sed primatus Petro datur et una ecclesia et cathedra una monstratur. | ut ecclesia Christi una monstretur. |
| Et pastores sunt omnes, sed grex unus ostenditur, qui ab apostolis omnibus unanimi consensione pascatur | |
| | Quam unam ecclesiam etiam in cantico canticorum Spiritus sanctus ex persona Domini designat et dicit : Una est columba mea, perfecta mea, una est matri suae, electa genitrici suae. |

| A. | B. |
|---|---|
| Hanc et Pauli unitatem [1] qui non tenet, tenere se fidem credit ? | Hanc ecclesiae unitatem qui non tenet, tenere se fidem credit ? |
| Qui cathedram Petri super quem fundata ecclesia est deserit, | Qui ecclesiae renititur et resistit, |
| in ecclesia se esse confidit ? | in ecclesia se esse confidit ? |
| Super unum aedificat, etc. | Quando et beatus apostolus Paulus hoc, etc. |

If we compare these three texts, we soon become certain that the text *C* is a skilful combination of *A* and *B*. Except the phrase *Quam unam . . . genitrici suae*, there is nothing in *C* that is not in *A* and *B*. The text *C* is, so to speak, a harmonizing text.

The text *A* is what English critics call a *conflation*. Given two readings for one and the same text, the copyist may choose the one or the other ; or he may transcribe them both one after the other. In the present case, the copyist of the archetypal MS. had before his eyes two parallel redactions of the same passage, and, in order not to have to make a choice, he merely copied them one after the other.

From this first critical examination we may infer that what was deemed an " interpolation," i.e. an addition introduced violently into the authentic text, is not an interpolation, but a variant. Now this variant goes far back into ecclesiastical antiquity. The twofold redaction preserved in the text *A* is given by MSS. (that of Munich and of Troyes) of which the common archetype may date from the sixth or the seventh century. Indeed we have guiding-marks that are still more precise : the text *C* is quoted by Pope Pelagius II towards the end of the sixth century, and the text *A* by Bede in the eighth century.[2]

Scholars are indebted to Dom Chapman for having thrown light on the character of this fact, which in itself had doubtless been previously observed : the text of *A* con-

---

[1] The words " *et Pauli* " yield no sense, not even if we try to find in them an allusion to some text of S. Paul (as Eph. v. 3-5) for *unitas Pauli* cannot signify " the unity which Paul preaches ". " *Et Pauli* " must then be a corruption, doubtless of *ecclesiae*. Cyprian had just said " *una ecclesia et cathedra una* ". He now resumes " *. . . ecclesiae* unitatem qui . . . qui cathedram Petri. . . .* "

[2] CHAPMAN, vol. XIX. pp. 249 and 361.

tains not a single word or expression that does not belong
to Cyprian's ordinary language and usage, and is not found
elsewhere in his writings:[1] so that we must conclude that
the forger either has contrived to make himself a perfect
facsimile of Cyprian, or else is no other than Cyprian himself.
This latter hypothesis is the more plausible because the author of the text *A* uses Cyprian's vocabulary with a freedom
that cannot be that of a skilful and learned imitator, doing a
kind of marquetry work.[2]   Dom Chapman can, then, conclude that most probably the text *A* represents an edition of
the "De Unitate" different from the edition represented by
the text *B*, both being the work of St. Cyprian.

We have not far to seek, continues Dom Chapman, for
occasions that might have evoked each of these different editions.   One or two months after the Council of Carthage in
May, 251, Cyprian is told of the return of the Roman confessors to the communion of Cornelius: he had sent them
his forty-sixth epistle to exhort them to return to the true
fold, and now he sends them his fifty-fourth epistle, together
with his two books "De Lapsis" and "De Unitate".   The
"De Lapsis" might enlighten them about the lawfulness of
the leniency condemned by Novatian, and the "De Unitate,"
which, according to Dom Chapman, was "written against
Felicissimus, might be used against any schism whatever."
But Cyprian felt the need of revising the central part of his
fourth chapter, to adapt to Rome what had applied to Carthage.   How much more forcibly "could he not appeal
to their love of unity, if he showed them that it was not
from an ordinary bishop that they were separating themselves, but from the see of St. Peter itself".[3]

We fully accept, with Harnack, Dom Chapman's attribution of both text *A* and text *B* to St. Cyprian; we cannot
however agree with him on this point of secondary importance, the date of text *A*.   It cannot be that Cyprian sends
to the Roman confessors the "De Lapsis" and the "De
Unitate," at the same time as his fifty-fourth epistle, since
he says in this very epistle that he had sent them these two
little books before their submission to Cornelius.   Referring

[1] CHAPMAN, vol. XIX. pp. 364-73.
[2] *Ibid.* vol. XX. p. 48.          [3] *Ibid.* p. 49.

in this epistle especially to the " De Unitate," he says to
the confessors who have made their peace with the Pope
" [*Hunc*] *libellum magis ac magis nunc vobis placere con-
fido :* I am sure that this book will be more acceptable to
you now . . . inasmuch as what we have written to you in
words, you fulfil in act, by returning to the Church in the
unity of charity and peace ".[1]  Since the " De Unitate " is
now more acceptable to them, we must suppose that they
had received it at a time when it was less acceptable—in
other words, at the time they were still outside unity
and in rebellion against Cornelius.  In fact, in his fifty-fourth
epistle, Cyprian does not say to the Roman confessors " I
send you " but I *had* sent you : " *Lectis quos hic* [at Carth-
age] *nuper* [in the Council of May] *legeram et ad vos quoque legendos pro communi dilectione transmiseram* ".  The
two words *legeram* and *transmiseram* suggest the simultane-
ousness of the two actions and lead us to think that Cyprian
had sent the " De Unitate " to the Roman confessors immediately after he had read it in the Council of Carthage.[2]

The " De Unitate," then—we may conclude—is syn-
chronous with the Carthaginian Council of May 251, and is
directed not against schism in general, but against Novatian's
schism at Rome.  We may add, with Dom Chapman, that
text *A* is not any kind of text, but a text that has in view
more directly than text *B* the faction of the Roman schismatics.[3]

---

[1] " Epistulae," LIV. 4.

[2] Nor do I think that Dom Chapman has proved that the " De
Unitate " is directed against Felicissimus.  The minute comparison which
Dom Chapman—vol. xx. pp. 30-3—makes between the " De Unitate "
and the " Epistula," XLIII., seems to me to prove, on the contrary, that
in the arguments common to both writings Novatian is substituted for
Felicissimus.  Thus (" Epistulae," XLIII. 5), the phrase " *Pacem nunc
offerunt qui ipsi non habent pacem*," which is most appropriate when
applied to the Carthaginian *lapsi*, is not to be found in the " De Unitate " (11), because it does not apply to Novatian's party.  But we read
some pages after (*ibid.* 13) : " Quam sibi igitur pacem promittunt inimici
fratrum ?  Quae sacrificia celebrare se credunt aemuli sacerdotum ? "
These words have a quite different meaning : the " peace " is the liturgical
peace, the " sacrifices " are the schismatic worship, and by " *aemuli sacerdotum* " illegitimate bishops are designated.

[3] CHAPMAN, vol. xx. pp. 40-5.

Text *B* lays special stress on the powers imparted by the Saviour to all the Apostles: "*. . . et dicat: Sicut misit me Pater, et ego mitto vos: Accipite Spiritum sanctum, si cuius. . . .*" It does not say merely: "*Hoc erant utique ceteri apostoli quod fuit Petrus*": it dwells upon and enlarges the affirmation: "*Hoc erant utique et ceteri apostoli quod fuit Petrus, pari consortio praediti et honoris et potestatis.*" Text *B* seems to insist on the equality between Peter and the other Apostles: to all the same honour, the same power. On the contrary, in text *A*, the powers of the other Apostles are not insisted on, but the authority of Peter is emphasized. To Peter and to Peter alone, it was said: "*Pasce oves meas*". On Peter, Christ builds the Church. To Peter He entrusts the feeding of His sheep. In the person of Peter, "*unam cathedram constituit*". And the first rank is given to Peter, "*primatus Petro datur*". Hence it is manifest that the Church is one, and that there is only one *cathedra*. This unity is more conspicuous at Rome, where the episcopal *cathedra* is that of Peter and where Paul came in person. Can the Roman who does not hold this unity "think that he holds the rule of faith"? "*Hanc . . . unitatem qui non tenet, tenere se fidem credit?*" Can the Roman who deserts that *cathedra* which is peculiarly that of Peter—that on which the Saviour founded the Church when He said *Tu es Petrus*—believe that he is in the Church? In other words, to abandon the *cathedra* of the bishop is everywhere an impiety but at Rome more so than anywhere else.

The conclusion we draw from these facts is the same as Dom Chapman's: text *A* is Cyprian's (as well as text *B*) and it has in view the party of Novatian at Rome.

But whereas Dom Chapman, thinking that the "De Unitate" was written against the faction of Felicissimus, has concluded that text *B* represented the original and the first edition, I believe on the contrary we may safely affirm, that the "De Unitate" having been originally written against the faction of Novatian the text *A* represents the original and the first edition. *B*—the so-called pure text—is a text corrected by St. Cyprian: these corrections are the result of a revision made by Cyprian in order perhaps to remove from his argument what was too special to Novatian's case, and thus render its bearing more universal.

## III.

We have seen how entirely Cyprian and Pope Cornelius agreed, and how, through his work "De Unitate ecclesiae," the Bishop of Carthage intended to come to the aid of the Church of Rome. At this particular moment—just a few days after the Council of Carthage in May, 251—there arose a cloud between the two bishops.

Felicissimus, going to Rome, had lodged with Pope Cornelius a complaint against the legitimacy of Cyprian's episcopacy, and Cornelius had thought it his duty to take the matter into consideration. This we know from the letter, full of dignity, which Cyprian writes to Cornelius to upbraid him for letting himself be intimidated by factious spirits. Cyprian in no way blames the Bishop of Rome for interfering in a matter that pertains to the inner life of the Carthaginian Church : the principle of the solidarity of the Churches—a principle so distinctly and authoritatively affirmed and put into practice by Cyprian—authorized in his eyes the solicitude of Cornelius. But he complains that the solicitude of the Bishop of Rome has been aroused by dishonest intriguers whose complaints deserved no attention. It was true that the party of Felicissimus had set up at Carthage a pseudo-bishop, Fortunatus (one of the Carthaginian priests who, as we have seen, had been an agitator from the beginning), but this Carthaginian schism was not of such importance that the Roman authorities should mind it : "*Non ea res erat quae in notitiam tuam deberet festinato statim quasi magna aut metuenda perferri*". Cyprian says to the Pope: " . . . *nec de hoc tibi scripseram, quando haec omnia contemnantur a nobis*".[1]

If we read attentively Cyprian's able letter, we perceive that the solicitude of Cornelius for the church of

---

[1] "Epistulae," LIX. 9.

Carthage somewhat troubles him. What has been the object of those adventurers? They cross the sea, they appeal to the chair of Peter, to that " *ecclesia principalis* " whence the unity of the priesthood took its rise, and yet they know well that the mind of all the African bishops is that causes be tried and judged on the spot, that bishops administer and rule the particular flock assigned to them, and give to God an account of their stewardship.

" Navigare audent et ad Petri cathedram atque ad ecclesiam principalem [1] unde unitas sacerdotalis exorta est [2] ab schismaticis et profanis litteras ferre? . . . Nam cum statutum sit ab omnibus nobis, et aequum sit pariter ac iustum, ut uniuscuiusque causa illic audiatur ubi est crimen admissum, et singulis pastoribus portio gregis sit adscripta quam regat unusquisque et gubernet, rationem sui actus Domino redditurus, oportet utique eos . . . agere illic causam suam ubi et accusatores habere et testes sui criminis possint, nisi si paucis desperatis et perditis minor videtur esse auctoritas episcoporum in Africa constitutorum, qui de illis iam iudicaverunt. . . . Iam causa eorum cognita est, iam de eis dicta sententia est, nec censurae congruit sacerdotum mobilis atque inconstantis animi levitate reprehendi. . . ." [3]

The case of Felicissimus has been tried and judged at Carthage by the bishops of Africa: if the appeal of a few condemned ecclesiastics can hold in check such a weighty

[1] These two famous words " *ecclesia principalis* " refer to the Roman Church, in which Cyprian recognizes the " *Cathedra Petri* ". We believe the meaning of the word " *principalis* " to be the one given already by Irenæus to *principalitas*, and by Tertullian to *auctoritas* (" Praescr." 36).

[2] Some have seen in these words an indication that the churches of Africa had been founded by the Roman Church. In reality, nothing at all is known of the origin of the Church of Carthage and of the African Churches. DUCHESNE, "Hist. anc." vol. I. p. 392. We believe that Cyprian is here recalling an idea on which he is insistent elsewhere, viz. that the Church built by Jesus on Peter is the Church to which all the other Churches stand in a filial relationship.

[3] " Epistulae," LIX. 14. The words " *minor videtur esse auctoritas episcoporum in Africa constitutorum* " imply that Felicissimus regards the authority of Rome as greater than the authority of the African council, in the sense that an appeal may be made to Rome from a sentence of the African council.

sentence, it is all over with the authority of the episcopate: "*Actum est de episcopatus rigore et de ecclesiae gubernandae sublimi ac divina potestate*".[1]

In his emotion over a case in which his own action was called in question Cyprian fails to estimate aright the competency of Rome.

\*\*

" The Council of Africa," Mgr. Duchesne writes, "had become a regular institution. The letters of St. Cyprian show that, except in times of persecution, it met at least once a year, in spring and sometimes also in autumn. These great periodical assemblies did much to maintain a uniform discipline. Their fame spread beyond Africa, and the reputation of the wise and illustrious man who was their very life and soul, added to their renown." [2] During the autumn of the year 254, the request of two Spanish bishops —the Bishop of Merida (*Emerita*), and that of Leon and Astorga (*Legio, Asturica*), was laid before the Council. These bishops—Sabinus and Felix—had succeeded respectively Basilides and Martialis, who had been deposed. But Basilides had gone to Rome, and obtained from Pope Stephen, for himself and probably for Martialis also, a sentence of restoration. The Council of Africa, before which the affair was brought, gave it an opposite solution: the African bishops confirmed the deposition of Basilides and Martialis, and the election of Sabinus and Felix. " It is hardly possible to decide which was in the right," says Mgr. Duchesne. We have no Roman document bearing on the question, but only the synodal letter of the thirty-seven African bishops announcing their judgment to the faithful of the two Spanish Churches.

But, was this a judgment, properly speaking? In the case of Felicissimus, had not Cyprian represented to Pope Cornelius that such cases must be tried on the spot, that the witnesses may be heard? The two Spanish Churches have

---

[1] " Epistulae," LIX. 2.

[2] " Hist. anc." vol. I. p. 419. With Benson, Harnack and Duchesne we suppose that the Spanish affair was previous to the baptismal controversy. But it is not unlikely that even at this date (autumn of the year 254) there was a rupture between Stephen and Cyprian.

written to Carthage in behalf of Felix and of Sabinus; these two bishops have joined their testimony to that of their two Churches; the Bishop of Saragossa, "*fidei cultor ac defensor veritatis*," has written in the same sense.[1]  The council of Carthage is asked, not exactly to judge, but rather to take cognizance of the sentence passed already in Spain, and to recognize the two bishops who, in Spain, are held to be legitimate.

The exceptional interest of the case lies in the fact that, Rome having pronounced in the contrary sense, we may suppose that the two Spanish Churches appealed in good faith to the Catholic world, beginning with Carthage and the Council of Africa.

At Carthage, this appeal was taken up with equal good faith.  Cyprian sided with Felix and Sabinus, because he deemed it well-established that Basilides and Martialis had been convicted of *gravia delicta*, and that, consequently, they could indeed be admitted to penance, but not maintained or re-established in the priestly order, according to the previous decisions of the whole episcopate and of Pope Cornelius: ". . . *cum iam pridem nobiscum, et cum omnibus omnino episcopis in toto mundo constitutis, etiam Cornelius collega noster, sacerdos pacificus ac iustus et martyrio quoque dignatione Domini honoratus decreverit*".[2]  What has been decreed by the whole episcopate must be observed.  But, we may say, it is hardly probable that Rome should think of setting aside such a wise and recent law: Rome then may have had good reasons for thinking that Basilides and Martialis were not guilty of the crimes with which they were charged.  Cyprian knew from his own experience that local intrigues and factions do not spare even the members of the episcopate.  But no, Basilides had gone to Rome to plead his innocence, and had deceived Pope Stephen: "*Romam pergens*," writes Cyprian, "*Stephanum collegam nostrum longe positum et gestae rei ac veritatis ignarum fefellit*".[3]

Rome was too far off, says Cyprian: but was the whole episcopate much nearer? we ask.

---

[1] "Epistulae," LXVII. 6.        [2] *Ibid.*        [3] *Ibid.* 5.

To this Cyprian replies that he must abide by the judgment of the two Spanish Churches. The *plebs*, he writes, that *plebs* which fears God and obeys the Lord's commands, must break with its bishop, if he is a sinner, since, after all, it has the right to choose worthy bishops and to refuse those who are unworthy: "*Plebs . . . a peccatore praeposito separare se debet, nec se ad sacrilegi sacerdotis sacrificia miscere, quando ipsa maxime habeat potestatem vel eligendi dignos sacerdotes, vel indignos recusandi*".[1] But, if an appeal to Rome imperils authority, is there not also a danger in granting to the *plebs* in every Church this right of deposing unworthy bishops?

There is something still more serious. We begin to discern in St. Cyprian's doctrine a tendency similar to that which we have noticed in Origen: upright and spotless candidates alone must be raised to the episcopate, because it must be certain that, when they pray for the people, they are heard of God.[2] The sacrifice offered by a bishop who is a sinner pollutes the people who partake of that sacrifice.[3] In a case which he deemed similar, that of Fortunatianus, Bishop of Assuras (in Africa), who had been deposed as a *lapsus* and yet persisted in exercising his priestly functions, Cyprian had declared that his followers must part company with him: "*quando nec oblatio sanctificari illic possit ubi sanctus Spiritus non sit, nec cuiquam Dominus per eius orationes et preces prosit qui Dominum ipse violavit*".[4] Cyprian confounds the lawful exercise of Orders with the power of Orders: a bishop, however great a sinner he may be, does not forfeit the power to consecrate the Eucharist and to offer up the sacrifice validly: the Church can take from him only the right to exercise this power; and

---

[1] "Epistulae," LXVII. 3.

[2] *Ibid.* 2 : "In ordinationibus sacerdotum non nisi immaculatos et integros antistites eligere debemus, qui sancte et digne sacrificia Deo offerentes audiri in precibus possint quas faciunt pro plebis dominicae incolumitate. . . . Eos oportet ad sacerdotium Dei deligi quos a Deo constet audiri."

[3] *Ibid.* 3. Cyprian ("Epistulae," LIX. 5) applies to the heretical bishops the text of Osee : "*Sacrificia eorum tamquam panis luctus, omnes qui manducant ea contaminabuntur*".

[4] *Ibid.* LXV. 4.

such is the doctrine held and professed at Rome, as we learn from a decision of Pope Callistus.[1] Cyprian, on the contrary, speaks in such a way that it may be inferred from his language that a bishop who has forfeited the Holy Ghost through his unworthiness, loses also, as a consequence, the power of Orders.[2]

\*\*\*

Soon after the affair of the two Spanish bishops, Cyprian received one after the other two letters from the Bishop of Lyons, Faustinus,[3] about the refusal of the Bishop of Arles, Marcianus, to follow the practice sanctioned by the whole episcopate in the year 251, regarding the reconciliation of the *lapsi*: Marcianus clung to the rigorism of Novatian. The Bishop of Lyons, together with " *caeteris coepiscopis nostris in eadem provincia constitutis,*" had denounced Marcianus to Rome at the same time as to Carthage, as a bishop who departed " *a catholicae ecclesiae veritate* " and " *a corporis nostri et sacerdotii consensione,*" and embraced " *hereticae praesumptionis durissimam pravitatem* ".[4]

Cyprian must have been somewhat disconcerted on hearing of the conduct of the Bishop of Arles, for it was in flagrant contradiction with his theory that the whole episcopate was bound together by a cordial understanding. That pseudo-bishops should be set up at Carthage or at Rome, did not greatly affect his theory of the Church ; but that a legitimate bishop, like Marcianus, and he the bishop of a great see like Arles, should attempt to disregard a disciplinary measure which had been adopted hardly four years before by the whole episcopate, that he should dare thus to insult the episcopal college, was a clear indication that the unity of unities, as described by Cyprian, was more precarious than he had thought.

Had he been faithful to the doctrine of his letter to the Spaniards, Cyprian ought to have written to the *plebs* of

---

[1] "Philosophoumena," IX. 12.

[2] On the way in which, because of his speaking thus, the Donatists used to quote Cyprian in their favour, see MONCEAUX, vol. II. p. 465.

[3] " Epistulae," LXVIII. 1. This incident occurred probably at the beginning of the year 255.

[4] *Ibid.*

Arles, and invited them to break with such an heretical bishop as Marcianus. He did nothing of the kind. Or, again, as, according to his theory, a provincial council judges supremely the causes arising in its province, he ought to have written to the Bishop of Lyons and to his *coepiscopi*, and exhorted them to excommunicate Marcianus and choose a successor in his stead. This likewise he failed to do. The step he decided to take was the one we should least expect of him, seeing the principles he had previously laid down : he wrote to Pope Stephen and asked him to intervene with the bishops of Gaul. " Facere te oportet plenissimas litteras [1] ad coepiscopos nostros in Gallia constitutos, ne ultra Marcianum pervicacem et superbum et divinae pietatis ac fraternae salutis inimicum,[2] collegio nostro insultare patiantur. . . . Quam vanum est, frater carissime, ut Novatiano nuper retuso et refutato et per totum orbem a sacerdotibus Dei abstento, nunc adulatores adhuc nobis patiamur inludere, et de maiestate ac dignitate Ecclesiae iudicare." [3]

" Dirigantur in provinciam et ad plebem Arelate consistentem a te litterae quibus abstento Marciano alius in loco eius substituatur." [4]

[1] By " plenissimas litteras " we must understand a reasoned and forcible letter. It is a literary expression.

[2] " Salutis inimicum " refers to the rigorism of Marcianus who refuses to reconcile the *lapsi*. Cyprian (*ibid.* 2) speaks of Christians whom Marcianus *annis istis superioribus*, had refused to reconcile to the Church before their death. Hence Marcianus was Bishop of Arles at least as early as the year 250. This inference tells against the statement of Gregory of Tours, according to whom St. Trophimus came from Rome to Arles, precisely in the year 250.

[3] *Ibid.* 2.

[4] *Ibid.* 3. According to Benson, Cyprian begs Stephen to write two letters : one to the bishops of Gaul, telling them to excommunicate Marcianus ; the other, to the *plebs* of Arles, who will choose a successor to their excommunicated bishop. BENSON, p. 318. But we need not thus divide the action to be taken : the Pope is to write " in provinciam et ad plebem consistentem ". The only delicate question is to know who excommunicates Marcianus. It is Rome, no doubt. Once the sentence is pronounced at Rome, it will be carried out by the bishops of Gaul and the *plebs* of Arles, who will choose a bishop for the see which is treated as vacant. Cyprian writes : ". . . litterae *quibus* abstento Marciano alius in loco eius substituatur ". Harnack ("Dogmeng." vol. 1[4], p. 494)

" Significa plane nobis quis in locum Marciani Arelate fuerit substitutus, ut sciamus ad quem fratres nostros dirigere et cui scribere debeamus."[1]

In the body of the letter itself, Cyprian enumerates the motives that should induce Stephen to intervene : it is necessary to rescue the souls Marcianus is abandoning and driving into despair through his rigorism ; it is necessary to uphold the discipline sanctioned by Pope Cornelius and his successor Lucius, and, since he is their successor, Stephen is more bound to see to this than any other bishop. After such good, but general reasons, why does not Cyprian personally intervene at Arles? Why does he urge the Bishop of Rome alone to move in the matter? The conduct of the Bishop of Carthage in this conjuncture is in contradiction with his previous declarations.

Does not this show that it was the Bishop of Carthage, and the Council of Carthage which acted under his influence, that had been innovating, in their previous declarations? Felicissimus of Carthage, when he lays before the Roman Church the complaint of his party against the legitimacy of Cyprian's election, attests that in Africa the traditional Roman fact is accepted and that it is deemed lawful to appeal in a case involving the deposition of bishops to the judgment of the *ecclesia principalis;* Basilides attests the same when he appeals to the same Roman Church from the sentence which had deprived him of the see of Leon, and Martialis of the see of Astorga. The Bishop of Lyons and the other bishops of Gaul have applied to the Roman Church to bring to his senses, or—if need be—to depose the Bishop of Arles. Cyprian's letter to Stephen, which acquaints us with this fact, expresses approval of the step taken by the Gallic episcopate. The Bishop of Lyons is faithful to the tradition of St. Irenæus, from whom he is separated by hardly two generations : what we may venture to call the ultramontanism of Faustinus, of Basilides, and even of the un-

admits that the Bishop of Rome has over the Bishop of Arles a power which the bishops of Gaul have not. So too do Sohm (" Kirchenrecht," p. 381), and Ritschl (" Cyprian," p. 228).

[1] " Salutis inimicum ". These last words imply that the case of Marcianus will be satisfactorily judged at Rome.

fortunate Felicissimus, appears far better authorized to call itself traditional Catholicism than is the restless and inconsistent provincialism of the Africans.

Gallicanism and Donatism—those two grave errors on the constitution of Catholicism—were, then, involved in these disputes. An action of Cyprian is about to cause the controversy to spread to the whole Church, and Rome is about to speak. We are come to the climax of the early history of ecclesiology.

## IV.

Cyprian caused a question to be put to him by Magnus, a layman of distinction, and he answers in an epistle which is less a letter than a treatise. Must those heretics who have received baptism from heretics, be baptized when they come to the Catholic Church? Magnus explains that there is no question of re-baptism, but only whether baptism given by heretics, and especially by the Novatians, is not to be regarded as a profane cleansing, whether we are not to hold that the Church alone imparts valid baptism. Cyprian answers: heretics and schismatics have neither the right nor the power to administer baptism.[1]

The question had already been under consideration. As we shall see, the absolute rejection of heretical baptism had been pronounced by the Council of Africa some thirty years before; a similar decision had been taken by several councils of Asia Minor, about the same time; as likewise at Antioch and in Northern Syria. On the other hand, at Alexandria, in Palestine, and especially at Rome, it was admitted that baptism strictly so called could not be repeated—indeed in those quarters, this was deemed a point that did not need discussion. What was invalid in such cases was the at-

---

[1] "Epistulae," LXIX. 1 : ". . . an inter ceteros haereticos eos quoque qui a Novatiano veniunt post profanum eius lavacrum baptizari et sanctificari in ecclesia catholica legitimo et vero et unico ecclesiae baptismo oporteat. De qua re . . . dicimus omnes omnino haereticos et schismaticos nihil habere potestatis ac iuris". This letter dates probably from the early months of the year 255. See A. D'ALÈS, "La Question baptismale au temps de Saint Cyprien," printed separately from the "Revue des Quest. hist." April, 1907.

tempt to confer the Holy Ghost through the imposition of the hands of heretics : this alone, it was maintained, must be repeated by the bishops in the case of heretics who wished to enter the Catholic Church.[1]

Cyprian would not have suggested to Magnus to put the question to him, had not this disagreement between Rome and Carthage, on a matter affecting the conditions of salvation, become a subject of scruples for many of the faithful. It is this which must account for the care he takes to enlighten Magnus. He enumerates the Biblical proofs which justify the African custom. The most conclusive text is unquestionably the one in which Christ says : " *Si ecclesiam contempserit sit tibi tanquam ethnicus et publicanus* " (Matt. XVIII. 17). From this text it may be inferred that heretics and schismatics are to be treated as pagans and publicans, inasmuch as in their rebellion against the Church they erect false altars, appoint unlawful bishops, offer up sacrilegious sacrifices, and lie in all that they promise.[2]

Cyprian did not allow himself to be restricted to the casuistry of the problem : he saw at once the far-reaching importance of the controversy that was then beginning. Whereas, in the " De Unitate," he considered only the unity in each Church and purposely confined the dispute within limits, he has now in view only the universal Church.

In fact, there is but one Church, and of this Church it is said : " *Hortus conclusus soror mea sponsa, fons signatus, puteus aquae vivae* " (*Cant.* IV. 12). The Church is this closed garden, closed against the profane and the strangers. Whoever is outside cannot approach this sealed spring, this well of living water ; those only can baptize with its water, who are within the closed garden. The Church is the ark of Noe : could any one be saved outside the ark ? St. Paul declares that Christ loved the Church, and gave Himself for her, that He might sanctify her, *purgans eam lavacro aquae* (Eph. V. 25-26) ; can any one expect to be cleansed in this bath outside the Church ?[3]

But, some may object, the faith of the Novatians is the same as that of the Church. Not at all, Cyprian answers.

---

[1] DUCHESNE, " Hist. anc.," vol. I. p. 422.
[2] " Epistulæ," LXIX. 1.   Cf. 3-6.               [3] *Ibid.* 2.

Their creed is not our creed, or they lie when they profess our creed; for the Church is mentioned in our Creed, but they have not got the Church; and forgiveness of sins is likewise mentioned in it, but they do not believe in this forgiveness through the Church.[1]  As to God the Father, Christ and the Holy Ghost, in whose name they baptize, we grant that they believe in them: but had not Core, Dathan and Abiron the same faith as Moses?  Still, not the less on that account were they struck by God, although they were less guilty than Novatian, since they only disputed the censer with Aaron, whereas Novatian contends for "*cathedram et primatum*," the chair and the primacy, and at the same time claims the privilege of baptizing and offering up the Holy Sacrifice, "*baptizandi atque offerendi licentiam*" (*ibid.* 8).

We may go still further: inasmuch as they disobey the Church and are stubborn in their disobedience, the heretics and schismatics show that they have not the Holy Ghost. Hence, even supposing they could baptize, they could not give the Holy Ghost.  But this is asserting too little: whoever has not the Holy Ghost cannot even baptize (*ib.* 10). For baptism forgives sins, and sins are forgiven only by those who have the Holy Ghost, according to the text: "*Accipite Spiritum sanctum, si cuius remiseritis peccata, remittentur ei*" (John xx. 22).  Now the heretics and schismatics do not give what they have not: "*Cuncti haeretici et schismatici non dant Spiritum Sanctum*".[2]  The Church alone possesses the Holy Ghost.

Cyprian had declared and defended his belief in his letter to Magnus: he succeeded in getting it approved in the Council of Africa held in the autumn of the year 255. He himself composed the synodal letter with his own hand. This document was addressed to eighteen bishops of Numidia who had, in a letter, laid before the Council assembled at Carthage, the question of the validity of the baptism of

---

[1] "Epistulae," LXIX. 7.  Here he falls into the fallacy of confusing baptismal and penitential discipline.  The mention of the Church in the baptismal creed is attested by Tertullian and by Marcion.  HAHN, p. 387.

[2] *Ibid.* 11.

heretics. These Numidian bishops, impressed by the contrary custom followed at Rome, had evidently misgivings as to the lawfulness of the custom followed in Africa.[1]

At the outset Cyprian states that the Bishops of Numidia, who have questioned the Council, keep what he calls "*veritatem et firmitatem catholicae regulae*," viz. the principle that the baptism of heretics is null. He urges also an argument not mentioned in his letter to Magnus: namely, that this principle is not new but had been laid down long before by the Bishops of Africa and had been observed by them.[2] This argument would seem to imply that the bishops of Numidia had alleged a more ancient custom than the one then prevailing.

Another argument which is hardly mentioned in the letter to Magnus, but to which the Council seems to have attached a decisive importance, is that, among heretics, the minister of baptism cannot confer it validly, because the baptismal water must first be cleansed and sanctified by the bishop: but how could it be cleansed by a minister who is not clean, and sanctified by a minister who has not the Holy Ghost?[3] Again, the baptized neophyte must be anointed with the oil of chrism sanctified by the bishop upon the altar: but how could it be sanctified by a minister who has neither an altar, nor a church, nor a Eucharist? Still more precisely: the validity of the sanctification of the oil and of the bread on the altar depends upon the intervention of the Holy Spirit: now heretics have not the Holy Spirit. "*Quis autem potest dare quod ipse non habeat, aut quomodo potest spiritalia gerere qui ipse amiserit Spiritum sanctum?*"[4]

---

[1] "Epistulae," LXX. 1.

[2] *Ibid.*: " . . . sententiam nostram non novam promimus, sed iam pridem ab antecessoribus nostris statutam et a nobis observatam vobiscum. . . . " Tertullian, "De Baptismo," 15, upheld the doctrine now advocated by Cyprian.

[3] *Ibid.* 1: " . . . quomodo autem mundare et sanctificare aquam potest qui ipse immundus est et apud quem sanctus Spiritus non est?" Hence Cyprian urges two reasons against the validity of heretical baptism: first, the unworthiness of the minister; secondly, the absence of the Holy Spirit.

[4] *Ibid.* 2. Cf. *ibid.* 3: "Si autem sanctum Spiritum dare non potest quia foris constitutus cum sancto Spiritu non est, nec baptizare venientem potest, quando et baptisma unum sit, et Spiritus sanctus unus, et una

Notwithstanding the arguments from tradition and from theological reasons brought forward by Cyprian in its behalf, the decision of the Council of Carthage of the year 255 met with opposition in Africa. This we see from the letter sent by Cyprian to a Bishop of Mauritania, Quintus, who had despatched to Carthage the priest Lucian, in order to learn what to believe. In reply, Cyprian sends him the synodal letter of the council of Carthage of the year 255, accompanied with a short commentary.

The point of fact, to which Cyprian had merely alluded in the synodal epistle, is now clearly stated: a Council of Carthage held under the episcopate of Agrippinus, about the year 220, was the first council to lay down the principle that baptism by heretics is always null.[1]

On the other hand, those African bishops who uphold the validity of the baptism of heretics, oppose to the authority of the two Councils of Carthage (the Council of the year 220 and that of the year 255) a custom which they believe to be ancient: "*Dicunt se in hoc veterem consuetudinem sequi*". Somewhat brusquely Cyprian sets aside this mode of argument, and, with Tertullian in his mind, ventures to lay down the principle, "*Non est de consuetudine praescribendum, sed ratione vincendum*".[2]

ecclesia a Christo Domino nostro super Petrum origine unitatis et ratione fundata. Ita fit ut cum omnia apud illos inania et falsa sint, nihil eorum quod illi gesserint probari a nobis debeat."

[1] "Epistulae," LXXI. 4 : "Quod quidem et Agrippinus bonae memoriae vir cum ceteris coepiscopis suis qui illo tempore in provincia Africa et Numidia ecclesiam Domini gubernabant statuit, et librata consilii communis examinatione firmavit. Quorum sententiam religiosam et legitimam, salutarem fidei et ecclesiae catholicae congruentem, nos etiam secuti sumus." Cf. "Epistulae," LXXIII. 3 : " . . . quando anni sint iam multi et longa aetas, ex quo sub Agrippino," etc.

[2] *Ibid.* 2 and 3. Compare the anonymous treatise "De Rebaptismate," 1 (HARTEL, vol. III.), which affirms that the Roman custom is upheld "vetustissima consuetudine ac traditione ecclesiastica," and "observatione antiquissima". *Ibid.* 3 : "Ad quae forte tu, qui novum quid inducis. . . ." *Ibid.* 6 : ["Utile est] tot annorum totque ecclesiarum itemque apostolorum et episcoporum auctoritati cum bona ratione adquiescere, cum sit maximum incommodum ac dispendium sanctissimae matris ecclesiae adversus prisca consulta post tot saeculorum tantam seriem nunc primum repente ac sine ratione insurgere." The treatise "De Rebaptismate" was written by an African bishop who upheld the

What was the decisive reason for the bishops who hold that the baptism of heretics is valid? There is only one baptism, they say. But Cyprian replies: Of course, there is only one baptism, and this is why we do not *re*baptize, but baptize; and if we baptize the heretics that become converts, it is because outside the Church no one can baptize, and because nothing can be received from him who has nothing to give. How imprudent are those bishops who honour heretics so far as to acknowledge in them the power of giving valid baptism, who "set the filthy and profane washing of heretics above the true and only and lawful baptism of the Catholic Church, not reflecting that it is written: "*Qui baptizatur a mortuo, quid proficit lavatione eius?*" (Eccli. XXXI. 30)."[1]

During the early part of the year 256, the discussion was still going on: the Bishop of Carthage had not been able to overcome the opposition which the African doctrine encountered even in Africa. The Council held at Carthage, a short while before Easter, had again to take up the question. The seventy-one bishops of Africa and Numidia, who were present, declared their accord with Cyprian and confirmed the declaration of the Council of the year 255: " . . . *Hoc idem denuo sententia nostra firmavimus, statuentes unum baptisma esse quod sit in ecclesia catholica constitutum* ".[2]

St. Cyprian wrote immediately to Pope Stephen and told him of this decision, which he thought well calculated to strengthen both unity and episcopal authority, the two principles which lay so close to his heart.

*⁂*

On their arrival at Rome, Cyprian's delegates were received as heretics: they were denied communion and hospitality; Pope Stephen refused even to listen to them. At Rome, at this time, Cyprian was treated as a false Christ, a false Apostle, a deceitful worker.[3]

Roman teaching on baptism: it was composed probably immediately before the Council of Africa held in September, 256.

[1] " Epistulae," LXXI. 1.          [2] *Ibid.* LXXIII. 1.

[3] As to the date of this episode, cf. DUCHESNE, " Hist. anc.," vol. I. p. 425.

This change of attitude on the part of the Romans would be inexplicable, had we not some reason for thinking that Rome had made a pronouncement a short time before, and that Cyprian, together with the Council of Africa, had ignored this decision, just as they had done previously in the case of the two Spanish bishops.[1] If so, Cyprian's epistle to Jubaianus (written in the summer of the year 256) will have been an intended censure of the doctrine as affirmed by Pope Stephen, especially of the underlying principle to which Cyprian thus refers : Let not any one, he says, plead against us, for the circumvention of Christian truth, the power of the name of Christ, or say : "*In nomine Jesu Christi*[2] *ubicumque et quomodocumque*[3] *gratiam baptismi sunt consecuti*."[4]

After speaking with this firmness, Rome could not allow that the question was still unsettled. Still less could it permit the Bishop of Carthage to send to Pope Stephen the following ill-inspired lines :—

"Haec ad conscientiam tuam, frater carissime, et pro honore communi et pro simplici dilectione pertulimus, cre-

---

[1] See " Epistulae," LXXIII. 4, an allusion to a (Roman ?) letter, which is no longer extant. DUCHESNE, op. cit. p. 424. Cyprian answers this letter in his epistle to Jubaianus.

[2] By baptism in the name of Jesus Christ, we must understand baptism given in the name of the Father, and of the Son and of the Holy Ghost : Pope Stephen could not think of any other rite. In his invective against Stephen, Firmilian writes : " Illud quoque absurdum quod non putant [i.e. the Romans] quaerendum esse quis sit ille qui baptizaverit, eo quod qui baptizatus sit gratiam consequi potuerit invocata trinitate nominum Patris et Filii et Spiritus sancti." " Epistulae," LXXV. 9. Cf. " Epistulæ," LXXIII. 18. Compare the letter of Dionysius of Alexandria to Philemon (EUSEB. " H. E." VII. 7 : τοῦτον ἐγὼ τὸν κανόνα κ.τ.λ.). FELTOE, " Letters of D. of A." (Cambridge, 1904), pp. 53-4.

[3] These two words—*ubicumque, quomodocumque*, do not imply that any form suffices, but that any minister, *servatis servandis*, suffices. Tertullian (" De Baptismo," 17) teaches that the bishop is the ordinary minister of baptism, but that in case of necessity baptism can be given by laymen : ". . . etiam laicis ius est ; . . . baptismus ab omnibus exerceri potest ". Pope Stephen abides by this principle, whereas Cyprian disregards it.

[4] " Epistulae," LXXIII. 16. Compare " De Rebaptismate," 10 : " Reddamus et permittamus virtutibus caelestibus vires suas," etc.

dentes etiam tibi pro religionis tuae et fidei veritate placere quae et religiosa pariter et vera sunt.

" Ceterum scimus quosdam quod semel inbiberint nolle deponere nec propositum suum facile mutare, sed salvo inter collegas pacis et concordiae vinculo quaedam propria quae apud se semel sint usurpata retinere.  Qua in re nec nos vim cuiquam facimus, aut legem damus, quando habeat in ecclesiae administratione voluntatis suae arbitrium liberum unusquisque praepositus, rationem actus sui Domino redditurus." [1]

These are painful words, especially in view of the contradictions in which we feel that Cyprian is becoming more and more entangled.  He holds, or at least he held but recently, that the doctrine of the nullity of heretical baptism is an article of the " catholica regula " ; now he declares this article to be one of those on which bishops may differ among themselves, without detriment to concord.  He disclaims any intention to impose authoritatively anything on anybody, since every bishop enjoys autonomy in his own territory and is amenable to God alone for his administration : it is strange that the Bishop of Carthage should speak thus after his action in the case of Marcianus of Arles.  It is strange, again, that he should speak of concord which is above all things, at the very moment when he claims for bishops the right to be discordant, and seems to withdraw all primacy from the Roman Church.

Stephen answered Cyprian in a letter of which the decisive passage alone is extant :—

" Si qui ergo a quacumque haeresi venient ad vos, nihil innovetur nisi quod traditum est, ut manus illis imponatur

---

[1] " Epistulae," LXII. 3.  Similar insinuations are found in the letter to Quintus (LXXI. 1) : " Quidam de collegis nostris malunt haereticis honorem dare quam nobis consentire ".  " Nec Petrus, quem primum Dominus elegit et super quem aedificavit ecclesiam suam, cum secum Paulus de circumcisione postmodum disceptaret, vindicavit sibi aliquid insolenter aut adroganter adsumpsit, ut diceret se primatum tenere et obtemperari a novellis et posteris sibi potius oportere, nec despexit Paulum. . . ." (*ibid.* 3).  These last lines reveal both the authority which Cyprian felt was armed against him at Rome, and the bitterness he felt about it. This was in the beginning of the year 256.

in paenitentiam, cum ipsi haeretici proprie alterutrum ad se venientes non baptizent, sed communicent tantum." [1]

We may place this sort of edict side by side with that of Callistus regarding penance: in both the same authority speaks in the same style. Unlike Callistus, this authority does not now address the Roman community; it addresses the Bishop of Carthage and all the African Bishops, and in addressing them lays down the law in such terms as to convey the impression that it expects, indeed is sure, to be obeyed. Writing to Stephen, Cyprian had said: "We neither do violence to any, nor lay down a law—*aut legem damus*—since each bishop has, in the government of his Church, the free control of his will, and owes an account of his conduct to the Lord only ". In answer to those imprudent words, Rome intimated to him the *law*.

It may be that Pope Stephen used harsh words in his communication to the Bishop of Carthage ; but all we know of the matter is from Cyprian, who, under the influence of too human an emotion, may have been led to find everything in Pope Stephen's decision "arrogant, irrelevant, contradictory, unlearned, short-sighted ".[2] Evidently the soul of Cyprian was more primitive than that of Fénelon ! It was likely that he would regard Stephen's allusions to the

---

[1] "Epistulae," LXXIV. 1. Cf. EUSEB. " H. E." VII. 3, who gives the true meaning of the formula, *nihil innovetur nisi quod traditum est* : Μὴ δεῖν τε νεώτερον παρὰ τὴν κρατήσασαν ἀρχῆθεν παράδοσιν ἐπικαινοτομεῖν. We must not make any innovation contrary to the tradition which has been held from the beginning. The same meaning is also assigned by Vincent of Lerins, "Commonitor." I. 6. The translation given by Eusebius is preferable to that given by Tillemont and Bossuet, according to whom, Stephen meant to say that nothing must be repeated except what tradition declares must be repeated, i.e. not baptism, but the imposition of hands. Compare the " *Nihil innovandum* " of the letter of the Roman clergy to Cyprian ("Epistulae," XXX. 8) and the " *Nihil innovetur* " of Cyprian's letter to his people ("Epistulae," XLIII. 3). The formula " *Manus illis imponatur in paenitentiam* " is understood by St. Cyprian as though it meant " manum imponere ad accipiendum Spiritum Sanctum ". " Epistulae," LXXII. 1. It must be confessed, however, that the formula of Pope Stephen, as we have it in the document above quoted, is ambiguous. So also is the formula in the " De Rebaptismate," 2-6.

[2] *Ibid.* : " Nam inter cetera vel superba, vel ad rem non pertinentia, vel sibi ipsi contraria, quae imperite atque improvide scripsit. . . ."

traditional Roman fact as arrogant and out of place; for to justify the Roman custom regarding baptism, Stephen had cited the Apostles to whom he traced it back.[1] He invoked the Apostles Peter and Paul, as his surest authorities.[2] But he appealed also to the authority of his own episcopal chair, not that of his Church merely: an authority he justified by the fact that, sitting in that chair, he was the heir of St. Peter. This we learn from Firmilian, who tells us how vexed he felt about it: "Atque ego in hac parte iuste indignor ad hanc tam apertam et manifestam Stephani stultitiam, quod qui sic de episcopatus sui loco gloriatur[3] et se successionem Petri tenere contendit, super quem fundamenta Ecclesiae collocata sunt. . . . Stephanus qui per successionem cathedram Petri habere se praedicat."[4]

Pope Stephen, then, affirmed the primacy of the see of Rome—a primacy dating back to St. Peter and giving to the Bishop of Rome a right over the other bishops of the Christian world.

The Council of Africa, which met at Carthage on 1 Sept-

---

[1] This argument of Stephen is known to us through Firmilian, "Inter Cypriani Epistul." LXXV. 5 : " Et quidem quantum ad id pertineat quod Stephanus dixit, quasi apostoli eos qui ab haeresi veniunt baptizari prohibuerint et hoc custodiendum posteris tradiderint, plenissime vos respondistis neminem tam stultum esse qui hoc credat apostolos tradidisse," under the pretext that heresies arose a long while after the Apostolic age. In his letter to Jubaianus, some time before receiving Stephen's answer, Cyprian had already refused to accept this argument based on the Apostles, " Epistulae," LXXIII. 13 : " Nec quisquam dicat : Quod accepimus ab apostolis hoc sequimur ". *Ibid.* 9 : " Quod autem quidam dicunt," etc.

[2] This we know also from Firmilian, LXXV. 6 : " Quod nunc Stephanus ausus est facere, rumpens adversus vos pacem, quam semper antecessores eius vobiscum amore et honore mutuo custodierunt, adhuc etiam infamans Petrum et Paulum beatos apostolos, quasi hoc ipsi tradiderint. . . ."

[3] A bishop speaks of his rank, *locus*, that is, in the *ordo* of the Church in which he has the primacy, *primatum*, over the priests, the deacons, and so on. On the contrary, Stephen glories in the rank of his episcopate, in comparison to the other bishops : *de episcopatus sui loco gloriatur*. This distinction is to be noticed, and agrees well with the claim to be the bishop of bishops.

[4] " Epistulae," LXXV. 17. We may recall the allusions of Cyprian (" Epistulae," LXXI. 3, quoted above) to the humility of Peter who was not so arrogant as to assume primacy over Paul, and so on.

ember, 256, under the presidency of St. Cyprian, took upon itself to answer the Bishop of Rome.

On opening the session, Cyprian had three letters read to the assembled bishops: the letter he had received from Jubaianus, the letter he had sent to Jubaianus, and the letter in which Jubaianus thanked Cyprian and declared he fully accepted the teaching of the Bishop of Carthage as to the nullity of heretical baptisms. Nothing was read from the correspondence of Stephen, his name was not even mentioned;[1] and yet there was no bishop more present than he to that Council of Africa whose members were greatly disturbed by the lesson the Bishop of Rome had just given to the Bishop of Carthage. The deliberation was opened: in acting as we are doing, Cyprian declared, "we do not judge any one, or deprive any one of the right of communion, if he differs from us. For no one of us sets himself up as a bishop of bishops, or by tyrannical terror forces his colleagues to obey; every bishop, in the full use of his liberty and power, has the right of forming his own judgment, and can no more be judged by another than he can himself judge another". Bishops deliberating in council begin by proclaiming their individual autonomy, so assured are they of their unanimity! And the Bishop of Rome is forbidden to make his voice heard: *"Neque enim quisquam nostrum episcopum se episcoporum constituit"!*[2] One after the other, the eighty-seven bishops gave their vote and stated its grounds: they held no other doctrine than that of Cyprian. One of

---

[1] See, however ("Sententiae," 8) the sententia of Crescens, Bishop of Cirta. The Council of 1 September met after Stephen's decree had reached Carthage. DUCHESNE, "Hist. anc." vol. I. p. 426.

[2] "Sententiae episcoporum" (inter Cypriani opera, ed. HARTEL, vol. I. p. 435 and foll.), prologue. The text is as follows: "Superest ut de hac ipsa re singuli quid sentiamus proferamus, neminem iudicantes aut a iure communicationis aliquem, si diversum senserit, amoventes. Neque enim quisquam nostrum episcopum se episcoporum constituit, aut tyrannico terrore ad obsequendi necessitatem collegas suos adigit, quando habeat omnis episcopus pro licentia libertatis et potestatis suae arbitrium proprium, tamque iudicari ab alio non possit, quam nec ipse possit alterum iudicare. Sed expectemus universi iudicium Domini nostri Iesu Christi, qui unus et solus habet potestatem et praeponendi nos in ecclesiae suae gubernatione, et de actu nostro iudicandi." D'ALÈS, "Quest. bapt." pp. 26-7, suggests a more favourable interpretation of Cyprian's words.

them, Zosimus, Bishop of Tharassa, made use of these words : *" Revelatione facta veritatis cedat error veritati, quia et Petrus qui prius circumcidebat cessit Paulo veritatem prae- dicanti"*.[1] Rome was summoned to give in.

But, at that very moment, Pope Stephen was forwarding to all the churches of Christendom the decision by which he acknowledged the validity of baptism conferred by heretics. Rome was sure of obtaining the adhesion of the Alexandrian Church, whose bishop, Dionysius, seems to have been sounded by Stephen, even before the Council of Carthage gave its decision.[2]  Immediately after the Council, Cyprian sent one of his deacons to Cæsarea of Cappadocia, to win over to his side Firmilian, the highly respected bishop of that city.   Was the whole episcopal body to be divided into two hostile camps : on the one side, Rome and Alexandria, on the other, Africa and Asia Minor?   Notwithstanding some affirmations to the contrary, Rome did not as yet excommunicate any Church ; but she spoke of severing relations with the Churches that would not acknowledge the validity of heretical baptism.[3]   In the name of the Churches of Cappadocia, Cilicia and Galatia, Firmilian replied to Cyprian in a letter which had probably been prepared in a council.   This document, which is the more important because Firmilian was an immediate disciple of Origen, is from beginning to end such a violent philippic against Pope Stephen that we easily understand why formerly the copyists hesitated to reproduce it in their MSS.[4]

---

[1] "Sententiae," 56.          [2] EUSEB. "H. E." VII. 2.

[3] "Epistulae," LXXIV. 8: ". . . haereticorum amicus et inimicus christianorum sacerdotes Dei veritatem Christi et ecclesiae unitatem tuentes abstinendos putat ".   Here Cyprian denounces Stephen as having thought of excommunicating the bishops of the opposition ; but the Pope did not in fact excommunicate them.   This interpretation is confirmed by a passage of Firmilian's letter (LXXV. 4) and of a letter of Dionysius of Alexandria (EUSEB. "H. E." VII. 5, 4).   BENSON, p. 354.   DUCHESNE, "Eglises separées," p. 147.   BARDENHEWER, vol. II. p. 462.   D'ALÈS, p. 38.   TURMEL's arguments to the contrary have not convinced us. "Hist. du dogme de la pap," vol. I. p. 157.

[4] As regards the authenticity of Firmilian's epistle, see BARDEN- HEWER, vol. II. p. 271, and BENSON, pp. 377-89.   Unquestionably Fir- milian took a great deal from the letters Cyprian had sent him, and

In Firmilian's eyes, the Catholic Church is primarily hierarchical. How great his error, how exceeding his blindness, who says that baptism or forgiveness of sins can be validly given by heretics. For whoever uses such language, abandons the foundation of the Church which was set by Christ on one rock, and forgets that Christ gave the Holy Ghost to the Apostles only :—

"Potestas ergo peccatorum remittendorum[1] apostolis data est, et ecclesiis quas illi a Christo missi constituerunt, et episcopis qui eis ordinatione vicaria successerunt ".[2]

The Apostles received from Christ a *potestas* which they transmitted to the Churches they established, and to the bishops who are their successors. Firmilian does not explain and would have found it very hard to explain how a Church, as such, is the depositary of this power; hence he adds presently that bishops are the ministers of this *potestas*, because they succeed the Apostles and hold their place. We cannot but be struck with the distinctness with which he affirms the hierarchical character of the Church and the apostolic character of the hierarchy: without the bishop, no baptism, no priesthood, no altar, no Church. Firmilian cannot forgive Pope Stephen the gross error of acknowledging in heretics and in rebels, like Core, Dathan and Abiron of old, the power to administer baptism validly, " *Maximam gratiae potestatem,*" and the other Sacraments of the Church, " *magna et caelestia ecclesiae munera,*"[3] of which the hierarchy alone is the dispenser.

re-echoed, in his reply, the words of the latter : this we learn from Firmilian's own testimony (LXXV. 4).

[1] Firmilian thus designates the baptismal forgiveness of sins. Cf. " Sententiae episcop." 17 (Fortunatus of Thuccaboris).

[2] " Epistulae," LXXV. 16 : " Qualis error sit et quanta caecitas eius, qui remissionem peccatorum dicit apud synagogas haereticorum dari posse, nec permanet in fundamento unius ecclesiae quae semel a Christo super petram solidata est, hinc intellegi potest quod soli Petro Christus dixerit : *Quaecumque ligaveris*, etc. [Matt. XVI. 19], et iterum in euangelio quando in solos apostolos insufflavit Christus dicens : *Accipite spiritum*, etc. [Ioan. XX. 22]. Potestas ergo . . . successerunt. Hostes autem unius catholicae ecclesiae, in qua nos sumus, et adversarii nostri qui apostolis successimus, sacerdotia sibi inlicita contra nos vindicantes et altaria profana ponentes, quid aliud sunt quam Core et Dathan et Abiron ? "

[3] *Ibid.* 17.

"Haeretici, si se ab Ecclesia Dei sciderint, nihil habere potestatis aut gratiae possunt, quando omnis potestas et gratia in Ecclesia constituta sit, ubi praesident maiores natu qui et baptizandi et manum imponendi et ordinandi habent potestatem " (LXXV. 7).

A heretic can neither ordain, nor lay on hands, nor baptize, because he is " *alienus a spiritali et deifica sanctitate* ". We defined, says Firmilian, this article of belief against the heretics a long time ago in a council held at Iconium, which was attended by the bishops of Phrygia, Galatia, Cilicia and neighbouring regions.[1]

On what does the unity of the hierarchy depend? That unity is a fact, Firmilian knows it well and his sense of it is as vivid as Cyprian's own. He rejoices to feel himself in communion with the Bishop of Carthage, however distant from each other they are, " *quasi non unam tantum regionem tenentes, sed in ipsa atque in eadem domo simul inhabitantes* ".[2] It is a "unanimity of faith and truth," and he gives thanks for it to God, its author.

" Quod totum hoc fit divina unitate. Nam cum Dominus unus atque idem sit qui habitat in nobis, coniungit ubique et copulat suos vinculo unitatis " (LXXV. 3).

Precarious unity! Like Cyprian, Firmilian is pleased to think that it accommodates itself to differences in all that is not essential. He recalls that there is diversity regarding the date of Easter " *et circa multa alia divinae rei sacramenta,* " thus probably designating the liturgy. In several questions Rome does not agree with Jerusalem: " *In ceteris quoque plurimis provinciis multa pro locorum et hominum diversitate variantur, nec tamen propter hoc ab ecclesiae catholicae pace atque unitate aliquando discessum est* " (LXXV. 6).

Firmilian is not concerned about this diversity, so convinced is he that unity is secured by truth, truth by tradition, and tradition by the hierarchy. He does not imagine that

---

[1] " Epistulae," LXXV. 7. Cf. *ibid.* 19 : " In Iconio diligentissime tractavimus et confirmavimus repudiandum esse omne omnino baptisma quod sit extra ecclesiam constitutum ". This Council of Iconium may have been held about the year 230. BENSON, p. 348.

[2] *Ibid.* 1.

a judge of disputes can be needed; hence his indignation on seeing the Bishop of Rome claim to be that judge. Unkindness, audacity, presumption, blindness, absurdity, foolishness, wrath—this litany of insults hardly suffices for the Bishop of Cæsarea to express his feeling.

"Quin immo tu haereticis omnibus peior es. Nam cum inde multi cognito errore suo ad te veniant ut Ecclesiae verum lumen accipiant, tu venientium errores adiuvas, et obscurato lumine ecclesiasticae veritatis tenebras haereticae noctis adcumulas" (LXXV. 23).

One asks oneself sadly what became of unity and peace in the midst of such invectives. The responsibility lies at the door of the Bishop of Rome, Firmilian declares: "*Lites enim et dissensiones quantas parasti per ecclesias totius mundi*" (*ibid.* 24)! To believe Firmilian, Stephen is alone in his opinion: he cuts himself off from all the other Churches: he makes himself "*a communione ecclesiasticae unitatis apostatam*" (*ibid.*); he is not afraid "*cum tot epis- copis per totum mundum dissentire*" (*ibid.* 25). Not even for an instant does the thought come to Firmilian's mind that the courage of the Bishop of Rome may spring from his certitude that he is standing by the true tradition, and that the authority as Bishop of bishops which he claims for his intimation of the truth is the legitimate authority of Peter's successor. For Stephen to recall the Roman primacy is, in Firmilian's eyes, a mark of pride and a usurpation.

After defining the law, Rome was forbearing enough not to excommunicate the Churches that questioned its legitimacy. All over the East, during the autumn of the year 256, episcopal synods must have been held which concluded for the nullity of the baptism of heretics.[1] The relations between Rome and the Churches of Asia Minor were doubtless suspended, as they were between Rome and the bishops of Africa. This distressing state of affairs lasted until 2 August, 257, when Pope Stephen died. "His successors," writes Mgr. Duchesne, "though they maintained the custom of the Roman Church, and tried to make it prevail as far as possible elsewhere, saw no necessity for being

---

[1] EUSEB. "H. E." VII. 5, 5, the letter of Dionysius of Alexandria to Pope Xystus (FELTOE, p. 50).

so rigid with those who differed. Dionysius of Alexandria, the Irenæus of this new Victor, though in his diocese he observed the same custom as Stephen, was not disposed to follow him in his severity. He had already written, in this sense, to Stephen himself and to two learned priests of Rome, Dionysius and Philemon, who naturally agreed with their Bishop.[1] After the death of Stephen, the new Pope Xystus II and his colleagues made it clear that the Roman *presbyterium* had modified its attitude. Dionysius of Alexandria, in writing to them, does not disguise his feelings as to the gravity of the attempt made by the deceased Pope, or as to the importance of keeping the peace, and respecting the decisions of largely-attended and important councils. His words helped to consolidate the unity, already restored by the mere fact of the change of Popes. Xystus and Cyprian renewed the relations between Rome and Africa, which Stephen had broken off. Correspondence with Firmilian was also resumed. Dionysius, the successor of Xystus, came to the assistance of the Cappadocian Church in its distress after the invasion of the Persians in 259, and with the alms of Roman charity, he sent a message of peace. Happy days, when charity was so fervent, and resentment so short-lived!"[2]

Pope Xystus II, whom the Africans greeted as a "good and peace-making bishop,"[3] thus calmed down the controversy. It had long, however, to wait before the many problems to which it gave rise received their final solution. Indeed, the final solution came only with the Councils of Trent and the Vatican.

*<br>* *

The baptismal controversy had aroused the discussion of principles appertaining to the very structure of the Church.

First of these was the principle of the validity of the sacraments. Outside the Church no sacraments, says Cyprian. At Rome, on the contrary, it is maintained that baptism can be had outside the Church, inasmuch as the grace of baptism is dependent on the rite by which it is ad-

---

[1] Euseb. "H. E." vii. 5, 6.    [2] "Hist. anc." vol. i. p. 429.
[3] Pont. "Vita Cypriani," 14.

ministered; so that, if heretics or schismatics use in the administration of this rite the ecclesiastical form, they administer validly. Cyprian's doctrine, which rests on theological reasons, is a deduction from the axiom : Outside the Church no Holy Spirit. Pope Stephen's doctrine does not deny this axiom; but it co-ordinates it with another traditional belief—belief in the efficacy *ex opere operato* of the baptismal rite. We shall not say that both doctrines are almost equally ancient, since all the lines of evidence converge to establish the priority of the Roman doctrine, and the greater solidity of its basis.[1]

In the second place, there is the principle of the perpetuity of the power of orders. Rome has given her decision only as regards the validity of the baptism of heretics, and has not touched on the cognate question whether the power of orders continues among heretics; Cyprian comes forward and boldly decides this question in the negative. Here again, the teaching of the Bishop of Carthage is a deduction from the axiom : Outside the Church no Holy Spirit; whence he concludes, no priesthood, no sacrifice, no Eucharist. A logician may go still further and conclude: the power of orders, then, can be lost, and bishops, invested lawfully with the episcopate, lose the episcopal power of orders, when they become schismatics, or heretics, or, we may add, public sinners, or even merely sinners; and thus we drift into Donatism, Wycliffism, Puritanism. But it will be easy for Rome to ward off these errors which the principle of her baptismal doctrine already condemns. Like the other axiom formulated by Cyprian, "*Salus extra Ecclesiam non est*,"[2] the saying: Outside the Church no Holy Spirit, has its limitations. But Stephen holds as much as Cyprian that the Church alone can impart the Holy Ghost, and this is

[1] D'ALÈS, pp. 42-4. Cyprian fully realized that he had only theological reasons to set against the tradition appealed to by Pope Stephen. See his declarations on reason, as opposed to custom ("Epistulae," LXXI. 3), and on the duty to learn (LXXIV. 10): "Oportet episcopos non tantum docere, sed et discere, quia et ille melius docet qui cotidie crescit et proficit discendo meliora". All this is appallingly rash and reminds us of Tertullian, after he became a Montanist.

[2] "Epistulae," LXXIII. 21.

why at Rome the laying on of hands *ad accipiendum Spiritum Sanctum* has to be repeated by the bishop.

Third principle: the Catholic Church is one.   How can Harnack say that the "confederation of Churches" was not fully realized and formulated before the days of Constantine and under his *régime?* or again that "the idea of the one exclusive Church, embracing all Christians and founded on the bishops was," in the time of Cyprian, "a mere theory . . . refuted by the actual circumstances"?[1]   For, so far from Cyprian being in advance of his time when he expresses the idea of Catholic unity with so much insistence and eloquence, his doctrine of the "empiric" catholic unity finds deep echoes everywhere.   Firmilian, in the name of the Churches of Asia Minor and beyond, returns the echo to the Bishop of Carthage from far distant Cæsarea of Cappadocia;[2] the same echo reaches Rome from Dionysius of Alexandria, not without an accent of discreet remonstrance, as though Rome had risked the shattering of that unity which all conspire to strengthen.

"Know now," he wrote to Pope Stephen, "that the union is perfect, after having been for a moment compromised, between all the Churches throughout the East and beyond[3]; and all the faithful are of one mind.   The bishops everywhere rejoice greatly in the peace which has been unexpectedly recovered.[4]   Demetrian at Antioch, Theoctistus at Cæsarea, Mazabbanes at Ælia, Marinus at Tyre, Heliodorus at Laodicea, Helenus at Tarsus and all the churches of Cilicia, Firmilian and all Cappadocia, . . . all Syria and Arabia, to which you daily send succours and have just sent some, Mesopotamia, Pontus, Bithynia, in short all everywhere rejoice in unanimity and brotherly love and return thanks to God.[5]   Be it remarked, this "unanim-

---

[1] "Dogmeng." vol. I[4], p. 422.        [2] "Epistulae," LXXV. 1, 3, 24, 25.
[3] He refers to the reconciliation of the *lapsi*, and the Novatian schism.
[4] After the persecution of Decius.
[5] EUSEB. "H. E." VII. 5, 1-2 (FELTOE, p. 44): ἀγαλλιῶνται πάντες πανταχοῦ τῇ ὁμονοίᾳ καὶ φιλαδελφίᾳ. Cf. the Syriac fragment of the same letter (FELTOE, p. 47): ". . . in order that we may be in agreement one with another, Churches with Churches, bishops with bishops, priests with priests".

ity " is that which had just excluded the Novatians from the Catholic communion. When we read one after the other the " Sententiae " of the eighty-seven bishops assembled for the council of Africa in the year 256, we realize how profound is the sentiment of unity conjoined with an intense hatred for heresy and schism, in the hearts of the bishops even of the most insignificant Churches of Numidia and Mauritania—Mascula, Girba, Buruch, Cuiculum.[1]

To say that this sentiment resembles imperialism is to misrepresent it. For the confederation of all the Churches —visible as it was and hierarchical—presents no analogy with the Empire, which is not a spontaneous confederation of cities and municipia. The geographical distribution of the churches throughout the Empire, their grouping around the metropolitical churches, is independent of the territorial divisions of the imperial administration. Besides, in the East, Catholicism goes beyond the boundaries of the Roman Empire. As we have already seen, Dionysius of Alexandria speaks of the churches of Mesopotamia as united with the ὁμονοία of all the other churches; some fifty years later, Eusebius will speak of the Christians of Persia, Media and Parthia; as early as the end of the second century, Pantænus had preached the Gospel in India, which means either South Arabia, or the kingdom of Axum.[2] In this its universal

---

[1] See the " Sententiae," 1 (Caecilius of Biltha), 2 (Primus of Misgirpa), 5 (Nemesianus of Thubunas : " haec omnia Ecclesia catholica loquitur . . . nisi in Ecclesia catholica quae est una salvi esse non possunt "), 10 (Monnulus of Girba : " Ecclesiae catholicae matris nostrae veritas semper apud nos, fratres, et mansit et manet "), 14 (Theogenes of Hippo : " unum baptisma quod est in Ecclesia sancta "), 17 (Fortunatus of Thuccaboris), 26 (Felix of Utina : " sinum matris Ecclesiae "), 27 (Quietus of Buruc : ". . . vitali baptismate quod in catholica Ecclesia est "), 33 (Felix of Bamaccora : ". . . Ecclesiae nostrae adversarii "), 37 (Vincentius of Thibaris : " Haereticos scimus esse peiores quam ethnicos "), 44 (Pelagianus of Luperciana : " Aut Ecclesia Ecclesia est, aut haeresis Ecclesia est . . . "), 46 (Felix of Marrazana : " Una fides, unum baptisma, sed ecclesiae catholicae cui soli licet baptizare "), 60 (Rogatianus of Nova : " Ecclesiam Christus instituit, haeresin diabolus "), 79 (Clarus of Mascula). Cf. MONCEAUX, vol. II. p. 61 and foll.

[2] HARNACK, "Mission," vol. II. p. 121. DUCHESNE, "The Christian Missions south of the Roman Empire," in " Eglises separeés," pp. 283-353.

dispersion, Catholicism is much more like Judaism.[1] Like Judaism, like Stoicism, it tends towards a cosmopolitanism. Who calls himself "catholic" calls himself "universal," whoever bears this title is placed, as God is, in a category where there is no further distinction of kingdoms or races.[2]

This sentiment, this ecclesiastical sense, this love of unanimity in catholicity, is a historical energy which is in full activity at the time of the baptismal controversy. If the Christians of subsequent ages forgave St. Cyprian his errors on many points, it was because no one before him, not even St. Irenæus, had spoken as he did of the unanimity of the Church and of concord among bishops. The controversy he had stirred up concerning the validity of the baptism of heretics might still remain open, and seem undecided to many bishops; but the subordination of such disagreements to the duty of remaining united, and the realization of the absolutely sacred and imperative character of this duty was above all—"*salvo iure communionis diversa sentire,*" St. Augustine will say later—was strong enough to end all conflicts, in the time of Cyprian as in that of Irenæus. It is surprising that the Protestant critics take so little notice of this historical energy which is, not only a great idea—ideas are cold and silent—but a profound and heartfelt sentiment springing from the Christian faith.

Hence the baptismal controversy served to manifest in Catholicism its theoretical and living unity. It recalled also its Apostolic, and therefore legitimate, origin. The Roman primacy alone seems at first sight to have come out of the conflict somewhat weakened as compared with what it was at the end of the second century.

When, indeed, Gallicans and Josephists seek some authority behind which to shield themselves, they may appeal to the Bishop of Carthage.[3] Anglicans and Old Ca-

---

[1] We may remember that the Christians appear to the Romans to be a race, like the Jews. Celsus says διὰ τὸ ἰουδαίων καὶ χριστιανῶν γένος. ORIGEN, "Contra Celsum," IV. 23.

[2] MINUT. "Octav." 33.

[3] BOSSUET, "Defensio declar. cleri gallicani," IX. 3-8, especially 4 : "Sancti Stephani papae contra rebaptizationem decretum, tota Sedis apostolicae auctoritate factum, et tamen concilii generalis sententiam merito expectatam." DUPIN, "De antiqua Ecclesiae disciplina" (Paris,

tholics will vie with one another in citing the unguarded expressions of St. Cyprian and St. Firmilian in their conflict with Pope Stephen, and in extolling the irritated independence of these "primitive saints" in their dealings with the See of Rome.[1]

But this is to forget that at a more serene epoch Cyprian had recognized (1) that "a special importance attaches to the Roman see, because it is the see of the Apostle to whom in the first place Christ granted apostolic authority, thereby to show with unmistakable clearness the unity of this authority and the unity of the Church that rests on it; and (2) that, in the history of Christian Origins, the Church of this see was the Mother and root of the Catholic Church spread over the earth. In a difficult crisis which Cyprian had to pass through in his diocese [of Carthage] he appealed to the Roman Church, to the Bishop of Rome, as if communion with this Church was in itself the guarantee of truth."[2] Conditioned by such a primacy the *concordia episcoporum* is no longer Gallicanism. That bishop does not ignore the traditional Roman fact, who tells us that the Emperor Decius, "*tyrannus infestus sacerdotibus*," would have preferred to "hear that a rival claimant to his empire had been proclaimed at Rome than that a bishop had been elected there, in the person of Cornelius:[3] he does not ignore the traditional Roman fact, who speaks on one occa-

---

1686), p. 344. FEBRONIUS, "De Statu Ecclesiae et de legitima Potestate Romani Pontificis," cap. VI. § 9. DÖLLINGER, "La Papauté" (Paris, 1904), p. 3.

[1] See REINKENS, "Die Lehre des heiligen Cyprian von der Einheit der Kirche" (Wurzburg, 1873), pp. 28-48. LANGEN, "Geschichte der römischen Kirche," vol. I. (Bonn, 1881), pp. 333-46. LIGHTFOOT, "Christian Ministry," p. 96. PULLER, "The Primitive Saints and the See of Rome," third ed. (London, 1900), pp. 49-72. GORE, "Roman Catholic Claims," sixth ed. (London, 1897), pp. 117-9.

[2] HARNACK, "Dogmeng." vol. I[4], p. 420. Cf. LOOFS, p. 209.

[3] CYPRIAN, "Epistula," LV. 9 : ". . . sedisse intrepidum Romae in sacerdotali cathedra eo tempore cum tyrannus infestus sacerdotibus Dei . . . multo patientius et tolerabilius levari adversus se aemulum principem quam constitui Romae Dei sacerdotum". HARNACK, "Mission," vol. II. p. 211. Recall too the fact of Aurelian who, at Antioch in the year 272, makes the bishops of Italy and of Rome the arbiters of ecclesiastical legitimacy. EUSEB. "H. E." VIII. 31.

sion of that "*ecclesia principalis unde unitas sacerdotalis exorta est*," and of the see of Rome as the place of Peter, "*locus Petri*". This was the language of tradition: Irenæus would have recognized in it his own declarations. Would Pope Victor or Pope Callistus have thought that Pope Stephen was introducing a novelty, when, as the vicar of the Apostle Peter, he claimed to be the bishop of bishops in the Church of Churches?

WHEN, on the morrow of the peace of Constantine, the Fathers of the Church looked back upon the three centuries it had taken for Christianity to conquer the world, they could not help seeing evidence of God's intervention in the rapidity with which this conquest had been effected.

Modern historians have likewise been impressed by this rapid conquest: " Seventy years after the foundation of the first Gentile Church in Syrian Antioch," writes one of these historians, " Pliny wrote to Trajan concerning the spread of Christianity through remote Bithynia; where in his judgment it threatened the stability of the old pagan cults of the province. Seventy years later still, the paschal controversy reveals the existence of a Christian federation of Churches, stretching from Lyons to Edessa, with its headquarters at Rome. Seventy years later again the Emperor Decius declared he would sooner see a rival claimant to his throne spring up at Rome than a new bishop to fill the see there that was then vacant. And ere another seventy years had passed, the cross was attached to the Roman colours."

Such a conquest of the old world had been attempted by Judaism. But, as we have learned from Origen, Judaism was a people by its race and by its law. When they spread among the heathen the fear and worship of Yahweh, the Jews continued to affirm that " righteousness " could be reached only through the perfect observance of the whole Law, beginning with circumcision: the Greek, to become a member of God's people, must become a Jew. As to Jewish Hellenism, it could indeed present itself as a " philosophy," but by that very fact it became a synthesis of incompatibles without a future.

The true essence of Christianity, its divine originality, manifested itself from its very beginning, in that it was

26 *

neither a " philosophy," nor a people, but a revelation and a Church. Christianity was the preaching by Jesus of a kingdom of God, not an apocalyptic kingdom of God, but a kingdom that was at once interior and transcendent, a kingdom revealed by Jesus and thrown open by Him. Christianity was a faith and a life. Jesus was the truth and the way, and it immediately became manifest that this truth was from God, and that in this way the disciples walked not as sheep without a shepherd, but, on the contrary, as a flock that follows its leader. The disciples were the "called " (κλητοί), the flock they made up was the ἐκκλησία. After Jesus had gone back to His Father, there was to be a shepherd to feed the sheep and the lambs : on Peter the Church would be built. To the gospel of the kingdom, was added the gospel of the fold. For the law of God was substituted the kingdom of God; for the people of God, a people of " flesh and blood," was substituted a supernatural and social communion, freed from every idea of race, the visible and universalist Church of God. All this was announced and established by Jesus.

Ecclesiology demands of us no sacrifice of soteriology : we distinguish the kingdom from the Church, we distinguish the Church from Redemption. Faith and baptism introduced the believer into a supernatural condition which made him a member of one and the same mystical, invisible body : he was reconciled to God by the blood of Jesus Christ, he was cleansed from his sins, he lived less himself than Christ lived in him, he was a new creature made for life eternal. But this interior justification would have left the Christian perfectly isolated in the world, for of itself it did not imply an exterior socialization, a flock and a shepherd.

The preaching of the Gospel by the Apostles had, on the other hand, the result of everywhere forming the Christians into visible and organized Christian communities, into brotherhoods in which there were no more Jews, or Greeks, Scythians, or slaves, but in which Jesus was all in all. The Christians were brothers by a brotherhood which was supernatural indeed, but was also immediately social. Individualism was never the law of the Christian religion.

Outside the Apostolic generation and in the course of

the three first centuries, it is a notable fact that the propagation of Christianity was not the work of missionaries. St. Paul, carrying the Gospel into Cyprus, into Galatia, into Macedonia, into Achaia, perhaps into Spain, is the Apostle *par excellence*, but he will have no imitators in the generations which follow the Apostolic generation. The successors of the Apostles are not missionaries, but the bishops. Henceforth Christianity advances gradually and obscurely, propagating itself step by step, along the great Roman ways. There is, for instance, no historical record of the evangelization of Roman Africa, or of that of Great Britain. Tertullian and Cyprian, who probably remembered the details connected with the Christian conquest of Africa—details that are unknown to us—conceived the propagation of Christianity as a kind of genealogy of Churches, a mother Church bringing forth other Churches which became her spiritual daughters. In truth, wherever Christianity established itself definitively, it established itself in this way: the spread of the Gospel was a multiplication of Churches, like to the prolification of cells.

However, the multiplication of Churches, unlike that of synagogues, was limited: it was subordinate to the law that there was to be only one Church in each city. Origen will most justly dwell upon the analogy between the local Church and the city. If there were for a while and among the "first fruits"—in the words of St. Paul—domestic Churches, these temporary institutions, which answered a temporary need, soon disappear altogether from history. St. Cyprian, and long before him, St. Ignatius, proclaims the law of the unity of the Church in each city. All these local Churches have the same hierarchical structure: the collectivity of the faithful, and over them, as a ruling authority, one *presbyterium*, one bishop. Even supposing that it took some time for the monarchical episcopate—as it is called—to find its explicit form, still it remains true that this term was reached by all the Churches during the second century. Whatever analogies may be found between the civil offices in the cities of the Empire, and the *ordo* of the Churches, what characterizes the ecclesiastical hierarchy is the fact that it is not an elective and temporary magistracy, but a priesthood for life.   The hierarchy did not depend on the charisms, or extraordinary gifts of the Spirit: it was a power inherited from the apostolate, a living *magisterium* which continued that of the Apostles.

One Church in each city, one bishop in each Church, all the Churches joined together by a constant exchange of guests and letters, of helps and warnings, all forming a species of confederacy, all firmly rooted in this unity by their intimate sentiment of unity.   Yet it was not these facts and conditions which produced the unity of hierarchical structure, or the fundamental unity of faith, worship and discipline: we do indeed find traces of efforts made to defend this fourfold unity; but of efforts made to create it, there is no trace whatever.   The circumstances which since Ritschl have been cited as having produced it account for it only by begging the question.   On the contrary, that actual condition of the facts is easily explained if each Church, proceeding from a mother-Church by spiritual filiation preserved an inherited tradition which imposed upon her her hierarchy, faith, liturgy, and discipline.

From all these characteristic notes, we must conclude that Christianity spread and established itself as a " religion of authority ".   It was not a contagion of enthusiasm, such as may be found in certain " revivals," an outpouring of the gift of the Spirit, of prophecies and extraordinary ways; these charismatic manifestations were from the first subject to strict control, as much as if they had taken place in Jewish synagogues.   The right to heresy existed no more for the Christian in his Church than for the Jew in his synagogue.   Heretics were separated from the Christian community, just as public sinners were separated.   The faithful ordered their belief and their conduct according to what had been received: what was new and not in agreement with what had been received, could only be foreign, and mere " tradition of *men* ".   But there was a tradition of God.

In spite of Renan's expression, repeated by Harnack, it was not mediocrity which in Christianity founded authority; it was the Gospel which founded authority.   Men became converts on hearing the words of the Apostles sent by

Jesus : the words of Jesus and of the Apostles, continuing the words of the prophets, were the words of God, as his Law was for a Jew. And as the words of the Lord and of the Apostles were not at first set down in writing, tradition became authoritative before the new Scripture. Thus there was a sacred inheritance, the content of which was the message of God. When the presbyters of the second century said in simple humility to the heretics, whose subtlety was on a par with their inventiveness: "We repeat what we have learned," they expressed the authentic and primitive conception of the Christian faith—which was never a "religion of the free spirit," but was carefully preserved as a deposit.

The religious map of the old world, could one hope to delineate it throughout with the degree of completeness which is possible for some regions,—for the province of Asia, for instance—would reveal most striking contrasts. The regional differentiations, which are so conspicuous in the pagan religions, are also strongly marked in Gnosticism, in which it is easy to distinguish the Syrian variety from the Alexandrine, the Asiatic from the Roman: Gnosticism is indeed a typical instance of a perpetually changing syncretism, assimilating to itself elements as various as are the countries where it prevails, and the men by whom it is taught. Montanism itself, although it came comparatively late and was influenced by the Catholic atmosphere far more than Gnosticism, is not the same everywhere: the Montanism of Phrygia differs from that of Africa.

Christianity, on the contrary, shows itself endowed with a prodigious homogeneity. Unlike Mithraism, it is not a religion for a special class of men, since it is propagated in all classes and is embraced by the slave Onesimus as well as by the ex-consul Flavius Clemens. It is true, most of its adherents belong to the humble and illiterate class, to the *tenuiores* and *simpliciores*. In the province of Bithynia, the refined mind of Pliny sees in these converts of all ages and conditions, and of both sexes, "nothing, except a depraved and excessive superstition"; and this is what it must have appeared everywhere to men similarly prejudiced. The wonder is that, sinking as it did so deeply into the souls of the pagan multitudes, it did not become corrupt, by syncretizing with the errors denounced in the Epistle to the Colossians, or in the message to the seven Churches, of the Apocalypse.

On the contrary, the greater the danger appears, the stricter does vigilance make itself felt in every Church. The Churches are armed and ready to defend the purity of the faith, just as they are to defend the purity of morals: in either case, the same strictness; the virginity of the Church depends on this two-fold continence. The faith which was the same everywhere met the Christian to whatever Church he went, as in the cases of Abercius, Hegesippus and Papias. In each Church, the ruling authority made each one of the faithful, not the disciple of a school, but the soldier of an army; he was bound by a pledge which was similar to the *sacramentum* or military oath, and he pledged himself both as to his belief and as to his conduct, of which he must always be ready to give an account to his Church and to its rulers. In all this, there is neither constraint nor oppression, for the profound reason that the faith implied such a unanimity, and that for a Christian to break away from it was a sign that he was abandoning faith and truth and salvation, to become a child of Satan.

This unanimity in each Church and among the Churches was rendered possible only by the control of an authority which was in the " presbyters," as they were called. The " presbyters " maintained the inherited tradition, the doctrinal and ethical catechisms that had been formed from the beginning, the "dogmas " of the Lord and of the Apostles. They cared little for the "persuasive words of human wisdom "; they claimed at most to give "interpretations of the sayings of the Lord ". Papias, amongst others, is a typical "presbyter" of the second century. When the great Gnostics, like Valentinus, made their appearance, the " presbyters," distributed as they were from Edessa to Lyons, did not need to meet together and concert plans; for a long time past the Christian community in every Church had known how to protect itself against the assaults of " false knowledge " and the " profane novelties of words ". Had she not been thus protected, what would have remained of her even as early as the years 100 or 120 ?

About the year 200, this homogeneity of Christianity in its hierarchical structure, in its faith, in its liturgy, and in the discipline of its Churches, extended to all the provinces of the Roman Empire, and even went beyond its boundaries on the East. The Churches and the "presbyters" had subdued the old world to a faith which, having been carried and established as far as the extremities of the inhabited world as then known, rightly deserved the title Catholic, which it had borne for almost a century. The words of Paul had been fulfilled: God had chosen the foolish things of the world that He might confound the wise, and the weak things of the world that He might confound the strong. By using the criterion of tradition, and invoking prescription against novelty, the "presbyters" had preserved the Churches from the baneful syncretisms that threatened them at the end of the Apostolic age and during the second century. The homogeneity itself of the faith of the Churches, the uninterrupted succession which connected that faith through the bishops with the Apostles, the assistance of the Holy Ghost promised by Jesus to the Apostles, these formed the threefold justification of the claims of Catholicism.

But there were further questions still demanding solution. Had not the Spirit a mission to suggest new revelations? Unquestionably another Gospel than that of the Apostles could not be thought of: but could not some new prophets arise? The Churches fixed the canon of the New Testament, by settling the hesitations entertained here and there about the canonicity of such or such an apostolic or prophetic book. It shows the rigour with which they proceeded in this work that a certain number of writings, like the "Didachè" which was highly esteemed at Alexandria, or the "Shepherd" which was held in great esteem at Rome, were kept out of the canon. When, in the time of Montanism, some new prophecies claimed credit in the name of the Spirit, the principle that revelation was closed universally prevailed.

But at least could not the canon of faith be expounded by some process of dialectics? For Irenæus and Tertullian Greek philosophy was simply a worldly and dangerous sophistry: the use made of this philosophy by the great

Gnostics, could not but predispose the Churches against it. Some apologists, however, like Justin, appealed to it, with the object of accrediting the Christian faith in the eyes of the heathen public.   Clement of Alexandria and Origen accepted, and—not without meeting with some opposition— succeeded in getting the Churches to accept the idea that philosophical propædeutics might be a fitting preparation for the faith, and that the revealed faith might mature into an ecclesiastical gnosis.   Philosophical apologetics and deductive theology thus became acclimatized on the Christian soil, just as later on, in the time of St. Thomas Aquinas, the Aristotelian philosophy, for which Tertullian has anything but words of praise, was to be acclimatized.   Christians entered, not without some regret, upon these paths of discussion.   It remained at least beyond question that the canon of the faith was the standard by which every thought had to be judged, and that the ecclesiastical gnosis was the legitimate gnosis.

The ecclesiastical rule of the faith was manifested by the unanimity of the Churches and of the bishops: that on which all Christians agreed in the whole world could not but be a tradition inherited from the Apostles.   The authenticity of the tradition was confirmed by the fact that in the "principal" Churches the succession of bishops was connected with the Apostles who had founded those Churches.   Among these Churches of Apostolic origin, the most illustrious was the one founded by the Apostles Peter and Paul at Rome, where their tombs were preserved.   The Bishop of Rome was the successor, not of Peter and Paul, but of Peter alone: he held the place of the latter, he was sitting in his chair. The witness of the Roman Church in matters of faith had as much weight as the witness of the whole Catholic world.

It was a fact, both in Greek Christendom in the time of Origen, and in Latin Christendom, that before the age of Cyprian, bishops were looked upon as the judges of the faith and the arbiters of controversies, and the Bishop of Rome was recognized as possessing a sovereignty, which no other bishop denied him.   In the affair of Montanism, both the opponents of Montanism and the Montanists themselves asked his decision: in the affair of the Quartodecimans, the

Bishop of Rome intimated orders to the whole Christian world. We have for the second century, the testimony of Ignatius and of Irenæus.

These facts and these texts do not constitute, it is true, the whole history of the Papacy; but, as by sudden flashes they light up the life of the Christian community and reveal to us the place which the *cathedra Petri*, as such, held in that life. The consciousness which Popes like Callistus and Stephen during the third century, had of this was not an innovation or a usurpation, but a tradition which had come down from the promise made to Peter by the Saviour Himself.

The rapidity with which Christianity was propagated during the first three centuries, and that under the pressure of the imperial persecutions, is not then the only fact that should make the historian wonder : the internal and organic development of Christianity is still more wonderful. Far from being, as is claimed by Protestant historians, a series of crises and transformations that could only have brought forth differentiations and dislocations, Christendom shows itself to be a catholicity, a unity, a homogeneity ; it is such in the year 200, and in the year 250, after an existence of two centuries. The monarchical episcopate has none of the features of a successful *coup d'Etat ;* the Roman primacy has none of the features of a high-handed conquest ; the unanimity of the Churches has none of the features of a slow and painful labour, with organized endeavours, successes, and, reverses. Neither the Roman Church nor any other Church was the chief artificer of this unity. The same must be said of the Roman primacy : the evidences of its existence come to us in the form of acknowledgments of it by others more often than as claims set up by Rome. After being extolled during the second century, it did not escape being gainsaid during the third ; and even then—as when she sent to Corinth the letter of St. Clement—Rome did not plead her own right which she knew to be divine : she exercised it. Catholicism grew like a tree (the comparison goes back to St. Paul) which expands in keeping with the law of its nature, under the continued assistance of God Himself, by whom it had been planted.

Many a woodman has impiously raised his axe against the branches of this great tree ; many a storm has passed over it, since the times of Clement and of Stephen ; but it is still erect in its rugged strength.  Now, as in the days of Irenæus and Ignatius, the Roman Church, the heart of the "great Church" survives uninjured; but how many Churches have been for centuries separated from her, how many sheep have been lost! The historian cannot think over these losses without emotion, when he remembers the nascent and conquering catholicity of the first three centuries. The present work would not have been written— especially at the painful hour when I wrote it—did I not believe this history of the origins capable of arousing in the separated Churches a yearning for unity, and giving to churchless Christians an intuition of the true faith.

# INDEX.

ABERCIUS (*inscription*), the Roman Church in second century, 175-178; "The Spotless Virgin," 177, 178.

Aeschylus, apocryphal texts attributed to, in interests of Judaism, 7.

Africa, Council of (256), 399; proceedings of, in election and deposition of bishops, 375, 376.

African Church, the, excommunicated by Pope Stephen, 395.

Allegorical method, used by Philo, 8.

Alms-giving, character of, in primitive Christianity, 31, 32; primitive Christian, an inheritance from Judaism, 31.

Ananias, conversion of Izatis by, 15.

Anastasius Sinaita, on Pantænus, 179, 181.

"Anathema," origin of term, 29, 30.

"Angels" of the Seven Churches, 120, 122.

Anicetus, dispute of, with St. Polycarp on the Easter Question, 169, 170, 222.

Antigonus of Socho and the Pharisaic Tradition, 9.

Antioch, Council of, condemnation of Paul of Samosata by, 328; "pillars" of the Christian community at, 57.

Apocalypse, the Johannine, 119, 120.

Apostle, Jewish, St. Paul as, 39.

"Apostle," meaning of term, 37, 39; Pauline use of term, 40, 41.

Apostles, function of, the "Didaché" on, 109.

Apostles, the Jewish, 37-9; attempt of, to undermine Christianity, Eusebius on, 37, 38; St. Justin Martyr on, 38.

"Apostles," term applied to the Seventy by St. Irenæus and Tertullian, 41.

Apostles, the twelve, authority of, St. Ignatius on, 138; decree of in Acts xv., xx., xxii., 60; equality of, St. Cyprian on, 358; as foundation of the Church, St. Paul on, 101; pre-eminent authority of, in the primitive Church, 41, 42, 53, 54; and the Judaizers, 60.

Apostolate, the, Catholic idea of, origins of, 52; not a charisma, xix; distinctly Christian character as institution of, 37, 39; Harnack on, 39.

Apostolic Succession, 410; St. Cyprian on, 335.

Apostolic Tradition, 409; Clement of Alexandria on, 251; "Epistle to Diognetus" on, 180, 181; Hegesippus on, 173, 174; appeal of Papias to, 172, 173.

Aristo's "Dialogue of Jason," 241.

Aristobulus, on the Greek philosophers as disciples of Moses, 7.

Arrian, on the conditions of becoming a proselyte, 12.

Asceticism, Christian, Origen on, 304.

"Atheism," Christianity regarded as, by the Pagans, 18.

Aurelian, the Roman primacy recognized by, 329.

Aurelius the martyr, St. Cyprian on, 338.

BAPTISM, Christian, formula of, in the "Didaché," 107; "Clementis Secunda" on, 182-4; forgiveness of sins after, Hippolytus on, 288; St. Justin Martyr on, 189; nature of, 67; *ex opere operato* efficacy of, Pope Stephen on, 397; as a "seal," 177.

Baptism, heretical: validity of, Pope Stephen on, 387, 389, 390, 392; invalidity of, Council of Carthage on, 381-6; St. Cyprian on, 383, 384, 387, 396, 397.

Baptism, Jewish, administered to proselytes, 11; necessity of, to becoming a proselyte, "Jebamoth" on, 12; as "a bath of levitical cleansing," "Gerim" on, 12.

Bigg, on ecclesiastical attitude of Clement of Alexandria, 263.

"Binding and loosing," force of terms in Rabbinical language 90, 91.

Bishop, monarchical, the first known, 122.

Bishop of Rome, the, as Bishop of Bishops, Tertullian on, 288, 290; as

413

Pontifex Maximus, Tertullian on, 288, 289.

Bishops. See under "Episcopate" and "Hierarchy"; first mention of, in Christian literature, 98; councils of, Origen on powers of, 322, 344-346; dignity of, "De Aleatoribus" on, 362; election of, St. Cyprian on, 335, 347, 348; election of, the "Didaché" on, 107, 108; right of laity to choose, St. Cyprian on, 377; equality of, St. Cyprian on, 362; as guardians of the Deposit of Faith, vii; as guardians of Scripture, Origen on, 321; of heretical bodies, 163; the Holy Sacrifice offered by, 336; Pagan and Christian, their independent origin, 98; "Pope," title given to all, 290; succession of, in Jerusalem Church, Hegesippus on, 175; successors of the Apostles, 393, 405; unworthy, power of orders not lost by—so Pope Callistus, 378; lost by—so St. Cyprian, 377, 378.

Bishops of Africa, the, St. Cyprian's primacy over, 345; of Jerusalem, the, Eusebius on, 239, 240; of Palestine, the, in synod condemn the Quarto-decimans, 240.

Bishops of Rome, the, succession of, from St. Peter, St. Irenæus on, 203; verified by Hegesippus, 174; successors of St. Peter, 411; authority of, attacked by Tertullian, 288, 289; significance of Tertullian's attack on authority of, 290.

Bousset, on Judaism in New Testament times, 1; on the transformation of Judaism into the Church, 1.

Burial Clubs and Christianity, De Rossi on, 34.

CALLISTUS POPE, on the Christian Hierarchy, 294; on Christ's promise to St. Peter as justifying the Roman Primacy, 291; Tertullian's polemic against, 288, 290, 291.

Canon of the New Testament, fixed by the Church, 400.

Canon of the Old Testament, inquiries of Hegesippus into, 173; inquiries of Papias into, 173.

Canon, the, principles of, in "Clementis Prima," 126.

Canon of Scripture, the, Origen on, 311.

Canon of Scripture, Marcion's, 235, 236.

Carthage, Council of, 344, 345, 356, 357, 373, 376; on validity of heretical baptism, 381, 383, 384, 386.

Carthage, third Council of, its reply to Pope Stephen, 391.

Carthaginian Church, the, officials of, in time of St. Cyprian, 337.

Catholicism, antiquity of, Harnack on, xxiii; attitude of Hegesippus towards, 241; conception of, St. Irenæus', 216; formation of, according to Protestant writers generally, 144; formation of, Ritschlian theory of, 237; formation of, Sabatier on, 145-63; fundamentals of, acquired by end of second century, 228; heresy as posterior to, Clement of Alexandria on, 260, 261; imperialist. conception of, 228; not of Roman origination, 229, 230; rôle of Rome in genesis of, Renan on, 157.

Catholicism, primitive, more like primitive Christianity than Protestantism, according to Harnack, x; resemblance of, to Judaism, 1.

"Catholic," use of term in Classical and Patristic Literature, 139; term first applied to the Church by St. Ignatius, 170; identical with "Roman," Harnack on, viii.

Celsus, "True Discourse" of, 193-6; Origen on, 193; on the character of Christians, 195; attack of, on Christians for forming unlawful associations, 36, 194; on the unity of the Church, 196; on the Gnostics, 194, 196; on the disputable books of Scripture, 247.

Cemeteries, the faithful buried in the same, 342.

"Cepha," use of word in the Targums, Hart on, 85.

Chapman, Dom, on editions of De Unitate Ecclesiæ, 371-2.

Charisma, the Apostolate not a, xix; of prophecy, prominent in primitive Christianity, 29.

Charismata, abundance of, in primitive Christianity, 29; authority of the Church the outcome of the evolution of—so Sohm, xx; "Clementis Prima" on, 123; criteria of, 68; not always due to supernatural revelation, 29; "Petri Prima" on, 113; St. Paul on, 29, 30; Renan on, 150; Sabatier on, 150, 151; prophetic, St. Justin Martyr on, 219; prophetic, St. Irenæus on, 219.

"Charismatic anarchy," primitive Christianity not a, xxii.

Charismatic element in the primitive Church, subordinate to authority, xviii.

"Christian," origin and significance

of name, 56; name applied by the Jews and Pagans, 56.

Christians, the, charged with the burning of Rome, 20; accused of unnatural crimes by the Pagans, 25; mutual love of, the Pagans impressed by, 31; persecution of, under Decius, 341, 350, 356; persecution of, under Domitian, 26; persecution of, under Nero, 17, 20; persecution of, by Pliny the younger, 22; probity of, in Bithynia, Pliny on, 22, 25; solidarity and duties of, St. Paul on, 68, 69; " a third race," 74.

Christianity, apostolic, character of, vi, vii; as "pneumatic anarchism," Harnack on, xiv; sources of authority in, Harnack on, xv.

Christianity, beginnings of, Tacitus on, 17; as a "catechesis," 64; "born Catholic," vii; social character of, in Bithynia, 23; growth of testimony to the divine character of, 411; definition of, Tertullian's, vi; of Edessa, 229; as taught by Jesus, 404; Judæo—two kinds distinguished, 242, 243; Jewish origin of, Sulpicius Severus on, 21; confounded with Judaism by the Roman State before 64, 3, 18, 19; when first distinguished from Judaism, 17, 28; detachment of, from the jewries, 34; Jewish tendencies in the earliest, 55; profession of, when first forbidden by Roman legislation, 22, 25; a "religio illicita," 35, 36; wide and rapid spread of, in Bithynia, 22; unity and homogeneity of, 408, 409.

Christianity, primitive, character of almsgiving in, 31, 32; character of, 36; character of, Tacitus on, 17, 20; not a "pneumatic anarchy"—so Sohm, xviii; regarded as "atheism" by the Pagans, 18; a brotherhood from the start, 31; abundance of charismata in, 29; not communistic, 31; and the collegia, difference between, 33-5; local organizations of, Harnack on, 153.

Church, the, as a social brotherhood in time of St. Cyprian, 341, 342; Canon of the New Testament fixed by, 400; character of, Jesus on the lasting, visible and spiritual, 80; corruption of morals in, Origen on, 299, 303; exercise of excommunication by, Origen on, 298; beginnings of, in the Gospels, Loisy on, 76; attitude of Gnosticism to, 210, 211;

hierarchical basis of, St. Cyprian on, 349; origin of idea of, Loisy on, 76; Kingdom of God, not identical with, 76; as a living magisterium, Origen on, 313; teaching of St. Matthew on, Wellhausen on, 83, 87; organization of, in the sub-apostolic age, 142; organization and worship of, the "Didaché" on, 107, 110; Origen's theory of, Harnack on, 307; powers granted by Christ to, Tertullian on, 292; as the one ark of salvation, St. Cyprian on, 359, 382; Synagogue, the, contrasted with, by Origen, 324; conception of, Tertullian's, 128, 277; testimony of, to herself, Möhler on, 144; transformation of Judaism, into, 4; unity and nature of, 405, 406; unity of, recognized by Celsus, 196; unity of, St. Cyprian on, 348, 355, 358, 359, 363-5; unity of, Firmilian on, 394; unity of, St. Ignatius on, 133-5, 138, 139; unity of, St. Irenæus on, 205-7, 216; unity and nature of, Origen on, 300, 322-5; unity and nature of, St. Paul on, 101, 102; unity and constitution of, Petri Prima on, 112, 113; source of unity of, Clementis Prima on, 123, 125; unity of, Hermas on, 186; vision of, by Hermas, 186, 187; origins of, Sohm's theory, Harnack on, xvi, xix-xxi.

" Church, concerning the,' Greek fragment entitled, 266.

Church, Jerusalem, the succession of bishops in, Hegesippus on, 175; corruption of, by Thebutis, 175, 240.

Church, the Pagan, contrasted with the Christian, by Origen, 323.

Church, Palestinian, the, St. Matthew's gospel, a work of, xiii, xiv, 81.

Church, primitive, the, character of, Renan on, 150; part played by the Episcopate in, 54; unity and solidarity of, Harnack on, 32.

Church, Roman, the, testimony of Aberciusn to, 175-8; "boundless charity of," praised by Dionysius of Corinth, 185; officials of, in 251, Pope Cornelius on, 337; as the test of orthodoxy, St. Irenæus on, 209, 210; St. Peter the founder of, 203, 362; as bond of union for other churches, St. Irenæus on, 207-10, 216; supremacy of, St. Irenæus on, 207-10, 216; wealth of, 185.

Church, significance of term in the LXX, 70, 86; in the Epistle to the Hebrews, 87; in St. Stephen's speech in the Acts, 87; in the

"Didaché," 110; as used by St. Paul, 70-3; Wellhausen on, 87.

Churches, African, the, excommunicated by Pope Stephen, 395.

Churches, Eastern, the, excommunicated by Pope Victor, 226, 227.

Churches, Gentile, the organization and hierarchy of, in first century, 98, 99.

Churches, Seven, the, "Angels" of, 120, 122.

Claudius, expulsion of the Jews from Rome by, 18.

Clement of Alexandria, date and life of, 246, 247; on baptism, 253, 254; on the unity and universality of the Church, 255, 261, 262; on the visible and invisible Church, 254; nature of Christianity of, E. de Faye on, 257; ecclesiology of, Harnack on, 246, 247; ecclesiology and theology of, 246-63; on the Ecclesiastical Canon, 248-50; on the Ecclesiastical Gnosis, 257, 258, 263; Ecclesiastical and Heretical Gnosis distinguished by, 259; on the "True Gnostic," 246, 259, 260; on Ecclesiastical Tradition, 258, 259; on heresy as posterior to Catholicism, 260, 261; on the Church as antithesis of heresy, 255-7; on the Church as the "best heresy," 287; on the powers and functions of the Christian Hierarchy, 251-3; Hypotyposes of, 247; on Pantænus, 178, 179, 181; "Blessed Presbyter," title of, 248; on the "Tradition of Presbyters," 248, 251; Stromata of, 250.

Clementine Homilies and Recognitions, the, Waitz on source of, 243; date and character of, 243; Duchesne on, 243.

Clergy and laity distinguished in "Clementis Prima," 127; remuneration of, by the Church, St. Cyprian on, 339; secular functions forbidden to, in time of St. Cyprian, 338, 339.

"Collegia," the, Christianity different from, 33-6; Christianity modelled after, according to the Pagans, 33; different from the jewries in legal status, 34; severity of legislation for, 35.

Cornelius the Centurion, visit of St. Peter to, 15.

Cornelius, Pope, on the officials of the Roman Church in 251, 337; on the fraudulent ordination of Novatian, 335.

Cumont, on the Pagan worship of the "Elements," 100-4.

Deacon, see under "Hierarchy"; election of, the "Didaché" on, 107, 108.

Decius, attitude of, towards the Roman See, 401, 403; persecution of the Christians by, 341, 350, 356.

Deposit of Faith, entrusted by the Apostles to guardianship of bishops, vii; in the Pastoral Epistles, 114, 116, 119.

"Didaché," the, date and character of, 105-7; on the function of apostles, 109; on the formula of Baptism, 107; on the functions and powers of the Christian Hierarchy, 107-9; on prophets, 109; on subordination of individual inspiration to authority, 106.

"Diognetus, Epistle to," author of, 179; theology of, 180, 181; on Apostolic Tradition, 180, 181.

Dionysius of Alexandria, letter of, to Pope Stephen, 398; on policy of Pope Stephen, 396.

Dionysius of Corinth, letter of, to Eusebius, 184.

Diotrephes, first known monarchical bishop, 122.

Dispersion, Jewish, the, centres of, 2.

"Dispersion," the, sole Christian use of term, 111.

Docetism, condemnation of, by St. Ignatius, 134.

Dogma, development of, Origen on, 321.

"Dogma," primary significance of term, 136, 166, 167.

Domitian, persecution of the Christians by, 26.

Duchesne, on Burial-Clubs under the Empire, 34; on authority of the Roman Church, as taught by St. Ignatius, 142; on the Church, 230; on the semi-canonical authority of "Clementis Prima," 187; on the Council of Africa, 375; on Marcion, 230; on the Domitian persecution, 26; on the Neronic persecution, 25, 26; on "The Shepherd" of Hermas, 187.

Ebionites, the, not representative of primitive orthodoxy, 154.

Edessa, Christianity of, 229.

"Elements of the World," meaning of Pauline phrase, 100.

"Elements," the, Pagan worship of, Cumont on, 100-4.

Eliezer, Rabbi, on the conditions of becoming a proselyte, 12.

Episcopate, the, see under "Bishop"

and "Hierarchy"; forfeited by penance, 345; originally plural, 54; identical with the presbyterate, Theodore of Mopsuestia on, 117; in the primitive Church, Sohm on, 54.

Ethnarch, Jewish, the, in Egypt, functions of, 4.

Eucharist, the, celebrated weekly, on Sunday, 67, 107; centre of new religious life, 68; use of bread and water in, by heretics, 249.

Eusebius, on the attempt of the Jewish apostles to undermine Christianity, 37, 38; on the bishops of Jerusalem, 239, 240; rebuked by Pope Julian for deposition of Athanasius, 328; on the letters of Dionysius of Corinth, 184; on Montanism, 221; on Pantænus, 180.

"Evangelist," original and later meanings of term, 51.

Excommunicated, the, reconciliation of, 343, 344.

FABIAN, Bishop of Rome, letter of Origen to, defending his orthodoxy, 328.

Fast Days in the primitive Church, 107.

Felcissimus, the case of, and St. Cyprian, 353, 354, 356, 373-5.

Firmilian, on the hierarchical character of the Church, 393; on the unity of the Church, 394; invective of, against the Roman See, 392-5; on the invalidity of heretical sacraments, 393, 394.

Fish, Jesus as the divine, 177, 178, 278.

Florinus, letter of St. Irenæus to, 167.

Fortunatianus, the case of, and St. Cyprian, 377.

GALILEE, when annexed to Judæa, 1.

"Gerim," on the initiation of a proselyte, 11; on Baptism as "bath of levitical cleansing," 12.

"Glossolalia," 30.

Gnosis, Ecclesiastical, Clement of Alexandria on, 257, 258; Ecclesiastical and Heretical, distinguished by Clement of Alexandria, 259, 263.

"Gnostic, True," the, Clement of Alexandria on, 246, 259, 260.

Gnosticism, character of, Harnack on, 214; pre-Christian origin of, Lightfoot on, 100; Hegesippus on, 175; historical significance of, 210; attacked in the Pastoral Epistles, 115; and the Symbol of the Apostles, 161.

Gnostics, the, appeal to Apostolic Tradition rejected by, 213, 214;

Catholic attitude towards, 212; attitude of, towards the Church, 210, 211; Celsus on, 194, 196; doctrines of, 211-6; St. Irenæus on, 210-3; St. Justin Martyr on, 190-193; treatment of the Scriptures by, 212.

Gore, on the "permanent process of ordination," 118.

Gospel, the, character and credentials of, St. Paul on, 64, 66.

Gospels, the Four, origin of, St. Irenæus on, 201; Origen on, 311; universalism in, 92-5.

HARNACK, on sources of authority of Apostolic Christianity, xv; on the Christian Apostolate, 39; on the nature of the earliest Christian community, 77, 78; on the relations of Jewish Christian communities to the Church, 155; on local organizations in primitive Christianity, 153; on the charismatic element in primitive Christianity, xviii; on the antiquity of Catholicism, xxiii; on the author's "Primitive Catholicism," viii - xi; on Sohm's theory of Church Origins, xvi, xix-xxi; on the unity and solidarity of the primitive Church, 32; on the causes of the unity of the Church, 152; on the ecclesiology of Clement of Alexandria, 246, 247; on the character of Gnosticism, 214; on Marcion, 237; on the origin and character of St. Matthew's Gospel, 81, 82; on Origen's theory of the Church, 307; on Origen's Doctrine of Apostolic Succession, 311; on the Reformation, xxi; on "Roman" as identical with "Catholic," viii; on Roman Catholicism in Clementis Prima, xi; on the causes of Roman Primacy, 152; on the relations of the Eastern Churches with the Roman See, 329; on Pope Victor's excommunication of the Eastern Churches, 226.

Hasmonæans, the Jews under the, 4.

Hebrews, the Epistle to the, on the character of the early preaching of Christianity, 29.

Hebrews, the Gospel of the, 241-3; commentary of Symmachus on, 243.

Hegesippus, inquiries of, into the "true tradition of Apostolic Doctrine," 173, 174; inquiries of, into the Canon of the Old Testament, 173; attitude of, towards Catholicism, 241; succession of bishops of Rome verified by, 174; on succession of bishops in Jerusalem Church, 175; on corruption of Church of Jerusalem, 175.

Helbo, Rabbi, on proselytes to Judaism, 17.

Heraclitus, as a disciple of Moses, 7.

"Heresy," origin and use of term, 115; Jülicher on term, 115.

Heresy, sources and characteristics of, Tertullian on, 265-76, 279, 280; combated in the Apocalypse, 119, 120; combated in the Johannine Epistles, 121, 122; genealogy of, St. Irenæus on, 215.

Hermas, as Prophet and Visionary, 218; "The Shepherd" of, 186, 187; "The Shepherd" of, forbidden to be read in Church, 285, 286; on pseudo-prophets, 218; on the unity of the Church, 186; his vision of the Church, 186, 187.

"Heterodox," term first applied to heretics by Origen, 316.

Hierarchical basis of the Church, St. Cyprian on, 349.

Hierarchical idea, the, recognized by Tertullian, SS. Cyprian and Irenæus, 349.

Hierarchy, the Christian, functions and powers of, 299-301, 303, 306, 307; Pope Callistus on, 294; Clement of Alexandria on, 251-3; "Clementis Prima" on, 127, 128, 129; "Clementis Secunda" on, 182; St. Cyprian on, 333-6, 338-47, 351, 352; the "Didaché" on, 107-9; the Ignatian Epistles, 132, 133, 135, 136; Lightfoot on, 98; the Pastoral Epistles on, 117, 118, 119; Origen on, 320, 321; Tertullian on, 279, 280; source of, 405, 406; Tertullian's attack on, 286-8, 290, 291.

Hillel and the Pharisaic Tradition, 9.

Hillel, School of, on the "uncleanness" of Gentile proselytes, 13.

Hippolytus, on the forgiveness of sins after Baptism, 288.

Holtzmann, on the date of St. Matthew's Gospel, 89; on the analysis of the Pastoral Epistles, 119.

Homer, apocryphal texts attributed to, in the interests of Judaism, 7.

IDUMÆA, when annexed to Judæa, 1.

Ignatian Epistles, the, v, 131-42; authenticity of, 158.

Ignatius, St. on the authority of the Apostles, 138; use of term "Catholic" by, 170, 171; on the unity of the Church, 133-5, 138, 139; con-

demnation of Docetism by, 134; on the Roman Primacy, 140-2.

Irenæus, St., life and teaching of, 199-210; on Apostolic Tradition, 202, 203; on the succession of the bishops of Rome from St. Peter, 203; Protestant theory of his role in the evolution of Catholicism, 164; on prophetic charismata, 219; on the nature of the Church, 205-7, 216; on the pre-eminence of the Roman Church, 207-10, 216; letter of, to Florinus, 167; on origin of the Four Gospels, 201; on the Gnostics, 210-213; on the genealogy of heretics, 215; intervention of, in the Paschal Controversy, 227; on St. Polycarp's relations with the Apostles, 204; relations of, with SS. John the Apostle and Polycarp, 167; on the Rule of Faith, 198, 199; letter of, to Pope Victor on the Easter Question, 169, 227; Victor's right of excommunication not questioned by, 228.

Izatis, conversion of, 15.

"JASON, DIALOGUE OF," Aristo's, 241.

"Jebamoth," on the initiation of a proselyte, 11; on the necessity of baptism to becoming a proselyte, 12.

Jerusalem, destruction of, its influence on Christianity, 154, 155.

Jewish community in Egypt, polity of, Strabo on, 4; communities, official names of, in inscriptions, 4; customs, penetration of heathen environments by, 14; theocracy, character of, 5.

Jewries, legal status of, different from that of the collegia, 34.

Jews, the, non-absorption of, in other peoples, reason of, 5; expulsion of, from Rome by Claudius, 18; expulsion of, from Rome by Tiberius, 3; under Hasmonæan rule, 4; hostility of, towards characteristic features of Pagan social life, 3; hostility of, towards foreigners, Tacitus on, 5; attitude of, towards idolatry, Pliny the Elder on, 3; monotheism and anti-idolatry of, Tacitus on, 13; legal privileges of, under the Empire, 3; aversion of, to mixed marriages, 3; the large numbers of, in Egypt in time of Philo, 2; "a race of philosophers," 7.

Johannine Epistles, the, heresy combated in, 121, 122.

John the Presbyter, relations of, with Papias, 173.

Josephus, on the theocratic character of the Jewish constitution, 5; on the wide vogue of the Sabbath in the Roman Empire, 14.

Josua, Rabbi, on the conditions of becoming a proselyte, 12.

Jubaianus, letter of St. Cyprian to, on invalidity of heretical baptism, 387.

Judæo-Christianity, gradual isolation of, from Catholicism, 16.

Judaism, golden age of, 2; resemblance of first century, to primitive Catholicism, 1; transformation of, into the Church, Bousset on, 4; date of expansion of, in the Greek cities, 2; geographical expansion of, in New Testament times, Bousset on, 1; Hellenized, 8, 9; Hellenized and Pharisaic, contrasted, 16; Pharisaic, claims of, 9; as a "wisdom" (σοφία), 6.

Judaizers, the, attitude of, towards St. Paul, 58, 59, 61, 63; not synonymous with Jewish Christians, 60; attacked in the Pastoral Epistles, 116; St. Paul warns the Philippians against, 9.

Jülicher, on term "heresy," 115; on character of St. Matthew's Gospel, xiii, 82.

Julius, Pope, Eusebians rebuked by, for deposition of Athanasius, 328.

Juvenal, on Roman proselytes to Judaism, 14, 15.

KATTENBUSCH, on date of the Roman Symbol, 160.

Kingdom of God, the, teaching of Jesus on, 75-7, 79; not identical with the Church, 76; in the Gospels, character of, Loisy on, 78, 79.

"Kingdom of Heaven, Keys of," force of the expression, 90.

Kreyenbühl, on Christ's Promise to St. Peter, 95, 96.

LAITY AND CLERICS, distinguished in "Clementis Prima," 127; rights and powers of, St. Cyprian on, 340.

"Laos," Jewish communities called, in inscriptions, 4.

Lapsi, the, question of, St. Cyprian on, 350-4, 378; refusal of Bishop of Arles to follow practice of reconciliation of, 378.

Lectorate, the, St. Cyprian on, 338.

Lightfoot, on functions and powers of the Christian Hierarchy, 98; on authorship of the "Epistle to Diognetus," 179; on the pre-Christian origin of Gnosticism, 100.

Logia, the, Papias on, 172.

Loisy, on the beginnings of the Church in the Gospels, 78; on the origin of the idea of the Church, 76; on the character of the Kingdom of God in the Gospels, 78, 79; on the nonauthenticity of John xxi, 81; on date of St. Matthew's Gospel, 89; on Christ's promise to St. Peter and the Roman Primacy, 91.

MAGNUS, letter of St. Cyprian to, on the rebaptism of heretics, 381-3.

Marcianus, the case of, and St. Cyprian, 378-80.

Marcion, Duchesne on, 230; Harnack on, 237; St. Justin Martyr on, 233, 234; Tertullian's polemic against, 235-7; his Canon of Scripture, 235, 236; encounter of, with St. Polycarp, 231.

Marcionite, the, Rule of Faith, 236.

Marcionites, the, Tertullian on, 233.

Marriages, mixed, hostility of the Jews to, 3.

Mithraism, its organizations and manner of growth contrasted with those of Christianity, 33.

Möhler, on the Church's testimony to herself, 144.

Montanism, rise and character of, 163, 217-21; effect of, on Catholicism, 163; condemned by the Roman Church, 285, 286; condemned by Serapion, 220, 221; opposition of all Christendom to, 221; regional differentiations of, 407; Eusebius on, 221; as a revival of the "Prophetic Spirit," Sabatier on, 148; as a "spiritual" movement, 28; Tertullian on, 283, 284; conversion of Tertullian to, 264; Tertullian's reason for embracing, St. Jerome on, 285.

Montanist, Tertullian as, 286-93.

Montanists, the, appeal of, to Rome for recognition, 222.

Montanus, disowned by the Church, 284; raptures of, described, 220.

Moses, the Greek philosophers as disciples of, 7.

NERO, persecution of the Christians by, 17, 20, 25-8: Duchesne on, 25, 26; Orosius on, 26; Tertullian on, 26, 27; reason of, Suetonius on, 27, 28; favour of, to the Jews, 20; suspected of setting fire to Rome, 20.

Novatian Schism, the, Novatian and Novatus, 356, 357; and St. Cyprian, 354-7, 361.

ORIGEN, on Christian Asceticism, 304; on Apostolic Succession, 310, 311; on Baptism, 298, 304; on the preparation of candidates for Baptism, 298; on the Baptismal Symbols, 312; on the Canon of Scripture, 311; on use of term "Catholic," 324; on Catechumens, 298, 304; on Celsus, 193; on the Church as a living magisterium, 313; on the corruption of morals in the Church, 299, 303; on the office of Doctors in the Church, 314, 315; on the difference between the Church and the philosophical schools, 298; on the Pagan "Church" as contrasted with the Christian, 323; on the Church as contrasted with the Synagogue, 324; on the nature and unity of the Church, 300, 322-5; on the results of Christianity being embraced by the Romans, 330, 331; on the Greek philosophy in relation to Christianity, 296; Christianity and Judaism contrasted by, 330; Pagan calumnies against Christianity rebutted by, 295, 296; on the universality of Christianity, 295: on the refusal of some Christians to enter Army, 330; on the high moral character of the Christians, 330; on the development of Dogma, 321; appeal of, to Ecclesiastical Tradition and Authority against heresy, 309-11, 317, 319, 320; on the exercise of excommunication by the Church, 298; on Esoteric and Exoteric Christian Doctrine, 314; letter of, to Fabian, Bishop of Rome, defending his orthodoxy, 328; on the rational grounds of Faith, 296; on the Four Gospels, 311; polemic of, against heretics, 316-21; relations of, with the heretic Paul at Alexandria, 297; on Christ's Promise to St. Peter, 308, 326; corruptions of the Christian Priesthood denounced by, 304, 305; deposed from the Priesthood by Demetrius of Alexandria, 327, 328; on the value of Greek philosophy, 295, 314, 315; and the Roman See, 327-29; on the spiritual sense of Scripture, 312; on Virgins, 304.

Orosius, on the Neronic Persecution, 26.

PANTAENUS, Anastasius Sinaita on, 179, 181; Clement of Alexandria on, 178, 179, 181; Eusebius on, 180; preacher of the Gospel in Arabia or India, 399.

Papias, appeal of, to Apostolic Tradition, 172, 173; inquiries of, into the Old Testament Canon, 173; relations of, with St. John the Presbyter, 173; on the Logia, 172.

Paschal Controversy, the, 222-7.

Pastoral Epistles, the, authorship and character of, 114-9; analysis of, Holtzmann on, 119.

Paul of Samosata, condemned by council at Antioch, 328; deposition of, intervention of Emperor in, 329.

Paul, St., defence of his apostolic character by, 42-7; as Jewish apostle, 39; as Apostle of the Uncircumcision, 47; use of term "apostle" by, 40, 41; denunciation of "false apostles" by, 42; relations of, with the Jerusalem apostles, 46, 47; on the Apostles as foundation of the Church, 101; on Charismata, 29, 30; on the unity of the Church, 67, 73; on use of term "Church," 70-3; on the solidarity and duties of Christians, 67-69, 73; on the character and credentials of the Gospel, 64, 66; attitude of the Judaizers towards, 58, 59, 61, 63; the Philippians warned against the Judaizers by, 9; teaching of, on justification, identical with St. Peter's, 61-4; martyrdom of, at Rome, 26, 277; founder of the Roman Church, with St. Peter, 203; sole reference of, to "The Twelve," 48.

Paulinism, approved of and encouraged by the Jerusalem Apostles, 57, 58.

Pella, Jerusalem Christians flee to, 240.

Penance, public, for grave sins, 344; remission of, by martyrs, 350, 351.

Peræa, when annexed to Judæa, 1.

Persecution, of the Christians, by Decius, 341, 350, 356; by Domitian, 26; by Nero, 17, 20, 25, 26; by Pliny the Younger, 22-4; by Valerian, 257, 333.

"Peter, the Preaching of," 243.

Peter, St., as Apostle of the Circumcision, 47; visit of, to Cornelius, 15; as founder of Roman Church, with St. Paul, St. Irenæus on, 203; connection of, with St. Mark, Clement of Alexandria on, 247; martyrdom of, at Rome, 26, 277; place of, among the Apostles in the primitive Christian community, Harnack on, xiv; adhesion of, to St. Paul's doctrine of justification, 61-4; conference of, with St. Paul at Jerusalem, 46, 47; prerogatives of, Origen on, 326, 327; primacy of, Weizsäcker on, 92; promise to, Christ's, xiii, 84-6, 89-91; Harnack on, xii, xiii; Kreyenbühl on, 95, 96; Origen on, 308, 326; Resch on, 84; Tertullian on, 291, 292, 359; Wellhausen on, xiii; as justifying Roman Primacy, Loisy on, 91; as establishing Episcopacy, St. Cyprian on, 352, 353; chair of, the source of the unity of the priesthood, St. Cyprian on, 374; the bishops of Rome successors of, 411; apocryphal epistle of, to St. James, 243-5.

"Petri Prima," date of, 111; on Charismata, 113.

Pharisaic Tradition, the, and its transmitters, 9.

Philo of Alexandria, use of allegorical method by, 8; as Hellenizer, 8; legendary meeting of, with St. Peter at Rome, 19.

Pindar, apocryphal texts attributed to, in interests of Judaism, 7.

Pliny the Elder, on the Jewish attitude towards idolatry, 3.

Pliny the Younger, correspondence of, with Trajan on Christianity in Bithynia, 22-4, 407; persecution of the Bithynian Christians by, 22-4.

Polycarp, St., dispute of, with Anicetus on the Easter Question, 169, 170, 222; relations of, with the Apostles, St. Irenæus on, 204; relations of, with SS. John the Apostle and Irenæus, 167; date of martyrdom of, 166; encounter of, with Marcion, 231; Epistle of, to the Philippians, 165, 166, 168.

"Polycarpi, Martyrium," 170.

Polycrates, intervention of, in the Paschal Controversy, 223-5.

Pontius, on St. Cyprian's conduct as priest, 337.

Pope (Papa), when first applied to the Bishop of Rome, 290, 304; originally title of all bishops, 290.

Prayer (προσευχή), term applied to a synagogue, 6.

Presbyterate, the, as identical with the Episcopate, Theodore of Mopsuestia on, 117.

Presbyters, College of, 117.

Presbyters of the Synagogue, 6.

Presbyters, see under "Hierarchy."

Presbyters, Tradition of, St. Irenæus on, 202; Papias on, 172.

"Prescription," use of term by Tertullian, 272.

Priesthood, Jewish, the, full control of, by the Sadducees, 8.

Prophets, the "Didaché" on, 109.

Prophets, Pseudo-, Hermas on, 218.

Proselyte, Jewish, conditions of becoming, 11, 12; initiation of, "Gerim" on, 11; "unclean," 7 days after circumcision, 13.

Proselytes of the Gate, Schürer on, 11, 15, 16.

Proselytes of Righteousness, 11, 13, 15.

Proselytes, Jewish, designation of, in inscriptions, 10; hatred of, for non-Jews, 15; large number of, 10.

Proselytism, Jewish, brief survival of, after destruction of Jerusalem, 16.

Pythagoras, as a disciple of Moses, 7.

Quartodecimans, the, condemned by bishops of Palestine in synod, 240; excommunicated by Pope Victor, 226, 227.

Quintus, letter of St. Cyprian to, on invalidity of heretical baptism, 385, 386.

Rabbinism, the essence of, 9.

Reformation, the, Harnack on, xxi.

Renan, on the nature of the primitive Church, 150; on Charismata, 150; on Rome's rôle in the genesis of Catholicism, 157.

Resch, on Christ's Promise to St. Peter, 84.

Ritschlian theory, the, of the formation of Catholicism, 237.

Roman Primacy, recognized by Aurelian, 329; St. Ignatius on, 140-2.

Roman See, the, first record of appeal to, 130; recognized by St. Cyprian as mother of the Catholic Church, 401; as the "Place of Peter," St. Cyprian on, 402; special importance of, recognized by St. Cyprian, 401; attitude of Decius towards, 401, 403; pre-eminence of, shown by the appeal of Felicissimus and Basilides, 380.

Rome, burning of in 64, 17, 20; the Christians charged with, 20.

Rossi, De, on Christianity and the Burial Clubs, 34.

Rule of Faith, the, St. Irenæus on, 198, 199; insufficiency of Scripture as, St. Ignatius on, 136, 137; Marcionite, 236; Tertullian on, 267, 273, 275, 281, 282.

Sabatier, on the formation of Catholicism, 145-63; on Charis-

# PRIMITIVE CATHOLICISM

mata, 150, 151; his "Religions of Authority," 145.; on Montanism as revival of the "Prophetic Spirit," 148; on the Symbol of the Apostles, 148, 160.

Sabbath, the, wide vogue of, Josephus on, 14.

Sacrifice, the Holy, offered by bishops and priests, 336.

Sadducees, the, full control of the Jewish priesthood by, 8; wealth of, at Jerusalem, 32.

Schürer, on "Proselytes of the Gate," 11, 15, 16.

Scripture, disputable books of, Celsus on, 247; insufficiency of, as a Rule of Faith, St. Ignatius on, 136, 137; heretical appeal to, Tertullian on, 267, 269; value of, as compared with Greek philosophy, Origen on, 314, 315.

Seneca, on the penetration of heathen environments by Jewish customs, 14.

Septimius Severus, measures of, against the Jews and the Christians, 242.

Septuagint, the, date of, 7; antipathy of the Zealots to, 7.

Serapion, condemnation of Montanism by, 220, 221.

Shammai and the Pharisaic Tradition, 9.

Shammai, school of, on lawfulness of circumcised Gentiles eating the Pasch, 13.

Simon Magus, St. Justin Martyr on, 190; as heresiarch, Tertullian on, 271; heretics connected with, according to orthodox writers, 215.

Simon the Just and the Pharisaic Tradition, 9.

Sohm, on Charismata, xvii, xx; on Christian origins, xvi-xxi; on the part played by the Episcopate in the primitive Church, 54; on "Clementis Prima," 130.

Sophocles, apocryphal texts attributed to, in interests of Judaism, 7.

Soter, Pope, charity of, 185.

St. Clement of Rome, "Clementis Prima," xviii, xx, xxii, 122-31; "Clementis Prima," principles of canon in, 126; "Clementis Prima," Roman Catholicism in, Harnack on, xi; "Clementis Prima," on Charismata, 123; "Clementis Secunda," 181-4; "Clementis Secunda" on Baptism, 182-4; "Clementis Secunda" on the nature of the Church, 183, 184.

St. Cyprian, life, teaching and times of, 332-66; on almsgiving as expiation, 344; on equality of the Apostles, 358, 364; on Apostolic Succession, 335; on Aurelius the Martyr, 338; on forgiveness of sins after Baptism, 344; on invalidity of heretical baptism, letter to Jubaianus, 387, 396, 397; on invalidity of heretical baptism, letter to Bishop of Numidia, 383, 384; on invalidity of heretical baptism, letter to Quintus, 385, 386; primacy of, over bishops of Africa, 345; on autonomy of bishops, 388, 389; on bishops' power of excommunication, 342, 343; philanthropic work of the Church in time of, 341, 342; on the unity of the Church, 348, 355, 358, 359, 363-65; on the Church as the one ark of salvation, 359, 382; on the remuneration of the clergy by the Church, 339; on the oil of chrism, 384; views of, on Episcopacy, 365; and the case of Felicissimus, 353, 354, 356, 373-5; and the case of Fortunatianus, 377; on heretics, 382, 383; on ecclesiastical unity as opposed to heresy, 358; letter of, to Magnus on rebaptism of heretics, 381-3; on invalidity of heretical sacraments, 361, 381-6, 388, 391, 396, 397, 400; on the powers and functions of the Christian Hierarchy, 333-6, 338-47, 351, 352; on the question of the Lapsi, 340, 350-4, 378; on the Lectorate, 338; denunciation of Marcianus by, 378, 379, 380; and the case of Martialis and Basilides, 375, 376; and the Novatian Schism, 354-7, 361; on Christ's promise to St. Peter, as establishing Episcopacy, 352, 353, 358, 361-3, 365; on St. Peter as founder of the Roman Church, 362; on St. Peter's Chair as source of the unity of the priesthood, 374; episcopal autonomy maintained by, 391; conduct of, as priest, Pontius on, 337; on nature of primacy of the Roman See, 364; on schismatics, 358, 360, 361, 382, 383; letters of, to Pope Stephen, 379, 380, 386, 387, 389; reply of Pope Stephen to, 388, 389; refusal of, to listen to Stephen's delegates, 386; "De Unitate" of, its date and occasion of publication, 357; "De Unitate" of, its argument, 365; "De Unitate" of, editions of, 366-72; "De Unitate," question of interpolations in, 366-72; Dom Chapman on, 371-2.

St. Jerome, on the Judæo-Christianity of Palestine, 242; on Tertullian's reasons for embracing Montanism, 285.

St. John the Apostle, relations of, with SS. Polycarp and Irenæus, 167, 204.

St. Justin Martyr, the Apologies of, v, 188, 191; his "Dialogue with Trypho," 188, 191, 193; on Apostolic Tradition, 189; rite of Baptism described by, 189; on prophetic charismata, 219; on the attempt of the Jewish apostles to undermine Christianity, 38; on the universal vogue of Christianity, 189; on the Gnostics, 190-3; on Marcion, 233, 234; on Simon Magus, 190; "Syntagma" of, 187, 188.

St. Mary, as "the spotless Virgin," inscription of Abercius on, 177, 178.

St. Mark, connection of, with St. Peter, Clement of Alexandria on, 247.

St. Matthew's Gospel, date of, according to various authorities, 81, 82, 89; origin and character of, Harnack on, 81, 82; character of, Jülicher on, xiii, 82; ecclesiastical character of, xii; teaching of, on the Church, 83, 87; a work of the Palestinian Church, xiii, xiv, 81.

Stephen, Pope, on the validity of heretical baptism, 387, 389, 390, 392; on the *ex opere operato* efficacy of Baptism, 397; appeal of Basilides to, 375, 376; letter of St. Cyprian to, 380, 386, 387, 389; reply of, to St. Cyprian, 388, 389; on the Roman Primacy, 389, 390; reply of third Council of Carthage to, 391; letter of Dionysius of Alexandria to, 398; policy of, Dionysius of Alexandria on, 396.

Strabo, on the polity of the Jewish community in Egypt, 4; on the functions of the Jewish Ethnarch in Egypt, 4.

Suetonius, character of, as historian, 27; on the expulsion of the Jews from Rome by Claudius, 18; on the reasons of the Neronic persecution, 27, 28.

Sulpicius Severus, on the Jewish origin of Christianity, 21; on Titus and the burning of the Temple, 21.

Sunday, celebration of the Eucharist on 67, 107.

Symbol of the Apostles, the, 160-2;

and Gnosticism, 161; Sabatier on, 148, 160.

Symbol, the Roman, Kattenbusch on date of, 160.

Symbols of Faith, Eastern and Roman, 160, 161.

Symmachus, commentary of, on the Gospel of the Hebrews, 243.

"Synagogue," original and derivative meanings of term, 69.

Synagogue, the, date of introduction, 6; hierarchy and polity of, 6; called a "prayer" ($\pi\rho\sigma\epsilon\nu\chi\acute{\eta}$), 6; president of, 6; presbyters of, 6.

Synagogue, the Great, and Pharisaic Tradition, 9.

Tacitus, on the character of primitive Christianity, 17, 20; on Christian origins, 17; on Jewish exclusiveness and hostility towards foreigners, 5; on Jewish monotheism and antiidolatry, 13.

Tertullian, date and life of, 264; on Apostolic Tradition, 269, 270, 273, 274, 276; on Apostolic Succession, 269, 274; on Baptism, 277, 278, 387; conversion of, to Montanism, 264; as Montanist, 292, 293; polemic of, against Pope Callistus in " De Pudicitia," 288, 290, 291; his conception of the Church, 128, 277; his definition of Christianity, vi, 36; indebtedness of St. Cyprian to, 332; on Ebion as heresiarch, 271; on the resemblance of Gnosticism to Greek philosophy, 265, 266; on the sources and characteristics of heresy, 265-76, 279, 280; on the heretical appeal to Scripture, 267, 269; on the functions and powers of the Christian Hierarchy, 279, 280; attack of, on the Christian Hierarchy, 286-8, 290, 291; polemic of, against Marcion, 235-7; on the Marcionites, 233; on the Neronic Persecution, 26, 27; on St. Peter, 277; on Christ's Promise to St. Peter, 359; " Prescriptione, De " of, 271-6; use of term " prescription " by, 272; on Rome as the centre of unity, 277; on the Rule of Faith, 267, 273, 275, 281, 282; on Simon Magus as heresiarch, 271; on the Valentinians, 333.

Thebutis, corruption of the Jerusalem Church by, 175, 240.

Theodore of Mopsuestia, on the identity of the Episcopate and Presbyterate, 117.

Tiberius, expulsion of Jews from Rome by, 3.

Titus, deliberation of, on the burning of the Temple, 21.

Toleration, religious, and the Roman State, 17, 18.

Trajan, letter of, to Pliny on principles to be pursued in all measures against the Christians, 25.

"Trypho, Dialogue with," St. Justin's, 188, 191, 193.

"Twelve, the," in the Acts, 50, 51; in the Apocalypse, 48, 52; in the Gospels, 48-50; St. Paul's sole reference to, 48; right of supervision exercised by, Weizsäcker on, 51; not exhaustive of number of disciples, 51, 52.

VALENTINIANS, the, Tertullian on, 233.

Valerian, edict of, and persecution of the Christians by, 257, 333.

Victor, Pope, as author of "De Aleatoribus," Harnack on, 363; excommunication of the Eastern Churches by, 226, 227; his power of excommunication not questioned by St. Irenæus, 228; intervention of, in the Paschal Controversy, 222, 223, 225-7; letter of, to Polycrates on the Paschal Controversy, 223-5.

WAITZ, on the source of the Clementines, 243.

Weizsäcker, on St. Peter's Primacy, 92; on right of supervision exercised by "The Twelve," 51.

Wellhausen, on the term "Church," 87; on St. Matthew's teaching concerning the Church, 83; on Christ's Promise to St. Peter, xiii.

XYSTUS, Pope, renewal of relations between Rome and Africa by, 396.

CPSIA information can be obtained
at www.ICGtesting.com
Printed in the USA
LVHW04s2340120918
590006LV00012B/110/P